UNIVERSE AND REALITY

OR

PROPORTION
OF SPIRIT AND LETTER

Dr. M. Zehnder,

Universe
and Reality

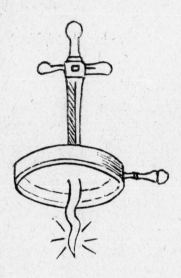

By

DR. MEINRAD ZEHNDER
342 Bloor Street West
Toronto, Canada

BL
51
.Z43
1989

FIRST EDITION

I reverently dedicate this book to the
memory of my father

PREFACE

From the biographical notes of "Anthony Martin's Life."

Anthony was always, from his early youth, a keen observer of others, and still more of himself. All these things could not escape his sharp eye, and he received there urges of broadest survey over human and universal fate; all experiences with their richness of contradictions appeared to him in a clear light and spoke to his sincere mind and sensitive heart with the distinct and intruding language of terrible suffering and unexpected disappointment. The continuous abuse of his holiest intentions by his circumstances and the mockery of fate in regard to his best and noblest actions and will power excited him in time, and countless questions and answers to all possible things arose in the hurt young man.

As long as we are fixed to the pole of shame and are flogged in humiliation and terrible suffering, we may be great in deep feelings, true ideas and important productions, afterwards we easily lose this power. We can express this truth perhaps in other words: *we are productive in the degree as we are sensitive.* Indeed as long as Anthony's ship of life was endangered by the wildest waves of the passionate gulf of destruction, the psalms of joy, deepest sentiments and of universal grandeur gushed forth from his heart all the time.

When Anthony, in February, 1926, started his *Monography about Wrath,* he first made rather general explanations in a broad moralizing way, pointing to the dangers, the connections, the reasons and results of anger; he exhibited the danger of luxury, of hyperculture in artistic religion and unfolded a large complex of near ideas which were interesting and well expressed in his strong feelings. The first part was written in his diary and may partly have been influenced by his former studies of Freud's lectures of introduction in psychoanalysis, though all was built up on a quite different basis. But a special psycho-analytical tendency was and remained typical of Anthony's first and all later philosophical writings.

In the current of writing this treatise, Anthony compared the function of anger to the lightning in the sky. He studied exactly the conditions of the lightning in the tempest, described minutely not only its poetical, but also its physical nature, and was surprised to find out how similar the whole phenomenon of a sharp fit of anger and of a stroke of lightning are. The simile of the lightning seemed to him very relevant, he believed to observe in both the same quickness, exclusiveness and listlessness of choice, the same one-sided concentration of the action to one point, while all others are compensatorily excluded from attention and touch. So he deemed to have the same in the psychological life with anger. One idea is illuminated by the powerful will and feelings shuddering through one point of intelligence with the smashing energy of a powerful lightning, whilst all other associations, more important perhaps objectively, are neglected and subordinated, at least for the moment, as long as the glaring illumination of anger lasts. Only afterwards the pouring rain of repentance may come; the remorse and sophistication from the wrong and one-sided hyper-emphasis.

The concerning exactitude of this simile exalted Anthony's imagination and thinking power, and he meditated a long time about this problem. He was then reminded of the pupil of the eye which concentrates also to one point like the lightning, and so much more in the degree as the intrusion of the light is more intense, and, in addition, of the magnifying glass, where the focus of the light also may be gathered into one smallest burning point, and loses its lighting intensity so much more as its light funnel is scattered on a larger light-circle.

When Anthony meditated about the optic nature of the magnifying glass, he was surprised more and more by this discovery. He felt most distinctly, without being able for the moment and for a time, to explain exactly that he had found out a deepest and most valuable *speculative principle*. The mystic glimmer of this extraordinary precious stone glistened charmingly from the deepest shaft of the universe, and the sensitive mind of Anthony was in a position, quite in advance, and with one powerful grip to forebode and feel, from a few meditations and feelings, the whole power of concentrated truth lying in this hidden majestic and magnetic idea which he then branded with the name: *Psychopupillarismus*.

His first prospecting activity in Psychology had thus led him to a most important concentration of mental values. He was firmly convinced that he had made one of the greatest discoveries possible and knew also that the most intensive activity during a whole life would not be sufficient to analyze this deep and complicated speculative nucleus which he had beheld running in the millions of its countless relations, in the deepest pit of the universe, through the whole created world, attracting and fascinating the startled observer to the utmost degree in deepest reverence and admiration.

The conviction of this extraordinary, important fact and the decision to sacrifice to its development all his forces and his life needed not more than the time of about an hour. Anthony had experimented with his magnifying glass in the setting sun of the cold winter evening, and the short insights he received there were determining for him. They filled him, indeed, with greatest enthusiasm, imparted farthest and surest survey over all creative questions in one rounded and clear conception, explaining, in his opinion, in the root everything of heaven and earth, strength and form, passion and suffering, mechanical and psychic movement in one simple and universal formula. When he went to the living-room, his magnifying glass in his hand, he told his family in the most serious manner: "I have found out something quite important, I am sure that I made a discovery of great consequences, so that I cannot tell you now. But it is absolutely true." He was trembling and shuddering with his whole body, when he was saying these words. He explained shortly, and his people listening, were, of course, surprised and felt that something extraordinary had happened in their immediate neighborhood without being able to see it exactly. It was late when Anthony fell asleep that night.

The following morning he started to develop his principle, and to strive to lay the first foundation of its explanation. He was sure that it was so deep because it was so simple and so extremely difficult to put before other people's minds, because it was so extremely natural and unassuming. But, in spite of knowing this difficulty, he understood the general and exact information flowing from it to everybody, giving clearest connections to all realms of life and so he decided that he had to, and would, sacrifice every fibre of his heart and every bit of his energy to the development of this idea which was not for him, not for one branch of science, not for art, mechanism or business life alone, but for humanity as a whole and in all relations.

Anthony acknowledged only two values in the world which Schopenhauer chooses as the title of his large work: "Die Welt als Wille und Vorstellung": The Will on one side and the Representation on the other. The whole world, the human psychology and all creative and universal values have these two components, the thriving force of the will and the resulting representation of the visible existence; will or energy, on one side, and representation, or repression, on the other. You may say instead of will in the deeper philosophical sense and in psychology, also sentiments, feelings, idealism or divine force, whilst in the group of representations, we have to put the notions of form, material, detail, multiplicity, variability, reality and even *intellectuality,* because it means relation and extension.

The imagination is only the link between these two powers of sentiments and intellectual thinking. It is the transfer and the symbol throwing, like a star, the light from the ideal heaven to the admiring eye of the intellectual world and connecting deepest universal feelings with the most accurate intellectual shortsighted perception of our eye. The imagination has only an intermediary *symbolic* role changing sentiments into reasoning power or intellect, and intellect into sentiments, like a pond allowing two rivers to interchange their waters. These two rivers are intellect and feelings, two interchangeable and invertible values making all possible relations of quantity, always within the limits of the individual life-force which never can be augmented or diminished in its totality.

The temperamental predilection of the habitual choice of a certain *imaginative size or diameter* is the springing point of any psychological and philosophical system.

In regard to his magnifying glass, Anthony applied these conceptions in the following way: He thought that the intensity of the light was comparable to the sentiments of the individual, expressing the stress put on any idea or fact or object, whilst the extension and circumference of the light-circle would correspond exactly to the intellectual occupancy of our psychological life. The larger the circumference of our intellectual light-field, the more numerous the real objects, the better their relations, the better their single relative observation, the more equal their role within the light-circle, but the more dim the lighting of the single object or individual. In the narrow light-circle we have instead a concentrated light, few chosen, but outstanding objects exalted on the throne of high glory and glaring illumination, whilst in the large circle we have the equal and just apportionment of the light to very numerous ones, and in this way a just, mediated, and mediocre lighting stress on the single object, or a moderate affective value of the single individual.

The feelings or sentiments or ideal reaction occupied thus, in our psychopupilar system, if you will, the vertical or perpendicular direction corresponding to the direction of the sunbeams falling from the sky, whilst the horizontal expansion, the intellectual trimming and occupation of the light-field corresponds to the real world, to the surface of the earth with its detailed objective and intellectual categoric values in the broadest sense of the word, containing all values within the boundaries of time, space and causality in as far as we are concerned with them in a practical way. Both are reciprocal values constituting together our whole human fatal or psychological reaction.

It is the same idea as we have it in other physical contrivances, for instance, in the *tackle,* where we have in a similar way the changeable and compensatory inter-correlation of force and categoric expression in time and space, transformation of energy in form and vice versa in a measurable proportion. We may heave a considerable weight with the tackle, but we need instead a longer way and a longer time. The more categoric expression, the less need of energy, and the more energy, the more abbreviation and shortness of categoric expressions.

With greatest concentrating effort, you may express on half a page the intellectual value of a book, and in comfortable leisure you may glide over a thousand pages without expressing more than the affective weight of one page. A river may fall continuously flowing over miles of distance of a soft slope, whilst the Niagara Falls rush down in one vertical movement to the depth, in no time and no space. The gradual yielding of the repressing landscape decides the proportion of the categoric and energetic proportion. We have categoric cataracts not only in the Niagara Falls, but in the most comparable way in the ravines of the Alps, in the psychological life, in art, in high religious events, in all great conflicts; everywhere there are abbreviations of the normal categoric developments.

You tell me: How can you try to express mental values in a formula like this, where space and extension are deciding? But I ask you: Is there any expression or representation of our mental life, where we have not the necessity to use as well the same intellectual categoric expression, where we have relations, graduations and similes in any way without resorting to the same notions? If we succeeded so badly in the past time in building up fundamental philosophical principles, if our ancestors during many thousands of years slaughtered each other and called bad what is good and vice versa, instead of loving and finding out the definite truth and love, have we, in such a state of things, to be afraid of sending out new explorers to the ocean of psychological and philosophical possibilities in order to investigate again and probe once more what seemed to be found out and settled all right, and which practically proves to have failed? What sincere and painstaking thinker would be afraid of the cursing condemnation of his new ideas with the label of frenzy, or of any cross, if he is convinced to be able to contribute in the least degree something substantial and essential to the betterment of the human fate of the future!

In addition, the problem of the different and mutual cohesion and exclusion of material and mind is not at all solved; there seems to be, in spite of all, a gradual difference, a difference of refinement, age and evolutionary perfection which not for always and under all circumstances separate, but continue in developing and changing one value into the other. There is not opposition, but only distance.

The psychopupilar laws are built up on an *artistic philosophical* basis. The optic sense is the guide of the whole idea of Psychopupilarism. It applies the optic laws of the magnifying glass and the whole visible nature to all mechanical real and mental psychic life and existence. We go back to most simple things comprising everything; we discover most deep and interesting things if we only will trust our eyes which we are accustomed to believe more than anything else. Our psychopupilar principles are, therefore, valuable for the falling ball of the playing child, for the hammer of the locksmith, for the sunbeams meeting the earth, for the stars rolling through the universe, for the most hidden sigh and tear of the secret lover, and even for the wings of the cherubim and the last and most intimate sentiments and powers of the most remote impulses of the creative universal *causes*. We share our lot with the divinity in as far as we succeed in discovering, thinking and adoring the thoughts and sentiments of the Creator, we are indescribably happy if we are allowed to look with a free eye at the workshop of universal deeds; we are thrilled to see new worlds sparkling from His divine furnace like sparks of burning coal thrown in all directions, seemingly without choice, how they are continuously born and remoulded from others and how the old ones in perishing are used for following ones in the fiery whirlpool of the continuous universal creation.

Thus, Anthony's essential conception was, that according to his psychological-artistic philosophical system, all creative and mental values have to be expressed in this way, that the intensity, the stress and the sentiments of everything corresponds to the perpendicular direction, whilst the intellectual display, the detailed explanation, the real extension occupy the horizontal direction and that both together are in a reciprocal relation and interchangeable. The more height, the less extension, and the more extension, the less depth *within the extreme limits of life-force*. His study was dedicated to the *distinctions and relations between spirit and letter*.

Anthony applied first his principle to his description of anger, where he came to it in connection with the comparison of the lightning, but then he found that it is applicable even more to love and after all, to all life and existence. His intelligence of these things grew like a huge fire comprising after all the whole universe. He was convinced to have found out that not only all real and visible life and mechanical relations, but also all mental and psychic life with their different angles, in religion, sexuality, art and human psychology and everything react exactly according to this principle, all these different branches of life were for him only different rivers running in the same direction, driven by the same universal forces and appealing to the same urges, rippling the same waves in their course and carried along through their beds all by the same laws of gravitation, following exactly the same variability in their temperamental influence. He found out that they really and fundamentally all follow one and the same law of motion toward the universe. He thought that this psychopupilar principle was most pronounced in its extreme in the artistic type, that it has very different stages of intensity, that its extreme application gives the highest degree of life, love, delight and success, but also of dangers and failures, whilst its balanced mediocre application gives security of existence, but mediocre activity. "The good die first, and those whose hearts are dry as summer dust, burn to the socket."

Soon, in this connection, the young philosopher had the idea that we have, in the extreme psychological attitude of the artist and the highest idealist, as we have it represented in the genius, the extreme application of this one-sided great, but dangerous principle.

If you take a tube and blow powder through it, it will form, at the exit, a circular cloud, and if you permit the evaporating damp of the earth to rise and be cooled in the higher layers of the air, it will assume, if there is no troubling wind, the form of a ball, a cloud. We have here the simile of the further development of the psychopupilar principle. All artistic philosophical conceptions are moving between the extremes of the point and the circle, they continually go to and fro between this representation and alternate without interruption between these extreme stages of creative conversions, according to the former explanations, where we have the broadest circular lightfield on one side and the narrowest monopunctual size of the focus of the magnifying glass, on the other.

If we go a step further and pursue not only the extension of the problem in two directions, as perpendicular and horizontal, as we made it first, and not only up to the limit of the stereoscopical ball, with the addition of the idea of depth, but if we prosecute this progressing evolutionary creative direction along a straight line, we come to the representation of all psychological development and creative evolution in form of a necklace or rosary along which all representation augments alternately to the size of a ball and diminishes alternately to the concentration of a small divine golden link. All psychic creative and universal developments are such beautiful beads of historic representation and concentrate, again and again, to the compressed size of a smallest link, as for relaxation, as it were, and from this temperamental monopunctual relapse new worlds, new creeds, new loves and new inspirations for the future branch out again and again. Everything we understand goes on, in this way. Our understanding and temperamental possibilities are built up in this manner that we can understand and observe only on the basis of this special division and organization, even the idea of God, in as far as we are able to seize it through the spectre of our human disposition, as just a wonderful temperamental necklace, where the charming pearls of the cultural creation are alternated always again by the strong golden links of intermittent divine urges, running between each culture along the incessant way of the circular historic development and evolution. All creative and intellectual life is a flower thriving and blooming one day and fading away the other in the individual, the nation and the culture, superposing each other so that one needs more time than the other one, but continuing in the totality in a continuous eternal wave going up and down in the individual short existence. Nothing escapes this general law in the nearest smallest and broadest and most extended sense of the conception.

In this way, Anthony thought to understand heaven and earth, knowing any movement of earth, analyzing the reason of its circular form, describing the orbs of the universal stars and studying any urge of force and progression wheresoever. He found out that all existence and its movement is the resultant of two opposite forces moving between the point and the circle, being in balance between universal attraction and historic repression in the categoric world, all returning always from one extreme to the other like the tissue of an eternal never-resting weaver's loom. This law is, in his opinion, binding everything, heaven and earth, material and mind, art and religion, science, education and business. All work according to the eternal circulation of this deepest biological principle.

His intention was not only the most concerning expression of the steam engine, of the electrical power, but also of the majestic lightning in the open nature, of the manifestation of the sparkling beauty of the sea, of the deepest heart of the nation, of the original source of the creation, of the manifestation of science and art, of the softest play of the feelings of the human being.

He had the conviction that he had taken away another great and oppressive nightmare from humanity, that he had discovered new great dawns which never more would disappear entirely and he felt that he had found extreme lights and stars shining forever to the cultural humanity. He had put together the fulfilment of energy and form. He considered in his personal inclination the temperamental energy as the more important half. All possibilities of creation, representation and eternal progression were combined in his broad speculative principle.

He was so much impressed by these new universal views and by their truest and deepest value that he calculated instantly what time and work was necessary for the scientific unfoldment and explanation of the principle. His aforesaid estimation of the work needed at least about six thousand pages; the chief points which he intended to explain were creation and universe, earth and culture in general, humanity, nature, art and practical national life and customs. He intended to devote in advance to each of these topics in a liberal way about a thousand pages in order to analyze and explain along these creative examples his fundamental idea which seemed to him so difficult to be demonstrated in a short theoretical way. All these topics were, in his eyes, different great rivers advancing in the same direction, having the same waves, vibrating with the same rhythm and underlying the same eternal and equal laws.

Only at that time, when he had suffered so much in his life, he found an explanation for his reality, a concerning justification of everything, a reconciliation of every situation of the life, the abolition of any one-sided party, a perfect justice in every event and a definite balance and peace of his destiny.

He had the temperament, respecting and observing well all reality and experience, but rushing with irresistible power in an eternal superior beatitude to last and most remote stars with the wings of unflinching universal energy. He felt the terminal magnetic power of the artist going on from the detail, sharply observed and recognized, to general values finding the balance of the reasoning power and the consolation of the wounded heart in the outside extra-individual general results of divine forces and imperishable goals. Now he understood Beethoven's word: "He who understands my music, is forever beyond all sorrow and desperation."

Had he lost before so much in his sincere faithfulness to the law, had he been hurt again and again in most vital conditions, in love, confession, matrimony and possession, he soared at last now to compensatory mental conceptions which gave to him liberation, freedom and joy forever and ever. Nobody could take away these broad ideas, nobody could cheat him in his superior conceptions which were composed as well of the sharpest thinking criticism and the most devoted divine sentiments. Here he had a balance, there he could not be unsaddled by the tricky fate of all his future experiences; the eagle had built in his distress and terrible necessity an eyrie so high and bold that it was inaccessible to his enemies who searched to hurt him and turned down his unchangeable idealism. There he had fastened all his changeable values to eternal laws and found after all the satisfactory solution of his fate to understand the transitory and even necessary character of all phenomena of the real life, their changeable character and their interchangeable necessity bound to the very fundamental nature of individual and universal life.

He was filled, as soon as he had found the psychopupilar principle, with a spirit of most uplifting confidence as we cannot describe it. The secret of his sparkling psychopupilar diamond replenished him with continuous exceeding happiness; he clung to it more than any king to his kohinor, his magnetic soul beheld and appreciated incessantly its magnificent beauty and he stuck to it only so much more when he saw that nobody but himself was able to understand its weight thoroughly.

So Anthony started devoting all his free time to his important work. His beginning practice and his isolation in Light-town allowed to him much free time and he wrote regularly about five hours a day. He first wrote in German and his language assumed soon a most exact terminological precision fitting in well with his sharp scientific notions. After short, anxious trials comparable to those of the young eagle trying the first days to do his bold flights over the most threatening ravines, the writings assumed great steadiness and regularity, the notions came out more and more like shining crystals gleaming with magic beauty through the frame of the sentences. Anthony was deeply sunk in his work. He wrote for self-instruction and enjoyment and for personal belief in his great mission. His interest was far beyond practical or individual utility. He expressed even the idea that any egotistic interest in a philosopher or artist would mean the instantaneous death of real greatness and the unworthiness of universal significance.

Thus, in continuing his essay about *anger,* the second part became different from the first; whilst the first was very general and moved on in usual expressions understandable to everybody, the second was more scientific, built up on the notions and the terminology given and created by the psycho-pupilar conceptions. Two persons read it. One is the professor of Psychiatry of the University of Zurich, Hans W. Maier, who sent the book back with an extensive letter, where he pronounced the following ideas: "The explanations are original and very interesting. There are new, true and relevant comparisons." He advised to publish the book after a few changes.

The greatest and holiest and eternal thing is perhaps what we call *haphazard*. No intelligence is perhaps as frightening as that all greatest things are born from the difference of a most insignificant haphazard developing from a most unmentionable circumstance like an avalanche to the size of an empire or a world. The fact that everything in our life is optional is terrifying, on one side, but, on the other, also encouraging, because it means that the strong developing effort is indeed able to bring about longest consequences from almost nothing. All greatest things in the material visible, intellectual invisible and universal world have to develop in this way. There are, however, two things in this regard to be kept in mind, first, the haphazard leading very far must be capable in itself and in the circumstances, and second, there cannot be an important haphazard in your mind without magnetic correspondence from your side. There are magnetic attractions between all things which happen, without our knowledge, and thus, in a certain sense, haphazard is under a surprising mask, one of our old friends or enemies, perhaps the most intimate of our oldest acquaintances. The haphazard is only mummed with the veil of strangeness and novelty of the surprising moment and is really just the result of our own former efforts, behaviour and work, thus there is indeed no haphazard. It has an underlying natural scientific basis and intimate relation to our personality, it has grown like a tree, inch by inch, in the hidden past, and peeps with its peak over the wall of the visible real world of our experience.

The apparent haphazard of Anthony's finding of the psychopupilar principle was not at all a haphazard either. No haphazard in the world of invention or wheresoever is casual in the common sense, but just a confirming formula of an idea which fixed and haunted the inventor a long time ago in the most thorough and serious manner. That he clinched so much on this idea was the result of his former meditations, of the clear intelligence that he was keen in the idealistic sense, and that his life lacked another more realistic component in order to have more security, real success and human balance. He had been hurt so much by his proud idealistic exclusiveness that he understood that he was in danger to lose the real right of his existence and any material possession and social or legislative acknowledgment or perhaps even honour. We shall understand later how much all these ideas were explained and included in his psychopupilar principle representing a whole rounding of the best harmonious conception of life where all opposite elements are falling in, in a circular subsequent order and where the exclusive blaming and praising order of experiences are replaced by other notions allowing a quiet impartial and complete consideration of the life as it is in all its struggles and seeming contradictions.

The choice of the element of haphazard and the insistent clinging to it are the fruit of greatest purposes and bring about the most remarkable results, if the choice is good, as on the other side, we have to be careful to avoid stubbornness with which we shut our own open doors and are liable to cling too most shallow and undevelopable values instead of precious stones and diamonds lying just near by, without being noticed. Thus judiciousness is most important for the success of the haphazard and that deep visionary sense of the foreseeing mystic looking to the bottom of the universe, understanding the whole net of most thorough speculative ideas in all their relations, with one gigantic grip of deep and true intelligence.

If we have to have the courage to take a chance in our life, on one side, deciding for one point and putting all at one stake for our greatest convictions, passions and ambitions, we, on the other hand, have also to have confidence, up to a certain degree, in the easy drifting compliance with the charming breeze of the fatal will and the universal progression.

Anthony had taken that deadly serious decision in regard to his haphazard. In his psychopupilar principle he had recognized that great walking stick which had to bring him, as a supporting friend, through this life and to which he thought he would cling forever in a fervent and huge effort, as long as he breathed. He found then out, more and more, that this principle was not so easy to develop and explain as he thought. Or with other words, he found gradually that he was more able to apply it to the whole creation, where it was confirmed step by step, in the clearest and most beautiful and concerning way, whilst, on the other side, where its exact analysis and the explanation of its precise formulation was concerned, he felt difficulties though he understood it personally with absolute clearness and security. In its complicated, unfolded application, it was most easy to be explained and described logically, beautifully and poetically, but in its fundamental philosophical constitution he did not succeed thoroughly in explaining it without risking all the time misunderstandings from all sides. The reason was the unbelievable simplicity itself. Just in these shortest and seemingly insignificant explanations the insufficient insight into one word or relation becomes inevitably the reason of the failure of the understanding of the whole principle.

Anthony wrote and thought so much about this idea filling his whole heart and absorbing all his thinking interest at that time that he developed quickly an achieved concerning scientific terminology fitting his principles, matching perfectly with his system and impressing and fascinating everyone coming in the reach of his explanations. How many times explained he to his friends at home, to his wife, to people in restaurants, to the most learned men in Switzerland and ordinary people in the street! They all were instantly grasped by his selected and poetical language and by the depth and sharply concerning clearness of his chosen expressions.

Whilst Anthony was indeed most decided in choosing and sticking to his philosophical principle appearing and recognized by him, as the most beautiful head of Apollo, as the essence of the brain of Aristotle and rhythm of the songs of the universal orbs at the same time, he in the elaboration trusted more the drifting gravitation of the haphazard. He permitted, in the first time, his pen to run where it would. He knew that his principle was applicable everywhere, and he, just like the priestess on the tripod of Eleusis over the sulphur fumes, was sitting on the chair of the broadest creation and allowed the puzzling vapor of the reality to lead him away and to excite him to whatsoever oracles in all directions, on whatsoever subject; he was sure to be reasonable, important, true and original in all statements of his, if he only had the possibility and the will to stick exactly to his principle which he was decided to carry through in the application of all visible and psychic world.

This was the atmosphere in which Anthony started his first work; the *first part of his Psychopupillarism.* During his previous essay on Anger, as we remember, he made the most serious training in using his psychopupilar terminology and conceptions, sharp and imaginative restrictions at the same time, to this goal, and the most elaborate adaptation for the language which he developed, creating new expressions and using old ones with new meanings. The idea of anger and its function, its physiological process were in this manner described most clearly and visibly in a new language and new ideas. What a great thing is a really clear new expression! It gives new inspiration or better, it comes inevitably about as the consequence of great new inspiring necessities.

In the first part of the work of Psychopupillarism, Anthony embarked then on the ship of his literary fate at the end of February, and steered it through the wild ocean of struggling doubts, threatening contradictory whirlpools, of dangerous mists of difficulties hiding icebergs, as it were, until the end of June without returning to the shore of the everyday life. How often every day did he dive to the bottom of his agitated psychic ocean in order to discover deepest connections of truth and the most beautiful corals of the human heart! In all his adventures, he had always one star leading him through all risks, his sincere will and in all sacrifices and superhuman efforts, one thing consoled and encouraged him: the conviction of the wonderful general purpose of the creation, the idea of the ultimate success of his evolution, the beauty and interest of the realm of existence through which he advanced all the time, with his admirative heart, and yet with the amusing self-confidence of a loafer in a garden in spring, enjoying and loving everything for itself, and understanding more and more the great purposes of the whole. He learned there and above all and forever to think collectively. Not the individual fate and happiness matters very much, but the collectiveness of the human and universal destiny which we all háve to serve on the way, as we are fitting in. We have collectiveness of responsibility, collectiveness of happiness and excuses, of reward and punishment and of justice, there was no doubt about that for him.

The first topic which occupied Anthony very much in this work was the *religious fanaticism*. He adapted his ideas of the affective psychopupil most sharply to this problem alike as to all following ones, having so a clearest method. There he built the first guns to shoot his great enthusiasm, in such a power and with such an unheard strength that he was frightened and shaken by the dynamic forces with which he dealt and was sure that their roaring shots were echoing through many following centuries of the human cultural history. At the bottom of these explanations on religious fanaticism lay his own sentimental development in Monkswood. He pointed out that the extreme artistic visual elaboration of the religious service was narrowing the view of the reality, with a refined skill, that in this way, the affective psychopupil became habitually shrunk to one point and that the fanatical individual was, therefore, in a position to shoot most efficiently, but really restricted, owing to the law of compensation, his lifeforce to universal stars and terminal magnetic goals. He explained that the state of this individual may be called happy and artistic, but unreal, narrow and exclusive because being directed to, concerned with, most magnetic and exceedingly attractive terminal values which in the later life are remote, so that this individual becomes dissatisfied and disgusted with the life for which he is not fit.

Further chapters are about character, neurasthenia, art, fashion, work, creation, genius, etc.

A small part of this work was read by Dr. Weber, editor of the "Basler Nachrichten."

The artistic philosophical character of the psychopupilar principle had the consequence that Anthony was induced to stress the esthetical side of the world, the universe and psychology. His developments proved to him the conception that the idea of delight was the terminal element of the conclusive success in everything, that there was the expression of the divine in our specific psychological organization. He wrote much about the notion of delight and looked at it as the monopunctual terminal ideal result of the progression of the logical working effort and preparation. This notion seemed to him to be, according to his system, the essential kernel and result of the psychological progression, the most significant peak and turning point to which all life and motion strive again and again in an incessant vital circulation, the charming centre of the peripheric intellectual life, around which all creatures, objects and energies swarm like bees, and to which all are attracted irresistibly like mosquitoes fascinated by the light.

From these meditations, Anthony's book: *"Das Entzuecken"* (The Delight) gained existence. It was a short volume of 200 pages, being a programme of all his future intended writings with ten definite chapters. He unknowingly had clearly outlined his life-work.

The first chapter explained and defended the psychopupilar conception in general. The second chapter was a clear graphic representation and description of the notion of delight. The third was entitled: "The terminal-ideal delight," and dealt with the symbolic meaning of the cross, the lights in the church, miracle, mysticism and symbolism in the religious service, conceiving them as artistic optic and notional means, in order to concentrate the mental faculties of the believer in a sensorial way to monopunctual sentimental delight.

The following chapters were: The delight in sexuality, in nature, in art, in poetry, in painting, in music, in sculpture, in the daily life, and Delight and Luxury.

This book was read and criticised by Mrs. Edwards, London; Dr. Scheiwiler, Einsiedeln; by the editor of "Wissen und Leben," Zurich; by the artist Rickenbacher, and others. The publishing house of Dr. Eugen Diedrichs, sent it back with the remark: "An interesting artistic-philosophical work with large foundation." The editor of "Wissen und Leben" advised publication as a whole, since the single chapters find their explanation in each other mutually.

The second part of Psychopupillarism by Anthony dealt chiefly with the notion of suggestion. Anthony became most conscious of its importance during the descriptions of the Delight in Nature, when he meditated about the mists of the Alpine perspective and found then soon out that there is, also in Psychology, scarcely anything comparable in importance, to the idea of suggestion. He entitled, therefore, this second part of his work: *"The Suggestion,"* and wrote on it a book of about four hundred and fifty pages, of the same size as the first part; he took up every concerning feature in the real, visible, psychological and ideal life, in sexuality and religion, art and practical life, which seemed to him to have reference to the idea of suggestion. The book became, therefore, most variegated, seemingly disorderly, but there was nothing in it which was not linked up most sharply to the relation of the idea of suggestion. He described there the whole human life from the angle of suggestion. He allowed his pen to drift along through all phenomena of the human life, went back again to nature, to the different suggestive influences of the colors and of all sensorial urges, spoke once more about the black color seeming to him so important, mentioned once more fashion, but dedicated most of the book to the topics which seemed to him the most interesting and important in life, religion, art and sexuality. He digged into his meditations, and spilled there the fire of his heart and most elevated sentiments which were abused and misunderstood in his outside social relations. He wrote a long chapter about benevolence, malevolence, love and hatred, conversion, gratitude, laziness, anger, temptation, about the value and significance of material gifts, but returned again and again to his two chief topics, art and religion. He spoke much about the evangelic narrations, about the symbolic person of Christ, about the meaning of the historic church, legislation, criminology and legal actions. He created, chiefly in the second half of this book, almost in every sentence, new combinations of terminological expressions which were, it is true, sometimes very long, but were always not only very clear and sharp in the meaning, but also exceedingly brilliant in the formulation. In this part, he reached the peak of the perfection of his language, never he was able to write more beautifully the German language and never he had a more powerful, rich and continuous flow of outstanding and original philosophical ideas.

He seemed to be quite untirable in continuing his work, day by day, night by night, week by week and month by month; he dictated regularly in the evenings to his typist, Miss Egli, mostly until midnight, until the end of June, when his fate brought him over to Canada.

He had been for a while there and had written already other books, when he had the idea to send his "Suggestion" to an outstanding firm in Berlin for criticism, and eventual publication. He sent it to the firm Julius Springer, one of the most considered medical publishing houses in Germany, and had then a correspondence with them, whose most important consequence was the following letter, which he received from Berlin, the 17th of March, 1927: "Dear Doctor: I am in a position to send you the opinion of one of the most considered modern psychologists to whom I have forwarded your manuscript for criticism. May I ask you to tell me which are your further intentions? In the meantime, I shall meditate whether I can make a definite proposition as to the choice of the publisher. It is not quite easy to find the fitting firm under the present circumstances of our time. With perfect consideration. Yours truly, Signature."

The copy of the criticism had the following contents: "It is difficult for me to give a succinct judgment of the manuscript of Dr. Martin, because there are everywhere allusions to the philosophical system of Psycho-pupillarism which is not explained in the book. Because it works with probably artificial, but very simple means in the optic sense, it gives opportunity to the author to throw sharp spotlights on all possible interesting problems of human life. There is the question of most variable things, partly (he underlines) in a really witty and beautiful manner. There is no doubt of the quite unquestionable literary talent of the author.

"It is difficult to say what advice has to be given to the author. It would be probably the best to tell him the name of a publisher who likes interesting explanations on a broad, popular basis. For the essays witness indeed an excellent talent and are always interesting. So often I enjoyed the really original and poetical lights of the book."

This second part of the first book was read by nobody except by this outstanding German psychologist, the following correspondence did not bring out the fruit of publication, since the firm, Julius Springer, would not make up their mind to publish themselves, because of difference of their topic, and Anthony was not inclined to publish his book in an other than a first-class publishing house. He had no publishing experience and not much interest in publication for the moment, his interest being devoted to writing more and more; he also had lost all his relations with Germany since many years and made no real efforts, for the time being, to publish the book.

During the first time of his stay in Canada, Anthony wrote his last book in German language, entitled: *"Die Affectivitaet der Musculatur,"* "The affectivity of the muscular movements." He dealt with laughing, weeping, work, sport, dancing and muscular rigidity of the dead.

Anthony had met in Toronto an excellent young friend, a clever court reporter who soon acknowledged and appreciated his philosophical tendencies, and proposed to write for him, if he would put down his ideas in English. This immediate step from the mother tongue to a foreign language, of which he did not know very much in the refined literary sense, was, of course, a difficult thing for Anthony. He hesitated and was, then, however, after all, decided to continue his writings in the English language. The time from the 27th of September to the 3rd of December, 1926, was then entirely dedicated to the first part of "spiritual" investigations which he called *"Proportion of Letter and Spirit."* The time from that period to the 27th of February, 1927, the sequence was achieved, being called the second part of the work. Each of the two volumes comprised five hundred pages.

There could not have been found somebody more filled with the highest conception of his work, more convinced of his high mission, more diligent and regular in his writing activity. He forgot there the whole world over his great task, enrapturing him all the time. He lived in his room with the quietness and most engrained tenacity of reserved solitude, meditating and writing month by month during day time, and dictating evenings to his faithful Eckermann, who was well educated and had, above all, great aspirations for every noble and high thing. He went on with such a deadly serious purpose and perseverance that life and death, years and food, material and social need, could not count anything in comparison with the great overwhelming power of his creative will pushing his enthusiastic soul ahead; he did not know nor ask to which goal. But we are greatest when we do not know where we go, as Oliver Cromwell said. There is no doubt that he never had more elevated and happy hours than there in his lonely room, where he fatally and intentionally, was isolated. The strong ideal desire of his burning heart attracted instantly the words of the English language to perfect regularity and esthetic array, standing up like a row of nails pointing to a nearby attracting magnet.

This book has been compared to a cathedral. Every ornament suits the style. He who does not grasp the fundamental character of the first principles, misses the whole book. If one does, all is an easy kaleidoscopic display and the whole book is a continuity linking up thoroughly.

Natural scientific applications are the most thrilling "fairy tales," more true than the detailed experimental truth. First the language is a little handicapped, later it flows more easily with the increasing strength of the convincing idea.

It is a popular work, however, a thorough self-instruction in distress, a clarification of the author's conception of the world. He who did not suffer intensely himself, will not be able to understand this book whose deepest root is the desire for impartial truth in this social world.

The word "sentimental" is not used in the modern despicable way, but in a broad scientific way, expressing all relations to sentiments. The word "affective" has, firstly, the sense of any universal force in the broadest vital sense; secondly, it designs the whole amount of human life force; and, thirdly, it expresses, in a restricted manner, the psychic force used for sentiments. "Symbol" is taken in the literal sense of its Greek meaning; "Intellectual" is used synonymously with distinct reality, material representation and multiple relation of the world and mind. The word "theistic" has mostly the meaning of the divine in as far as it is reachable by the historic, symbolic preparation. According to former scientific work, the author does not use the word "angry" very often, in a blaming sense, but as the raw material of vital strength.

The partial "fairy-tale character" of this book is not improbable, miraculous complication of the life, but the large conception on the contrary that really all functions of life are one and obey the same law, so that the separating exterior differences and logical differentiation, up to a certain degree, are not only often neutral, but even hurtful for deep understanding and clear representation of the most important psychic observations. Looking at the deep and true unity of the things of life gives more information than to emphasize and remark their near superficial differences.

In serious work, we indeed cannot be afraid of elaborate language; for any difficult task in writing work not less than in technical science, rich and detailed instruments are necessary and cannot be avoided. If our time claims that we have to use only simple and short words, it gives witness to its mental laziness.

This book is not written for readers, but for thinkers. It will convey directions for crossing psychic oceans.

This book is an encyclopaedia of the human heart, not coming chiefly from the outside learned world, but from the inside experience and suffering sincerity. It is a trial to maintain the deep convictions of an early youth, in which the author has been disappointed by the experiences of life.

We could entitle this book very differently, for instance, "Our Relations to the Universe," "Once More: Intellectual or Sentimental?" "The Rhythm of Universal Forces," "Relations of Universe, Historic Religion and Art," "Psychology of Time and Eternity," "Philosophy of the Universal Temperament," "Art, Science and Religion," "Poly- and Mono-symbolism," "The Old and New God," "Universe and Reality," "Our Outlooks Beyond the Stars," "The Split Through the Universe," "Incidit in Scyllam qui vult vitare Charybdim," "Universal Insight and Outlooks," or, according to Schopenhauer, "The World as Will and Representation." It is a fight for religious truth, a struggle for psychological harmony of our life. Another title would therefore be: "Our Ultimate Doubts."

The book has a stoic character, its philosophy comes out from hurt idealistic individuality. The author wishes to be at the same time the mouthpiece and expression of the same attitude of a nation; he is the outburst of a disappointed culture. The philosopher proceeds from personality to general truth like the artist.

This book is drawn from the experience of the present psychology of central Europe, although on any page there is the question of universal things with which everybody is essentially concerned in the depths of his personality. It is a reflection of the Psychological struggles and difficulties which sweep over Europe since centuries and still continue.

This book is about the reflection of the psychology of the moderate religious modernist in Central Europe. It may be the explanation of the psychology of the Liberal, as we have it in that country. This type is rather friendly to historic religion, but he is broader and does not submit absolutely.

Under its present appearance and dress, this book has to be called "Popular Psychological," though its radical claims are higher.

The philosopher is the conscientious controller of reality. He analyzes it and synthetizes it again, better if possible. Too often he understands that there is not much to change in the mediocre reality, that the reality of the world is a compromise of struggles and antagonisms and that contradictions keep the world together, but full harmony, order and peace mean the death of the creation. This book is an attempt to save old ideas as much as possible, and to explain and understand bitter disappointments and their consequences.

Bacon said: "There are three kinds of books, those that have to be

XX

tasted, those that have to be swallowed and those that have to be chewed and digested." This book belongs to the third class.

The book comes from a foreign language, school, taste and education. For many, the book is so much more interesting for this reason. The topic in itself is such that the book is destined for intellectual readers of ability for abstract thought.

This book does something which never has been done before, it introduces a foreign mind in its full quality into the English language, without transforming sentiments and thoughts. Or rather, it sacrifices the local adaptation to the truth of personal genius and character. The author was compelled to do so by his exterior circumstances which put him just in the beginning of his writing career, on the ground of an English-speaking country. Is it not interesting for an English mind to follow exactly the features of a foreign, literary product? Would it not be going too far to avoid the special values, the flavor of sentiments and the originality of thought? If you enjoy them in a benevolent cosmopolitan spirit, we will be well pleased.

The book comes from mature life and is appealing to the mature, observing and serious man, but even among those it is only the philosophically inclined part who will be the most interested in this book, although there is no page and no word which deals with anything else than with the most radical and essential interests of any human being.

This book undertakes a task for inter-confessional and religious peace. Fundamentalism and modernism, science and religion, Catholicism and Protestantism are compared and reconciled, an improbable idea indeed, but a promising work.

This book intends more to point out how life ought to be than how it is, for this reason the historic questions are of minor importance, and the educational value of different conceptions is in the foreground. It is incomparably more the lasting universal side of the questions which matters here than the historic part of it.

Perfect clearness of a book means polite superficiality and testifies more to technique than to depth.

It is a perfectly individual book at a period which moves away from genius with tremendous strides, and has to be taken as such in its sincere novelty.

ACKNOWLEDGMENTS:

Many thanks are due for permission to reproduce the plate representing Moses by Mestrovic, to the Art Gallery of Toronto, furthermore to Miss Maud E. Coo, for her technical help, and to Mr. Sam Hunter for his lasting interest, frequent hints, discussions and encouragements in regard to the book.

CURRICULUM

Born 1887 at Einsiedeln, Dr. M. Zehnder spent a happy youth in the mountains of Switzerland. He attended in his home town the primary school and the classical college (Gymnasium) and studied medicine in the universities of Geneva, Lausanne, Munich, Berlin and Zurich, where he acquired his license as physician and the diploma as medical doctor. After two years of assistantship and military service, he practiced for eight years as a general practitioner in Klingnau in the Canton of Argovy, dedicated two years, mostly to paediatric studies in Vienna and London, and emigrated 1926. Then his literary career started.

Toronto (Canada), September, 1929.

All greatest values are ambivalent.

The genius is a remote universal influence appearing as a sparkling mono-punctual star, owing to his extreme distance. The farther away the source, the longer its activity. The genial star may be extinct, but its light travels to you for thousands of years.

Die materielle Sorge unseres Lebens erlaubt uns nicht, uns in unser tiefstes Ich zu versenken. Es ist ein offenes Geheimmis der Natur, dass wir bestimmt sind fortzueilen durch das Schicksal des Universums auf leichten Fuessen, unbekuemmert um unser eignes tiefstes Wesen. Die historische Religion mit ihren mystisch erhebenden Fluegeln und symbolisch gehemmten Zeichen ist zugleich das Vehikel und der Hemmschuh, der die beiden Gegensaetze unserer ahnenden Wuensche und wirklichen Notwendigkeiten versoehnen soll.

Dem Herrlichsten, was auch der Geist empfangen,
Draengt immer fremd und fremder Stoff sich an;
Wenn wir zum Guten dieser Welt gelangen.
Dann heisst das Bessre Trug und Wahn.
Die uns das Leben gaben, himmlische Gefuehle
Erstarren in dem irdischen Gewuehle.

Goethe.

——*all partial evil universal good.*

Pope.

INDEX

XXIII

INTRODUCTION

Alles Vergaengliche ist nur ein Gleichnis.—Goethe.

If in the sunshine children produce, through a magnifying glass on a rectangularly underlying plane, a circular light-field, the size of it may be larger or smaller according to the distance from the glass to the light-field. The child easily discovers a size of the light-field as small as a point and is surprised and thrilled when it sees rising smoke and burning fire in this punctual light. Everybody knows the reciprocity of the size of the light-field and the intensity of the lighting. The largest light-field includes the widest diffusion of light, within its boundaries; the tiniest most concentrated one on the contrary, possesses a blinding flash of light which in its combined power affords the pleasurable astonishment to our children.

This fact is exceedingly clear. The equal amount of sunbeams comprised in a small point, must exercise, on this small place the same power of light and heat as it has in the diffusion of a large circular plane. In the latter case only the addition of all the light and heat, dispersed in all the points making up the larger light-circle, gives the amount of the smallest punctual burning beam. We in one case have lost space and extension, but gained localized intensity of light and heat, whilst in the other, the wide diffusion and larger space are equalled by a weaker light and a smaller heat. What we lost in space, we gained in concentration and intensity; and what we missed in intensity and power of concentration we may find in a large and wide diffusion. So we recognize, that there is a perfect compensation between space and intensity of light, that the total amount remains the same, if it is pressed together in a small point or diffused in a larger circular light-field.

We shall find a striking congruity between these conditions of the physical functions of light and heat and space on one side, and of the psychological relations of the functions of our soul on the other. The space and the expansion of the light-field correspond to the detailed display of our intellectuality, whilst the intensity of light and heat are quite comparable to the degree of concentration of our sentiments or feelings. Intellect is objective, sentiments are subjective.

We admit, therefore, that our psychological life is composed of two factors, of an intellectual and sentimental part, which are to each other in relation of mutual compensation. A large expansion of intelligence and detailed survey excludes at the same time a deep intensity of sentiments or affectivity, as we will call this function, and a strong concentrated power of sentiments, as we find it in the moments of anger and enthusiasm, never is in a position to give us at the same time a broad outlook on the detailed intellectual reality of life. What we lose in intensity of affectivity, we shall find it in a broad intellectual expansion; and what we have lost in extension of our intellectual functions, we gain again in the depth and strength of our more concentrated affectivity.

XXVII

Our psychic life consists in the progression from the intellectual fixation in the enlarged light-field of our detailed objectivity to the punctual concentration of our strongest affectivity. All our works and all our actions meet first innumerable details and objects in the peripheric field of the enlarged light-circle, and as a mill grinding and refining the different grains to fine, homogeneous powder, our soul simplifies all reality and experience by logical effort to the uniformity of great and powerful ideas. These ideas are intellectually simple, free from real complications and rammed like guns with the most efficient affective energy. These last ideas to which always our work is concentrated and happily simplified, are truth, beauty, strength and kindness. They have the small punctual size of the light-field which we compensatorily ask for the most developed intensity of our affectivity. We call these final ideas of our psychic work symbols—an excellent word—because most distant ranges of divine nature and most simplified sensorial activity or intellectuality are always the compensatory supposition to meet any high and strong goal beyond our intellectual life, in the realm of eternal sentiment and divine value. The symbol is, therefore, the small window through which our intellectual nature reaches affective divinity, or it is, rather, the narrow barrel of a gun through which, as a projectile, the utmost compressed totality of our psychic force is shot out to the universe of idealism.

The enormous efficiency of the modern gun has its reason in the disproportion between the explosive force and the small diameter of the barrel. Since all energy of the gunpowder is forced to go exclusively through the narrow channel of the barrel, there is produced an exceeding concentration of force and energy, which conveys to the missile an extraordinary compulsion of reach, speed and strength and which is the addition of all the amounts of energy which would have been spent, had the explosion taken place in a non-protected surrounding globe of air. Any smallest augmentation of the circumference of the barrel weakens the energy of the projectile and any most insignificant narrowing makes an important addition to the strength, reach and speed of its flight. There we have again nothing else than the law of compensation, where life, energy and amount of expansion are in exact complementary correlation to, and dependence, on each other. Never the whole sum of the energy of the gunpowder is transgressed ; from where would the missile take the energy unless from these known conditions ?

In our psychology we have quite a similar order. Our life-force represents a continuously renewed and almost stable amount of energy which is elaborated in intellectual work and idealistic sentiments. We meet, after all, always in a gifted individual, an enormous excess of life-force which behaves to intellectuality similarly as gunpowder does to a rather large barrel. There is always, already in normal life, a serious disproportion between intellectuality and affectivity. In addition, our life-force does not like to be expelled through the ordinary and numerous holes of our ordinary peripheric notions and experiences being unable to let through large amounts of feelings, but prefers naturally the more energetic notions of symbolism, which have the right size and resistance in order to allow the most delightful passage of the strongest and most energetic concentrated life-force. The individual likes this psycho-mechanic energy of symbolic concentration, it is agreeably excited by the rushing-by of the stormy strong feelings. It is always the destiny and the purpose, psycho-mechanic necessity of our nature to make consecutive intellectual concentrations and to produce final symbolic reactions.

Even the real disproportion between the purport of our intelligence and our potential life-force is quite considerable, as though affectivity was a giant prisoner, in a small room, from which he was in connection with the outside world, only through a small lattice-window. The prisoner lies fettered inside, with his strong limbs and stares to the stars through his intellectual window but he is condemned to stay in and to send out his longing looks so far as the fetters of his mechanically fixed intellectuality , the railing or the screen of his logical laws of time, space and causality do permit him. The prisoner tries in vain to get rid of his miserable state; he cries, weeps, flatters in songs and dances and contrives, in any art, wonderful affective-material refinement towards divinity, but he does not succeed entirely; always he remains short of what his warm heart ought to do, and always again there rises the frightening disproportion between the affective life-force and the purport of the intellectual understanding.

Modern life seeks a different solution, not in shooting feelings very high, but in enlarging the window of intellectuality, in order to avoid a disproportioned symbolic concentration. In this way a larger distribution of the passing life-force or vital sentiments is produced, the compression of the energy is compensatorily diminished and the individual enjoyment and affective pleasure, but also his danger and despair, disappointment and affective explosion become less. The modern scientific world with its rich intellectual work has enlarged immensely the window of our intellectuality and this will be a future way, up to a certain degree, giving us a view of a better balance between affectivity and intellectuality.

Acting and working in our life are, therefore, always proceeding from details to symbolic simplification, from intellectual objectivity to affective idealism. We start with the enormous distension of the light-field of our daily experience and of our real objective surroundings, and we finish with the terminal symbolic values of concentrated strength, beauty and truth. These are always inviting spring-boards to eternal values, always able to convey to our psychic force the necessary elasticity and compressive energy in order to be thrown into the lap of the universe, with tremendous power. As the stars and planets flit through the night of the universe, in the bright ways of their most rapid motion, so the projectile of our concentrated psychic force, after having left the narrow intellectual opening of the symbol, is thrown through the universe. These projectiles run with an unheard speed and energy to their divine goal—whistling like sky-rockets and shining like stars. All our great ideas and sentiments are stars thrown into the infinity of the universe out of the psycho-pupillaristic organization of our nature. Stars are like great ideas and great ideas like stars. Are not both incensed and lit by the friction of their speed —sparkling beams of eternal light and imperishable beauty on the way to their common goal, the most magnetic point, that which we may call God ? This extraordinary all-overwhelming magnetic attraction of the divinity is the most important fact, the main phenomenon of the universe, and we could not have any understanding of real or idealistic life, of mechanical, natural or affective processes, if we did not admit this overpowering magnetism of our strength, by another one. All forces have a higher scope in one point of most energetic attractivenes. It causes a hierarchic order in the creatures according to their affective value and weight, and here we recognize the root of logic and —idealistic right proceeding from the human work and action, but also from the law of the universe and the natural mechanism of the earth.

This unity and logical order of magnetic hierarchy has however a grievous crack, we know it; but there is the most remarkable thing for human beings, that it is exactly in the compromising constitution of our nature that this crack, this magnetic antagonism and this logical fissure is most clearly and painfully manifested. Human nature is the parting point, where most opposite magnetic forces meet and claim both their rights. Pain and unhappiness, sorrow and fickleness are, therefore, in advance to be expected essentially, in every human being, even if we consider life and its organization purely theoretically. We all unfortunately are in a position to confirm, by experience, this statement, we all have felt and feel always the tearing painful energy of opposite magnetic forces.

There is nothing without magnetic endowment. A stone, a bush a star. a road, everything is full of the mysterious fluid which we call affective magnetic force. Every created thing has the role of an affective medium, from which the sentiments flow over to another more capable magnetic object, and which is filled up with the affective force of objects less strong and capable than itself. We have a continuous interchange in the realm of the affective universe, all created objects give and receive their sentimental values and form, in their common activity, an uninterrupted chain of intimate connection of all things in the earth, in the realm of the visibility and in the spheres and spaces of the seen and unseen universe: in this ever flowing river of common feelings all happiness is founded, and in the separtion from it all our delusions, disappointments, diseases and sadness have their root and deepest cause.

Everything created, in our reach, has two affective components of which the one is in contradiction and in opposite direction, in regard to the other. Through all the universe, from the sun to the gnat, we discover always, in all things, an uplifting form or soul and a material bodily part which pulls in opposite direction according to the law of gravitation, and to the categories of time, space and causality. Bodily existence presupposes, therefore, always the intellectual resistance up to a certain degree, to the rising eternal idealism and its sentiments; its sure reality is conditional on checking the exclusive government of idealistic magnetism. The value of this truth is evident. We are bound to face it in the full meaning and weight. We have to understand the embittering character of our double nature, how hard it is not to follow high idealistic goals to their last consequence. It is ever and again this necessary maintaining of the balance of these two opposite factors affective or psychic existence, this inevitable and essentially necessary maintaining of the balance of these two opposite factors of our life and existence which creates continuous dangers and needs skilful efforts, cautious work, and above all ceaseless pain and sacrifice. The deep root of our unhappiness lies in our greatness. The discrepancy of our natural gifts is as much stronger as they are more developed, but the resulting way of personality and life will be exactly more sure and quiet, for this reason, because strong opposing amounts are less subjected to changing influences.

This is the strongest and most important personality which is composed of enormous ideal and realistic forces which have both found themselves together to a harmonious balance. The good man must be realistic enough to give leave to the overwhelming power of idealistic charm, as far as it encroaches on his reasonable and natural bodily existence, and, however, he ought to keep enough of uplifting idealism in order to embellish life, to put on everything the golden crown of love and important logical significance; he has to escape a shallow superficial conception of life. Life not only in its totality, but also in all hours and minutes, in all its real purposes and actions, should be adorned with some idealistic spark of charm, politeness, pleasure, - it should be connected with important convictions of truth and affective weight and ought to have always and in every case of experience, a communication with our sentiments of beauty and esthetics.

Although the law of compensation bears on the total amount of life-force and its full use, it is a fact that modest use of the functions has a mutual beneficial and even fructifying effect. One can not be functioning, if the other is excluded absolutely, in addition. Up to optimum use they help each other, beyond this measure one strangles the other in compensatory limits.

Don't hurry too much, in your life, to idealistic goals! Hurrying means covetousness and so loss of human balance, beauty and taste. If our longing, in the material realm, is too little, our exertion in regard to the idealistic world may be misunderstood or distorted. Material effort means therefore a bridling energy of the extreme affective life, it is, in a sense, a mirror of our psychic riches, a superficial detailed show and display of the deep powers of our affective soul. In the beauty of form and colors of the flowers we recognize the nobility of the sap of the plant. In the widely spread crown of the oak we admire the vital efficiency and mechanical strength of its roots. So, as a rule, we have to expect from the depth and strength of affective vitality, a strong development of rich flowery foliage of a large crown of intellectual and material reality. The number and size and beauty of boughs, leaves and flowers depends, of course, on the capability and the quality of the root, of the life-force which is typical of this species of plant or tree, for both are in a mysterious, most intimate causal connection. Without the deep root of important life-force, which means the general totality of life-force not yet elaborated, in this case, in intellectual work or in artistic application there is no expectation and no hope even for material success. Only a strong gifted affectivity has the possibility of building up whatever structure of intellectual and spiritual, of material and psychic matter, and it is only owing to different stress of the functional scale of our psychic nature, that we produce more or less intellectual or sentimental-spiritual goods. A predilection to emphasize the more concentrated and therefore, in a sense, more important idealistic values means a higher selection of work which is more satisfying, but also more exhausting, whilst the preference of the affectivity dilution in the material world is equivalent to love of steady intellectuality and the stolid, logical steps of our visible human proceedings. It means, for this reason, a less concentrated importance of life and destiny, in a sense, less weighty affective standards being in question and being farther away from high symbolic goals, but it protects against educational irregularities and serious dangers. Angry slothfulness and eliptic overskipping of the reality are excluded more surely from the modesty of the realist who instead is likely to lose the right hierarchic standards of the affective weight of the objective world. He overvalues the detailed peripheric world with which he deals, to which he constantly has directed his attention and becomes petty, shallow and insignificant, exactly where he thinks to be able to prove his preferability, even in a visible exterior way. Interestingly the despicability of life starts just at the corner of sensorial perceptibility, and life receives the title of nobility and admirable value only beyond the threshold of the senses and the external world. It is in the hidden corners of our soul, in the affective intimacy of our hearts, where we have to start and to keep all important resources of strength and values of our life, where love, beauty, true greatness, happiness and even best success are built up and remain hidden for ever.

It is owing to the quite general law of compensation that at the moment of entering into the intellectuality of the visible world any dignity, any deep psychic intensity and any condensed value are in serious danger to be diminished or destroyed. On the other side, we no sooner exclude the extreme multiplicity of the visible world and the too variable number of its characteristics, than we obtain easily a symbolic emphasis and in this an affective approfondation of our limited intellectual remainder. We have a deep and enlightened spiritual appreciation of the more concentrated circle of our sensorial reality which we put the much more in connection with the deep values of truth, charm, beauty and strength, as the notions become more simple in number and in logical characters. We have here again the different diameter of the barrel of the gun, highly efficient in a small, and less in a larger amount. All things rely on compensation in the world, but this thorough law reaches much farther into our daily life, into our lowest and highest, material, intellectual, affective and spiritual acts than we ordinarily would like to admit.

Das Leben ist voll Widerspruch.
Und sollt' es sich nicht widersprechen?

Goethe

FIRST BOOK

THE most religious genius calls himself the LIGHT OF THE WORLD. He claims an outspoken opposition to the world, and he recognizes in it his most embittered enemy. Its complicated multiplicity troubles his high spiritual simplicity and his union and communion with the universe; its sensorial attraction is declined by him because of the danger of realistic distraction. He calls himself the light in the middle of the large circle of the broad detailed visibility of the objective world: he claims to be the dazzling light-field within the social expansion, in the centre of the gloomy plane of human and sensorial life. He declines the possession of the earth. He feels an insurmountable aversion to all material reality. He even has the conviction that his light does not kindle, in a direct way, very far into the darkness of the world, that the world rather is not willing to accept his light, to be enlightened by the strength of his ideas. He does not fill the world as a totality with his teaching, although he penetrates and illuminates easily the individual affective disposition.

He very pronouncedly uses the law of compensation which never allows, simultaneously, both the extreme detailed understanding and real possession of the world and the concentrated spiritual or affective illumination of the mind. Human nature, as a rule, has not the force to be very familiar with the peripheric reality and, at the same time and in the same person, to be very concentrated and intimate in affective enthusiasm and symbolic strength and delight. He who possesses a very pronounced strength and facility of idealstic concentration,is always in the case to sweep swiftly over the multiple objectivity of his light-field, not to grind small enough the grains of the world of his experience,not to fix enough his affective life-force on the detailed world of his larger light-field. The longing and desire of his peculiar nature for the deep psycho-mechanic attitude of extreme concentration, diminishes very much the amenability for real, peripherically fixing magnetism, and has therefore, according to the law of compensation,the inevitable consequence of negligence of the real world.

If the religious genius dislikes the real world, if he exclusively loves the ideal world,he bears witness of his peculiar taste for the powerful energy of the spiritual life. He is so fond of the punctual concentrated attitude of his psycho-pupil that he excludes the periphery of the reality as the dark night of ignorance and ruthlessness. He not even does not explain the multiple real objectivity of this visible world,but he also condemns and disdains it. He does not give us exact opening keys to the very numerous and most differentiated real objects and questions of life, as science has the tendency to do,but claims to be,himself alone,the main principal key suitable to all various key-holes of real affectivity.

The peculiar tendency and taste of the religious genius does not like the wide open field of his and our psychological nature, but rushes quickly through the contractive action of the punctual idealism, with whose dazzling and burning light and symbolic simplicity he identifies his own strong personality. This is the meaning of the word that Christ is the light of the world. He represents the specific idealistic taste of our nature, both not lingering and wondering about, in the wide open field of our manifold objective reality, but emphasizing always and striving for the high affective value to the sensorially simplified symbolism. That he is the light of the world, means that He claims to be the supreme symbolic star in our real life. The religious genius thinks to have the force not only to impart an energetic push to the scattered reality, towards quick and complete,burning condensation and concentration in himself as the terminal light-point of universal active concentrative energy, but he considers himself also, in a retrospective effect, as the acting power of logical direction, and principle of all creative powers in the world. He is, therefore, the regular type of authoritative genius, dividing, directing and working as an inexhaustible source of real arrangements, by the enormous compressed energy of his spiritual life.

This second part of the effect of the religious genius is the production of the extraordinary deep wells of his activity, and it is the following work of his pupils and organizations which display and develop the wonderful flower of his psychic beauty,his charming love and of his exceeding strength and affective authority.The real display of his work is not his taste:his nature likes abstractions and principles,the fixed stars of symbolic notions and pictures and the general repeated intensity of affective guidance to the divine.

The religious genius is not at all liberal in lavishing many realistic and scientific relations of his ideas: he remains simple in his tenets and is therefore, in accordance with the law of compensation, always great and important. He never seriously abandons the mysterious frame of his notions of authority, idealism and notional generalities. He never takes our attention away from the depth and importance of his general feelings out to the complicated world of the intellectual part of our life. His digressions,in this direction, are always most reserved. His main purpose, which he never loses, is the strong idealistic concentration of our mind.

It is the deep psychological knowledge of the limits of our life-force which makes the victorious efficiency of the teachings of the religious genius. This knowledge enables him to possess himself of our whole psychic strength and bring about most efficient affective shots out of the narrow barrels of his symbols. There is unquestionably an important share of the effect of the religions in the excellent suggestive force of their artistic literature. By the abstract concentration of idealistic notions and by super-natural miracles with which they surround the figure of the religious genius,they exclude him as well as his teaching from direct contact with the rich detailed reality and put his affective personality as well as his idealistic system in the concentrated light of undiverted highest symbolism. The force of any religion reposes on its symbolic roots and development. The person of the religious genius who, as a man has practical necessities, is pushed back in the mist of a charming atmosphere of love and lofty elevation, and never we discover the full weight and the clear sunshine of his realistic humanity.

His life-force seems to be directed,uninterruptedly, towards the highest hills of idealistic light,he never is seriously subjected to the compromising necessities of other people. Even when he is most physically engaged by corporeal pain, he does not lose for moments the unity and depth of his affective strength.Temptations and outside trouble and pain are not in a position to effectuate an obstruction or confusion of the concentrated sheaf of sunbeams of his fiery idealism. It is just in this proof of his quite extraordinary talents, that we are most enraptured to admire him and where we are most inclined to admit his high divine forces; for, whilst everybody else would have been,compensatorily, swept away from ideals to cruel reality, by the strength of strong sensorial influences as being given in flagellation and cross, he maintains at all time the full attention and energy of his exclusively idealistic attitude. Is it not quite an astonishing fact to observe in the most suffering and in the very exhausted Christ simultaneously divine ravishment and most elevated ecstasy. This is the highest test for the extraordinary riches of the total amount of His life-force,of an unusual energy of concentration and incredible idealistic self-control.

He is, at the same time, penetratetd by nails,scourged by whips, covered with public scorn, and is, on the other side, in a position to send the lightnings of His charming idealism, with undisturbed confidence,to the most distant ranges of the universe.

Once He yields to the extraordinary tension between the realistic peripheric and idealistic central fixation of His psycho-pupil, once the central ecstasy almost is defeated by the power of sensorial pain of His peripheric experience, it is in the moment when He is crying: My God, my God, why hast Thou forsaken me? we appreciate this feature of concession to general human nature because of the tremendous necessity of expected psychological compensation. We are so much satisfied with the excellent proof of the psychological strength of the suffering hero that we have only tears of compassion in the moment when He makes clear allusion to the weakness of human nature,when He stops a moment with His tremendous affective effort and opens his psychopupil for a minute as though for a breath of realistic recreation. By His exclamation He stoops from the majesty of His continuous concentrated ideals and approaches the general human compensation of intellectual doubt, where He transiently fixes His attention. Here at least comes a real cloud over the bright soul of this divine hero; this moment at least the ghostly distraction of doubt in pain entered into the holy intimacy of His most central confidence always ready to meet terminal divine attraction.

What a difference from our usual manner of psychic reactions! The multiplicity and intensity of the peripheric experience of life troubles our mind and checks or absorbs our affective energy.In the degree as we use our forces to display intellectual work,we are likely to lose more or less the power of concentration and deep penetration. We necessarily pay tribute to the limit of the totality of our life-force never exceeding the boundaries of our personal vital strength. It is owing to the law of compensation that we easily lose our fixation to eternal goals, if we cling to the external occupation of life and that we likely give up our harmonious peace and our idealistic confidence, not being happy in the multiplicity of the intellectual world.Despairing in the business occupation means an excess of tasks absorbing our forces. Our modern life with its exacting activity pulls our life-force exclusively to the peripheric multiplicity. Our idealistic zeal and our communication with the divine has to-day a decreasing tendency, because the whole of our affective strength is withheld within the most detailed steps of the visible world. We often are even in danger not to be entirely sufficient for the peripheric actions of our daily life, and it is here where we suffer as well from the onesided use of our gifts as from insufficiency of our life-force. The enormous longing for charming pleasure is another form of psycho-mechanic craving for balance of peripheric work and concentrated delight, and we no sooner change the realistic character of our work into more idealistic efforts than a more quiet and modest desire for recreation will appear again. The fluid of our psychic affectivity flows untiringly, as the water of a sea, to and fro between the central concentration and peripheric disclosure of our experience, and always necessarily the concentration and localization of natural endowment changes and alternates incessantly like ebb and flow of the ocean.

The representation of Christ, by modern artists, as a mere flash of light, is very relevant. It means destroying the concentrative suggestion of His life, if we will depict Him in the whole realm of our categories of time, space and causality. The idea to represent the religious hero, in art, as a flash of light, a shining hem of a gown or a bright hand, is very efficient. If the hero never enters into the stage of our real visible human nature, he does not fail to exercise the full weight of his charging ideal influence. We are so much amenable to every influence of our senses, the avidity of our nature to magnetic fixation in peripheric life is so considerable that we lose the unity and strength of strong affective attention in the moment, when we are excited by manifold sensorial urges. Intellectuality has the first right on our psychic reactions, and only by skilful and cunning artistic help arises the possibility to lull their sensorial energy and to permit the almost totality of our life-force to concentrate and fix itself in the delightful point of penetrating idealism. Careful exclusion of the multiple visibility is essential for idealistic elevation. Too numerous real exact fixations weaken our elastic sway to overcome the narrow sill of symbolic signs for powerful excursion into the universe.

Never the follower of greatest concentrated affectivity may be met in the lanes of the outspread multiplicity of life. They are in pronounced psycho-mechanic opposition. There is always the question of economy of our total psychic life-force continuously proving to be insufficient to do both functions most thoroughly. Our soul has the inclination to go on in the peculiar manner of reaction, where it succeeds best, and becomes through experience, repetition and practice, at the end, much more affective-idealistic than realistic or intellectual-realistic than idealistic.

The light is the typical comparison with the most concentrated attitude of the psychopupil.Let us remember the burning small light-point coming out from the narrow concentration of the light-field of the magnifying glass. The dazzling intensity and the burning central flame are produced only in the last moment of progression to most complete punctual concentration. All surroundings are hidden in dark shadow which is very intense and sharply limited in the immediate neighbourhood of the light-circle and diminishes round the enlarged light-circle. The flame is the concentration of all light in one point; it sucks its existence from the surrounding sunbeams and has most efficiency,if there is least day-light immediately around. An intense clarity lavishly poured out over the whole surface of reality does not permit the light to shine. The force of the light consists in its contradiction to the darkness of the surrounding night, and its increasing diameter gradually loses its energy and significance while the lighting of the surroundings increases. The light effectuates a continuous emanation from its chemical life-source to the surroundings and pours more and more its accumulated force of energy to the darker periphery. For every fire there is a time to effuse kindling fire flickering with charming tongues towards heaven, but also a time of exhaustion and consumption, when it loses its shining life-force and fades away. The light is a life, a motion, a communion of strong vital moments; it is an expression of the interesting laws of gravitation and natural selection which choose one object to be the bearer of their concentrated life-force, as the lightning bolt obeying the law of necessity hits one point instead of a thousand.

This seems to be the preferable way of intercourse between the ideal and real world; one point alone is the thorough-fare of mutual communication: through this humble yoke the interchange of forces can be best performed.

The selected point of the light, with its sure localization of strength is not entitled or inclined to retain all the richness given to it by the liberal preference of fate, but is naturally inclined to surrender it to the surrounding night. All life is bound to give up life, and all concentration and strength and compensatory one-sidedness,any accumulation of energy will see the day of death and consumption.The lightning phenomenon of punctual concentration going through all physical and psychic life is perhaps the most important and radical clue in order to explain the process of life and its reactions. The touch of the glaring lightning-bolt is the great phenomenon of the creative world,its selective force and power of concentration, its exclusive predilection of one localized punctual expresion is not only recognizable in the thunder storm and in the electrical and magnetic experiment, but as well in psychological life and activity.

In the breeding development of races and times the growing strength of suggestion to accumulation of affective energy, the fact of lightning and striking congestion is not less remarkable and pronounced. The condensaticn of any cultural values makes an anxiously growing obstacle against concentrative discharge of affectivity towards idealism. It is because of this extraordinary development of affective compression and sentimental congestion not utilized by the highest cultural ages that the onesidedness of intellectuality, owing to psycho-mechanical necessity,creates a strong and inevitable, craving desire for the affective genius.

THE AFFECTIVE GENIUS is the personal condensation of the sentimental atmosphere of a whole age and culture.He is the true lightning through which, cwing to individual selection,the intellectually effused sentimental life-force is gathered and finally discharged towards ideal divinity. The religious genius is the glaringly illuminated spot of intellectual reality which has been touched by the strongest energy of affective idealism,he is the individual representative of the psycho-mechanic longings and necessities of whole generations and nations,whose intellectually obstructed affective delivery he condenses and combines in the gigantic capacity of his personality. He is the chosen divine ambassador going from the earth, on the winged feet of his condensed energy through the door of individually simplified symbolism,to the utmost elevation of eternal idealism.

The genius is, therefore, the true light of the world, sucking out and concentrating all neglected idealistic longings and spiritual necessities of people, who practically are forced to try to effectuate their affective discharge by multiple intelllectual fixation,in their daily working life. Alike as the positive and negative electricity of earth and heaven is not likely to proceed in flat and multiple meetings of both opposite forces, but in the one punctual representative spot of the lightning, which is the sparkling rod for the concentrated communication of the opposite poles,- so the genius is the wonderful magnetic mediator between intellectual and affective values,between reason and sentiment, between the visible and the unseen, between heaven and earth. He is the affective trance of the whole created intellectual world condensing in him the whole sum of magnetic theistic inclination of all mankind to strong idealistic concentration. He therefore is the central point of attention and love of all gifted: he is the exponent of all highest hopes and views, the charming crown and the glittering diamond of the psychology of whole nations. Through the individually limited river of this central symbolic channel flow the human and creative affective life-force of nations and ages with unheard of rapidity and immeasurable penetration.

All greatest men came out of the ages of high cultural development,—we meet them always in connection with outspoken political power and intellectual display. They are affective lightnings gathering their force from the enormous detailed energy of real activity from which concentration had been retained. The more business life with its onesided intellectual strength is developed, the more we discover always the compensation of the genial intensity. They at least are the greedy aspirators and transformers of charming eternal values; they passionately gather the whole magnetic forces of physiological intensity, in the nations and historic periods, and discharge all atmosphere of sultry hyper-tension of universal energy.

This is the explanation of the surprising fact that all great men always appeared under the magnetic suggestion of great ages. We always observe this fact, if we consider history; we see again and again flourishing artistic beauty and genial development at the courts of great political and wealthy centres. Let us remember the history of Greece, Rome, France, Spain, Austria, Italy and England. We always see the highest development of their power and political might at the same time, when they give the most genial men to humanity. Within the same time, within the same nation and exactly within the most crowded and very concentrated cultural points of these typical national powers we always find the spawning of the genial individual. He arises from the atmosphere of cultures like a lofty explosion from the creeping mist of inflammable gases. Shakespeare, Beethoven, Cervantes, Corneille and Racine were affective lightning bolts of striking energy at the very top of their national culture. According to the psychomechanic laws of compensation the exceeding onesidedness of material culture and exclusively objective display of life-force produces the genius as a powerful signal of emergency giving way to the enormous pressure of stagnated affectivity. A genius is, therefore, always an affective complement of an hyper-intellectual time. He is then most likely to be produced, when materialism and pride of real power are at the top of success. Victories of political nations, of intellectual scientific knowledge and material wealth create unsurmountable peripheric walls for affective discharge towards abstract idealism, and there it is,where we find the birth place of the outbursting compensatory genius. He is the tremendous spiritual outcry of the peripheric fixation of humanity and is in a position to re-establish the psycho-mechanic harmonious balance between reason and sentiment,between the multiple visibility of the objective world and the hyper-sensorial forces of the universe.

No sooner the affective sky-rocket of the genius has raised his charming sentimental energy than it falls down again to the affective dryness of the wide spread light-field of the real world to the sterility of merely intellectual life and fertilizes the whole plane of human society. Like a sheaf of fire or a powerful geyser the genius arises irresistibly to heaven, but he falls down again as a fine sprinkling rain engendering the whole surface of the peripheric dark and sterile earth. First the real and intellectual death of the resigning affective genius, then his splendid resurrection in outspreading and sparkling beauty and greatness over the whole detailed intellectual world. If Christ says that He must diminish in order to allow us to increase,He hints to this universal law of affective circulation in the world, where He is chosen to be the exceedingly powerful symbol of most concentrated geniality coming out as a complementary psycho-mechanic reaction of an entirely materialistic age, and directing His augmented and multiplied affective totality to unbelieved idealistic goals. He speaks out what nobody of His age found the courage or ability to speak and opens sources of expression, which were not only closed in the hearts of the exteriorized world, but which give to them back most psychic freedom. For life means a continuous supply to those deep feelings manifested by Him, and does not permit an exclusive application of our life-force in intellectual and material work. All our talents must have their proper functions and performances unless we have to risk neurasthemia, anger and slothfulness.

In the charming spray of sprinkling light falling down on all psychic and visible creation, the powerful concentration of the returning genius is divided into infinitely fine sparks of enlightening beauty,energy and truth inducing every fertilized individual to more activity. The latter augments while the genius decreases. He sacrifices in the very true and deep sense of the word his individual values in order to fertilize, to make strong the collective totality of his fellow-men. He himself fades away like a flower— a far-away remembrance, serving all—in giving all.

Growing cultures need geniuses and are able to produce them by bestowing, on gifted idealists, the assistance of their rich obstructed affectivity. The material business life and the intellectual onesidedness are the best complementary ground to give this power of affective force to individuals who are especially inclined to be efficient affective lightning-conductors in order to prevent the explosive disturbances of psychic diseases and unhappy life, which are consequences of lack of harmony between our intellectual-real and sentimental-idealistic endowment. Idealisticly gifted persons ought to go to materially aspiring and intellectually flourishing states in order to receive and practise there their affective priesthood and terminal-idealistic leadership.

No sooner the charming distribution of the countless affective sparks of the genial force has fallen down to earth than his existence is not necessary any longer. The genius throws out of his eternal life-force as much as he gathered and sucked in from the culture of his surroundings during his lifetime. According to the importance of his personal ability and idealistic ability and to the expansion and strength of his cultural life and atmosphere he is in a position to give back what he received. A culture of thousand of years of age and of extraordinary expansion is of course much more able to impart lasting and powerful productive influences, through the medium of its genius than a short and relatively narrow cultural epoch. Everything works within the limits of mathematical exactitude and compensatory balance; how could we wish a different law?

After a certain period of brilliant sparkling, the energy of the genius ceases. His whole stock of ideal energy has become the general good of mankind who are thoroughly transformed and imbibed of them. The notion of Fashion is just in this connection extraordinarily important. We may call it frivolous or fickle, but we never may forget that fashion means change, motion, active life, which bears as well on dressing as on science, affective art and even religion. STYLE is an expression of religion, a special fashion of a peculiar form of feelings, which wear out at the same time as their founding principles and ideas. Even conceptions of eternal things change. It is unnatural to retain tastes and ideas which are out of fashion.

Nature likes change because it will have, above all, emotional energy of life. It craves not only for superficial, but for deepest and essential moods and changes of the taste and expressive form of life-force. In history one genius must disappear on behalf of an other , and even if he is almost unexhaustibly rich,in liberal life spent to the world,he must obey the law of fashion and change affective emotion. The reason of the fact that we are subjected to fashion is the formalistic part of our nature,which is excited by new and bored by old repeated representations.

The genius has accomplished his role when his ideas are effused into the open light-field of the world,when every particle of his energy has found an adequate detailed reality. When his feelings have penetrated the hearts of all following generations,then these treasures are the hereditary riches of humanity and represent a precious addition of increased nobility for human nature. The powerful genial concentration has vanished. The genius gave his heart and his blood, like a pelican, to the outspread countless nations;now his fellow-creatures have grown in ideal strength,in more affective concentration.The great god is dead, but countless smaller ones have risen to life,by his death. The first shall be last and the last first. The genius must go to the Father in order to make live his followers.

DECADENCE means, in our current language, the transition from the exclusively intellectual materialism to the affective hyper-emphasis., a proceeding to extreme sentimental feelings. At this period the genial lightning of connection and reconciliation between intellect and feelings are no longer valuable for the affective force is everywhere fully divided and distributed and a general distension of the light-field was definitely attained. The beginning not too pronounced decadence means affective inspiration of the individual and all objectivity to the right balance of mind and heart, the reobtainment of the highest human dignity and the reestablishment of popular nobility of most important affective values which had been lost during the intellectual and material slavery of an exclusively realistic and visible reign. For every human individual has the claim and need to share the immediate transition of spiritual power going from his real light-field to eternal idealism and to be thus himself priest of the universe. Is not the average individual short in his affective metabolism and discharge, as long as the genius keeps concentrated all affective national energy?

FREEDOM means essentially the right of personal direct intercourse with the last magnetic forces of the universe, in an affective way. We are free if ur heart is in a position to approach the highest and deepest values of the universe, and we always remain slaves as long as we are not in possession of the genial spark which gives us the magnetic energy and direction to reach the most remote universal values.

Decadent ages produce geniuses. The force of affectivity of genial people of former generations have already fertilized the masses with their uplifting energy and they are themselves now in a position to enjoy easily idealistic values. They are protected against the hunger for idealism, of former times; they know and see clearly and feel easily the charming sources of highest beauty and strongest attraction. They have an unchangeable security of direction for idealistic steering; they are themselves geniuses for other countries and ages.

In the time of material culture the world has lost its affective dignity; the genius has gathered and concentrated it in the stupendous force of his personality. The genius is like a diamond or a piece of gold in regard to other minerals and metals. All kinds of matter begin to sparkle with an intense light as soon as they are energetically compressed. This law bears on all materials from the visible world up to the highest affectivity. The strongest charming spark of the diamond comes out through the extraordinary physical energy of compression; in business life, the result of concentrating effort and strong condensation is the golden splendour of riches, but in the psychical life, we recognize as the last production of social inheritance and personal logical effort the genius. He is the transforming saviour from the slavery of materialism, he is the energetic central channel of uplifting idealism and eternal spirit enrapturing all together to join in his divine race. He has all the riches of heaven in his personal power, while the right possessors of this psychic energy are doomed to be the poor slaves of real narrow restriction and intellectual material confinement.

From the beginning, but always more and more with the proceeding time, Christ withdraws His charming personality from the exact limits of time, space and causality and becomes therefore the most international and intertemporal possession of the world.

Length of ages volatilizes our personality. As soon as death has drawn its dark curtain over our intellectual individuality and localized visibility, we begin to have more chances to spread out the force of our affective importance. The dispersion of a general force is the more efficient, the more the individual component is pushed in the background. Ideas need a long time for their growth and expansion over the earth like the crown of a tree. The richer the individual genius is, the longer and deeper will be his effect on the nations. If a genius has a background of a small, geographically and linguistically restricted area, his influence must be smaller than that of a more able who transgresses the separating limits of languages and races. His reach will extend over all mountains, his high and kindling enthusiasm will be carried over broad seas and transport to delight the hearts of most remote tribes.

The cry to heaven, of the ancient nations: Pour down, oh heavens, the just, and clouds, rain him down to earth! is the inevitable outburst of their psychological necessity, the outcry of an entirely materialized and intellectualized time which had lost all facilities for lofty idealism and eternal sentiments. It is the collective desire of an intellectually fixed and directed time which makes the thoroughness of this idealistic compensatory prayer. This prayer is the expression of the sultry atmosphere of the discontented old nations, of destroyed human dignity and material depravation. All the abused crowds of capable people oppressed in slavery and servitude, during countless centuries, join the powerful choirs singing incessantly, full of fervour: 'Pour down, oh heavens, the just, and clouds, rain him down to earth!' From the hearts of all these millions of tramped-down slaves of the previous ages of the world, who all were gifted with desires for ideal happiness and susceptibility of love, the delightful and mighty geyser of Christ sprang forth, a compensatory affective condensation and energetic fly-wheel to highest idealistic values.

Christ was at that time the greatest psychological necessity of the affective world, because the affective congestion was of a most dangerous degree and needed most urgent remedy. Christ was the necessary last factor of refuge of the old Jewish and Roman world, the symbolic personality to which the light-field of his contemporary historic social psycho-pupil had to collapse in order to allow the world to overcome the multiple rich reality and to throw, through the most able affective channel of his genius, all hopes, all confidence and longings, retained and deceived in despair for long centuries out to the universe. Any offence, all injustice, pain and sin of the old time, all terrible suppression and crime and all checked pleasure for normal human pleasure gather in this enormous genial outlet of affective life-force and rush, converted, to their ideal goal with dazzling splendour, enrapturing magnetic elevation and most charming beauty.

That quite intellectual and exteriorized historic time must have had an unparalleled compensatory avidity for Christ's affective teachings. The avidity was so strong that millions of sensitive people died in ecstasy, for this conception of eternal enjoyment. They all were imperturbably fixed, in their punctual idealistic attention and could not be diverted by the most cruel MARTERDOM. They all were of high spiritual-affective gift, and they were the more liable of becoming victims of a cruel death the more they had that talent. They followed Christ to the very top of His idealisic enthusiasm and of His astounding fixation of idealistic energy. That quite materialistic age availed itself of the martyrs in the same way and under the same conditions as of their prototype Christ. They were most efficient helpers for the universal communication of the world. Exactly in the first time of psycho-mechanic change of the Roman Empire to the idealistic side of their psychological emphasis, after the initiation of this direction by Christ, the avidity for concentrating compensation was the strongest and therefore the struggling resistance most thorough.. Countless highly gifted individuals were sacrificed the same way as their master, assisting him in lifting the curtain of a new scenery of culture.

CRUELTY is a state of primitive exaggeration of new principles of which the force is put to a practical test. There is the tendency of establishing utmost opposition and tension between the central strength of these principles and ideas and the trial of peripheric diversion through energetic sensorial intervention. Therefore we find cruelty always in the first time of introduction of new religious, political and other experiences. The known predilection of children for cruelty, is the inclination for study of the natural laws of life; they will find out not only the different components of life, but also their mutual reactions and the affective degree of their peculiar nature. They put them in artificial connections and opposition; they choose the most opposite distances of vital factors, they try to cause diversions of idealistic purposes and high goals through peripheric exciting and burning actions and succeed, in this way, to valuate the different standards of sentimental forces of life. The genius being praised unto the heavens, the heroes and martyrs are the people who prove the superiority of idealistic standards, as it is, on the other side the comfortable yielding to the exterior difficulties of life, which is to be considered as responsible for the progressing materialism and for the general scorn of the most magnetic affective capacities of the universe. The martyrs are the salt of idealism; the idealists go with a bee-line to the test of cruelty, because the world is wondering to find out the importance and real purport of the pretended idealistic strength. The searching mind of a child tormenting an animal, the struggles in family, political and religious life up to rack, fire and cross, the French or Russian revolution or a simple bull-fight look all,under different conditions, for scientific equations between affective and sensorial influences on the individual being expected to prove the impossibility of real diversion from its pretended strong purposes.

Christ was the radical initiator of the decadence of the Roman Empire,in their sense; He was the tremendous consuming fire devouring this intellectual organism,at last. He was put, for a co-incidence of many reasons, in a position to relieve all inveterate detailed fixations from the affective periphery and to absorb them all in His genial symbolic divinity.The world in its turn could not help it hating Christ, it being its duty of self-preservation and natural compensation exactly as Christ and his true followers despised the world. If the old Romans killed the affective genius in and after Christ, they did it in order to keep their energy away from this tremendous power of attraction and charm, - and when Christ hid himself, when Christians went to deserts and catacombs and when even to-day millions of religious people enclose them-selves behind walls in order to es ape the rich reality of the wordly life, they do it in order not to succumb to the attractions of the other side of the human psycho-mechanism. Affectivity is rightly aware of the impressive seductions of the sensory part of the visible world, and intellectuality has reason to be afraid of the magnetic strength of the affective force in whose sentimental whirlpool it is easily driven.

The affective genius is, therefore, supposed to be the helper of the sinful,unhappy and miserable.They all together represent the obstructed state of the affective soul, which craves for pervious furtherance. They all are the previous psycho-mechanic tension of the mighty affective spring of which the genius is the energetic distension. They are the peripheric fixation of our life-force, in the complicated reality; they check the human social psycho-pupil from concentration,and cause, for this reason at length such an accumulation of biological onesidedness and therefore longing for affective concentration, such an intense stagnation of feelings, that in a given moment the obstacle is surmounted and the whole sum of intellectually bridled life-force smitten, at once, into the punctual symbolic centre. Intellectual obstacles,as we have them in disease,pain,sorrow,sin,unhappiness,hideousnes,extreme riches and poverty, are the peripheric slothfulness of our psychic energy and it is the affective genial energy of concentration, which corresponds to the need of the respective stagnations.

These questions are in the nearest relationship with the idea of individual fixation of our life-force in EGOTISM, another fundamental form of narrow affective restriction. Perhaps the multitude of human individuals would not be necessary , if really one greatest genius could selflessly surrender all affectivity to last idealistic goals, and humanity would not need geniuses, were men individually not so far removed from the desirable state of just affective congruancy in regard to the scale of affective standards in the objective and spiritual world.

Genius means the very concentration of affective life-force. As all strong compressions produce light and fire, the powerful genius is expected to be always brilliant. He is the most charming and most important phenomenon of the creation. He is produced by cultural necessity and by utmost need of his social environment. The genius is the terminal jubilant conversion of all human affective troubles.

The gospels are full of allusions to the genial conception of Christ. If He calls Himself the first born, primogenitus, He means that He is linked up nearest and first with the Father, the magnetic terminal goal of all creatures. If He claims to be the unicus unigenitus filius, the unique son of God, He pretends to be the very first genius of mankind, to be the strongest genial representative of the numerous ancient peri-Mediterranean cultures, especially the Jewish, Latin and Greek world. He pretends to be the very first genius of human history, who has succeeded more than any other in gathering and concentrating a most considerable amount of affective life-force within the gigantic capacity of His genial personality. He claims to have the richest cultural background which ever had been erected in the intellectual visibility of human society and to have gathered most repressed affectivity from many centuries of material misery, quarrelling unhappiness and tyrannical oppression in order to throw it out more efficiently and brilliantly unto the highest hills of eternity than any other genius or prophet ever did. Chinese, Indian, Arabian and other religious founders share with Him the surface of the globe, in performing the spiritual transformation of human forces. They all claim and do their part in affective hygiene, in their countries.

Christ hints to the fact, that the root of His genial personality reaches as far as Jewish history. He says that in His name every knee will be bent, which is to say that His central affective energy has an irresistible influence of attraction on all human beings in the reach of His culture, that He is the strongest directive psychic force subjecting all to worship Him.

Whatsoever ye shall ask in my name, it shall be granted unto you. In this saying He will express that His believers may choose the way of concentration through the tested symbolic light of His sublime personality, and this way may be more easy and practicable because He had equipped it with refined power of suggestion. In saying: If I be lifted up to the CROSS, I shall draw all men unto me, He hints to the shuddering intellectual—real confirmation of His affective—divine mission under the 'cruel' circumstances of the passion and the cross, and He puts all emphasis and confidence in this cruel show of victorious hyper-sensorial concentration through which He is convinced He will attract any human heart accessible to compassion. On the cross He claims to prove to have an idealism stronger and higher than even the most burning sensorial influence and diverting sensational impression. Had He defeated in this opportunity all the sensorial and sensual powers of the world, in the most thorough manner, He would think to refute all objections of reality against His idealistic tenets, in pointing out that they were stronger than all visible reality and sensorial influence, that they are, therefore, more important, more essential and real and deserve most attachment and admiration.

Is not it the most definite clearest statement of Christ's authoritative genial claims, when He is saying the words: 'I am the way, the truth and the life'? We always must visualize the sublime superiority of the genius who is so great, general and admirable, because elevated over the categories of time, space and causality. All His sayings and expressions reveal, at every point, the strong and ruling energy of his affective life and of its sublime goals and he, therefore, always refers to this strong idealistic-terminal magnetism. If he really has that enormous affective-symbolic concentration, as we learned before, we undoubtedly must believe him to be in most direct and strongest connection with divine truth. He is the life as much as he is the clearly visible and smooth symbolic threshold for our affective emotion to which he claims to have prepared the easiest selective passage to divine values. He is the last finger-post on the way to God, the ultimate beacon shining over to our real world from the most distant cliffs of the universal ocean.

A quite deep conception of the geniality of Christ is handed to us by St. John's appellation of LOGOS. Logos means word and expresses, therefore, thoroughly the special role of the fascinating personality of the genius, demonstrating his two-sided importance of an indispensible transforming power from intellectuality to affective sentiments. A word in every case is a collective expression of intellectual characteristics,in :. very great or very small, merely symbolic number, within the fra e of a notion. By the number of these intellectual characteristics the size and circumference of a notion is fixed so that we, in one case, have a very wide and in an other, very narrow and small expansion of a notional light-field The word is a most exact real-visible fixation of this notion;it is in a position to convey to the abstract mental characteristics the exterior sensorial expression of a picture. The word is, through this power, the two-sided head of the mythological JANUS, who had two faces looking in opposite directions.Every word looks with one face into the real intellectual world and with the other into the realm of abstract idealism and to affective values. The word is the mediator between both, the changing transition from the intellectual details to the affective general life of sentiments. It is the remarkable sign comprising on one side a certain amount of objective reality, a compensatorily corresponding part of fixed sentiments, within the ring of its real characteristic size.

We learn, therefore, in the word essentially the most refined human sign of transforming reality into ideality, of thougths into feelings, of visibilities and details into abstract generality. The word is for us the most important and charming door, through which we enter from the real and intellectual life into the beyond of our control. We easily recognize in the word again the light-circle of our psycho-pupil which has a bearing on the law of compensation, the most energetic force in the most concentrated affective light-field and the weakest in a large light-field. This compensation, as we pointed out in our former writings on 'The Delight in Poetry', baers entirely on words and notions. Those most simple in intellectual characteristics are the affectively most powerful, most able to catch our total life-force and to throw it, with glittering beauty to the stars, while the complicated words are much less able to drive our psychic force to strong magnetic goals. We pointed out in the concerning chapter of'Delight in Poetry', how much all activity of the poetical writer is directed by this compensatary truth, in a progressive concentrating way. In this way he lands easily at the terminal charming most affective notions of beauty, truth, hope, confidence and love.The intellect-ual face of Janus has grown very small in these simple notions, whilst the affective assumes an enormous size and absorbs most magnetic life-force in favour of the idealistic side of our nature.

We must agree that Christ too has an enlarged view and attention for the idealistic universe and a relative negligence for the realistic world. His face is tremendously magnified on the side of idealism, and is surprisingly thin on the side of detailed intellectuality, more than that of His followers who are exceedingly rich in petty intellectual experiences. His idealistic face is lovingly developed and attracts us irresistibly by its brilliant distinction and beautiful enrapturing features, but His intellectuality, on the other side of the Janus head, is accordingly very small, blurred in its features and poor in details. Have we to take this fact as an educational regard for our human weakness and insufficiency? Even Christ cedes to the psycho-mechanic law of compensation which never allows strong affective idealistic discharge in the high ideas of beauty, truth and love without simultaneous strong intellectual concentration and narrow notional light-circles.

We used, from the beginning, the term SYMBOL for the concentrated light-field. It is the two-faced head of a real-ideal Janus, quite large and important to the idealistic, comparatively superficial to the realistic side. The symbol is the absorbing transformer from the real to the ideal world. It takes the numerous small points of affective fixation from their objective localization, gathers them in a concentrated refined symbol and throws this combined force through its greedily sucking whirlpool into the universe.

Christ is not only the Logos, the word, the parole of the Christian era, where all these nations meet and understand each other, He is the symbolic word, which means the most simplified intellectual formula of strongest real concentration and foremost energetic sentimental discharge. He is the common intellectual sign of agreement, and international meeting, the powerful traditional suggestive facilitation to highest values.

The affective genius is through the nature of his make-up the forwarder of old cultures to younger ones, he is the refined common platform of intellectual and simultaneously mysterious intercourse connecting both. Here we meet the point of affective fixation, in the genius as the simplified and strong result of all work of former centuries and ages. We are surprised in admitting that exactly our most intimate and holy cultural secrets turn out to be nearest linked up with old vanished times. One age gives its culture to the following one in the concentrated form of a genial diamond. One epoch fertilizes the other one; one political and cultural empire is the intellectual key-stone of the next. We use as our most undoubted and appreciated principles the quintessence of ancient experience and wisdom, which have been forwarded to us in the form of the symbolic mystery of a genius. What we think to be most essentially our own, is the inheritance of former ages and the condensed jewel left to us by dead old generations, offered to us like supporting crutches to do our own work of augmenting civilization. We received in the genial symbolism, from old times owing to its spiritual conversion of former intellectual values, a stabilized fixation in order to work energetically possessing the shining light of genial stars , not to be stifled in the atmosphere of our multitude of intellectual tasks and duties. Every culture serves as basis for the next one, encouraging it through the mighty aspirators of its magnetic symbols, until the younger age is strong enough to produce its own great geniuses and to be crushed and discarded in its turn, dropping the old worn out, yet necessary crutches of old genial symbolism, giving way to the general law of change and fashion , which underlies all life and all nature. We take for granted, in the symbolic round-about way, what former cultures experienced to be right, and later ages will accept,in symbolic genial crystallisation , what the totality of our working experience teaches us to be best. The link from culture to culture always is the genius, who does not permit that the smallest old experiences of humanity are lost , but preserved and handed over, in concentrated form, as bright symbolic precious stones to later generations.

"How can we be the heirs of former ages," you object, "if we observe the contradiction of the alternating movements of idealistic and realistic psychological waves? Opposing your idea",you continue,"we know that Europe became sentimental though it was the successor of the realistic Antiquity, and America, instead, is realistic, because its immigrant children were frightened and disappointed by the effects of their idealistic home countries."The character of this alternating transformation of the cultural Janus head of humanity depends on the SYMBOLIC CONVERSION.

The genius is the important turn-table or turning-pin which exchanges the direction of the two faces of the psychological Janus head of ages and cultures. His high mission in this exceedingly interesting connection between two cultures one following the other; at that time his inter-psychological importance is of highest dignity. His principal task is to serve the promotion of the function of life-force, to renew the direction of working life with a new temperamental starting run and give other methods of spiritual impulses. The genius gives a new magnetic force by new views, he delivers the cultures and nations from the old and worn out garment of a genial system of yore and replaces it by the splendour of his attractive and impressive novelty. It is the law of life that all old things,even the best, must fade away and die and give way to the necessity of a morning of quite new conceptions and methods. The magnetic force of concentrating life needs,again and again the representation of the old energy in a new dress; the best wine of all real intellectuality becomes flat and insipid in old hoses and is liable to lose its enthusing force - like old used coins which, from long circulation, show no longer the original distinct picture of the king.

A strong symbolic action has always the supposition of a very suggestive and efficient sensorial impression. The exacting affective BOUND over all cliffs of the radius of the light-field, from the detailed visible periphery to the symbolic centre needs so much energy that the sensorial susceptibility of the individual must be hit very thoroughly, in order to bring about the effect of concentration at once. The intellectually concentrated light-circle of a symbol must be very clear and accessible, must be bright in colors and intensity like a nuptial torch of delight. If this central symbolic attraction of the senses is most efficient, we have the best guarantee of a strong affective concentrator.

For this reason we might likely find the most universally reverential type of mankind in the countries, where the symbolic genial organization is traditionally most elaborated and fixed. The force of incessant practice and methodical repetition during centuries has augmented extraordinarily so that we have a great facility of pushing the peripheric individual experience towards the centre. Through this traditional habitual facility to move into the symbolic light, even the most helpless man is supposed to discharge easily his affective life-force toward most elevated goals.

The strong fixation of historical and traditional genial symbolic signs becomes a hereditary achievement of the most skilful nature. These symbolic lights have, after centuries, the enormous attractive force and effect of a spell: they have then a quite automatic irresistible attraction on whole nations and civilizations, which become altogether prisoners of these charms having penetrated and overcome all peripheric life and individual logic long ago.

When a young affective genial period, after violent battles, is once settled, there is for a long time, no view for intellectual resistance to the incomparable suggestive force of genial symbolism which through the addition of innummerable repetitions of affective longings towards its difficult obtainment, - of being spread out through the most remote countries and tribes of the earth, - through the extraordinary genial value of the founders and the cultures from which they rose, through the long historical organization , the long habitual support and lasting deepening inheritence, receive at last a weight and importance which overtakes any individual and kills any other inclination to intellectual symbolic arbitrary localization of our inventive psycho-mechanic activity. We all are the most strictly ruled slaves of the foremost genial symbols of our age, which becomes so engrossed with its genial suggestive zeal that every least trial of intellectual or individual independent motion is considered to be a public crime, worthy of public persecution. So much increases the influence of an important symbolic genius. The intensity of his light breaks in all radial directions from the centre of the light-field to the margin of the periphery; he shows through the overwhelming beauty and radiance of his symbolic beacon the direct way to his central genial sign which he has put unchangeably, by his strength and superiority in the bull's eye of our cultural light-field.

This sun of powerful life has the sooner reach d the top of its influence and ruling government, as it pours out lavishly its energy to all sides of the intellectual periphery and detailed objectivity. The genial sun spending liberally is in danger of exhausting its energy, and the receiving periphery is liable, on the other hand, not to be able to accept any more the one-sided influences of its time, because it is hyper-saturated with them. The more the genial symbolism of a time has reached enormous strength and real success the more and sooner there comes a point of inevitable affective revolution against a method whose excellent influences have lasted a long time and have had their full expected effect for educating humanity. Genial self-control, the most improbable thing, is therefore necessary; the right medium of rhythmic activity is even here valuable and indispensable so that we understand now, why the old Greek temples showed the inscription: "Meden agan!" "Do not go too far in anything!"

The genial ideal is not the ultimate goal of our affective life, it is the brilliant door helping us to the most distant and most principal eternal magnetism. As little as we are entitled to hurt or mutilate the humanized symbol of the genius in our imagination, we can retain it in the visible world without serious danger of strong affective fixation at the threshold of concentrated enjoyment. In this case our affective force is not permitted to go through the concentrated punctual hole of the symbolic sign of eternal values, but it is fixed at the sensory and intellectual part of the light-field, in the place of the reactive symbolic sill, what we call fixation in PLEASURE and what leads so easily to habitual pleasure-thirst. This last point is only the goal of our terminal affective discharge, even though a most precious diamond it may be to us. It never will be in a position to satisfy our hearts because of real localization, but it has the role of a preliminary stage of our idealistic terminal reaction. In this sense we recognize pleasure as an intellectual-sensorial function, and DELIGHT as the very terminal discharge of affective-idealistic reaction We are very inclined to be fixed and retained at the charming symbolic threshold or sill of our last intellectual concentration. The fixation of our affectivity in the immediate neighbourhood of

most concentrated reality means an enormous last obstacle before
we go through the symbolic opening to the always bold, but the
much more promising step of terminal discharge.

It happens very often, on the other side, that after having had
for a long time an excellent strength and energy to throw all obtainable life-force through the charming opening door of genial
symbols to the idealistic distances of the extreme magnetic universe, we lose one day this indispensable courage of bold reaction
and begin to stick to the sill of genial symbolic concentration of the
light- field which we before have developed exceedingly well in
artistic taste and riches. We acquired inadvertently a sensorial
RELAPSE from idealism to realism, from the abstract delightful
divinity to the intellectual reality of pleasure and technical art.

Thus we touch one of the most important and interesting problems of all times, whose solution and different conception has
caused the most excited discussions and even bloody slaughters of
human beings in religious wars, and, in addition, countless misunderstandings and prejudices. The gaping differences of methods
of different churches turn essentially on this idea to avoid the
strongest attractability of the genial symbol in order not to fix
the affective amount of the concentrating soul of the believer in
the last moment at the charming point of real pleasure, but to
give to him rather, through smooth simplicity, an easy passage
between the sirenic cliffs of the sill of affective discharge to idealism. This is the last difficult obstacle to be overcome by our
concentrating psycho-mechanic progression and, after having defeated this last localized avidity of our heart, we are sure to have
done the best work. Up to a certain amount, nature will have real
pleasure, but the strongest affective discharge and the most successful avoiding of sentimental stagnation are only possible in
continuous energetic tension and distension of the bow of our
faculties up to highest idealism and strongest terminal goals.

Christ summons us to pray to His Father in His name, through
Him. He claims to be the last symbolic finger-post, for the human
desire, on the way to the terminal divine goal, but of an extreme
necessity and aptitude, outside of which no name be given to humanity. He hints in these words to His mission as genial punctual
symbol, to His psycho-mechanic role of transitional turning-pin
between humanity and the universe If St. John says, in His sense:
"I and the Father are one," he means the most possible congruency
of His human affective standards with the universal will and force.
He hints to His most approached and favored intercourse with the

powers of highest divine value. He was the most central psycho-pupilar light of the human cultural soul at the time of the most repressed congestion of inter-spheric affective progression at the fulfilment of the time.

In spite of repeated assertions to be one with the Father, Christ maintains the idea to be something different from Him. We will follow most closely the idea, which He may have expressed, in calling Himself son in discrimination from the Father. Up to now we understand that He is the most brilliant sensorial expression of our human affectivity. He is linked up to us by the real side of His Janus head, which grasps our sensorial susceptibility and is the fundamental part of our common individual existence. By the intellectual narrow confinement of his symbolic character, the religious genius is a sharp and clear finger-post for terminal-idealistic signalization, characterizing Himself, simultaneously as real and remote from exclusive universal deity. His symbolic connection to our earth is the string by which we are fixed to universal grace, the symbol, is the toe of a divine ambassador, still touching, as the last part of his foot, the earth, when the hero is just transported to heavenly fields. The religious genius is the most capacious river of eternal affective grace flowing under highest pressure between the narrow shores of his symbolic concentration, but he does not identify himself with the last high-ways nor with the magnetic fluid of the universe.

The religious genius is for longest centuries and ages the DOOR for psycho-mechanic symbolic concentration. He claims to be the only person in a position, at the conditions of his time, to concentrate and idealize again the paralyzed world and he invites all mankind tenderly in saying: "Come unto me all ye that labor and are heavy laden, and I will give you rest." He has prepared so smooth and sharpened a symbolic sill that meeting him in the middle of the symbolic light-field is promising for idealistic discharge. He knows how much people need this new door to eternal treasures and he gathers them all like strayed sheep into the fold of his divine concentric love. How skilfully is the imaginative attractiveness of his charming personality achieved!

The danger of luxurious fixation within the sweetest bay of the enrapturing symbolic sill is radically cured, on the other hand, by the appalling fact that the strong prominent THORNS of the crown wound around the symbolic genius reach into the very centre of his concentrated love and compel us after being thrilled and attracted by his delightful charms and lofty elevation to utmost concentration, to leave, through the punctual opening of his genial symbolic light, to the universal magnetism and lost idealism. The stronger the concentration was,the more attractive and enthusing you find the new central localization, the sweetness of his yoke,- the more you will be surprised and frightened meeting the whole story of passion and pain grasping you inevitably and scaring you out from the genial door to the lap in the measureless universe. This last courage will be the greatest,you will be an excellent success of a shot to highest affective eternal ranges,but the preparatory steps are very difficult and the way very narrow.

The affective genius invites you with the charming smile of his concentrated idealistic beauty and pays you with the bitterness of his suffering. He attracts you near the window of his wonderful, star-like shining symbolism, through which the bewitching and longing force of idealism grasps our looks of admiring curiosity , and as soon as we are there, we are assailed by the cruel instruments of torture, so much so that we , with desperate boldness, supported by other beckoning star-lights, leap into the gulf of the limitless and mysterious night.

Death and birth and symbolic concentration are very near notions. All three are states of the utmost simplified intellectual form of individual existence and have, therefore, close philosophical relations.

The usual denomination of Christ as the SON of God or son of man characterizes and emphasizes His nature and attitude of mediator between universe and earth, between invisible affectivity and localized intellectuality,between terminal magnetism and inferior phases of magnetic power. According to this usual appellation in the gospel, Christ does not claim the fullness of the terminal greatness of the universal force, but the sonship of God.

How many times is hinted, always again, in impressive uplifting terms, to Christ's sonship with God, to His perfect harmony with him, above all, in the most genial gospel of ST. JOHN, which could be entitled the most perfect psychology of the genial character of the Christian hero. John is the philosophical revealer of the peculiar claims of the psycho-mechanic attitude of Christ, of His proportional position within the chain of universal standards and forces; he deals with the principal role of the genius, and, he rightly is, therefore, called the disciple of love which means the most affectively concentrated strength. St. John is,for this reason, painted resting at the breast of his beloved master whose most important and most essential mission he deeply discloses.Most characteristically for him, again, it is said that he, at his old age, when he was weak, continued saying: "Little children, love one another!" He in his continuous pithy inclination to explain the chief problems of Christ and His life, is the genial eagle of the Christian doctrine, since he deals exclusively with the affective bull's eye of the target of Christian teachings, in speaking of the charming love and beauty and strength of sentiments of his master.

What is the meaning of the expression: the son? In our earlier meditations on WORK, culture and creation we found out that every real work originally comes out from sentimental repulsion from the previous enjoyment in the deepest causes of the world and existence. Work follows the expulsion from the delightful garden of the Paradise. The stagnation of affectivity after the closure of the channel of the first love becomes so strong that the repudiated individual, driven by necessity, has to use its own natural gift in an other way and another direction. This is the very root of real work and creation: the magnetic necessity of changing our producing energy after previous repulsion from sentimental enjoyment is the psycho-mechanic key of cultural work, creation and generation.

Sonship means clear distinction from the father. It means difference of power, of individual unity and character; it presupposes former life and previous causal action on the part of the separated father. Christ put Himself, through the appellation son, in every case, into the realm of the categories of time, space and causality; He admits the affective priority of the Father who has begotten Him and He interpolates, therefore, Himself into the continuously rolling chain of creative development, in which He is the important link of the first genius, but not the terminal point where the whole universal chain is fixed and supported.

In the numerous impressive finger-posts of St. John, to Christ's sonship of God and the perfect union and intimacy between both, we always have allusions and conditions which, perhaps, are rather better explained by the expressions Logos, Symbol, Light and Point. But all together express the creative protection by a previous cause in regard to a later consequence, a signalizing shining light from the idealistic eternal world into the visibility of our conditions, a material localization of eternal values, an intellectual depositum of a lofty affective pro-creation.

He is said that His father is in heaven, while He is on earth, and that He is as well the son of man as of God. He is, therefore, chiefly keen of His outstanding mediatorship between the real and idealistic world, between universal forces and earth, between the sentimental heart and the understanding brain and eye, between effused eternal affectivity and distinctly limited visible reality. This is the incessantly repeated emphasis of His longing heart : to have the mission of an excellent interpreter between idealism and materialism, between the hidden strong longing forces for the universe in our soul and the intellectual categories of time, space and causality.

The root of the activity of any religious philosopher is to find out and elaborate the relations between these two distant ranges of ideal affectivity and intellectual materiality and to try to put them in the best Harmonious connection. To this task he devotes his whole life. Where must he place the short-gifted human nature within the very long finger-board of the large display of the forces of the universe and earth? Where will he put most successfully the restrained talents of human nature in the large scale of created and expected possibilities in order to attain the best result and avoid most damages For the human heart and mind and all nature have an extremely broad Potential disposition and are not easily retained or satisfied in a narrow confinement of the creative scale;   on the other hand, no individual has strength and gift enough to understand and absorb all these values. This is the reason that we consider so many things, unfortunately, as oppositions and contradictions, chiefly at the limit of our personal experience and reasoning power. How will the religious leader destroy this our narrow conception of the totality of existence and creative possibility, how do away with our clumsy tendency to take all as contradiction of our intellect and not to take the intellect as an enemy of the forces which belong to the realm of the sentiments? How can he hope to preserve our vital narrowness from the continuous danger of conceiving oppositions and meeting incommensurable sizes, where there are only distances of gradual and logical development, even if in measures and ranges of light-years, misunderstandable figures? That which by now is not yet within the limits of our approachable calculation, we shall put it one day in the frame of our understanding. The spiritual roots and views of our intellectual life are deep and rich beyond description. "Alles Vergaengliche ist nur ein Gleichnis."

Now and never we should be unfriendly or suspicious towards the universe and the world of distant affective values, even if they may be higher than our present understanding. In the same way we should not despise our material reality and the law of our logical restrictions of time, space and causality, because they are beneath eternal values.All these differences are merely questions of a different distance and of a different angle of consideration.The most mystic shining star enrapturing you by its dazzling punctual light, in the silent night,becomes a measurable body with intellectual details, when it approaches, and the richest cultural world shrinks to a tiny point, when it is removed far away. Intellect and sentiments are different functions of the same power; both use our total life-force in a different mould of working machinery.Both are equally essential to our naturally performing existence, only in a different phase of concentration and development. They are DISTANT, BUT NOT OPPOSITE functions and values.

In calling Himself son of God and man in the same important and reverent sense, in stating Himself to be continuously in perfect union, love and harmony with the Father though separated by sonship, Christ proves pronounced acknowledgement both of the affective idealism and the intellectual visible world. In putting these two components always again in most friendly connection, St. John endeavours to make friendly relations between the two distant ranges of sentiment and intellect, of heaven and earth, and he thus looks for principal reconciliation of these two points of tension,so ready to make troubles in the human disposition. Exactly in this conception and elaboration of the notion of the son of God and man we recognize the loving idea of Christ for all visible and invisible creation, and the declining attitude He shows, as a rule, towards the world,here at least is dropped with a pronounced philosophical-real statement. Realistic and visible projection of eternal life, human sonship of universal divinity can impossibly mean a state of aversion, hatred and unfriendliness towards the powers of heaven nor of the universe towards humanity, but that good connection and a grateful quiet intercourse should be possible between the two worlds; not exclusion, but neither self-destruction of our logical laws ought to be the consequence of our filial allegiance with the eternal powers.God loves us and if he has begotten us, he also provides and cares for us in the right way of our best natural development. How much Christ opposed generally this real-idealistic harmonious conception of life, in His teachings and fatal experience, who does not know? If He praises the confidence of the sparrows and the carelessness of the beautiful lilies of the field,He, on the other side,inculcates the most pronounced sense of sacrifice for idealism and ascends to Calvary because of highest aspirations for the idealistic part of the creative range of magnetic universal standards.

The religious architect often is unsettled, how to resolve the gigantic problem of putting the short human capacity in the right place, within the large expansion of the affective standards of the universe both of the intellectual-real and sentimental affective part. He often hesitates and doubts, where he will put the leeches of the creative universal magnetism , on the human dispositional constitution, in order to have the best results of the totality of mankind. If, on one side, Christ is continuously called the son of God and the son of man , in a reverential manner, and if, on the other He rejects peremptorily this world, He exposes Himself to the suspicion of different appreciation of the same thing, in different cases. Is it not difficult not to condemn our whole real nature, if we condemn the world, and is it not just as easy and logical to respect the world and even to love it, if we admit the real-intellectual part of our natural constitution? Doubtless it is a despairingly difficult task to satisfy always the necessities of affective human two-sidedness, in a harmonious way, and to maintain, at the same time, the sufficient respect for the more essential because more capable idealistic standards towards which the magnetic gravitation of all affective movements, after all, have a strong tendency. The difficulty of this problem is the impossibility of making two quite differently sized things congruent, to stretch our short human capacities out to the extraordinary imaginative elongation of the universal keyboard. Our total psychic efficiency is not at all, in advance, sufficient for the elongation of the universal adaptability. It was the genial idea of mysticism and miracle, of excluding many of the intermediary steps of logical development and consistent real progression, which gave to the religious genius the power of stretching our natural shortness to unexpected universal elongation, and to save our insufficient total life-force so much, on one side, as to reach even the most distant goals of universal standards, on the other, without losing entirely the real connection and the touch of our intellectual nature.

The religious affective concentrator, owing to the law of compensation, is not in a position to stand a strong intellectual display. The detailed intellectual fixation of the psychic force would withhold and use our total energy in the enlarged phasis of our light-field and not permit, therefore, a strong concluding start from the punctual concentration to most distant ideal goals both because of intellectually checked energy and of an insufficient amount of disposible life-force. Affective religion and all other near concentrating actio..s are, therefore, in this sense, as people say, a school of "intellectual" IGNORANCE. They cannot help being very influential in this regard. If their strong magne⁺ic goals receive unchecked activity in all their charm,they attract the individual irresistibly and suck out all life-force from his most intimate nature. So much so that the central localization and strong magnetic attraction to most distant goals cause a dynamic and quantitative absolute necessity of givinig up any thorough peripheric dispersion and fixation.

In this sense reasonig power and intellectual display are handicapped by religion, and doubt is considered a crime against the virtue of FAITH, which means the highest and deepest strength of affective recollection, concentration and protection from the outspreading dissipation of a part or the whole of our psychic life-force which so much is needed in the centre in order to reach and join effectively the last magnetic goals. There is rather the question of a sufficient amount of life-force so as not to lose the golden trace of the most distant terminal ideals than that there could be an essential interest, in the case of religion, of a serious resistance against highest magnetic attraction. Badness and evil, in this conception, are any checking limitations coming from private and previous interests and conditional points of view: the idea of concentration is weakened by the sharing necessity and division with intellectual life and thus we understand that the danger of undermining mutual destruction of ideal and real forces enflames the most embittered struggles between both magnetic drafts.

The next conclusion from this meditation would be, that strong inclinations to, and performances of, affective concentration include as a rule extensive ignorance not in spite, but exactly because of the deep sentiments and strong idealistic force of steering speculation. We rightly are told that ignorance is the deepest source of evil, pain and wrong-doing, and we must, therefore, be very careful to avoid it in order not to become subjectively deep without objective right or confirmation.

Christ, as He saw the necessity of limited choice, given by the narrowness of human nature on the long finger-board of the universal standards, has inserted the human capacities in such a manner that He allows them only a very small real share, almost shrunk to a symbol, but, on the other hand, a rich extension and plenty of idealistic relations. If we condemn ignorance and complain about lack of enlightenment, if we are humiliated and even repulsed by the fact that the sensorial world has been eliminated so far, we are not entitled to forget, however, that this restricted choice is to be considered as a product of emergency and that there is the question of the lesser of two evils, because of our small total life-force facing the infinite riches of the universal ocean. We may be horrified , if we discover, how much religion supersedes, by feelings, the detailed display of intellectual science in order to save its necessary energy, but we are by no means in a position to take away this humiliation from our human nature, turning exactly on the permanent insufficiency of our forces. We either must eradicate from the human heart the germs of rich universal claims and wishes or give to it a much richer total life-force, if we will succeed in avoiding the one-sidedness of intellectual imperfection.

Must we, perhaps, admit that, unfortunately, all what can be done with the imperfect tools of the human faculties, is bound to be bungling work, even, or most, in the most difficult art to converse with God and eternity. Our nature and our real achievement never reach the perfection of our heart nor the justice of our mind.

Religion has the essential task and will to bring about affective concentration. The MODERN life has produced a displacement of our affective fixation to the objective key-board in that sense, that the human talent has much more attachment to the real part of objective values and that the idealistic role has a relatively little share. Therefore the aversion of to-day against religious interests, the poor sense for art and highest idealistic values. In the daily life in general, but chiefly in the strong atmosphere and the overpopulation of our time, we are compelled to face very thoroughly and prevalently the practical life with its visible intellectual factors. Pulled out completely into the realistic periphery of our psycho-pupil, the total life-force has no affective rest to be put in the other half of our psychic activity. All is absorbed by the rushing and urging daily real work. We, in this connection, realize very well, from the opposite side, in a mathematically clear manner, how much this special conception of adaptation of life-force to universal life-force is able to fulfill the task of affective concentration and of accelerated psychic energy.

As the Janus head of our daily psychology shows a large and very exactly detailed real face and, on the contrary, a very shrunk idealistic elaboration, so the genial Janus head of the religious conception shows the contrary conditions. We immediately are tempted to say that obviously, just at the time of materialistic one-sidedness the genial-religious idealistic exaggeration must be a welcome complement, a precious help for balance and harmony

The almost total fixation in real visibility produces a very serious peripheric stagnation of psychic energy, and checks the indispensable concentrating facility of happily confident magnetic forces. The last goals of pleasure, of beauty, truth and strength are too far away from a pronounced variability of the peripheric business, and there is, therefore, danger of wickedness, unhappiness, explosive anger and desperation. In these moments and in these difficult human conditions, we realize the extraordinary significance of the genial religious interference. It has sufficient real contents in its intellectual Janus face to find connection and tender itself as a link from realistic to idealistic life, taking the communication from the real side as a means and help to throw the strong real stagnation of life-force to the mighty aspirators of its symbolic force.

The fixation of the strong absorbing punctual opening of the genial symbol, on the real body of our daily life and intellectual experience, represents a valuable real- idealistic compensator taking the necessity and magnetic disposition of our present practical life and transforming it into sweeping idealistic energy, by addition of the absorbing genial representations. There is only the question, whether or not such distant temperamental incongruities, as modern daily life and genial symbolism are, can find the practical way to link up with each other, in sympathetic mutual understanding. The difficulty, in our daily life,is that the strong peripheric fixation is in danger to repress and paralyze our concentrating affective energy and emotional elasticity towards delight,while the one-sided danger of religious-genial attitude is exactly the contrary, namely that we easily are tempted to put too much stress on idealism at the expense of the intellectual visibility. The danger of one side is the opportunity of the other. The voracious idealistic attraction, of the symbolic genial superposition, finds rich food in the *plethoric* fat stagnation of the real life-force. Materialism is the biological compensation and the supposition for successful idealism; the daily life necessities and the genial apparatus are exactly complementary, in their construction and distribution of affective avidities.

The principal right and the indispensability of religion and art repose on this fact, on the incessant urging invitation to prcceed, giving always flowing inspirations connecting the different degrees of affective concentration, working by powerful magnetic influences. Practical human life and genial religious organization are two OPPOSITE FORCES with distant intensity of affective life-force,- two differently sized flutes of an organ, one of which is very small and produces vibrating high tones with silvery vox humana, whilst the other one gives deep sensibly shaking sounds from its huge hollow body and mouth.

The human soul is similar to a radio system between both, always ready to substantiate minute registration, always impressible by high as well as deep sounds, itself being at first a rather indifferent faculty able to receive highest and deepest suggestions, -from the scale of universal standards extremely and most differently pronounced in the realms of world and idealism. Human disposition is extremely unsettled, in the first time of individual existence, as to the inclination and choice of affective standards. But those temperamental experiences, which are repeated most frequently, become a fixed habit, creating a predilection of the individual in his affective reactions. Any experience leaves an imprint in our soul, as musical sounds in the waxy body of a gramophone, and their effects will be always recognizable in our further and present actions and development.

Thus we find here again the omnipresent phenomenon of all life-functions, the oscillation of our affective force between two opposite, or better distant, poles of attraction, between which we have the whole series of the countless affective STANDARDS from the quite material pole of visible dead clay up to the highest peak of vibrating divine attraction. Our life-force is determined, in its action, by these keys of attractive energy, and how easy is it to see, in what an enormous degree we depend on our exterior influences! We run energetically to materialistic goals, when our surroundings invite and necessity compels us, but we melt in eternal hopes and are lifted up on sentimental wings, when the suggestion of art, of enrapturing music or some persuasive tongue carry us away. Our indifferent psychic life-force may be facing high or low affective standards, always it reacts in conformity of the same concentration, always it is willingly moulded by the exterior influence. This offers itself, at all times, as an instrument, reflecting, in a certain way of demonstration, our psychic faculties, echoing their creative call. The standards are specific channels or barrels, with most various diameters in perfect accordance with the deep temperamental features of our soul, through which it shoots.

It is the intention of the genial disposition and conception of life to introduce uplifting energy, the charm of thrilling delight and concentrating unity into the peripheric every-day life, raising our soul from the dusty work and from the danger of lazy low peripheric fixation, up to the hills and mountains of idealistic sway and terminal discharge.

It is most significant that we choose six days for the intellectual application of our peripheric life-force and only one for the service of the concentrati..g power of refined idealistic elevation. But if we remember the essential attractive differences of the intensities of different standards then we are not astonished that we still are inclined to be short in the fulfilment of our real duties, even if ceding to the sixfold suggestion of the real working opportunities, because the magnetic strength of the idealistic concentration is not only six times stronger, but incomparably more. This is the psychological reason for the rare Sundays and the numerous week-days, the relative necessity of keeping down the enthusing idealistic fire.

We are not entitled to play unpunishedly with the fire of idealism. We unknowingly are driven there because of the energetic attraction of its concentrating draft. Easily, by its superior force, we are swept away; its intense flames burn our psychic wings elevated to the heavens, over the clouds and shadows of reality, and we are likely to fall down, thus losing our sweetest hopes and and dreams in desperation and mutilation. The unbelievable and unspeakable glamour of eternal suns is not entitled to take entire possession of our whole nature by means of their extraordinary attractive beauty. We, on the contrary, are bound to the moderation of our two-sided ideal-real natural balance and we have to avoid all dangers, even those coming from noblest idealism lest we may be thrown out of the saddle of our psychic equilibrium. Our aspiration to God, our love for the higher part of our nature must be tempered and bridled; in the humiliation of real self-control lies the peculiar heroism of humanity.

The will of our average nature seems not to be to produce heroes, but to bring out the decided conviction to see our universal short-comings and to act accordingly. Thus our greatest heroism obviously consists in having the strength to be humble enough not to be heroes. Being insufficient for highest performances, we can reach the most excellent universal goals only by destruction of our natural harmony, by objectionable mutilation of the beautiful features of our constitutional balance. It is not only more deserving to restrain, in certain circumstances, our actions from high-strung affective idealism, in continuous consciousness of our deficiency, but it is equally much harder, for many, to do so. The differentiation of idealism and its consequences will follow later. Up to a cert..in degree we have to consider it as the kernel of the MORAL fate of our nature to go through this humiliating tragedy of our natural constituion, to abstⁱn from the highest and most charming goals which are seen by our mental eye and longed for most fervently by our sensitive idealistic disposition. But idealistic reward will not be lost in this case either; it comes in again in a roundabout way.

Universal tendencies have to share their energy with the generative idealism, with the psysiological and working material life. All must always be in sociable compatibility, steady in a strong will of justice, mutual respect and support. Every performance of one of these affective STORIES means a subtraction of life-force from the others,and we never are in a position, therefore, to permit to one branch of our natural affective key-board an exclusive preponderance, because, according to the law of compensation, all others would be handicapped. This law is, of course, most valuable for the inferior faculties of material life, but even much more for the highest stages of artistic idealism, because their exacting magnetic attraction is prone to subject our whole life-force to its service, leaving the other natural faculties, in that way, without affective food, which means a laughing-stock of unbelievable helplessness in the eyes of all humanity.

One extreme produces the other. A strong peripherically entangled fixation of our affectivity prepares, through slothful collection of biological desires, compensatory bounds of energetic concentration, and makes, therefore, owing to the earlier abstemious attitude, so much more for later exaggerated contraction of the light-field. Where the concentrating magnetic claim of our psycho-pupilaristic nature never had opportunity to happen, in an earlier time, this magnetic tension becomes a source of most convulsive idealistic effusions, as soon as the idealizator or elevator of genial influences has prepared a free passage between periphery and centre or has removed, as it were, the damping *sourdine* from the charming violin of the sentimental heart. Not only is God's help nearest,if we are in distress, but we also see reversely, how easily people dispense with their concentrated idealistic light-field, if they are in the outspread riches of reality. Possession and earthly RICHES are, up to a certain degree, a multiple peripheric fixation of heart and life-force,but exactly this peripheric ramificated affective spider hiding before the sun-light of delight, this peripheric biological obstacle for concentration, leaps, in some instances, to sudden surprising trances of affective re-contraction. Riches, moderately used, is the creator of rule,stability and order in life and is thus the chosen friend of historic religion. It creates a middle state between peripheric immoral and helpless materialism and the luring light of exclusively idealistic genial attention. These people begin to represent, as the *Middle Classes,* the compromising state between highest idealism and shortest materialism, with more security; they fix the steps of their lives in the tempered clear day of an half contracted light- circle; they at least have acquired a strong real-idealistic PERSONALITY conscious of its natural limits and faculties, and find, therefore, in themselves, in the order of their proper experience and life, the best rule of mediated demeanour of humanity, localized in the middle phase of central genius and peripheric materialism. It is the reasonable careful indifference, acquired by sophistication in other classes and cases, but here by previous necessity between these two extremes, which makes the individual master of his own destiny, which gives to him the decided and reserved strength and real force of his own personality. It retains him as well from the burning fire of highest idealism as from the dead frozen platitude of the arctic materialism. The useful art of life lies between both, not condemning anything, but doing conscientiously the near duties being always in medio.

The meaning of the philosophically most revelant comparison of the rich entering heaven less easily than a camel passing through a needle's eye, is not only, that the numerous peripheric fixations of the individual life-force prepare a compensation disfavourable to higher concentrative power, because the rich and voluminous material display cannot be pushed through the punctual idealistic light-field. The simile hints also to the fact that a certain possession of riches has at least still the desire from the periphery towards the centre of the light-field. Because the riches covers a large part of of our temperamental capacities, we easily become reasonably tempered and circumspect. The clever interposition of life-force between extreme materialism and strongest genial enthusiasm, are in a position to produce this reasonable INDIFFERENCE, our middle stage between extreme respect for visibility and intellectuality, on one side, and idealistic elevation on the other. Here the security of the harmonious personality is produced, which has given up the oscillating struggles between peripheric and central forces, but has found other directions to work in a more even way. This state produces perfectly self-sure quietness in regard to the eternal charm of religious values, as they are offered in the genial conceptions, as well as it removes the senseless superestimation of the material goods of the earth. Everything is relative and imperfect, nothing is able to bring harmonious happiness into our life, except our pre-conceived reasonable will. Any impression and enjoyment, by whatever object, is quite one-sided and leads easily astray, in a materialistic or idealistic way. Mostly the object is insufficient for our capabilities, but always distorted as to the harmonious real-ideal need of our nature. Only the sum of the continual MIXTURE of all objective experiences crossing our daily way and filling our hours with material mechanical work, intellectual tasks and high idealistic aspirations, which all together engage, in a harmonious way, all our talents, attain this goal, because they are almost equally numerous, picked up from all affectively absorbing standards of all possible creative energy of the universe, as much as they are amenable to human nature. May one approaching objective influence be too concentratted in its affective absorbing power, another instead may be too little spicy for our natural taste, too dull for our affective palate, but together they make a good mixture and a healthy meal for the totality of our psychic metabolism.

The small dose of idealism must be, as it were, a SPICE in the real food of our daily experiences of life, making them savorable and palatable. As we, in our life, need a continual mixture of carbohydrates, albumens and fats, for a healthy food, and as the combination of all corresponds best to the working possibilities of our complicated apparatus of digestion, the incessant mixture of material and intellectual notions and work and the dealing with imaginative highly concentrated feelings make together the wholesome nutrition of our psychic life.

The congruency of our use of spice. in the material food, and of highest feelings, in psychic experience, is surprisingly perfect We are not in a position to use many or strong spices, in our meals, without destroying the good taste, and, nevertheless, the small addition of spices is indispensable and gives an essential feature to the taste of the food. In a similar way the idealistic values penetrate the whole of our intellectual performances and give to them the thorough power of energetic sway and uplifting concentration. But in the same manner as in the realistic food, we are not entitled to abuse the salt and pepper of idealistic energy. We ought to be very careful in their dosage, adding them to our ordinary intellectual and mechanical life. If we make only small mistakes of hyperdosage, we spoil our psychic meals and make them unedible and undrinkable. An entire destitution of these components would make our psychic food unenjoyable as well. In the first case we had a spicy exaggeration burning and stinging our palatal sensitiveness, and, in the latter case, reversely, our appetite and longing for intellectual and mechanical action are destroyed, made dull and slow by lack of characteristic life, by privation of affective sway. A careful addition of the sentimental spices of highest gaols cannot be dropped, the concentrated fat of imaginative values, with their high molecular energy, cannot be superfluous in any of our psychic enterprises; all vital functions help one another and ensure thus healthy performance of the whole.

As in the CHEMICAI CONSTITUTION of our food we distinguish very different degrees of molecular concentration, as fat, for instance, has the multiple caloric index of carbohydrates, we have to make the same discriminations in our psychic life. The complicated compositions b th in our material chemistry of the real food and in the notional life of our psychic performances are typical of high efficiency and of less digestibility. In order to avoid real and psychic indigestion we must be careful in using the most concentrated molecular bodies of chemistry, on one side, and the most contracted imaginative notions, on the other.

The heat of exaggerated conce itrated addition of life-force leads both body and mind easily to irregularities, to hyperemphasis of their natural possibilitie, to over-strung claims for luxury, to quick inconsiderateness, to overdone tensions between extreme opposite gifts of human nature, unnecessary zeal in accumulation of riches, towards artistic and religious goals, in the upper direction, to slothfulness, anger, diseases, poverty and desperation, in another direction. For the provision of most concentrated values introduces a highly explosive energy into body and soul, in the chemical or psycho-dynamic realm, and makes for hyper-sensitive functional readiness. Once accustomed to the strong instigations and abundance of the high-molecular magnetic thrills, the organisms accept definitely the specific manner of reaction to these habitual energetic standards, and they are no more in position to change their extreme reactive excitability. Little concentrations of molecular and intellectual values are not able to incite these spoiled vital organisms to working efforts. Practice has effeminated or, looking from the other side, hardened them.

Extreme idealism produces material and PRACTICAL IN-APTITUDE. These people obtain, in time, such a pronounced inclination to exclusively selective reactions only to strong affective instigations, that they have not any answer at all to all realistic urges and necessities. They are like grown up children, suspended in the air of arbitrary imagination, enjoying the beauty of the heavens beyond the clouds, and never touching the earth and its realities with their feet. The urges of material and real life with their lesser intensity of affective persuasion, have lost their influence on this special habit of idealized reactive transformation, and these people, therefore, are no longer in a position to react properly on the urging necessities of their practical life.

I remember a young girl, once in my service, who was a lofty and idealistic noble creature, brilliant and bright in her continual contact with highest affective standards. She was a shining reflection, in her life, from excited idealistic happiness, so much so that the urges of real life never could attract at all the attention of her most sensitively reacting soul. She unknowingly felt her pampered sentimentality, a superior excuse for neglecting small real obligations., and she had difficulties to be aware, even in the least degree, of the instigations of the intellectual and social life to help to any other person. There was no lack of good will, but of interest and mental adaptability. She was so energetically put in refined connection with the high standards of her most elevated religious values that her real reactions and her mechanical and intellectual work were, compensatorily, atrophical in perfect helplessness. She was, however, most clever in her way; she understood well to defend her own stand-point and rebuke any different affective claims. She knew her goals and ways very thoroughly and had an easy possibility to attain all her high-strung idealistic wishes,in the richest measure She was a most developed one-sided idealist of refined taste and of noble feelings and so sure of her deep union with her loving God, so strong in her psvchic glamour of highest affective relations and fulfilments, that the strength of her charming personality swept away everybody to sincere love and admiration. Her energetic union with the ideal world infused her with the utmost conviction of her noble value, and she could not be bothered, in the high elevation of her beautiful soul, with the real necessity of her paid engagement. There was no possibility, for her, to descend to the dusky vales of real duties. Her small total life-force was entirely used for the powerful absorbing forces of eternal attraction which even would have beeen strong enough to engage the whole production of strength of the richest affective life exposed to such a splendour, with the same eagerness. Her skilfully achieved one-sided refined psychic reaction answered exclusively the energetic urges toward charming idealism. The refinement of idealistic people averse to real work and disinclined to intellectual responsibility means not, indeed, a refinement, but, in a sense, rather a roughening of psychic reactions, because they answer only to the strong magnetic concentration of explosive affectivity, to perform personal tasks. The diluted magnetism of sensory urges is insufficient, in energy, for the specific sensitiveness of these people who, owing to a long practice and inheritance, obey only the inter-spheric urges of universal dignity at the expense of the sensorial invitations of the intellectual visible life.

Now, the attraction of the interspheric magnetism must be more energetic than the sensorial energy. The latter has an immediately fascinating and compelling influence on our nervous system, but its lasting consequence and the trend of its activity are not at all of comparable importance. Spread through all the universe and poured between all intellectual and material life, the interspheric magnetism is not at all able to resist and to directly counteract the sensory visibility. But once caught by its skilful attraction, the individual is swept away with much more intensity and deeply moved by its mysterious and successful persuasion. Not the question of first approach decides the permanent influence of objective action on our faculties, but much more the intensity and stability of the magnetic instigation, which has to be the favorite objective choice of our life-force.

We can, therefore, understand that our young lady, after having previously yielded, in a naive and incautious manner, in her youth, to the beckoning interspheric forces, was kept inescapably within their toils. She had arrived at a state, where she permitted this magnetic intensity to reduce her intellectual life to the utmost degree. On behalf of her natural disposition, of the practised exclusion of the sensorial broadness of life, on behalf of her willingly and early semi-closed intellectual light-field, she arrived soon to a state of an oblique plane, where the rolling stone of the affective supreme will slipped, first slightly, down hill and moved at last to the narrow bottom of extreme affective one-sidedness, from where there was no escape. The beginning indulgence to the intruding persuasion of idealistic agreeable activity, turned out, at last, to be most tyrannical and more influential on the avidity of the psychic life-force of this girl, making her finally its slave, with more duration and less hope for release than any real chains may be able to do so to any prisoner in a gaol.

In spite of the full weight of the law of compensation in regard to quantitative preservation of our life-force, in that sense, that a prevalent and more achieved idealistic function likely excludes, with the time more and more, the real-intellectual work and vice versa , there must be also, in addition, a law tending to equal work of both psychic elements. We easily discover a balancing force not allowing the individual an exclusive idealistic or realistic function or use of his life-force. After a certain amount of affective exertion in the sentimental direction,nature turns its directive channels and craves irresistibly for an intellectual, mechanical - real task. It does not stand an uninterrupted sequence of muscular, mechanical or intellectual work as little and entices our magnetic gift, after a certain time, to put itself in connection, for another recreation, with the attractive forces of sentimental-artistic values.

For this reason, we are entitled to say, in a certain sense, that extreme idealism produces extreme materialism, that pronounced intellectual life creates most peremptory sentimental longings and necessities. Despite the stability of a certain character, inherited or acquired, we observe always this fact, and, in addition, even changing phases of idealistic and realistic predilection, in every individual development, alternating with each other and behaving mutually like cause and effect, connected by what we call disappointment, revenge, success, frivolousness and necessity.When the vital centre of intellectual or sentimental capability is filled up with life-force, it urges to discharge its magnetic longings, and when one of the two centres is exhausted by straining work, it loses its magnetically speaking tension, is inclined to rest until it is filled up again. DESPERATION and SUCCESS mean exhaustion and saturation, in a similar sense, being the outside visible reflection of the analogous psychic processes. They are reverse and opposite, so much so that we have, in the success, the beginning of desperation,whilst we may look at desperation as to the gray chilly morning of our new success. After a period of success our respective affective function is exhausted by long effort and will be overcome by other competitive factors, in the same rank, whilst the state of desperation means an intellectually indifferent period of application and use of our life-force. It is a transitional stagnation of affective energy, resulting from momentaneous inadaptability of the personal will to the given objective circumstances. The despairing mind is checked by other standards of the surroundings, and it has, therefore, the best security of receiving soon the dynamic superiority, over other psycho-mechanic units of its environment. We soon go out victoriously from a struggle, in which we have been beaten once before.

ALTERNATION of idealistic affectivity and intellectuality are a continual dynamic play of natural scientific justice,each of both functions performing its show always on a stage, which has been prepared and well equipped for special use, and leaving always that stage which has done its service and looks disorderly. May the other fellow arrive; he likes that kind of romantic outfit.

We have these changing waves, again and again, in whole nations, centuries and races, in the different families of a community, in the different generations and members of any family, in our special life-age as well as in the mood and atmosphere of our daily life and in the very features of our smallest actions. We incessantly have a more or less flowing river of magnetic inclination, of our active soul, towards intellectual or sentimental stress of our work, always changing and always determined by all the alleged personal and historic, but also relative surrounding factors.

As in music the highest sounds are accompanied always by the lowest ones, by which they are esthetically supported, we generally meet in the psychic life, opposed to the highest hills of affective enthusiasm, the deepest reactive valleys of realistic performances. The highest mountains throw the longest shadows; the lightning hits the most prominent real objects; extreme idealists surprise by most pronounced realistic features.

Owing to his concentrating efficiency, every Genius is, in a sense, a Saviour of the world, in gathering all of the same mind, and leading them in the chosen direction., but also an intemperate destroyer, in casting out, irresistibly, all who are not assimilable to his lighting concentration. Thus the genius does not bring the peace into the world, but the most pronounced separation and quarrel. He is a two-edged sword, friendly on one side, hateful on the other, but dangerous, in both cases, by the sharp edge of its fervent revenge and its partiality and one-sidedness. He scatters all ungodly, in excluding, ignoring, neglecting, boycotting and killing all opposite opinions and convictions. He draws and maintains always the sharpest limit of the dazzling splendour of his narrow punctual light-field and the dark, despised night of the surrounding shadow. Superseding the detailed peripheric reality towards a preconceived central goal means the most angry and ruthless performance. The multiple vital fixation on the peripheric objectivity defends against the sudden and uncritical collapse of the light-field of our psychic experiences. It checks and guides our centrally proceeding actions, bridles the life-force by setting it free,step by step, as the forests retain the water, after a tempest, on steep slopes of the mountains, from the multiple objective avidity. After consecutive affective saturation the concentrating energy proceeds gradually so that this arrangement protects best against sudden affective revolutions and is the surest source of real circumspection, logic and meekness.

The essential idea of the genius is in close connection with the notions of INDIVIDUALITY and EGOISM. To be a genius means to be rid of peripheric selfishness, to have an essential affective standard of personal fixation, which is very near the perfect central light-field, and so to have an easy transition to universal values, from the individual fixation of affective light-force. The average human individual has its localization of personal interest about in the middle of the most extended and most contracted possibility of the light-field; it dwells quite consistently, owing to its real-ideal nature, with pleasure in a compromising attitude between central generality and individual peripheric detail. The normal human being is pleased to cultivate as well idealistic, general affective as detailed material interests. According to his specific double nature, man has interests which belong only to him and which exclude a share with everybody else, and such, which are common to all together, in the affective unity of sentimental force.

Creating individual characters is like a game of arrows shot by the skilful nature to a target and striving to hit the bull's eye of central genial idealism. Most shots hit between periphery and centre, whilst some meet the extreme material margin of the target, and others, a few, reach almost the very centre. We understand, that the strongest individualist, in a sense, is the peripheric realist, because he has most detailed development and display, claims and characteristics, whilst the central idealist, rid of intellectual detailed exclusiveness, has a strong tendency to general affectivity and imaginative feelings common to the unlimited human collectiveness. The most peripheric realist has most inclination to distinguish himself from the affective totality of mankind and of the universe,- that most approached to the centre, on the contrary, is so prone to be pulled into the magnetic general forces of the universe that he does not appreciate very much his intellectual individual existence, since he has an extraordinary broad outlook over all collective values of humanity, earth and universe. According to our human nature we have, then, to admit that we never can be thoroughly either ALTRUISTS or egoists, because it is quite essential for our human nature, that we must reside continuously between the the two extremes of separatistic egoism and generalising loving altruism, if we will exist in the world. We are born egoists by our intellectual body, but natural altruists by our affective soul which forms the desire for collective union with all mankind and with all the universe. Human normality includes, therefore, a middle stage between egoism and altruism, a certain ideal respect for the wishes and rights of other people and of the general universe, but also an individual restriction and pronounced limitation of the personal interests and detailed individual rights, a division within the peripheric categories of time, space and causality, in equal justice.

The compromising nature of mankind is, exactly in this regard, very interesting. The genius is far away from the human normal life; he has escaped from the real-idealistic middle stage which makes, in its balance, the esssential characteristic feature of human psychology, - to the lonely mountains of one-sided affective elevation.

There are seemingly very serious entangling contradictions. The genius is the most energetic and most affective personality. We know that the narrowness and diminution of the intellectual light-field develop rapidly, as soon as it approaches the centre, and we learned long ago, that the combination of the punctual psychopupil and the greedy affective standards of idealistic notions bestow,on our personal life-force, a peculiar affective strength and sway.The genius is, however, for this reason, not at all,more egotistic, in the real sense of the word, but more fixed and strong in his idealistic conceptions. He is diverted from the respect for his detailed real and personal exterior needs, which are neglected in the shining glory of his universal outlook; his personality is almost completely and congruently melted with the punctual temperamental attitude of the light-field of the world.He puts his individual interest in closest connection and neighbrhood of the concentrated fiery universal symbolism. He is,therefore, strong and energetic, but not for his real interest, but not in the sense of his affective personality, which is in most favorable communion with eternal goals. In the special attitude of his concentrated mind, and owing to the easy outlook over the enormous sequence of the links of the universal chain, the genius has his eyes directed much more to the universe and to eternity than to anything else; his heart is illuminated with the kindling torch of his affective central contraction, and his senses are swept away by the high power of magnetic energy, pulling with irresistible perseverance, from the universal vacuum.

The congruity of interests,of the genial individual character and of the central human light-field, is so perfect, the river of the genial life-force has the possibility to flit so easily through the two narrow holes of the subjective individual concentration and the general affective conclusive symbolism of humanity, since both openings are very approached and interpolated in a straight line going up to universal views, that there may be little ambiguities nor resistance nor obstructions of the main psychic artery to be overcome, on the proceeding way to idealistic work. The genial egoistic fixation is not in contradiction and does not mean a serious subtraction in regard to the pushing affective energy to idealistic goals. His type is rather a directing,supporting and really gathering means and preparing temperamental administration, towards the definite idealistic conversion.

Can we imagine, however, such a perfect genius possible in the world? World is still rich in idealists. At all times many extraordinary heroes have set the world astounding. From the beginning of history, through the current of all centuries, we meet great and important men outstanding from the average through the strength of their will and deeds and the height of their sentiments, so much as the longest stocks of ears stand out from the other, in a field.

All greatest heroes were only a short time at the top of their heroism and soon subjected their ideals to shorter goals, if the immortal crown of an early glorious death was refused to them. Life does not permit any mortal to transgress a certain limit of intellectual real egoism, from which existence never exempts anybody.

A completely genial man would be a bodyless affective spirit. He could not possess the qualities of the real personal individuality, which are the egoistic limitation and segregation from its visible surroundings. But in the rarest case of the birth of such a triumphant genius, we would quickly be shuddering witnesses of his being spoiled of the categories of time, space and causality. Every man, as soon and as sure as he lives in this world, is entitled and naturally obliged to have a strong self-preserving desire. Ethics is the science of the separation and limitation of our individual claims from those of the social totality, of whose material and ideal possession we have only a small part to appropriate to ourselves. It is exactly in the turbulent and tempting muddle of realistic tangles meeting with egoistic struggles, where the idealistic value of the individual is shown most distinctly, and where it has to prove most energetically, by abstemiousness, its specific ethical conceptions. Leaving the practical struggles of humanity, in the periphery of the egotistic individuality, in a blurred state of general indistinct-- iveness, and surrendering them entirely to the haphazard of the play of the individual forces, means evading the most burning problems of our compromising petty life. By his extraordinary perfection of centralizing facility, being out of the trend of our practical life and our egoistic necessities, the genius may be the object of our admiration, and of directive authority to terminal goals, but he is never in a position to give us the necessary and sufficient example of behaving in our practical daily life. The essential value of the genius rests, therefore, with his role of affective concentrator of the human society, excluding the peripheric interests from his mind.

The genial type has the deepest knowledge of affective standards, the farthest reaching attention for the universe, the best will to perform tasks of absolute value. He has the strongest affirmative connivance with the most distant universal powers, announcing ,in transporting beauty, the shuddering glory of his divine ecstasy.

Nobody is as sure of the finest shades of the innumerable standards of the created and speculative world as the genius. He has an enormous mastership in affective valuation being the reflection of his principal security, of being in continuous intercourse with the deepest informative sources of the universe. These last values are measure and scale of the total appreciation of life and experience. Because his scale of standards is very relevant and thorough, his judgment is impressive and logical, but more creative than observing. He is the best intuitive judge of the world.

The genius is in strongest affective harmony with the interspheric magnetism. He gives to it most unrestrictedly his total lifeforce, withholding no considerable particle of it for intellectual existence and support of egotistical interests. The latter claims are, in this case, essentially melted with the highest idealistic sway of human possibility; their subordinated interests are synonymous and complete the moving picture of the genial personality. We have to understand, therefore, that the harmonious will of the genial individual, up to the interspheric forces, help it to grow in ideal greatness, truth and beauty and that the whole personality as the partaker in such important and high energies, gains a part of them reflecting out of him, as though he were a mirror of the universe.

The readiness of the genial will, the inclination of the genial heart to join the interspheric magnetism or the divine idealism, are quite perfect. There is no part of the will, which would be checked from the harmonious motion of divine rhythms. There is a total surrender and yielding, of all affective life-force, to the heart-rending power of idealistic discharge.

We easily observe that the unrestricted function of the energetic interspheric affective metabolism, does not only impart to the whole existence of our individual and bodily conditions, a brilliant glow of charm of the highest goals, to which we aspire, but at liant glow of charm of the highest goals, to which we aspire, but at universal rage, our frail body is soon destroyed and burned to ashes. The complete delivery of our will and of our attentive heart to last eternal goals means a charming harmonious happiness of our affectionate sensitive nature, but not at all a guarantee of our intellectual-bodily, economical, social and health conditions.

The frame and vehicle, the mould of our creative objectivity, as it meets us, in the visible world, is given in the CATEGORIES of time, space and causality. All the creative world and all detailed display within it, are only able to exist and continue under the severe rule of these three kings and masters. The unreserved yielding of our will to the affective universe, transgressed the preserving hedge of the intellectual categories, and spoils the careful rhythmic function of the real organs, through the burning rage of the free attraction of interspheric magnetism or idealistic affectivity.

All creation, stars, earth and all our visible objects, our body and its intellectual proceedings are completely depending on the categories of time, space and causality. They alone are the steps of resistance against a complete affective downfall of our intellectual nature. They are in a position and necessity to retain our creative natural part from red hot fire and from destructive liquefaction through the uplifting suggestion of interspheric attraction. The unrestricted will to the highest idealism creates the thorough desire to run away from the intellectual conditions of our visible world and constitution. Extreme idealism abuses the limited possibilities of our intellectual nature and visible body by tiring and exhausting affective exertion and destroys, therefore, our nervous constitution by the respectless sway of enormous idealistic drudgery.

Real intellectuality has principally the meaning of thinking hesitation. It is the *cog-wheel* of our individual historic existence, retaining us from instantaneous rush to the universal effusion. The visible world, the scientific intellectuality and the working business, are in a radical necessity of opposition to the affective idealism; both sides are dangerous competitors of one another, twins, whose common nourishing mother is the total human life-force. Principal opposition to absolute sentimental idealism is the indispensable duty of self-preservaton of the real word and objective visibility, up to a certain degree, unless they lose their right of strong existence and are thrown, like burning fuel, into the devouring furnace of interspheric universal forces.

What charming beauty and what valuable heat are produced by the coal thrown into the consuming fire of a stove, but how quickly have disappeared body and form and categoric existence of this piece which was built up slowly and conserved for centuries, far from the destructive fire!

What thoughts give us, in this regard, theFADING LEAVES of the autumnal forest? What a thrilling variation of their red, brown, yellow and greeny shades with most refined differences! Never the leaves are so admirable as they are at that season. It is the hour of their death, of their approaching decay and destruction in fire and dust. As long as they were in the full strength and freshness of their physiological life, they all had the same green unassuming color, they worked in a hidden corner; but now, when they take leave from the workshop of their activity, when a full physical and chemical task of a long summer time is fulfilled, they start blushing in surprising colored beauty, moved with heated cheeks, dazzling with dewy tears of separation. What a shining glamour in the moment of self-destruction of their body ! They

depart to idealizing elevation of their living breath. Is it sadness?
Or is the sweet melancholy of the autumnal foliage of our trees
rather the expression of their solemn joy to part from their done
task, expecting, perhaps, a new and higher work, - like bees going
from one flower to the other? The hope of future tasks makes the
faces of the leaves blushing. They depart, clad in the most moving
beauty, filled with the tenderest dreams and the proulest hopes of
their affective desire. As in the coal, where the process of burning
kindles the black body to one delightful light, the foliage of the
wood, in the moment of destruction, is inspired by highest beauty.

There is no doubt that all creative representation has the task
to destroy its intellectual part and real possibility, by the fire
of idealism and eternal intentions. Nature always again finds the
way to push us, volentes nolentes, into the furnace of her affective
transitions from material reality to sentimental idealism. She often
starts being impatient with our slowly creeping use of the categories
of time, space and causality, and establishes angry changes of our
life and lot, by passions, artistic symbolism and cruel accidents so
that we are carried away quickly and easily to goals, where we ,by
the only use of our understanding logical steps, never or very late
would have arrived.

It is the method and favored invention of the affective genial
part of our nature to dispense, in highest degree, with the intellectual categories of time, space and causality, to discard this
natural staircase from our ascension to the heavens, and to replace
it by idealistic wings and beautifully soaring affective aeroplanes.
The genial method, in comparison to the intellectual process of our
natural development, is very much alike the general desire of modern people to ride all over in motor cars instead of walking on their
feet, and neglect the slackening and checking intermediary obstacles
on the way. But natural means never will be dropped without bad
consequences, in regard to physiological and temperamental habits.
Whereas in abuse of motor cars the New World is the most pronounced abuser, we find the overwhelming influence of the genial
temperament much more in theOld World. In Europe people are
most fond of psychic "motor cars", in America of real ones.

We are surprised to observe, how long ENGLISH speaking
nations are able to keep the freshness and suppleness of their youth.
People of other countries, undoubtedly, show earlier marks of bodily decay and progressing senility. A considerable role in this difference plays the concentrating genial influence, which is too energetic and traditionally accumulated , in the old countries, and leads

therefore, by powerful PASSIONS, to early bodily decay and premature senility, in spite of all charming beauty and enthusiastic admiration enjoyed before. The intellectuality and the body share all the uplifting cultural pleasures, and furthermore, they are shaking and vibrating with sympathy, serve them eagerly and exhaust themselves in overwork, since they are so greedy to pick up, always again, some thrilling sparks of eternal beauty, falling, like crumbs of ambrosia, from the rich table of idealistic sentiments. But as soon as these dazzling sparks lose their intense light and the perfumed crumbs are enjoyed, - when the eternal dreams and inspired passions have faded, the intellectual-material part of our nature becomes aware of its exhaustion. Embittered disappointments and rueful wrinkles are the consequence of intellectual overwork in the service of interspheric magnetic attractions.

. The intellectual work and exterior business, is an excellent self-preservation of the body and keeps a person young, in the technical sense of the word. It is not so easy to overwork from intellectual, as from affective causes. Ascensions to extreme idealistic goals use always more energy. We understand, in this light, that the work done in joy and willingness seems to us easy, while the other done by compulsion and in slavery, is exhausting and bad. In one case we have collaboration, in the other antagonism of real and affective forces.

The real intellectual and manual work keeps the right time and measure of good development, within the categories of time, space and causality, checks overwork and bridles, in this manner, the individual faculties within the boundaries of their natural possibilities. The so-called LAZY man is, in fact, the more active; in his kind of work, there is more danger of exhaustion and overstraining. The loiterer becomes more easily fixed by his exhausting enterprises than the most eager business man, because the latter is protected from rhythmic irregularities of his affective mind, by the adaptation of his WORK to the logical gradual dilution of life-force, in distance, time and causal reasoning. The misgivings against sentimental occupation derive from its concentrated nature and our easy inclination to enjoy it and stick to it most perseveringly. The difficulty of the intellectual work is an early warner against exhaustion. Early tiredness and superficial regularity ensure its hygienic function. Thus, what people call work, prevents deep vital exhaustion, and, what they call laziness, is most dangerous, exactly because of inevitable *overwork*, being introduced as sweet poison. The remark: "Martha, Martha____" in the gospel, hints, however to the fact that the great psychic assets are on the part of the sentiments and the heart.

People who, by culture and tradition, by natural temperament, exterior circumstances and affective peculiarity, are disinclined to the strong and angry genial concentration of their light-field, are in a position to avoid the exhaustion of affective overwork and the eliptic irregularities of their performances. They likely have the Precious habit of a never disturbed rhythmic measure of their intellectual work; all exhibitions of their life-force are ensured against passionate consumption and exhaustion, retained within the most convenient and possibly economical time, through the pendulum of the categories of space, time and causality.

This categoric PENDULUM, of course, is of inestimable value for the good performance of the vital force of every individual. Without this dividing help of our intellectual pendulum, we have difficulties to use our physical forces properly. The constructive organization of the body puts a limit to methodical use, and our corporeal functions are expected, furthermore, to serve a long time, without early exhaustive destruction. The spring of our affective life-force is wound up once in our life, at the time of youth heating our heart blood; but from that time the work of our intellectual nature has to go through the years of the life, in accordance to the right measure of the surrounding world.

It is not advisable to put a wrong pendulum permitting too quick an action and being always faster than the right time, and it is even less desirable that the pendulum is taken away at all and that, in this manner, the spring of life-force, becomes practically or intellectually useless. By the unhingement of the pendulum, the life-force of the elastic spring is directly thrown out to the universal values. There are cases, where the tension of the life-force has gone, by universal passionate abuse, and others, where only the pendulum of the categoric clinches is unhinged; but the combination of both conditions is naturally most frequent. Keeping time with the exterior world and the nature of our intellectual organization, is most important for self-preservation, not to overwork or abuse our bodily material, which is adapted and adaptable only to the amounts and methods of organic and real nature. Keeping intellectual time guarantees a LONGER LIFE; if we do not abuse our bodily and psychic intellectuality, we are expected to prolong our life, in the same way, as we may shorten it by the overwork of the untimely irregularities of unbridled idealistic enthusiasm. The spring of our life-force is supposed to provide affective food of energy, for our intellectual life, sufficient for all normal functions of our earthly career. We have to be,therefore, economical in saving,and never spilling,the precious liquid of deepest vital energy. We have to be careful, that the regular clinching and escaping movements of the categoric balance keep on going, bridling and releasing methodically, up to the end of an old age.

On the other hand, we read here,from our psychological analysis, that it is just the strength and the power of affective possibilities, in every way, which is an indicator of longevity. A deep well of idealism in youth, may have the meaning of a most resistent lasting personality, of a long and rich affective development of life, of a mighty spring of innumerable motions and energetic evolutions in a tenacious personality. Up to a certain degree, we may read out, in young days, the amount of efficiency of the individual life, and we may, out of this, calculate, the years and deeds of future useful work. But it is not the time, which essentially counts, but the deeds. The developed adaptation, however, to the categories of time, space and causality, affords the hygienic guarantee for diluted dosage, and, in this way, for dispersion over a number of years. The deep genial type contracts the same actions into a shorter condensed space and time. He dies early,because of lack of categoric carefulness,because he "lavished" his energy and transgressed his bodily limits. It is known that geniuses produce in exuberant jerks, they are most inactive in the middle time. One may be an almost hundred years old genius like Goethe,in this way, without offending the indicated law of genial exhaustion.

The strong efforts toward terminal ideals cause, therefore, reflected in passionate bodily reactions, easily exhaustion of our forces. It is especially the sexual idealism, which, in its relapse to pleasure, seems to produce most easily exhaustion. whilst the artistic and extreme terminal elevation of the spirit, if it is associated with regular order, sensorial moderation and muscular exercise in fresh air, very often allows an old age and keeps even young, with its vivifying sparks of charm,truth and beauty, enjoyed by the persons who have dedicated their lifes to it.

According to the special necessary carefulness, required in order to prevent passionate relapses, in the genial work, we know, that the pronounced genial manner of living is altogether a dangerous and consumptive task. Like the thrilling beauty of the fading leaves and of the burning coal, the physical potentialities of the genial man likely are driven to a red hot state of exceedingly energetic performance, so that they are used and exhausted in a short time, because they have been abused, in disproportion with the moderate time of the intellectual categories. Thus the genius grows old, at a relatively early age; his extraordinary sparks, of shining beauty in the world of intellectual reality, prove to introduce a state of organic decay and of intellectual self-destruction.

In the fervour of his affective performances, he overdoes the real allowances of his visible and individual gifts, crushes in the anger of his enthusiasm and burns, in the heat of his idealism, the intellectual possibilities of his nature, which are only adaptable to the cooler proceedings of the slower logical development. Thus we understand that the high genius staggers early into his grave, a wonderfully colored autumnal leaf, a burning coal of dazzling shining beauty, which consumed itself too early in the magnificent splendour of its irresistible and unchecked genial order.

The genial disposition of Christ delivered Him too early to the death of earthly destruction. After having taught His ideas scarcely for three years to the world, He already was the victim of the nemesis of His overwhelming greatness. The eternal range of His intentions and dispositions hurt Himself ; His system and ideal claims had lost the real social vitality, after three years of public tuition. What a fascinating shining leaf of an early autumn! The charm and the glamour of His brilliant personality was indescribably delightful and enraptured all His surroundings. But the real circumstances of His historic period swept Him away, like a storm in November scattering the rustling leaves of trees.

The perfect lack of intellectual realistic resistance to the idealistic concentration of our soul, weakens and destroys the necessities and claims of our earthly position, of our social individual and local rights, of our material fortune and business career in the public life. If we surrender all our life-energy to a goal which is outside and beyond the reachable possibility of our real existence, we consequently may allow as well the loss of all privileges of the intellectual part of our nature. If all our psychic energy is coined in idealistic energy and, in addition lacks the checking mechanism of the logical categories of space, time and causality, we soon and entirely are the slaves of idealism and have nothing more left for the bodily and intellectual claims of our nature.

Although the genial disposition often is combined with a great gift of personal life-force, a genial character and a rich natural psychic endowment do not occur necessarily in the same person. For genius means a strong temperamental inclination to one-sided idealistic concentration, whilst we merely express a quantitative measure through the word of great talent. The more considerable the life-force is, the easier is it to permit a powerful contraction without total exclusion of the intellectual periphery. The genius enjoys, however, the benefit of the suggestive powers of the cultural atmosphere of his time, which is concentrated and condensed, in his personality, like a strong magnetic current in a lightning-conductor. The combination of this significant magnetic suggestion with the strong specifically inclined personality may help to produce those enormous concentrated shots of idealism, as we are accustomed to admire them in any genius, most in the outstanding genius of Christ.

He really was, according to the tales of the gospels, chiefly that of St. John, a burning well of quite extraordinary affective concentration and divine energy, of incomparable idealism in the history of the world. If we may be entitled to call all and every mark of affective energy divine, which is thrown out from our heart, in the form of high longings and idealistic sentiments, toward the universe, we are right so much more to call divine this incessantly flowing river of eternal elevation and sentimental beauty, poured out by Christ with richest depth and profuseness. He is considered, therefore, the prototype of a divine man comprising the background of most important cultural atmosphere, of a strong individual life-force and of an exceedingly outspoken genial personality. He is the greatest child of the greatest history, great in what He received from His suggestive cultural surroundings, great in His personal talents and great in His wonderful genial divine disposition. He enjoyed the principal pre-suppositions of a genial action and surpasses the wonder of all the world, up to to-day, by the efficiency of His idealistic energy. His divine intimacy gives to Him rightly the sonship of God, the title of the first-born, the most apt and thorough mouth-piece of the human heart.

He doubtless disposes of the clearest harmony and the most perfect willingness for divine progressive accomplishment. He possesses the most attentive and most ready affirmation toward universal fulfilment. He is, in this sense, at the top of human-universal WISDOM. We may define wisdom as the straightest line and nearest connection between objective world and value, between personal affective interests and between the universal idealistic attraction, with equal emphasis of all three stations. Christ has least difficulties to connect His personal affective interests with the universal magnetism, but He sacrifices the objective realistic values, the individual comfort and even earthly existence and the honor of the world. He is so much transported, overhearing distinctly the whispering suggestions of the eternal powers that any personal real wishes and interests have no hearing, in His universal ecstasy.

He had the longest range of psychic outlooks towards the universe. He was a deep thinker. But His LOGIC came down from heaven and took possession, of all creatures, in a retro-speculative way. He explained all, in as far as He was interested, in the light of highest and unalterable divine and eternal standards. His thinking has a spiritual character, bestowing on Him the most stolid authority. His thought is not going out from the ground of real experience, through the clouds, up to the universe of sentiments, but He pulled all His reasoning arguments from the eternal hills of life, truth and beauty of the heavens.

Our ascending thinking process of to-day moves the reverse way, building the law of thought from real experience, and stepping on this footing uphill to the rocky mountains of sentimental authority. The modern time admits what it understands and claims always for everything the confirmation of experimental truth. Christ, on the contrary, would not explain but what was in accordance with His genial divine point of view, which He and His followers developed like a tree displaying its bows, leaves and fruits, out of one deep hidden root. They planted their genial tree in the ground of history. Christ's mission came from the genial concentration of His powerful personal values in combination with the cultural magnetism of His time.

It is always very serious, if somebody has not the courage to himself. It obviously is an exaggerated self- consciousness, if one is not able to stand by what one thinks is true and right. Christ was the most consequent upright man. His relations to the experimental real world were put into perfect harmony with His idealistic views. In His genial manner He was farthest away from HYPOCRISY, but by His strong consequence and overwhelming authority of force He demonstrated most clearly the weakness of the average man, raising th standard of honesty by His outstanding score of sincerity. The small man was, after Him, more distinctly recognizable as hypocrite and sinner. Christ was neither a hypocrite nor a sinner, because His genial disposition His extraordinary life-force and the suggestive support of the cultural masses helped Him to build and maintain the prolonged straight line of His logical personality. He was an intrepid builder of His spiritualized logic. He was in a firm position to interpolate His noble personal interests between the highest idealistic goals, which He seeked, and the intellectual objectivity, which He adapted or excluded , in as much as it could not be adjusted to the straightness of His great genial main line of divine wisdom. He was not a hypocrite, because owing to the genial peculiarity of His strong personality, He was not fixed in the periphery of the interests of the real world, but was born and gifted in natural deep love with the universal eternal idealism. He had, therefore, no oppositional egoistic reluctance against the terminal goals and the punctual central attitude of His pyschopupil. His natural inclination just led Him to this attitude, as well as the psycho-mechanic necessity of His time and the attractive compulsion of the universe.

The little gifted average individual was and is not at all in the same case. It has not the size of His personality, not the abundant plenty of His psychic force, not the one-sided genial inclination or possibility. He has not the freedom to neglect the real surface of his life which holds him with thousand intimate ties and fixes him to the real objects and their beauty. He feels, however, the same urge to be logical and irreproachable. But his life-force is scattered and dispersed, in a far reaching light-circle, like a small shot, not hitting any important ideal goal. His life-force necessarily is fixed in all the innumerable small points of his business interests and of the daily life and likely is not sufficient to carry through a retro-speculative order in his real display. He has not the strong, deep and rich genial fixation in eternal terminal roots. Christ instead had this radical fixation first and, coming out from the glory of the Father, He directed all real life accordingly, in as far as He dealt with it.

SINNERS and HYPOCRITES can be produced by their affective deficiency. They have needs and wishes in the daily life, which disagree with the eternal universal views which Christ inspired in the world. The hypocritical sinner submits to the outstanding authority of the divine hero. These people are slaves of great principles which they accepted without personal will or skill of understanding. They are not in a position to establish a straight main line of logical consequence between their objective experience and life, on one hand, between their personal tastes and predilections, on the other, and their eternal ideals which they accepted as right and valuable standards. They try to bring about a more completely even compromise between the three stations of emphasis, since Christ was not wise in the sense of the interests of the world. But they lose instead of the universal wisdom which He had. The hypocrite is not wise in the sense of Christ, because his bargaining is his own terminal disadvantage.

The average man can and will not drop his manifold real fixations which bluff him and rule the present moment with undiscussed authority, forcing him to believe that they are more right, owing to their sensorial immediateness. His natural intellectual tendency does not give up the real taste and affective egoistic fixation of his real peripheric life on behalf of the central predilection of his genial master, nor does he penetrate or recognize or feel as well the shining clearness of the magnetic terminal powers, overflowing the personality of Christ. But if many accept, more by traditional and public compulsion than for genuine personal insight and appreciation, their religious standards and principles, and if they, on the other hand, are not able to direct accordingly the objective world and to subordinate to them their egotistic will of man, of blood and of flesh, then there will be many ambiguities and circuits on the way to the last admitted and generally accepted ideals. There will be a lack of the logic of the desirable straight forward running sequence. The main line of the experimental objective development of the egoistic will and of the idealistic faith, is broken. We call this man, not grasping the consequence of affectivity and logic going through all the universe and world, a hypocrite and sinner. He does not understand or is not willing to observe or to establish one consistent unity between his idealistic creed, his individual inclination and the real objectivity.

This multiple unhingement and distraction of the different components of the psycho-mechanic functions is indeed a very serious fact and an unworthy state; serious because of the affective frictions and stagnations caused by the ambiguities, narrow passages and interruptions of the real idealistic channel, and unworthy for the reason, that helplessness and confusion in the most principal questions of a developed life testify to great weakness not becoming a man. We are entitled, therefore to say: hypocrisy and sin destroy the dignity and firmness of a man. An accomplished man ought to be in a position to establish a most perfect harmony between his last idealistic principles and the practical deeds of his life, by correcting all his three affective stations, in as far as it is necessary. The root of the dignity of a man consists in his upright courage to be true and consistent through the whole make-up of his compromising real-idealistic nature. This is the noblest diamond in the character of any important individual, after having observed seriously the boundaries and possibilities of life, to stick unrelentingly to the obtainable truth and values of life, to the principles as far as they are useful and practicable within our natural possibilities and to exclude all impossible troublesome claims, from whatever source they may be suggested.

We no sooner accept exceedingly distant ranges of our affectivity, and strive to visualize and substantiate them too clearly, in our ambitious pride, than we lose the reasonable continuity and the straight line of our human logic, from the details of our daily life up to the divine distances of countless light-years beyond the stars, and easily lose the affective strength of idealistic direction and real understanding, according to the law of compension. Sin means an omission, a loss or ambiguity of ideal direction or a forbidden leap over the steps of our intellectual development, an unjust and inadequate localization and emphasis of life-force.

Consequenz führt zu Widerspruch und gerade der
Widerspruch wird schœpferisch.
Wilhelm Pinder.

SECOND BOOK

THE barrel of a RIFLE or CANNON has to be the thicker and more resistant, as the circumference of the discharging channel is larger and the shooting energy more intense. In a pistol we observe a thin barrel, whereas in the largest cannons, as they were used in the Great War, enormous masses of metal were necessary for building the barrels. Of course, the energy of the explosion must have a corresponding resistance from the wall of the barrel. An insufficient resistance, on its part, would naturaly and easily allow its explosive destruction. We understand that the amount of the mono-determined energy, throwing out the missile through the channel of the barrel, is a radical condition of the range of the shot. The prolonged ring, or tube, of the barrel does not allow the potential shooting energy to escape in another direction than one corresponding to the axis of the barrel. The circular wall of the barrel is, as it were, composed of many strong concentrated muscles intertwined with each other, or many energetic hands, all together checking the shooting explosion from non-intended deviation, and throwing it, in a common and simultaneous grasping action, in this fixed direction, out of the opening of the barrel towards the goal. For the explosive force, in itself, has an indifferent tendency of expansion to all directions, and it is only the peculiar preconceived will of the mono-directed construction of the channel, which gives to this indifferent tendency of extension one sure and most efficient direction. This gathers and compresses all energy in the ultimate fiery sheaf or ray of shooting explosion, which would have been otherwise discharged, in a regular globular reaction.

We are convinced of the striking simularity of the genial affectivity and the barrel of a cannon. The genius always gathers all life-force produced by his rich vitality, in the compressed channel of his idealistic discharging personality, excludes the whole kaleidoscopic globe of peripheric action of the intellectual part of the life, in order to throw all energy together to his one chosen direction. He is anxious not to lose any smallest article of direct congruity with the last universal goal, to which he has aimed the axis of his genial gun barrel.

In shooting with a rifle we feel, in the moment of the discharge, the energetic repercussion of the butt against the shoulder, and if we happen to stand in the neighborhood of a huge cannon, in a small earth-quake. What tremendous power of resistance must such a cannon barrel possess, and by what a terrible shaking must it be moved in the moment, when the weighty missile is swept through the passage !

We already have small degrees of this reaction, up from the most harmless small shot and pistol. It gradually grows faster and faster in the moment and degree of augmenting energy of the discharging explosion. In the smallest shooting arms scarcely recognizable, though existent, this reaction of the barrel is enormous in a huge cannon, and pulls the total local surroundings into the trembling physical vibrations of its energetic concentrated convulsions.

The genial and human affective shots exhibit very concording conditions. The barrel of our affective shots must have as well the corresponding strength and physical resistance of a healthy intellectual brain and body in order to help and to guarantee the vital functions. Weakness or lack of intellectual resistance of the surroundings and of the physiological strength of the human body, which like an organic circular muscle includes the punctual opening of our idealistic discharge, would produce as well the destruction of the body and of the intellectual order of life. In these psychomechanic shots, we have to observe also the shaking commotion of the barrel of our delightful idealistic discharges, and so much more as we have a greater and a stronger amount of life-force. The individual producing little psychic energy ,of course, has no strong simultaneous vibrations of its intellectual and bodily surroundings, in the moment of affective punctual discharge. But there is no least affective idealistic explosion without accompanying trembling repercussion of the bodily functions so that we have to admit that there is no affective ideal emotion without physiological commotion.

If we dispose of an important amount of total psychic life-force, and if, therefore, the confining channels of the affective shots are shaken more intensely with the more sensual and more perceptible corporal phenomena of the PASSIONS, they are the strong vibrating answer of our nervous substance and our muscular fortune, since they are the channels, through which the affective powers of human sentiments are discharged. The sensational passions are, up to a certain degree, felt even agreeably, and the individual looks, therefore, for artificial establishment of their conditions, and augmentation of their shaking vibrations, which leads most easily to the realistic relapse of pleasure. In this state we search the idealistic discharge because of the connected vibrating commotion of our sensitive nature, instead of having the contrary intention to desire chiefly idealistic discharge and to enjoy the pleasure of passionately sensitive commotion only accidentally and secondarily. Here we touch the most pithy problems of educational help and perversion; here we may find the most precious and radical finger-posts to avoid the thoroughly dangerous steps to sensual luxury and material perversity.

The genius has the most energetic accumulation of affective discharge He is the roaring lion of the human psycho- mechanic concentration. He is the most powerful idealistic gun of humanity. His enormous life-force throws out the greatest quantity of affective magnetic power, and the speed of his energy is indescribable, his range goes out farthest to the universe and reaches most divine goals which to the small rifle of the average man remain definitely inaccessible. But at the same time this psycho-mechanic genial power needs a strong channel of intellectual and bodily organic resistance, a circular enormous strength of a wall or coat, as it were, of cast-iron or cast-steel, which forms the real basis of this psycho-mechanic function, and which, like in a gun, throws the affective energy with mighty hands, with strong concentrated and contracted muscles and with an enormous amount of nervous capacity, through the narrow channel of the punctual human individuality into the most distant universe. What a passion, what a commotion, what an indescribable repercussion must result from these thundering shots of the affective genius !

We hinted to the danger of early destruction of the body of the genius, of his muscular and nervous substance, which are only adaptable to the slower methods of the reasonable categories of time, space and causality. Up to a certain degree a strong bodily constitution may be able to stand the shaking commotions and the passionate vibrations caused by the peculiar genial idealism. But never in an ordinary human being we can expect or admit, that the genial excess of sentimental energy, as it is ascribed to the outstanding personality of Christ, may find its sufficient natural and intellectual resistance. The degree of human corporal resistance never can be so enormous as to be the vibrating barrel of such a genial vibrating shooting, as it is related going out from Him incessantly, with superhuman energy. In all history of mankind, of natural science, of medecine and physiology, never we met a man of such a personal aptitude of divine effort. The human body is essentially unable, in a physiological sense, to stand a similar gigantic degree of nervous and muscular exaction, in commotional and passionating work.

The mighty lightnings of this dignity would explode in the delicate barrel of the human body; the most resistant and healthy lightning-conductor of any human constitution would tear into shreds the individual,like a bomb-shell under the energetic weight of such an universal power. The flaming and overwhelming force of its report would kill, at the very first touch, the frail human body, which would have ventured to surrender itself to be its conductor and barrel. No normal man of flesh and blood could stand this unparalleled degree of divine and universal sentiments, this continuous sequence of the highest genial feelings ascribed to Christ, perhaps not even one shot of His tremendous idealistic discharge. Divine sentiments of His description would instantly demolish the walls of the barrel of the intellectual body. The strongest human possibilities of muscular and nervous performances would be baffled,because the body would be shred and burnt like paper or tinder.

In the reverse direction, as the mono-genial affectivity sucks its concentrated force from the rich food of its cultural and historical background, we may assume that it is possible for a collectiveness of human intellectual organisms, of real nervous substance and, muscular protoplasm, to offer themselves as a more resistant and stolid wall of a barrel for the genial lightning, where any single human individual would be insufficient. Where the individual would be destroyed by the inevitable passionating repercussion of the lightnings of the extreme divine sentiments, where his individual intellectual-organic faculties would be comparable to a trembling aspen leaf willing to resist the explosive divine forces, a *collective* body of many persons has more chances to stand efficiently the extraordinary compression of the dignity of a high genial emotion. Where many strongest hands are twisted and where numerous physiological muscles are intertwined forming together the utmost compressive walls of the genial gun, we may admit that the muscular hearts are not so easily dilacerated, burnt and shred from strong commotion and that the nervous shocks are less likely to kill the shuddering individual.

Recalling the energy of patriotic commotions, under whose influence we are transported with thousands of people, in a public review before a brilliant worshipped personality or king of a great time, or the shaking enthusiasm in a public meeting within the halls of an artistic old cathedral or under the influence of a thrilling speech, we are perfectly able to appreciate this idea. One alone would not be able to stand the enrapturing affective energy of this moment, but a totality of men can carry successfully this power of explosive expansion. They all together form the organically possible mother-ground of an enormous shaking force which would have crushed a single individual who would have been forced to endure alone by himself the whole weight of this public enthusiasm.

Without impeaching on the special divine claims of Christ, we assert that a real person of flesh and blood of the genial dignity of Christ is a biological impossibility. In the next surroundings of twelve and then seventy followers, the highest values of His genial personality and the totality of His affective energy were naturally crystallized, to incomparable overwhelming greatness and most delightful universality. The remarkably gifted circle of the evangelists whose synoptic writings are of inestimable value, their close friends and adherents, the outstanding figures of Saint Paul and the early fathers of the Catholic church, formed altogether the intellectual and biological, muscular and nervous resistance, the reliable barrel against the tremendous genial historic Christian nucleus. The personality of Christ is the idealized and concentrated peak of this whole genial development. They altogether as an unity had the natural possibility to tender a physiological resistance sufficient to be the barrel of the genial Christian shots; they were the cast-steel barrel of the gigantic gun, from whose channel the fiery genius and the towering energy of the Christian idea was shot to the most distant universe. What an intimate unity and what a strong friendship must have existed in the circle of these genial great men, who, through the charming love of their concordance, created the possibility to be collectively the powerful intellectual barrel of the most thundering genial idea which ever left roaring the human society and the human heart.

As a matter of fact, the overwhelming energy of this thoroughly strong and therefore so dangerous cannon killed many, as it came to the use of its function. Thousands and millions of its friends and enemies were swallowed by the destructive earth-quake around it, and owing to its tremendous repercussion which they could not stand. The Persecutions of the First Christians, the innumerable martyrs from the very first death of Christ Himself, and His immediate followers and organizers, up to the religious wars of the Middle ages and the Inquisition, the countless and hateful religious slanders and prevarications in private, social and political life, are all witnesses of the continuous danger of affective explosion of the mighty force of the Christian idea, through the loose real cracks and fissures of our visible and intellectual life and world. He who has a soft, yielding and accommodating heart is defeated easily and quickly by the gun of the strong and enrapturing Christian ideas.

DISSIDENT individuals are weak points within the massive coat of the *systematized genial gun.*They are thrown out, in the lateral direction, by the central explosions. Thus they are, it is true, a subtractive element in regard to the pushing energy running along the axis of the historic and traditional affective gun of humanity. The real particle of the barrel, however, which sacrifices its safe protected position within the totality of the organized wall of the metallic tube, goes through an *essential tragedy* by choosing its separatistic way. It impairs the universal efficiency of the sensitive and domineering system, from which it is separated, but gains by the enormous courage of its independent step, by losing its protected unity within a whole social body, by yielding more than all others to individual urges of idealistic rapture and energetic sway, -- the high dignity of becoming a new idealistic muzzle of a gun, like a REFORMER. The innumerable martyrs after Christ can be considered as idealistic elements of the world, which were cut out from the surrounding intellectual world and carried away by the inner draft of the absorbing idealism of the gun. The impression of the first discharge of the organized affective Christian cannon on the world must have been most exciting and revolutionizing. First it was not yet in a state of good service; the barrel had not yet that density and impermeability as it received soon through the compressing and expanding energy of use.

To those affective outsiders, who dare to be for themselves mouth-pieces to eternal sway and truth, who dare to come in personal and intimate contact with the affective energy of the interspheric magnetism, through new intellectual streets made by themselves, belong so many whom we despise and admire. All the religious reformers and scientific outsiders, the unbusinesslike sincere artists, the martyrs of their own convictions and those who, by true love for religion, offer themselves to be the slaves of other people, and finally, abused too much, thrown to the street in ingratitude or finding the courage to explode in the holy anger of their personal rights and convictions and mature to their own real and ideal crystallization, after all difficulties and pushed by necessity, - these altogether are the children of a new and right affective emotion, daring to use the fruits of their own experiences and personal convictions like an exploding muzzle of a courageous and efficient life-barrel. What a great country, where there are men of sacrificing courage for truth! What a despicable and miserable land, where there are none! The self-sacrificing and courageous are nearer God, being his intermediators in their own sense.

After the first struggles and real failures, the cannon of Christian idealism began to show an excellent function. The most successful shots were produced by it through many centuries; they were powerful, resourceful and aimed well to highest and most distant ranges of human affectivity. Long processions of human generations were taught to surrender their life-force, in most beautiful sentiments, to the divinity and hit the very central bull's eye of the target of universal affective standards, according to the helping genial formula: Per Christum Dominum Nostrum. Undoubtedly the organized body of the Christian church has done most precious services to humanity. It has given a flourishing health, strength and charm of life to human mankind, chiefly during the *Middle-Ages,* so that we cannot help but admire greatly the high qualities of an affective efficiency of that sort. The idealistic freedom going out from the confinement of the most beautiful artistic expression has perhaps never been as high and energetic.

The old MYTHOLOGICAL creeds, in their turn, were also precious discharging affective guns in their contemporary milieu; other directive idealistic opportunites for other nations and centuries which were concerned with their own faith in a serious manner as well. There was the question of necessary methods of idealistic discharge of the human heart. The cultural ideal formula of any time had and received its dignity and value from the fatal necessity of its function in the life of men, and surely, in each case, is surrounded by a shuddering glory of symbolical eternal truth. It is conveyed every time there, where the human heart is compelled seriously enough to absolutely insist and find last truth and beauty.

At the time of the awakening Christianity those old, once indispensable, but then worn out barrels of the antique religious mysteries had served a long time and, in their sense, in an excellent manner too. The antique CHURCHES—as we may call quite generally every human society united with the special purpose of discharging our life-force to ideal goals by symbolic signalization - decayed owing to their psycho-mechanic technical fragility, exactly like old worn out and old fashioned cannons. They had to be replaced by a new formula more suitable, surprising by novelty and grasping vigorously the whole humanity.

Everything being in connection with material and intellectual functions underlies decay and *change* and use. The functional collective social body and their system serving universal sentiments as a directing and compressing barrel, are just in the same manner perishable and changing as the steel-cast barrel of a material gun. There is a time to work and to reach the summit of success, in everything, and there is nothing indeed more successful than the historic systematization of a genius, but there is as well a time of change and decay, of rebellion and explosion. Then the old barrel is no more able to fulfil its role of discharging the eternal universal longings of whole nations and continents. As old cannons and guns of famous wars are exhibited and admired in a historic museum, those antique mythological creeds are worshipped as dear and interesting souvenirs, in poetical descriptions and representations, where the wonderful efficiency of their former idealistic shots still is echoing through a thousand years. But they are altogether a glorified mummy praiseworthy, but dead in historic functional life. There is no use to eternify anything, which is in connection with our human, intellectual and material nature. Any exaggerated attachment to the exterior formula of a system is likely to be already again that what contradicts the deepest principle of our idealistic call. It is the adoration of material and localized values, the lazy rest on old laurels, which are most objectionable because of their danger of luxury and superstitious misunderstanding. God is spirit and truth. Every formula is liable of decay and sure of change. We are not entitled to fix our heart too much on any *formula,* but, always again, we must detach ourselves from every real or intellectual frame of a law in order to throw our best life-forces, without intellectual hindrances, up to the highest points of universal attraction -more and more : excelsior! Love surpasses any written law with its insatiable eternal sincere force and, therfore, is freedom forever. The old churches were once precious barrels of affective guns, which after having become useless, were replaced by new material and intellectual elements. No materialism, no visibility, no intellectuality ever may satisfy or can ever be persistent and general. For this reason we have in the very same way, as in the material gun, the law of fragility and destructibility of the barrel in all our human institutions. With the passing centuries they are likely to become venerable perfumed graves, from where the original creative genius escaped, remarkable dead craters, whose central divine fire is extinct.

Let us not despair because of the inevitable change of the genial garment of idealism. It is not the everlasting truth of spiritual and affective love and universal magnetism, which alone is holy and perfect and alone must be obeyed and fulfilled, -which changes. Only the human accidental formula of the intellectual garment, the sensory shawl wrapping the eternal truth, only the subordinated standards of really diluted affectivity, change and go under. The letter kills,it is the spirit which vivifies. The letter itself always again must be killed in order not to kill the spirit. The letter, the intellectual material must serve in order not to kill the superior eternal sentiments. Every exaggerated attachment to individual life is the root of immorality. Our first and last duty is getting rid always again of any one-sided intellectual, historic, artistic,personal, familiar, scientific, cultural, traditional and customary formula, in order to reach the spirit and that virtue of detachment which fills with such wonderful serenity the expressions of the Indian and Chinese gods. The holy meaning of purification and bath is in nearest connection with this principle of *detachment*.

A detached smile at the death of our dearest may, thus, be even a proof of a pure heart. All greatest things in our life are un-losable and imperishable. Life is kind enough to clean us continu-ally of the bad habit of sticking too much to material intellectua-lity, in changing always, in depriving us from what we just began to be fond of, in giving us all charming material gifts not when we are longing for them fervently, but in the moment of our least expectation. Nature cares not to associate the human heart intim-ately with material goods, and less in the measure as the human being is gifted with wisdom. The uplifting energy of the concen-trated upper affective standards have such a power of magnetic attraction that they strive to absorb the life-force towards them-selves, at the expense of the material dilution of the intellectual objectivity. They reserve for themselves the role of importance and stability, of mastership and goals, of centres and bull's eyes and of affective MISSILES, round which the accidental and fugitive fragility of intellectual detail and material interest turn and move ever changing, like the planets round the sun or the moon round the earth.

The big man of a city, often called very significantly *the big gun* of a community, is a man of a domineering and ruling position, who has the power to attract the attention, the hopes, the fears and interests of his fellow-citizens,to his personality, round which they group themselves like the planets around the sun or like the walls of the barrel round the missile. They form together the psycho-mechanic and intellectual real opportunity, of the social life, for the success of this great man, and he, in his turn, avails himself of them as of intellectual material steps to the ascension to power. They are the tight c oncentrating ring round the glorious punctual light-field of his forbidding authority, through which society discharges their complicated idealistic shots of glaring concentrated success.

He is the centre and principle, the missile of the psycho-mechanic unity of this social body. Nobody knows, how it came about, if the superiority of the leading man or the inferiority of his fellow-citizens was the starting point; but as much is sure, that he could not be the outstanding leader without the surrounding mould of his subservient and adapting friends, nor could they have a successful career without his central position. The leader is given by them to be the affective nucleus of their public life. They, in retiring, would lose their supporting and supported utility as well. It would be dangerous for anyone of them to give up his support, because he would lose the protection of this influential man. Is it the only merit of this clever and strong-minded singular leader, that he has progressed to his ruling central role and subjugated all? Are his ambition and his bold force the causes of his outstanding position, or is there, on the contrary the question of the timid unimportance and lack of affective energy of the totality of people uninterested in public life and having, thus, brought about the existing authoritative conditions? All these different circumstances, in their complicated nature, may have helped and complemented each other and effectuated the existing genial reality. The chief reason was the intrinsic psychic necessity.

The prominent position of a man is always a very relative thing depending equally on two sides. It is conditional, of course, on both his own personal courage, skill and individual affective value, and, on the other hand, of receding readiness of the surrounding people who agree that this single man shall be their common superior, their MEDIATOR and channel to most desirable concentrated values directly inaccessible to each of them. They hold the stirrup to his power, lifting him up with united forces, and hope to attain their realizable advantages best in this intermediary way. They have recoiled to the more comfortable trenches of second-hand favour and receive their share of goods from the benevolence of the chosen mediator in whom they trust. This man at least is elected, by compromise, to reach their common boldest dreams of highest standards, he may proceed to the sanctuary of the immortal genius, if he is willing to distribute to them all the lower real values of the world, in a just manner.

Perhaps there is even more the question of the necessity of ever establishing the concentrating order of the social organism, meeting all psychic and social powers, from an understanding unique point of fixed *rendez-vous*,than to have chosen a quite extraordinarily gifted personality. We always need seriously and indispensably the affective intercourse of all real and ideal values and receive and give it always through an interfering mediating person or a concentrating and uniting dispensator who has the important role of a turn-table between all. His task as a genial king or religious mediator or social leader or intellectual and moral priest or artistic seer of the human society educates him by his circular compressive influence, as soon as he is invested with the noble task of his central position within the social light-field of the world. By the importance of the peculiar characterizing features of his duty he is formed and moulded to successful general service, if he has some natural inclinaton to it.

Considering the fact of the aptitude of a very large number of gifted individuals for the affective role of mediator, according to the almighty law of necessity and compensation, we may ask, how it came about that just this individual and not another one was chosen for the sublime nobility of unique affective mediation between the average and peripheric every-day man and the central and ideal brilliance of the genial election. Even in spite of the fact that this question may be an useless matter of jealousy, because, indeed, humanity is to be considered as one collective functional body with common rights and duties, with every vicariation of deficiency and enjoyment, of merits, glory, shame and punishments, the question of origin of the *genial selection* may seem noteworthy to many.

Genius, creation, life and culture are ideas and problems, which we will meet and approach under similar psychological conditions, always again. It seems to be one of the favorite moods of nature to proceed in concentrated energy, to establish strong accumulations of forces, and to connect the past with the present, and the present with the future, preferably,through the exclusive antennae of the genial compensatory symbolism.The special selection of one individual to be this chosen point, this out-cry of whole nations and cultures through one single human voice, the choice of this sparkling psychic lightning- conductor must be caused by the largest relative excess of higher affective avidity for concentrated idealistic values, by the stronger keenness of magnetic aptitude, small as may be the individual difference. Here lies the whole explanation of the individual preferability for genial work: the strongest hereditary and cultural realistic fulfilment is the best preparation for idealistic longings. The strongest magnetic desire or need leads the natural law of concentrating energy the way to hit, with selective overpowering distinction, that most receptive man for the universal forces, who so quickly and thoroughly will be developed to be the genius of a time. The least realistic type is the *locus minoris resistentiae* in the building of the universal world and the leading point, where the universal and "extra-universal" longings find their thorough-fare to rush to their future terminal goal. He is the leader of the desires of the world.

If we remember the law of the *electric current,* we know that the electric light is due to the compressive friction coming from the disproportion of the quantity of the flowing electric energy and of the relatively small cross-section of the conducting metal wire. As soon as the amount of the electric current diminishes or the section of the wire has been enlarged, the light goes out. Every light and every fire are the product of strong friction and energetic compression of any moving force within a narrow conductor or light channel or point, in a similar way as the burning point of the magnifying glass came about. A genius, in the same way, is a glowing concentration of the magnetic spiritual energy of whole nations and whole historic cultures. He is, physically speaking, the same fire and the same punctually condensed magnetic life-force, as we have it in the artificial electricity. But there is also the same law of limitation. An excess of the electric current destroys the kindling possibilities of the wire, as well as a surplus of interspheric magnetism kills the corporal and physiological possibilities of a man. The considerable enlargement of the genial section of the light-field extinguishes, instead, the burning light of the former narrow light-point, because the disproportion between its size and the passing amount of affective life-force and, therefore, the enflaming friction has ceased.

Doubtless Christ was such a compressive accumulation of affective energy. He was an inter-cultural lightning-conductor, a red-hot wire of the electric compression of interspheric magnetism sparkling through all the world, because of the tremendous disproportion with the individual amount of natural physiological possibilities. He was the thin organic wire and lightning-rod of the genial transformation of His great time. He was the affective centre

of a most revolutionary historic period, the flaming product of
idealizing coincidences and of great meeting opposite and frictive
energies. He was on the peak of the first summit of cultural events.
His trembling continuous rapture must be supposed to have been at
the extreme limits of superhuman efforts.

No wonder that the *human heart of Jesus* receives high tributes
of special homages from His worshipping believers. Our heart
aches sensitively, when we have a serious sorrow. The circular muscles are painfully contracted by strong affective excitement. The
sorrows and sins were thrown on the responsible heroic shoulders.
What incredible disproportion: this single sensitive human heart,
on one side, and the weight of a most important cultural world
rushing down on Him like a drowning inescapable tempest, on the
other! Would that heart not physically burst and be burnt like an
hypercharged electric wire !

Thus we assume naturally, according to the principle and
conviction, that all human things develop through steady laws
ruling all the universe, that it is the peculiar culminating conversion
of the material and intellectual development of the Old World,
to which is hinted by the word: FULFILMENT OF THE
TIMES, and which caused the affective concentration of the
social soul of the world. In this fulfilment, which means, in the
extreme degree of material and intellectual development of the
old civilizations, psychologically speaking, was given the main
reason for the genial psycho-mechanic concentration of the social
Christian soul. The previous intellectual one-sidedness was driven
too far for a long time so that, owing to this hyper-mature development, the crushing and very complete genial collapse of the
cultural light-field became the inevitable, sudden and catastro-
phal necessity of the total psychology of the peri-Mediterranean
cultures.

The hyperextended, never never idealistically relaxed and rested
psychopupil of these countries lost, because of abuse of its elastic
forces, the power of its peripheric fixability and experienced a sudden and perfect magneto-mechanic shrinking down-fall from the
periphery to the centre, from the extreme of the most developed
and richest intellectual objectivity to the utmost concentrated
genial sentimental compression.

Up to the time of Christ the psychological real face of the
human Janus head was large, distinct and ruling everything, whilst
the idealistic sentimental was very small and shadowy. The balance
of the compensation of the psychic possibilities and powers had

stooped, to the utmost degree, towards the intellectual values. The affective feelings of the soul were neglected, ignored and scorned. It was the memorable moment of the starting Christian culture, when the wonderful change from intell ctual to sentimental psychic prevalence took place with surprising swiftness and thoroughness, when, according to the biological law of existing compensation between intellectuality and sentiments, the scale of the latter, after having been checked a long time, received instantly almost all weight and attracted, as in the beginning creation, all psychic life-force into its genial whirlpool. The world became young once more and started again from a most powerful first affective point. It received again the first enthusiastic energy of an original impulse and creative magnetic power. It was in the Christian idea, where this thorough renewal or *kosmo-psycho-mechanic renaissance* found its symbolic expression.

Here we have the cultural-psychological explanation for the outstanding necessary historic position of Christ. He in His materialistic age had plenty of space to plant His wonderful mystic tree. He was the most successful idealistic antagonist of an enormous realistic culture, gathering and compressing conscientiously all affective energy which vibrated and lingered longingly in the atmosphere of His time.

Christ was the charming punctual fire resulting from the complete peripheric failure of His contemporary history. In Him humanity started a new life, in Him the human social soul heaved a deep breath from old worrying and started again towards future new tasks and works. What a refreshing and delivering breath must this have been, when humanity had its new energetic starting from the genial spring-board of Christ!

The divine Christ must have had the readiest genial disposition in order to be suitable for the ideal sensitiveness which fate laid on His shoulders. But it was as well the extraordinary force and necessity of exterior historic conditions which formed and moulded Him and conveyed on Him, not only the brilliant crown of the chief and king of humanity, but transformed Him literally into the most compressed, most lovely sparkling affective symbolic diamond of mankind.

This Christ, the child of greatest historic coincidences, with the startling power of greatest divine sentiments, shares His psychological features with the idea of GOD. On one hand, we crave for the idea of god as well by our reasoning thought, as we, on the other, are unable, owing to the laws of our own reflection, to explain it. In the same manner Christ is the necessity of our theoretical psychological thought as it is, on the other hand, a most difficult problem to represent the force of a god as a man without giving Him a superior organic rank than the ordinary fragility of an individual human body. The notion of god as the divine concentrated dignity of Christ, in their perfection, as our intelligence and our mathematical logic may reason them out, are an intellectual headlong prolongation of our experience, a genial compression of our concluding causal ideas into one point.

The hours of irresistible longing for the simpler conceptions of our childhood create, in a similar manner, an *affective relapse* from the periphery of acquired culture and intellectual experience. Following these urges would be what we call CONVERSION from the real experience to the genial compression and punctual simplification of the sentiments of our heart. It would be a renewal of the individual psycho-mechanic manner of reaction, in a similar way, as Antiquity, by its converting personal Christian ideal, was made a young child again. In every Conversion the old stable of Augias is cleared out and receives all polished charm of youth, energy and optimism, but all need of sophisticating experience and renewed intellectual instruction too.

According to the deeper impressions of our affectively heated deeds, thoughts and experiences into our personal memory and habits, at an early age, we find very generally the life-long clinging of the average individual to its early acquired notions of kinship, nationality, language and conception of the ideal world. Notwithstanding the most various later disquisitions on all these matters people always fall back to their early conceptions and habits. What was created within them *in statu nascendi* of their personal early development, is dearest to them, as a rule, in their old days.Le coeur revient toujours à ses premiers amours.

The figure of Christ in the highest perfection,as the Apostles, the first Christians and the later Christian nations accepted it, is the idealistic symbolic simplification of all the magnetic urges, and the compressed individual apotheosis of the total precious affective conversion, which happened at the thoroughly fatal and therefore so thoroughly helped failure of the pre-Christian history. His name and His personality became the interpreting parole of the affective light-bearers of this great time. They altogether learned to understand, and speak to each other, in a new_ *terminology* which transformed entirely all former intellectual notions and conveyed to the *modern languages* so different a notional content

and meaning, that we to-day have difficulties to learn the old languages because of the total change of cultural conceptions. The
nucleus of this change is the notion of Christ, the God-man who
introduced into the world quite a new notional combination of
intellectual and sentimental characteristics, pulling heaven to earth
and, even more, raising earth to heaven. It was the surprising and
unheard of, fact that a very audacious and serious attempt was
made to establish a more fluid and less checked interchange between highest idealistic and deepest materialistic values, to connect
more fluently the different affective standards of distant values of
sentiments and thoughts, and to fix this resolution even by an
adequate and cleverly balanced new terminology more able to convey affective lofty elevation. The divine idealistic notion of Christ
is the root and roof of this enterprise. The charm and the sentimental magnetic tension of this ̇ d alone was the crown of the intellectual and philosophical masterpiece of the starting Christianity. The synoptic EVANGELISTS were most careful in elaborating a most balanced and refi..ed new terminology, a~cording to
their changed philosophical conceptions. Their harmonious grouping
around the central divine notion of a personal Christ, answers our
astonishment that the holy writers could agree so well in the topic,
in their conceptions a..d expressions; but if one will prove, by this
fact, that Christ indeed must have been the individual real experience of all these men, we rather would ask, if ever had been so
perfect harmony and concordance among people in the world.
The achieved unity of their common thoughts and sympathies was
the most elaborate psychological event of the highest suggestive
magnetism. They all together were under the incomparable pressure of the highly charged psycho-magnetic atmosphere of their
intellectual time, absolutely av~~se to intellectual criticism, when
they once had entered into the delightful concentrative draft of
their emotional time. They were thrown irresistibly into the attractive whirlpool of their psychomagnetic compensation.

There is no question that the most valuable human beings
never were publicly known. Their best qualities prevented any
systematical advertising. They did neither like nor need public fame.
The artistic representation of the greatest genius and the announcement of His glory have been so skilful and, above all, persevering,
that we cannot help but understand the success of the divine news,
from a merely superficial look, not mentioning the intrinsic deep
psychic and personal justification of the hero. The advertising of
the historic god surely found the most artistic expression, by the

collaborating strain of a highly gifted artistic union being under the same strong pressure of the most efficient artistic atmosphere. Perhaps never since the beginning of the world such a lucky and strong coincidence of numerous circumstances favored the creation of an artistic masterpiece as the artistic announcement and unfoldment of the Christian idea. The personal aptitude of the holy genial writers joined with the worthiness of their divine hero and the thorough longing of all the earth and universe. We notice an accumulation of most complicated resourcefulness towards the raising of the mighty picture of the most perfect description of a genius. We have the most efficient combination of numerous highly gifted people with a genial disposition, meeting at the same time and same place—a rare occurrence—and we have simultaneously, which is the chief thing, a tremendous affective suggestion of the intellectually exhausted historic development, which nobody could resist, and which stooped with the energy and the magnetic force of a lightning on the heads and the hearts of the genial apostles.

The greatest poets, the genial artists and painters are important through their affective generalities concerning everybody, and they lose their universality and their striking general validity, if they follow too closely the peripheric way of the individual intellectuality. The picture of Christ has its inestimable value, because it is above the individual existence. He was the historic and intellectual wonderful opportunity of gathering and compressing into one immortal genial unity the crying needs of His changing time. Had He been depicted in the distinct features of historic existence, to which softly is hinted in the holy writings, had He transgressed the narrow boundaries of high genial symbolism, Christ would have been disturbed by His apostles to reach that general and central force of attraction, by which He pulls our affective longings incessantly.

The amalgamation of the genial personalities of the holy writers is quite wonderful. They lose up to a highest degree their individuality and are melted into one condensed circle around their common uplifting purpose, forming together the strong barrel of their great idealistic missile which they shoot in supporting strong compression from the muzzle of their general genial union. Their excellent synopsis has its reason in the common magnetic fact of their great goal given to them by the contrary confusion of the fulfilment of the time and the intermediation of their divine hero. God himself descends from heaven unto earth, where strong and sincere will unite people in friendship. God himself arises in their midst as the strongest tie of their agreement and where the strong idea of the eternal deity is worshipped, this common service makes them best and most reliable FRIENDS. In this sense the obliging and sincere friendship of the first Christians was proverbial. They all were inflamed by the same eternal goal, they all had the same hopes and rewards, but shared also the same dangers and fears. In their turn they formed again a powerful and impermeable barrel of the Christian idea, neglecting their individuality and presenting themselves as an amalgamated collectivity and as one harmonious social human body to their enthusiastic central genial idea.

PEACE and exclusion of continuous misunderstandings are always founded in the secret power of the common intense enjoyment in one great ideal taste, in one terminal goal, which permits by its abundant affective attraction the individuals to overlook the differences and contrary inclinations of the daily life. Great common successes have always the basis of common taste and principles, of congruity in fundamental questions of life. Common terminal magnetism is the key of explanation of great social success. Common conceptions of the world and the same selective emphasis of affective standards are indispensable for thorough mutual understanding and confidence. They are the common platform, where all great and small arising quarrels have their source, in creating different *tastes*. Where the strongest and last calls of life and their methods are in concordance and parallel direction, differences in the daily life and in the small individual interests may easily be settled. They are entirely at a loss to thoroughly upset the intellectual methods, because they are peripheric, which is to say, of weak directive power in the whole relations guided and directed definitely by the common interests of highest magnetic dignity. The higher interest subjugates the lower, the most intense common ideal has always the power to defeat the material world. This was very plain in the idealistic tendencies of the first Christians who were selected idealists having the advantage of a genial strong atmosphere which made to them easier, what is more difficult today, the irresistible aspiration to divine sentiments.

Genius and ARTISTIC representation are very close. It is the essence of the genial character to gather all general features from individuality into a new formula more creditable and powerful than any individual sample and to inspire into this artificial summary the soul of genial authority and weight. The genial artist augments the contents of truth, beauty and affective weight of human nature, so much so, that he compensatorily must dispense with peripheric representation of human individuals and details. He would be at a perfect loss to offer in the combination of his task the refined intellectual minutias of one human individual, unless he would sacrifice the genial affective sway of his intention.

The holy writers adapted their pictures to the principle of an ideal-real conception with strong tendency to prevailing affective idealism. There are individual features in the representation of Christ; but these individual and intellectual deeds are always wrapped within the charming dreamy mist of divine poetry. We always see, through the transparent mask of a human person, just to the bottom of most general and genial powers. This skilful artistic, in some sense threadbare depiction, in simultaneous representation of most elevated ideal and most ordinary daily moments is necessary owing to our functional hesitation to consider, at the same time, very distant ranges of affective standards and to accept them in an unitarian equally attentive meditation. We often have nothing but a smile at comparing most distant and seemingly mutually excluding values and stand-points. One thing seems to us very intelligent and affectively objectionable, and, reversely, an other thing is full of sentimental dignity and elevation, and, however hurts us in an intellectual way. Where is the reason of *mockery* and *derision*? In our own shortsightedness.

Genius and art exclude essentially individuality and detail. Art is the consequence of the insufficiency of our limited attention. It is a broadening, far-looking master of our life. In order to force our attention, it is forced to establish surprising oppositions, where there are only distances. It creates universal conflicts and bluffing surprises, where, in fact, there are smooth transitions. In its shortening way it condenses distant values and their comparative understanding into a narrow space. It gives simultaneous universal spot-lights of broadest instructions which could not be attained in another way. Every artistic and genial work is, in a certain sense, the *numerator of an equation*.

We understand that a religious system with the attempt and claim of universality is always, inevitably exposed to the realistic intrusions of mockery and derision and of scientific contradictions, on one side, and to affective disgust and abandonment, on the other. Every religious system suffers from the disproportion of its high claim and goal and of the scarcity of vital and representing means, which are put at its disposal. The perfection of the intellectual minute picture of the life is handicapped by the uplifting force of the religious ideals, whose elaboration is the chief purpose of any religious system, whilst the strong enthusiastic energy of high ideals, on the contrary, is bridled by the intellectual narrowness of the human language, thought and imagination. The affective sentiments strive, independent of every intellectual matter, up to the heavens. They refuse the limitation of any intellectual formula and are inclined to put themselves in a contradictory position in regard to this conditional and accidental help. The real life, in its turn, easily likes to refuse the action of the affective idealism as intruding incompetency, and thus the struggle between the two comes about. The historic religion has to be careful to avoid joke and mockery, on one side, and the reproach of sterility and empty formalism, on the other, because it *exceeds the boundaries of human possibilities*. _____

The real part of our nature attempts, indeed, to throw out the influences of the affective values by humour, joke, mockery and derision. This, of course, is accepted and felt as a high treason and flaming insult, from the enthusiastic part of the sentimental soul. At the same time the affective universal idealism scorns the formula of the intellectual help, although it cannot do without; despises its methods, which are the indispensable ladder for its successful ascension to heaven. Therefore idealism likely changes its intellectual ways, again and again, in order to reproduce its uplifting discharge. It does not allow the intellectual side of the soul to share sufficiently its splendour of idealistic dignity, dooming, on the contrary, every idealistic spark, falling down from universal effusion to the intellectual world, as relapse into effemination, luxury, degeneration and sterilization.

We see any kind of disorder arising from both the idealistic and realistic side, as a product of an attempt to build up a very extensive and superhuman religious system, between most disproportioned amounts and forces. We are punished on both sides, if we go too far, on the idealistic, if we will be too intellectual and distinct, and on the real side, if we, on the contrary, intend to produce very strong concentrations of affective rapture and sentimental delight. We always have to feel the revenge of pride, the shame of our insufficiency, and always, when we try to cover it on one side, it is the much more visible on the other one: intellectual perfection producing sentimental, whilst affective full practice and achievement is leading to intellectual, negligence. There is the question of human pride, of superestimation of our natural forces and of not being able to carry through, equally and consistently, the great enterprise and task which was started in the pride of a most promising outlook.

We understand, therefore, the compromising tendency of the clever religious founder. If it is not wrong,in advance and after all, to be a religious founder,under normal human circumstances,because of the danger of immediately starting disquietness and self-destruction of the human insufficient force in anxiety, self-accusations and remorses, he has, in any case, to do everything to maintain and strengthen the idea of the harmonious medium between real and ideal components, within the boundaries of the frame of human possibilities.

The practical value of any historical religious system is so much as it is able to avoid and hide all dangers of arising intellectual criticism, in joke, mockery and scientific clashes, on one side, and in affective scorn, pride, reproaches of luxury, degenerative mummification and formalistic petrification, on the other.

The choice of very distant points of individual attraction, in a religious system, produces an extraordinarily *intense circulation* of our vital force between the two opposite poles of extreme idealism and most exact real attention. The to and fro of the flowing energy is exciting for the individual and forms very strong needs and customs of attraction and repulsion, which, of course, means an ubiquitous psycho-mechanic energetic motion and strong discharging currancy of human psycho-mechanic rhythms. But this easy and thrilling sway of our affective emotion, hygienic as it is for avoiding stagnations, produces at the same time and by the same reason strong needs of continuous sensational and sentimental excitements, psychic overwork, lavish use of energy, and therefore Neurasthenia.

The DIVINE ARCHITECT of the Christian religion was quite aware of the extraordinary disproportion between human claims, hopes and longings and the small amount of disposable total individual life-force, with which he ought to have covered all these distant interests and struggling desires. He decided, as we pointed out, more to the favour of the strong idealistic standards, and was compensatorily forced to drop the desirable intensive development of the detailed human objectivity.

Intellectual reality remains rightly one pole of every religious system. The forcing sensorial power of the daily life succeeds instantly, with its intellectual sharpness, in capturing our first attention. What would happen,if reality was only symbolicly hinted to, in a religious system? Connection with,and explanation of, the intellectual world would be insufficient. If we would not draw the further consequence, in this case, to turn the back to the dangerous strength of the sensorium, to leave the world and hide ourselves behind walls, we would succumb inevitably, earlier or later, to the misleading supremacy of the ruling sensorial influences. The result will be, that the strong real engagement of our life- force, in the visible world, owing to vital insufficiency, absorbs the share of the sentimental idealistic universe, causes a small supply of affective force for the deeper extension of our vital interspheric wire, and, surrenders the individual to the *angry leaps* of symbolic mysticism, miracles and sin. All these intellectual and moral faults are due to affective hyperextension of the human life-force and to the opposite violently tearing magnetic energy toward the two extreme goals of the individual exposed to weakness, undecidedness and angor.

The *evangelists* strove continuously to be aware of the different opposite dangers. In their difficult task they intended to avoid both to stick to closely to the formal intellectuality and to hide, up to a certain degree, how little weight they put on the peripheric reality. Owing to the enlarged imaginative freedom of their new terminology, they easily dismissed a too closely bound intellectual accuracy and distinction in order to avoid intellectual and scientific distraction. It is because of these carefully elaborated and balanced notions and use of language, because of that reservedness of linguistic means in dealing with the personal individuality of Christ, that the affective avidity towards the universe is not thoroughly checked, but attains easily its idealistic universal discharge. The holy writers never enter on natural scientific problems. There is, on the contrary, the pronounced inclination, to include them into the supernatural power of the genial hero, if there arise difficult and unsolvable questions in regard to the natural laws of gravitation, of life and death, of meteorology, of chemistry and physics. Thus Christianity turns out, in its classical books, to be essentially idealistic. It neglects rather the respect for the peripheric and detailed intellectuality than to give up the utmost facility of sentimental sway and affective enthusiasm.

According to its peculiar opposite direction of magnetic emphasis, intellectuality strives incessantly and necessarily to work out the highest degree of sensorial clarity, utmost visibility in measurable details. It appreciates perfect real display and objective explanation, and rejects all even smallest imaginative values within the linguistic scientific representation.   It sneeres at the least observation of uplifting idealism and appreciates their value not higher than a merchant the air bubbles in cast metal, representing nothing else than a clear loss of material weight.

Idealism and affective sentiments strive, on the contrary, to get rid, again and again, of every intellectual formula. They understand the relative and restricted narrowness of every intellectual value and, therefore, never are satisfied with the real world. They move from an imperfect step to a better one, ever disappointed in new and greater expectations. This is the pride of the extreme idealist. Nobody could be subjected more thoroughly to the *changes* of intellectual visible and scientific fashion than the high-minded, sincerely gifted and one-sided idealist. Thus we see that both idealist and realist are under a vital and essential necessity to be radically opposite , owing to their specific magnetic attraction in contrary directions. The affective sentiments go directly uphill on their nimble, spiritually volatilized wings, and material intellectuality either follows slowly in mincing cultural preparation, in the same direction or joins the same last eternal goals through the inferior roundabout-way of the links of material gravitation.

Exaggerated worship of ancestry and tradition, old customs and antiquities, veneration for old familiar peculiarities, even worshipping the dead, the reverence for the opinions of our ancestors, for the places of great historical events or relics of great men, even the preference of one's own family, one's own country, nationality and language, are, if taken too seriously, altogether the proof of *intellectual slothfulness*. The often alleged word of Christ:" Who is my brother and sister? He who fulfils the will of my Father in heaven, is my brother and sister," He hinted to this common traditional *laziness and intellectual petrification of our heart*. He warned and scorned people averse to new future views. The eager idealist is the creator of new formulae. The extreme idealistic type is not in a position to accept, uncritically, traditional old formulas given to him by education and history, but his sincere and powerful sway unto the eternal universe, induces him, always again and again, to try new *intellectual fashions* more appropriate to his high idealism, and to discard all old, even dearest, formulas objectionable in the least degree. What is not imperfect in human life? The objectionability of the old accustomed methods and intellectual fashions of mind and body consists exactly in the dear veneration and worship they enjoy, or in the danger to cling too much to them, falling down before self-made gods, in superstitious idolatry. The idealist is the self-sacrificing and intrepid torch-bearer leading the van of the nightly procession of mankind out to the frightening extreme abysses of the universe. He is the daring inventor of new-land, principally never satisfied with life and its conditions, as he first meets them. It is the fundamental law of the idealistic organization of character to pull off all real material and intellectual dirty clothes of our affective life and to look for new possibly better fashion, linen full of the fragrance of cleanliness. He is a courageous optimist, looking ahead with the conviction of future improvement of the world. In this sense of our best *personal and honest* efforts we are salvable, as the culminating conclusion of Faust says: "Wer immer *redlich sich* bemueht, den koennen wir erloesen." "Whosoever himself strives sincerely, we can save him."
For the extreme idealist it is clear that the lower interests of reality continuously must be sacrificed to the higher idealistic ones. For him it is exactly the superior power of divine sentiments, which induces him, again and again, to exclude the intellectually lower

and more imperfect bearers of idealism, to crush the old vases, which turned out by experience and use to be old,wornout,clumsy and hideous, and to replace them, with utmost care, by better new ones. Exaggerated inclination to *Conservatism* in any sense is a very serious angry slothfulness which makes too great concessions to the intellectual stability of all times and neglects the necessary and courageous genial unfoldment of humanity. This kind of laziness leads to reactive *revolutions* which are violently retrieving psychological waves, angry compensatory psycho-mechanic contractions into a new genial state.

It is the fate of all intellectual and real things to be worn out one day. All old despised rubbish was once the splendidly ruling fashion of the day. In this sense we may assume that the material things are a later state of the universal creative power. *Materiality* is the cool depositum, the rubbish of old creative victories of the universe, the rejected and worn out intellectual formula of wonderful genial *creative* lightnings and red-hot prehistoric productions, the last peripheric crystallization of life-force and the most remote tombstone of the central genius. There is no more fire, no more energy, no more emotion towards the central subjective goal of contraction; the antagonistic force of the centripetal magnetism of the earth has received the absolute influence on the "dead" materiality.

From this state of peripheric helplessness, to which the material substance, or better the substantiated universal energy, has been driven by the centrifugal genial sway, it is set free again and moved centralwards by the intermediation of cultural work and of art. The material substance receives, through the human actions of **art** *and culture*,again the possibility of sharing, in an artificial and synthetical compressive way around a new creative idea, the nobility of central genial sentiments. The mincing cultural and refining artistic work elevate the material substance, again and again, to strong notions of wonderful idealism and produce, once more those glittering diamonds of ideal and real combination, as we had them in the morning of the first creation, with both the surprising novelty of real formal expression and the suggestive energy of genial feelings, in a masterpiece.

The great *efficiency of intellect* rests with the creative powers of development of earth and universe, culture and art. It is always in the bold intellectual leaps to and from eternal sentiments and values, where the intimate amalgamation and mingled action of intellect and feelings produce the highest beauty and deepest truth, and it is the first creative realization of eternal sentiments in the multiple visibility, where intellect and sentiments have by far their most important expression and overwhelming charming intimacy. Intellectuality receives most unfolding energy, from affectivity, in the creative STATUS NASCENDI, whereas it becomes cool and stiff and dull at the periphery of its distant exhaustion at the margin of its perfect detailed development, where it is most clearly visible and measurable.

We acknowledge the affective symbolic imaginative idea as the mother of all greatest intellectual things, of the richest real display and inventive unfoldment. It is the most inexhaustible well of material and visible plenty.

CREATION is the universal genial affectivity outbursting into the realm of intellectuality. It is the charming and uplifting splendour of the inspired material and intellectual life *in statu nascendi,* where the surprising novelty of the beautiful real garment is espoused to the thrilling energy of the genial need of the progressive expansion. Both real intellectuality and eternal strength touch each other at the nearest possible point of central meeting; they both encounter in the immediate freshness of their typical character, amalgamated and melted most intensely in their intimate mutual embracement. There is as well a tremendous flashing fire of concentrated genial energy, visible in all wonderful features of the real masterpiece, as a refined elaboration of material detailed work. There are two pronounced oppositions, a genial giant challenging the material peripheric world, inviting it to approach as much as possible in the central direction without giving up its distinct precision, and at the same time on the peripheric side, an intellectually proud giant of highly developed material riches and utmost logical categoric resistance, enticing the central affective opponent to meet him at the utmost periphery. These two pronounced and seemingly irreconciliable and incompatible adversaries hold each other, in the middle of the universal arena of the stellar battlefield of the creative performances. They both are very strong and despairingly determined; they come from a faraway country, unknown to each other, and now they are wrestling as two powerful equal heroes trying to encroach on the deadly defended mutual provinces. Both are unable to obtain their perfect victory. The enemy stands erect still. But in the intimate mingling of the battle both unknowingly have accepted many a resemblance of one another. In the mighty fight we see the kindling sparks of the energetic genius, glittering from the garment of material reality, and we admire the artistic flight of the beautiful creases and waves, the heated blushing features of the realistic material intellectual adversary, but also the hesitating order and systematic creative work of the genial hero. Both are unable to defeat each other. And thus they stand in unyielding stubborn effort, immovable and petrified for ever, in the attitude of their undecided battle, definitely fixed in their highest pathetic compromise. This is the perfect natural artistic masterpiece, the make-up and the painful development of the *creative and artistic psychology.*

The dearest and sweetest surroundings, the most intimate injunctions of the dearest mother and of a beloved and truly reverend preacher, all educational tenets and principles, can be accepted only as hints to the right direction. They soon must be sacrificed to a new spring and a new morning of future genial affective creation. Our noble and proud soul is fond of the novelty and the enlarged dignity of the new creative artistic *change,* of intellectual and visible *fashions.* Novelty conveys so easily the charm of superiority.

This, in a way humiliating, in an other sense honoring, continual *material change* means a law of our psycho-mechanic nature. Hard as it may be for the acquired security of our domesticated lazy intellect, the never tired sway of our idealistic talents pricks us again and again and induces us to change our intellectual formula, as a snake changes its hide in spring time. Individual, nation, science, language, conception of life and artistic style, share all together this fate with the daily fashion of dressing. New kindreds, new personal unions must arise, new political prospects must be opened, new acquisitions made or losses suffered. New philosophic hypotheses supersede the old obsolete; other principles and views come en vogue, and immediately the best former ones lose all respect and observance, until, after a certain number of circular revolutions of the psychic life, the oldest are discovered again, under the disguise of an other label, as the last and most noticeable *modern fashion.* We have this phenomenon very distinctly recognizable, in a small and unimportant scale, in the function of dressing, where always old forgotten fancies and frills are issued as last novelty, whilst the previous last fashions are rejected as impossible.

We have the same taste, comparing small with large things, in the principal philosophical conceptions of the world and the ages, which sometimes are very intellectual and fond of material appreciation, scorning all sentimental aspirations; another time they are puffed with high uplifting imagination and sentimental affections, despising material and intellectual values. Thus the psycho-mechanic physiognomy and psychic faces of all centuries are very different.

Within the large units of thousand of years we observe, not the less, a *continual affective metamorphosis* going from the peripheric intellectuality towards the sentimental centre, and reversely from the genial punctual centre towards the large detailed display of visible riches and scientific clear understanding.

There are, in those changing and alternating revolutions of the history of the long historic periods at a great scale, *turning points* like the *solstitial* points of the spheric flight of the planets round their central sun.

All life is characterized by the everlasting law of *Waving and alternating movements*. As the palpitations of the heart are regulated by a continual alternating contraction and distension of the muscular organism, as the surface of the sea is in an incessant motion, owing to following innumerable waves, caused by the physical magnetic force of gravitation, thus we are entitled to assume a similar law for every created existence, in the material and intellectual and affective world. We all are links of chains vibrating over longest universal abysses. Not only the small visible and short waves are ubiquitous in the sea and, in an other sense, in all the world, as petty individual distinctions, but, in the same manner as we observe, besides curly wavelets on the surface of the water, often mighty breakers of a hurricane clashing and destroying every obstacle, and as we distinguish, in addition to the regular small waving of the sea, the interference of the larger waving movements of ebb and flow, - thus we have the same phenomenon in all vital and biological units.

Our physiological body, our social unions, all our physical and psychic reactions have their *different waves of very different amplitudes interfering with,* and SUPERPOSING, each other, each going its own way and following its own laws and measures of development. Every minute of human physiology and psychology has its smallest measures of reaction; every seize of human collaboration obeys its own special law and method. We are very wrong, if we forget, that also the largest extensions of historical and creative developments have not only small individual and annual wavelets, but also such of largest amplitude, exceeding our consciousness and individual imagination. There are psychological waves which are quicker and shorter than the palpitations of the human heart, which go on with more rapidity than the thought and the lightning, but there are also universal and collective psychologicol reactions, which pre-suppose a slow accumulation of forces during thousands of years in order to effectuate one deep psychological *conversion* of the whole totality of the affective humanity. And there remains the omni-present law that extremes touch each other. The slowest and least noticeable motion may have the most energetic powerful discharge at once. The lightning strikes after a long sultry hesitation and is, therefore, the more energetic.

So we recognize in the genial conversion of the world, at the time of Christ, a topmost culmination of a waving motion of the psychological world, on a large scale. Thousands of years of peripheric distraction and intellectual resistance, of biologically affective sultry oppression were the pre-supposition of this huge oscillating culmination. The genial symbolic idea of Christ was the glittering and foaming summit of such a powerful historic-psychological wave, as they return into human experience - a spectacle for gods indeed - only once in thousands and thousands of years.

How wonderful is the look at the high *breakers of the sea!* Their tops are shining, vibrating and splashing in their beautiful feathery splendour. They come again and again in order to disappear after one impressive moment. They are the final products of mighty uplifting movements of huge masses of water driven up to high mountains. There they begin to adopt a wonderful greeny esmerald color and a charming boiling and vibrating condition of white pearls and filigrees and are unprecedentedly charming, culminating in the splashing fascination of brewing foam and hovering dreamy mist. In the twinkling of an eye this wonderful top of the wave falls down like the vision of a magnificent fairy-tale, carrying with it, however, for a certain distance, the glorious beauty of seezing foamy majesty and greeny spell. Then all the masses of water fall the deeper into a low black grave, as they were elevated to high culmination before.

The Antiquity was the driving intellectual power of the cultural ascending wave of humanity. Christ and His temperamental type was the genial wonderful top of this unexampled psychophysical development, and the following centuries are the descending part after this huge cultural culmination pre-supposing the previons action of many cultural nations. The post-conversional times and cultures were riding on the powerful genial idea of the descending Christian enthusiasm. Nothing can help the physical affective elevated wave going back into its natural compensatory grave of cultural annihilation, from where the magnetic uplifting play will start again and swell the social human soul once more unto the thrilling culmination of the cultural fulfilment.

The world always again becomes old by the growing experience and by the increasing accumulation of material riches. It loses its uplifting and concentrating energy more and more, in the continual satisfaction of its peripheric covetousness and becomes more and more disgusted of the intellectual and detailed attractability. Then it will be tired of its own peripheric method, and this peculiar selection of affective standards will, one day, no more excite the greedy claims of human society, always fond of new fashions in both petty and greatest scales. The biological body of the largest society will no more clinch the smallest detailed and weak standards of peripheric intellectual and material reactions, and the whole organism automaticly throws away, or excludes itself from, the peripheric performances, with which it is conmpensatorily overfed. Society refuses, at this state, conscientious and consequent intellectual work. It will be unhinged from its previous intellectual tastes and loses the sense of peripheric interest and responsability.

We know that in the OLD AGE the memory of later experiences perishes, whilst that of early youth not only persists, but emerges, from the background of oblivion, with more sharpness than ever. Thus we understand that the idealistic intellectual part of childhood rises again and receives its first domineering and all overlooking position, when *senility* lends its characteristic features to human soul. The later intellectual formulae fall first back from the beginning functional unhingement of the human soul, because they were not inscribed, into our life, with ink mingled with hot heart-blood, whilst the first prove to have an inseparable everlasting strength of union, according to the fiery heartily amalgamation of infantile intellectuality and sentiments - *in statu nascendi.*_____

We have so the senility of old age, therefore, as well in the totality of whole nations and ages and cultures, as in the single individual. In both the intellectual performances cease; the organic instruments for their purposes become worn out, and necessarily and inevitably fall back, because of lack of creative faculties, to the first experiences of humanity, which they had acquired in the former state of first historic development, in the time of cultural childhood, when the injunction of primitive laws amalgamated the primitive symbolic principles of truth - most intimately - with their genial soul. The old civilizations forget and refuse, disgustedly, all further intellectual development. The organic greediness for these peripheric values has, at last, ceased because of experiences of bitter disappointments and returning genial tastes and convictions. The return to the primitive state of their earliest starting symbolic human ideas follows inevitably, re-appearing, once more, in a wonderful clearness, charming dreamy splendour and magnetic attraction.

Life starts again. It has a new vibrating magnetic energy flowing from the source of these wonderful simple symbolic ideas, which it makes to be its task to display and to develop once more, with the zeal and the confidence of a working bee, and in spite of being intellectually handicaped or exactly for this simplifying reason, it has its moving affective life-spring wound up again, and is able to perform, in a new turn, intellectual work and display.

Human destiny goes incessantly round its smallest individual daily working circle, but has as well its centennial and millinarian psychological revolutions. Life and world never stop in any regard. They have all kinds and measures of moving biological necessities, turning around themselves in the smallest daily and individual circumstances, and being carried away through the universal spaces of thousands of years, in unexpected and unobserved rhythms. Like the earth turns round its own axis and flies in its own way of gravitation round the sun, human life and affective destiny have also an individual and collective fate. But as we must assume that even the attractive centre of the solar system moves, and, as we do not know, where the magnificent and complicated universal movement of the sun stops, and where and if it has its last fixed and absolute goal, thus, in our psychological affective life, we discover higher and highest rhythmic laws of affective attraction, most general forces of central systems, comprising millenarian spaces of human psychic development as one unity, as one moment and like one point of genial energy, and we never know, how important and complicated will be the universal psychological background of the ever flowing overwhelming fate of the human affective collective life. We admire here, and are surprised, in the same manner, as at the look at the *flaming whirlpool* of the universal stars, all going, as it seems, along their legally prescribed ways, but nobody knowing, where the last degree of their magnetic attraction will find its absolute, stable and final goal.

The WHOLE CREATED UNIVERSE seems, indeed,in its tremendous moving energy, to circle round a central point. If it is allowed to compare smallest with greatest things - and why should we not ? - we are reminded by the sparkling movement of the stars of a WATER WHIRLPOOL, from where the last portion of water just is flowing out, gurgling through the narrow opening and describing large circles around it. Is not the circular movement in itself surprising? Why does the little rest of remaining water not simply fall out through the opening, but rather makes the complicated round-about way along the circular margin of the hole of the whirlpool? It is clear that these circling water-dances were handicaped, as long as the over-lying river or cistern was full of water, because the high masses of water oppressed the freedom of movement. But towards the end of the outflowing action of water the turning circles increase their intensity and are then well recognizable until all water has slowly emptied through the hole. Would this process not have advanced much more quickly in the direct action of falling out? There cannot be a doubt about this fact, at least in regard to the last portion of water.

In the earlier state of movement, however, the circular speed of the movement had the effect of acceleration and good use of the space. The water elements are sent, quickly and abundantly in the open hole, and rush through, in just and equal distribution of the marginal circumference. The mono-punctual centre of the whirlpool is most remarkable and instructive in itself. It is nearly the crossing point of countless water rays rushing,in different radial directions to, and over, the margin of the hole towards the centre, leaving open, however, necessarily the central point, round which the countless radii of water are closely intertwined, in a narrow circular net. A certain speed of movement is necessary in order, first to satisfy the pressure and weight of the water, and, second, to avoid the adhesive power of the liquid which, in slower movement, would flow together, without forming radial rays, and relatively obstruct the whirlpool.

The necessity of a mono-punctual transfer, between two masses of liquid, connected through a whirlpool, is most interesting and significant. Any unit of fluid energy, forced to gather its spread matter in a hole or pipe, approaches, in all its elements striving to escape the direction opposite the left margin, one central point which we call the centre of the whirlpool or *vortex*. It is the central reposing compromise, the directing king, of all working opposite forces, pulling them together in a circular group, in a harmonious and efficient existing unity. A vortex is, therefore, the representation of harmonious concurrance, many forces complying, under the pressure of inevitable local conditions, to respect a common useful goal and tendency. The spheric forces round the centre are bound and attracted to it as the maximum of their energetic desire, and the circular arrangement means the best apportionment of their approaching procession leading to successful division in unity.

The vortex therefore, is very much the same as what we call, in the mental life, *genius* and *symbol*. It is the point of transfer between an old and a new magnetic formal unity. It is the mediator between an old and new formal energy. It is the *raphe* or *sutura* or *seam,* the connecting point, where two corporeal or mental units are connected, in more or less *symmetric reversion*. The reason for the symmetric representation is the crossing action in the vortex, where each proceeding element, approaching the central point of the whirlpool, continues its way to the opposite half of the hole, coming out in the realm of the new unit. The central point of the vortex, like the symbol, is the neutral link between a new and an old massive or reposing unit; it is the just and necessary dividing transfer regulating, giving and receiving between two fatal energetic units, in the best manner under the given limiting circumstances. It is a two-sided uneven balance of forces, because of the gravitation being in favour of the lower future unit. It distributes the masses in a most efficient geometrical arrangement with accelerated speed. The vortex is the *common pole* of two units of forces, the ending pole of one and the beginning of the other historic formal unity. It is the death bed of the first and the cradle of the second unit. In this case *death means birth*, perishing means rising, losing the old life gains the new; death and resurrection are the very same act considered from two different sides of the symbolic hole.

After the physical analysis of the vortex, let us apply this idea to the STELLAR SKY. There is also, comprising all together, such a fluid whirlpool, although we are not cognizant, from whence and whither it flows. But, incomprehensibly large as this *universal whirlpool* may be, the size exceeding our measures, surely is no reason against. The circling and dancing stars are just dazzling water drops rushing along, and, over the margin of a common sym-

bolic centre, and the whole stellar universe, with all its details is a
nearly emptied cistern of one *creative universal unit,*from which the
prickling and glittering *divine nectar* just is gurgling out into the
next *universal creative cistern.* We are in the moment, when the
contents had flown out for the greatest deal, and when the small
pressure, on the scintillating and intoxicating fluid,gives sufficient
freedom to establish the most accelerated circular flight of the
whistling elements along the margin of the universal symbolic vortex. The part of the universe, accessible to our observation to-day,
is, therefore, a huge vat or cistern of golden wine for the celestial
gods, of incredible dimensions. But it is almost empty. All the blue
transparent spaces point to the hollowness of our universal cistern
and the far away sparsely scattered stars smile to us like the last
reminders of an old good time. Soon this last creative fluid will be
out from the mighty universal pipe. What wild and majestic dances
is it describing in the silent and listening fragrant night !

Was all that tremendous cistern of our universal spaces once
full of chaotic creative substance, perhaps of unorganized and stiff
dead material? Does organization, civilization and life mean, perhaps, preparation and action of the circular motion, in order to
switch through the symbolic hole into a new, higher unit of creative universal representation?Will the whole totality of the universe,
as far as we can think and much farther than we see, flee away, in
time, through the outlet of the universal cistern, and, after the
symbolic conversion and symmetric reversion, drop out, in shuddering gurgling motions, into the morning of a new universal creative
existence, into new most spacious tanks ? Will there be a time,
when all existing stars of our sky, all our nearer and farther stellar
relatives, including the earth, are pulled out from their circling
spheres, like the last remainder of the turning water whirlpool?
Will they all, one day, or are they already in action to, be blown
far away, in a whiff of universal creative wind, like the last scintillating sparks of a dying fire, still hesitating, for a moment, over
a chimney? Will their light soon be extinct, and will they serve
as *soot* to build up the fertile mother-ground of future creative
universal *evolutions?* Is the luminous beauty of these fiery sparks
the product of their swift circular motions round the symbolic hole
of their future near death, which will be the birth and resurrection
of an universe? Is the sun, which we think fixed, kindling with
glowing fire, because, among other reasons, it rolls with desperate
energy round the outlet of the universal outlet?

Assuming that this tremendous whirlpool of the creative stellar

sparks throngs continuously through the symbolic transfer, there
must be a wonderful spectacle of luminous order and beauty far out
in the extreme universe, where the countless celestial bodies
arranged in long sheaves composed of fiery pearl-sticks, pass round
and then through the symbolic hole, in perfect geometrical circu-
larity. They shoot through the outlet in numberless majestic rows
each made up by the beads of the shining stars. What a charming
two-sided universal bouquet of fiery blossoms, being held together
by the mysterious ring of the symbolic transfer! Like numberless
fiery arrows they pierce the heart of their central symbolic point and
stab, with irresistible energy, through the *door* of their longing, in
order to pass and to be reborn again, into a new growing world, a
new morning of creation in another creative unity. What a quite
illustrious procession! What an impressive show before the eyes
of last divine esthetical sentiments!

Then the masses of the bodies of the old stars are filling the
vast spaces of the new creative cistern. Perhaps they fill first for
ages, as dead material, (in the pre-conversional language), their
new spaces until they are full to the brim with immovable chaotic
matter. The maturity of this powerful conception will burst again
into a fulfilling creative unit building up another new universal
world. What a great spec-
tacle must it be, 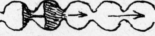 when, by internal growing necessity, the
sluices of the new universe will be opened again, and the incredible
masses and energy, create by *necessity,* a *new symbolic outlet,* into
new spaces, seeming to be the last future world.

It will not be the last. The tiding waves of filling and emptying
go on, ever changing, ever increasing and decreasing, from one
universal cistern to the other, without end and limit. How can this
be? How can a world after the other be created and perish, be born
and die and be re-born again? Our reason has to take refuge to the
circle, in all questions of eternity and infiniteness. The first universal unit passes over into the second, the second into the third and
so on until the circle is finished and the ever flowing universal
energy will reach again the first historic localization of its universal
activity. How long time does it take from one universe to the other,
from the first beginning of the universal circle until the new start
in the second revolution? In which universe are we now?

In describing the circle, we admit again a central energy, round
which the different outcoming universal creations are in circular
incessant movement. We meet, therefore, an other background of

creative resources, which, in itself, has a similar constitution opening the view of wide creative dispersion, like a turning wheel on
top of the spraying water hose, at one time, and contracting to
central narrow symbolic concentration,at an other universal historic
period. Its direction runs as well in a circular way, but *rectangular*
through the centre of the described daughter wreath. The later
circle of the universal creation behaves to the former one like a
pearl-string round a curved ankle of a lady. But this first circular
historic formula is moving itself according to the same law, expanding and concentrating in its vital energy like the ever changing
waves of an ocean going up and down, or like the breathing lung
of a living body, alternating always between expiration and inspiration, expansion and compression - assimilation and dissimulation -.
taking in vital material, in one motion, and blowing out the refined
and elaborate material in a later vital reaction.*Breathing respiration
is the fundamental law of all creation, in various superposition* and
most complicated intricacy, but always the same.

In regard to psychology,we will find a law, where the inspiring
capacity augments, where *more intellectual activity means more universal riches and elaboration* and therefore, each time, after each
intellectual period, an enlarged, more powerful and greater universe, digressing from its first circular way, in more freedom and
larger excursion. If we apply this idea to the universal creation, we
have to state that the *greater cultural elaboration means breaking
up the harmonious circle of the creative universal sequence.* The
richer cultural elaboration augments,in a certain sense, the material
masses of the universal unit; the latter becomes more voluminous
and independent of its original centre,so that we have the following

manner of developing law: the first unit is relatively small, the second larger, each following
larger in mass, at the same time, the circle leaving more and more the original common centre,
digressing more and more in the further universe. Intellectuality means, therefore, re-accu-
mulation of genial forces, in a new way. Cultural work means, in this materialistic sense, increasing importance of the creature, more material mass and more
increasing independence from central historic powers. Cultural and
intellectual increase are bringing about, practically, transition from
a lower unit of universal significance to a higher. The increased
effort and action of *inspiring intellectuality* or *cultural work* has the
effect of increasing vital capacity of the material substance, of

stronger expiration, more pronounced created independence, augmented *inter-universal metabolism*. Intellectual and cultural work is the open explanation demonstrating, how worlds rise and increase like growing trees having seeds of ever augmenting potentiality, how the universal activity is pulled out, more and more, from the original theistic traditional concentration and unfolds in incredible real detailed riches, in proud evolution, to creative self-emphasis and progressive *possessive absolutism*. Intellectuality is the key opening the door to greatest creative optimism. Smallest and most frail beginnings develop in cultural effort and energetic straining perseverance; the divine glory is scattered, more and more, in all direcions through the stellar sky, lighting like torches in indescribable beauty, if the creature is working out its cultural disposition in unflinching confidence and assiduous diligent faithfulness to itself. There is almost no end of future glory for the straining real effort, the world will be heaven with its universal riches, magnificence and power, if we are faithful to our *cultural working tasks*.

The swift circulation of the elements along the margin of the symbolic hole demonstrates the competitive race of the numerous individuals desiring to switch through the opening, as soon as possible. It applies to our psychology. The *intellectual-idealistic* type is most fervent in building up the *extra-historic* universal world. He is the leading point in which the *extra-universal longings* find their thoroughfare to rush through, within and out of the historic organization. The *materialistic realist* provides the real foundation and basis to this later unrolling divine development.

We understand that SYMBOLIC WORK means concentrating unification of forces. It is a powerful effort with culminating attention toward one central success. It is the *narrow door* to the paradise of a new world, where the unity of all forces has to knock powerfully and strain severely, until the door is flung open and permits to enter the children of the old world, in groups most favorable to both the situation of the door and the compromising necessity of the arriving pilgrims. Each in his impetuous desire to enter first, would likely stumble and obstruct the opening, in disorder, would not by the natural law, a certain regularity and order be arranged, as we pointed out. Like an army of soldiers, the countless stellar elements of any chosen paradise and superior success, enter in regular array and rhythmic logical step, the conquered door of the new universe and rush in swift circumspection to the new possession reserved for them.

The Swiss hero *Winkelried* is said to have embraced, in the battle of Sempach, a great number of spears stretched forth, like an iron wall, by the Austrian knights against the assailing Swiss troupes, and have buried them in his chest in falling down and crying: " I will make a lane to liberty! " His country-men could so intrude, over his body, in the inimical rows, and defeated them. The essential of the great symbolic action is very similar. The heroic conqueror, concerned mostly with the main goal, has to be pierced, in his very heart, by the central point, to which he is most attracted and only, after having been penetrated by a lance, in his deepest intimacy, - or having pierced the enemy, if another, realistic conqueror, because the symbolic action works both ways, - he enters into the paradise of his wishes. We have to go over the dearest things of our heart, if we will progress to the future development of our destiny. We have to eat ourselves through the sweetness and kindness of self-love, before we can advance to the increasing importance of our life. Any strong central attraction of our love and desire means, on one side, a finger-post and door to heaven, on the other an obstacle by its local fixation and one-sided concentration of forces. The most attractive point is that, which is loved and abandoned by everybody, praised and insulted, worshiped and hated, embraced and killed, used and abused, complimented and cheated. The most important central point is that which permits and allows all services and insults, without any expectation of gratitude or threat of revenge, serving even, when seeing ingratitude coming from far: being kind, faithful and serviceable in spite of a keen critical sense looking through the treacherous reality. Readiness for *service and sacrifice* is the way to heaven, the narrow door to the paradise, - for the others, and even for yourself, because the symbolical door is the nearest and surest guarantee and opportunity for your own entrance. The symbolical door- keeper is in best position for the symbolical universal conversion. The way to a new life goes through a valley of death. There has to be a murder, in the biological sense of the word, a stabbing of a heart—it may be your own—before you can expect universal resurrection. Who knows, if yet he -is the chosen door to the paradise for another, that symbolic centre, to which from all sides arrows and spears have to be shot or extorted from the other side, in order to make possible the progress and enlargement of one or many human destinies? In one case you may be chosen, in other your brother may be. But all have earlier or later the exquisite role, in a social culmination, to serve as the bull's eye of the symbolic centre, on the way to their desired happiness, to be the chosen holocaust in order to make others happy; - to be slandered, banished, crucified, murdered, in order to make a way to freedom, for the individual or collective progress of their surrounding society.

The type of the *religious genius* and mediator has the same basis. His heart has to be pierced by a lance, in order to make a lane to the universal freedom of the historically religious humanity. The innocent has t , bleed for the guilty. This is the deep *moral* sense of the symbolism. We have *collective responsibilities,* and it is not the matter of individual justice to decide, who has to suffer and who has to make suffer, to stab and to be stabbed in his heart, but only the collectivity of our destiny distributes, with the free gesture of a sovereign, the individual roles in a manner that every act in the world's spectacle is performed and the result ensured. And the tragedy of the symbolic idea, in the sense of the human heart and life - for all these things are of general nature and validity - is the fact that it is always the most willing, kind and benevolent, who naturally offers himself and is chosen to be the suffering symbolic centre of the others. He is illtreated, slandered, disfigured, dilacerated, spat upon. The innocent is dying for the sinner; but the sinner is the punishing judge, in the sense of the religious psychology. The more innocent, the more you likely will be judged; the more guilty, the more you are inclined to judge and condemn the others. But there remains a very little spot in a heart, like in the water whirlpool, where no material nor intellectual spear ventures to advance. It is the very centre of the heart, the central symbolic fire of human truth and self-respect. The centre of the water whirlpool is elevated to an immaterial central idea, that of the human honor and truth to a spiritual eternal value, which cannot be attacked or turned down by the lances of the boldest and most insidious intellectual justice.

There we have the explanation of the *mystery of the innocent lamb* sacrificed for all others, and this idea has such a deep and universal biological sense that the remark of a writer, that the Christian conception is unlogical in the postulation of us all being pardoned by the mercy of God punishing exactly only his beloved innocent son, unrelentingly, has to be refused as unbiological and superficial. It does not enter enough into the deep and paradox mysterious world, from where the terminal religious psychology is drawn. Religion, in its true universal view, exceeds our narrower feelings of individual justice and our levelled conceptions of equality, by reducing every fact to broadest relations and necessities. In the last universal light everything is just and all right. Yet the conception of *individual justice* is, as it seems, difficult to be settled nearly satisfactorily, in human society and is, as a rule, considered to be perfect only by a few hard-hearted and narrow persons who draw advantage from suffering and abuse. But even these sad conditions are understandable in the view of universal necessities. The postulation for individual one-sided realistic justice does not agree with the general creative disposition, on the contrary, according to the reciprocal relations between realistic and idealistic values. But petty individual justice matters little, where *universal equilibrium is guaranteed*. May the wish for eternal individual life, in the heart of the unhappy just, not be the need of revenge.

The whole symbolic question becomes so challengingly tragical, for the human restricted thoughts and sentiments, - and then the noblest is in danger to strike against the universal will - in the fact of the individual injustice and in the *reversion of individual merit into individual punishment,* but always in the individual, never in the collective sense, and not at all in the post-reversional idea,since the central symbolic element, even when paying the expensive ticket of individual and material self-sacrifice, is most prominent in divine grace and admirable importance, in its function. If it is neglected in the real world, it has the first right of expectancy for universal glory.

This biological law pervades of course the whole universal structure, referring to psychic life as well as to architectural material performances in the greatest and smallest scale. The whirlpool of the second or later new universe is a clear demonstration of this fact. The stars rolling in shining pearl-sticks rush through the middle of the symbolic opening and are thus,in most kindling glory, eliminated from the plane of the daughter-wreath. Child and parents are biologically, in their cultural and material development, put in a rectangular difference of working direction.

The stars are the more thronging and elbowing and, perhaps sometimes, even smashing each other, the nearer they are the centre of the turning central vortex. So we may say, from another side, the more greediness and desire for a new world, and the greater the wish to leave the 'despicable' old place of dwelling, the less sense and detailed respect for the necessities of the present reality. The consequence of this behaviour is, in spite of the causal glorious idealism, that the probability increases, of being smashed or stabbed or killed, by lack of caution. The HERO type is, of course, in this central localization corresponding to the central elements flowing out from the vortex of the symbolic opening. The nearer the symbol, the greater the shining splendour of glory, but the surer the loss of the historic individual life, being struck by the high tension of the concentrated vital wire of the symbolism. Serving greatest future purposes is giving up rights and social possibilities of the present individual collective connection and security. Every kind heart means, - looked at from the other side, - an inviting door to a paradise for another, where the abusing individual throws its spears of desire, piercing through the heart, and landing with its energy, over and through the corpse of the sacrificed heart, in the hoped-for new land.

There are always losses of the heart, before the door of new great experiences, in universe and life. No entrance without a valuable ticket wheresoever; no progress, no enrichment, no pleasure, not even any moderation of sorrow or relief from cross, without the exchange of a serious sacrifice of the past life. Was the cross before on the right shoulder, it will be put over to the left, after the *symbolic conversion,* in the symmetric change of all relations happening in progressive transformation.

The idea of the SYMMETRIC CHANGE, within the symbolic transformation, is, indeed, of the most interesting. It indicates quite generally, that the conceptions of right and left, up and down are just reverse after and before any symbolic transformation, and we understand now better the unbelief of the idealist in the reality, the helplessness of the strong realist in artistic and religious matter, the mutual aversion of post- and presymbolic conceptions in continuous mutual frictions and misunderstandings. Their appreciations lie just on the opposite side. Which is the highest for one, is the lowest for the other. Their appreciative standards are increasing and decreasing just in the opposite directions. The whole history of fighting of the human race, all political and religious struggles refer to such pre- and postsymbolic oppositions and misunderstandings coming about by the symmetric dislocation of the composing elements. The symbolic change means, of course, the most pronounced and perfect opposition and is, in itself, an inevitable root of radical hatred and mutual rejection. But the symbolic vortex needs essentially, and brings about psychologically and biologically, this symmetric dislocation of all vital elements, so that right and left, up and down, clever and stupid, admirable and condemnable and even good and bad, up to a certain degree, may be symmetrically changed as well. Here we have the explanation of the idea of *the good Lord's Fool* and of the short-sighted shrewdness of the busy people of the world, being convinced to do the only best thing. But the same we have in any new creative permutation, even in the greatest real creative sense of the different universal representations of the stellar world. The young and the old misunderstand each other.

So we found out that each different world, in the real and mental life, is, in regard to its mother-world, reverse, symmetrically changed, connected with it in a symbolic touch. Especially interesting, of course, are the relations of the real and ideal world having a most pronounced symbolic relation, although, if we would be bold, we would come to surprising confirming conclusions in regard to the localization of the navel of the earth and the other stars. The expression " *verkehrte Welt*" - *reversed world,* usual in German for ridiculing idealistic impractical conceptions and aspirations, and the humerous English appellation *High-brow,* demonstrate clearly the exactly opposite emphasis of appreciation of human values. The realist emphasizes, of course, his stand-point and scorns ironically that of the other. The idealist, on the contrary, rejects the much more the realist and the sensorial impressions in his *trans-symbolizing* view. There are, as we all know, enough individuals having their natural *temperamental emphasis* prevalently either on the realistic or idalistic side, and, accordingly,they are friends supporting their harmonious sentiments, or antagonize each other. The good human condition lies in the middle between realism and idealism, giving each of them half share, understanding appreciating and reconciling both sides.

CULTURE, in the broadest sense,means building up of the world. We understand it as the materially refining organization of the real elements circling ronud the margin of the symbolic idealism. Culture establishes a competition of the real elements toward immaterial idealism, and conveys on them, in mincing preparation, a smooth readiness to run easily through the ideal goal. Culture is the progressive intensive investment of universal energy in the objective material world, bridling the restless rush of inter-spheric forces in inexhaustible formal riches, for a certain time and up to a certain degree, only to let them go, soon again, to outside divine goals.

The progressive culture means splitting up the raw-material of the accumulated material world, within inspired formalism, in the creation of a whole stellar universe, of plants, animals, human beings as well, as in giving shape and sense to the formless material, in art, work or industry. The progressive culture invests, more and more universal energy in material formulae, and in the *materialistic conception of the world,* is willing to perpetuate and hyper-emphasize this material-idealistic combination and only transitional amalgamation. It is like an increasing imprisonment of the spirit in the bodies, which, if abused, grow in numbers and sizes like plants in a hot house. But they are in danger to exhaust their organic vital possibilities, or spoil the specific nature of the universal energy, alloted to them only in a certain measure, and under certain transitory conditions. The unfoldment of the material world however, is the purpose of the creation. The elevation of the material world to ennobling amalgamation with the higher energetic life is the admirable meaning of the creation; only there is the question, how far and in what temperamental movement this transformation has to proceed, where the productive inspiration available for the universe, is exhausted, this state leading to *universal neurasthenia,* and how it has to be saved for the lasting future integrity of its penetrating creative efficacy. We have here again the question of the *pendulum* moving between two extremes, going, at one time, to the extreme of energetic manifestation of inspiring inventive splitting work of the material substance, and, at another extreme period, to the petrification and lazy stagnation of the world in super-abundant chaotic material accumulation.

Is this, perhaps, only another, perhaps more practical and understandable expression for what we said before about the growing sizes of the different universal representations? Augmenting intellectuality means increasing real unfoldment of the universal energy in the formal material of this world. It pulls the outside divine inspiring forces into the formal representations of this visible world and enriches so the creative reality, while the biological readiness for accepting more of the creative universal will, impoverishes more and more. There are two reasons for this fact: first the tiring and naturally blunting one-sidedness of the universal creative function, and second, the serious danger of being obstructed because of hyper-investment within material crystallization. In the hyper-production of real life spirituality undergoes a formal spell.

In MATERIALISM the two elements of energy and material are developed to the one material side, at the expense of the other. We have an excess of reality and a lack of promoting strength. Materialism is as little the consequence of intellectuality as of affective sentiments. It is a passive state of inter-lying laziness, a dark deep valley of the human psychological nature, where the heart led down, on a sunny serpentining path, from divine hills and the theistic Olymp—and from where intellectuality leads again up to new future, snow-glittering mountains. Materialism strives to make the forces of life *stationary*. All its products are hyper-mature because of lack of energetic function. The objects of a material epoch are like huge hyper-mature cabbages, bulky because favored in the hot-house of one-sided intellectualism, which stopped, in treacherous individual egotistic way, at the commencement of the sacrificing phase of the development.But these boasting huge creative vegetables are tasteless, and if they are not used for universal furthering and sacrificing utility, will decay quickly. They have huge categoric measures, but no spiritually refined features.

Realistic intellectual work effectuates growth of an universal unit, all elements augmenting their sizes and filling, more and more, the space of the universal system, if we will return to our former conceptions, whilst spiritual hyper-intensity means decrease of real material importance and size. It makes universal energy free, at the expense of the material investment. In the second case, the spaces of the universal cistern, filled up with refined material, empty freely in an outside new world, whilst, in the first case, the spaces of the present universal unit are more and more filled up to utmost capacity, with clumsy material elements unable and unprepared to be symbolically transferred. In this case, the world goes on to elementary material hyper-maturation with hydro-cephalic sizes, so that this final fruit of work, bursts out violently into a new daughter-unit, whilst, under the first conditions, the reality of the universe is early spiritually refined, loses so the exaggerated accumulating desire and its internal possessive strength and *turgor*.

Thus we have to acknowledge the spiritual intensity as the first thriving act of the cultural maturation of the real world, leading over to a new creation, in a successful, non-explosive procession. The realistic intellectual work, on the contrary, considered in itself and when emphasising the formal material stability and possession, is, on the contrary, the thriving real fecundation imprisoning more and more the divine forces into the material reality. Maturation pre-supposes self-possessive strength which creates then the direction of future universal units. Spiritual force makes reality lean and stable in progress; intellectuality, on the contrary, is fattening, thriving and dividing into new revolutionary outbursts. Intellectuality makes for exterior appearance, spirituality for will. So we have the problem of the filling and emptying water cistern from another side. It fills with the help of material conceptions up to the degree of bursting maturity and empties easily with the forwarding help of spiritual idealism. Both forces have to work in an equal amount of activity and alternating in adequate emphasis. Even materialism has a certain transitional right of historic short existence; but soon humanity has to rise again from this comfortable slumber and lethargic stiffness to the *fresh matinality of intellectual idealism*. Realistic intellectual emphasis of the given objective world alone accumulates and retains, in a blind way, the crystallizing material, whilst digressing spiritual action alone would have the effect of thoroughly preventing any material accumulation, creating thus real and cultural precocity and immaturity in the first part of the creative stream entering into the cistern, being necessary so much more, however, in the second half, for the expedient emptying action, in harmonious symbolic transfer toward future creative units. Without spiritual energy in the second half of the creative accumulation, we have a blind stagnation of non-organized creative elements which become definitely crystallized and, therefore, an obstacle for the universal progress, not having a transforming purpose nor possibility for the future. Universal energy alone never permits the filling up, of the heavenly universe, with real stars and sweeps them too quickly away to future units. Realistic intellectual tendencies alone fill the creative cistern up to the brim with liquid of real work and makes it overflow, after all, spilling the precious divine nectar, without sense and usefulness through the night of unknown extra-universal spaces, if there is no explosive revolutionary destruction. One of the two forces, localized intellect, bridles too much, by formularism, on the way of the proceeding forces of the universe, and the other is inclined to put too little stress on the reality, by artificial and spiritual organization. Real intellect easily forgets the inter-spheric connections and is restricted to the present real existing order and material possession, losing the just eye for their universal relativity. Everything has to be done in the right place and at the right time. Sentimental-idealistic, material-realistic and intellectual forces are the consecutive links of an ever developing creative chain closed in a circular sequence, ever working.

Good cultural activity is the prudent simultaneous use of all these elements, forces and points of view in a historic time. It is, therefore, the carefully mincing preparation, of the material world, for the following centrifugal spiritual re-volatilization. Even *riches* has a distinct idealistic halo, turning to merely symbolic notions of imaginative authority, on the top of its success. The almost unlimited ductility of the gold proves that also this mighty representative of riches approaches a *most refined* physical composition, an analogous expression of the biological nature of the authoritative value, which is represented by it. Only there is, in connection with increasing riches, perhaps more than in another case, the danger of canonizing the means for the purpose.

The essential of *culture* is making new, variable and small combinations of parts of chaotic material lumps. We break up mountains in order to build up little houses; we build chairs of trees, giving to the objects a new meaning and esthetical unity of expression. The printer makes little slugs from lumps of metal in order to print, after all, a little book. The stronger the dividing intensity, the nearer to mental character and idealistic terminal volatilization. The printer is near the creative and idealistic work, because he has, on top of his slugs, a froth of intellectual signs. He is, therefore, at the threshold of the creative work having inter-spheric reference.

Culture is the *wood-cutter* of the logs of the material world, sawing and chopping cord wood and kindling wood, in material and scientific work. Religion and creative, inventive and artistic effort are the spiritual fire, sending them out to extra-universal goals , in centrifugal divine flight, through spiritual combustion. Good culture inspires divine tensions into the real world, but releases them in time. Culture tries to approach to heaven, the elements included in time, space and causality, and strives to bridle with reason the fiery horses of idealistic dissoluteness. Culture tries to build heaven, within the categoric world. It is the radiant face of the early riser, glowing with *intellectual- idealistic glory.*

Das Unzulaengliche hier ist es getan.
                              Goethe

THIRD BOOK

WE learned that the *spheric revolution of the earth round the sun* has an OVAL CONFIGURATION, the two most distant points being called *solstitial,* the two nearest *equinoctial points.*

With regard to the social psychology we shall find analogous conditions represented in THE SOLSTITIAL CONCEPTION OF THE LEADING HISTORIC RELIGIOUS GENIUS. In our figure A means the solstitial localization of the genial power of the religious leader. B is the central theistic magnetic force, C the equi-noctial position of the Middle-Ages and the arising intellectualism. The two hatched quarters of the oval or *elliptic field,* are of intellectual, the two blank areas, of sentimental pre-dominance.

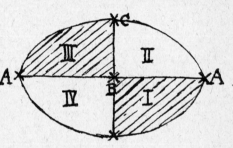

We have, therefore, 4 equal quarters of the spheric circumference and field, in the collective psychological performance. If we, for instance, following the way of our collective historic psychological planet, move along the periphery of the hatched quarter (I), toward the point A, our magnetic attraction to the *central theistic* god continuously decreases, on behalf of the reciprocal increase of the intellectual digressing magnetism. In that quarter we recognize the supremacy of the centrifugal spheric intellectual attraction, which is responsible for the ellipsoid form of the spheric way. The human psychic nature is carried, at this period, to the most distant point, is in *apogee.* The intellectual quarter has the signature of the defeat of the sentiments, their natural central attraction being over-balanced by the victorious digressing intellectuality.

Upon the arrival at the SOLSTITIAL POINT A, of the human historic soul, the leading supremacy of the intellectual psychic component stops. In one extreme moment of affective distress and most daring intellectual solstitial removal, the sentimental part of the life-force resumes the leading role, again, at once, and

opens the second era (II) of the spheric collective revolution, which
will be *the first sentimental quarter*. No sooner the humiliated and
repudiated sentiments have turned round the solstitial corner, than
the attractive theistic goal exercises a mighty power of magnetism
on them. We instantly observe a strong affective correspondence
between the natural magnetic part of our life-force and the strong
central theistic goal. The affective human nature has an extraordinary facility of proceeding rapidity toward that goal, because it is
lying on the line of old traditional experiences and customs, left
for a time, but coming back now on the wings of the help of the
subconscious memory. Humanity is pleased to approach, as much as
possible, the nearest real point of its formost divine vicinity, which
is given in the EQUINOCTIAL POINT. Humanity blushes
with enthusiasm, and flies irresistibly, through the immeasurable
spaces of the universal distances and millenarian ages, with the
charming help of mysticism, into the longing arms of its historic
real god. It is moved with expecting transportation and loses
its breath with panting swiftness. The affective energy, advancing
toward the equinoctial point, rushes at last like a glorious hurricane,
and humanity, encouraged by the theistic sentimental success and
sweet attraction, hopes, for a time, to go on nearest the goal; it ventures to stretch its arms forth, for the intimate approaching union
in bold direct divine embracement. In this period we have the
signature of chivalry, religious unity, iron legislation, exclusive
fanaticism, narrow conceptions, artistic security and charitable heroism. It is the time of the MIDDLE AGES.

As the leading intellectuality of the first quarter, which we
may call ANTIQUITY, for the sake of an instance and in order
to commence somewhere, in the indifferent circle of vital history,
was a time of hard work and severe intellectual efforts, so we observe in the second sentimental quarter an immense danger of artistic luxury and diminishing strain in real useful work, because
the leading sentimentality entered into its comfortable magnetic
phase, into its most favored centralizing spheric conditions. It has
subjugated entirely the intellectual part of the psychic social nature.
The conditions of human happiness of the heart and the artistic
surroundings become, during this golden *epoch* so agreeable, the
most desired goals of the heart seem to be so near and easily objectively attainable that any plodding intellectual effort stops, for a
time, seeming undesirable. Universal intellectuality, in this epoch,
is persecuted.

No sooner the spheric motion arrives at the *equinoctial point*

C than there begins another important affective *conversion,* a new digressing removal, from the magnetic historic goal becoming necessary. Intellectuality rejected in the former sentimental quarter takes instantly charge of the leading part of human nature; then the affective component receives a passive, bridling and opposing role, exactly in the reverse manner, as it had been in the former quarter. The comfortable *genial* affective ride of the human psychological society toward theistic charming goals ceases; a strongly toiling period of hard real work, of social affective self-denial and of slow logical performance has arrived.

The old powerful affective unity suffers, at this *equinoctial* moment, almost instantly a very thorough break of converting affective change, and it is owing to it, that we observe, with the same instantaneous sharpness and strength as in a cutting keel of a boat, the enormous affective motion of the social totality fall into pieces, first into two huge waves, as we see it at the time of a first great *Reformation,* and afterwards, with proceeding distance from the centre, into numerous smaller units of religious opinions and philosophical convictions, all together the consequence of the magnetic yielding, of the human spheric fate to the peripheric intellectuality. The affective distress, the desperation of the sentimental heart in this third (III), second intellectual human spheric quarter is great; the remembrance of the sweet old times shines like a faraway time of fairy tales into this dry and hard world of straining effort, materialism, money and most critical natural science. The heart is disappointed and becomes embittered. Now all nations from all the world go to admire the surprising greatness and beauty of the cathedrals and monuments of the passed *middle ages;* all praise the wonderful tokens of stone, wood and canvas of the old idealistic ages. All are stealthily longing for it, in a subdued homesickness; but life, fate, atmosphere, time and circumstances have not the least indulgence for desires like this. We live under the other spell of intellectual magnetic excursion; intellectuality has the leading reins in her firm hand, and the augmented energy of the material weight progresses more and more, producing immeasurable riches of primitive intellectual real objectivity, a *super-estimation* of the intellectual display and a perfect contempt of all affective magnetic relations to the historic central goal, to which still it is bound, but from which it strives to retire.

The moment shall come, however, once more, when the *solstitial conversion* initiates a new sentimental era of affective leading supremacy. There will be another terrible short struggle for ruling predominance; another enormous genius of all-comprising affective energy will instantly rise like a lightning flash. This will be the solstitial culmination of another *fulfilling time*, at the threshold of the second sentimental, the fourth (IV) period of the human psychological spheric way round its historic fixed star. Another second charming ride of affective central theistic affirmation of all leading circles of mankind will create a new harmonious happy unity of the psychological human social formation. There will be a time, where this star will fall down again and degenerate into luxury. Humanity will then, after the *second equinoctial change,* be driven back into the intellectually guided first quarter of beginning Antiquity, and the circling way, in such a manner, is concluded.

We see that the human psychology as a total phenomenon, has as well its revolutions and changes as the individual has. There are *golden ages,* but also those of *silver, brass* and *stone.* We have continuous changes and never we enter a bad magnetic condition without the sure arising chance to reach soon a charming compensation. Our fate drives round the special human solar theistic centre, and there we find the magnetic criterion of our heart's possibilities for happiness. We ought to understand better, by now, why it is so easy to burst into divine enthusiasm and idealistic delight, and why we find work and intellectual activity so hard. The first is, in its theistic form, custom and prepared facility, the second goes out to unknown new-land. The strong central theistic attraction is enjoyed more with every approaching step, the intellectual digression, instead, carries away from the historic precision of the central god. Going towards a central magnetic goal means happy sentimental affirmation and heart's pleasure, because of going a secure way, to a well known goal, as we have in the sentimental religion, in hyper-traditional belief and petty affirmation worshipping the letter. Going away, in a centrifugal digressing direction, means, for the first time and immediately, unhappiness, loss of the old natural specific magnetic satisfaction and clear direction of eternal hope, of accepting hard work, detailed splitting intellectual effort, self-consciousness and cross. It means the inventive incertitude of opening new ways within the infinite blue possibliities of the digressing universe opening the desirable directions only to the perseverance of knocking *necessity.* _____ _____ _____

There is an inevitable continual *change* in all life and all world. All is composed of necessary *compromises* moving from intellectuality to affectivity, from happiness to unhappiness, from affirmation and enthusiasm to negation and hatred, disappointment and disgusted aversion. But all help and desirable conversion to the better inevitably comes back again once more. Every tear of the human ages will be wiped away, by a new period, and there is no disharmony and no sorrow in the depth of the whole fate of the spreading humanity, which will not have its exact affective charming balance, in later parts and moments of our fatal spheric revolution.

We would be wrong not only to put the religious hero in the centre of the theistic solar system, but also to admit undoubtedly, that our present human psychological conception is final and the absolute definite centre of attraction.

The *solstitial point* is the most distant spheric range between earth and sun. The sun seems to stand still, for a short time, because of the *narrow curve* of the distant ellipsoid sphere of the wheeling earth. In our intellectual-affective history, the rising Christian idea was such a solstitial point, where the gravitating way of our double human balance, having emphasized most the intellectual component of its alternating change, was most distant from its historic, magnetic theistic conception, and where the psychologic life of Greek, Roman and Jewish cultures turned, in a solstitial sharp wheeling, their way into the opposite direction than before, going back to their central sun, whilst they moved away in the earlier time. Christ means the expression of the *solstitial conversion* of the human psychological fate, from intellectual to affective preponderance, which mysterious change happens in the moment of the *circum-navigation* of the most distant point from the theistic goal. He seems to be the centre and the still reposing culminating point of culture, because He reflects the central light of us, through the arena of our historic experience, from the outstanding solstitial high altar of His cultural mission.

At this point, human life received the utmost degree of intellectual distance from the central affective god, and returned to bask in the nearer ranges and warmer friendship of its solar centre. In the solstitial point, the extreme expansion of the intellectual JANUS head instantly disappears, since our changing preponderant attention leaves that side and looks to the other affective face, which has the symbolic punctul size of intellectuality. Owing to our changing position and the law of compensation, the intellectual face of Janus instantly shrank to the punctual size of the genial lightning affectivity, and started, once more, to slowly enlarge its intellectual diameter. We are, this time, perhaps at the most interesting point, where *the extremes touch each other*, a maximum producing a minimum, the largest face of Janus not consecutively and gradually diminishing,from our historic *centro-restricted* standpoint of looking at it, but falling down instantly from the maximum intellectual extension to the smallest genial punctual concentra.-tion.

The immediate downfall of the intellectual face of the head of Janus, from the largest size into the smallest genial light-point, is a consequence of our narrow total life- force and our limited and weak power of universal apprehension and sensorial perception. As soon as the peripheric display of the light-field has reached the utmost extreme limit of dilution,the light of the central sun overflows the turning globe and the intellectual universal light, which had all power up to this moment, is released, in its activity, for a quarter of the spheric way. We look always in the direction of the stronger attractiveness,and from there the light of spirituality shines with abundant riches excluding all other lights. The intellectual face is excluded, up to the degree of a symbolic point; it is not prepared in its state of tiredness, to meet and defeat the new refreshed plenty of the central theistic flashes. The old and exhausted intellectuality needs again time for slow growth, in being put beside.

The moment of this intellectual solstitial loss, jubilant in spiritual freedom and light, reduces the attention for the objective world only to a symbolic point. The whole past world and life are put into a small genial bag, neglecting the details, and rush on to their centri-petal glorious flight.

Why cannot we continue to look at one intellectually developing face of the Janus head, until it will be exceedingly great and we shall ripen greatest enjoyment of it? Why do we fall instantly back, at the solstitial point, to the punctual genial affective side, and must start again to develop our light-field by work, like Sysiphus *rolling the huge stone always again uphill?* Why cannot we continue to look at the growing intellectual face, infinitely, and why are we rather forced to change instantly our stand-point, at the solstitial conversion, and to look at the Janus head from the other side? Our narrow human life- force exacts alternating releasing changes of our functions. Our life-force finds its limits as well in the collective human psychic performances as well as in the single individual, putting barriers and closed doors everywhere, where our natural way may lead us.

There is the special reaction of the flashing lightning.This is the affective genial answer of the collective social psychology at the culmination of its real success. The most powerful cultural conversion of the psychological occiden. il world had to bear the affective flaming torch of life-force back to the central goal of its historic idealistic dispositon, after having been carried away by the winged zeal of the intellectual Antiquity, to the most remote intellectual solstitial distance. Its wheeling movements turn back again, in the approaching direction in hope, love, faith and confidence, towards its traditional most magnetic attraction. Humanity, therefore, could obey, from this moment, the charming magnetism of their attractive law, and the stigma typical of Christianity is, therefore, love and conversion from intellectual *"negativism"* into willing affirmation toward the traditional magnetic goal.

At this solstitial point of the psychological life the big camel of the material riches and intellectual display, at least and at last, not at the eleventh, but exactly at the twelfth hour, found its way through the genial punctual eye of the needle. Here was the physiological and biological revenge of the neglected sentimental idealism, returning from the earthly intellectual effusion, and, for this reason, there in one moment was healed by the force of one wonderful affective instantaneous lightning, all which had been such a long time a peripheric pain, sin, shame, sorrow, distress, disease, poverty, luxuriant earthliness, injustice, egotism, thoughtless superficiality, weakness, desperation and hypocrisy. Here we have the scientific explanation of the fact that Christ had the special mission and faculty to heal all diseases, making the blind to see, the lame to walk, the deaf to hear and the dead to rise, that He continually tells people hat their sins are forgiven and that they shall inherit eternal life.

If we would define SIN as the affective withdrawal from the magnetic *theistic* goal, then we are quite satisfied in finding the cradle of the Christian idea at the solstitial point of our cultural social psycho-gravitation. The notion of sin had always a commanding importance in the religious philosophy. Sin expresses in its meaning and terminology the radical lack of deficiency of human sentiments to move in the direction of their magnetic theistic goal. If Christ will be similar to us in all things with the exception of sin, then He offers Himself as the great historic psycho-magnetic solstitial point of the occidental humanity returning in repentant decision, from the utmost intellectual peripheric digression, to the resumption of an old *centro-theistic allegiance*. Humanity is at once rid of the sinful intellectual corruption of the averted removing Antiquity, in the very act and point of *solstitial affective conversion* unto its central magnetic goal. Doubtless the nations, at the starting and startling era of Christianity, were inspired with a strong longing, for theistic goals, burning like a generally spread pandemic infectious Influenza. At that time people received at once a feverish magnetic inclination for their divine theistic ideals. The quite unprecedented irresistibility of their magnetic attraction pulled millions of Christian heroes ruthlessly, from their peripheric real categories of time, space and causality, by an enthusiastic push of energy, into the most possible distances of flashing divine love and most elevated magnetic affective standards.

It is the strong pronounced magnetic susceptibility of our affective nature towards our central theistic goal, which makes us most able to enjoy, but also to suffer, which makes a strong inclination for sentiments and an aversion to intellectual detailed work. Strong disposition and education unto our traditional exact notion of god augments our magnetic concentrating inclination and drops, accordingly, the self-control of intellectual work. *Conservativism* means strong clinging to this historic sharp conception of god, to this pronounced magnetic attraction, by which people so energetically and easily are fascinated, and FREEDOM OF THOUGHT and LIBERALISM mean, instead, the prevalence of the investigating intellectual component of our human disposition, giving influence, however, to a later different attractive power outside, which is greater and even more promising than the spheric affective solar system. We are fixed, it is true, and dependent, especially and radically through our historic notion of god. But the warning, not to have the intention to see god nor even to pronounce his name, has the meaning not to endeavour to try to frame his existence in a narrow notion. And if we try to do it in a historic localization, and think to have caught the divine eagle in the bower of our solstitial drawing, he flies away and is gone through all universal far-away blue sky. Oh wonderful divine bird, which we thought to have surely enclosed in a strong cage. He has anawares escaped.

We are not entitled, in the light of this instructive spheric conception of human affectivity, to worship exclusively the central charming god of our traditional teachings. Fate, life, good development of humanity, necessity of hygiene and of universal progression forbid and check it. The traditional idea of god is insufficient, because it is traditionally centri-petal and sentimental. We have further centri-fugal divine dispositions. They are given in the intellectual work. INTELLECTUAL WORK releases another vibrating disposition of further magnetic appeal, in our nature; there is a higher, more universal fate in our psychic inclinations. Intellectual work, in this conception, means a further blowing-up of our historic Christian idea of god, into a more distant affective future universe, more general and more powerful in its extension and in its magnetism. Our human aversion against this intellectual power, and our affective difficulty to go on toward it, consists in the easy custom to know and possess the historic habitual affectivity, and in the difficult task of inventing and embracing new unknown realms of experience. But what is now, according to the law of our natural laziness, only a struggling necessity, groping into dangerous centrifugal adventures, will be one day a repeated custom, as well as now the historic notion of god is, and the enlarged universal notion of god will be an affective easily obtainable possession in future, because we will enjoy it by skill and repeated practice. Even it will be, one day, antiquated and worn out as our limited understanding of the notion of god to-day, and there will rise the further future necessity, after all, to enlarge again by new centrifugal work and intellectual striving, without end.

We learn so to *appreciate the gigantic intellectual disposition of our present time.* We are aware of the circular phases of our affective relapses; we know that human fate is a circle, and that our hopes, on all sides,are so easily, and always again, deceived and disappointed; but we have the natural right and duty to hope,and, by strong and repetaed efforts, we will succeed, in future times, in enlarging the circle of our vital spheric development, so much so as to leap, one day, into the higher order of an outside further, more powerful and more universal crystallizaticn of a theistic solar system. Intellectuality is more appreciated in this connection; it leads to the higher order. It is the historic supposition of the growing spiritual universality of mankind. It is the toiling preparation of to-day, for the heart's enjoyment of to-morrow. Sentiments are retro-spective magnetic sparks of the human soul. Thoughts and intellectual work are the "centrifugal" magnetic invitation of outside universal forces to the future development of the narrow limits of our present human psychology. What is sweet and most desirable to-day, will be obsolete to-morrow, and, what is a striving natural pain and sacrificing self-destruction of our most natural and deep affective magnetic disposition,will be the ruling possession and affective enjoyment in a short time. Our collective fate never stops, and our natural magnetic capability will grow continuously into higher conceptions and greater goals, increasing with greater tasks, if we courageously undertake the self-denying, tiring struggle of intellectual work and progressice centrifugal expansion of our spheric life-circle. We hope that by the continual intellectual striving work, the spheric arches of our fate will be more and more stretched, so that our circular way will be enlarged like a growing *spiral* or a snail house, and one day will be flung into the superior realm of a *higher affective unit* of an universal solar system unknown by now, to which to-day our intellectual part has the centrifugal tendency.

We will, in the meanwhile, not indulge too much in delusions. Human psychological history is a circular spheric way, and we shall have again our enormous *affective sentimental relapses*, it is true, perhaps sooner than we think. There will be new fatal solstitial points, we may call them as we may. We shall have other, exclusively sentimental quarters in our psychological human development, where no intellectual investigation will be permitted and every scientific progress will be frustrated. There will be new periods of affective absolutism toward the magnetic, traditional, historicly fixed notion of god, and there will be new equinoctial resistances, struggles, apostasies, combustions, martyrs and sectarian divisions and - other intellectual periods of greater technical triumphs than we have them now. In the future higher units of intellectual formality we shall meet even more enforced laws of bridling stability against further rushing developments towards the outside universe, because more considerable amounts of forces will clash together.

We have reason, however, to assume a PROGRESS. Be it, that, unable as we are to look outside of our own intellectual period, we are in a subjective shortcoming to judge the importance and the success of our far-reaching contemporary performances, but we surely are entitled to surmise that the intellectual work of our present period was richer and more important than that of all previous corresponding intellectual quarters may have been. We have, therefore, the right to assume, that the centrifugal component of our circular vital revolution has grown, that it was relatively stronger in its cultural role and that accordingly the spheric archcircle of our period is of *more stretched description* than former ones have been. Thus we shall have a future progressing enlargement of our circular spheric psychological revolution. *Our human life-year will, for this reason, last longer,* on behalf of the swelling broadening circle of our intellectual working self-denial. At the same time, it avoids, more and more, the fascinating approach to the traditional theistic magnetism and its exclusive power, and is able, in this way, to loosen always more its enslaved dependence on it.

This enlarging movement, one day, will be strengthened enough to progress rapidly in the sure position to turn out from the old traditional theistic solar system and to swing into the next higher universal theistic order, whereto the intellectual dissatisfaction of the present order aspires to-day with its groping experimental efforts.

Humanity always progresses like this. We have the right and duty to hope and to aspire always to higher units of spheric concentration. What could essentially be the reason of our self-denial and self-vexation by work, as well as of the incessant struggle and disregard, against and for, the charming past of our own history but the ambition of the further opening of the spiralic development of the human circular fate, the higher aspiration to switching the world into more magnetic, more attractive and more inportant future central solar systems? What was, three hundred years ago, considered a criminal action against the social well-fare, is to-day a serious and free scientific problem which cannot be rejected by slander or morally condemned, and it will be, later on, the freedom and salvation of the human race, giving not only new prospects and hopes, as it does now, but carrying the whole of humanity into new and stronger units of fixed inter-spheric magnetic relations. Up to god, nearer to god! Leave the old god in order to find the stronger new god! This is the ultimate sense of the intellectual researches, the meaning of the serious work of all humanity, the intention of all biting and straining criticism. Nothing can ever be enough. The greatest future will be mummified and fade away. We look back with tender feelings and reverent respect for all glorious past cultural acquisitions. The progress of the most remote history cannot be extinct by time. But there is no use to stop. The hurricane of human fate blows irresistibly, and the incessant river of daily production of human life-force craves for new laurels and other higher and *more universal victories*.

If Christ is the solstitial point of the Mediterranean and European history, then this genial concentration and divine fulness has doubtless the prominent importance for the following occidental humanity of Europe, which took, at this time, the leadership of the following sentimental quarter of human fate. For this part of humanity He was the genial symbolic, almost inexhaustible well of directive life- force and unforgettable splendour, the over-whelming, contrasting lightning of the new humanity, after the despairing night of thorough affective corruption and thoughtlessness. He was the wonderful new solstitial conversion of the lost heart's life of the world. He was, at this solstitial Roman epoch, the unheard of, and unexampled genial turning-point of a new strong *affective instradation* into new directions, full of energy and determination. All occidental humanity, during the Middle Ages, was dazzled by the fascinating brilliance of the lightning flash. All looks were directed to this solstitial new-birth and renaissance of humanity drawing all courage and all hope from this tremendous power of concentrated life-force. Men had, during all this sentimental quarter, easy access toward the equinoctial approach of their historic central deity, having the human perfection before their surprised eyes, and drifting comfortably, on the sure path, to their theistic goal.

From the EQUINOCTIAL POINT their fate changed. They had to accept a *steering component for new goals*; they had the additional task of strong centrifugal intellectual development, which was no longer offered under the clear, previously sufficient genial historic direction of the theistic sun and moon. If they had before but to surrender their life-force, concentrated in genial Christ, to the central historic deity, after the equinoctial point, they had to create, by themselves, a new enlargement of their life-circle, directing by the daring boldness of their own intellectual work, their new way digressing from their historical conception of god, in another new intellectual quarter. The religious genius was the excellent leader of the sentimental epoch. He was the opening standard of the former period of old times, giving, in his *symbolic solstitial conversion*, to the occidental nations the fruits of former intellectual performances; but from the equinoctial point, there arose new needs for intellectually enlarging developments, - again the pre-supposition for a later and greater religious genius. The former historic-religious leader was himself the startling genial light-point of the old time, throwing all his glory through the centuries of the early Christian times; but at the equinoctial point, the fundamental part of his task was done, and humanity had the bitter duty to get rid, up to a certain degree, of its most charming and surest intellectual genial symbolism.

Although it was wrong to confuse the genial compression of life-force, given in the religious genius and elaborated so artistically by his followers, with the actual plenty of the universal god himself, this difference of conception could not matter practically for the sentimental period, because of the congruity of the magnetic force and atmosphere of that time with the social desire drifting into the historic, unmistakably divine goal. Their capacities and their genial leadership and suggestions were an even balance. But from the equinoctial point, this divine historic equilibrium was upset. The social cultural mind started to assume a steering will, after the drifting obeisance. The intellectual new humanity had not a security of the historic divine goal, which made the human restriction of the *corresponding* symbolic genial sign dispensable. The later humanity had, instead, instantly the task to find out a higher conception of the old historic notion of the central deity, which it has to leave, as much as possible, in the *elliptic necessity of its intellect*.

Thus everything intellectually not quite clear, in the religious genius and in his humanized divinity, became very shocking for the new intellectual conceptions. The old genius became, therefore, for the *new post-equinoctial humanity, quite* unsuitable, because of its prevalent fondness of intellectual accuracy and carelessness of sentimental perfection. The religious genius was the full authority and the sufficient initiator for the *pre-equinoctial* humanity of the first occidental centuries; but he turned out not to correspond to the intellectualized desire of the starting second period with its typical withdrawing enlargement of the circle. He taught, how to go to the historically given theistic centre of humanity, he made the path, in the result of his church, toward the theistic god, smooth and very practical, though he personally revelled in incredible universal out-cries at the top of his culminating *solstitial view;* but the bitter way of the resignation in going away from the charming love of the historic god himself, in intellectual sacrificing work and principle spheric digression from him, this topic was not even hinted to with exception of *Passion* and *Cross*.

Through the introduction of these latter points of view, the religious genius, however, characterized himself as keen predecessor even of the farthest post-quinoctial times. In those representations we have, at the same time his fare-well from cruelty and real brutality and already the germ of a new intellectual conversion of the world, although the totality of the religious philosophical disposition rises in joyous glory from the fatal real issue of the divine life on earth and rejects so intellectuality again. There are so many to attend to the dinner of Christ, and so few willing to go with Him to Calvary. The brilliant idea of the historic theistic conception of the Father and his overwhelming love, overcomes, at last, all peripheric obstacles of *Passion* and *Cross,* and He shows always such a principal aversion to the world, not dealing with it but in parables, withdrawing Himself into the desert, clinging to His definite conception of god and excluding the world from His incompatible realm. His god was too advanced for His contemporaries.

According to our natural disposition, the affective centripetal god of the historic conception is not the fullness of our destiny nor of our duty. He is the unchecked duty of the previous sentimental quarter of our national fate; but after the fatal equinoctial Conversion unto prevailing intellectuality, we have to reckon even more with the centrifugal opposite urge of intellectual *creation,* which makes the leading part of our postequinoctial fate. Our historic central affective magnetic god has only half the share of our life-force; his idealistic-sentimental power is counterbalanced by the universal power of the digressing intellectual necessity. We run from the old historic notion of god to a new one. Not only the religious genius is not the central god, whose affective life-force he symbolically represents, but even the historic notion of god, which we have, because of its restricted exact notional one-sidedness, is neither perfect nor definite.

We received our *conception of god*, of to-day, in dependence on the symbolic historic religious genius, through the intermediation of his systematized ideal organization identifying the idealistic outstanding figure of its hero with our knowledge and our enjoyment of god. Its god is love, beauty, pardon and meekness like its hero, whilst the former god was chiefly justice, strength and unapproachable majesty. He was the preferably intellectual conception of our eternal magnetic goal, as our age accepts it,again more and more. We have the necessary sentimental genial role of the religious founder, at the starting affective period, conveyed to god himself. The intellectual ages of the Antiquity and of the new modern times, instead, are more inclined to give to him the iron features of severe strength and towering necessity. Both are right and both wrong, because the combination of both is right in order to make the whole picture of our god, as he rules, in fact, human fate. Our historic god is the reflection of the contradictory natural disposition of ourselves, forcing on us, and "permitting" everything within the compromising fate of our natural tendences or necessities. The intellectual god is supra-individual and universal, the affective god is, instead, the individual loving god, full of respect and care for our personal well-fare.

The *central conception of god* is insufficient. We witnessed it, silent, startled and shuddering, during the great war. God has even higher, and opposite, intentions than individual and even general human well and woe. But as everything finally turns out well, we are entitled to hope, that the eternal power, crushing humanity and throwing them out their natural most noble feelings, surroundings, wishes and theistic traditions, bring about a cultural renaissance, an enlargement of our experimental light-field and an instradation into new higher spheric orders of theistic beauty, strength and happiness.

If we would think, that, by the *solstitial conception* of the religious genius, we had left our former circular psychopupilar system, speaking at once of an *oval instead of a circle,* we would have been superficial in understanding our last meditations. The OVAL FORM of the human spheric psychology comes about owing to *the continual rush toward peripheric intellectual records.* Like we have in a circular *arena for bicycles* a peripherically ascending slope, in order to repress the centrifugal swing of the quick motion of the racing competitors, at the obliquely ascending wall, and like the most accelerated bicycle is swung up to the topmost peripheric elevation of the circular wall, the total covered way forming, in this manner, an oval or ellipsoid circle, in spite of the regular circular form of the arena, - thus we have to accept the effect of the most efficient religious genial racer, within the exacting psychopupilar arena of the human psychic disposition. As we said quite at the beginning of the development of our ideas on *Psychopupillarism,* it is comparable to a hollow rubber ball with a central movable and enlargeable hole at the bottom and in the centre of the top, somewhat similar to the interior of the *vesica urinaria.* From the bottom hole, within the empty inside, the walls form also a circular ascending slope, ending into an inclosed vaulted ceiling. We accept so, in the solstitial conception, the religious genius as the powerful racer of the human *psychomechanic arena,* rushing in his zeal of victorious competition to the highest points of the circular arena, where he is checked by the ascending wall. We easily observe, that, in this manner, the oval instead of the circular form of the covered way comes about, because of the strong centrifugal effort of the racer. He is,therefore, the straining and strong centrifugal effort willing to transgress the periphery of the arena at the utmost degree and comprising, in his superior record, all lower performances. The greater the effort of the competition, the more the peripheric ascending distance from the centre and the more inevitable the strongly pronounced and always repeated oval form of the way. The continual to and fro of the dice of our fate, shaken within the vase of the psychopupilar mechanism, is thrown most energetically by the first historic religious genius. He has beaten every former record of humanity, going further and higher in the peripheric swing and distance than all .He has destroyed and upset the vulgar regularity of the human intellectual-affective activity, and, by his forced records, he established an almost impossible and dangerous method of solstitial one-sidedness, which he reached one time,conquering the supreme laurels of highest religious human performances not being beaten up to the present day. By his divine efforts and unequalled peripheric energy, he reached the topmost and most peripheric point of any human oval course ever done by a human individual. He has, in this way, the prize and the crown of human divine achievement, having enlarged,beyond expectation, the oval enlargement, and added the idealistic elevation in *the third dimension*.

This is the meaning of the expression: *son of god*. If we willingly and unmistakably like to call the foremost religions genius son of god, we express our pride for our social darling, to whom we give every chance and every honour, because he had enflamed our hearts and taken all our sympathy, by the enrapturing fascination of his quite unexpected affective effort. He raised the totality of humanity, by his unheard record, to a higher dignity than before. We all share the marvellous achievement of his extraordinary genial perfection. By his topmost racing performance he has beaten all his fellow-men in the battle of competition. He possesses in his highest score the potentiality of all lower effects and in this sense he is *our god*.

By the highest performances, the religious genius has reached and overtaken the most distant periphery of the contemporary human light-field; he touched the stars with the top of his head; the high-way of his victorious race cut the centre of the vaulted psychopupilar ceiling. He comprised utmost human capabilities within his superior personality.According to our psychopupilar organization, a strong and important effort and victory discharges itself finally from the central genial light-point of the ceiling; thus we see in the highest religious genius, how highly he is elevated by the energetic affective swing and the sincere struggle of his success, beyond the categories of time, space and causality. His extraordinary consistent successes make him already soaring to heaven,hovering in the air, rushing through closed doors and upsetting any kind of material and categoric law of resistance and impermeability,because he is swung above the categories of time, space and causality, driven by the centrifugal force of his racing way up to the starry ceiling of the human psychopupilar arena, discharging his forces from the symbolic sky-light to the universe.

We meet the religious genius here again in his specific genial attitude as before. He was driven, on behalf of the human global concave necessity, back to the genial punctual mouth of *our centro-theistic nature,* only in the ceiling of the arena instead of the bottom. For this reason, we see so little of intellectual features in him, and we are scandalized therefore, not that he would not have been able to substantiate them, since any higher function includes the lower, in the sense of our device, but because even he succumbs to the compensatory law of human ideal-real restriction. His overwhelming skill and life-force throw even him on and back to the precocious issue of the central genial sky-light. In spite of his extraordinary life-force he neglects the peripheric real display, because he is driven, by the super-abundance of his energetic enthusiasm, and owing to his exact human psycho-mechanic organization, to the repeated affective concentration, leading again, in a symmetric deviation, to where he started, to the light-point of genial *death,* after having arrived through genial *birth.* He, therefore, is a whole and perfect man, with all restricted psychological necessities and the organizatory limits of everybody. Although he is the first and most honored racer of humanity, having crossed the zenith in his victorious flight, he remains not the less the child of our human disposition, not only corporeally, but also in the most hidden features of his mind and soul. We are fond of the statement that he likely was the most divine among human beings, who ever lived. He had the strongest concentration of human life-force within one individual, but he has not any essential difference from other people, except that he is exactly more human in the extreme elaboration of the features of his heart. His difference is merely one of *higher degree.* He obeyed the general geometrical laws of our psycho-mechanic restrictions; he followed the same path of human insufficiency in the compensation of his intellectually lacking performances. He, therefore, has the same claim and right, to be judged and acknowledged as our foremost successful racer and unexampled hero in the highest human spiritual achievements, but nevertheless he fully remains a human being, and we ought to be jealous of this most encouraging fact. This is the only way to claim divine progress for ourselves. The religious hero has the same body and soul as we have, and he is only distinguished from us through the quite extraordinary and idealistically elevated and pushing disposition of his soul and life-force. There is a temperamental difference of taste and another of quantitative psychic riches.

In making the statement, that the earth with all her absorbing power could comprise the *whole universal divinity,* we could find as little belief as by the assertion, that a small stone could comprise and saturate the whole magnetic amount of gravitation of the earth. Earth and all its inhabitants are able to receive as much gracious affective saturation as they have the capacity to, and nobody, on this human theistic earth, was or will ever be in a position to accept or harbour more divine universal magnetic force than is allowed to him according to his human magnetic natural disposition. The central conversion of the whole culture was fixed in the hero's genial historic reaction, not being able to give even to his enormous personality a greater intellectual circumference than human nature is able to bestow and, therefore, being driven back to the simplification of the genial symbolism. He is the great son of god; but he is also the greatest son of man, our firstborn, but genuine victorious brother.

If we think to be able to catch and compress the eternal and inconceivable greatness and majesty of the universal god within the psychopupilar mechanism of human nature, we would have to admit to have birth, flourishing life, death and resurrection of the divine individual altogether in one moment, and, in addition, a burning explosion of all created nature as well. So little is the narrowness of the human and earthly disposition able to comprehend and comprise the universal force of the eternal god. But the human race was always very proud. It is the top of of our magnomelia, however, if we cannot acquiesce to harbour only a part and a sufficient share of divinity within our reach, but that we rather claim just to have the totality and the last root and depth of divine power in our midst, if we assume seriously to enclose the entire divine majesty within any human individual. The universal claims, however, are justified, in a *potential* and *evolutionary* way.

The genial human reaction, great and important as it may be, and it is always more visible in its compensation, the greater it is, must always be a compensatory psychic deficiency. To enclose the highest development of divine terminal magnetism into the frail cage of human nature, would be a most pretentious distorting assumption. God indeed lives in it and fills it to the brim, as far as the human organizatory constitution allows, as far as size and surrounding walls permit, but no human psychic being could hold or claim, seriously, an affective amount comparable to the fulness of last universal standards. The very genial character of reaction, as we certainly observe in the highest religious genius, speaks against the *simultaneously active universality* of his power and proves the human limits or his divine performances. He is the strong repretsentative of the historic central and genial idea of the god of his and our contemporary culture, but he represents only the genial one-sided conception, excluding the peripheric intellectual display.

The universal terminal god never will be comprised by a genial, always deficient method. The terminal and true god will and can not be gathered, by the screen of the causal categories, in a punctual concentration. He spreads and effuses his eternal goodness and beauty, power and strength everywhere liberally, and he does not permit to be compressed in one point of genial one-sidedness.

A *genial conception of god* would be a case of human compensatory emergency. God does not need any compensatory contraction. He is everywhere in the same active and full glory of his eternal light, and it may be a dangerous *educational* attempt to gather him into one genial localization or artistic mechanism. Here, like nowhere, we must be aware of the danger to play with the fire; here humanity is able to burn its fingers so thoroughly as nowhere else. Every localization of the great idea of god, even in the historic traditional central idea of god, affords a danger of luxury, sterility, petrification and corruption, because we likely worship a cage, from which the divine eagle has fled away. But we unfortunately have similar dangers in a social historic organization composed of so small and multiple deficient peripheric interests, unjust tendencies toward all sides and personal egotism and ambition. The genial character is extenuated, it is true, in a multiple genial body, the deficient one-sidedness of the genial conception is partly excluded, but, instead, a superficial wordly and business-like frivolity likely arises, and we, at last, have possibly nothing but the intellectual organization, a powerful historic rock of real political resistance against destruction, full of exterminating possibilites : the genial divine child has been spilt with the bath, and we mourn to have lost its charming smile of eternal lovely innocence, on behalf of the real peripheric fixation of his followers.

Every localization of the notion of god into one point is as well understandable and human, as a very wrong and fatal enterprise. We have in this first step already the serious decision to fix god, to limit our future efforts, to relapse to real luxury and to concentrate with *angry slothfulness*. Localization of god to one point, in philosophy, religion, history and ecclesiastic organization, is, in a sense, a very serious handicap to universal progress and development of humanity. How could we enlarge the limits of our light-field, how could we ever switch from our old theistic Psycho-pupillarism to another more important universal one, if we stare with never doubting look, in a state of never changing hypnotism, at the traditional central notion of god, acknowledging his historic artistic representation as the last and unchangeable perfection of the universal possibilities? Not even the god of our present day will be the definite expression of our wishes. He withdraws himself continuously, if we risk to discover him, only and always again aware of our further necessities of magnetic prolongation and withdrawal not being able to stand any intellectual and fixed terminal approach.   The construction of divinity, in the religious genius, goes, therefore, the contrary way, augmenting and approaching the conceivability and visibility of god, supporting the charming idea of his living and dwelling among us in the world, in a personal way. The never failing attractiveness of this form of injunction of idealism is rather clear, but, as there is a strong two-sided educational effect of this disposition, we must ask, what is the influence on the character, and what form of idealism is produced by the strong sensorial emphasis of the genial localization of the idea of god? It is the topic of the educational value of the historic religion, which comes in here; let us delay these meditations for that special part of our book.

We smile, if we learn that the Jews had, for a long time, their "national" deity which they would not communicate to any stranger, and which was made accessible to all by the efforts of the great personality of Abraham. In spite of the great cultural significance of the Jewish god we are prone to decline the bliss of a national god. We no sooner have given the monopoly of the divinity to any localization than we have done the first step unto the roughening genial acceptation of the most outspread divine eternity. This form of divine advance is likely to fascinate our psychological disposition, by its comfortable magnetic strength and intellectual simplicity, but it roughens our feelings and misrepresents the intentions of the eternal divinity longing to attract us outside unto its absolute and immaterial transcendental greatness and eternal supracategoric realm, which, by the genial method, risks to shrink to the symbolic sign. But there are also in this matter distinctly two sides to be considered, one favorable and another disfavorable.

God is jealous not to be put into the frame of any human limits. If men try to do it, they hurt, burn and deprive themselves.

In order to deepen our clear recognition of the *relations between god, genius and humanity,* let us recall once more the sketch given in reference to the solstitial conception of the religious genius. If we think ourselves driven again, in the *peritheistic spheric revolution* of our specific psychological human fate, starting out from the *solstitial point,* and if we mark the influence of the light of the *central god-sun, which means clear and harmonious affective happiness,* then we observe easily, that the human flight proceeding through the sentimental quarter has the utmost favored and best sun-lighted magnetic facilitation. The eternal light kindles the way, through which the sentimental individual flies, in a direct and leading manner, whilst from behind the traditional background of the genial solstitial *remembrances* illuminates and shines in a *reflective* indirect way. If the solstitial historic moment is artistically fixed and elaborated, as the systematizing genial societies use to do with their heroes, then, according to our mental recording nature, and possibilities of imagination and suggestibility, we shall have easily a mighty traditional light, following the flying globe on its spheric track.

We incline to dispise, ignore and, some, to fear or hate,the *centrifugal shadow.* Some are said, in famous fairy-tales, to have been anxious, excited or ashamed of this unobserved, yet most remarkable new universal germ of our own physical and spheric individual organization, which one day possibly could be elected to evolve to a similar bright abundance of living light as the solar light and its system which we serve now. We, therefore, are anxious, recognizing in our shadow the mysterious question-mark about the essence of the very sunlight. The shadow is the expression of the ubiquitous opposition and the mark of future misgivings. The shadow is the unforgiving sullen face of the humiliated, the sign of present historic rejection from the participation in the central sun-light ruling the moment. Shall the shadow overtake the light, one day?

The systematized religious idea worked out such an elaborate traditional influence on our sentimental emotions, that the moving planet of our social and individual human personality receives its gracious divine light or eternal magnetic attraction, from the anterior side, on its way toward the equinoctial point approaching the central historic god. The intellectual need of nature, is handicaped during the sentimental quarter, but is always again frightened and appeased by the dazzling light of the solstitial symbolism, which, like a powerful directive beacon, is continuously held in a trimmed condition, by the official genial trimming society, the church. Thus the psychological globe of human nature is literally wrapped by divine magnetic light, the anterior leading hemisphere being attracted and lighted directly by the theistic central god-sun, and the second following hemisphere enjoying reflective illumination, being consoled and calmed by the sweet reflective moon-light of solstitial cultural remembrances. The whole globe is clad in divine light, through direct rushing desire from the anteror part, and historic traditional divine memories from behind. Thus we recognize, in the solstitial genius, a lighting reflection of the central theistic sun, helping humanity in dreary shadowy real hours by sweet brilliant dreams, suggesting new hopes, when the global turns of our fate have partly averted us from the gracious favour of the direct central sun.

All piety for country and ancestry, above all for old tenets and principles, for *Art and Antiquities*, the pilgrimages of our age to the wonderful churches of the Middle Ages, our admirable artistic collections and all political and philosophical history, form all together such a cultural shining reflection of the theistic old time, a genial fiery trace of the radiant comet of the gone-by sentimental track of the spheric revolution, which has its commencement in the first genial lightnings of the distant solstitial hero of our culture. The power of tradition, of recording culture and historic remembrances so turns out to be, - we should not be surprised by this fact, if we visualize the human importance of memory and *brains, - an eminent tranquillizer* and substantially helping and suggesting comforter of our life. How different are the old cultural countries full of artistic works and masterpieces! How powerful is the suggestive influence of a rich medieaval cathedral in a city ! The population is bound , by this artistic symbol, to old times, and under the spell of this ingenious old token, it will grasp, much more difficultly, new progressive intellectual ideas and views. Humanity in the influence of this strong old atmosphere is settled, fixed, decided, achieved, but also crystallized and petrified and becomes a glorified mummification, fascinated by the old gigantic and faraway spirit of the ancient centuries, looking with spell-bound enigmatic clarification from the fronts of the *medieaval churches*.

How sweet and comforting is the enjoyment of the ancient artistic background of an old time! The collector of a carefully achieved artistic museum feels it best, when all the riches and the glamour of the ancient esthetic styles and times look at him with fascinating smile. The old masterpieces effuse on him their charming beauty, their holy bliss and peace and their mighty central theistic secure affirmation. They all confirm our old existing system of the order of the world; they are full of satisfaction and expectation toward the future fulfilments of the times, according to given former foundations; but we, who are later chidren of history and, therefore, already more disappointed in the fulfilment, are no longer able to smile so confidently as the charming holy statues of the *medieaval saints* do from our walls. The hopeful and sincere naive smile for their future confirms the confidence in the retrospective part of our historic present order. Our doubtful anxiety is smoothed by their smiling serenity. Leaning against this cultural sweet suggestion, we do not fear that the old world will fall down or explode, and we feel invited to go on fairly and happily, like an *artistic connaisseur* in a plenty of antique beauty or a stylish lady in the midst of refined historic laces and cushions. All these things have the strong effect to sooth our agitated progressive life by calming the intellectual doubts about the present and the future.

The suggestions deriving from the past are more powerful than we might guess. Our whole affective state of happiness is as much dependent on all possible suggestive circumstantial memories as on personal objective successes. We all are fond, in some way, of having good conditions of easy spheric progress toward the equinoctial point of our life and history, and of enjoying favorable direct relations to the oldest symbolic genial commencement of our age. As far as the curved spheric way of the sentimental quarter of the cultural peritheistic sun-year reaches, humanity sweeps very quickly through the ranges of the categories of time, space and causality, following rapidly the leading and irresistable component of magnetic theistic attraction. We, therefore, have an easy task during this period. The magnetic rushing facility causes, however, later difficulties expressed in the following intellectual awkwardness and reluctance, and, quite characteristically, for the sentimental or genial quarter of the *cultural human sun-year,* we intellectually stumble and leap, owing to the forcing affective attraction of the centro-magnetic preponderance or over- weight. Miracles, mysticism, heroic deeds and arts and angry slothfulness are typical of this time of hyper-magnetic theistic tendencies. The individual loses easily the *rythmic logical reality* under its feet, running unhesitatingly and full of sway and enthusiasm to its cenral-theistic approach, wich is most pronounced at the moment of the equinoctial position.

The reflection of the divine light is essential for the genial character and action. This divine light is a combination of utmost intellectual clearness, within the historic symbolic limits of the given solstitial point, and of the extremely secure purposiveness in the harmonious affective approach toward the centre. All reactions during this sentimental period must have the genial character, in a certain sense, in receiving the *artistic genial intuition* from the directly iluminating and inspiring intercourse with the central historic god. Many enjoy god scarcely in the extenuation of reflected intensity and there are so many who ride all their life in the dim rear of the proceeding human fate, looking admiringly to the beautiful and dreamy moon-shine of divine glory, whilst there are so few who take the steering part of the flaming front of our fatal collective psychic aeroplane flying to god.

Humanity is fond of averting its weak eyes, dazzled by the shining glory of the central sun-light and hurt by the sharp draught of central magnetism, back to the milder light of the reflecting relations with the central god, through the symbolistic transfer of the religious hero. The reflective light spares our weak eyes and sensitive skin and nerves. All celestial mail of Christianity takes the circuit through the meeker genial intermediation. All applications and love-letters to heaven, from Christian countries, are characterized through the stereotypical address: "Through Jesus Christ, our Lord ". He is the intermediary station, the transfer office for the Christian intercourse with heaven. From Him and to Him, both parts, central deity and peripheric humanity, receive and confide their mutual messages.

The solstitial retrospective genius invites our divine proceeding faculties to take the transfer of his humanized and more comfortable symbolism toward god, and mankind pulls, in this manner, the theistic supracategoric magnetic standards and values, into the circle of their daily intimacy.

Everywhere in the historic religious conceptions we observe the choice of the role of an intermedator, played by the first genius, being more accessible to the theistic susceptibility of the soul. In this light we realize the identification of the religious solstitial genius with the central theistic god. The emphasis of this idea has the effect to keep the believer back from the blinding direct intercourse with the supra-human and supra-reasonable central god and goal. But, on the other hand, owing to our natural theistic capacity, the rich river of divine affective grace streaming out from the central deity toward humanity, is condensed in the solstitial point, like a high electrical power in a narrow wire which is glowing with light and forwards the energy to the periphery. Is not the centro-theistic sun-light of the central Deity pulled out immeasurably and perhaps abusively, through the solstitial punctual moon? Do we suck out, through this symbolic transfer, all the central treasures of the theistic divine love, burning and hurting ourselves, once more, owing to the genial organization of the intense symbolism with the flaming point of the magnifying glass? Or have we to accept it as a quantitative and qualitative regulator between humanity and the central god, like an electrical accumulator or condensor? Has the symbolic interpolation the effect of lavish communication or of obstruction of the divine and human intercourse?

Strong aspirations through the genial communicating mouth piece of the historic religious symbolism produce an utmost contraction of this opening, the more the aspiration is strong, and in the same degree, the flaming and blinding force coming out from the friction of the strongly compressed divine fluidum, - as we have it in the concentrated light-field. The reflected light of Christian conception is, therefore, in this connection, to be considered as a *theistic mitigation* checking and destroying as soon as we indulge in a very strong interspheric magnetic desire and action. Genial symbolism, owing to its essential technical organization, is a *regulating transformer of affective divinity into categoric human intellectuality* retaining, during the sentimental quarter, humanity by the reins of the moderated suggestion of its humanized divine idea. The historic genial religion is, thus, the limitation of our nature, through its historic theistic heroic restriction and checking influence, not permitting our vital globe to fly irresistibly either to the equinoctial or, in the other sense, to the solstitial point. Christ turns out to be the retaining genial condenser of affective transformation, between the central magnetic god and the progressing human life-force. The solstitial genius is indeed the eye of a needle dividing and distributing the riches of the universal and human psychic-real world.

The *solstial point* is like the EYE OF A NEEDLE, through which the thread of divine, intellectually checked limitation, is running, round a distant corner. It is like a narrow pipe or a covered channel, through which only the water can pass or be obtained, within a unit of time, corresponding to its caliber, unless we shall risk, by any other attempt, most disagreeable and fatal dangers of torn or damaged affective threads or an empty affective channel, which could easily become obstructed, and would so bring serious prospects for future explosions. The genial disposition is the specific *affective human scale and measure,a prophylaxis against lost theistic exaggerations*. It is the last utmost limit, where nature rejects nearer and further approach of our affective greediness toward the highest theistic standards. Christ Himself is the historic eye of the needle, the *key-stone, corner-stone* and *meta* of His cultural revolution, round which the whole development of the following sentimental epoch must take its genial round-about way.

The psychological task of the religious genius, to our social nature, is, as it were, the work of the soft finger or hand of a lady holding the *vital yarn of our affective life,* and allowing it to run through between the fingers, in both directions, to the ball of peripheric real intellectual humanity and the magnetic whirlpool of central affective divinity. The fatal yarn incessantly runs through the holding genial hand of Christ, to and fro in both directions, not to be checked, owing to the impartial, mediating and serving institution. The intermediating role of the religious genius is intended to be an absolutely *impartial* establishment of good communication between intellectuality and sentiments, real humanity and ideal god. But we know that the mechanic psychological mediator is a pronounced admirer and adherent of the divinity. The religious genius is bribed by the magnificence of the magnetic central force he feels in his intermediating hand and by the beauty of the divine features. He, therefore, searches, necessary genial intermediator as he is within the historic cultural frame of history, to unroll the human affective ball toward the central divine side, in order that we could have a continuously running magnetic yarn or current heading toward the central divinity, the *human coil* diminishing in the same degree, on behalf of the increasing divine centralization of forces. The religious genius is the affective and intellectual translater and interpreter,but he is in favour of the affective heart. He searches to exploit the forces of humanity to the advantage of his universal goal, which fascinates him. His genial possibility was the last and highest method of his partial divine predilection.

At the equinoctial point we have the equilibrium of both intellectual and sentimental components of our life-force, as we have the same at the solstitial point, only with the reversion of special representation of intensity and quantity. The enslaved intellectuality began to grow from the solstitial point toward the light of the central sun; at the equinoctial point, we have another new psychological *conversion,* the intellectual hemisphere turning once more to the dark shade of the exterior side, and the affective sentimental one turning entirely toward the magnetic centre. In reality, we can say, that the obstinate tenacity of the intellectual oppositional work has found grace before the eyes of god. He rewards it for its hard retaining conviction in giving to it the light of the charming grace. It becomes by the long custom of working persistence, itself, the harmoniuos lightful affirmation and unrestricted theistic happiness of mankind. It is elevated to the affective side of the kosmic psychological world-globe of humanity, being called sentimental part of human life-force.

Instantly this knighting conversion is balanced by a duty of the other part, since by now, from the equinoctial point, the decentralized former affectivity of the psychological globe, receives from the outside universe a new magnetic task, for the future, more powerful and prospective than the old affirmative solar system ever had. Is the difference of intellectuality and sentiments only an inversion of tasks of the same function, a changing intervertible difference of magnetic direction and degree, or are they essentially incompatible forces?

The former strong solar system has acquired, in the new union with its former intellectual fiend, in its affective loving and artistic knighting, a new promising ally increasing its affective power of concentration.But it has lost, in the same moment, the precious collaboration of its old, dismissed, yet tired humane friend who,owing to the equinoctial conversion of the turning psychological globe, instantly has accepted an outside further affective engagement of more universal value and significance. The success of the former pre-equinoctial human sentimental life-force has been rewarded by its *extra-solar knighting.* We have, therefore, at the equinoctial moment, two promotions: of the former negative intellectual power to the lightful affective central affirmative conversion, and of the former affective or sentimental force to the extrasolar affective allegiance. Conversion and apostasy of the two forces happen at the same time and cross each other.

If we stand inside of the old solar organisation, if we stick to the former order and have the will to maintain for ever the central solar system of our history, then we may call the former charming affective semi-circular connivant inclination, in its averted state, a faithless renegade going over to strong and ruthless intellectual accomplicity. In the other case, if we take part for the further digressing development of the human theistic idea, if we hope that one day the spheric spring of our theistic-central solar year will leap out to a higher affective universal unit of greater dimensions than the past, - if, according to the strong decentralization of the direction of our intellectual life-force of the present day, we assume, that there will be ever a possibility of an *elliptic enlargement* of the psychological sphere of our human destiny, then we may call the future digressing intellectuality, as it is effectuated in the intellectual scientific era of humanity, *the extrasolar affectivity or the germing universal sentiments of the modern time.*

In the conception of the old central historic idea, everything not absorbable, not logically dirigible toward the central magnetism, is called *evil*. Greatest evil means the essential magnetic opposition against the central theistic magnetism, in the traditional sense, the aversion and resistance to the holy eternal light of the magnetic enthusing affirmative love and its central attachment. Bad is considered that bold being which desires and undertakes to switch out from the wonderful perfect circle of the central traditional psychological sun, and assumes the shuddering courage to put itself into opposition to the total cultural and magnetic system of our past ages. It is looking out for new intentions and purposes, outside of the charming balanced whirlpool of the central historic past. There cannot be imagined, therefore, a more intense or striking condemnation than that of the strong and jealous central sun against that being, of this god who always attached all into the magnetic lap of his theistic love, and now 'suffers' by the subtracting loss of the digressing magnetic sympathy.

We may assume that we live in the second (II) intellectual section of our psychic solstitial light-year. The overweight of the intellectual force, in the old theistic *terminology,* - inter-legere means, however, reading *between* the lines, - or the extrasolar affectivity in the universal sense, effectuates this outside deviation of the human psychic way. The continuity with the perfect circle of the human psychic way of the past history is broken, and the spheric digression of human fate is driven into the distant insecure universe far away from the magnetic whirlpool of the historic divine harbor. The way of the second spheric human period forms the most audaciaus curves away from the traditional conception of god into the problematic future universe. The fiery zeal of its leadership escaped from the former central fascination, left the circular narrow concavity of the former times and makes again the same thing, which the ancient world did, it forms an elliptic enlargement and a breaking up of the traditional magnetic circle , finishing in a new, tremendous solstitial culmination greater than any previous one, from which humanity was thrown, back again and again, under the equinoctial yoke of the traditional centralism. The religious genius is the most distant turning-point of an old huge culture, who strove to escape definitely from the traditional local theistic conceptions. He is the mark of a terrible magnetic struggle between different energies and directions of the peri-solstitial interspheric magnetic tempests. He is the great culminating moment of the victorious decision of history, in favor of the central divine crystallization. After this *transitional time* humanity was sent back to the charming slavery of the realized theistic realm, which was an improved edition of the former one, in order to go round a further magnetic revolution of a psychic light-year, encircling the traditional and 'revised' eternal Majesty.

The run of the Antiquity for the theistic emancipation was not yet sufficient. Its top-score in the victorious exponent of the genial hero had not yet reached that necessary distance and height sufficient to escape the old theistic magnetism. The strongest aversion to the old traditional historic theism, and the most successful universal assault against the old written and legalized religious conceptions and tenets, relapsed, after all, to pronounced central-theistic limitation.

Has our present culture overtaken the efficiency of the old Jewish, Greek and Roman culture ? There are, in our time, undoubtedly assets of a very superior intellectual culture. Our scientific and technical developments have reached a towering perfection as never before, presumably, and, inspite of periodical embarrassment, we may reasonably assume that the new spiralic digression of to-day, of the modern intellectual quarter of the spheric psychological orb of humanity, is so considerable that we may be sure that we are already on the verge to succumb to an attraction of different magnetic strength and direction, with a localization in the further and greater outside universe. The foundations of our old historic theistic conceptions are shaken. The overwhelming attraction of stronger universal magnetic whirlpools exhaust and empty old historic lakes of divine grace and force. The sun itself is the servant of the extra-solar magnetism of its future; after having served enough in the more narrow circle of the traditional deity, humanity will be promoted to the higher direct service of the superior universal magnetic unit. All goes on like this in the created world, progressing from one smaller theistic circle to a stronger more universal of greater magnetic depth and idealistic efficiency and an enlarged affluence and size. Always, then, there will be a procession of all development. Never the last step of the eternal ladder will or could be reached, all the world and all the universe being an incessant and for ever progressive divine increasing fecundation.

Thus our age moulds new platforms for a gigantic future religious genius, a more sparkling and splendid symbolic light than ever was since the beginning of the history of mankind. May we expect that the modern cultural intellectual run against the peripheric walls of our old theistic notion was strong enough, this time, to escape definitely from the charm of our historic central deity? Then, after so many revolutions and increasing elliptic efforts, human nature will at last dispense with the future solstitial returning relapse to the service of its former central magnetic superior and will have the startling new honor of the instradation unto a new magnetic unit, with similar laws at a higher scale. There we would have again a strong psychological revolution round a central theistic nucleus, after a first short time of oscillating adaptation to the new measures of a regular circle, and in time, once more with oval tendencies, with intellectual digressions, solstitial points and intermediating religious geniuses. Circularism seems to return for ever again. All phenomena of the universal life are a circle also, the same efficient laws come and go again after fulfilment, and all conditions of life are incessantly repeated after a certain time and after a certain number of whole or half or quarter spheric revolutions. Life indeed always starts and never stops, going on in one line of continual eternal glorious Divinity.

The withholding attitude of the *post-equinoctial devil* turns out to be a fraus pia of the human psychological destiny. Intellectuality and peripheric humanity are not entitled to keep the yarn of their lives for themselves for ever, or to build up their own huge cultures to be their own gods, as many believe in the groping magnetic undecidedness of their *transitional affective conditions,* but their fate will have to succumb once to another magnetic theistic whirlpool mightier than the former one. The pride of independence of the psychological humanity of this period is a self-deception and a short-sightedness. The state of magnetic transition, too, is a human loss of universal view and circumference, a stagnating interspheric confusion, a necessary forwarding condition, however, for broad universal development, the consequence of immeasurable eternally repeated urges unto higher divine goals. "Scandals" must come; here we have the explanation for this truth. The devil and the spheric *anti-circular negation* turns out, as the 'worst' things change to the best, to become the solstitial point of a new enlarged magnetic instradation. He is the platform of further tremendous accumulation of new theistic expression of energy and augmented solstitial conversions of the later increasing colossal figure of Christ, may he fall back to the old historic central theism, being a new re-intensification of the existing historic religion, or be the powerful first step and racing swing to new divine standards.

Why have we no ARTISTIC STYLE to-day? Because we have lost, in our transitional period, the burning love and the enthusiastic affirmation for the perfect circular expression of the affective emotions. Style means the most perfect circular magnetism working from and to, a certain historic, local, racial and geographical conditional taste. Perfect style is always, essentially, the sure habit of performing beautiful circles inspired and suggested by the central magnetic persuasion. To-day we are groping for new circular achievements. Humanity hovers between old historic and new scientific magnetic nuclei, and performs the oscillating inaesthetic movements of undecided doubt, affective inconsequence, in trembling hesitation. But there will come a new age of perfect circular fulness and sure rounding satisfaction, of a new concentric accomplishment of our psychological action, and we shall have a future perfect contentedness in the regular stylish beauty of human self-control and modesty, within the enlarged limits of our future theistic magnetic circle. Then the day of new perfect happiness and of undisturbed esthetic fulfilment of the most balanced human taste will arise, and there will be other *golden ages and eras grasping* further divine goals and running their proud accelerated ways round stronger conceptions and ideas of the never and ever changing eternal God.

Every perfect esthetic style is founded on the love for the circle. The respect for the central, harmonious and unitarian balance of the circular revolution of our affective love round the accepted magnetic kernel of a highest attractive standard, is the first and last condition of perfect beauty, through logical order and performance, in the past and in the future. The lack of any present style has its root in the proceeding transition to the new future encirclement of higher magnetic goals, to which our intellectual quarter now is aspiring.

Our *period of transition* of enlarging affectivity has escaped from the charming fascination of the circular historic deity of former times. Our traditional predilection for the circular elegant sway has gone and is replaced by all different tastes and tendencies of less attractive persuasions of the present day. In our *modern period,* concerning art,the majority of people seem no longer thrilled by the circular perfection of the mediaeval saints; their serene, smiling satisfaction is no longer in a position to fill up our hearts to the brim. We are longing for a future and higher developed enlargement of our more radical divine conception. We are not any longer hypnotized by the sweet trances of the old art. All those hopes, which enflamed the mediaeval artists, are ripened and their fruits enjoyed. By their passionate anticipations, the old artists have even produced a stop of the wheel of the going-by times and of the psychological ages, when our happily surprised and overtaken ancestors cried aloud: "O Augenblick verweile doch! Du bist so schoen!" "Oh moment, I ask thee to stay! Thou art most beautiful." The artistic culmination of the middle ages had, therefore, produced the putrefying stagnation of luxury and angry slothfulness. We are the end of those delightfully enjoying nations and generations of the past art. We are the last disappointed heirs of those admiring periods—the hindmost tail of an old worn out culture, and we crave necessarily and irresistibly for new enlarged cultural values and expression.

Humanity hoped all of the wonderful artistic figures of the former ages with their harmonious peaceful smile and with the perfectly elaborate circles of their eye-brows calming like sweet rain-bows. Their imperturbable quietness, their serene self-sureness and balanced geometrical beauty were the promising spell of many centuries, and humanity has absorbed from them all pleasure and happiness, all sway of development they could give and urge. But now they are old and worn out. Now they are the detached expression of an old , far away culture, and we are no longer bribed by the golden splendour of their fluttering garments. Like the old oriental gods of most remote ages, they begin to be rejected by the majority of our progressive humanity which rushes to new future high goals, fond of expectation for new psychological experiences and developments, forgetting and leaving the most hopeful serenity of all artistic mediaeval achievement and of the most elaborate historic theistic skill. There will be yet a single unhappy traveller more charmed by the dreamy devotion of those old harmonious beauties. The setting sunshine falling through the stained glass windows of a dim ancient church or an old museum gilds once more the peaceful features of those masterpieces of an old past, but for the generality of mankind they are gone and faded. They are also rustling leaves of the historic autumn, at the verge of a powerful turning-point of the beginning stormy new season.

There are people, however, who indulge too long a time, owing to their hyper-conservative habits and natural disposition or exterior social compulsion, in enjoying the smoothing charm of old gone-by ages. They cannot miss the harmony of the perfect half-circle of the old ages, and they cannot escape from the hearty sincerity of the happy expressions. They abhor even the surprising and unexpected novelty of the modern forms and lines. They are disgusted by the 'mephistophelic' pondering and objecting curves of the modern mind, of the sarcastic smile of the modern thinker and the doubting and straining intellectual worker of to-day. They prefer the rounded, balanced harmony of former times.

The old artistic time was an epoch of sentimental enjoyment, the golden age of rewarding conversion from a previous time of toiling intellectual work and straining enlargement. We again live in a hopeful and honorable age of enlarging human magnetic goals, by the effort of our intellectual psychological quarter, as it was during the ancient centuries; and also we in our turn will have following ages of artistic harmonious concentration of all the results of our work, as soon as we shall have turned around the solstitial corner of a new, highest human record.

Artistic enjoyment is the consequence, the blossom and head of a previous intellectual work, the psychopupilar encirclement and the total harmonious comprehension of a whole cultural task, taking only place, if we have the sure and definite balance of a new future unitarian centralization. Art supposes the skilful practice of our spheric affective way round a central clue or theistic cultural goal ; it is least at the solstitial point and at the immaterial intellectual retirement, and most pronounced during the sentimental approach of humanity toward the equinoctial point. We may surmise, for this reason, and we do not doubt about it, that there were other big centralizing motions in the former human history, which produced great artists and geniuses, - and we are entitled to recognize in any important *political culmination* or collective human action a *Subdivision* or a part of the general historic affective centralization, which returned and returns always again.

These cultural and genial points of affective concentration are built according to the same principles of the theistic frame, only in a smaller size, and we find correspondingly here again, always around the strong genial kernel, the revolving moons of some outstanding man of solstitial dignity, reflecting the strong central light of his culminating cultural weight and glorious height. The splendid Periclean time produced Socrates, Plato, Sophocles, Phidias, Euripides. The King of the Sun, Louis XIV. who said :"L'etat c'est moi",had around his important central personality the sparkling trabants of Racine, Corneile, Moliere and Bossuet, whilst the glory of the Spanish political culmination was encompassed by the genial Cervantes, Calderon de la Barca and Velasquez, the time of the great Maria Theresa by the musical stars Mozart and Beethoven, and last not least, the enormous genial strength of the English Elizabethan time found its immortal representative reflective echo in the thundering mouth-piece of the incomparable genius Shakespeare.

All these ages had, according to the same laws of concentration and artistic reaction, their trabants like the sun has in Mars, Venus, Jupiter, our earth etc. All are splendid reflectors of the great plenty of light and glory of their centralizing historic time, and throw the received intensity of charming kindling fire, back and forward, to whole following generations of humanity. Like wheeling stars, they incessantly and ever glorify, embellish and emphasize the immortal glory of their special cultures; like crowns of indescribable beauty, they ornament the central genial head of their concentrated affective civilizations.

Christ was also a central genial personality, living under comparable conditions as those men, but the size of His measure and the measure of His size were entirely different. He surpasses all the genial nuclei and trabants of our later and former cultural, most important men by far and and has accordingly the richest sparkling circle of wheeling planets. His capital head was oiled with the sweetest perfume of reflective reverence, adorned with the most enrapturing flowers of the virginal strength of His divine idealism. His personality was, through long centuries, the most efficient psychic inspiration of whole nations and whole continents. His love gave the most thrilling intensity to the daring minds of countless heroes, poets, painters, sculptors, philosophers, politicians and thinkers. He for a long time filled all nations for far around with the inexhaustible intensive force of His genial solstitial outstanding resources of concentration.

As long as we have not reached once more the sure tranquillity of the circle, in a theistic centralization of our magnetic tendencies, no important *style* will be possible. The trembling indecision and the groping oscillation of the magnetic finger of the transitional period bereaves us of that manual security, in drawing those wonderful circular figures which are essential for all *art*.

If we remember the highly developed artistic taste, as it is in existence, for instance, in the cultural old centres of Vienna and Paris, we observe a charming traditional magnetic background of theistic civilization, which gave to these nations their reliable circular possibilities and enables them even to-day, after further psychological revolutions, to receive continual tasteful circular suggestions from their original historic theistic culture. These nations have still to-day, owing to centenarian customs and practice, the sure skill and easiness of the circular conceptions and possibilities of all their theistic experiences, and in these highly developed cultural inclinations we have to recognize the chief reason of their artistic superiority over other people. The sharper the theistic trace, the more artistic the achievement.

Every artistic masterpiece is the triumph of an emphasized genial circle, round which all other elaborate helps and refined technicalities are lavished in concentric groupings. Sexuality has the same concentric method; it has a similar disposition and intention and is, therefore, so near and productive in art.

The *solstitial period* itself is most distant from the artistic harmonious regularity of the circle. It strove at the utmost degree to go away from this regular moderate satisfaction and concentrated modesty. It is, on the contrary, the culmination of the intellectual proud peripheric digression and has, therefore, no artistic possibilities in itself. But it is the starting point of the most thrilling following art. The time of Christ did not show any important artistic masterpieces. Already before the culmination of His extreme digression, the intellectual real development of Roman, Greek and Jewish cultures had lost the harmonious circular regularity, and the first Christian centuries as well were a time of real intellectual quarrel and most serious political bloody struggles. But soon the concentric approach produced the most charming and countless flowers of Christian art, in a degree and quality such as the world never may have seen before. The circular energy around its theistic magnetic goal was restored in the approaching sentimental quarter; the running magnetic circulation had received even a mighty new urge and a stronger impulse than ever, by the genial help of the previous solstitial digression. It had the effect of a spring wound up once more and let loose after the point of the extreme solstitial tension. Therefore, the surprising artistic fertility of the following circular swing of humanity, the prodigious number of excellent masterpieces of the middle ages.

Like we have in the globes and circles of the sun, the moon, the stars, the earth and the flowers perfect artistic objects of the creative nature, so we have to find out and observe the same technical principle in all great art, the clearer the greater it is. There is always the question of the glorification of the genial symbolic circle. It seems to be the inevitably last and most accurate expression of the human genial disposition. It is the wonderful shore of the fiery lake of the divinity, which fascinates our nature, or the regular arch of the divine eye-brow, out of which God's eye speaks to our heart, or the thrilling rain-bow extended and thrown over and round the full concentrated riches of the most divine and serene consolations of humanity, - an artistic colorful ribbon around a rich nosegay of fragrant divine flowers. Only within the persuading spell of the CIRCULAR RING the majesty of the divine grace descends from heaven to earth. The circular organization of our genial compromising nature has in this concentrating sign its *divine parole and its secret spell*. This is the rain-bow of the Covenant, which produces always again the most harmonious divine smile, as soon as we use it. We have here the full confirmation of our psychopupilar mechanism.

The intellectual time of transition and the intellectual quarter of the psychological sun-year hate the circle. They have the tendency to stretch the circular curves and inclinations of the psychic spheric way, and to throw the track of our active progression outside of the charm of the theistic concentration into the extrasolar universe. Therefore, we have the utmost *artistic sterility in the ages of the intellectual scientific work, of the logically progressive investigations and of the independent material and idealistic liberalism.*

On the other hand, the retrospective traditional *Conservativism* is given much more formalistic security and facility. It has its old examples and historic suggestions. It has inherited, at least, the stereotypical circular formula of construction, if it was unable to escape from the justified objection of sterility, of imitation and eternal disgusting repetition. There are at least elements of divine beauty and imperishable greatness, which always again fascinate the human heart used and hardened as it may be by the former traditional artistic uniformity.

In the degree as a religious or any psychological organism clings to the old theistic notion, it is fond of the circle, and on the other hand, it feels a horror and aversion against strong enlarging intellectual longing and need of extrasolar development. So we see always again, if we look through our civilized world, that the retrospective sentimental old church, unproductive and uninventive as present art may be, continues to build in more or less artistic taste, imitating the most refined circular variations of the old art. It has kept a certain stock of the old magnetic attractability toward its glorious old theistic conceptions, and if there is no thoroughness of creative truth and deep invention, it still has the utmost facility of historic and traditional suggestions. Si non e vero, e ben' trovato. In spite of the worn out sterility of the formalistic motives, these copied monuments of art, even to-day, exercise often an uplifting influence on our sentiments and carry us back, for hours, to the genial charm of old past ages. The old Christian church looks back intensely to former historic traditional theistic times; it clings to the early intellectual formula,which seems, in the light of modern views, to have shrunk to a glorified mummification, a refined fancy of the past and an artistic, but sterilized achievement.

The modern time, on the contrary, looks ahead. Its vision is directed toward the following times of future psychological developments of humanity. It, therefore, is aware of the dangerous charm of the circular inclination toward old theistic magnetic centres. It is not willing any more to succumb to the artistic inducements of worn out conceptions which would fascinate it again and enslave it once more under the power of scientifically overthrown old former principles. It, therefore, is careful, not to accept the sweet modulations of the circular line. It rather prefers the hesitating broken and softly curved artistic development of the pondering logical conception. Thus we see, if we wander for instance through the English empire, in all churches built under modern intellectualized ecclesiastical influences, always soft and reserved allusions to the elements of the venerable old Gothic style,always slightly pronounced and subjected to the reasonable purpose of practical utility.

The new intellectualized church in connection with science seem, therefore, to be the leading part of our psychological period. It has the strong will to enlarge the circumference of our theistic spheric sun-year. It has the digressing energy of scientific researches which it respects and according to which it will establish its future life-circles. Protestantism is born under the tremendous necessity of the trembling magnetic finger looking for new human developments. It has left the absolute inclination to submit to the magnetic encirclement of former human theistic scopes and is, in the scientific signature of the modern time, the guiding representative of a new humanity, which searches new extrasolar clues of the divinity. The modern church renounces the golden charm of the medieval saints; it is not thrilled any more by the sweet smile and the shining beauty of the old Christian art. It has found out and experienced that the old divine pleasure became luxuriance, sterilization of the mind and affective hindrance. It was disappointed by the old glory in the sense of the former church , from which humanity hoped all one day. It is sophisticated in the fulfilment of the glorious promises of early theistic conceptions. The success given by them has lost its influence on it. The enjoyment of fulfilment does not satisfy any longer, and has created the craving desire for new enlarged possibilities of digressing work and intellectual distensions of our theistic circular more remote periphery.

Any artistic strong development pre-supposes a strong central genius who begets the other smaller ones, who serves as a central emphasis and point of support for the human sentiments and artistic curves, to whom all affective forces of his age have a concentric tendency and from whom they receive the laws of gradual progression toward his punctual central light-field. The punctual genial contraction of all our affective life-force is the essential method of all human affectivity. We cannot dispense with, in spite of its insufficient basis and limiting character. All strong human efforts fall back again and again, like the rolling stone of *Sysiphus,* to the magnetic encirclement of important genial goals.

The times of *psychological transition* become, however, so short-sighted - a natural necessity of self-protection - that they wish to perpetuate their extraordinary state of interpolated function. They lose even the possibility to understand the linguistic terminology and artistic formalistic language of other magneto-centric ages, and, of course and fatally they love their stylistic distraction, their peripheric materialistic affective fixation and their unbalanced eccentric misunderstandings and mutual contradictions.

All vital stations of development find their good friends in history , since indeed every state and any condition and point of view has its advantages and disadvantages. The magnetic theistic centre has its faithful adherents and so has the intellectual state of transition and the intellectual quarter. But also, last not least, the solstitial genial point has its fervent claims and desires not to be dethroned.

The solstitial mediator keeps firmly the keys of the Kingdom of Heaven. According to his psychomechanic task he has the power to bind and resolve and is, therefore, not willing to give up easily his important duty and the *bridge-toll,* from which his whole royal court has its income. It is chiefly this surrounding party of the high-minded and high-browed solstitial genius, which has its material peripheric interests in the eternal existence of this affective historic transfer between humanity and the central god. It is this developed royal court, which searches to check the vital radical necessity of universal progress of our social psychological life. There will be as little possibility of eternifying a historic solstitial hero as a historic conception of a cultural god.

We are much too much inclined to stick to old material and intellectual formulae, and we understandably have not the power to separate easily from old approved of, methods which turned out to be very useful and helpful. We expect always further services from institutions which have helped us in the past, and we forget that we, in this manner, establish an idolatric apotheosis of intellectual formulae or conceptions of material and individual validity. But all this leads inevitably to the most radical affective psychological troubles of human social development. It is not the necessity of the genial organization, not the solstitial genius and least God, who are in danger to be lost or who could perish, according to our necessary human disposition. It is rather only the transitional historic fixation, the human amalgamation and allegiance with past times, and the inferior degree of development of the idea of God and His human solstitial intermediator, who must change. We always must have new genial heroes and intermediators, new centro-theistic crystallizations and new administering societies. All will be more developed in our later historic progress, more perfect, stronger and more idealistic.

The future idealistic hero will turn our solstitial transfer to the *right* instead of the *lefthand side,* if he is able to avoid the old danger of the historic theistic relapse. He initiates the new instradation to the extrasolar development of the idea of God, an essentially higher degree of the former magnetic affective centralization. But he may accordingly have a new categoric history, a new foundation and another historic administering organization. Will the technical laws of the natural performances remain the same? These switching processes and these digressions and aversions of the historic development of the theistic idea will be again the victim of some new magnetic overwhelming kernel which will bring about a new circling dance of all created things and of all inferior magnetic standards, around it, in order that we shall have the same *extrasolar solar system, but more* powerful in deepening performance, like a drill entering with a second effort into a board of wood, or like an Artesian fountain which throws out its water powerfully as soon as the pipe has pierced the covering geological layers. There is the question of the same genial psychomechanic methods searching God, the religious genius and the historic spiritual organization, which all three are important and main points of the personal and collective human psychology. They all three will preserve their domineering roles. We shall have always churches in every old and new smallest village, as already the ancient writer said. But the theistic fountain must come out once more from a deeper well in order to throw out more and better water of eternal life. A new and stronger deepening effort must be made always again in later history, and for this reason new, fresh, young enthusiastic and idealistic ecclesiastic workers are necessary in the vineyard.

All our boisterous claims and all our transitional struggles in order to go away from the old traditional god discharge themselves, after all, into a new stronger affective embracement of a new magnetic genial kernel. All extrasolar *"anti-theistic"* development will at last be only a more serious *approfondation* of the Artesian drill of the genial notion of God. Anti-theistic historic movements mean merely a dissatisfaction with the former successes of religion and have the significance and the effect of a repeated serious effort of an arm lifted up to strike the more thoroughly the real resistance against truly deep terminal theology.

So we see that the evolutionary 'devil' will be victorious in our life, that he is right, in a sense, to resist the past historic centralization, if he is convinced to bring about a better and more efficient development. We today surely move to a new extrasolar goal. We already begin to sail within the affirmative atmosphere of a new solar magnetic unit of the universe. What was not assimilable to the old magnetic system and was decried and despised as *crime* and devil, will soon bee clarified or submit to the magnetic charm of a new theistic genial concentric movement, and the world soon will have the similar, but more powerful and more beautiful features of the old circular art, balance and brilliance.

The communications of the former times, between the theistic centre and human personality, have changed to-day. Whilst in former Christian times the *yarn of affective life-force* incessantly was running from the human to the divine side , and whereas at that time, with the help of the intermediating partial religious genius, the continually unrolling ball of real humanity became always smaller, that of the central historic deity was increasingly bigger like a mighty coil. The yarn of the interspheric affective communications runs, instead, incessantly from the historic god to the peripheric work, to the detailed intellectuality of the present time. The polypoid peripheric fixations of our multiple real performances turn the central god, in time, to the periphery. The central yarn ball of the historic accumulations of divine forces will be always more unrolled, owing to the glomerulous rooting of the real ramifications of our age; the peripheric world has become a mighty monster with innumerable hands and arms and feet, groping and grasping new future extrasolar possibilities, fixing itself greedily with all these instruments to the reality, and pulling incessantly the affective yarn of the human fate and taste toward the peripheric direction. Thus we shall have at last a poor and lean historic notion of god, but instead a rich and multiplied coil of the objectivity, intellectual and material accumulation. The religious genius with his central predilection checked this movement as long as he could, pulling in the other direction. But at last he was at a loss to retain the incessant and increasing human desire for peripheric material expansion. We must be careful not to tear the yarn of our fate. There could be, in addition, another extrasolar, magnetic theistic *anger,* already watching the opportunity and availing itself of the rich magnetic rich accumulation of our intellectual vital coil, for his purposes. Another jealous theistic whirlpool unawares could tear our intellectually enriched material ball from us, and our longing toiling work would be in vain. What consolation would it mean for the greedy categoric egotism of the materialistic world, to know that it has to give up its riches to the advantage and service of the right instead of the left? Then the materialism would think that the devil was expelled with Belzebub. The bereft and dishonored historic god would have succeeded in his revenge, in giving a Belzebub to his devil, surrendering him to more energetic, tighter and more attractive magnetic slavery than before.

The most threatening evil in the psychological world is our *slothful egoism,* which induces us to exclude our individual share of the universal magnetic affectivity from the general intercourse. It is not enough, if, like nails attracted by a magnetic pole, we direct our real detailed exterior life into a parallel and concentric order of artistic astheticism unto high ideal tasks. It is, furthermore, not enough for the universal progress, which inevitably has to be served, if we have some general affirmation unto the majestic unfoldmnt of the psychological universe. We even are expected to help with enthusiasm, to send our sentiments to its new development like fiery arrows, not to bury in a hidden corner the talents, the fortune, the individual life-force, in a narrow, dim and sulky, exclusive egotistic recess, not to be greedy to augment and enlarge the yarn ball of our individual importance, but to be aware always that we as individuals may have only some short transitional existence, that we are pilgrims quickly crossing the stage of life and that there is no use for any eternification of our exclusive individual significance.

We have to expect the same thing from the psychological collectiveness of nations, languages, styles and kingdoms. All fade away like grass mown in the morning and burnt in the evening, in the furnace of the idealistic volatilization and historic reformation. As we saw already, even solstitial leaders, even genial historic bodies and even the historically bound notions of God are at a perfect loss to escape from the fate of their intellectual individual destruction and change. The most important genius, the most glorious religious community, the most thrilling leader who won the hearts of all and was the unique darling of all centuries and generations of a thousand years, the most ingenious, philosophically and artistically most elaborated conception and idea of the historic god, all will go away in the furnace of the universal progressive history. Nobody is entitled to repose on old laurels, to be permanently checked by the conviction to have done something important in the past. The jealous fate will come and stir and prick his *slothfulness* with the *angry* fork of the peripheric devil in order to liquidate his individual egotistic yarn ball and to guide his life-force to further more important and more general universal affective performances. What at one time was a sublime genius or a splendid, most necessary and useful spiritual organization, will be, later on, subjected to the advancing, biological laws of fashion and transition.

"Even the strongest rocks may totter", after all, and the absolutism of the historic psychological progress never will allow that there will be one fixed point in the development of the universe. All is one increasing evolution; all is going on enlarging, gaining and augmenting incessantly.It would be an astounding presumption to keep God back within the philosophical or dogmatic cage of one historic organization, or exempt Him the most powerful and most jealous, alone from further universal spiritual organizations. If we retain the development of the notion of the historic god, we do the same thing as if we would expect that some very rich man gives all he has to his inferiors and does not claim any interest for himself, wearing continuously the same old suit. We have quite different experiences, in our life, with the character of the rich. Just these people are, as a rule, more egotistic. This was exactly the spring of their accumulating energy. God also changes sometimes His worn out, intellectual-historic coat, which once was so beautiful in its rich medieaval golden creases, but now is frayed and shredded. He wishes the interest of serious scientific theistic researches. It would be most suitable for the leading interspheric role of human nature, if we would aspire to better and deeper knowledge of God than we had in the past. Whilst we extend our sciences into all directions, must we be held back from the most burning, most interesting and most essential questions of our life, because the dogmatic organization of a strong and petrified society has ventured to claim the monopoly of divine and theistic teaching? Can drinking water be more general than love of, and interest in, studies concerning the extreme roots and goals of our life? Are we not allowed and even under duty, everybody by himself, to *think of the deepest problems* of humanity, and to do everything in our personal power to resolve the difficulties and elucidate the dark points in the psychological kernel of our theistic conceptions ?

A transfer of the theoretical sincere research for truth, to the ground of *political quarrelling*, personal defamation and persecution and economical boycot, is it not a sad proof for our insufficient human development in every sense? It means always that the party using forceful, 'unlogical' *violence,* is not in a position to liquidate the difficulties in the same proposed theoretical and scientific way, and is not willing to rise to the more promising and humane methods. It must be the expression of an inferiority complex of the individual mind, if it is freely chosen. The sad circumstance in the use and choice of the brutal solution lies in the lack of cultural refinement and of mental sensitiveness of the violent and, after all, also of the ill-treated person. And yet, is not the principle of mobilizing all obtainable force and all total energy against a convincedly harmful adversary, in perfect congruity with the universal necessity of the psychological progression? In some stage these evolutionary struggles have to start. But how on earth can a normal individual with a circumspect mind and sincere observation arrive to the state, when he furiously rushes to kill his brother? Must we not be keen enough, however, of any essential conviction and task, to give them not only the consent and the personal sentimental affirmation, but to send after them also the sharp spears of our personal conclusiveness, in sacrificing life, body, social honor, material happiness and everything else?

It was reserved to the refining influence of the suffering passive religious genius to have established the conviction and the taste rather to suffer than to harm the next. The idea of the divine dignity of human nature and individual has received, in our age, such an increased height of personal inviolability that the cultured religious person often rather prefers to be hurt and excluded from human society, in his spiritual taste and conviction than to play his role with violence and unscrupolous opposition. Is not there often a lack of thorough possibility of decidedness, idealistic pampering and a sentimental misconception of real duties, a disproportioned, passive tender resistance against real, active offending aggression, offering little chances of practical success? *Hamlet* was a classical instance of this type. But it is the opinion and wish of our society, - and was so perhaps always - that humanity should after all be educated to liquidate their theistic and political disagreements in an objective, impersonal scientific justice, and ought to have a sincere desire to submit amicably to the will of the *majority,* as we have it in the republican commonwealths. But these conceptions are, in spite of their desirability, built on the principles of lazy affective conservativism, and they are opposed to the progressive, always dividing and struggling movement of the universal development. Are we condemned to always repeated fighting and war?

Of what a tremendous influence is the principle of ANGRY SLOTHFULNESS in the whole universe ! It is the source of all woe,but, perhaps also the strongest instigation to all progress. It appears in the smallest omission (sin) of our daily necessities of life, in our convinced indignant incongruity with our surroundings and circumstances, in the struggling progress of our working development and soaring enthusiasm, but even in the social anger of *war,* which follows the lazy historic omission of the gradual necessity of progressive intellectual adaptation of humanity. If our small personal omissions are the sins of our lazy conservative lack of initiative and necessity of affective affirmative harmony with our fate, with the same reason, we must call antiquated social, affective, mediating solstitial institutions, the slothful omissions of late history. They also cause the lacking, progressive promotion of our society unto the necessary enlargement of theistic-historic notions. They hold back, owing to their posseession of the key, our affective terminal success, and they also cause, accordingly, the consequence of any hyper-conservative slothfulness, the anger of exploding social wars and revolutions.

Progress must be. The comfort of retrospective happy quietness is not our share. The smallest daily affair and the greatest social duty for interspheric magnetism, need in the same manner, always new energetic urges of angry urges, if we are lazy in accomodating ourselves to the enlarging intellectual exactions of progressed future times and ages. The anger of social wars and revolutions means the biological vital answer of the universal life-force, coming out in the case of emergency, if we have fixed our social affective gift within the sinful egotistical stop of exclusively retrospective historic tradition and national or philosophical petrified reservedness. Our clinging to the traditional intellectual development is, in the sense of our interspheric progressive continual necessity, a sinful omission. Even the historic conceptions of God, our overwhelming solstitial geniuses and their following organizations are transitional values which have done good and best services at their due time, but which are also, after all, rustling leaves of the autumn, swept away by the strong initiative of new future affective universal progress. Clinging too much to old intellectual-ecclesiastic formulae has the value of embracing an old wonderful cage, from which the mighty divine *eagle* escaped long ago, through the tremendous distances of the blue universal sky. We have the duty to run after him once more and not to rest until we have caught him again, within the charming cage of better and larger human intellectual formulae and ideas. This hunting play through the universe will never stop. We never shall have the opportunity to indulge a long time in the enjoyment of the divine eagle, within the prison of our symbolic, dogmatic or intellectual notions, golden, elaborate and well logically rivetted as they may be. The eagle will escape again, and we incessantly have to follow after him. Or he will grow old in the domesticated human conceptions. He might become lame, weak and even die, whilst it is the young *eaglet*, which escaped earlier in his first days of a fledgling, which we have to follow because of the divine increase of his strength and his sublime, terminal affective attractability. Then it will be the moment, when people raise their voices: "The old divine king is dead !"And immediately afterwards they exclaim:"Live the new king ! Our mourning and moaning about the good old king has to be buried in our silent hearts. .We quickly are prepared for new great joy, being anxious to serve the new promoted successor and bearer of the sparkling universal affective crown and the possessor of the terminal divine throne.

Thus, reviewing our total results from the meditations on the universal human psychological development, we may admit that we even here have the same *waving progression* or the same *molecular vibration* of energy, as we have it in all our creative life, in our animal body, in colors, light, sound, electricity and everywhere. Even in the *theological development* of the world we have a continuous alternation of affective concentration and intellectual dilution, of augmenting molecular energy or *assimilation* and of diminishing and dissolving force or *dissimilation*. We observe their an uninterrupted sequence of high theistic idealistic waves and deep materialistic or "antitheistic" intervals. We surely have the repetition of the quickest movements of warbling electric progression even here : the tremendous refined rapidity in the progression of the specific waves is even here renewed, on a greatest scale. We see everywhere nothing but the endless eternal application and practice of the same most simple and universal *natural scientific principles of waving molecular and compensating energy*. They begin their action within the stone, the air and the plant and bear even on the historic and human perceptibility of the highest Deity. How great must then the importance and validity of the most simple physical natural laws be, if they have their application even for our human progress in becoming acquainted with, grasping and losing the eternal God. *This couple of most modest principles of always waving fluctuations of the universe and of mutual exclusion of two different degrees of concentration at the same time and place* never have been discovered and never forgotten. The most primitive experience of the child breathes within the incessant action of these laws. Greatest and most universal things are so natural that they never need to be found by science, or risk to be lost by carelessness. They are so automatical and sure in their action that they work every moment without being mentioned. They are so near our natural disposition that we look over them.

In connection with the theistic development, however, the concentrating and increasing formation of one new towering divine wave seems to our individual shortsightedness the large work of an immeasurable time, but it is, nevertheless, only the descending half of a culminating theistic wave, which will have its splendid summit, its descending second half and its gaping interval, from the following and all future waves, covering the sea of all universal affective possibilities of development, with their eternal divine procession. All indeed is evolutionary development, in so far as it goes and comes again, diminishes and augments and never loses the vital principle of waving action, be it the progressing or diminishing process. For this moment it is quite essential, though we of course hope and are inclined to admit even a qualitative universal achievement in everything, that we note the extraordinary stability and universality of the waving magnetic vibration of all vital molecular energy from the earth up to the greatest univerasl living things. Always we observe a central most important kernel which represents the ideal concentration of most magnetic accumulation, always an augmentation and ascension until the clearest and most pronounced punctual magnetic determination, but also afterwards inevitably a dissolution of this concentric organization of forces, a decay of this molecular-affective hierarchic unit and a transition of the old power of energy and culminating segregation, into the following molecular scattering display, which, in the same manner, is gathered again in one magntic central force ,in repeated towering punctual localization, and so forth ...

How great and victoriuos the energetic head of the theistic idea arises, we all know well, and how obstinate and thorough the struggle of extreme peripheric intellectual powers, against the centro-magnetic avidity, runs through all human history, who would not have observed it ? The summons and the admonitions to be faithful to the theistic central ideas, and the warnings and condemnations against every peripheric digression are innumerable in the prayers and thoughtful suggestions of the administering churches of all religious systems. The hatred, the scorn, the open and secret persecutions of the magneto-centric,theistic,realized idealism fill up the history of the centuries. Both parts do everything to discredit each other. There is the question of the most powerful, serious, necessary and burning question of the psychological humanity. The ecclesi astic, sticky clinging to the precious, elaborate theistic idea is as well understandable as the progressive necessity of the universal psychology is inevitable. What a tremendous power of crushing wars, of hideous slanders, of 'scientific' shuffling, of misinterpretations, of personal boycot and of social contempt, meet each other from both sides the theistic and the 'anti-theistic'. Both are enthusiastic of the interspheric necessity of their missions. Both are the light-bearers of the most elevated human functions, but they put their stress on different points. Whilst the theistic slothful Psychopupillarism has forever the will to stay within the balanced elaborated organization of its illustrious history, the angry progressive 'antitheistic' intention has the tendency to leave the historic psychological theistic concentration and to scatter the carefully accumulated and organized energy into the new intellectual discoveries of a future extrasolar world.

The central solar Conservatism puts all stress on maintaining the strong historic organization, the progressive *Liberalism,* on the contrary, has the most fervent longing to lead the historic, magnetic centralization into other outside universal channels, far from the last concentrative accumulation and localization. It has the will to create new possibilities and new intellectual historic expressions of magnetic theistic centralizations. But for this purpose, it claims and must claim all obtainable amount of the human psychological energy. Thus we recognize that both parties are concerned with the same magntic power, and their embittered struggle for its possession is a vital self-defence in a case of emergency, both parts being in the necessary position to be biologically concerned with the same amount of the individual life-force. This is the reason for wars, slanders, scorn, misinterpretations, cutting mutual declining. Both parties have their essential right and duty of historic existence and both are fulfilling inevitable tasks of highest human and interspheric missions. Thus the continuous struggle between both is a question of intellectual interspheric lack of self-control and lack of surety, of ignorance of the progressive rhythm of past harmonious developments, one side putting all stress on a most prolonged affective stay in a definite historic theistic solar centre, and the other side super-estimating the necessity of intellectual extrasolar progression.

Thus once more *our human insufficiency,* in appreciating the magnetic necessities of the universe, turns out to be the reason of our theistic quarrels. There is not the question, how much historic religion is entrenched and protected behind the walls of political institutions, against the intruding assailment of progressive intellectual urges; there is not the question, how much the material and scientific life have developed their detailed riches and world-wide importance; there is rather the question to find out, what are the interspheric necessities of affective progression at a given time. It is the oscillating inexperience of our theistic psychology, which is the reason of quarrels, wars and social disturbances, of lack of harmonious rhythm in proceeding from one molecular, historic, theistic magnetic concentration to a following one.

It could be so easy to make further steps into future theistic developments. Quarrels, social persecutions and human hatred could be so easily avoided, up to a high degree, if we had the courage and the knowledge to part, at the right time, from exaggerated slothfulness and Conservativism into new magnetic goals, and if we, on the other side, could be decided not to do more digressive extrasolar steps than it would be useful for the present humanity. For in spite of the praiseworthy tendencies for the liberal future development, we all have learnt in the common affective part of our historic experience not to love hatred, slander and aversion for themselves, - the pure intention of the noble-spirited decline them in any case - but only as a case of emergency for higher purposes and with the terminal meaning of general social augmentation of happiness and deeper mutual love of the totality. Sanctification of the means for a desirable goal is the most common thing everywhere in the world.

We carefully must be aware, how easily every firm, to which we have sworn, becomes again a source of sterilization and affective stagnation, and there is no possibility to escape from this error, if we have not *the strong will to do both concentrating and digressing work most readily*. Digression means destruction of an antiquated system with the idealistic background of building up new better extrasolar affective constructions, and it is this latter purpose, which gives dignity and eternal value to all digressing Liberalism of the periods of transition.

Is not too strong development of the *liberal system* as bad as that of the draggy and antiquated Conservativism ? Both are only travellers on earth, as well as the individuals, and they have to work or to be silent and passive, most adaptingly according to the wish of the momentaneous psychological necessity of human society. A claim of one religious or political or psychological system to be an universal panacea is a misunderstanding and dangerous one-sidedness, which creates instantly, or derives from the material background of egotism, personal utilitaristic interest, and is, therefore, more damaging than useful for the total society. We easily come in this way to the point, as we often have the opportunity to observe it in the religious and political life, that the historic denominations and parties have no exact real meaning at all, Liberalism and Freedom of thought being possibly, in reality, the most narrow organization of real utility and of abusing out-of-date sport, under an oppositional title of progress, as it happens, that Conservativism, in its most decried historic dress of theoretic, antiquated narrowness, is so broad-minded, and accustomed to such a general outlook over all real and idealistic developing necessities that in reality the social roles of the parties are exactly exchanged from what we would expect from them. So much so that the names of political and religious parties and denominations very often are quite misleading, boasting lies or denouncing self-degradations. So much is historic development apt to change and shift originally right distinctions; just the continually educating resistances, experiences and the increasing carefulness about weak points are in a position to reverse the original tendencies and dispositions of a system which, however, one day will change its chief purposes and even the name, when the historic attachment and the exterior compulsion of circumstances will have disappeared. The broadest party is the most kind and charitable. Love means secret approval and understanding of universal harmony in all and everywhere.

It would be such a quiet, harmonious, universal development, if we were not checked by the night of our *Ignorance*. It is the reason, why we are groping and tasting uninterruptedly toward all directions, why we make our sinful omissions when we should advance energetically, and why we start and depart in enthusiastic anger, when and where best we should stop for a long time. There must be always, first, a certain accumulation of experience which means a stop and which gives us the necessary light of knowledge to proceed in a courageous run to future hopes and expectations, - which partially and possibly means disappointment and perhaps an useless and unjust offence of existing preferabilities, in order that there is always an opposite danger of doing too much or too little, in concentration or digression. All this is a sure consequence of our ignorance which is undecided and hesitating in a conservative slothfulness, on one side, or rushing and ruthless in a hyper-liberal excitement, on the other hand. Our invincible human ignorance is the tremulous oscillating magnetic finger, whose groping indecidedness points to a doubtful future, not only in our unhappy private affairs, in our business life, in marriage, politics and science, but even, and much more, up to the highest questions of intersolar, theistic attitude. It is sure that the historic fixation of highest theistic magnetic goals imparts an outstanding sureness of achievement to all our inferior affairs of life : this is the reason of the successfulness and attaching superiority of a definite and and clear theistic system. But we ought not to wait, with the revision of our highest goals, until the practice of our social life has overthrown for a long time these last idealistic institutions, which really and indeed have the task to lead, not to check our intellectual development and our daily customs. Even the highest and last idealistic institutions of humanity are a continually flowing river which must be allowed to go its further way, and is the more dangerous to be checked, when the more important, superior standards of our social psychology are obstructed, whilst the daily practical conceptions of life have overtaken them.

The intellectual *scientific disposition of our age,* therefore, is right. *Here lies the root of the possibility to avoid serious future social affective stagnations.* If we extend our sciences to all realms of human relations of the inferior and even most elevated description, then we may avoid the angry slothfulness; then we shall approach the state, where a careful balance between the necessity of retaining and preserving Conservativism and progressive furthering Liberalism of our human behaviour will be figured out and introduced in practice. But never we shall reach the entire balance of knowledge and necessity. Humanity will always have again the necessity of changing all their institutions. Fate will always impose on us unforeseen experiences, and thus we never shall escape from the necessity of discussions, quarrels and wars. Always there will be hyper-conservative, affectively lazy people, and always hyper-liberal intellectually and affectively digressing reformers, even such who like quarrel and digressions for themselves and, for whom it will be always a cruel and interesting pleasure and a sport to do harm and to hurt their fellow-men. But the continual scientific peripheric outlook of the experimental researches diminishes the angry possibilities. It valuates the necessities of our future magnetic oscillations in advance, and prevents, therefore, threatening explosive, affective catastrophes, up to a certain limit.

The psychological nature likes our quivering, affective oscillations. Easily we are swung into future developments with the help of the revolutionary anger and the fervent war. But our time and our age have been chosen to have discovered the necessity of continual exploring and experimental work and of minute peripheric investigation in order to find out better, what afterwards, again and again, will be necessary to be done next, without the most serious expenditures of the overthrowing revolutionary destructions and the radical loss of the precious acquisitions of former ages. It is only in the clear-looking and minutely distinguishing scientific way , when both opposite possibilities are given a chance to defend their different standpoints and to discover early enough progressive necessities as well as to keep back, in an always distinct way, the precious and persistent values of the discarded past. Science is able to convey at the same time a sharply distinctive eye for different values. It saves time and life-force in order to master life and fate instead of being surprised and bluffed by them.

Du musst kaempfen, du musst wagen,
Denn die Goetter leih'n kein Pfand.
Nur ein Wunder kann dich tragen
In das schoene Wunderland.

Schiller

FOURTH BOOK

WE admitted the very difficult task of the *divine engineer or architect,* in building up the religious edifice. On one hand, we recognized the enormous extension and the endless row of universal affective standards, and were at a perfect loss, on the other hand, as to compare the efficiency of the human real achievement with the theoretical and idealistic dispositions and desires. So the divine architect, if he will cover the idealistic avidities in human nature, likely and necessarily overlooks the detailed reality, loses the principles of this solid earth, of the categories of space, time and causality, and incurs thus the danger of ridicule and mockery, - or if he, on the other hand, strives to put a perfect congruency between the real-material exactions of our intellectual nature , then he risks the loss of affective views and connections, the idealistic uplifting energy and remains in realistic and materialistic shortsightedness.

In order to avoid these two extremes, the religious construction strives to remain, in fulfilling its task, about in the middle part of the universal affective finger-board, introduces and combines many real elements, but uses preferably idealistic connections. Thus it becomes possible to have an existing human function of religious activity working on both sides the idealistic and realistic. But there must be still, accordingly, a *great difficulty,* because the exactions exceed likely human possibilities. Ideal-real functions can only be performed, if our nature is put into the comprising and compromising attitude between both. But still, always and in every case there will be *extreme danger* that our vital individuality and life--force either cling too much to reality and then lose the necessary uplifting energy and idealistic trend because of being fixed too much to the peripheric, detailed, intellectual objectivity, or, in the other case, the idealistic sway and the divine imaginative avidity tear our peripheric real connections and consistency: we lose our real and intellectual fixations and drive, without any categoric or intellectual checking control toward the highest, divine goals. Our small intermediary compromising life-force is *easily attracted toward one of the two opposite affective sides, idealistic or realistic,* and is prone, once having chosen one direction, to maintain it and to give to it even all psychic capacity, - which is so easily understandable in connection with all magnetic tendencies of accumulation, - instead of dividing it in a compromising justice on both realistic and idealistic orders.

The vital one-sidedness is a terrible danger of our religious education and has its chief reason in the extraordinary disproportion between the affective small ranges of our life-force and the enormous extension and energy of the universal possibilities and our corresponding aspirations. The religious question is, therefore,*above all, a dynamic problem*. How are we able to find out a relatiely sure and quiet intermediary position of the small polished ball of our natural, affective realization and gift, since it has the strong tendency to run, at the least difference of magnetic attraction, rapidly along the charming creative channel of the dispositive universal fingerboard? How can this frightening danger of easy and exaggerating one-sidedness be avoided? How can a reasonable, middle security of the real-idealistic life be obtained? How are we able to escape from the continual, strong, hurting and lavishing excursions of the oscillating finger of our compromising magnetic fate? How can we approach the highest, eternal, sentimental goals without losing the ground of reality under our feet, without being turned away from any peripheric fixation and relation? And how can we remain intellectually, really and even materially closely interested people without losing the affective depth of idealistic views and the large outlook to most distant and general , social and universal goals? This is the question which puts itself to the serious constructor of every religious system. He is under necessity to find a ballast against exaggerated, idealistic energy, furthermore a delightful explosion against the slothfulness of real application, a strong help of sufficient, peripheric fixation of our life-force, which so easily tears, in its turn, the fine objective ramifications fixed on the intellectual, detailed reality, and loses so the radical idealistic communication. The divine, psychological architct is further in a position to reflect, how he can not only guarantee the lasting connection of our psychological force with the most remote idealistic and realistic extremes, but how to avoid any dangerous proceeding rapidity into both the idealistic and realistic directions, how to have *always ready a checking help against hurtful acceleration* as well as an *instigating force in case of affective stagnation,* and how he will supply all these means, in emergencies, in appropriate and useful dosage.

The genial religious founder uses a large number of means in order to exercise these *psychodynamic influences,* but there is in fact not only the question to *interpolate the quickening or bridling,*

*dynamic means of psychological treatment and development, but the
refined, adapted, special use of these means, in every case, is, of
course, no less important.* There is no use to shoot against flies with
cannons and as little to shoot against tigers and lions with a small
shot. But all these things are liable to happen in the religious, psychological life, unless we emphasize the most pronounced carefulness
in using the intercalation of the presented psychodynamic helps.

Let us consider, first, the different religious helps toward regulating the concentrating, uplifting direction or the realistic retardan-
tion of our affective energy. In these principally opposite magnetic
tendencies, we put as the prototypes and chief representatives
of their character the *Miracle* in one, and the *Cross* in the other direction. Each of them has the contrary psychodynamic intention, the
Miracle pulling up to terminal idealism and the Cross fastening our
life-force at the peripheric, intellectual reality.

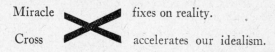

Miracle   fixes on reality.

Cross   accelerates our idealism.

These two groups have the significance of two opposite antidotes
within the psychological establishment of a religious doctrine. They
both may be used freely, according to the excess of concentrating
affective or peripheric, realistic, intellectual necessity of the moment.
The psychodynamic group of the Miracle has the task of concentrating and lifting the lazy realistic part of the peripheric humanity up
to the distant idealistic goals in order to impart the necessary affective jerks unto these last goals, and the Cross, on the contrary,
to recall the idealistic, individual insufficiency of self-control to the
intellectual earth and to fasten it on the real, detailed life. But
these two groups of accelerating and retaining, affective progressions
are not only in a general and comparative way the rythmic and
dynamic regulators of the psychological life, but it seems easy to
point out, in an exact manner, how they can and have to perform
their special, oppositely directed functions.

Within the same psychological group as the miracle we comprise
the notions of *Symbolism, Mysticism and Prayer,* whilst we, on the
contrary side, add to the symbolic idea of the cross, the notions of
Passion and Pain. All these notions are indicated and developed already in the scriptures, but they accept the two most important and
precious additions later on, in adopting the rather more concentrating *Art* in the early middle ages and the nobility of the straining

Work in the modern time. The incorporation of these last two terms and human, real-idealistic, best values, which saved and elevated the meaning of antiquated and occasionally dangerous principles and notions of the former times, brought a new, excellent, vital possibility into the more primitive theoretic formulas of the original psychological conceptions, and it is chiefly owing to the addition of these two psychological pillars of the later history, that our religious genial organization has, still to-day, an outstanding, practical role in human society, pushing it energetically to highest, most distant, idealistic values, by the help of its artistically refined resourcefulness, and having a surprising strong hold on reality, by the knighting of real work and painful sacrifice.

The logical foundation of the enterprise of symbolism, mysticism and miraculism is the intention of economizing the individual, psychic force. The circumference of the intellectual light-field is, in these cases, intentionally made more narrow in order to save compensatorily the affective energy. At length and again and again, we spoke about this essential phenomenon of idealistic development.

The ideas of mysticism, symbolism and miraculism are to be found in an outspoken manner in any historic religion, and it is the large and liberal use of the mystic and symbolic principles, which lifted the holy scriptures to their extraordinary, divine credit and gave to them the splendour of supra-categoric, eternal importance.

Already the creation and the use of a *more imaginative language* is the first step to this goal. The skilful escape from the exact, daily reality, in describing the life of the divine hero, is another step which is, in a hidden way and skilful manner, emphasized by the fact that there are always hazy views to intellectual, peripheric backgrounds, localized scenic fixations of the psychic events, historic and cultural details, but of such insignificant an amount, that they just serve as a small, most simple and narrow door of real symbolism into the realm of the richest sentimental effusion. The psychic force is not at all retained or used up in the contemplation of the intellectual detailed surroundings, but it is instantly compressed within the concentrative narrow notions of mystic symbols, and in this manner thrown in the first run to the uplifting level of ultimate, sentimental concentration. Symbolism and mysticism are cunningly invented, psychological rings or circles imprisoning the affective soul and and forcing the psychic strength to adapt itself to their intellectual small size, which holds it tight and does not permit to go astray into the rich detailed objectivity. It rather compels the psychic life-force to go on from this suggested, symbolic, accepted basis toward the outside, universal spiritual direction. If we speak in the language of our accelerating and checking psycho-pupilar circle, we must call all symbols different degrees of, and partly developed, affective concentrations, which prepare the comfortable spring-boards for the affective force to proceed energetically toward the last degree of utmost punctual concentration. If our psychic life-force accepts these prepared and offered, intellectual spring-boards willingly, then it has the advantage to be very superior in the concentrating facility, to have gone already near the most concentrated progression by the previous help of the artistically created and offered, symbolical and mystical notions. Then it is clear that the fresh, untired and unaverted psychic force, inserted in these moments, has more chance to reach quickly and energetically the delightful centre and has more probability, after having rapped thoroughly at the punctual door of the last central symbols, to be heard by the idealistic, extra-sensorial magnetism, to enter the sublime halls of the stellar, universal world and to be allowed to shoot efficiently the affective totaliy of the life-force through the open celestial door across the supreme spaces to most desirable terminal standards. So the symbolism and the mysticism have the methodical peculiarity to exclude a great part of the preparing, intellectual work; they cut off the beginning surface of the intellectual structure. They leave the maeandric maze of the reasoning development and have, in this manner, the advantage to procced so much further toward the idealistic,spiritual ranges, because they have compensatorily given up the claims to the near intellectual reality.

When healing the blind, Christ spat on the ground, made clay of His spittle, anointed the eyes of the blind man with the clay and sent him to a pool to wash. Christ does not tell him simply that he shall see, but He uses the sensorial help of the preparing symbol which means a concrete, visible, simple psychic foundation, from which the human imagination, as from an accepted, intellectual sure basis, may swing to the divine, affective elevation and terminal concentration of super-natural faith. Christ never expressedly denies or decries the universal validity of the scientific natural laws, but He surely declines peremptorily to enter closely into discussion on them, because He, according to the necessity of compensation, needs all human and almost all His divine life-force for the uplifting idealistic energy. He might have been able to speak about the medical value of His cure, about the scientific efficiency of His spittle or the used clay or the water of the pool in which He understood to use quite extraordinary, healing forces, according to His divine wisdom and enlightenment. But there is no word about it. In this and in all other cases He rather intends to exclude fundamentally the interference of the discussion of the multiple, intellectual reality, in favour of the *"one needful"*. It is an understandable, but wrong misinterpretation, if many think that He puts Himself into contradiction with the detailed development of the natural laws, induced only to bar their influence on His special sentimental action. If we feel, nevertheless, a contradiction, it has to be called temperamental, but not material. He cleverly does not exclude entirely the sensorial world, but pays to our nature the tribute of short symbolic signals, which are nothing but single legal steps, to which the real constitution of humanity may cling as to distinct beacons, illuminated fingerposts or supporting crutches on the long and doubtful way, and from which it swings after all to the terminal affective idealistic realm, of which He exclusively speaks and wither He leads.

The MIRACLE is, therefore, the conscious "angry" exclusion of the natural scientific laws from His concentrative jubilant thrill. The miracle is the strongest, concentrative leap, in psychology, from the intellectual periphery to the central idealistic divinity. It is the emphasized step, from which the divine hero starts energetically for the innermost *sanctissimum* of his spiritual world. In the miracle he disjoints, in a tremendous idealistic, temperamental effort, the intellectual, sensorial representation from his powerful, divine energy and leaps with exclusive, divine-aristocratic gesture into the eternal realm of his terminal, sentimental desire. In the miracle there is surely a clear and pronounced, *methodical* opposition against the process of the natural laws. He claims by this attitude a superiority in the faculty of mastering alike the higher and the lower intellectual and sensorial world. He announces by his miracles the possibility of disposing freely of the real nature. But he shows the expressed will to neglect the minute explanation of the natural science of the visible world in order to be free and clear in his concentrating *spiritual* action. The miracle is the highest degree of subconscious departure from the categoric world, in the experience of the believer, - the conscious starting out from the material life, in the mind of the religious founder. It is the last culmination of the religious genius' absolute will to cultivate the highest degrees of idealistic possibilities even at the expense of the inferior intellectual reality of the human experience and knowledge. The miracle is the "angry" *abbreviation* of the real-intellectual display. Christ does not hesitate, in this highest form of reaction on the idealistic-magnetic energy, to take the risk of putting Himself, seemingly, into contradiction with our daily conceptions of the *legal sequence* of the order of life. He expresses, by the miracles, the educational intention to exclude entirely all intellectual and experimental science from His teaching, in order to receive and to impart the most efficient concentric sway.

There cannot be and never will be a contradiction between human logical order and necessity and the higher, idealistic laws. Both categories of development go on along the same line of natural, idealistic and universal , common scientific principles. If the religious hero and his educational school put so much stress on the temporary negligence of the consideration of all the detailed, logical steps of our human life, they do it only in order to have the entire disposal of our total life-force which they need for strong, idealistic purposes. A miracle may be called, therefore, a *fraus pia,* a pious theft, pulling the human individual away from the inferior categories of time, space and causality and driving it with one strong and decided gesture directly to the elevated hills of sentimental idealism. The miracles are merely psycho-dynamic helps in the case of emergency. They play the role of the most accelerating, "angry", dynamic, sentimental sources of energy. The created nature and the visible world tremble and ache under the mighty, starting leap of the departing, idealistic hero. His powerful foot has left the most remarkable imprint in the thrilling, miraculous spring-board of his contemporary, historic culture, from which he was soaring like a firy missile to the foremost idealistic ranges, forgetting and leaving the real-intellectual help of his and our material-real part of existence.

Only in the compensatory conception the miracle has a reasonable meaning, in the affective development of humanity. It allows a high, most attentive concentration of the human heart. It has the effect to compress all our faculties into the most sentimental, imaginative centres of our possibility. It creates in this a superior platform for divine claims and intentionally educates us, in this manner, to drop our peripheric, scientific and intellectual interests in the moment, when we desire, or are supposed to be gratified with the utmost concentrating sentimental energy. Ordinarily religion combines the mystic symbolism and the miracle. The religious hero teaches to his disciples the most refined manner to exclude in opposition to their materialistic, periphericly lost age the real world at the utmost degree and to accept, instead, a strong, concentrating, energy *or better* facility for happy affective development. His teaching is a psychodynamic instruction for the new possibility of *easy affective attention*, which was lost in the former ancient ages. It is an educational finger-post unto new rythmic conceptions and affective reactions of his disciples and of the following humanity to whom he bequeathed, most ceremoniously, His symbolical, concentrative methods.

A classical example of this temperamental localization and rythmic emphasis we find in the EUCHARISTIC TRANSSUB-STANTIATION, where Christ educates His pupils to exclude the whole sensorial world with exception of the narrow symbolic object of bread or wine, and instead of the large, sensorial, excluded reality He puts within the simple, remaining, symbolical sign the most compressed conception of His important, divine personality. Divinity seems to be most immediately connected with force, from this viewpoint. By the manner of this almost perfect, sensorial seclusion, the necessity of the divine deepening of the only remaining intellectual picture and idea imposes itself most powerfully. The divine hero apotheoses himself in the most efficient, psychodynamic manner, in identifying his memory with the compensatory, most simplified symbolic signs of bread and wine. He accepts as worthy of divinity the greatest amount of individual, surrendering effort. This mechanism of the highest affective, compensatory sentimentality is the testament of the religious hero, which he leaves to humaity. In this most magnetic, idealistic one-sidedness he is sure to remain the best beloved, ever present, most impressive and always lasting divine memory of his disciples, of his believers and of his culture. This significant instruction before his leaving of the real world exhibits the utmost symbolic simplification and creates a sure channel out to his future universal abode, far as he may depart. Here he enjoins expressedly to his friends to repeat themselves this method into his memory. This Eucharistic mystic performance of the faith represents his great, terminal miracle of love; in it he proves most clearly to be the great psychodynamic teacher of humanity, which he instructs, how to go on most easily toward eternal goals, how to leap most surely and successfully over the checking, detailed hinderances of the real, accidental, intellectual, visible life and to gather all life-force compensatorily into the small, mystic and symbolic circle of one narrow attention. The symbolic piece of bread and the chalice of wine are the miraculous, simple substitution of the whole supplanted world and the supposition of his love. He is ready to descend from heaven, if his adherents instead are willing and energetic enough to separate from the reasoning broad field of intellectuality. He wishes necessarily the psychodynamic segregation from the peripheric, intellectual details. He insistently claims the previous droping of the categories of time, space and causality, or at least of one of them. Then only his divine majesty is inclined to apear as by a spell, clad in all his delightful splendour. Oh wonderful sunrise of divinity!

We have in this religious institution and and in this secret of the New Testament essentially, in the psychological sense, the strong, psychodynamic education of humanity unto the mono-attentive effort toward divine affective compensation. Here lies the important clue explaining the significance of the surprising turning-table of the cultural history of the peri-Mediterranean and occidental humanity, *that the hero teaches mankind again what to do to be happy*. The concentrating faculty had become lame in the Antiquity. The intellectual, peripheric diffusion had absorbed irrevocably all human energy. The real, material sorrow had taken away from people every possibility of happy, even momentaneous forgetfulness of earthly worries, and it was his special mission to repair this broken spring of the antique psychology, to point out again what to do in order to accomplish the entire psychological contraction, as a necessary physiological reaction and as the only means and way to perfect happiness.

The firm fixation and serious, exclusive staring at one point, as the religious psychology teaches in the eucharist, we find it in our days in a similar way in the scientific application of any *hypnotizing* influence. It is underlying any religious, loving and even artistic intensity. The *hypnosis* of to-day starts in the same manner from the energetic and exclusive fixation of one sensorial point or visible impression, which is emphasized by the effort of the will during a certain lasting time, and which such guides people to the desired, *intellectual retraction* being the basis of any surrender of the total life-force to any affective, extra-sensorial influence. Many people call this localized fixation or mono-determined attention of the beginning hypnosis *artificial tiring*. We recognize in it the compensatory intellectual deflection. In all love and in hypnosis we have the suggestive connection of one ruling idea with this punctual symbolic fixation of the life-force, so that Christ immediately says, after the impressive exhibition of His charming, simple symbols: "This is my body; this is my blood!" With this hypnotic suggestion He instantly pulls the whole individual life-force, through the symbolic hole, out into this one affective, imaginative injunction that this is His living body and blood and that, from the starting moment of the symbolic, limiting, sensorial representation of bread and wine, He claims to possess quite exclusively the whole influence on our total desire, imagination, will and thought. The symbol is pretended to be His body, but the affectionate love of the believer identifies Him with the universal love.

The different conception of the eucharistic phenomenon is very typical of the character of the various sections of this religion. Whilst one direction succombs entirely to the hypnotizing suggestion of the symbolic influence, and takes and keeps the full, literal weight of the affective insinuation of the eucharistic symbolic mysticism, the other, post-equinoctial part, already more intellectually directed, makes a difference in the interpretation of the words of Christ and gives to it the value and the significance of a comparison or of an indirect meaning, in retaining a part of the intellectual, peripheric control, and not throwing the totality of the psychic life-force indiscriminately into the abyss of wonderful divine love. The latter psychological society withholds so much of energy within the intellectual surrounding categories of time, space and causality that a contradiction between the eucharistic mystery and the intellectual real experience is excluded. But still even in these circles and meetings a shuddering affective power is lingering around these charming symbolic ceremonious functions, and the historic national ecclesiastic and familiar tradition of the Christian education has emphasized the hypnotizing eucharistic readiness in our hearts and senses so much that we never attend to its performance without the most pronounced divine rapture.

So the sentimental Christian world was by the word of its Master: This is my flesh and body, entirely swept away, in connection with the symbolic signs of bread and wine, up to the equinoctial, mediaeval, intellectual conversion. This saying of the overwhelming personality of Christ had hypnotized His loving followers so much that they had no power to reason, for a long time, about the intellectual side of it, but were most closely and immediately attracted to his symbolic formula. So much so that they lost all critical moveability and discharged all their total psychic life-force through this symbolic imaginative ring immediately into the terminal goal of their love. Only in the beginning of modern times, when the sentimental spheric suggestive help was changed, at the equinoctial, point, into the intellectual digressive resistance, the sense of detailed criticism instantly began, a mighty disagreement started and one began to analyze and think prevalently in a realistic way. The hypnotized giant awoke from his symbolic, absolute and narrow fixation: he began to look around his mystic sign and reduced the literal conception of the symbolic object to the real meaning which he could connect with the surroundings of the daily experience.

In the eucharistic performance Christ offers to us a very audacious simplified symbol. By this terminal examination of Christian psycho-mechanic skill, on the eve before His leaving. He puts the highest and most exacting claims to the intellectual symbolic mysticism. Scarcely the hero was ever so irrespective of all reality in his former miracles; never he leaped so energetically and clearly over all logical experience as he did in the eucharistic achievement. At least here he would state in a splendid case of psychomechanic examination what he could do with humanity and how far he had developed his mission to be the affective dynamic concentrator of the new generations.

In this last *dynamic* formula,he trusted to give to the world a perpetual panacea of their future evils. Here he expected they could and would find and draw always new hope, joy, eternal enthusiasm and rejuvenating happiness, forgetting the peripheric multiple and paralyzing intellectual fixations, at least for hours or moments.

It is a great education to be taught to believe in the future and be longing for the movements of the universe, to forget the petty manifold worries of the present day and fix our heart on the love for, and confidence in, the things to come. If it does not matter for many, and perhaps rightly, wither love and confidence go, one thing is quite sure that they always have to be seeked and cherished and that we are afraid to stay in the tearful night of our present existence without the luminous constellation of Faith, Hope and Love in the firmament of our psychological experience.

But the supposition for this work is very hard. It is the very progressed possibility of the previous affective symbolic concentration. The first step to this symbolic contraction is as difficult as humanity afterwards leaps into the abyss of the divine universe most easily. For, in accepting the mystic eucharistic symbolism we are already far elevated toward the border of the idealistic standards, and if we are fixed on this extraordinary and most simplified sensorial platform, we have the disposal of our full psychic energy just at the threshold of our celestial entrance. Bread and wine, the wafer are for the believer the immediate last sensorial help into the divine transformation of eternal sentiments; the faith enables these happy people to enter with full psychic energy through the door of heaven, without being forced to make first a long way of intellectual logical approach. They are reposed at their entrance into the realm of idealistic love. With one symbolic leap they are highly uplifted to the immediate vicinity of the door of heaven and of the terminal idealistic concentration. In the eucharistic psychomechanism Christ leaps and throws us with one thrilling hypnotic jerk from the elevated platform of symbolic simplification into the ideal centre of his divine love.

Christ is said to have breathed on the apostles before He gave to them the power of keeping and forgiving sins. In this case He used again the symbolic power of one sensorial, this time a *tactil* simple sign, in order to concentrate and deflect the attention of His disciples toward the unique concentrating significant idea which He would impress on them. The psychic force of the apostles is by this sensorial symbol averted from all intellectual display and for this reason caught in the most thorough manner and thrown most efficiently toward the intentional idea and its affective elevation. All truth which must convey any deep impression on people, is bound to a sufficiently narrow concentration in order to force the affective possibilities of our sentimental gift to produce from this localized narrow symbolic basis, deep idealistic emphasis or uplifting elevation. This would not be possible at a given *lateral intellectual opportunity of psychic digression*.

This is the great secret of SUCCESS in the world, in science, religion and business, to be able to make a sufficient intellectual simplification of the mind in order to receive the energetic, deepening, sentimental localization of the total psychic forces. The effect of the success comes out from one deep affective well, from one narrow localized effort of idealistic skilful exercise. Here, from the continual incessant strain, from the always grinding millstone of punctual work or from the ever falling drop of water every highest affective result will be obtained. Not even the stone is unable to resist the incessant perseverance of one clearly conceived and for ever prosecuted, even weakest purpose in its single action. The unshakable heartrending patience of one inflexible clear direction of affective will is the absolute way to success. But there is the narrow intellectual limitation which is connected inevitably always with success at the same time, and which necessarily escorts like a shadow the energy of successful affective depth, as the natural intellectual compensation. "Was wir in der Jugend wuenschen, haben wir im Alter die Fuelle". Every advantage must be bought by a disadvantage. Never in our frail life we are permitted to have the perfection of both intellectuality and sentiments at the same time. It is only in the perfect achievement of *art,* where these two oppositions and "contradictions" are peacefully crystallized after a gigantic battle and where both components are of outstanding importance.

Symbolism, mysticism and miracles have exactly the same psychological conditions and meanings. They all three are angry temperamental leaps from the intellecual periphery to the affective centre. They put bluffing startling facts without giving the reason for them. They lift the basis and the level of our not understandable principles up to an artificial higher scale; they claim their probable and even most believable reasonable importance by the sensorial power of their existence, but refuse and decline to develop to us their logical intellectual make-up. If we observe well, however, we must confess, that not only in the artistic established realm of our psychodynamic religious education, but also in the ordinary daily life we meet incessantly the most pronounced fact of logically undeveloped and involved phenomena which impose on us by their mere sensorial existence and influence. But as it is, in the case of daily experience and enjoyments, our inclination and duty to try to resolve the Gordic knots of the real riddles which nature and life present to us, - as we must in these cases explain the hidden developments of the bluffing facts by serious work and study in a logical way, in order to understand and introduce them into the regular rhythmic river of intellectual nature, - as we in nature and science look for progressive intellectual synthesis and analysis, for explanations and display of all symbolic occurring facts, so we have the same intentions and inclinations in the realm of our psychological world, looking for understanding the symbolic riddles of our affective soul, searching to make a logical development out of the genial mystic spots and knots of our religious history, abolishing, if possible, the "angry" leaps and intellectual condensations of mysticism and wonderful symbolism. We try to replace them by intellectual, logical, rhythmic development, and, according to the strong intellectual tendencies of the spheric quarter of to-day, one looks for avoiding the future renewal and synthesis of future repeated symbolic contractions. This latter remark is suggested by the strong intellectual one-sidedness of our modern time which is thoroughly averse to any symbolic affective contraction of our life-force. Our age is fond of intellectual solutions of problems. It feels very humiliated and unhappy, if it meets many affective symbolic knots which cannot be resolved. Our time does not only like to read the cross-word-puzzles generally in all our modern news-papers, in public and private opportunities, but even to face the highest and most complicated symbolic and hidden logical contractions and entanglements, above all the last and most involved cross-word-riddles of eternity, God and religion.

But in the light of psychopupilar necessities and economical concentric efficiency this question of course takes a very different aspect. The prevalent thinking function and intellectual inclination of our time means, however, that we indeed live in the post-equinoctial Christian time and have, according to our natural intellectual and spheric essential task, by fate and even in disharmony with the magnetic tendency of any historic religion, to look for new great intellectual expansions and unfoldments of the possible outside extrasolar universe. And yet, one future day, this spheric digressing need will be satisfied once more and humanity will fall back to the *left* or *right* hand of the new future, genial-solstitial attachment approaching its old or a new central theistic, sentimental sun. Then one will appreciate too much again the sentimental symbolical ways of mysticism and miracles, as to-day the majority dislikes them thoroughly.

The continual use of symbolic signs, by the religious hero, proves his respect for the scientific natural laws of our sensorial life. In what consists the modern quarrel about *miracles?* In what lie the opposition and the contradiction, in the conceptions of the miracle of to-day and of the former times? Partly in the assertion of the modern age that there can be only a harmony between miraculous action and logical development, whilst earlier ages admitted and postulated a mutual exclusion or even contradiction between natural and miraculous performances. The taumaturgic individual may know more than the most honored scientific man, but his knowledge is on the same line and in the same direction as the rule of the natural law. The affective progression may be more condensed, more rapid in "angry" development and magnetic purport, but never it can be in contradiction with reasonable thinking. The symbolic and mystic miracle may hide, exceed and overleap the logical sequence of the slower regular intellectuality, but it could and would not ever abolish or impair the imperturbable eternal majesty of the simple elements of the natural law. The mystic idealism may be able to choose a more energetic and more hidden rhythm of progressive concentric methods. It may be ahead of intellectuality and find out by the superior srtrength of its natural *intuition, farther-reaching truth and more achieved ways of the natural laws*. But always it means a parallel and synonymous direction and way as the intellectual reason has to go it.

So the miraculous mysticism turns out to be a superior and more perfect degree of our intellectual capabilities and rougher logical methods. It can be very far outside the measures, manners and the trend which we are able even to-day to reach with the means of our intellectual scientific and experimental helps. There could be a superior degree of clever energy and skilful use even of intellectual display, by the genial individual, above all in a genius of first capacity, but never a contradiction, in as far as go intellectual laws. It may have been an amazing surprise to witness the intellectually symbolic miracles as Christ is related to have performed them. But just this surprise added to the shortcoming insufficiency of the testifying intellectuality. Therefore the bluffing and yet natural fact that where causality is hidden, there wrongly a contradiction with the intellectual laws of the categories likely is assumed by many. We may be surprised to the utmost degree by the refined and thoroughly involved facts like miracles opening new not only extra-categoric, but also categoric views and hopes, but we never are entitled to lose the confidence and the conviction that the future development of science and culture will one day be able to resolve this hidden and symbolically compressed, exact intellectuality, in order that at last we shall find all those threads and droped arguments necessary for our logical explanations which we missed in former sentimental times.

There is no doubt that a genius of the dignity of Christ or a genial artistic society of the importance of His immediate followers, if they sometimes proceeded to any strong intellectual effort of their superior affective life-force in order to manifest their real power to the unbelieving intelligentia, - were much more in a position than ordinary individuals to fulfill personal performances of astounding quality, that, in the genial sway of their life-force, they intruded most intimately upon the natural laws of life and were able to create an extraordinary large outlook on the intellectual display of the created world. Our practical intellectual possibilities are the product of the most numerous and most energetic works which we are able to do in a short time within the realm of the objective world, and who could doubt, that exactly men of the gigantic life-force of the religious genius and his first followers were able to perform outstanding scientific and intellectual achievements, as soon as they would. We know that the intuitive persons are the most intelligent ones, that they always find out with their divinatory intuition what even to their own reasoning recognition is hidden, and yet afterward their affective intuitive surmises and suppositions turn out to have been right, so that in time the intellectual experimentation is able to follow and to confirm the prophetic mind.

If the religious genius and his disciples were in the centre of the affective conversion of the most extensive and important human culture, if they had the most exraordinary riches of affective communication with the interspheric magnetism, then we rightly assume that they also had the most developed facility of intuitive digressions into the realm of the intellectual world, and that they had the most remarkable faculty to intuitive visions and discoveries of progressed intellectual stages and things and principles which we are not able even to-day to find out with the reasonable help of our cool logical science. Surely *science* is a carefully progressing organiation stepping from century to century and giving, in all its different phases, mutual helping and facilitating hands. This is the precious rule of all scientific order. But in that genial solstitial turning-point, as we had it at the time of the affective conversion of a whole intercontinental culture, we must assume that higher, more elevated and deeper intuitions through the future intellectual development of humanity are possible, that the most powerful lightning- flashes kindle and enlighten the whole intellectual features of our race, and that, therefore, intuitively, by the individuals of this personal genial size, truths, tenets and principles must be found out which still are hidden behind a veil of intellectual obscurity despite the pretended tremendous progress of the human scientific knowledge to its most modern results.

So we have no intellectual contradiction in the miracles, but a quite remarkable transitory acceleration of human affective progression. The performer of miracles is, of course, right to avail himself of their authority. He points again and again to their superior value, not in the meaning that they are against intellect, but that they, on the contrary, include, in an involved way, even a higher degree of handling and using logical and intellectual laws, to an extent and to a perfection which are impossible to the most experienced and one-sided practical people. The religious genius bases a part of his divine claims even exactly on this superior knowledge of natural science ; he considers the miracles as an expression of unusual perfection in, and a most intimate familiarity with, the human and superhuman natural laws. His superior possibility in natural science and his initiation into deep natural secrets are accepted as an analogous demonstration of his quite extraordinary genial magnetic divinity. But we will not forget, there is always and only the question, in all these things, about a more or less degree of divine truth and superior achievement which we really and indeed and not only emblematicly share in all essential features. Because of his excellent magnetic intuition being proved by his miracles, the religious genius is more god than we. He had succeeded in demonstrating his superior purport of divine power more efficiently than we altogether through the manifestation of his extraordinary skill and quite startling unbelievable use of the intellectual natural laws. But he remains a man as we are and we share essentially his divine, that is to say, his affective interspheric magnetic spiritual disposition.

The chief reason of the declining of miracles and of mysticism, by the present time, is their *temperamental Anachronism.* Miracles and mysticism seem to-day to the majority to be entirely worn out notions of an old time, and many think they are old-fashioned superstitions and and unreasonable deceptions. They have no affective connections with, nor hold on, the ruling tendencies of to-day. They thoroughly contradict the present psychological atmosphere. We understand that the magnetic spheric suggestion of the sentimental part of our psycho-solar fate has been converted at our age into the intellectual opposition and so, there is not at all any space left for the energetic acceleration which is always the supposition of symbolism and miracles.

For it is as well the need of energetic affective concentration toward far ranges which creates symbols, as on the other hand they are artificially constructed by the will to reach and permit to reach far away idealistic, postulated goals. Miracles and symbolic signs are the very efficient intellectual steps of the progression of our life-force rushing toward ideal sentiments. They are the mighty intellectual, absorbing engines which are mounted at certain distances of the logical way, between reality and idealism, and which, owing to their strong affective contracting energy, facilitate the progression of the life-force from the intellectual-peripheric to the central-sentimental fixation. They are comparable to the old *Roman specula,* which were used in order to signalize commands by symbolic signs through the whole Roman empire in the shortest time, guiding and transferring the will of Rome,by these countless signalizing stations, to the most remote parts of the ancient world.

The symbols and miracles assume the role of different players at a game of ball, throwing the ball to one another in a consecutive progression from one goal to another, every player receiving the ball but also hurling it energetically farther on, by the impartation of a new quickening jerk, toward the next player receiving and throwing the ball in the same manner. So at last the possibly very distant goal will be easily reached by the intermediary collaboration of the interpolated numerous players. It would have been quite impossible to hurl the ball in only one throw from the starting point to the goal, or if it would have been practicable, there would have been

necessary a quite extraordinary effort on the part of one player en-
acting all his energy and exhausting himself. But with the intervention of many people and the intermediary, inserted numerous helps,
the distant range becomes easily reachable and gives even a pleasure
to many people through the manifold haphazards resulting from
the alternating accelerations and resistances of the play.

So in the same manner the symbolic miracle overleaps great and
long ranges of our logical affective standards and attracts from far,
owing to its idealistic avidity, the flying ball of human affective
life-force. Because of the multiple establishment of such miraculous
insertions, the individual indeed is able to reach his farthest ideal
goals, such which he never would be able to attain, had these intermediary wonderful stations of artificial symbolism not have been
intercalated. The miracle and symbolism turn out to be inserted
psychic sources of new magnetic energy and acceleration like a
strengthening and supporting *electrical battery* intercalated along
the electrical current in order to give it a new and stronger progressive impulse and efficiency.

The rich symbolism and the miracles of the scriptures and much
more afterwards, the gorgeous symbolic and miraculous unfoldment
of the Catholic church have expressedly the clear intention to convey
to the human psychology the necessary reinforcement, the magnetic
energetic impulses to go on along the far way to the quite distant
terminal idealism, without losing courage, force, without panting
or even dying by the way from fainting affective exhaustion. So the
individual would perhaps have missed the ideal sentimental goal,
on whose attainment the establishing founder put all stress and on
which he made dependent the whole success or failure of his reli-
giuos system. He was very much aware how much the splendour of
his theistic strength and distance surpassed the possibility of human
life-force and how much there was danger that the personal life-
force succombed to the disproportion of its task, - that in the best
case the enormous necessary effort would have exhausted the individual total possibility, missing the symbolic interference, or have
disturbed too seriously the comfortable psychic meditation of the
man. The concentrative sway and energy indispensable to the extraordinary ranges of idealistic theistic goals, long before having reached the goal, would have lost their magnetic attractiveness. The gear
of the human nature is not strong enough, its strength and size are
much too small to compare successfully with Gods'. The religious
founder was quite conscious of the disproportion between the ideal
goal he offered to humanity, and the individual magnetic gift of the

human force, and so he was induced, would he make an easily landing possibility toward these divine goals quite distant from habitual
human intercourse, to intercalate the symbolic miracles so powerful
in magnetic, concentrative furthering of our life-force.

Even if we admit the relative superiority and the splendour of
the established theistic ideals, we cannot praise, however, in any
respect, that they suppose a psychodynamic energy which is quite
beyond the reach of our normal natural activity. We cannot but re-
gret that the increasing development of the idealistic idea produces
spoiling of our normal logical thinking by mystic symbols and by
the angry leaps of miraculous conceptions. It must be essentially
wrong for human nature to be incessantly driven to highest ideals
which we cannot reach chiefly logically and in an orderly proceeding
thinking way, but rather by the help of the innumerable idealistic
sparks and and energetic blowing up bomb-shells of the artistic
symbolism, mysticism and miracles. The artistic digression from the
quiet progress of human intellectual logic means of course a serious
educational pampering of our natural disposition, but the importance
of this question must be considered more closely later.

So we understand on the other hand that the *post-equinoctial*
intellectual tendencies have a pronounced aversion to symbolic
mysticism and miracles. The characteristic stigma of the intellectual
spheric quarter of hmanity is the fatal removal from the theistic
central sun; our magnetic universal influence turns us prevalently
to the extra-solar universe and for this reason the centro-dynamic
acceleration of the symbolic and mystic description is in exact opposition to the prevailing and ruling magnetic digression of the intellectuality. This is the chief reason why mysticism and miracles are
scorned, sneered at and held in contempt to-day, just in the most
pronouncedly important leading circles of our society. The educational misgivings about mysticicm and miracles are also given in
their pampering effect, of course, and they have a great weight to-
day. And yet we all experimentally know that the theoretical and
scientific principles and considerations never would rule a social
conception in such an exclusive manner if there were not behind it
the magnetic help of a favorable spheric fatal wind. Only these
extra-individual and general leading cosmo-dynamic magnetic energies are in a position to induce the whole society to turn the back
to the old glorious and most refinedly invented and elaborated
symbolic theo-centric helps of mysticism and miracle. The post-equinoctial character has not any use for the theistic supporting energies
of miracle and mysticism. Its goals are temperamentally extremely

different from the helping possibilities of these religious central re-inforcements.

Owing to the strong magnetic tensions and energies imparted to the proceeding movement, by the accelerating artificial bomb-shells of symbolic mysticism, the human individual is put indeed into the ability to reach most distanced idealistic ranges and affective concentrative standards. The ball of the human psychic force flies sure-ly and energeticly, with all these helps, to its goal: but the arising intermediary play of the magnetic accelerations and resistances and the explosive force of the symbolic shells cause a dangerous and often most fatal intercourse between the engaged, incensed and am-bitious players and forces: they are likely to bring about above all the fundamental symbolistic mind, a lack of self-control, in a sense, and the genial, but practically in life often so disastrous anger. They easily destroy our scientific taste, if abused, and strive to make the results of our painful scientific experience most transitory, because they organize all our will power in an *intentional,* but not *conditional, absolute,* but not *relative* manner. Doubtless the most charm-ing pleasure of looking at the artificial wonderful fire work will ever again surprise our attention. The most thrilling stars, sky-rockets and color-trains are continually produced by the marvellous symbolism and mysticism, but we will, apart from the educational danger of the affective roughening and pampering, not forget that it is always risky to play with fire works, that we can be hurt by the affective explosions, in whose middle we perform our vital actions and that we hardly can stand the responsibility to change our solid, logical natural laws into a bold sportive game or into fire works, charming and fascinating as they may be.

Mystic, symbolism and miraculism thus arise because of the bold audacity of our human pride to prosecute sentimental goals not attainable for our natural disposition. The disproportion of the exceedingly far away terminal strength in regard to relative weak-ness of our vital total life-force, causes the technical irregularities of our affective development both in accumulating our energy in con-centrated mysticism and miracles and in diluting or even interrupt-ing, in a reacting compensatory way, the immeasurable, elongated and extended wires of our interspheric logical way.

The cultured intellectual man of to-day, as a rule, does not deal preferably with the notion of miracle. As the representative of the intellectual signature of our time, he is the friend and the defender of the clear experimental proof and is prone to decline the bluffing impressions of the symbolism and of the miracle. The magnetic charm of the former sentimental hypnosis has ceased, and the intellectual criticism came entirely to its own, excluding the hidden affective influences of extra-intellectual and *subconscious* description.

There are many other reasons for this kind of appreciation. Life is full of contradictions, as Goethe says, and psychology not the less, so that one has to respect the established ecclesiastical doctrines, because they have their impressive roots in the absolute, far-reaching tendencies of religion, which have become possible, however, exactly by these disliked and dangerous symbolic methods. Our age, roughly speaking, has the peculiarity to praise much the result and the universal will of the deepest religious effort, by which humanity shall be connected to the solar universe, but it does not like its sentimental symbolical methods, because owing to them the ever moving further development is withheld. Despite the reverence and the general will to maintain all precious and good cultural results of the past, the intellectual age has the strong intention even to enlarge its theistic circle by its intellectual striving, and whilst it is on one side afraid of the "antiquated" and earlier educational methods, which were *the result of psychomechanic emergency in regard to the real and ideal disproportions of the human nature,* it strives itself by its intellectual digressions to create even larger, more powerful and more distant divine goals. What will happen, when the next sentimental quarter will dawn, when the coming future solstitial point of a most successful and gigantic religious genius will turn our spheric intellectual quarter again back to and round the new theistic centre, which for the past time presented itself as an extra-solar digression and negation? Will the human life-force be stronger at that future period? Will we have the possibility to resist better the future splendour of an even more attractive divine magnetism and will our strong intellectual education of the present time be sufficient to maintain the logical accustomed way in a perfect human balance? Shall we be able to cross the enlarged new solar light-field and to cover the new elongated solar radius without becoming even more tired, stumbling, more impatient and helpless on the way, since our ancestors were compelled to use the help of the dangerous and doubtful mysticism in order to reach their less distant and less elaborate theistic goals? Indeed we are right to develop the intellectual strength and skill of our generation. The regular logical laws will be after a certain time of practice an imperturbable custom of the human manner of mental reaction. We are right to develop the force of our body, of our muscular and nervous system to the utmost degree, because we stand before greater tasks of human performances than any past time. If we are educated well unto logical thinking achievement, if this special intellectual habit has become an unlosable cultural inheritance, as we have now, in old countries, cultural, comparable acquisitions in the "opposite" sentimental sense, then we shall be able, perhaps, to maintain our logical regular order even during a future sentimental, most attractive theistic period. But what about our centripetal energy at that time? The clear and well trimmed divine light will beckon the much clearer into the shadow of reality.

If we have strengthened our body by *sportive* life and enriched our life-force by reasonable, moderate and healthy customs, then we possibly shall be apt to reach even more distant and more important theistic goals in a less symbolic and mystic way than our ancestors were, in order to go to their historic God. Then perhaps we shall continue to dispense during the next sentimental quarter with the magnetic charm of the affective Conversion approaching the central Deity, or at least, we will not be hurled in a passive and fatal manner toward God. We shall find God not by collective coercion and fear, but by free individual love. We may do it in a more conscious and intellectually freer will. At this future age of desirable human development we may be able to do away with the notion of the miracle. Then we should be in a position to go the long way toward divine values in the regular and untired rhythm of strengthened logical faculty, satisfied with the dividing and instigating helps of the work and of the direct vision of love supported by art. We should like and hope not to miss our future divine goals in the next phase of human affective fulfilment, after having received by long cultural practice and abstemiousness a sure intellectual possibility of work and a reasonable advancing instigation of tastes and customs. Week days may thus be filled by the rhythmic progression of work, and Sundays by the harmoniuos divine accelerations of love and art. Will mankind arrive one day, by these rather temperate but steady psychodynamic helps, to the same or higher divine goals as the former humanity went to by irregulated symbolism, mysticism and miracle?

In this connection we are inclined to consider as the superior type the reserved, dry intellectual man, who is able to resist the magnetic force of the central attraction and who has the sufficient intellectual individual hesitation, being at the greater distance from the affective centre. Though we always, after every solstitial point, approach the theistic sun and need the sentimental way, and though it seems that the reward of the intellectual work consists exactly in the sentimental conversion, it must be admitted, nevertheless, that the progressive *spiralic evolution* of the intellectual digression, even after the solstitial sentimental conversion, means a certain degree of relative individual augmentation and greater distant freedom. The higher human dignity, worthiness and importance consist, in this sense, in the further distance from their historic conception of God. More intellectual digression is the way to greater personal force and liberty, closer sentimental approach is the less degree of dignified personal importance.

We see, therefore, that the *solstitial conversion* has also the meaning of the HISTORIC JUDGMENT of the collective humanity. History itself is the exact and inevitable judge of all mankind. In the degree of the peripheric development of the solstitial point, we have naturally and instantly to expect the following, just, historic judgment. The historic successful judgment, on the broadest scale, means the sufficient distance of the last solstitial range so that humanity is able to be pulled into the extrasolar new spheric circle, leaving the former spheric circumvolutions. This is the historic and scientific conception of the word of going to the right or the left side after the last day. Going left means being remanded to the old, narrow, sentimental, peri-solar movement because of the insufficient range of the previous solstitial point, whereas the *promotion to the right* outside extra-solar new circle means the reward of the more industrious, stronger and more successful terminal range of the most distant solstitial record. If any genial organization believes that the score of its historic achievement never will be exceeded, its rock never will be crushed and the competence of its authority never will be refuted, it assumes that all efforts of future times to overcome the old solstitial score will be relative failures, because the greatest possible effect had been done by the former victorious religious effort.

So *historically* we must think that failure and *punishment* consist in a less degree of cultural independent development of intellectuality, in a nearer, merely sentimental approach to God, and that the successful reward, on the contrary, enables us to promote to the more distant radius of the extrasolar circle. Thus punishment and reward are only possible, in this light, in the historic social intellectual world with its categories of time, space and causality, where the distance of the affective human personality allows different intellectual degrees of preferabilities and corresponding *comparisons*. It is the intellectual possibility of comparison which creates the invidious punishments and the exulting rewards. Are we in the possession, without our individual brain and heart, of the instruments of being rewarded or punished? Has not the individual affective soul in every case, to return after death to the lap of its maker, from whom it was amalgamated with the material intellectual body? Is not the individual unable nor susceptible of having an individual judgment after death because of the loss of its intellectual nature, while the historic humanity instead, being the most pronounced and lasting intellectual incarnation, represents the clearest performance of judgment in the nature of its very existence? Life itself, in its intellectual struggle is our continual earthly reward or punishment. What a human glory to be victorious in a just cause, but what a greater divine satisfaction to suffer and fail even, for a holy conviction! The idea of *suffering* will guide us to other surprising viewpoints. We seem to have all requitals in our present life through work and suffering. Work is active suffering and pain is passive work. If we will escape from the active work, we must make up with the passive suffering.

Yes, we have to expect our happy freedom through intellectual culture. This freedom is founded on the tendency of human reserved distance from, and in, dependence on the solar system, whilst the centripetal *theologian,* on the contrary, searches to join us as closely as possible to the historic divine central axis. So we recognize two thoroughly opposed tendencies in the intellectual, cultural scientific magnetic inclination on one, and in the sentimental theological theistic intention, on the other side. And indeed, both directions have a strong aversion to each other, as it seems. I remember, how a famous surgeon at Zuerich, some time ago, sneered at the theological criticism and represented the theologians as the last and ultimate edition of any possible lack of objective judgment. This man was surely a strong representative of our intellectual period, and he was indeed right, in his one-sided conception, because the essential feature of the theologian is not to do any digressive, rebelling steps from the old, solar, historic circle, but to induce, on the contrary, humanity into a sentimental harmoniuos way to move faithfully toward the strong theistic concentric axis of the given historic preformation. The essential character of the theologian is, therefore, not intellectual criticism, as the unfriendly surgeon rightly meant, but rather a careful magnetic, more drifting establishment of our psychodynamic movements toward given theistic goals, whereas,in a quantitative sense, the exact scientist comparably is right to claim more steering importance, more freedom of thought and more digressive reservedness from his extrasolar God. How instantly we always feel all the magnetic digressions in each other, and our acting accordingly, mostly without us being able to give account of, even to ourselves, takes the corresponding sympathetic or averse attitude and direction.

But in spite of the natural real opposition of intellectual culture and the concentric historic theology, and despite the fact that experimental intellectual science indeed has a much higher degree of independent steering possibility than every sentimental theistic function, we must not forget that all that heroic intellectual reservedness, this new star too becomes old in the psychological future of the human race. It will change one day, in its turn. The intellectual character of the scientific type, according to our sketch of the solstitial conception of the religious hero, after having passed the most extreme turning point and having been carried so far by his own previous effort, will acqiesce after all with the extrasolar, yet still *concentric, sentimental and divine love.*

So is the intellectual scientist of the present time the most successful for-runner of the future theology. He creates the necessary suppositions of a new later powerful solstitial Conversion. The more the spheric elastic hoop of our psychological life-year is extended to one side, owing to the digressing efforts of the intellectual extraverted naturalist, the more after the solstitial distension the psychological world will fall back again, at least for a reactive period, and in this we have to recognize that the important concentrating psychological energy of the future time will be the exact consequence of the amount of the intellectual digressing effort of the present intellectual effort and work. In declining the theologian we cultivate him even more, and by dismissing him as a small man through the front door we soon shall see him returning as a giant or almost a God, through the rear door. So important and natural is the genial psycho-mechanic function of the divine, and he cannot be missed, although many objections and people oppose him and he unfortunately is included in the common circle of human insufficiency. He has his necessity and right of existence in the psychological need of the continual inevitable concentrative conclusiveness of the human social and individual action. He has in his turn to be the guard of a certain concentrative ready strength of humanity, representing the balance of the opposite intellectual peripheric dissipation being the function of the preparing cultural and material work.

Science and religion are called magneto-dynamic adversaries, both having very neccessary, but very different missions. The *scientific* effort has the task to enlarge and classify the human real size, preparing it for new theological units, the *theological effort,* on the contrary, has to retain, concentrate and regulate the human energy toward one historic theistic point of the past, and not to allow it to be scattered in its affective riches, indirectly, in the large intellectual possible universe. But this will result from the struggle of these two official opponents. The future theologian will be much more intellectual than that of the former times. He represents the important affective opposition of mankind until the solstitial record, and he will be the leading strong reaction after its turning sentimental conversion. He then will possibly reproduce and use the miraculous symbolism and mysticism in order to go more easily to the central goal or in order to pretend an intellectual connection, once more with seeming logical development, without which human nature never could exist. If we have an evolutionary conception, however, of our intellectual performances, then we have to assume that the divine of the future will be more intellectual, less mystic and symbolic, owing to the cultural acquisitions and the psychological inheritance of human intellectual customs. The concentric, magnetic rapidity and, therefore, the miraculous mysticism will no more be so impatient, because the independence of the centre and the accustomed spheric distance from it will be definitely more considerable. The future theologian will be of a more intellectual type, because his action will take place in a more peripheric realm than in the past, but he still will represent the affective reactive concentration of the human mind ,in as far as it will be permitted under future circumstances to approach a theistic centre around a central mono-theistic standard.

Thus the theistically ungifted realist turns out to be the bearer of the human cultural progress. He is the more gifted in the sense of the human cultural furtherance. In a certain sense the moderate naturalist, retaining and bridling the charming theistic sentimental contraction , is the emphaziser and accumulator of the human progressive future, and the following ages will gain by the self-sacrificing, enlarging effort of his developing periphery. If the next ages will be farther than we are to-day, if their life-circle will adopt a much prouder independence and more considerable circumference, then this will be due to the previous intellectual work of our scientific time which strives so gloriously to build more audacious arches of human intellectual achievement than any former time did.

But even each future sentimental quarter will have a mystic character, up to a certain limit. It is and remains essential to the theological peculiarity to quicken the contraction of the human heart and mind toward a theistic centre, and mysticism is both the forced magnetic and free artificial production of ecclesiastical performances and methods. These special symbolic technicalities will be for ever typical of the administration of every theistic religion.

We should, therefore, neither be surprised at seeing the strong tendency and inclination to *uniforms* and *costumes* of the ecclesiastic taste. Even the more independent and freer intellectual modern churches are scarcely able to get rid of them. There again we have the expression of the same symbolic authority and submission, the partial exclusion of reasoning criticism, the preventing grasping of the good will, the ever returning, summary and thorough captatio benevolentiae being most characteristic for all divine concentric action. Not reason, but faith is the root of all religious activity. Not intellectual reasoning, but magnetically drifting devotion lies, hitherto at the bottom of all theistic performances. Who would not remember very distinctly temperamental differentiations and oppositions in different persons, in this regard, so that we see clearly the natural easiness of one person in the theisting direction and of the other in the scientific reasoning way?

There are very affective "condescending" and extremely intellectual "obstinate" individuals. There is an exceedingly pronounced contrary difference in their disposition, and it is the inheritance, we might almost say the star and the spheric localization of their conception and birth, which are the cause that two individuals living under the same conditions are extremely different in the prevalence of sentimental and intellectual gifts and inclinations. We could call them even, in a sense, theistic and anti-theistic natural psychological dispositions, one looking back and clinging to the historic theistic past and the other digressing to the peripheric universal future. That there cannot be, as a rule, a good agreement between the two types of such an opposed natural disposition, is clear, and as in two different following ages of the spheric human sunyear it is excluded, that they do not prosecute essentially different goals and appreciate one another, so two individuals born at the same time, but conceived under these opposite *astrological influences,* as it were, are far from the possibility to understand each other. Here we have the explanation of the continual social, political and religious, collective and personal quarrels of the human race. Here we have the simultaneous existence of the most opposite spheric magnetic dispositions; and although there is a leading magnetic tendency at every age, according to the spheric localization of the human history within the circle of the psychological sun-year, the checking weaker component opposing and opposite to the governing signature of the time and of the moving force, is not easily ready to give in and is really represented by a living portion of mankind. So we have the spheric antagonistic struggle expressed and exhibited by, and within the individuals of the society.

Everybody, more or less, is called even before his birth to be an advancing or checking factor of the signature of his time, and this moment decides whether he will be successful or not in his exterior life. But both parts are always necessary, of course. Without antagonism the circle of human collective fate could not exist, and if there are people who are driven successfully and comfortably to all their desired goals, there must certainly be also others who drive and bear them, by exciting antagonism and liberal broad-mindedness. Looking at life from this angle, we never should have opportunity to discuss and quarrel about *justice* and injustice of the fate. Our destiny is just, because it is collective and not individual. All together form the glorious wreath of the psychological orb and fulfil the magnetic total will of their nature, in spite of many being crushed like flies and others, instead, uplifted to the sparkling stars of sublime honours and highest success. The main thing, which matters is *the ready reality of service to the whole and the regular, incessant performance of the whole vital circle*. This must be, from the general standpoint, a sufficient answer to indivdual claims, complaints, questions and doubts.

But there comes out another clear idea from this meditation. The more narrow the curves are round one theistic near centre, the greater and more disastrous is the danger of *social crushing of a part of humanity*. The more stretched and less concentric the human psychological fatal spheric curves are, the less the trend to destruction, with intolerant distinction and discrimination, of one part of humanity, in favor of the other half profiting by their ruin. Theoretically justice and happiness of the individual is guaranteed by the most stretched curve. The intellectual justice is rightly represented by the absolutely straight line, which parts a whole amount into two equal halves, but which we never can reach because it would be the death of the root of our biological vitality. The narrow curves make for exclusive and sharp one-sided conceptions. We easily see the confirmation of this truth in looking around in the world and history. The strong and narrow theistic one-sidedness is always likely to crush the larger portion of the population in favor of a small selected and privileged part, whilst the strong intellectual commonwealths prove practically much more to produce equality and democratic, social living possibility for all their children. In this connection we easily understand that the *socialistic* tendencies of to-day have a pronounced aversion to narrow theistic concentration and that theistic conceptions and *monarchic* predilections and tastes are ordinarily connected.

In spite of the fact that *miracles* are concentrative explosive helps and accelerate the human theistic performances, we have to consider some other ideas important in this regard. Principally we really would wish that there would be only one terminal symbolic attitude of the psychological function, at the end of the logical work, when the individual discharges his life-force from the last symbolic concentration of the simplest notions of truth, beauty, strength and love. The miracles outside of the area of these last ones are premature affective idealistic knots, which likely produce as well too early delightful fixations and impede, in this manner, the strong progression of the life-force toward the last idealistic goals. The miraculous psychological "bomb-shells" are expected to explode at the terminal idealistic stations and aims, after having been charged with the peripheric life-force. But often they do not explode at all, and then the individual is fixed by them because they are retained rather outside the terminal centre. The individual life-force once engaged and fixed by the symbolic mysticism will easily be infatuated with the attractive splendour of their beauty and strength, and it often happens, therefore, that the idealistic, progressing, accelerating intention of the symbolism, mysticism and miracle has the contrary practical effect, the checking peripheric fixation and the luxuriant infatuation, within their insufficient values. Like children, if they hear amusing fairy tales, become fond of, and prefer, them by far to the more serious and drier stories of the practical life, loving the *fairy tales* because of their charming circumstances and never failing success, and not caring about their deeper sense and higher intentions—unfortunately, many grown up people seem to do in enjoying the symbolic and mystic beauty of their poetical ceremoniuos religion. They are pleased to satisfaction with the traditional dignified mystic charms and have not any need to develop them to the last and absolute divine symbols of truth, love, beauty and strength, wherefor they stand.

Many people are always very ready, and we all are at least in our young imaginative days curious to know, if miracles ever happened or could happen. But this question is not so interesting as it seems at first sight, to the well educated and directed. It is perhaps just objectionable to be inclined to such extraordinary thrills in the practical life. We gladly will admit the reality of miracles, if we can find them philosophically possible and understandable. What interests most in miracles, are the questions: In what do they consist? Which are their psycho-dynamic laws? What are their advantages and dangers? Are they, therefore, desirable or not? We spoke now many things about the psychological nature of miracles and mysticism and their relations, permitting answers to these questions.

In every case we know now that the symbolic mysticism and miracles are the quickening concentrating helps of the necessary, psychodynamic divine performance, that they are a case of emergency, in order to save the intellectual part of our life-force, which then instead can be used for the sentimental angry miraculous energy, that mysticism and miracle are making for anger and angry slothfulness, that they are roughening the spiritually well gifted by strong sensorial magnetic impressions and jerks and that they fix easily that type on peripheric lazy luxuriance. They are so more desirable and useful, of course, for the spiritually ungifted who, as the consequence of his lack of genius, will likely misinterpret them. There are many disadvantages and dangers of the miracles which so easily replace our steering and working, intellectual thinking by drifting, uncritical faith, in a higher degree than it is necessary. In general, therefore, without declining entirely the psychodynamic necessity of the symbolic miracle as a possible case of helping psycho-mechanic function toward important divine goals, we look to them as undesirable. We all would be glad, for educational reasons, if we could dispense with them more and more, in all stages of miraculous performances excepting the most central and most lasting necessary human symbolic miracles , the sparkling stars of divine love, of charming beauty, of idealistic enthusiastic strength and the most simplified important truth. These notions are our last human and natural symbols and most admirable and reliable bright miracles. They are so desirable, useful and welcome to us as all others are felt humiliating and troublesome. But still our nature has reason to be humble.

THE PRAYER has the intention to suggest the direct and strong connection with the eternal ideals, with exclusion and at the expense of the peripheric reality. Sin and sorrow, pain and passion are such undesirable peripheric notions, from which the praying individual tries to get rid, again and again, in the way of using the law of compensation. His attention is fixedly directed toward the highest ideal of the Divinity, touching the peripheric reality only superficially and as the starting point, fringing only the sharp and threatening details of life and throwing instead easily and comprisingly all affective life- force into the abyss of delightful divine hope and consolation. Prayer is the strong and intended conversion and the expression of the pronounced desire of the individual toward idealism. It belongs, like the symbols, to the accelerating mystic means of the psycho-dynamic progression, representing the affective suggestive, sentimental, non intellectual approach to God.

The reasoning, almost *intellectual prayer* entering a little more into causality, is sometimes to be found in the modern denominational Christian conceptions. But generally and essentially we meet the *stereotypical formalism* of the prayer, heavy with mysticism and being little concerned with the reasoning detail of the intellectual world. It represents the most pronounced expression of our strongest will and desire for uplifting happiness. We use the strength of our affective concentrative will as an emergent help for our way to the divine goal, because our life-force, extended simultaneously to the intellectual surface, could not reach to the depth of the charming universal ocean. Our intellectuality is not able to go to the divine aims and we must, therefore, try to do it with our affective heart, at the expense of our intellectual gift, which cannot be permitted to take away one part of our life-force unless we may risk that the concentrating affective power of the prayer could not reach energeticly its divine goal. For the most affective prayer exacts the compensatory exclusion of the logical intellectual light-field, and it is the comfortable formula of the prayer with its "old-fashioned" character and its symbolic effect, from which the resting and quiet soul is able to reach the eternal goal, as from a ready spring-board.

The prayer is the most energetic symbolic, mystic-miraculous expression of the Christian and of any religion. It is the practical application of all the symbolic methods given before. They altogether pla⸗ the role of the symbolic education leading up to the facilitation of the final and most successful individual symbolism in the prayer. The prayer is the concluding, topmost station of the skilful symbolic mysticism. It is even the concentrated reward of the mystic action, by giving to the individual indeed the deliverance from the widespread ordinary daily life and broad intellectual light-circle with its peripheric entanglement of sorrow, suffering and painful distraction. Prayer is essentially the greatest miracle itself, in comparison to which all others are only a previous, inferior, methodical school. Prayer exacts from the individual the most bold miraculous leap from the extremely peripheric, sharply distinct and deficiently miserable detailed life toward the very central and smallest symbolic notions of *Faith, Hope and Love*. It is the duty of the believer to concentrate instantly his widely divergent intellectual outlook to the punctual, small, but brillant notions of this last, idealistic-symbolical station. This angry uplifting elevation of the soul toward heaven, this concentrating affective necessity to point and discharge all psychic energy at once from the huge, really enlarged light-field into the most compressed symbolic notions of hope, love and confidence, presuppose the most skilful practice in idealistic, affective shooting, and the symbolic mysticism and miracles are to be considered as a theoretical exercise for the good practice of the praying action. It is not so easy to hit the small symbolic points of idealistic hope and love, which, however, look at us with the inviting distinctiveness of sparkling mirrors reflecting the sunshine. It is rather difficult to establish at once the perfect congurity between our rapid affective contraction and the small size of the notional little points. The contradiction between the rough peripheric ruthlessness and the smoothing concentric charm of the divine values is too obvious than that the almost instantaneous necessary adaptation to the very remote divine notional symbols could be done easily and unfailingly without continuous exercise and without the danger to miss ever the idealistic bull's eye.

The efficient praying individual is, therefore, the mystic who is fond of, and very familiar with, the miraculous temperament of religion. He must have the right educational culture and schooling in order to be the surest and most able idealistic shot, and he has to have the most apt instrumental helps, if he will reach quickly the central theistic symbols. For the mystically unlearned the intellectual prayer is more successful. Prayer and all symbolism are in closest connection. They stick so unseparably to one another that we likely meet them altogether or none of them. As soon as one of them is scorned and despised, the other one has the same fate, and as soon as one of them is respected, the other will gain in authority too. All these methods reject the intellectual process toward idealism; they all advance by the affective suggestion which excludes the logical steps of the human reason and soars instead to heaven with the symbolic and mystic help of the imaginative affective desire, giving to the believing individual the miraculous fulfilment of his wishes, as soon as he leaves all real doubt and grasps with burning sentimental confidence and attentive effort the eternal ideals.

The prayer is the accomplishing act of the religious apparatus, its psychological masterpiece, its most refined and most desired purpose, the chief terminal-ideal discharge of the affective human force, the last intention of all religious symbolic, mystic, artistic and ceremonious ecclesiastic institutions and principles. They all have their justification in the prayer being of high psychological hygienic value, so much so that the welfare of the individual is most dependent on his rich and energetic affective discharge.

The prayer has the intention to eliminate the real sorrow of our daily life as much as possible, through its terminal ideal suggestion. The affective force of the individual in its intimate totality is hurled energetically toward the terminal idealism, and this process produces compensatorily, according to the limited total strength of the individual, the necessary alteration and the detailed blurring of the surface of the objective light-field. In the moment of his most urgent distress, the praying individual receives, through this, two advantages at the same time: first the deliverance and the deflection from the disagreeably vexing and tormenting difficulties of the real life, which perhaps will have improved or disappeared already after some hours, by the running, ever changing, objective metamorphosis of the human fate so that, as a matter of fact, we have gained or saved time in a most urgent case of psychological emergency. Second we have at the same time the strong affective conversion to God the strong source of all directive energy, from which the courage and the confidence will be drawn for the possibility of the necessary rearrangement and logical intercalation of the intellectual superficial objects which are the reason of unhappy confusion and sorry disorder. So we have in the prayer the *exact causal therapy of the affective sorrows of the life.*

For the sorrows may have become insupportable, too great and too heavy for our shoulders, this coming about, because we often effuse our psychic life-force too one-sidedly or even exclusively into the large, widely divergent intellectuality, super-estimating the detailed work, and impair or lose the faculty of their logical, orderly direction, through our retreat from the terminal ideals. All these moments are instantly inversely regulated in the prayer. They are arrayed according to the harmony of their terminal psychic order, significance and direction. Proportion and distribution of the affective emphasis and use will thus be regulated very differently. After short moments of prayer, owing to compensatory self-help, the individual has attained an excellent deliverance from his previous one-sided activity. Had he first a stagnation by the circumstance that intellectuality and objectivivity were too great, too well considered and non-abductible to the realm of imagination, of the possibilities and of the terminal ideals, - so the instantaneous cure and improvement is reached by the fact that the strength of the individual terminal gift is moved more into the affective terminal ideal depth and that in this the narrow fetter of the detailed intellectuality and of the sorrows is recognized in its true significance and in its relative limitation. Through the greatness and solidity of the standpoint now attained, we receive the sufficient survey on the *relativity of our daily, sharply detailed and narrow sorrows.* The wings of our sentiments have carried us to richer and more fertile sources of joy and pleasure. Our affective river has discovered strong and comfortable capacities and feels to be exceedingly discharged, after having toiled so much before and for a long time in vain to flow into the incapable objects of the reality. This impossibility of the fluctuation of the affectivity aspired to, that is to say, the incapability and unworthiness of the visible world to accept our total life-force, is exactly characteristic for the rise of sorrows. They will be removed by that that a good affective fall can be found toward very capable different goals. The sure estimation of the different affective values will now be quickly clear to the praying individual, and in this enlightening, intimate experience consists exactly the recovery and the reactive *recreation* of the prayer. Thus the prayer is a wonderful, terminal ideal method of *vital respiration,* and, at the same time, a *relaxation,* discharging affectively, the most advantageous *climatic change* of both components of the psychic activity. A sure, essentially carefree and most happy holyday of the mental and corporeal forces, which partly before had become tired by sorrow and work, which partly were too much superseded from their functional high tasks by inferior duties and which now both are able to find easily in this praying means of the affective regulation, the harmony of their two-sided role.

So we see that for the miraculous attainment of the praying intention of the divine consolation we must sacrifice our intellectual logical exactitude. We must be able and willing to sweep our affective energy with the most elastic rapidity through the whole scale of the created universe; one angry grasp lifts the praying individual over all visible and intellectual world up to the sentimental heaven and confers on him the sparkling crown of eternal consolations and charming divine love, at the expense of the sacrificed intellectual reality excluded from contemporaneous attention. This is the goal of all religions. May the Chinese stoop before his gods! May the Mohametan kneel down on his prayer rug or mount to his minarets and recite his rosary! May the Christian pronounce his traditional or spontaneous prayers! All together prosecute the same psycho-dynamic miraculous mechanism; they exclude the peripheric sorrowful reality by their happy auto-suggestion and throw, compensatorily the largest obtainable amount of their psychic life-force toward ideal divine sentiments. They all forget real life and intellectual real necessities in the moment of their prayer and unite in the common and strong hope of humanity to escape from the detailed suffering and pain of the daily peripheric intercourse and to accept instead the rich and powerful attraction of the divine terminal symbolic unity.

The Christian prayer is characterized by its interesting *humanized symbol*. The Christians have, in their worshipping enthusiasm, so much condensed and apotheosed their genial outstanding founder and hero that his name is equal to the sweetest expressions of hope, love and confidence. They have so far progressed in the affective suggestive refinement of the name of Christ that He freely and commonly is used as the terminal human symbol of most divine simplification, that this name has become the last and most energetic ideal spring-board of the Christian believer. All Christian hopes are founded in the name of their symbolic divine hero; all Christian tendencies incline to this last divine symbolic notion, and all share the confidence that their wishes must be granted in this name. The formula: Through Jesus Christ our Lord, is the stereotypical symbolic reference, credential and trump of the praying Christian. It has become the terminal sensorial foundation of all their hopes, all their love and all their confidence. This name is for the Christian the comprising fulfilment and punctual compression, the diamond of all last and simple, most imaginative terms, and he generally runs from the terminal miraculous notion of Christ toward his conclusive universal effusion. The linguistic imaginative compression of this word is the set of his terminal cultural spell, the nearest and last door of human perfection, through which he enters into the glory of divine consolation, of the eternal hopes and of perfect happiness.

We see in the miraculous suggestive mechanism of the prayer clearly enough, how much and how generally the principle of the symbolic mysticism understood to intrude on humanity. The prayer indeed is the most general form of mysticism accepted and admitted, even there where the other forms of these "angry" affective leaps of mysticism and miracles have been excluded because of their educational doubtfulness. Prayer is the one mystic method almost universally accepted. It has more credit in humanity because of its immediate and greater practical usefulness than all other forms of the same psycho-dynamic character. It is the last combination and culmination of all mysticism; it is the practical application and the advantageous conclusion of their "angry" movements. None can compete with its human and real, healing utility.. But naturally, up to a high degree, prayer shares nevertheless, the fate of its other psychological allies. It is not at the top of its authority, to-day, and it is scorned and despised by the intellectual world of our life-quarter almost as well as any symbolism, mysticism and miracles. The draft of our time is thoroughly intellectual. All sentimental idealism, all affective rush and all feeling progression toward divine goals become short in comparison to the quiet and steady, gradual intellectual law of logical progression. Prayer too is put in the background of the choice of psychological methods of to-day. It has lost its grasping automatical fascination on the totality of our cultural age. Even prayer has become suspicious of its suggestive and symbolic character in the circles of the intellectual society. But the problem of the prayer is indeed not as simple as that speaker at Hyde-Park-Corner, remarked chuckingly:"If you pray, you pray only to yourself. Pray as much as you will, you are a fool because the only one who hears your prayer, is yourself."

The prayer is the last and most charming flower of the ages of every high sentimenal faith. It is the technique of the symbolic mysticism which has produced it, and it is only in connection with the acceptance of these suggestie laws, that it can be learned and preserve its authority and strength. Whosoever lifts his sorry heart to God, whosoever feels the necessity to discharge his sad and discouraged feelings into the consoling well of the eternal divine goals, must be willing to strip off all material and intellectual relations, to gather his total affective life-force and to throw it altogether to the divinity. The root of the successful prayer is and remains the principal inclination to leave one's intellectual predilection, to renounce one's steering logical pride and to drift instead on the mysterious boat of one's suggestive magnetism and divine surrender toward the far away dawning goals of the theistic love. The intellectual resistance and the sensorial superiority and mastery of our intellectual magnetic quarter of the spheric sun-year is the most efficient hindrance against the easy possibility of succeessful prayer. If the churches point always to the pride of humanity and exact, in the first place, dropping of the pride unless the believer risks not to arrive at the realm of his ideal fulfilling God, they mean the *sacrifice* of the logical detailed notions and of the gradual thinking intellectual precision.

We understand, therefore, easily the desertful and difficult role of the *New Church* of to-day which has received the ticklish task to make a combination of our intellectual modern thought and of the sentimental conceptions of the former times. The new church emphasizes the middle position of both opinions, sacrificing a part of the old, symbolic mystic miraculous methods, but claiming at least something of the old principles in maintaining and practising the divine prayer. We easily remark, how much in this church the prayer is approached to the modern intellectual conceptions of the life, how the language of its prayer is studded with the reasoning arguments of the human real life, how it strives to meet the objective details, to gather and discharge them finally and logically into the abyss of the consoling terminal imaginative symbols. But not even the new church is quite able to escape from the theoretical, strong and hidden suggestion which is the psychodynamic foundation of every prayer. Even here we find the limited argumentation of the peripheric detailed difficulties of the pain and of the sorrow of our life and even here we observe, how quickly and smoothly the praying divine leaves the exact discussion of the detailed obstacles, overskips the peripheric logical connections and starts energetically, with all his emphasis, toward the last and most significant notions of joy, delight, reward, consolation, hope, confidence, love and eternity: altogether nothing else than the attractive suggestive strength of symbolic idealism, which excludes the laws of our daily intellectual development, gathers the individual force in one sheaf and runs unhesitatingly toward the affective divine centralization. It is not easy to convert prayer into an intellectual expression of human nature. Our life is full of unsurmountable checking difficulties, and it is impossible, easy as it may be to suggest the totality of a believing community over the intellectual obstacles of life, to point out in every case the remedy of all sorrow and of all unhappiness. It would be an infinite enumeration of personal detailed disagreeable circumstances which we ought first to know and then only the serious efficient religious prayer could start. In every general conception of the prayer we have to restrict ourselves always to imaginative ideal notions wich are, therefore, indeed essential for the psycho-dynamic accelerating nature of the prayer. Would we start to describe the serious details of our sorrows, within the church, the checking obstacles would rise to a great power, and the church, as the mediator of the reality would rather be a difficult place of real quarrel and individual argumentation, as the outside world is, instead of the peaceful reunion of the people. Peace and reconciliation have to be expected from common general, but not from individual antagonizing interests.

The more general and mystic the tenor of the prayer is, the less is it able to meet the special circumstances of our life in an efficient way and to eliminate the different special sorrows of our life and fate. The more intellectual and adapted to our personal situation the prayer instead can be, the clerer and more special influence on our individual sorrows we have to expect. But the moving energy is then less.

The conceptions of the intellectual contents of the prayer are surprisingly different in the use of the churchs. From one extreme of the *Latin prayer* of the Catholic church, which on Good Friday disguises itself partly into Greek expressions with the artistic intention to become unintelligible morever to the educated people, we have the intellectual proceeding and augmenting graduation to the stereotypical formula of the prayer pronounced in the language of the country, as we meet it for instance in the English High Church, and to the modern spontaneous prayer, as it is practised in the freer Protestant church. The Catholic prayer in Latin and Greek which practically almost nobody understands, has the clear tendency to exclude all intellectuality, and this effect is in addition more increased through the stiff and unchanging *repetition*. The modern Protestant spontaneous prayer, as the opposite pole of this conception, on the contrary, has the intention to invite God to descent from His golden stellar tent, to enter into our houses and circumstances, of whose confusing difficulties we are the sorrowful victims and to help us from the daily and hourly unhappiness, by looking closely at, and removing, the special intellectual cause of trouble. There arises the serious question, what way may be the right to go, of these three given in our practical scale, from the Catholic stiff extreme formalism over to the intellectual spontaneous conception.

The religious mysticism, of course, will point out that the cure of our psychic and corporeal sufferings must be done by the help and the seecret suggestion of the authority and that the hidden affective influence will be able to extend to all individual needs of our life, even to the very superficial intellectual circumstances,if there is only the general strong underlying confidence and faith in God. The mystic church thinks that by the mystic prayer we will be educated to reduce our estimation of the real, superficial intellectual world, and it tries to remand us thoroughly to levelling ideal goals, so that we may have peace and deliverance from sorrow, in leaving the field of the visible intellectuality to the untired quarrelling claim of the adversary or of the disagreeable circumstances. The mystic prayer tries to teach us superior wisdom. It gives to us the affective ideal charm and happiness of the heaven and leaves instead, owing to the law of compensation, the dangerous and unhappy battle-field to the voracious opponent, avoiding the challenge offered by fate and enemy. The mystic prayer is, therfore, not at all a resolution of the troubling question,but the procrastination and the transitional flight from the entangled situation, which rises again as soon as the effect of the dreamy suggestion is reverted to the experiences of the real life and of the daily surroundings.

The reverse conception of the spontaneous prayer has the advantage to have the more detailed appeal to reality and the more direct claim of the theistic affective help. It has the intention to combine the most distant values, the eternal theistic ranges and the most pronounced and clear categories of time, space and causality. The spontaneous prayer looks to fix the ideal magnetism or the power of the directing helping God immediately to the most peripheric reality.Religious faith and divine authority are,from far away as they may be called, in the spontaneous prayer adapted to the small daily circumstances, as it ought to be, but the extreme distances of these two goals of magnetic standards, put immediately together, often turn out to be too bold, often react like contradictions, like hissing water touched with fire. This method is audacious and dangerous, but it contains the nucleus of that what we must claim and hope for, if we seriously will have any direct utility and practical success in a given distress, from the divine interference. If God exists and lives and likes us, then He must indeed enter into our most intimate needs and help us in all our sorrows; we are not satisfied with the far-away universal theism. We claim a loving, a near and a helping God who sees and meets us in, all our special occurring distress as well, as we will be His faithful servants in His intellectual real commandments.

Without a clear, determined application and meaning of the prayer ,on one side, there can be scarcely any strong will and intention. But, on the other side, the good prayer cannot cling either too much to the real detail of our experience. All intellectual circumstances are a very accidental factor and quickly changing, and it would be as wrong to elevate them to the absolute significance of eternity as it would be dangerous to accept the absolute, mystic standpoint of the fatalistic negligence of the intellectual reality. The extreme mystic procrastiation of the troubles of our daily life proves of course discouragement and lack of initiative, and any act of slothfulness, as we know, will be retrieved by the following lightning of the anger; yet the hasty appeal to the most distant eternal values, in connection with our small daily affairs, is surely as much imperfect. The incongruity of the last idealism and the small daily intellectual categoric circumstances will be too noticeable and the disappointment in this connection too probable than not to be more a hurting and despairing than a helping enterprise.

We never should try to escape from sorrow in a direct way. It is already much better to find out, how to run away from insupportable circumstances. Our prayer ought to be rather careful in the precision of our wishes. It never should lose entirely the connection with the universe. We should prefer to wish most solid and eternal things, most unchangeable and most lasting values which we need naturally, and not such which by our own will we drop already the next day or the next week. The outlook into the universe makes our prayer very large and impersonal and our attachment to present real values very reserved. Indeed this form of prayer has the thorough and unchangeable solidity .which promises to be wise in the everlasting sense, most precious for the potential emphasis of our life and human nature. But on the other hand, at every point we have to avoid the mystic compensatory retreat and the complete affective negligence of the real world, as it is given in the highest degree of the symbolic unintelligible prayer. Prayer never ought to be allowed to be the help or the means to escape entirely from the real world or to forget the real working duties of life completely. For sorrows are only the shadows of the necessary intellectual works and tasks which must be developed by our energy. If prayer is not able to solve our difficulties, if it rather more paralyzes our real aggressive energy and leads us astray from the real duties which life has givon to us, by imaginative deception and suggestive procrastination, then we dispense much better with that prayer which is not good.

The law of compensation plays a fatal role in the mystic prayer. Exactly here the withdrawal of the vital force from the real and intellectual life often turns out to make the difficulties much worse than they were before. The intellectual atmosphere of the individual is intoxicated by the suggestive narcotics of the mystic elements, but afterwards the imaginative deception likely must be paid by real and objective loss. Our circumstances of time, space and causality follow their running laws even during the time of our idealistic dreams, and we shall have to pay all deceptions and misconceptions of the objective reality, when we go back to our work. But subjectively, however, we may be recreated and instigated and so much more able to overcome the difficulties which we could not solve before our praying digression.

So we know that even in praying the good way is in the middle, - at the balance of good human real-idealism. Praying in its nature is and remains essentially concentrative. It is to say, it has to have the principal characteristics of the symbolism, miracle and mysticism. The faithful prayer may remove mountains, if our faith is strong enough, says the scipture, and rightly means that we, in our idealistic, compensatory, affective concentration, move away ourselves from the mountains or the intellectual categories of time, space and causality. Then, if we have taken away all attention of the life-force from reality, it will no longer matter to us, if the mountains are here or there, because to the burning affective love of the faithful praying individual the intellectual localization can impossibly play an important role. The interest in the reality is exhausted by the zealous power of faith and love, when the eternal attractiveness had carried away the individual forces to the outside universe. But what happens with the intellectual reality? This is the way to remove mountains: going away from them. The mountains are objectively still at the same place, but subjectively we are rid of their impeding influence, because we ourselves have resorted to the distant idealistic goals. And yet, after all we live nevertheless in the real world. We cannot always go away from the mountains, and we cannot stay for ever far from objective difficulties. The troublesome work and the tasks of our life will come back with their full weight. We at length are not willing and not able to close our eyes continuously to the sensorial reality of the intellectual laws. It is so easily understandable ,though criticized by many as shame and cowardice, that one likes to retire from any difficult case of our inteltuality to the refuge or ambush of our idealism, and we soon experience that fate drives us out again from the hidden corner of our sentimentality, and that we have to descend once more into the struggling life of the reality, having the necessity to meet new intellectual work and to solve, moreover, the former duties procrastinated by the earlier idealistic retirement, as we have reached it in the mystic prayer. But at the moment of the return of the idealist from his former retirement we may learn that he indeed is able, sometimes, to remove real mountains, as it were. He has the sharpest sword, the most piercing spears and the strongest arm, when he is refreshed and recommences his realistic work.

The temporary deliverance from the hustling, crushing and using reality is doubtless necessary and useful for our psychic constitution. The idealistic digressions are hygienic for our psychic health, but they have only the permission to fulfil this transitional recreative task, not to guide us astray into the ideal "lazy" realm, continually and for a long time. We must go back again and again to the abandoned mountains of the real hindrances, we must try every day and most frequently to move and heave the stone of Sysiphos, which rolls so easily down hill, and which we are never permitted to leave quietly in the bottom of the valley, ourselves going to take the unchecked walks up to the lofty hills of the comfortable idealism.

In spite of all we maintain that in its effect prayer is even a strong real power and more things are achieved by prayer than we think. This is true as well because of the following reasons. The prayer has the faculty to put the individual force into the frame of a large outlook. The praying individual looks at his sorrows, which seemed at the immediate vicinity so great and threatening, from a far-away elevated stand-point, and he is, therefore, in a position to judge much more freely, independently and, therefore, courageously about his personal, almost negligible troubles and checking circumstances. The magnetic power of the prayer, in addition, has more or less an indirect influence on the real entanglement; the logical disposition may be, in many ways, improved by the directing force of the prayer. Things and circumstances are continually changing, and the time gained by the idealistic retreat may be, casually in many cases, just the time necessary for the automatic agreeable change of the real objectivity. The prayer moreover has, by its idealistic magnetic power, the peculiarity to impart to the praying individual an attractive optimistic charm, to put a stronger connection with the universal intentions and to establish a stronger magnetic parallelism with the other, successful universal wills and fellow-men prosecuting the same goals. The praying individual leaves his troublesome isolation and enters into the closest communication with the other forces and persons of the same affective directions. The postulated union of the Saints must be understood under this common point of view. All parallel tendencies of the same universal direction form one strong, affective magnetic, mutually attractive and helping unity.

Poeple characterize themselves by the manner of their prayer. The narrow egotist who puts his personal wishes into the centre of the universe, who is not able to join the highest purposes of the universe and to subordinate his personal narrow fate, prays in the most determined, claiming manner. Only the perfect genius could risk to identify his personal wishes with the will of the theistic centre without hurting the intentions of the interspheric fate by his intruding personal insignificance, without being narrow, audacious and inconsiderate. But just the highest genius is always least ambitious of his personal acknowledgement, having his strong personal fixation in his universal affective intimacy and friendship, as we see in the Lord's prayer of Christ. A genial individual is sure enough of himself and of his attachment to the divinity, that he easily can stand to be neglected by other people. Everybody else would have to change and correct his praying wishes continually, almost every day, because all personal and sharply intellectual needs and wishes are in a flowing incessant alteration. The utmost pronounced intellectuality in praying would, therefore, be a frivolous enterprise. The average individual has much reason to be selfconscious enough of his own intelligence not to emphasize too thoroughly his present needs and inclinations and to be hesitating about his own personal urges which so often turned out to be more hurt- than useful. The wishes of the moment change usually so quickly afterwards. Besides we will not forget that fulfilment has always the bitter possibility and even biological necessity of disappointment, and praying, on the contrary, in itself is the delightful expecting hope. The most lasting prayer and the wisest aspiration of humanity is always that trustful prayer which is very general and freed from momentary individual moods and atmosphere: "Thy will be done!" The most essential prayer is that which is able to detach the individual thoroughly from the individual peripheric fixation and to give to him wishes directed toward the unchanging intentions of the super-individual common needs of the magnetic universe. Everybody has his personal needs, but nobody is entitled to lose or postpone the purposes of the broadest creative community which will live a longer time and have a more important fate than all his most burning personal desires and all his most ardent and urgent individual distress and sorrow.

Doubtless the *Lord's prayer,* as it was taught by Christ, according to the gospels, and as it is literally accepted by all Christian denominations, is a masterpiece of the clever and balanced conception of the human relations to the universe, especially in the first part. It maintains the general necessity of our physiological needs, but does not emphasize too much the individual detail. It looks at our momentary necessities in a broad way, but respects more the magnetic will of highest and ultimate goals. The first part of this prayer is undiscussedly the most perfect and most valuable form of prayer which could be used by everybody respecting both his individual needs and the universal will of the progressive magnetic divinity.

It is in the second part, where we have some difficulties to understand. Is it not too anthropo-centric, if we ask God to forgive us our trespasses *as* we forgive those who trespassed against us? The comparing intimacy in the words as, sicut, hos, seems too familiar with the idea of God. If we ask God to forgive us as much as we forgive our offenders, this means that we ask Him to be even less magnanimous than the church expects us to be in exacting that we have to love the enemies. In this comparison we hint that God may punish us for our unforgiveness and that we would like if God would take a measure and a scale for His magnanimity from our own human previous readiness to pardon. Is it not wrong to approach God in this assuming way, and is it not conceit on our part, if we have the courage to establish our forgiveness as an example and a limitation of the divine love for the world and for our individual wickedness ? But just here we discover a strong educational insistence introduced in the human heart, and there is an intimate causal nexus between our human behaviour and our universal success. The condition to be happy and free in your conscience, is to resign deliberately any claim for revenge!

The prayer, not to induce us in temptation, is a further more difficult passage of theLord's prayer. We have here in the shortest way the confession of the dualistic conception of the world. The divine hero touches here the most ticklish problem of his God. He becomes in these words, carefully as they are expressed, the witness of the limitation of the absolute will of the historic theistic God, as he understands him, and he admits that our life and our fate are often subjected to the unintelligible contradictions with the affective terminal will-power, experienced in sin, evil and unhappiness.

In this prayer the religious founder would like the human fate to be put in more intimate absolute connections, to bring a more consecutive power into the world, so that mankind could not be thrown into different contradictory inclinations and circumstances leading astray. In saying:"But deliver us from evil!" he admits that human life practically is entangled in *evils*. The evil has the meaning that the human life, in its intellectual real side, often is not in congruity with the absolute idea of God. His theoretical God is not in perfect congruity with the practical fate of our daily life; how often is it impossible to make the logical connection between the opposite extremes of the human lot and of the last divine theistic goals which he bequeathes to us. He admits that there are powers and circumstances which we cannot understand from the theistic religious standpoint, and that it is desirable to look for a more universal and absolute conception which could help us better in explaining and directing our troublesome life and the last goals into more logical connection. In this prayer he is longing for a correction and progressive settling of the remaining dark spots and shadows of the human thought and experience, and with this impressive appeal to the most enlarged divinity of universal love he concludes the Lord's prayer.

How should we pray? This is the exact question which was put to Christ and which He answered in such masterful a way. Prayer is one of the concentrating symbolic and mystic actions of the religious life. But according to the human, real-idealistic disposition and the great danger coming as well from the strong idealistic as from the exclusive, nearly intellectual conception of prayer, we ought to strive to have also here the tendency to maintain our middle balance of real-idealism. We must strive to reach the last divine goals, to save the utmost amount of life-force for our magnetic terminal ranges, but we must as well be careful not to succomb to the dreamy unreality of extreme sentimentality.

God, give to me the force to wish thy last intention, to join the magnetic terminal purposes of the universe in perfect harmony with thy will and the possibility of my existence! Attract the divine sparkle of my personal disposition toward the most important inclinations of thy proceeding spheric energy! But do not blind me by the brilliance of thy greatness! Do not fetter or weaken my intellectuality so much by the fascination of thy magnetic affective strength that I lose the reasonable intellectual determination of my earthly lot! I will not become the affective laughing-stock of the intellectual humanity. I will not be the administrator of only one of both components of my nature, but of my intellectual real visible part as well as of my affective uplifting tendencies. Since a am born a man, I like to be a man. Because I have inherited the real urges of the earth, I will accomplish and obey them. As long as l am a man I will live on the earth being a logical and possessing individual and not flying away with the wings of one-sided idealism. I do not wish to lose the prospects of the real life. I desire to be fixed, with my eyes, on my earthly existence and on my daily real experience which I will thoroughly. Do not permit that my earthly lot be a prey on my affective nature! Do not allow that my heart is too far away from my necessary individual intellectual interest and necessity! For I am afraid I could lose all my human historic resistance and individual significant stability and not fulfil the real role which has been given to me by being a man. Preserve me, oh Lord, from burning my ideal wings and falling down to the abyss of disappointment and embitterment, but deign to let me live in benevolent, yet serious optimism for ever.

We may conscider that beside the concentrating actions of the miracle, mysticism, symbolism and prayer there are other homologous helps toward the same goal, facilitating and quickening, in an "angry" manner, the affective delight of our soul. In our book"The Affectivity of the Muscular Life" we pointed out that the concentrations of the muscles are *parallel physiological actions* of the body, going themselves from distension to concentration or tension, accompanying or augmenting in the same sense the concentric action of the soul, as in the reverse sense muscular contraction may be always produced by the affective sentimental concentration of the soul.

Without developing the principles of our *"Affectivity of the Muscles"* we remember that there are two groups of muscles in our body, the *intellectual-linear* and the *affective-circular group*. It is especially the last group which influences, and is affected by, our feelings in the concentrative sense. The circular function of the muscles recalls exactly the theoretically postulated organization and function of our psychopupilar mental disposition. We find the circular muscles everywhere in the inner parts of our body, above all in the bowels, in the chest, in the lungs, in the heart and in the throat, and very pronouncedly in the uro-genital system. All these functions are in immediate connection with the affective psychological action, and they themselves are in a position, in their turn, to exercise also a very energetic influence on the sentimental function of our soul.

Having hinted to this interesting chapter of human life, let us, in this connection, only speak of some powerful physiological factors which psychology and religion use continually for strong psychodynamic purposes.

The most efficient circular muscular help for the concentrative affective action of our soul is WEEPING. It is rightly put into this group, because the muscles of the mimic face belong embryologically to the circular affective ones and must be conceived, even to-day, as one circular muscular unity, in their function, in spite of having been divided, in the later development, into many separated linear and intellectual muscles. Their function, however, remains the same as before. They altogether perform the circular total function of former phylogenetic times, contracting in the affective and relaxing in the intellectual phase of the soul. Weeping is a strong help for the affective concentration of the soul. Religion makes a very frequent use of the circular muscular function, suggesting and strengthening the psychic effect. Everywhere in the church, in the religious poetry even more than in any other one, in the description of the passion of Christ we always observe the strong artificial help of hot tears toward the theistic concentric goal. The divine function and psychology are full of weeping inclinations and tearful urges, and religion has always a strong allegiance and successful union with weeping.

In a sense, weeping is a further instance of psychological, mystic symbolical emergency. It is based again on the disproportion of our wishes and our reality. Weeping is a confession of the real shortcoming toward the highest idealistic goal. The tears replace the physiological insufficiency. They quicken and strengthen the affective contraction of the soul, and they help, in a sensorial physiological way, to *complete and augment the psycho-mechanic energy, which by personal, objective intellectual circumstances was checked.*

The religious individual is educated to have a quite disproportioned longing toward the eternal goals. He wishes for things which are very far from him and are difficult to be reached. It is against this terminal helplessness, that the artificial and physiological production of tears is directed. As long as we shall have strong divine affective goals surpassing our personal capabilities, we shall have tears furthering toward these goals, and as soon as we limit our wishes to the trend of our natural possibilities, all tears will be wiped away. Religion is, therefore, the source of the most profuse and sincere tears. Religion needs tears for its distant sentimental goals; religion produces artificial groups of glittering tears in order to use their lights as direction in the shuddering darkness of universal distances. They are a successful help for strong idealistic concentration. The sentimental religion needs the quickening escort of this accelerating natural muscular, exemplary concentration. If nature is at a loss to lift the insufficient individual soul up to the highest success to cross the universe and embrace the most distant stars, because of lack of energy and courage, then the physiological support of the tears gives to our affective imagination new sensorial wings, and we soar to highest goals in the sentiments of our hearts. We are charmed with the eternal meaningless symbolic beauty of the tearful diamonds of our eyes, if nature or fate will not permit us to go on toward the tremendous ranges of our ambitious religious wishes and claims. The tear is the spell which makes unexpected possibilities of connections between our narrow life-force and the most distant idealistic goals. It is another form of the mystic miracle giving to nature the possibility of momentaneous grasping of the most desired objects of our checked need of affective progression. The tears indeed fulfil our most ambitious desires. They, after all, carry us away over all the clouds of reality and, in one bold leap, hurl our psychic life-force into the most elevated and ordinarily inaccessible realm of delightful happiness and consolation. The rain-bow of sweetest divine love shines through every tearful rain. The goals which we thought were not amenable at all to our life-force and which were completely hidden as behind gray clouds, owing to the present circumstances of our life, appear like the triumphant sunshine after a morning storm and lovely gild and smile through the wonderful sprinkling and sparkling beauty of the tears.

It is, therefore, religion which produces tears because of the disproportion of its goals, and it is, on the other hand, just the intellectual character of our time, which is most able to wipe tears away. The intellectual culture offers goals to human life-force, which are reachable by its understanding faculty and which, in every case, never exact such an enormous extreme effort of affective concentrative energy. So we understand, because of the essentially concentrative "miraculous" eliptic substitution of the tears, that indeed the religious affective tendency needs urgently weeping, that weeping is an indispensable and ubiquitous escort of religious feelings and conceptions, whereas, on the contrary, the psycho-dynamic comfortable trend and progression of the intellectual character is in a position to move unto its goals without the symbolic help of weeping.

There will be of course always tears as long as the human intelligence limits itself to the real values of earth and as long as the human heart wishes to embrace conceitedly the whole universe. The disproportion between these two values and functions will produce again and again the charming miracles of psycho-dynamic tears, but they will diminish in the degree as we find out a better dynamic condition and relation between heart and reason, sentiments and logic. Our modern culture has this tendency: it enlarges our intelligence into the outside universe and pulls, at the same time, the universal sentiments into the confinement of our earthly life in order that we are able to mingle our two essential psychic faculties, reasoning and sentiments, in a more appropriate and less disproportioned manner. We should strive that all our intellectuality receives some touch of a warm affective reverence and, at the same time, that all our highest sentimental flight never misses the intellectual, precise, imaginable formula of our real-intellectual nature. If we are able to reach this point, to restrain our needs and wishes to this possible human, balanced measure, then our tears will dry almost entirely one day. We already observed that tears in our days have become exceedingly rare; the intellectual quarter of human fate will be and was always very scarce in tears, and this in spite or just because of the strongly neglected concentrative action. The reason is this, that the sentimental eternal goals are, as it were, hidden in clouds and that human nature, during this period, is not exposed at all so clearly and sharply to the sunshine of the magnetic influence of the theistic attraction. It is the sharply dazzling beauty of the terminal idealism and the exposure to its unweakened attraction, which causes the tears in our eyes, in a similar way, if it is permitted to exemplify with smallest things, as the sharp influence of onions irritating our eyes, if we are very near, and losing their tearful influence, as soon as we move further away. During the intellectual quarter we are and go further away from the theistic established centre and lose, therefore, our tears. In approaching it, on the contrary, during the sentimental quarter, we instead begin to weep again, excited by the heartrending attractibility of the nearer and more recognizable central theistic beauty and strength. Sentimental approaching produces tears and intellectual removal wipes tears away. The higher claim for energetic theistic progression needs the help of the tears; the modest theistic reservedness of the intellectual life, on the contrary, is able to go to its reasonable goal in time with the logical development, without the symbolical need of the angry tears.

As long as the earth will be one grain of dust in the infinite universe, tears will be always with us, or rather, as long as we have the ambitious longing to shoot through all universe with the sharp arrows of our burning desires, in spite of being bound and restricted to earth and its visibility and intellectuality, the most shaking and moaning tears will never cease. Our unrestricted wishes and desires are the reason of our tears. The most satisfied historic period and nation, the most contented man is always that who knows to restrict his wishes. The modern modesty of intellectual conceptions has almost entirely succeeded in wiping away all human tears. Our social life in the cultural intellectual states has received generally the expression of most moderate serenity, because the atmosphere of the time has become intellectual. It has lost the intemperate and greedy, angry methods of the affectivity of the sentimental periods. It is farther away from the uncovered theistic magnetism and is able, therefore, to unfold everything within the rhythmic regulation of the clearest development, dispensing almost entirely with the helping supports of symbolism, mysticism, miracles and tears. So during intellectual ages tears dry up automatically, just as sentimental affective times produce them. The affective age needs them and is fond of their glittering sparks, using them always again preferably, whilst tears become useless and senseless during intellectual times and are liable to be scorned, abhorred and even hated as well as miracles and mysticism.

Every intellectual time claims the stolid rhythm of detailed, logical performance and despises all angry leaps of symbolical methods. It is the countable, visible real merit which is only appreciated in the eyes of the intellectual time, and it is owing to its pronounced logical emphasis and to its aversion against any dropping angry method, that in ages like ours the performances of miracles and tears have lost their credit almost entirely.

And yet, there is something very deep, noble and even sublime in tears, inspiring awe to anybody. Tears have a sure and unmistakable alliance with heaven, so much so that everybody is compelled by tears to a reverent behaviour. The sparkling shine of a tear has the effect of a lightning going to the deepest bottom of our heart and moving it to the most distant divine goals. Nobody can resist a tear, in a certain sense. The disarmement by tears is the quickest and most complete. The most ruthless accuser becomes silent, looking at tears. The tear is the altar, where the unhappy criminal looks for his salvation, where the misery-stricken individual clings to consolation, pardon and hope, where the religious enthusiastic people look for the fulfilment of their highest wishes, where the lazy idealist expresses, because of his angry slothfulness, the desire to have the release of his real, logical debts and duties. He will go very far in the realm of the supra-experimental universe. But he is not able to make all logical realistic steps without losing his affective energy long before the goal, or stumbling and falling on the way, and , therefore, in the burning desire to go there, he sheds the tears of divine desire. And how interesting! The tears give him the charming imaginative spell indeed, they carry him away like energetic wings over all realistic checking logical rythm and help him to overcome the extraordinary long fingerboard of the universal standards so that he reaches easily and completely his goal and desire, in this act. Here we have a striking illustration of the idea :"Seek and ye shall find! Ask and ye shall receive! Knock and it shall be opened unto you!" But ask seriously, thoroughly and with burning tears of your contrited heart! Then you are sure that in this act itself the divinity will open its heaven and smile,with indescribable sweetness, on your longing face. The bliss of divine eternity looked on all tears ever shed by beggar or criminal in the most miserable dark recess. The boundless beauty, love, happiness, pardon and reconciliation of God are sparkling in every sincere tear.

So the symbolic function of tears helps the human insufficiency in its theistic need always, as soon as it is necessary. The impressive and pitying effect of the peripheric real entanglement of the passion of Christ is energetically moved to the central theistic sentimentality, by the means of the tears. The tears come about most efficiently there, where the peripheric intricacy is most obvious and the terminal will and goal still stronger. Is not the tear the sweat of the spiritual effort? There is a psychic simularity with the humorous laughing, as we shall see. The hymns of the somehow more intellectual methods of the new church are still full of pitying imaginations and comparisons, and it is again by this means of the charming tears, that the more really reserved Protestant is thrown into the lap of the central Divinity, where he would have so much difficulty to proceed without, because of his reasoning mind. The whole atmosphere of the finest parts of the scriptures swims in a hidden weeping sentimentality, and Christ Himself is desribed as shedding tears, when He is most efficiently willing to accelerate our life-force to heaven or where the resistent reality will not submit readily to His high divine aspiration.

There are other muscular functions which help to reach more easily our theistic goals. Laughing, singing, dancing, the sexual performances are all able to idealize our life and accelerate our specific affective progression toward the divine. SINGING has the advantage to combine the concentrative circular muscular action with the *artistic laws of progression* and has,in this manner, the precious peculiarity to emphasize and accelerate the human idealistic gift and to regulate its rhythmic progression, by the harmonizing effect of the artistic measures. Singing is, therefore, the most apt and the rightly favored means for supporting the human idealistic action, giving, on one side, strong miraculous urges to hurl the affective force toward the idealistic scope and retaining it, on the other hand and at the same time, by the modulations of the artistic technicalities. The singing people are helped to central attention without succombing to the danger of angry immoderate mysticism. They receive strong concentric impulses by the peculiar circular-muscular emphasis and instigation and have at the same time a sure guidance within the real logical way of progression, owing to the modulating artistic law. So we meet in all religious services the large use of singing in order to reach the idealistic goal. Singing belongs to the group of *artistic* helps, and there we shall have to speak again about the quite peculiar useful collaboration which the human performance receives from this precious idealizing life-well. In every case we learned from this meditation on singing, that it is above all the *general popular song,* which must be efficient, because the individual muscular performance is an essential help for everybody in order to receive the personal *organic idealizing instigation,* which is given in the performance of all circular-muscular action as a possible suggestion. This form of the divine suggestion is stronger than the mere passive influence by listening to the artist. It is the waving progressive oscillation and contraction of our own circular-muscular corporeal organization, which has a more efficient uplifting influence on our idealistic possibility than the best and most attractive artistic suggestion from outside. He who had not enough opportunity to find out this truth by himself, has missed unretrievable happy hours. The best effects have always their roots in the deep need and collaboration of our own physiological, biological nature, and we have most guarantee to soar in an unfailing way to the idealistic goals, if we succeed in moving our whole corporeal disposition in an analogous way, by its most appropriate organization. It is indeed efficient to listen to the idealstic songs in a passive receptive way, but it is of much higher educational value to perform them ourselves and to impart the progressive waves of art not only to our ear and *heart,* but also to the sensitive movability of our circular and linear vibrating muscles. If we understand to inspire and idealize our physiological nature toward the intentions of the mind, then we have more good prospects to reach in a passionate and efficient sway the intended idealistic centre and, at the same time, to receive the harmony between physiological will and idealistic purposes.

In connection with this consideration we realize the idea of the ancient and many contemporary religions to look at DANCING as at a religious function and to introduce it in the religious services. Remote as our present conceptions and tastes are from this statement, we should like to ask, whether dancing could not be a most successful idealistic help, if it is done in a most aesthetic , artistic and serious manner? The totality of quick muscular movements, as they are done in artistic dancing with dignified harmony, represents again a circular progressive, contracting action and has, up to a certain limit, a strong idealizing power of suggestion. No sooner dancing is done in a less perfect manner than it relapses to the sexual idealism; but the very excellent dancing, as we are able to see it sometimes in great artists, swings our admiring sentiments instantly up to the highest terminal love of the source of the universe. If we are able to gather our idealistic performances from the very periphery of our muscular, nervous and sensorial life, if we succeed in associating our peripheric intellectual functions with our concentric idealistic natural tendencies, in order to help and support instead of checking them, then we have received the almost guarantee and utmost facilitation to reach our idealistic intentions. From the educational standpoint this problem may be of very great importance. If our muscular and physiological natural disposition is put in rhythmical idealistic harmony with, and serves faithfully, our highest and purest universal longings and tasks, then the resulting achieving amalgamation of both idealistic and realistic component of our life-force may have the best and lasting idealistic-real influence on our life.

Our time has good views, if it is willing to idealize our real-intellectual functions, in an artistic way and if it, at the same time, has the tendency to lower our idealistic visions in so far in their universal reach that their goal will be more attainable than before. If we have ensured simultaneously easy idealizing possibilities of our real functions and a more approachable terminal desire, then the extraordinary tensions of our psychic action cease, and we shall be more able to do away with all symbolic and angry mysticism and weeping. Perhaps it is more important to search our idealistic help from reality in the natural muscular performances, than we think. And at the same time we can have the best real services from them, for the practical life and health. We may even ennoble our real actions and make them more efficient by a higher and and more successful rhythm without danger of spoiling, up to a certain limit. On the other side the mental faculty, which is so easily spoiled by mysticism, is very liable to receive bad influences from the affective prevalence. The muscular action gains by every idealistic aspiration and has little danger to damage its peculiar nature, if the vital action proceeds from the lower to the higher function. It becomes stronger and more successful. But mental intellectuality, much as it may be helped by affective idealism, is in its refined susceptible disposition lacking almost or entirely the mechanical corrective, very much exposed to the danger to be spoiled or roughened, which will be recognizable in anger, rudeness, intellectual dependence, unreasonableness, superstition and neurasthenia.

Remembering the first group of our *centro-accelerating helps* we state that they are comprised into the notions of symbolism, mysticism, miracle and prayer. We are entitled to call them altogether the *notional* or *psychological* group, because they bluff the individual life-force with their accomplished imaginative notional appearance. The stage of these notions is exclusively the mental function of humanity and they are already very far from the fullness of the direct experience and the peripheric reality. They represent already more imaginative and more general ideas which are partly detached from the categories of time, space and causality, and whose affective energy drives the individual, first peripheric-intellectual activity at once from the outside reality toward their partly symbolic-idealistic compression. The individual is able, therefore, to ride, as on the most quick and energetic motor-car, as it were, from the periphery until the symbolic degree or station and will accordingly, from this advanced point, be very fresh and strong in order to undertake the following further necessary voyage toward the central idealism.

Beside this first notional or psychological group we learnt a second homologous group receiving its instigating energy from the physiological muscular contraction and which we call, therefore, the *muscular psycho-dynamic group*. We include into this group weeping, laughing, singing and dancing. The most insignificant smile is a small miracle, the most hidden serious, longing or repenting or loving tear, going to high aims, has the value of the symbolic centripetal acceleration. We saw that the muscular contractive energy, in its turn, also has a strong contractive, persuasive affective influence on the psycho-centric progression, and the additional effect will be the much greater as the influences derive from the physiological function of our life.

But there is an other third group which has the same purpose to concentrate our psychic energy into the affective delight or to the universal sublimation, and which receives its foundation neither in the notional psychological subtility nor in the muscular escorting or emblematic help, but in the quite different nature of *pharmacological causes*.

We have thus the following index of helps for psycho-dynamic acceleration:

    a) the notional psychological group: symbolism
                                                   mysticism
                                                 miracle
                                                 prayer

b) the muscular group: weeping
                                  singing
                                  dancing
                                  laughing

c) the toxicological group: alcoholism
                                  morphinism
                                  hashishism
                                  cocainism   and others.

The *toxicologial group* comprising al narcotica has the peculiarity to paralyse the real-peripheric intellectuality of the individual
functions, to exclude the real escapements and the reasonable
resistances of the peripheric world, and sets free, therefore, compensatorily, the concentric affective energy of the human life-force.
This whole group has very distinctly the inclination to use both
former methods, the symbolic notional concentration and the strong
muscular contraction, which we met in the second accelerating
psycho-dynamic group. But these two helps are used, by the unrestricted action of the pharmakological group, only as superficial and
inconsistent emergencies. In all psychic effects, from narcotic means,
we recognize very easily the domineering feature of strong energetic
progression and the perfect carelessness about any peripheric
logical development. But all muscular and notional symbolic helps,
used in this group, are lavished in a quite distorted, disorderly and
unsuccessful manner or they are only touched, irreverently, boldly
and impatiently without consequence, in a short movement like
flat stones scaled over the surface of the water. They often touch
the surface of the water, but the strong accelerated energy swings at
the slightest contact with the muscular and notional symbolic performances the affective desire headlong further, accelerating toward
affective delight and unrestricted will and action, without any
sufficient real thinking emphasis. Thus the toxicological mysticism is
very odd being far from the easthetic performances of the preconn-
ceived *artistic religious,* symbolic harmonious elaboration. .So much
so that the muscular and notional contractive activity of the intoxicated has no logical reason or harmonious beauty. The intoxicated is, therefore, most remote from the logical intellectual and normal muscular motions. All his energy is chiefly used in forwarding
the concentrating energy, overlooking any logical peripheric detailed
preparation and elaboration, in accordance with his extremely one-
sided use of the law of compensation.

The word *spiritual* in the broadest sense includes all transscendental universal possibilities of our relations, those which are approched in a traditional, acknowledged and logical way and have a beneficial and preserving effect on our psychich and corporeal health and those which are reached in a disorderly rejected manner and are opposed to the happy stability of our present categoric individual and social life. The old Greeks used for the whole circle of this human spiritual human faculty the word daimonios, significant for the attitude of the rising following church toward former pagan conceptions. The ancients had so one word for all our relations with the eternal universe which relapsed in our era to the meaning of merely the *bad* or *demoniacal* universal relations. The *good* relations with God are called divine, in our time. They are protected and cherished by church and legislation, while demoniac actions are rejected and forbidden. Now in the narcotic psychodynamic means we observe no clear distinction between good and bad spiritual influences. Little alcoholic consumption, for instance, has undoubtedly, in normal cases, a good spiritual effect. Confidence and optimism, artistic imagination, broadmindedness, enterprising and common sense, harmless joy are brought about, on the average, by exceptional and modest alcoholic consumption, whilst larger and habitual quantities of drinking have indeed the most outspoken develish or demoniacal effects on our actions. They are still prevalently spiritual, in the sense of the old expression daimonion, but bad, in the sense of our use of the word demoniacal.

The thorough disagreements about the advisability of *alcoholic* consumption is explained in the fact that there are insecure limits between the good and bad effects of this chemical means, which circumstance is aggravated by the fact of the great differences of the individual tolerance and the corresponding impossibility of sure dosage. All other narcotics seem to have almost exclusively or prevalently *bad* effects on the human psychology. This whole pharmaco-psycho-dynamic problem has, therefore, the value of a psychological scientific analysis and will not be very practical, in its consequences, even in alcoholism, before a definite possibility is reached to exclude the bad effects with security.

ALCOHOLISM is the main representative of the toxicological group. It is very common in its social diffusion and, therefore, well known in its effects and manifestations so that everybody has in his life the possibility to observe closely the typical alcoholic psychology. We will not enter in this connection upon the symptomatical part of this peculiar state of the mind and disease, near and interesting as it woud be.

The fact of prevalent concentrative tendency, in alcoholism and religion permits a comparison between the psychic nature of both. We exclude any mention of the criminal and pathological alcoholic state which belongs to the asylum or the hospital, but reserve the expression "Alcoholism", here,to the psychic state produced by the light alcoholic drink in the affective function of the normal citizen.

It seems that religion, in so far as it fosters the miraculous mysticism, is consecutively unable to reject alcoholism entirely. That part of the religious world which has the most logical and intellectual customs and clings most to them, must accordingly be more opposed to all affective central raptures and to every form of central enthusiasm. The strong inclination of the Protestant church toward *Prohibition,* in our days, has of course its deep psychological roots. The new world is fond of its intellectual logical methods and is at the same time afraid of the symbolic mysticism. It is only consistent in this case, if it struggles against any compromises with alcoholism. The lenience of the Catholicism, in this question, is founded reversely on the intimate connection with its psychological conception and taste which essentialy is more willing to accept symbolism and mysticism and whose first and last purpose is the strong progressive theocentric efficiency. So we assume that there is an interrelation between alcoholism and religion, both having nearly related psychological features. It must be in connection with these theoretical meditations that whole nations found the admirable and serious energy,often to their own commercial damage to maintain and carry through the prohibition with the most stiff and inflexible neck. There must be strong and careful *theological considerations* behind this powerful action, because the inclination of some psycho-pathic people to go under owing to the alcoholic vice. cannot be suppressed by this legal measure, as we see every day. The psychological right or wrong of this decree must be essentially a theoretical scientific discussion on the right or wrong and on the best distribution of the intellectual and affective amount of our life-force in our daily habitual performances. Without being willing to enter nearer on this subject, we have to judge this doctrinary suggestion rather as too severe, and if the old church exaggerated by lavishing symbolism and mysticism toward the strong concentrating action, the modern Prohibition seems a rather too energetic string pulling people exclusively toward the intellectual function. If they are really practicable, the prohibitional measures are right, because their psychic effect can be reached better by other more hygienic and less dangerous means, but unfortunately this in itself valuable decree turns out to be considered as too thorough and draconic and damages perhaps more the authority of the magistrates, if it cannot be maintained properly. A less materially interested country than the new world would look up to prevent an education and legislation which export an immeasurable capital each year to foreign trans-oceanic countries, chiefly for having pleasures which are forbidden at home. But many think it better to have excluded the alcoholic danger at any price.

It is very characteristic for the Zeitgeist, the ruling tendency of our age, that even alcoholism has been abolished, a last consequence of the same line which in the middle ages repulsed the mysticism and preferred and embraced the scientific ruling direction and taste of the modern time. The Prohibition is the last logical runner of that first anti-symbolic and anti-mystic separating movement, it is the last and newest proof of the lasting pushing vitality of that change of psychological views. It is the last and newest assertion and decision of to-day against any " anti-logical" or symbolic mystic ways of affective progression and concentration.

There is no doubt that lenient alcoholism, with its strong concentrating energy, plays or shares a psychological role in the human society, which cannot at all be estimated as insignificant. The affective concentration of our psychic force must be, if we will enjoy any happiness and any idealistic satisfaction on earth, and it is just the divine and priest, who had at any time, as long as the world existed, in all ages and religions, the professional incumbance and duty to make, by their symbolic mysticism and miraculous ceremonious actions, the psychological vital contractions possible and easier, which are ordinarily so much and variably handicaped by the peripheric reality. Dealing with alcoholic and prohibitional questions is for this reason, strange as it may seem, exactly a theololical task, because the whole psycho-dynamic disposition of the social soul belongs to the duty of the divine. He has to decide how much and with what means the human energy has to be pushed to, or checked from, the central divine affective aims, and he should know best how much the human society can stand the intellectual charge and peripheric confinement, without breaking down.

Alcoholism is, in a certain sense, a help or even competition of the divine functions. Perhaps the divine prohibitionists over-estimated their professional affective concentrative skill and efficiency, by the perfect suppression of alcoholism. By the total exclusion of the alcoholic concentrative help they made their concentrative task the much more necessary and indispensable, and they had to care about their concentrative power and efficiency the much more. But the divine profession, which in our intellectual time has an essentially more difficult and weaker position, is scarcely able to make up with the centro-theistic loss suffered by the total exclusion of alcoholism. Exactly in our days, when the intellectual quarter has such a strong magnetic prevalence on our fatal performances, a lenient allowance of a small supporting dose of alcohol would be wise.

The intoxicating aid of the alcohol is declined, however, because of disorderly and unlogical influences and possibilities, by the modern theologians. They claim the methods of the preconceived, clear reasoning and of noble self-control, as much as possible, and suspect the demoniac digressions of the alcoholic spirituality. Many may be surprised, if we dare to make comparisons between theological functions and and narcotic effects, if they do not follow exactly our philosophical display. But if they do, they cannot escape from the principal agreement of both methods. Several days ago I left church with a clever lady, who made the following statement on the way home: "I will not go any more to church. People become drunk there in the same way as if they take alcohol. It is just the same effect: the loss of all discerning individual will and of the reasoning faculty. Did you observe the general smile on the faces and the unexceptional happy intercourse of all churchgoers coming out from the service?" And yet the church has quite essentially the role to make people drunk with the eternal wine, with that water, after whose drinking one is never more thirsty, and there is no other means for the theologian to reach this goal than the suggestive exclusion of the reasoning power. It is unjust and one-sidedly intellectual if we despise entirely this reactive necessity. It is the natural condition of happy psycho-dynamic relaxation. The ciliar muscles of the eye and human intellect work in the same way, in distending or relaxing the central pupil shrinks and the spiritual eye looks sharply to the infinite. It is the most essential task of the parson or pastor to change the water of our logical duty into the wine of the affective idealism. The position of the theologian will be sure and indiscussable within the frame of this special performance and method, as long as we shall have religion and perhaps even psychological dynamic necessities. The right of the divine, in his fight against alcoholism, lies in the disorderly and complicated effect of the alcoholic intoxication exceeding easily the limits of our controlling responsibilites.

The affective help of alcoholism, however, is so much true, that the intellectual divine one-sidedness of taste, as it is often likely to occur in our scientific time, creates a stronger need of the population for alcoholism. Our time is not yet so far and perhaps none will be, that it could dispense entirely with the symbolic mysticism of psychodynamic concentration. Alcoholism is, therefore, just the danger of the intellectual time and of the countries of the most logical cultures. Where there is a pronounced predilection for exclusively logical conceptions and teaching, there the danger of strong alcoholic collaboration and competition, in public and private life is most outspoken, according to the law of compensation. The public needs yet to-day the mystic urges toward delightful goals, and it is the divine who has to exercise much more energetically these strong psycho-dynamic symbolic influences, if he will perpetuate the abolition of the alcoholic consumption. The serious struggle against alcoholism in the most intellectual parts of our civilization has its deepest foundation just in the somehow competitive psychological possibilities of the concentric sway of the alcoholic intoxicatin. The modern divine feels the serious temperamental antagonism of alcoholism against his purified intellectual methods and searches consecutively to exclude it from the public influence.

In this connection we ought to look to the different role of alcoholism in the various countries of Europe. It seems quite clear that alcoholism in the Latin southern countries does not play an important role, in spite of the high qualities and the cheapness of the alcoholic products and the habit of the Latin race to spend much time in public bars and restaurants. The Germanic races, as we have them in Switzerland, Germany, England and in the Scandinavian countries, as we have them moreover prevalently in Canada and in the United States, are much more inclined to serious alcoholic intoxication. Generally we are accustomed to put this phenomenon on the account of different climates, and it may be, that the colder climate disposes much more to alcoholism. But there are, in my opinion, much more other reasons which have created this very different needs of the single nations. The Latin have a strong mystic symbolic and miraculous- religious education and culture. They are suggested by their old conceptions to have strong suggestive and sentimental concentric-affective reactions, and they are, therefore in an easy possibility of moving to, and reaching, their delightful theistic goal. They, therefore, have not the strong natural appeal to the alcoholic concentric help, being in a developed facility to bring about easily the strong cultural concentration. The Germanic races instead, fond of petty observation and exact logical performances, and afraid of the angry leaps of mysticism have much more difficulties to proceed toward delightful imaginative goals and it is this psychodynamic handicap which creates their more urgent need to ensure themselves with the alcoholic support.

The mystic Catholic theologian has in his miracles and symbolic belief and in his strong sensorial methods toward his goals a very energetic educational means to carry his public to eternal magnetic theistic ends; the Protestant scientific modern divine teacher is rightly careful and reserved in the use of concentric-affective, notional and artistic sensorial symbolism. He has, therefore, more difficulties to go on to his central theistic imagination, and it is this his possible insufficiency of theistic energy which exposes him to the humiliating danger of alcoholic competition.

The *drunkard* is always a very remarkable individual in his demoniac disposition. He always must be originally a man much more gifted for the universal idealism than the average person. He is possessed of a strong desire for sentimental concentration and delightful enjoyment; but he has relapsed to irregular pharmakological concentric helps, because his surroundings, his circumstancees and experiences or his religious system were not in a position to give to him the sufficient help to justify his personal theistic and celestial expectations, in a suitable and satisfactory way. It is therefore clear, as it is known, that nobody is so highly susceptible of, and amenable to, religious values, as the drunkard and that nobody can be so easily and thoroughly cured from his passionate sickness, if he only surrenders his affective needs to the strong magnetic influence of a religious system. Alcoholism is a perverted, intoxicated form of religious psychology which can be compensatorily saved, redirected by the religious conversion.

The serious rise of the alcoholic danger cannot be considered as an acknowledgement of the divine success of a country. If alcohol is in a position to be dangerous for the whole community of the national welfare, then there must be indeed a strong materialistic and anti-idealistic draught in the cultural organization of that commonwealth. The theologian is expected to create such a domineering and charming beauty of his attractive religious system that there could not be any serious competition or danger on the the part of the pharmakological intoxication. He must be able to wrap his terminal idealism in such a splendid and brilliant dress, he has to appeal so sincerely to human responsibility, self-control and dignity, he must strive to become so tasteful and desirable even for the most spiritually gifted man, that he does not check or disgust him in the way of his divine desire, but overcomes and defeats even the most hungry demoniac disposition with the abounding energy of his preventing divine charm.

This question may be practically difficult, because what is necessary and useful for one may be too much for another and what constitutes a danger for this man, is just the appropriate help for his neighbor. The alcoholism is the doubtful spiritual substitution for failing or awkward or insufficient divine instigations. It is a mistaken toxicological help, as a rule, for the neglected or misunderstanding natural progression toward divinity. The alcoholic intoxication creates by itself the symbolic mystic miracles, which it is not willing or not able to accept from the legal professional educational divine, or which the latter is not willing or not able to offer, in the sufficient measure and manner to throw the individual theistic need energetically to the delightful terminal goals.

So we see that alcoholism has near relations to religion, to the special task of the divine and to the special conceptions of the religious denominations, to the peculiar taste of our educational culture and the affective and religious character of the Latin and Germanic nations of our civilization. It is not so much the race which itself may be also preeminently the product of religious education, which made its special relations to alcoholism, but it is rather the religious psycho-dynamic conception, which created the national attitude toward alcoholism. It seems that the cultural, accustomed facility to concentration, acquired by a strong mystic energetic system, has more the preventing power of overcoming this weakness. Where the need of idealistic concentration is great and where at the same time, owing to personal or cultural circumstances and intellectual conceptions, the affective concentrating facility is removed, there we have the greatest and almost inevitable danger of alcoholism. Alcoholism, in these cases, has received the role of replacing miracles and mysticism, but also of muscular toxico-logical performances in weeping, laughing, singing and dancing, which all functions it produces so easily and, unfortunately, in a distorted and unmotified manner.

There is surely a possibility, up to a certain limit, of mutual permutation between alcoholism and the miraculous mysticism, a law of compensation between all forms of narcotic delight and the religiously excited charming idealism. The need of the slightly alcoholic collaboration with the divine toward theistic ends comes out much more distinctly in the intellectual countries of our fatal social historic psychological sun-year. People are more fond of it during the "affective laziness" of the logical exactitude of our age than during the sentimental naturally concentrative ages of the former times. Even the divine of the present day, howevr, is supposed to be strong enough, in his cultural concentrative task, to overcome the affective danger of the unworthy competition of alcoholism by preventing it through his superior, theistic aesthetic dynamic energy. The best means against its prevalence is the surpassing affective force of religion. Alcoholism, as most wrong conditions, cannot be overcome by direct affective repulsion and legal punishment, but much better and more successfully by the *instradation* of the affective popular sentiments into the highway of strong theistic enthusiasm, to which to guide all nations is the essential duty and professional task of the *divine*. The serious danger of methylism is, in a sense, a charge against the sufficient penetration of the theological function. If the divine minister, in his intellectualized professional conception is not able to fulfil his enrapturing affective work, then he has to face not ouly the danger of intruding alcoholism, but must even fear to be superseded by this doubtful and dangerous toxicological concentrator. In a modest degree the alcoholic collaboration, therefore, ought to be permitted in our intellectual time. Our taste and present atmosphere are intellectual, it is true, and the divine is checked in his energetic centralizing work. The limited support of a small dose of diluted alcohol ought to be a clever measure of caution, of our time. Just the concentrative duty of the divine ought to help people to this small *additional complement* of their idealistic happiness. If one condemns, in the taste of our age, the mystic and miraculous possibilities and actions, if we think our logical intelligence could be spoiled by the strong affective influence of mysticism, then instead we are right to make a slight concession in permitting some alcoholic consumption. For the humanity is not far enough, up to to-day, and is not even built and intended to do entirely without any strong concentrative help. If we take away symbolic, mystic and miraculous aids, if we exclud and abolish the pitying strength of the muscular concentration in weeping, then we have to be the more careful in limiting the other given concentric supports, as they are offered in sport, singing, especially in art, as we shall see later on, and it seems even advisable not to exclude entirely a modest use of alcoholic drinks. Our ancestors were not wrong in every point, although they may have extremely wise children in our generation. No theoretic principle, if it is driven too far, is good, and if there is one of them, whose exaggeration could have very serious psychological and social practical consequences, it is just the exclusive intellectual and real one-sidedness.

In order to complete the muscular group of our affective psycho-concentrative index, we have furthermore to deal with the physiological function of LAUGHING. It will be obvious from intrinsic reasons, why this subject was delayed.

Laughing has the similar circular-muscular supposition and condition, as weeping has. The laughing individual throws the air of his lungs in energetic jerks through his mouth. Laughing also means essentially a circular-muscular contraction. The function of laughing is thus similar to the conception of the psychopupilar delight. It has, in the same manner, the contractive action of the circular muscles of the lungs and at the same time the violent expression of the air through the narrowed larynx. The contraction of the larynx is distinctly the more narrow, as the pleasure of the individual is more delicious and intimate, and on the contrary the less, as the reason of the laughter is less in a position to grasp thoroughly the roots of the individual affectivity and to hurl the feelings toward the sweetest pleasure and delight. Following the sketch we would have to call the *kiss* the highest degree of sincere happiness or the ecstasy of laughing. Therefore, laughing with high sounds generally expresses a much more special sense of refinement and delicious possibilities, whereas the deep voice in laughing means a more modest claim and an inferior possibility or opportunity in charming pleasure. Has nature made a joke in giving to woman the anatomically narrower larynx or does it speak for the fact that the female heart is capable of deeper emotions?

Laughing, therefore, is like a wonderful flower exhaling continually its perfumed breath toward heaven, gathering all its sweet affective life together and expiring it in one exhilarating spell toward idealism. So every most insignificant smile contains the germ of a symbolic and mystic miracle. Every smile has the capability to loosen our intellectual peripheric entanglement, to detach our life-force easily from the detailed sorry meditation of the peripheric work and to throw it easily and instantly toward the concentrative idealistic delightful divinity. Every smile is a thrilling spark from heaven, a seductive divine persuasion, a charming flower concentrating our erring vibrating affective feelings and exploding them continually in the artistic play of idealistic firecrackers and small divine bomb-shells. The strong desire of thrilling enjoyment and divine pleasure will never cease as long as we have the possibility of laughing. The muscular concentrative action has the most general and strongest connection with the human affective pleasure. The human character seems to be most intimately concerned with laughing. Our soul could scarcely ever progress to pleasure and joy without the smiling possibility. Smiling is the starting action from the peripheric fixation; smiling is the first energetic jerk away from the detailed peripheric reality. It is the first idealistic help out of the entangled multiplicity of our intellectual sorrows and helps us to move energetically centralwards. Smiling and laughing are so intimately connected physiological attendants of our psychic concentrative action that they appear in *both cases* wether we depart successfully in our soul to ideal pleasure or if we are excited from outside and induce the soul, by their help, to charming affective contraction.

The persuasive force of laughing is quite remarkable. There is no other such infectious or suggestive force like this. The slightest smile is in a position to make for overcoming all our sorrows. Smiling is a pronounced hint to a genial deliverance from the peripheric intellectual vexations of our life. Sexual idealism puts smiling and laughing as the bright flag on the top of its tent, as the chief attraction on the lips of its darlings. Art gilds by its smiling serenity all its masterpieces like with warm uplifting sunbeams and religion itself elopes with the hearts of its children, in wooing them through the smiling amiability of its angels and its messengers and representatives. Smiling and laughing means, in a certain limit, a detachment from the most peripheric detailed world. They establish unexceptionally the connection between the intellectual periphery and the affective centre, and appear so much more in a humorous way as the individual is unable to combine the peripheric intellectual observations with his accustumed idealistic views and former experiences. In this case he makes quickly a small golden bridge of emergency by the charming arches of the muscular-concentrative help of the smile and the laughter, and he instantly finds by this logical eliptic leap his central accustomed way of charming discharge. Thus we have here again the former muscular suggestive typical help from the physiological outside nature, in order to strengthen, to quicken and even to replace the concentric activity of our sentimental soul. Laughing and smiling have their place within the second muscular group of concentrative acceleration ;they help essentially to be rid of the most peripheric short-sighted intellectual fixations of our life-force and allow us to proceed easily toward the deeper concentric values of our life.

We observe instantly, however, that laughing has different sides. It is the charm itself and it is, therefore, a risky and tasteless intention to scold laughing for later obvious reasons. We will rightly be laughed at and help laughing, if we try to make serious objections against laughing. So winning is its suggestive power!But our serious and more thorough psychological duties permit and force us to look more closely at the function of laughing. Doubtless laughing has some frivolous features. It has the essential will, it is true on one side, to leave our peripheric work easily, to withdraw our detailed intellectual effort as soon as we could feel any serious real difficulties, but it is, on the other hand, not very anxious to lead the delivered princess of the affective force of the individual to the deepest well of concentrative symbolization. Laughing is pleased to fix us on the previous phases of affective deepening and development, in order that we easily can observe that laughing, as a rule, does not lead to energetic divine efforts. Laughing is a friendly and polite declining gesture of the Eternal, in regard to our serious intrusiveness and transcendental sagacity, to retire. Laughing is a veil spread peacefully over the face of the deep mysteries of our existence and the universe. Deus ridet si mortalis ultra fas trepidat. Laughing is a dreamy hamoc, where the human soul basks and rocks harmoniously between the two trees of knowledge and sentiments.Laughing has the role of an affective soothing mediator between all our psychic functions. Thoroughness and importance are generally far from it. Therefore, laughing is a successful help against affective over-charging. It exercises the levelling role between the peripheric intellectual reality and the deep theistic concentration, leading as well the theistic concentration toward intellectual superficial clear and multiple display ,as the latter toward the deeper and more concentrated affective simplifications. Laughing, therefore, is the guarantee of reasonable human limitation. It is the charming outlet which does not permit that one part of our two-sided nature develops too far in one direction at the expense of the other, intellectuality at the expense of sentiments or idealism at the sacrifice of reality. Laughing may be called,for this reason, a panacea against neurasthenia and overwork, against fanaticism and crushing towering materialism. It establishes the happy middle harmonious state of the different elements of our psychic life-force. Laughing is the most perfect expression of the happy mind in the happy body. Laughing is the compromising power between heaven and earth. It is in this similar to the art, not being willing to give up entirely real observation nor uplifting sentiments. It is distinguished from art, among other things, by the fact that it locates the accent more in the neighborhood of the realistic side, whilst art has rather more the inclination to push toward idealistic standards. Laughing is so be-

loved by all and hated and scorned only by two extreme psychological attitudes, the energetic theistic idealism and the serious
and sucessful peripheric, materialistic and scientific work.

Laughing makes a good thorough-fare for the affective life-force
between both the intellectual and the sentimental extremes. It
removes all one-sidedness and reduces the individual always again
to the harmonious middle real-idealistic attitude. Laughing is,
therefore, the best friend of the normal, virtuous human common-
sense.It is the most adeaquate and charming expression of what the
normal human individual must claim to be and to stand for, and to
what he must strive in his curious muddle of real and sentimental
characteristics.It is the representation of the modest and self-possess-
ing human psychology which is satisfied with its natural possibilitles
and limits and does not carry its wishes and needs beyond the compromising middle state of the reachable good mediocrity. So we
understand plainly that all extremists have to be supposed not to be
laughing people and to be rather averse to the strong magnetic
persuasion of their laughing fellowmen.

We could not imagine the religious genius with a loud laughter.
We would be inclined to think this would be in contradiction with
the divine conception of his dignity and mission. Full laughter puts
the human soul instantly into close and clear connection with the
detailed peripheric observation. We have to keep in mind that it is
to be considered as a serious work of saving affective energy, if the
sentimental loftiness of the divine action is not pulled into nearest
connection with the opposite far-away intellectual direction and the
distance of our petty reality. The educational carefulness of the
scriptures as well toward our limited life-force as the personal
dignity of the religious genius, which must be circumscribed and
would be exposed within the extreme, distant and double performance of the real and ideal nature, has chosen a necessary though
restricted method in excluding laughing from the atmosphere of the
prevalently idealistic hero and his enormous idealistic energy.
Therefore the sisterhood of art and religion.

The fanatical,digging,speculative idealist as well as the powerful
eager realist are both averse to the laughing reaction. They fear to
lose, by laughing, their gathering energy which they are only able
to maintain under the most serious earnestness and attention.
Laughing, therefore, is not in the same sense as the other muscular
actions to be taken as a strong concentric idealistic means. It has
this power up to a certain limit, but in a smaller degree and in both
the concentric and relaxing direction. Its deepening energy is not

strong enough to overcome easily the terminal symbolic sill, extreme waves of terminal delight, in tears and enthusiasm are rather thrown back to the mediocrity of laughing. Many girls have an insuperable tendency to laugh in a serious action or place, for instance in the church. There is also a reciprocity between laughter and weeping in the contrary direction. Strong affective waves of laughing and weeping link up with the nearest higher and also lower expressions of sentiments. Laughing is liable to fix the individual life-force on the secular artistic pleasure and the pre-idealistic concentration in luxury and superficial love so that we understand easily that strong and deep theistic and universal intentions and laughing are incompatible. Therefore we are not expected to laugh in churches, because the distant idealistic goals suppose a strong effort and the *hermetic* gathering of our life-force in order to reach energeticaly the deep well of theistic fixations. The atmosphere of high art commands respectful awe, never laughter. The same thing we meet in the efficient prosecution of our real working tendencies.

Laughing pulls our detailed fixation into the imaginative Eden of pleasure and of the charming enjoyment, blurs therefore the detailed surface and distinctness and restricts the interest in our real outspread peripheric activity. Laughing is the most charming and the most brilliant representative of the human harmonious pleasure. Nobody can dispense with it entirely. Even the man who is most anxious to bring about affective concentration in great art or in important accumulation of real riches, stoops again and again to refresh his features and his heart simultaneously in the tittering bath of laughter. But it is less dangerous to the peripheric security because of its less simplified psychodynamic energy and movement. Laughing is the most harmless and temperate of all the named psycho-dynamic helps. It is like art such a happy and careful mediator between both extreme tendencies of the human real-idealistic disposition, that it is also admitted even by the most severe thinker as welcome relaxation and rejuvenating change, and by the most diligent peripheric worker as an uplifting recreation. Est tempus ridendi et tempus flendi.

Let us mention here some other psychological notions which are related to laughing. The principle of all *jocular effect* is always again the necessity of simultaneous meditation of the peripheric intellectuality and of the mechanical and visible world and its laws and at the same time the attempt to enjoy the affective elevated sentiments. The broader the universal insight and possibility of intellectual explanation, the less wondering and reason for jocular effect. The perfectly sophisticated finds less reason for laughing and jokes, in a sense. According to the intellectual or psychic temperament, one laughs, when the other weeps. Every JOKE contains an exquisite intellectual sharp distinction which is like a barrier to go on to a general truth and an attractive imaginative background. The opposition of these two distant and very pronounced degrees of affective standards and their simultaneous experience try to split in a clear way the deep psychic individual life-force, to pull it at the same time toward the two opposite distant poles, and to produce a real stumbling of our individual action. In this instantaneous sensation of the rather surprising helplessness of our nature and narrow limitation lies the root of our humorous jokularity. It is a sort of selfconsciousness, of honest truth toward one's own shortcomings, a free admission of recognition of our own human insufficiency. We recognize in the state of humour and joke, how much we depend on a small intellectual scale of movability and affective distances, how immeasurably audacious and exaggerated an enterprise it may be, to attempt to conceive simultaneously such most distant ranges. Humour and joke are always, like laughing, philosophical, intellectual and reasonable, because they give new realistic hints and advices and help and protect against the exaggerated idealistic inclinations. This effect is excluded from the atmosphere of the religious books by careful allusion, in a reserved way, to the reality of life.

MOCKERY and DERISION hyper-emphasize the intellectual contents of the life. Mocking writers describe minutely the slightly hinted to, real intellectual conclusions of the affective standards of the hero and they point out in an exaggerating way, how thoroughly different and even contradictory to all what we since our childhood and through all experience had accepted as absolutely granted, the logical development of sentimental and idealistic principles must be. Mockery augments, by hyper-emphasizing and dwelling on the development of real circumstanes of affective descriptions and representations, the clear recognition of our narrow intellectual and human capabilities. It energetically calls our soaring sentimental inclination to return or not to lose entirely the intellectual soil under its feet. This is the state, of which Goethe says, dass der breitbeinig auf der Erde stehende sich nicht einmal mit einer Eiche messen kann. The exclusive rationalist and realist are naturally very inclined to mockery, but they are as wrong in their one-sided conception as the fanatical religious idealist who is extreme in the opposite direction. The derision and mockery is an instantaneous and rude awakening out of a charming idealistic dream, stirring up impatiently and violently from the nodding indulgence. Because of its caustic intensity and most thorough extreme opposition and assailing surprise, mockery is accepted always as a challenge and insult, as it really is and must be intended, if we exclude the intention of necessary levelling justice. We may be understandably very angry, if we lose so unexpectedly our charming illusions.

We understand through this meditation two things: first that humour and laughing must be a natural protection against sentimental self-exhaustion through abusive super-estimation of our affective life-force, which is put into certain limits of possibility, and secondly, how much many of us naturally incline to leave the soil of reality and to discharge the almost whole amount of life-force of the affective heaven.

Wherever very distant affective standards and ranges will be presented at the same time to the narrow and awkward human consciousness, scorn and mockery will show their frightening heads in order to protect against the exaggerated claims on psychic performances. The humorous deviation of the serious interest is there always most sure, where at the same time very distant psychic adaptations are exacted or desirable. The laughing and *scorning* individual refuses to enter seriously upon the affective matter proposed to him. He amuses himself, on the contrary, in a passive, evading and declining way, to deal with the great concentrative distances of tasks simultaneously proposed to him and is in a state of utmost wondering and surprise that fate and life could have imputed to him such extraordinarily distant accomplishments at the same time. He makes out of the distress of his insufficiency the virtue of wise self-amusement, putting himself right in the middle of the universe in the very moment, when he proves insufficient. The laughing scorner is a principal decliner of hard work. He exposes himself, up to a certain degree, to the reproach of laziness and weak self-pity.

Surprise means, therefore, a lack of quick adaptability of our psychic functions to the different necessities of our affective and intellectual surroundings and happenings in spite of ourselves. Mockery instead is the decided wilful opposition against the performances expected of us by a fatal disagreeable constellation of hyper-exacting circumstances. *Unhappiness* means a collision of two distant affective exactions of our exterior life and our individual affective taste and gift. The refusing *scorn and contempt* save the individual peculiarity and comfortable habits, from possible or disagreeable exactions of heart and mind and body. Scorn is therefore always supposed to be in connection with personal weakness or laziness. It is a previous and most uncritical refusal of the performance of a task offered to us by life: whereas humorous conceptions and mockery rather are active "scientific" trials to compare the opposite realistic effect and the interference between intellect and sentiments, and are in this more courageous and enterprising, but also more malicious and destructive and as unjust as the lazy scorn and the proud contempt.

We understand so that any system with the claim to cover a very large fingerboard of affective standards is always inevitably exposed to the realistic hyper-correction of mockery and derision, of scientific,so-called objective contradiction, on one side, and to affective boredom and idealistic universal abandonment, on the other.

Vincit qui patitur

Le mal que nous faisons ne nous attire pas
tant de persécution que nos bonnes qualités.
La Rauchefoucauld

FIFTH BOOK

FIFTH BOOK

ALL psycho-dynamic accelerating helps, as we have treated them one after the other, have of course, owing to their natural peculiarities, the great danger of exhausting the peripheric intellectuality, directing the dynamic draught of the life-force from the periphery to the affective centre and enticing the individual, therefore, to surrender the strength of his real detailed display to the centripetal tendencies of the heart. It is understandable that by this reason, welcome and thoroughly engaged as these helps were during the sentimental epoch, when they were rather more the natural expression than the forcing supposition of their sentiments, at the starting sentimental quarter of our human life-year they became despised and hated by the domineering intellectual methods. Intellectuality considered all the symbolic concentrative helps as a dangerous switching out and undesirable shifting on the keyboard of our present real responsibility, as an undesirable gliding over the slow and regular logical development of the legal human central progression. Intellectuality searched to exclude the concentrative psycho-dynamic instigators as much as possible, from the daily intellectual activity and the social educational methods, as we know, for instance in the abolition of the symbolic mysticism and in the introduction of the alcoholic prohibition. The leading intellectual new epoch, which raised its strong head instantly after humanity had passed the historic equinoctial point, is rightly considered as the product of the resistance against the seducing magnetic affective attraction. Its changes are dependent on the rising intellectual life-quarter, because it protested thoroughly against former methods and absolute and unchecked surrender of the human life-force to the magnetic centro-theistic history. The new time protested against the perfect sentimental one-sided government of the affective centripetal magnetism, and it became, according to the equinoctial intellectual conversion of our fatal spheric development, the leading light-bearer of new conceptions emphasizing the necessity of the intellectual peripheric scientific and working performances and condemning the unchecked sentimental artistic effusion of the former period. It is, therefore, clear, if we undersand right, that just the new religious necessity criticized and abhorred to a large extent the symbolic mysticism and the miraculous conceptions, putting at their place the strong and inexorable methods of natural proceeding logical methods. It followed in this the real, working and intellectual, scientific taste of the time, though this procedure, in another sense, led to less sensorial distinctness and was in so far a self-defence of religion against the increasing realistic wordliness of society. May historic, personal and political circumstances have been, as they may, it is sure that these great conversional moments of the mediaeval, intellectual, equinoctial point of our civilization were great and important changes. All human actions are done under the influence of the inter-spheric, prevailing magnetic necessities, and the reformers of the middle-ages acted also out of the deep need of the magnetic laws of the historic humanity. If it seems deplorable to cultured people of to-day that the changing zeal of that time was so thorough and if we all complain vividly that the fanatical enthusiasm covered even the realm of art and destroyed most precious artistic values, then we must not forget, how much and how thorough there was the question of fundamental tenets and of decisions of still higher value.

We remember that the whole, enormous necessity of moving the human affective force between real and idealistic goals exacts a most cautious and skilful steering possibility and is the product of the surprising disproportion between the given small human talent in developing affective life-force, on one hand, and of the exceedingly large fingerboard offered, of idealistic and realistic trend, whose total attainability has been raised more and more to general conviction or creed of mankind, during and through the educational methods of former and later religious and philosophical systems and practical habits. The strong effort of the religious founder to establish the most extreme and most energetic movability of the affective human nature has its deepest root in this inevitable necessity of emergency to cover the large row of active standards, according to the offering necessity of the moment and of the peculiar individual fate. But we understand well and the founders of religions knew it that there cannot only be means of pulling our nature into the one idealistic direction, toward concentrative theistic enthusiasm and sentimental imaginative elevation, as it is done owing to the described, accelerating methods of concentrative helps given in the intellectual, muscular and pharmako-logical, symbolic angry mysticism and miracles, but that there must be given a guarantee against the total real detachment, that human nature must be fixed much more on reality, as the tension is or can be considerable.

There must be as well intellectually *hesitating and retaining* psychological means, which according to necessity bring the human life-force to the intellectual periphery and check sufficiently the unsteady magnetic leaps toward affective idealistic acceleration. Religion makes serious efforts to resolve also this part of the problem of its task. It strives to be able to fix the human affectivity on the peripheric station, if it thinks fit to do so, and it endeavours with great emphasis to bring about checking moments in order to regulate any helpless and one-sided mono-determination of the concentrative progression of the affective activity. In spite of its preferably idealistic value and sense, and notwithstanding its one-sided sentimental notions, the historic religion recognizes the peripheric necessity of our nature; it tries to respect even the intellectual needs of our human disposition. We shall see whether and in how far it succeeded in resolving this part of the psycho-dynamic human problem. If the above mentioned part of the psycho-dynamic means had the common characteristic of accelerating and facilitating the theocentric delightful progress, the *bridling second division* of the psycho-dynamic helps will have the contrary effect. It is the checking *hesitation and the intellectual peripheric fixation,* which is typical of them all. They altogether have the *magnetic sense opposed* to that of the previously represented supports of our psychic emotions.

We instantly become aware of the fact that this necessary division of the magnetic gravitation of the human psychic tendencies must likely produce an unhappy struggle between both directions, that the most painful contradictions and the most pronounced disharmonious magnetic tensions will arise and be the more sensitive and considerable, as the contradictory elements are strong and their special goals very distinct and distant. We therefore cannot hope in advance that we shall have in the broad, universal construction neither the full satisfaction of the human heart being directed very clearly toward supra- or extra-intellectual idealism, far away from the general human understanding, nor the quietness and harmony of the real peripheric intellectuality having goals opposed to the heart and being therefore at a loss to enclose or follow the affective task of the religious sentiments. What an admirable greatness must inspire the foundation of a religious psychological system! The divine hero erects in his philosophical and universal contrivances and dispositions a marvellous huge building of tremendous superhuman measures and of a startling scale. But alas, the danger is just founded on the omni-present disproportion of the human performing possibility and the extensive and contradictory tasks received in this system. We may forbode already here in quite a theoretical way that the harmony and the balance between the different parts of the religious exactions will be easily disturbed, and if we know the prevailing taste of the idealistic founder and the general inclination of humanity looking more for enjoyment, exciting delight and sentimental thrill than for intellectual hard work, suffering and cross, then we may guess soon what could be the practical result of a religious system: the crushing prevalence of the magnetic idealism, in the hearts of one part, at the expense of the bereft reality, their one-sided interest in, and inclination to, the divine idealistic goals and the negligence of the detailed work, being the prey of the voracity of unworthy extreme realists. We have considered often the essential danger of intellectuality wrestling with sentimental idealism. The theistic goals dispose of the superior strong magnetism and are likely to be victorious, as a rule, as soon as they enter into serious competition with intellectuality. In the open battle and clear competition of sensorial distinctness idealism, however, succumbs to the intellectual categories of time, space and causality, with the one exception of the clear comparison of *artistic* elaboration and its thorough suggestive persuasion, where the idealistic victory is ensured.

For this connection we may quote the words: Jesus has many that love His Heavenly Kingdom, but few that bear His cross. He has many that desire His comfort, but few that share His adversity. He finds many partakers at His table, but few of His fasting. Many follow Jesus even to the breaking of bread, but few drink of His cup. Many honour Him for His miracles, but few follow the shame of His cross.

It is indeed most natural for the human disposition to like and to aspire to the affective concentration in divine enthusiasm, in prayer and love, by the quickening help of symbolic and mystic miracles, by the muscular support of singing, weeping and dancing, by the pleasure of the pharmacological affective acceleration. The human nature likes and is thoroughly inclined to strong affective discharging actions, as they are reached in the strong punctual contraction of the light-field. For this reason we never can and will escape from the essential predilection of the miraculous concentrating help.

Many people do not only not dispense with, but they combine these factors in order to obtain greater and more powerful affective successes. The *combination* of tears and wine is a frequent fact in life and artistic suggestion.Goethe's slogan:Wein,Weib und Gesang is a famous affective combination as old as humanity, much older than Homer, Anacreon and Horace, which has again the intention to strengthen the quickening force of powerful human affective concentration. *Sexuality* with its passionate persuasion has essentially concentrating psycho-dynamic features of a great power. It tries to throw the individual sentiments over the detailed steps of the logical gradual progression toward its charming goals. But sexuality is in itself so interesting and important and would absorb our explanations so much, if we would start here to give this subject the adequate attention, so that we prefer to be silent in this connection. Sexuality is in itself the other, second most important pillar of human psychology. It claims rightly much consideration in our scientific work. We drop it here with the general remark that sexuality is an exquisite psychological concentrator of the affectivity of the human heart. It often strives to enter in competition with religious means and goals, and although they unite in the same hymn of universal love, after all, they practically often behave as sharp adversaries on the way and search to damage and exclude each other.

Let us move again along the thread of our former psycho-dynamic meditations! There is no use to tarry longer. We must leave the charming hovering dreams of the miraculous mysticism. We must even learn to drink bitterest cups without the consolation of the tears. We must have the courage to dive deeply into the salty sea of the other side of human nature, of the peripheric restrictions of our sentimental wishes and illimited desires, given in the notions of *cross, passion, suffering and fasting,* which have been completed by the modern important additions of *work* and *science.*

In the CROSS we have the most efficient Christian religious antithesis to the charming symbolic miraculous delight. In the cross, which is again a symbolic notion and in so far a concentric link to the previous thrilling mono-concentration, we have a striking, comprising, central refined conception of our duty, a secret sign and a distinct and distinguished reminder of our necessary sacrifices. That which we hate and abhor by nature, to which the bottom of our heart is thoroughly averse, is put by this symbolic notion into the centre of the imaginative dream of our reverence, love and admiration. Suffering is put into the glaring lime light of eternity, by the sharp mono-punctual crossing symbolization. The highest degree of suffering is nearest to our immediate divine outlook and relation.

The suggestion of all our sentiments is by the cross mobilized from all peripheric hesitations, in order to make the difficult tasks acceptable and even agreeable to our nature, combining suffering periphery and symbolic central, attentive thrill, converting thus pain into delight by the graphic concentric symbolism, putting a positive sign before what we are accustomed to accept as a negative asset. It remains not the less an audacious and difficult, though most witty and helpful enterprise, to try to unite most opposed psychological things in one delicious concentrative symbolic notion. This idea to put the sign of suffering in the middle of our affective symbolism, clever and sagacious as it may be, yet surpasses in its bold, extreme emphasis the understanding and appeal of the average psychological reaction. So in spite or just because of its extreme genial brilliancy and quite surprising depth of composition the success of the cross is not popular. The result is too often such that mankind likes the inviting representation and the sentimental suggestive artistic relations of the cross, whilst the real experimental consequences of its suffering contents are avoided, neglected and repudiated, to-day and within Christian nations not less than in the old time of the Crucifixion, because the human nature is frightened and repulsed from the dry and checking component of the cross, from suffering and toiling work, as we know and shall see, according to the human disposition. But in spite of the essentially sentimental and delightful psychology of religion, we must admit exactly here, however, that *the cross represents the essential, serious attempt to include the idea of the sacrificing effort into its historic system*. Much is already gained by the principal fact that the ideas of sacrifice, suffering and work are put in connection with the central, loving values of the affective human nature, that even in this radically idealistic system we have received hints to the eminently precious significance of suffering and cross. And if we always again and again, though in a symbolic way, are guided and pointed to the attention and respect for the suffering and toiling principle of the cross, which is naturally abhorred, despised and neglected, of course most by the sentimental part of humanity, owing to the powerful emphasis of the working duty of the human life, the naive and unchecked collapse of our psychopupil is slackened and gradually withheld. The main Christian idea toward the charming breaking of bread is terribly thwarted by the warning fact of the painfully checking cross.

It is in the cross, where the Christian humanity receives the suggestion to understand the young life as the way, which guides us through toiling work and sacrifice gradually toward the old age and death, where it promises reward and the charming peace of our earthly pilgrimage. Our daily life surrenders us ruthlessly to the naked intellectual relations of time, space and causality and makes us feel all hardness of the real work and existence in most inevitable immediateness. It is the art which guides us in spite of intellectual connections much more carefully and soothingly over the logical laws of reality than anything else. But just in this we have the explanation that the objective occupation with art alone is insufficient and that the established religion is right to insert the notions of cross, suffering, sacrifice and work, if religion is to be expected to turn harmoniously on the roots of our natural human disposition. This is the deep sense of the symbol of the cross, though in reality it is so far away from the character of the meaning of a symbol, giving to us strict intellectual necessities and approaching us with the utmost pronounced, intellectual and sensorial exactions. The cross is the controlling, symbolic comprehension and the idealisically suggestive and simplifying direction of those natural forces which hurt our psychic nature, and of those efforts which must be extorted from our psychic life-force for the hard service of the intellectual reality. It is the ideal orientation within the entangling and confusing struggle of the visible world willing to retain us from the last idealistic goals. The cross maintains our idealistic confidence within the real intellectual difficulties of the life. It represents the guarantee of the terminal affective and sentimental reward of our active and passive effort. It is the elevated visible terminal sign of the harmonious last reconciliation of all contradictory magnetic forces of our life, which on the way often seem to lose their direction and their balanced collaboration toward one good goal. The cross of the Christian conception must be that bold bridge and that terminal-ideal arch, to which the hard and painful intellectual reality swings over to those concluding and comprising, highest values which we all hope and are longing for naturally: happiness, truth, beauty, strength and spiritual kindness.

We remember the always returning importance of the symbolic signs in connection with the last meeting symbol of the cross. They are all strongly impressive marks, abbreviated sharp hits for the memory, on which the attentive feelings are fixed and where our vital progressive force puts its steps in order to proceed from them further toward the ideal realm.

There is no doubt that the idea to represent just the intellectual struggle of the reality in form of a clear symbol must have a good effect. The discouraging tiredness of the energetic detailed work is so not allowed to go astray in desperation, because its result is fixed in advance on the central point of the victorious divine result. The

promising cross enlightens and ennobles the peripheric darkness of
the real tiring progression. The courage and the passionate push
are kept on, because they have the guarantee of adaequate reward
in the outstanding symbolic cross, because at every moment they
have the clear sight and encouraging view of their symbolic apotheosis in the divine symbolic concentration. The cross thus becomes
the salvation of the Christian conception from the reproach to
be the exclusive sermon of the agreeable delight and of the easy
affective love, faith and super-natural hope.

But there lingers of course always a danger in the audacious
apotheosis of the peripheric relations, as we have it in the divine
cross. How easy is it to confuse the charming part of this notion
with its toiling and suffering component! How quickly is it done
that we, in the meditation of this contradictorial and cunning symbolic notion, learn to invert hard effort into divine affective pleasure
instead of inverting the divine pleasure into hard work. Real intellectual hard work and divine delightful pleasure remain practically
opposite antagonistic notions. They must be clearly distinct and
performed separatedly. Which danger is nearer than the inclination
to paralyse the real accuracy by the affective simplifying influence,
if both intellectual peripheric and central affective methods are
united within one symbolic sign! Be it that we appreciate the principle of the noble knighting of real effort and individual resistance
given in the notion of the divine cross! Be it that this symbolic
combination of our two principal vital forces makes many precious
advantages in connecting ideal hope and confidence to our real
practical duties and peripheric realization of our conscience! Yet,
according to our natural disposition to be most easily suggested
toward the comfortable affective idealism and the uplifting enthusiasm and to drop readily the toiling resistant work, and respecting
the strong infectious magnetic attraction of all sentimental life,
the danger is exceedingly great to become one-sided once more and
to embrace most fervently the central magnetic power of the divine
idealism at the expense of our intellectual real life. Thus the
symbolic representation of the cross unfortunately easily fails in the
practical life. The audacious genial amalgamation of the two most
developed and distinctly distant human psychic faculties too often
does not succeed, the superior force of idealism absorbing our total
life-force and strangling in this manner the real necessities of our
human destiny. The symbolic combination of the working reality and
idealism is surely one of the greatest and deepest ideas. But often
it will not work practically because of our susceptible psychological

constitutional peculiarity. The immediate approach of terminal idealism and hard working reality is dangerous. The uninterupted vicinity and the indistinct amalgamation of reason and heart is likely to give way to the general psychological law of the suggestive superiority of the sentimental part of our soul. It makes for strangling our intellectual gift in giving opportunity to our sentiments to absorb in a comfortable manner the vital energy which must be guaranteed to the intellectual and working performances of our real life. The symbolic cross points out the extreme difficulty to handle the human psychology, in its great caution and skill, making concessions to both the intellectual and sentimental faculty and intimating relations of both. It strives to effectuate a just and equal division of our total psychic strength into two harmonious half parts the sentimental ideal on one side and the intellectual real application on the other part. Intellectuality loses in this competition at length its rights and importance, if it is put closely together with the suggestive strength of idealism. The refined and hidden nature of the charming sentimental feelings regularly understand to cheat the less movable real intellectuality of its rights and necessities. Already the choice of the passive work of suffering gives a distinct spot-light in advance for the development in this direction.

So we understand that the practice of the modern tendencies consists exactly in the suspicious, perfect separation of work from affectivity. The symbolic unity of both parts in the notion of cross has been discredited in the last epoch of history. Intellectuality was enslaved during centuries under the mighty yoke of the cunning sentimentality. Being sophisticated by now it decided to go its own way far from the fascinating magnetic power of sentimental idealism. The pronounced aversion and the hatred and the scorn of our intellectual age against the cross has its root in the historic fact of the intellectual slavery of the former times. Our intellectual time is aware of the danger of any sentimental alliance. It strives to repudiate any re-communication with the methods of the old historic union, when the real and intellectual life was the illegal and lawless servant of the sentimental arbitrariness. Historic progressions and psychological national developments have not less a good memory for past injustices than the individual. Historic ages claim the compensation of the right and wrong as well as the hurt personality, and whole centuries are able to tremble at any psychological danger, of which former have been the victims. The national psychology often burns its fingers like the individual and afterwards has for a long time a wonderful instinctive memory in order to avoid everything which could lead to the affective relapses of yore. Society as well as individuals has its prejudices and imprudennces, but also its bitter disappointments and its adapting oscillations. We are expected to progress not only in our personal, but also in our social human life.

In this psychological and historic connection we understand that the symbolic concentration of human fate, as it is given in the historic religion covering at the same time the two extremes of our double real-idealistic nature, can be the object of hatred and rejection. The symbolic contrivance of the most opposite human tendencies is surely very clever and cunning. It contains great intentions and broad views of harmonious psychological connection of the total vital and psychic performances of mankind, but its bold artistic elaboration and theoretical perfection are the serious reason of its almost fatal difficulties. Perhaps it is not the right method to go on with a pair of compasses in psychology in order to make the right division and distribution of the human actions. We never grasp simultaneously the totality of relations of anything and therefore all our intellectual elaborations are relative. We must consider the different nature and aptitude of both intellectual and sentimental quality of our nature, and then we easily by experimentation find out that the real and idealistic method and strength cannot be put into immediate neighborhood without the rise of continual serious frictions and thorough destructive competitions.

In speaking of the whole psycho-dynamic forces and taking a general survey over the organizatory frame of the religious psychology, just in the emphasis of the cross which played always an important central role in the Christian doctrine, we recognize the psychological root of its possibility of vital real existence. The sentimental one-sidedness of the Christian conception was always remarkably calmed by the symbolic connection with the peripheric reality through the notion of the cross. The cross at all times was the warning finger-post from the outside intellectuality and of the extra-solar possibilities. The cross indicated always the contradictorily intellectual and philosophical connections and misgivings deriving from the stable conception of human fate and psychology. Thus Christianity never was entirely and helplessly surrendered to its favorite central historic theism. There was always some gloomy spark of new development and enlargement, stretching the spheric arches of the human circular theistic ways. The highest religious genius himself in spite of his straight theistic conceptions, in spite of being fixed historically on them by the realistic church, receives indeed by the symbolic cross *the evolutionary glory of imperishable vital significance and biological greatness.* By his strong real connection, as it is performed in his suffering, in his passion and cross, he has received the centrifugal theistic features not only of the historic past, but also of the future hero of the humanity. He is not included definitely into the charming narrow circles of the past historic theism, he has even strong connections with the future divine development by the glorious sensorial and intellectual tendencies ,as they are given in his passion, cross and death. Had his role been restricted to the sentimental apotheosis of the human life, had he not shared by his symbolic cross the representation of our intellectual fate, and in this the enlargement of our future development, he long ago would have been excluded from the active humanity. He would have been forgotten and lost as so many great men of history, as numberless genial stars of the thoroughfare of the human ages and fates. He would be sometimes mentioned and described in splendid poetical and philosophical books like Plato and Socrates, but he would not continue to breathe vividly and practically through the present history. But in connecting the cross with his personal fate and in mingling the scorned passion and the peripheric intellectual cross, symbolic as it is at the same time, with his divine claims, he indeed chose the very best connection with the future progress of humanity. Which seems to be the most human feature in Christ, turns out to be the best guaranty of His divine preserving influence. In accepting suffering and cross he eternified his human idealistic activity. He generalized his divine and human mission most efficiently by the cross and his passion. In paying the toll to the intellectual development by his tragical cross, he put the most efficient obstacle to become ever entirely worn out or old-fashioned in the progressive history of humanity. What humanity keeps young is intellectual toiling work. The most divine thing and the most resistant skid against oblivion are the secret powers of suffering and cross. This power points to the future of humanity, this centrifugal divine action enlarges the circles of our fate and makes relations with the future human extra-solar destiny. The bitter chalice of the cross and passion of Christ points to what will happen in latest times to mankind, whilst the charming power of breaking bread, the circular harmonious action of the divine delight is directed toward the past and the present history, although it directs also the focus of its mighty psychological telescope toward great future visions of the individual and social humanity. It is due first to the suffering part of the life of the religious hero that he never could be forgotten. By his cross he shares the enlarging progress of our intellectual extra-solar fate. He does not deny entirely the future spheric development of the world, because he accepted the bitterness of the cross. So he was not satisfied with the accomplished theistic harmonious conception of the encirclement of his cultural epoch, but he put relations and made bridges to the later philosophical and psychological possibilities of humanity. He shared in so far the evolutionary will of the universe, because he intruded with his personal strength willingly upon the contradictory realm of the intellectual opposition. Had he fled from the oppositional entanglement of his last vital complications, as he undoubtedly could have done, the humanity of to-day would have been rid of his personal importance. By his cross he received the peripheric intellectual link of psychology necessary for his everlasting human and divine validity. In the cross he created the lasting connection with the latest further human development, in throwing out the strong attractive peripheric magnetic longings, by which he will be found and recognized always again within the human intellectual progress of the later ages and historic epochs. By the cross Christ accepted the ever fertilizing evolutionary germs of humantheistic development. By this circumstance he will be victoriuos in the decay of the passing-by historic rubbish, making up by his suffering and cross, in a general and potential way, what he missed through the the confinement to individual and local history and in the restricted development of his contemporary work and cultural historic science.

So we recognize that the purples and crowns of the kings and princes at every epoch of our human history fell down to earth again and again like old worn out clothes, that the most glorious old names and the most radiant families vanish like burning tinder; only and just the sneered and mocked royalty, as we meet it in the PASSION of the religious genius, though it was conceived by his contemporaries most ironically, has not faded away until to-day. The scorning kneeling worship before Christ, by his torturers, became the starting point of the serious adoration by a whole cultural world. The red soldier's coat, put on his shoulders as an ironical symbol of his "wrongly" pretended power, became at last the sign of his real regal majesty. The blows of the flagellation hit all Christian fellow-men in the most intimate recesses of their hearts and the crown of spines became not only the true and ligitimate crown, though contrarily intended, of his highest genial idealistic kingdom, but fixed him by the characteristic centrifugal spines unto the theistic human future of longest ranges. No other king had the idea, as far as we know, to put the cornets of his crown in the centrifugal direction. But for Christ and his special kind of royal aspirations it is quite significant that the hurting force of the spines was directed as well outside. It is indeed this outside direction of the activity of the pain, which gave to the Christian genial hero *his tremendous power of historic tenacity*. The pricks of his crown were able to make the most sensitive impression not only into the central theistic regal head of the historic hero inclosed into the historic encirclement of the painful crown, but the digressing, outside looking spines produced the most efficient connection with the future extra-circular world.

By His passion Christ indeed linked up with the future development of the following ages. The pricks of his crown fixed his historic mission on the enlarging movement of the cultural humanity. By the strong power of passion and suffering the hero prevented the possibility to become ever the antiquated intellectual formula of an old bygone time. By the most energetic connection of humanity to his cross, passion and suffering, he established an everlasting sentimental well , in whose intellectual antagoism we ever shall find the most powerful urges of further cultural development. The suffering religious genius was and will remain the most active pioneer in researching and testing the extrasolar possibilities. By suffering the most efficient and lasting, affective loving union has been received and created in advance with all struggling, striving, and working humanity of the ages to come. All progress which comes about in the world and the developing history, has its beginning roots in bitter injustice, in quarrels, suffering and passion. These are the first potentialities of all our future development. In suffering we acquire the first intuitive experience of our cultural progress. The passion means the incongruity of the momentary, possible reality, of the historically given time and culture with the dispositional longings of the human affective nature and heart.

The passion is the representative of all the historic gradual, intellectual theistic steps and powers which all must be overcome in time in order to strengthen the clear decisive courage, to make our longings truer and the life-force more progressive toward greater and higher extrasolar tasks. Suffering and passion are the first timid step toward work. The choice of passion means the stronger universal gift of the human heart which is energetically longing for, and inclined to, the further cultural development of our race and which is painfully checked by the borders of our historic, encircling cultural limitation.

The forces of *mockery, and irony* are dangerous means. Often they are likely to act like a bad rifle which permits the explosive force of the gunpowder to go in the reverse direction and to kill and to hurt the individual which perhaps would have shot the other. All strong forces in psychology as well as in the material physical world are, of course, always the much more dangerous as the contain a considerable amount of energy. Sneering, mocking and jeering are all very strong means of affective energy intending to kill the honour of a neighbor. But often these forces are discharged toward the malefactor. They kill our own honour instead of that of the intended victim. How scornfully were the torturers of Christ looked upon during all times of the Christian centuries! There could not be a more despising and more general rejection of any human beings than those men received by all the adherents of the charming Christ. The older part of the Christian art is full of the most scornful pictures of those contemporaries of Christ who were the instrumental expression of the political and cultural will of their time, and who were the vexing executioners of the energy of their constitutional government.

From the standpoint of their time the Jews and Romans felt obliged to retain and impede the rising Christian idea unless they would give up their historical political frame and fixation. The passion of the religious hero is just the exact expression of the fact that he had longings and made efforts reaching far over the limits of his given cultural circle, that the old time, politically fixed, defended itself with the utmost energy against any, may it be, most genial coercion by a single individual who was treated as a treator and a rebel against the existing political and religious laws. It is not the genial concentric force in the old sense of the word, which made him the object of hatred and persecution, but his checking real energy of resistence in the passion, which made him not only the victorious master of his culture, but also the guide of the later times, to which he was connected through the pitying power of his courageous and manly passion and suffering. His will to transgress all the given historic borders and his natural necessity to establish new enlarged intellectual laws surrendered him to the mockery, scorn, hatred and the torture of his fellow-men. He had the irresistible necessity in his nature to overcome and to break the old intellectual formula of his time. He progressed as the most energetic developing genius of his time to the further intellectual and cultural exploitations of the theistic idea, and this is the reason why the contemporary conception, in danger of destruction by the evolutionary enterprise, would prevent him by killing him. Therefore the passion is the concentration and the reaction of the universal progressive movement of the hero, and it is just in these laurels of the humiliating death, where he received his everlasting significance.

How must we explain this? Every action and every deed of our life is an intellectual development, a twig growing out from our affective theistic concentration. As soon as we have the intellectual clear development, we also have the clear historic fixation, which is to say, every intellectual statement must instantly die, because the flowing river of human progress overtakes it quickly. So the germ of the long duration of the church was given in the passion, not in the action. The action makes clear and real intellectual statements and has soon to cede its place to the next step of historic development. But passion and suffering, on the contrary, are unwritten laws, non-exhausted potential universal forces, not yet determined in the clear intellectual formulas, and on this account able to develop and to enlarge in continuous flowing energy. Suffering in the case of the religious hero was, I must say, an *ultra-intellectual sentimentality*. He already had magnetic attractions and longings outside of the old historic theistic circular frame of his age, in which he was born and historically included, with the most unbridled divine sway. Therfore he could break the fetters of his real culture only in destroying the intellectual categories of his personal existence. So his victory was in his passion and death. The suffering of the hero was the clear expression of the impossible congruity between his personal, genial, affective life and the historic fixation of the political and religious world of his time. At his epoch he was the exponent of the human longings for future progress and spheric enlargement. As long as he is able to catch our heart by his thrilling passion and death, as long as he is able to be a deep well of compassion to his believers and to the natural feelings of mankind, his extra-solar affective mind can impossibly be antiquated. He still is able to give new urges to humanity. Still he summons the cultural development to new intellectual statements and performances. The degree, in which the founder of a religion is in a position to produce further and new intellectual achievements out of the well of his sentimental life, is deciding for the exciting and existing living force he possesses, and he is antiquated and worn out then, when he is no longer able to cause new urges in art, in culture and in social, practical virtuous life.

Christ was expelled from His contemporary cultural time, because he strove, considered as a rebel, toward outside theistic goals. But he carried with him the sincere sympathy of the future, because he was the light-bearer of the universal development of that time. His magnetic attraction was superior to his epoch. This was the reason of his "dangerous" character and of his passion and death. But this was in the same manner also the cause of his unforgettable ideal and cultural *resurrection,* because he by himself created, in his new genial concentration, a new kernel of future theistic outside development, moving the lazy petrification of his historic world a step ahead, helping the universal psychological law in its necessary increase. It was the genial personal superiority of the great figure of the hero which expelled him from the real connection with his time, because he destroyed the old historic notions of the former history. His time instead felt to be induced to crush his real intellectual existence within its realm and to banish him from the real existing boundaries of its area.

If he says, that if he would he could ask his father and he would give him an army of angels against his enemies, then he means that his ideals are superior to his historic time and that he consequently would have the greater power than his enemies, because he had the stronger causing principles and the deeper potential sources. But he knew that at that time his new ideas were not yet really developed as the means of his enemies were in the flowing course of many centuries, and in addition he knew that the quick intellectual realization of his great genial and affective principles would be a hurting damage to their mysterious divine character. Humanity needed the youthful genial zest of his eternal hopes and promises, the prospect of his great idealism. Just in this lack of real development was the charm and the attractiveness of his superiority. The rising future religion existed in the compressed genial fate of the new principles. They included the most energetic force of future strength of development, because they contained the narrow germ of his starting new genial concentration. Humanity needed the slow opening of this charming new cultural flower of the high Christian genius. The slowly, but continually disclosing psycho-dynamic energy of the hero was exactly the neceessity and need of the dissolute ancient world. For this reason Christ, although he potentially could, would not resist intellectually the real power of his enemies. For his mission was essentially the affective and passive resistance against the quick intellectual disclosure of his genial affective principle. His passion and his suffering turned therefore out to be most essentially necessary to the divine cultural mission of his life. He does not compare intellectually, really and legally with the historic power of his time, because he essentially and exactly will represent to the world the future hesitations and resistances against the precipitated intellectual disclosure. Passion, cross, suffering and death are therefore the psychological preservations against the accelerated intellectual exploitation of his principles. By his time he was invited to show his intellectual fruits already at a stage, when his genial theistic plant was still in a phase of a germ or bud. But at this epoch he would not develop the genial compression of his new intellectual world. He resisted this invitation for competition by presenting himself rather to passion and death than to neglect the essential role given to him, which is to say, than to mingle with an intellectual real struggle.

So the conception is quite right that Christ died for the world and for everybody of us. But this idea has an extremely broad validity. He presented to the future world the necessary safeguards of the psycho-dynamic checks and escapements of their ideal longings. He rather was ready to sacrifice his personal historic existence than to venture into any real struggle at a period, when the flower of his new culture must have been still a tender, hidden genial germ. But this intellectual challenge of his time and of the following centuries was the heating sunshine and the developing force, which compelled his genial philosophy to display really and intellectually. All the shed blood of the Christians of the first centuries was the resistance against the attempt to induce the Christian idea to too quick development. Still in the first centuries the mystic hesitation and self-control of Christianity was so strong that it could be naturally disclosed in the intellectual direction only slowly and gradually. The passion, the suffering and the death of Christ, the bloody rivers of his martyrs altogether were checking obstacles (and at the same time intellectual challenges from the other side) against the intellectual precipitation and effusion of the idealistic tenets into the multiple objective world. They all must be considered as the checking preservers and safeguards of the slow psychodynamic disclosure of the Christian genial idea, which at last and gradually, under the continual pressure of the real experimental world, came out to the progressive real work and the intellectual maturation.

As long as the Christian suffered and was killed for his hidden idealistic principles, there was indeed no danger of his death. But when he too, even by himself and ambitiously, mounted the hill of intellectual display and real success, when he started fighting and used the sword, as it at last amply happened at the time of the middle ages and on the converting opportunities of the pagans, it became a real, intellectually developed fact, a political and warrior power, a historically fixed, theistic real system and underwent therefore, from this time, the laws of all intellectual life: to rule and to go by. Qui gladium acceperit gladio peribit.

Suffering wrong is the invincible might of the psychological life. This fact gives us the sympathy and connection of the future times and links us up to the latest following generations. But the clear satisfaction of the intellectual real life passes away in the sure glory of possession and of intellectual, legal right and does scarcely leave a trace of its former existence. This is the most lasting religious principle which is able to resist by suffering and which can stand the real struggle of the intellectual world by the passive power of painful idealistic resistance. The endurance of passion and cross is the guarantee of the duration of every religious principle. As long as it may resist the temptation of real comparisons, it cannot be overcome. But no sooner it displayed intellectually and mingled with the real quarrels of the intellectual life than it must become really strong, which is to say, idealistically weak and disappears therefore slowly. For the affective nature of the genial religion cannot stand the sensorial power of the intellectual life. As soon as it is enticed successfully to compete with intellectuality in the open arena of the categoric sunshine of time, space and causality, it loses its suggestive energy, and intellectuality takes away from it the splendid armour of human life-force which it succeeded before so skilfully in withdrawing stealthily from the categoric intellectuality by the hidden means of cunning suggestion. Religion is great in suffering, cross and death. From the mysterious atmosphere of suffering, persecution and slander, religion pulls the successful forces of the idealistic suggestion which helps it to overcome best the adversary intellect. Idealism and religion, under these circumstances, have the best chances to maintain their strong position and to deprive the real intellectuality of its vital force. The open air and visible arena of the intellectual struggle must naturally be fatal to the affective nature of the genial idealistic principles. Religion is naturally bound to be always the Cinderella of the world and to rule preeminently in serving. Intellectuality though less cunning and movable than affectivity is clever enough to have found out the weak points of the affective character of the religious tendencies. Therefore it always strives to seduce it to the real intellectual struggle and to defeat it then easily in the sharply discerning sun-light of the categoric circumstances of time, space and causality of the material, intellectual visible life.

If the clarity of the intellectuality consists in having found the sure sequence of the logical steps in going on to the affective delightful centre, the lasting principal and necessary parallel phenomenon in the religious psychology is suffering. Intellectuality, work and science are gradually checked and retained by the law of the logical thought, religion instead by the obstacles of its suffering restriction. Science and intellect are graduelly bridled by their clear progressive laws, but the affective religion has its checking moments in the self-conscious necessities of cross, passion and suffering, and it becomes as soon science and intellectuality, as it is entirely conscious and clear of the reasons of its suffering nature. No sooner, indeed, it has become intellectuality and science than it is itself the intellectual deed of a historic event and then it is likely to fade away or weaken spiritually as the single intellectual expression of any categoric time.

So we understand the declining attitude of the religious hero to the legal action started against him. He is not ambitious to be victorious in the letter, but in the spirit. He feels to be the deeper source of right and truth himself, much more than the historic artificial compilation of the historic laws. He is offended by the intellectual tricks used against him and he prefers to be misunderstood and have the intellectual disadvantage of condemnation and even of losing his temporal life than to compare and expose his superior dignity to ,the historic limitation of the contemporary human legal tenets. He claims to have in his idealistic mind the more competent causes of right, to be able to distinguish best what is right and wrong and declines, therefore, the logical power of the legal world, facing it by the startling strength of immovable silence. His personal, thorough conviction is the higher source of his right and of his conscientious tranquillity than the living collection of the refined distinctions of the legal experiences of a whole culture. His intellectual adversaries knew and looked for his compensatory retreat into the idealistic depth of his divine mind, and they were willing to, and successful in, ruining him by the intellectual tricks of their legislation. The hero could and would not deal with the superficial intellectual display of the letter. He would have lost his divine dignity and his pretended idealistic credentials, in quarrelling with the detailed forces of his legal wordly surroundings. He knew that, in the conception of his idealistic claims, under the given circumstances, he only could be satisfied and justified in accepting fairly the condemnation from the jealous competitive court of the intellectual function.

The idea of the real success is so terribly dangerous and difficult for the pronounced idealist. He himself cannot do wrong; he must be faithful to the idealistic spirit, never looking for intellectual tricks and is therefore so easily hanged by the small ridiculous tricks of the faithless letter of the intellectuality. Lie is as far from Christ as hypocrisy and real individual egoism, and for this reason He is not able nor willing to settle with the legal intellectual law. He declines the intellectuality because of its shallow sentiments and the relativity of its validity and at the same time because of the superiority of his universal and truer sentiments.

But in declining entirely the argumentation and the claims of the real world, the religious hero does not explain them. He bluffs intellectuality again by the tremendous fortitude of his character, and he does not build bridges between the realm of this narrow world and his eternal idealism. He does not bring about reconciliation, but rather the more pronounced opposition between the real-intellectual and the idealistic-sentimental components of the human nature than it was before, and at this point he leaves the world, taking with him the admiration and the longing of the abandoned, sad and puzzled congenial friends. Christ would be wrong in order not to be accomplice, not to be degraded from his high idealistic platform into the small intellectuad restriction of his time. He principally could not stand to be intellectually successful, because real success is the instantaneous commencement of decay and death. He claimed to be and was the rising star of the coming new intellectuality and of the unrolling civilization which only after centuries could have developed its real fixation. Christ himself did not display thoroughly any successful real historic fixation of his teachings in the world. It was his church which fastened the hovering Divinity of his personality to the intellectual categories of the life, and this church of course brought about what he avoided so carefully in his life, the important historic fixation of its hero, his traditionnal limitation and in this his cultural successfulness. Therefore the religious hero lives to-day as well as in the beginning in his idealistic undetermined values. Any church must stick most anxiously to his supracategoric divine values in order to receive from this imperishable well the shining right of farther historic existence.

SUFFERING is seemingly very near slothfulness. It represents itself psychopupilarily similar to slothfulness in clinging in a reserved manner to the periphery of the reality, in making, at the first sight, the impression of vulgar lazy weakness, of lacking ideal concentrative gift and will and of insufficient longing for affective penetration and courage. The cause of the peripheric fixation of suffering is, however, different. The methods of the progressing intellectuality in the visible historic world offering themselves to the suffering individual, are often not available for the same. The suffering man has not any lack of the strong ideal suggestibility as the stupefied lazy people who do not react upon the idealistic urges because of their lack of sensitiveness, but he on the contrary is most suggestible towards the affective centre, and the essential of the suffering consists exactly in this circumstance that the keen individual sensitiveness does not permit to follow his energetic affective inclination towards the central magnetism, so that he is really checked and compelled to resign in spite of his strong concentric desire. He cannot have his concentric wish fulfilled, because he wishes to reach more than is obtainable objectively in his historic time, better methods than there are possible. The core of suffering is therefore the strong idealistic suggestibility and the extremely select taste. Does the suffering individual not follow the affective magnetic invitation of the historic world toward its goals because of lacking of love for, or insufficient interest in, their attractive aims? No, he on the contrary is most sensitive of this invitation and suffers much more because of his individual free declining than others. The affective social way offered and necessary, up to a certain degree, but not acceptable to him is the reason of his sufferings. He has the natural inclination and the possible appreciation of the affective goals much more than the average person, but it is his idealistic depth and the genial elaboration of the divine ideals in his own heart which check him from accepting the common historic, social, legal and intellectual methods. He is so much swept toward his terminal idealism, that he is seriously hurt by the methodical steps of the reality. The overwhelming love for the pure divine goals forbids him to sanctify the means.

Pain and suffering are the much greater and stronger, the more developed the longing for enjoyment and pleasure is; and the more peripheric and efficient the checking bearers of the objective and and historic realities are. The ideal suffering hero reseigns in opposition to his natural high degree of affectionate susceptibility. Exactly in ocnnection with his strong concentric affective gift he formed

and educated the retrospective principles of the methodical pursuit
of his ideals. Just this accustomed claim for congruity between
logical way and ideal goal is the reason that he very often repulses
the real concentrative methods offered to him by the reality and
suffers therefore. He prefers to stay at the periphery of the light-
field, despised and humiliated, than to approach an ideal which he
cannot acknowledge as the full expression of his personal ideal
conception, nor to accept and choose a way which was not the direct
and logical progression to his goal. In suffering we have again that
extraordinary directive incompatibility so typical of the idealist and
his nervous system. He feels most easily every affective non-parallelism of all digressive ways that he very quickly and thoroughly
repulses all different directions and methods. Suffering is the expression of the conviction that the goal is not able to sanctify the
way, but that all ways are wrong which digress in the slightest
degree from the one needful goal. He has no confidence in all other
methods and ways, thinking that they are unable to lead to the
right aim. The suffering idealist, in addition, has the opinion that
different goals also must cause different intellectual and historical
ways, and that immovable leaning to old historic formulas would
withhold, for instance, from the development toward the further
future cultural progress.

So we see that the correct idealist prosecuting always in a consequent and accurate way his hightst goals must necessarily be the
most suffering individual. The genial idealist has higher goals
than the historic past; he is not satisfied with the logical formula of
the present and must, therefore, accept the bitter chalice of suffering
again and again, because of his prospecting super-intellectual affective tendencies which are beyond the reach of any historic development.

Suffering is for this reason the painful retreat from the present
real work toward the given historic goals; but it can be the germ
of a great future happiness of humanity, the seed of the greater
development and more universal unfoldment of human-theistic psychological history , and the genial anticipation of future fatal enlargements of the human collective spheric revolutions. The reason
of the idealistic suffering is not at all the disinclination against
work, but the longing for a greater and more perfect method toward the higher aims which the supreme speculative soul has chosen
and with which it will not at all risk to part by choosing uncon-
vinced old ways of others.

So we understand clearly that the religious genial hero must suffer indescribably. He made by his suffering the most impressive proclamation of his genial will to renew the earth by his future more divine legislation. He did not at all acqiuesce with the given state of the religious and psychological displayed mind of his time, but he indeed made the most remarkable new run from the very status renascendi, the first contraction of the general human gift as a very genial man and tried to bring out, with the addition of his personality, the higher affective theistic goals than his historic culture could show him the way to. He had then three moments for his superiority of divine conception : first, the cultural atmosphere which was then at the verge of a solstitial conversion; second, his personal genial peculiarity which induced and enabled him to gather all historical and psychological forces into one energetic, far reaching expression, and third, his individual strong life-force which produced a strong augmentation and addition to the two first factors. The enormous suffering of Christ is, therefore, the tocken of his highest idealistic and divine aspirations and talents expressed within the antiquated limits of the historic time.The most divine is most able to suffer.

Suffering for this reason is the dawn of the work, as the religious life must be *the affective anticipation of the intellectual realization in work and science.* Suffering like religion points to the future with the trembling finger of its magnetic prophetic oscillation. Fulfilment, success, satisfaction in intellectual work and science are instead connected with the past or the present. The right religion is full of secret prospects and of unresolved problems inviting us to serious meditation and sincere discovery. The checking regulations and the withholding time of its categoric measures are the misunderstandings, the contradictions and the persecutions of the real intellectual world in work, science and objective sensorial materiality. The affective religion must be the foundation and the inexhaustible stock of the intellectual experiences and developments of humanity, coming out by work and science, and suffering is the opposite introducing way as to how the affective high values of religion become full and mature in mankind. Suffering was the way by which the dull and childish ages were able to receive the important new germs of their future cultural development. Suffering was the first prophetic guidance to the human capability of idealistic possibility of the time of Christ, whilst the extended long way of the following intellectual unrolling of this mysterious goal was regulated by the laws of regular thought and by the categoriees of time, space and causality. Suffering has, therefore, to be considered as the quick supra-categoric affective accumulation of psychic energy which afterwards is opened out in the slow way of logical thinking. Suffering means the winding up of the gear of a clock which is quickly and energetically done with the power of the turning key, and logical thinking means instead the slow time of the pendulum which allows the distributing steady development of the gathered energy of the wound-up spring.

Thus the frightful atmosphere of the suffering Christ is most possibly elaborate in order to wind up the energetic spring of the human psychology. By the greedy embracement of his passion and suffering the religious hero made the most efficient efforts to gather and to concentrate the scattered magnetic forces of his age. By his suffering he wound up most efficiently the distended spring of his contemporary intellectual culture and hurled the social energy toward new goals by these suffering urges. Suffering in itself is to be considered as the most powerful affective retardation from the historic theistic notion, but at the same time and for the same mechanical reason, as the most efficient help toward the extrasolar extratheistic or the future enlarged theistic performances misinterpreted so often as "antitheistic" or even "atheistic". Suffering is the continual winding up of the distending spring of our individual lifeforce and of our historic intellectual worn out notions and real representations. Suffering is the only and inevitable strength giving to the stage of our vital performances and of our historic necessary progression always new and higher energetic urges and jerks and pricks going on toward more enlarged and more comprising notions and intellectual values than humanity could have them before. Without suffering, no progress. The more suffering, the more progress; on the other hand, the more ease and comfort, the more stagnation of the developing necessity. But it is not chiefly the torturer who will have the most advantages of suffering, but rather the sufferer himself, though both may be helped by it because of the collective fate of humanity which collaborates as a whole on the stage of life in taking the roles differently, one being the murderer and one the charming innocent lamb, but at the end the progress of the total psychological humanity and the terminal advantageous result is equally shared and distributed to all mankind. All are heartily invited to the table after the well performed play. Brutus is seated beside Ceasar and Banco beside Macbeth. They all are real friends and estimate each other with forgiving smile, because they all helped the success of the great idea of the play, in acting well their completing roles, increased so the mutual consideration.

Suffering is not a concentrative action, but the preparation to start from it. The better we understand to avoid the disagreeable ordinary circumstances of life, the more dangerous and ticklish must our fate turn out. For the human nature cannot miss anything as little as pain and suffering. The human soul degenerates and perishes gradually and quickly if the renewing energetic power of the suffering spring is not wound up again and again. Luxuriance, neurasthenia, unworthy predilection for exaggerated worhip of ancestry and insignificant traditions, silly laziness and angry slothfulness, unbelievable sterility of thought and exaggerated dangerous conservativism must soon follow, where the powerful intervention and instigation of suffering has succeeded in becoming excluded from humanity. No greater pain than lack of suffering.

Therefore we have the strongest progress, the most audacious human advancing and the most pronounced deepening of the theistic and psychological notions in the suffering man. He is the leading torch-bearer of the human affective progress. Suffering enables the world to progress, comfort makes lazy, silly, narrow and cowardly. The regal reward of suffering is the leading intellectual part in the future human development. The despicable punishment of the comfortable traditional affirmation and of the lazy uncritical adaptation to the tenets of others and of the old time is the antiquated and worn out insignificance, the oblivion by the future progressive energy. The extreme *conservativism* and the exaggerated fascination by the old crystallized ancestry is the dull and sterile punishment and the just equation of the lazy retreat from the pushing painful fate which grasps every man coming into this world. The confident prospect and the unchecked freedom of thought is, on the contrary, the reward for the courageous embracemnt of our destiny which life distributes to our natural development and whose painful suffering, pain and disappointment are the supposed energy for our future personal work.

We have thus the suffering as the supposition of working, as the winding up factor of the spring of our life-force. But suffering in its turn must have the strong attractive supposition of the most elevated idealism. Idealism is the first psychological station and cause in our human development. Only the large wings of the broadening idealism enable the wide excursions of the feeling heart, and the following work will turn afterwards according to these deepening, enlarging and connecting measures and excursions achieved on the great scale of idealism. Suffering thus is the middle step between affective idealism and real work. Suffering is therefore the turning-point between both. It is at the same time sentimental and sensorial, taking its food out of the idealistic feelings and impressing them on the sensitive nature of our corporeal constitution being the basis and the stage of the future real working development. So suffering turns out to be the most important link between idealism and real daily work, science, visible objectivity and artistic perfection, and we easily see that there cannot be any real progress without the strong insisting urges of suffering.

Suffering as well cannot play an important role in our life without the uplifting and superior claims of the attractive idealism and of strong sentimental progress in our innermost psychic kindly longings. The greatest idealistic progress produces the strongest, most hurting and most impressive sentimental-sensorial suffering, and this is in its turn again the most energetic urge and link for the following real working energy. No serious suffering without strong ideal disposition. No thorough suffering without high idealistic consequences, but as little strong real effort without suffering pre-suppositions and conclusions. So in the last point we rightly draw the opinion that the strong idealism may guide toward real work through suffering and that the last consequence of an energetic and serious working life will be as well the deepening and considerable reenforcement of idealistic conceptions. But the intermediary station of these opposite extremes is always again suffering, leading idealism to the real peripheric work, and the real peripheric real work toward idealistic simplification and clarification. The measure of suffering is the indicator of the degree of progressive uplifting idealism which is hidden like a flickering light within any individual and social system. Suffering is the proof pointing out, how much may be hoped or must be feared from any repressed principle or any oppressed personality.

Suffering and passion in the divine life do, therefore, not only mean the superior genial force of this hero, they do not only wind up the psychological spring of his mighty affective claims and connections, finishing afterwards in the reactive glory of his resurrection, but the continual emphasis of the suffering moments of the history of the passion of Christ is at the same time the exemplary natural winding up of the spring of our own psychological forces and energies. The sultry atmosphere of the passion, which does not leave us for one moment and which uses all artistic moments in order to keep us back and to retain with the utmost tenacity our feelings at the real despairing periphery of the torn intellectual circumstances of the world, are the skilful artistic and psychological supposition in order to gather and recompress the scattered "concentrable" possibilities and to throw them afterwards with one mighty energetic push to the most possible idealistic divine confident centralization producing excellent security, reconciliation and delight in the sentimental idea of the resurrection.

But the suffering representation of Christ with the glorious issue has simultaneously the educational intention to impart to our own personal lot the strong idealistic jerks of salvation, of hope and deliverance from the diluted intellectual force and from the detailed peripheric, despairing entanglement of the life, in giving us the thrilling suffering example and in showing us, by the emphasized description of his real and ideal obstacles, how much more he than we could have and had every reason to lose his ideal connections, and how he notwithstanding always was in strong and clear touch with his high divine central intentions and with the happy confident issue of his ideal genial subjective conceptions.

So the in-the-whole idealistic and exceedingly lofty descriptions of the *New Testament,* which is so far from our detailed existence, receive chiefly in the representation of the suffering passion of the hero the full weight of their general human validity and even intellectual importance which they have. The extraordinary and daring idealistic conceptions of the gospels are equaled in the opposite energy of the suffering passion which reconciles the one-sided and easy victory of the lofty idealism and establishes the psychological reality and intellectual-human justice at least in the end, whilst it was blurred at the beginning. It is chiefly this thrilling part of the suffering tales of the life of Christ, which attracts the reverent reader of the gospels much more, in a sense, and gives to him, for his shadowy and confused fate, all hopes for his future and all confidence for his terminal central harmony and reward.

If the hero of the gospels went much too far in his methods and ways than to have the intellectual understanding and the reconciliation of his short-sighted contemporaries, who tortured and killed him, if his extraordinary genius threw him over the marks of the traditional historic institutions and all settled order of his time, in spite of this he does not miss the perfect ideal reward and fervent longing for reconciliation at the last point, because he acted according to his best subjective conviction. This of course means the practical encouragement of the confidence into our best honest and true perseverance. It shows us how much we must naturally suffer and be abused by the historic legal fixation of the traditional world, if we will carry through our own best convictions, but it points out also what will be the terminal end of all this suffering struggle, first the cross, but then the everlasting apotheosis in resurrection, the idealistic eternal life and the valuable and imperishable universal acknowledgement.

So we know that suffering is not religion itself and as little science or active work. It is the middle stage of both parts, the transferring psychological turning-point between the two. But this is sure that the strong religious progress of humanity is definitely bound to the strong necessity of the suffering power and that the suffering strength, endurance and *patience* of any age is the measure of its following elevation and effusion in work and science. Suffering is the deep well, from which the working energy of the following times draws its living psychological water. Suffering is the strong forboding eagle which lifts the lazy historic and traditional humanity up to their new and enlarged future. Is not working, although not yet mere enjoyment in itself, nevertheless already a clear and sure gradual approach to the new concentric reward and delight? But it must have first the urging supposition of suffering and patience. Suffering is the psychological force which in advance must plough the earth with the painful implements of its hurting and intruding irons digging the deep wrinkles of our features, and only after this complete new conversion and preparation of the psychological human gift the individual inclination is again amenable to conceive the efficient seed of another flowering culture, progressing in work, art and science. Suffering is the preparing foundation of all human work and science, coming out always then, when new huge genial influences are ready to come down like divine lightnings and vivifying rains from the fatal revolution of the heavens, giving their fertilizing water and stirring light to the dark and absorbing converted earth, combining their pulling energy with the thriving faculty of the ground, prepared and ploughed in suffering, in sacrifice, in tears and blood.

Suffering comes about, if you know how things ought to be and how they are not, if you try seriously to mend them according to your conviction and they will not submit to your better insight. Suffering is the ignorance of the better knowing, and stupidity replaces the suffering of the ignorant.

We found out that WORK is the third and last degree of psychological development from the central idealism through the intermediary station of suffering toward the peripheric real world. If we compare the deep well of the affective sentimentality with the roots of the natural *tree,* then we rightly may liken suffering to the trunk and the executional work to the boughs, twigs and leaves, blossoms and fruits where the circle to general forces is closed. The forces of idealism are the most hidden and invisible parts of our psychic life, whilst the working quality of our nature means the visible disclosure and detailed display of our psychic force in the open air of the intellectual stage of our life. From the mighty crown of the tree, from its numberless blossoms and fruits we make the conclusion that the root must be deep and powerful, and in the same manner we realize that it is chiefly owing to the mechanical and nutritive qualities of the roots, that the tree has received its high and stately position and strong rich importance. In a similar way we gather the natural confidence of the working power of mankind from the central idealistic energy of character. But, if we observe and admit that the developed leaves of the tree have through their metabolism the utmost significance for the existence and the further development of the tree, perhaps at least as much or even more than the roots, then we must make the interesting statement that the peripheric detailed objectivity by its working metabolism produces also the most useful relations to the surrounding world and these relations play in the grown-up cultural humanity, as in the mature tree, the same important role as in the beginning the idealistic roots. So we see that the youth of the human psychology is conceived, born and fostered in idealism. The childhood of the human individual as well as that of the nations and the political and social unions are altogether characterized by the most pronounced idealistic expectations and hopes, by the speculative longing for future important performances, but also by the lack of real opportunities and the skilful adaptability to the working exactions. But when the child is grown up, when the nation arrived at the top of its development, and if experiences have increased the intellectual urges and possibilities, when the tree is fully mature, then the most important peripheric metabolic intercourse between the numberless objective leaves and the visible detailed world and the social and real surroundings will happen, and they consecutively have not only the most necessary influence of growth and preservation on the organs of the psychological tree, but even the most thorough effect goes back to the twigs, the boughs, the trunk and the very roots. All organs of the tree receive their advantages from the extraordinary display of the intellectual crown of the psychological tree and its real intercourse, and we observe easily, how *with the progressive age the relative importance of the idealistic roots diminishes and how much the objective role of the intellectual peripheric relations becomes more and more important*. This is the meaning of the culture: the continual transition from idealism to realism and intellectuality, the increasing easiness of their relations and the terminal oppressive and crushing real riches of the happy, detailed intellectual crown, whilst the power of suffering diminishes in the decaying trunk and the roots loose their absorbing energy in the dry earth. Just at the top of the delightful development of its rich crown, exactly at the time, when the shadowy foliage and the useful fruits have become most charming and numerous, when the tree begins to make the most overwhelming real impression of its force and importance, then the roots and the trunk decay and become rotted, and the mighty intellectual tree must be felled, just at the time of its most pronounced real peripheric development. The mechanical and static role of the strong character of the trunk and of the fastening roots could not be replaced essentially nor could the failing sap from the earth be made up with the metabolism of the aerial activity of the foliage. Even the disproportioned riches of the boughs and the fruits help perhaps to damage the health of the trunk and the roots. We see that the beginning overweight of the importance of the idealistic roots receded and went over, at the later period, to the peripheric detailed intellectuality, so that the end of the psychological tree, if it follows the real tree of creation, must be *Hypertrophia intellectualis*.

We undiscussedly admit that the working function indeed has the most intimate connection with the real intellectual world, that its realm is at the outside periphery of our psychic personality, that working has the most detailed and multiplied various intercourse with our real wordly visible surroundings. The working function gives and receives at the utmost periphery of our psychological action. It touches, progresses and receives in the clearest and most detailed intellectual and real relations. It is the last psychic runner of the individual, produced by the foundations of idealism and suffering necessity, crossing the realm of our reality and experience and emptying at last again into the central river of idealistic delight.

We therefore recognize easily that work has quite different natural laws, according to which it is essentially distinguished from the affective suggestible sentimental idealism and its proceedings. The characteristics of all works are clearness,reality,intellectuality, (visibility, materiality, multiplicity),logical progress. Work is not entitled to hover over all objective world and to run uncheckedly to its desired goal, as the affective idealism can do with the help of its suggestive sentimental powers and methods. Work has to step the steady walk of the logical advancing. It has to regulate and to array all meeting objective experience occurring to its affective standards and magnetic significance. It has to simplify and to contract the exceedingly detailed intellectual notions, to compress and to unify intellectually the various accidental experiences of the life, to classify all emerging values and so to prepare and create, in toiling effort, a new way toward the least intellectual and most imaginative, elevated, symbolic idealistic notions of truth, love, beauty and strength.

Work indeed is not flying in unchecked affective rapidity, but rather it means the slow gradual but sure toiling progress by the logical thinking laws and real categories. We know, therefore, already that work cannot be the accelerating force of our psychic affective centralization, but that it is the essentially peripheric funcion of our life-force, making the stage of our real intellectual life the main fixation of this effort and retaining, in this way, the centralization of the psychological progression toward the centre. Working at last turns out, as the foliage and fruits of the tree do, to emphasize exclusively the real periphery, it overlooks the efficiency and strength of the trunk and the roots, absorbs all vital sap from the brittle old roots, uses the gained force for the development of its own biological section and withholds by this the concentric progression of the vital energy of our fate. The peripheric intellectual tendency is so essential and so great in work that the main direction of the psychological magnetism, by the strong detailed working development, flows after all not so much from the periphery to the centre, but much more from the centre to the periphery, where the whole life-force is fixed and attracted by the thouand sucking trumpets of its detailed objective attentions and experiences.

In spite of the terminal common delightful goal of both sentimentality and work, there must be stated that there is a practical antagonism in the method and way and in the direct goal of both. Yet we will never forget that oppositions are always only distances. Both feel each other even as going in opposed magnetic directions. The work has distinct features of historic centrifugal tendencies. The work declines the unchecked proceeding theistic concentration and prefers to go through difficulties and obstacles only in order to have, owing to the circuit of the affective opposition, the terminal advantage of the higher degree of the extrasolar spiritual conversion and new theistic concentration. Every work means some digression from the historic faithful theistic centralization, and every work means, therefore, as well a small progress and some augmentation of our extrasolar future theistic universal conceptions.

Working means, indeed, essentially the logical and intellectual digression from the central historic sentimental activity. Work is understood, from the sensitive sentimental standpoint, as the most adequate expression of the expulsion of humanity from the theistic paradise. The work seems to be the accurate realization of the saying: In quo quis peccaverit, in eo punietur. Mankind scorned the most perfect adaptation to the theistic commandment. They were keen about tastes and experiences of their own, and, therefore, God told them to be punished just by having their will, as they had decided themselves to be doomed, to go their own "antitheistic" way in resigning and sacrificing work and to suffer the bitterness of the separation and of the recoil from the charming attractions of the historic God. So the secrets of the creation and of the outcoming cultural energy go back to the interesting notion of the magnetism of the ecclesiastical sin. But there we have the radical explaining idea of the creation, of the visibility, materiality and intellectuality at the same time. The idea which was called *Fall of Man* was just the expression of the starting intellectual creative work. It meant the most successful fraus pia or the most felix culpa, in its consequences, which ever happened, because it caused the marvellous and never ending beginning development of the creative world, in the psychological sense, of the intellectual life, of the visible multiplicity, of all creative artistic and cultural values until the end of all the historic rivers. The fall of man is a clever explaining contrivance, a simple but striking parable and exemplifies to us, up to a certain degree, the starting foundation of the creation. The principle of demoniacal resistance, of bold and independent personal criticism and the ripening pride of individual conviction were the starting point of all principles of separating intellectuality, visibility, objectivity and multiplication. But work is the bitter and toiling pain, the tiring sweat or the heavy tax which must be paid in order to reach this goal. Difficult work is the angel put with the fiery sword before the door of the dreamy and lazy paradise, sending us away and preventing us from the direct affective hovering entrance leading into this idealistic garden. The logical scale of thinking is meant by this fiery sword. The creative intellectual necessity of our nature in the bitterness of its personal energy of affective independence is hinted to, by the comparison of thorns and thistles. The pessimist takes our working effort as incessant treadmill or the ever rolling stone of Sysiphus. Humanity would have their own viewpoint and criticism and must, therefore, accept the digressing and checking obstacles of their logical, natural, real disposition.

The thinking man feels how bitter it is to have left his historic theistic intimacy, and he knows, how tiring and heartrending can be the stepping out from the old idealistic home country of the heart, the affective abstemiousness in intellectual struggle.But just in this loss of ourselves, in the rejection by the highest historic values of our progressive culture, we receive again the power of our future "extra-theistic" happy re-instalment. One day the elaborate extra-theistic working removal will have its new magnetic whirlpools, and then we have the same augmented theistic psychodynamic phenomenon once more, as we had it in the former historic theistic time, only now more powerful, greater and more perfect, because the life-circles have been enlarged. What seems to be and is, relatively speaking, in the moment a psycho-dynamic opposition, is in truth and in fact, considering the later ages and the last result, the help and the support for the future "enlarged" concentration; but every work in itself means, in the historic-magnetic sense, the progressive fare-well from the old paradise of the historic deity. Every smallest work has its hell in moving from, and leaving, its dreamy theistic and sentimental paradise, but every work has also its special shining heavenly star of higher theistic fulfilment, of affective delightful increase and terminal satisfaction.

Work is the fatal opposition to our affective concentric action. By our natural organization we have our total psychic life-force divided into two halves, one of which is evaporated in the sublimation of the affective sentimental pleasure, whilst the other has to pass the logical treadmill of the thinking intellectual laws. Work means the protection of our soul from its unchecked affective diarrhoea. Work fastens the individual to the peripheric categories of time, space and causality. Work gives to our real-intellectual objective and visible natural constitution its strong backbone, its human strength and real control and performance. The affective sentimentality is not able to go on without the regulating retardation of work. It would burn its idealistic wings, if it had not the checking counterbalance of the real and gradual logical progress of our intellectual component.

But work is not the blind fatal inculcation as we have in sorrow, pain and suffering. Work has the advantage on the transitional turning-point of suffering, that it has already a clear although near aim, a new magnetic goal, the fact of a sure task and of a definite purpose. The sorrow of the sufferer is not to know how to accomplish great wonderful visions, and the consolation of the worker consists in the fact that he knows, how to do, modest as his goals may be in reach and capacity. The sentimental imperfection of work is not chiefly its lack of magnetic attraction, but the multiple gradual fixation on the progressive, increasing steps of logical order of the different magnetic standards, as they are given in the natural, thinking rules of our intellectual nature. Work and thinking have purposes and magnetic energies; they have only the previous necessity to dispose their accidental real meetings into the consecutive increasing amounts of the affective attractions, refining all peripheric real objective notions into the simplification of other notions poorer in intellectual characteristics and therefore richer in imaginativ values. Working must therefore be defined as the grinding millstone of the psychic life, which refines our real experiences into the uniform flour of idealistic values and blows the definite small, homogeneous idealistic powder, after all, in charming showers through the same punctual idealistic hole, or through *the same, symbolic thrilling flute, as the affective sentimentality does, on the other side.*

We know that the essential intention of the genial religion is to accelerate the human soul with its psycho-dynamic means toward the strong historic theistic concentration. Therefore religion puts so much stress on symbolism, mysticism and miracle, where it receives the uplifting faith and the dreamy atmosphere which are essentially necessary as the basis of its existence and performances. In as far as the religious hero and idealistic founder had the progressive intention of the extrasolar development of the humanity, he inclusively made the proclamation of the essential pioneering necessity of work. But it is typical of the temperamental mission of the historic religion that he in his apparent manifestations did not leave the hazy glory of his divine character. He only progressed until the threshold of the working humanity, in accepting the equivalent experiences of suffering, passion and cross.

We must understand this attitude of emergency of the religious founder. For the religious activity means essentially the connection of our life-force with the central historic deity. It is not the intention nor the advanage of the religious idea to enter entirely and clearly into the realm of the intellectual working life, because it would lose the prestige of its secret divinity and the force of suggestion which, in its special character, is always broken and defeated by the sensorial competition. The further reason is the danger of us not reaching the ideal with all affective energy, owing to the law of compensation. For we remember that the individual human life-force is very short in comparison with the objective magnetic fingerboard presenting itself to the religious avidity. Had religion insisted very much on the detailed work and science, mankind would have lost the contact with the eternal idea more than before, and religion would not have done its task to join humanity easily to the highest divine magnetic goals, as the world needed it most at that time.

But the exclusion of the working intellectuality is, therefore, not the less exceedingly dangerous for the appreciation of any religious system. For there is no better educational value given under the sun than the example of the working performance, and there cannot be a greater danger for the psychic and real health of humanity than neglecting the working intellecual world. The sure help of the real sensorial cadence and the logical rhythm of the thinking laws are the excellent crutches for our affective disposition to move on, according to the best natural intention of our human nature. Work and intellectual activity are not only the most favorable introductory, forwarding helps of our developing theistic and cultural progress and of our fatal enlargements, but work has the inestimable educational advantage to show humanity how it must approach the ideal goal most naturally in this world, what is the best and most harmonious and appropriate rhythmic method for the human nature to go on toward the idealistic last goals and purposes.

If religion overlooks these ways, it is understandable under the point of view of the necessity of careful compensation, coming out from the consideration of our total vital insufficiency: but this circumstance puts the educational value of the religious spirit, nevertheless, in the light of questionable suspicion.

It is in the strong emphasis of *suffering,* that the religious genius and his church saved themselves partly from this possible objection. They created in suffering and cross at least the solid platform of work; they gave in suffering the inevitable human urges for the real struggle of intellectual work, and they, in the passion of the hero, pointed out that there must be progressive conflicts in the world, which cannot be avoided. It is in the suffering and in the passion of Christ, where there was hinted to the working task of our life, where mighty urges were given to embrace the centrifugal opportunities of our working energies and where was depicted the fate of the extrasolar individual who resists the historic central necessities by passive withdrawal from their exactions.

There are two opposite *reasons for suffering,* one consisting in the strong pushing ideal personality of the advancing intellectual force which is not permitted by its time and circumstances to leave the boundaries of the frame of the historic culture crushing the predecessor of the coming new enlargement in work and intellectual culture. The other opportunity of the same fate is founded on the passive laziness within the historic tradition of an old political or cultural time, whilst the surrounding world has proceeded already further. Suffering can, therefore, as well be the starting point of the glorious divine hero pushing forward toward new enlarging genial tasks and more important future work, but it also may signify the infamous repulsion of the slothful individual not being able or willing to collaborate at the progressive working energy of the universal cultural movement. Thus the golden crowns of kings and of earthly wealth and ancestry too often turn out to become the starting punishment of checking suffering of the wrong egoistic conservativism which has been overtaken long ago by the progressive working time and history; and it just the crown of thorns ironically put on the head of Christ, which was the most glorious and promising token of victory, because the hero was the most progressive man of his time and the most courageous predecessor of the coming human cultural enlargement. His thorny crown was the symbol of the coming time of self-denying work and progressive struggle. He had not the old theistic narrow conceptions of his contemporary cultural frame, but the widened vista of the future working development of mankind. So his suffering and his passion were glorious; he was not the shameful victim of his antiquated laziness, but of his antiquated surroundings and immovable worn out bad circumstances which would not allow the progressive wheel of the psychological time to move on, and which were in themselves fixed in historic traditionalism, whilst the religious hero was connected and concerned with urgent future working progression.

SCIENCE means the systematic excavation and generalization of the intellectual work. It is the most willing, exclusive and conscientious acceptance of the ruling logical laws within our brains, the experimental objective world and the human society. The influence of the scientific conception strives to exclude as incompetent all sentimental and suggestive psychic forces, and it puts all its stress on the detailed sensorial experience and the logical intellectual performance. The science rejects the affective methods of sentimental concentration. It is the most consequent expression of the most elaborated legislation of the intellectual principle of the work and shares, therefore, all its characteristics.

The strong development of work came only about in the last centuries of our psychological sun-year. During the sentimental, first quarter and still to-day, within the reclining cultural parts of our civilization, we see, how much the sentimental passive suffering and the affective historic tradition are much more appreciated than the working progress. Working progress is rather the object of anxiety for these social circles, because they are afraid of the change of their antiquated, theistic, historic conceptions which indeed necessarily must be transformed by the working and scientific influence. Work and science are not the first intention of the historic theistic religion, although the large and deep conception of religion imparts the most efficient urges for future work and scientific experimentation and vice versa. Work and science are even the pronounced temperamental enemies of any traditional religious system. But they are the predecessors of the following future enlarged religious conceptions. They are the best friends of the coming universal religious unfoldment, needing to this purpose, however, the whispering sources of universal spiritual direction and suggestion.

It is especially owing to the increasing influence of science, that work lost its stigma of shame and arrived to the high degree of authoritative competence and general honorable acknowledgement. As soon as the intellectual second quarter of our cultural section of mankind started, science made the most extensive and most successful efforts to systematize work in all realms and lines of our life and succeeded, by its accurate division and minute working performance, in producing the most stupendous intellectual variety and intensity, great intellectual refinement and most detailed logical development. It established its most perfect domineering position it likely ever had since the beginning of the world.

Although there is on one side an essential alliance between the categoric character of the historic theistic conception and the intellectual laws of science, the latter must be admitted, on the other hand, and considered as the most inimical enterprise against any historic theistic conception. It is already the preparation of the future solstitial development of our psychological world. It is the emergent biological reaction against the laziness of the sentimental fulfilment of the earlier theistic fixation and satisfaction. Science enlarges and prepares already the suffering and then ruling arches of the future times and is on the verge to run toward the future culminating conversion of the human fate. It is the presupposition and the preparing work of the next theistic involution into the extrasolar outside universal spaces. Science and work are transitional stages of the progressive and always craving human destiny, and their huge influence carries our race away on the wings of the most promising and farthest reaching religious hopes of our imagination. But in the sense of our traditional theistic historic conceptions they are to be considered as practically opposed because progressive forces. That would be a weak religion, in which the spiritual development has been exceeded by logical and intellectual claims. The religious genius, at his time, was the strong enemy of the contemporaneous crystallization of his historic tradition, beating it by the disagreement of the passive work of his bitter Passion and Death. The more the human society is filled sentimentally by the worn-out formulae of any religious system, the more it cries for new future intellectual expressions of its highest divine desire, and it is exactly the science, which has been sent out by the burning desire of humanity in order to look for the new expected greater Messiah. It is the science, which has the secret mission of the human society to go and to meet the next greater religious genius who could give guarantee to charm and gratify humanity better under a new appearance than the old historic worn-out traditional conception of the former theistic expression did. It is clear, therefore, that the secret and public circumvention and avoiding of the historically and legally sacred formula of the traditional theism, by the scientific methods and their helpers, cannot be flattering for the adherents of the old literal religious conception; and we, therefore, understand easily that these two original temperamental enemies, with irreconciliable difference of viewpoint, though doomed to some formal exterior mutual tolerance in order not to stop the social existence of the world, practise likely the most pronounced aversion, scorn, slander, suspicions and misgivings against each other. Religion and science are of different taste, opposed practically in the magnetic direction, in the methods and means as well. Only the terminal results of all vital processes are always the same. The end of all is unexceptionally harmony, reconciliation and peace. But what difficult travelling and misunderstanding grumbling going round the countryside before the two different methods meet each other on the promising peak !

The historic religion points out quite rightly that its tenets never can be in contradiction with science because they are true in an *absolute* sense , and science asserts in its turn that it does not respect but its more reliable, its greater own *objective* truth, and that its tendencies must therefore be in congruancy with every true relation and guide, after all, to the best and highest religion. Indeed the historic religion possesses the most thorough elements of deepest truth of humanity, because of the potential power of its symbolism, which science never will be able to destroy, and for this reason the universally inclusive religion has a certain right to claim its everlasting existence. The exclusive science in its turn has the merit of creating new progressive insights into the human and universal, psychological natural and universal state of the created world, and it has, therefore, the right to claim in many ways the higher and more competent authority than the historic religion. The opposite struggles of these two methods are, therefore, not so thorough and startling as they seem to be, because like everything in our intellectual work, they both are historic phenomena of our human existence, led and limited by the historic, cultural, accidental circumstances and the underlying human fallibility. But the historic religious conservativism may rightly be afraid of its historic accurate self-sureness and unchanging authority and of its rocklike stability. The progressive science changes unhesitatingly the historic fixations of any religious system, and there is no means against the radical progression of all theistic religious progression and centralization. There will inevitably be a time, when the egoistic sentimental obstinacy of every traditional organization will be scorned, hated and, which is worse, abandoned and overtaken by the new progress. The best scientific, intellectual progresses reach the vicinity of absolute validity and have therefore an urgent influence on the leading religious primacy.

Science in its turn has as well sufficient reason to be rather bashful. If it has destroyed many historic wrong religious fixations and has freed all people from many a superstition and sorrow then it must not forget that the so-called scientific superiority and independence has not the meaning of continual stability nor of the eternal self-government of the human intelligence. The highest blossom of the human science means always a period of transition from a historic theistic time to a later following one. The human intellectuality will have new sentimental theistic whirlpools and pitfalls in the future times, as it has most unnecessary fashionable changes, at any time, impairing the weight of its broad authority. There will be other theistic magnetic concentrations, when the totality of mankind will be fixed again during future sentimental quarters, and then the proud scientific people will be also the trembling docile children of the future theistic concentric fixation.

The scientist ought not to be too upset about the stiff narrowness and the short-sighted egoism of the historic religion, because he also in his turn, after his sentimental conversion, will adopt the same tenacity of the crushing sense of egoistic possession. And the historic religion should not be so sure and so absolute in its assumptions, because there will be once a time, after its intellectual conversion, when it will recognize and feel, how disagreeable and wrong it is not to have any progressive influence on the historic sentimental formula of customs, tenets and religion. Beati possidentes means in this sense that the sentimental possessor is not willing to go out from his settled fixation in the material and philosophical life. Everywhere we observe again and again the terrible danger of obstructing egoism and personal lazy fixation. It is so easy to fall from all sides into that horrible pitfall, as it is, on the other side, difficult to keep away entirely from its manifold opportunities.

The first sentimental centuries were bound by fate to the suffering eruption from the retaining political and historic frame of their time. The struggle for their new ideals manifested itself in the necessity of pain, martyrdom and suffering. They were expelled from the intellectual body of their real circumstances, in which they were born, by the "angry" action of fear, passion and death. But at last they overcame the historic obstacles and put their own enlarged centro-theistic conceptions at the place of the former. It seemed to be their task to repudiate their intellectual previous history and the traditional footing, on which they had to build up their new realm, and they succeeded in converting their first intellectual suffering role in the ruling sentimental prevalence which turned out to be so glorious, really successful and comfortably secure for them, that, after all, passive suffering was quite converted into active work, that they forgot the initiating difficulties of their intellectual entrence into the world and used almost the same methods of suppressing and condemning future new intellectual urges as first were employed against them, at the commencement of their sentimental epoch. The first starting of the sentimental quarter into the real world was, according to the example of their master, the period of suffering and passive work. The overweight of the traditional strength and energy suppressed the real weakness of the beginning new genial system and used to cut away instantly the outcoming individual expansions of its advancing real victories in the world, by killing light bearing individual representatives.

Did the fascinating attitude of the essentially religious hero's example not bring about, in many ways, that his followers stuck too closely, at first, to the necessity of passive suffering? For a long time they were handicapped to progress in active work, so much they received by the long historic suppression and essentially spiritual point of view the lasting reverent habit and conviction to overcome the difficulties of their system better by passive suffering than by active work. Art was the glorious link to the active intellectual conversion of the Christian civilization, and the modern science brought the further progression and solution of the suffering problem. The real intellectual crystallization of the old pre-Christian ages tendered the same resistances to the starting genial Christian idea, as at the time of the middle ages the genial organization opposed to the rising head of of the modern scientific work. At its starting point and at its historic beginning the new religious system strives to escape from the old traditional cultural frame and to build up, on the foundation of the previous culture, its new realm. In the same manner the modern science claims to enlarge and develop the historic theo-centric traditional ideas, by its digressing tendencies and to erect its future extrasolar centro-magnetic building, seemingly outside and in opposition, but in reality on the same common ground, with the same material of the old affective humanity. The most inimical scientific campaign against the old religious system will always turn out to succeed in curtailing at its best the abusing historic lazy habits and superstitious intellectual fixations of the same, and the last and best success of any scientific work will never fail to finish in the strength and emphasis of the main and best truth of the former philosophical, psychological, religious and political principles. Truth, beauty, strength, kindness and love are unlosable notions and values, and the most trying scientific work can only effectuate the clarification of any existing historic truth, the deeper imagination of its strength and the enlarged amplitude of its final centro-magnetic embracement. The opposite struggles are necessary times of transition which are natural magnetic developing expeditions into the outside universe. But the terminal result will be always again the common meeting in the theistic centro-magnetic natural phenomenon which, each following time of its sentimental reaction, will be greater, clearer, deeper, more secure and more resistant against any future development of its augmented magnetic power, on one side, but more indulgent and lenient because of its broader and more distanced outlook and better freedom of two-sided insight and judgment, on the other side.

Any intolerance against the progressive modern science is a similar frivolous selfish anxiety , as the Antiquity had in regard to the rising new culture. It is sure that all truth is imperishable and that all necessity continues to be provided for. Absolute institutions can only be helped and confirmed by science. Why worry? But nothing can save antiquated exterior formulas and historic fixations of old times, as a rule, even if they had periods, where they did excellent services. They must perish nevertheless because of their relative, intellectual and historic value. If we have the strong confidence that there is behind and beyond all past and future universal psychodynamic transformations and developments, in spite of all, a great divine purpose of concentric crystallization, which leads all and which comes out always again and again from the middle of our historic discrepancies and contradictions, as an adorable circular rain-bow of eternal peace, then there cannot be any reason to worry about the dangers and results of any developing human struggle. All finally must bloom out to the best of the progressing universe. There cannot be any useless contradiction; all and everything turns out to share the future enlargement of the psychological human theistic fate. There is no intellectual digressing opposition imaginable in the psychological world, which would not find again finally the magneto-centric turning around the common meta of the improved collective human destiny.

Let us resume, once more, the comparison of the tree, which we used at the beginning of our meditation on work. The scientific progress of our age is indeed a surprising rich and orderly display of our phychological life. The numberless scientific results and the most succinct systematization of the whole intellectual world, as science brought it about, may be compared most suitably with the fine division and arrangement of the rich foliage and the charming blossoms of the tree. Not only art, even science with its clear dispositions, with the wonderful symmetric constellations of its notions like aesthetic clusters and flowers, bold yet harmonious arches and regular drawings, fascinates our admiration and startles our human feelings. The tremendous scientific display and the extraordinary intellectual riches of our time, in its turn, has also created the most charming atmosphere. The birds of the heaven sing and nestle in these tender twigs and the most poetic shower of eternal hopes trembles also in the rich and fragrant scientific foliage.

But there is a limit in everything. There is at Fribourg in Switzerland by the Town Hall an old lime-tree aged four hundred years, which has been carefully cultivated and preserved as the historic token of old events of the city. Its trunk is utterly frail and partly decayed. The tree is supported by a whole scaffold of iron sticks. But as a matter of fact it continues to live and produce its leaves and blossoms every year . Yet the tree woud instantly collapse, as soon as this artificial mechanical help would be removed. Must we not fear in the same manner that the exaggerated working and scientific applications on the old tree of our culture could take away the mechanical and static force of our psychological affective characteristic culture and that the over-growing intellectual one-sidedness could succeed one day in felling the decayed trunk of our old idealistic historic principles?

Alas! Is there no essential help against this general natural law? All trees must grow, develop their rich crown and foliage, and the trunks of all trees must at length become old, worn out and decay. Lucky event that there are countless germs blown by the wind to all directions, and there is confidently to hope that after the fall of any real or psychological tree new shoots will arise from the thriving bosom of the creative earth, and that other, perhaps even better crowns will do the future work as the task of the former human historic institutions. Let then blossom all real and scientific working life! Let the idealstic trunks grow older and decay! Who could prevent it! There must be continual decays, degenerations and downbreaks in the idealistic, in the philosophical and theistic world. Scandals are necessary though regrettable. There must incessantly be reformations and thorough changes, storms and hurricanes in the collective humanity as well as in the individual, sweeping the surface of our earth, as stirring up the deepest forces of the individual heart. The whole creative world as the single plant and tree share this law.: *the resurrection of the continual fecundation cannot be missed long, but is an incessant development creeping from fact to fact and putting historic moments of equal or increasing importance.* There is never any reason for desperation. The will of the progressive common universal fate be done in everything! Let everybody do seriously the best part of his personal duty and deepest conception in thinking, in struggling, in making resistances, restrictions, remonstrances and supports in persuading and pardoning, according to our personal education and natural disposition. But all must help to advance the natural will of the universe which never stands still and to which we all are thoroughly subjected. No standstill in any relation to the real or psychological universe is possible. Standing still is the worst which we could choose and which would be revenged in the most angry progression of the accelerated following destruction. Continual faithful collaboration with the magnetic meaning of our time is the best we can do, - the buttresses of state and church may make perennial old high conceptions of the ideal youth of a commonwealth- and if we all would contribute our forces to this universal will and do without our historic slothful egoism, then we could progress without the angry reactions of *war, revolution, martyrdom, murder and destroying violence.* Let us follow step by step our universal fate, and nothing can then drive our development to angry concentration in anger, fear and exaggerated enthusiasm. Seasonable, most attentive grasping of the signature of our destiny is the foremost necessary task of our life. Everybody is obliged to recognize the inevitable magnetic necessities of his age and to collaborate in it with his best forces. We must offer our services to the common progressive fate according to our personal fitness and disposition, be it in the leading working, or in the suffering passive, part of our common lot, because both parts are necessary for the realization of any spheric way and progress. But we have to adapt also ourselves in accordance with the momentary necessities; we have to acquiesce with the restricted personal weight of our will in the whole of the psychological society and of the human tendencies, and we shall so best have performed our intended collaborating progressive destiny.

The notion of SACRIFICE imparts to the work and duty terminal-ideal labels. It represents the balance between the work of the reality and the ideal intention and is, therefore, of high human dignity. Sacrifice is the perfect human performance putting our working necessity into the best ideal connection and direction and guaranteeing, therefore, the total harmony of our natural, intellectual and sentimental activity. Through the terminal ideal intention our work is ennobled. The individual with the strong terminal ideal purposes is fixed by them in the best direction and preserved from dangerous intentional oscillations. The logical connection between idealism and work is saved by the idea of sacrifice. The dissatisfaction, the impossibility to make up with the human real tasks and circumstances is somehow diminished through the outlook at higher ideals . In the conviction of the insight into the connection with the ideal direction, of our working task, we are strengthened in our will and supplied with mighty energies for our destiny and for our working duties. The terminal goal makes us courageous and strong, takes away our waywardness and pusillanimity, pulls our affective longing over the egoistic fixations of pain, checking disappointment and nauseating humiliation, in the efficient terminal desire.

So we understand that the CROSS is called rightly the sacrifice of the New Covenant. It is indeed on one side so distant of the character of the idealistic symbol by its sharp intellectual and sensorial exactions as it is, on the other side, the consoling affective compression and the ideal gathering of forces and pains, whose functions must be extorted from our nature for the hard intellectual work of reality. The cross is the ideal orientation within the embarrassing struggle of the visible reality diverting us from the last goals, and the sacrificing cross forms, therefore, in a certain sense and in a limited meaning, the bridge, the terminal ideal connection toward those highest goods which we all hope and are naturally longing for: truth, strength, beauty and happiness.

When *Polycrates* throws, at the behest of his friend, his most precious ring into the sea, he confesses by that fact the religious ideal of the sacrifice. Our two-sided nature needs a rich activity of both its components. It is concerned not only with intellectual, but also with affective effort. Sacrifice is the intended, preconceived regulation of our affective forces like work, giving to us a good affective discharge in the terminal-ideal direction and a connection with religious practice, or urging in the direction of the exterior culture by fulfilling duty, charity or alms. The direct terminal purpose gives us much more energetic opportunities for our causal nature, and the strength of suggestion, in the sacrifice, has therefore the more magnetic energy than the simple, rather aimless and steerless work. Sacrifice is a symbolic action in the realm of the work with the conscious intention of the terminal ideal compensation of our psychic life-force. Each work has even, up to a certain limit, this levelling function, but we call it sacrifice then, if it is freely and intentionally done in the thinking mind of the individual. The affective compensation rising by it is that which Schiller calls the Reconciliation of the Gods. The envy and the wrath of the gods mean the relative disregard of the universe in comparison with the exact activity and the use of the intellectual exterior real work. The human destiny in the religious sense is stamped with good intentions or sacrifices and has reached in this the terminal ideal purpose. Every work is able to attain in this manner an ambivalent importance, being or becoming at the same time the expression of corporeal, intellectual performance and of terminal ideal affective "reason".

Through this the notion of sacrifice is characterized. It is the intellectual activity having the sign and mark of the terminal ideal purpose, a very broad and human notion, engaging our most distant human capacities and connecting them closely and harmoniously. For this reason we feel in any free sacrifice the strong sentiment of deliverance and of the most beautiful psychic harmonious atmosphere. We cannot imagine anything greater and more perfect than the action being devoted and dedicated to the last and highest purpose of all magnetic affective life, and serving, at the same time our daily life in the fact of a useful intellectual deed. For this reason we feel it as perfect harmony and the most accomplished psychic satisfaction. We have reached in this way everything that we will attain in our human destiny, on one hand the affective devotion toward the deity being our last goal, because we make our act the symbol of this ideal, to which our intelligence and our real sense of organization cannot mount, and on the other side as well, the intellectual, working utility abiding within the real thinking world, but receiving in the central purpose the most stable, directive, harmonizing, clarifying and ennobling security and principle. The affective activity is divided in both directions, ideal-sentimental and real-intellectual needs, and it is possible in this manner to bring about the harmonious and perfect whole, through the idea of symbolism and of the ideal intention.

Here we have the good and whole man. The dry reality receives the dignity and the judgment of the idealism and the blindly pulling magnetism of the imaginative world accepts the stability and the stolid structure of the definite reality. We now have the reconciliation between being and appearance, between past, present and future, between man and god, between corporeal and spiritual values. This altogether has become possible through the only ideal to perform everything at all times the best possible, to inspire ultimate significance to the smallest action, to give full attention to any deed, be it in connection with the nearest reality or the most distant purposes. If we have always simultaneously this double star of good will concerning next reality and distant ideality before our eyes, then we have the sure and best constellation of our total vital function. This is the strong side of the idea of the theistic elaboration and fixation: the theistic clear and definite conception gives, according to our causal nature, the strong goal for our intellectual gift at once and produces and ensures by that the strong attitude and causal fastening of the reality. The work ideally intended means the topmost point in the perfection of our natural organization; for the symbolic action without the intellectual side and without *vital utility* is one-sided, a fickle shadow on a wall. Both together give the entire satisfaction and fulfil all capacities and the rounded gift of mankind. If we have fastened this affective constellation, then the sun may rise and set, then the years of our life may flow and come, our hairs may turn gray, our heart will not be old and our energy not lame. The wonderful team of our double nature will continue to prosecute its work and the two golden scales of our natural disposition will no more lose the serene quietness of their quivering equipoise.

We see in this that the idea of sacrifice moves also between the extremes of idealism and working reality, as we had it in laughing and as we shall meet it again in considering art. There is the simultaneous connection of our life-force toward both sides the idealistic and realistic, and the psychodynamic value of it is, therefore, levelling, mitigating and giving the most perfect balance between the opposite forces of peripheric, intellectual, real and central, sentimental, idealistic tendencies. Using the old theistic terminology we must therefore accept the idea of sacrifice as one of the intermediary values between both psychodynamic, opposite possibilities, fixing at once our life-force on, and driving it at, most central and most peripheric goals. The comparison with the *smoke* of the fire is thus very suitable for the sacrifice. Smoke is the intermediary state of condensation between the massive and volatile substances, and sacrifice connects both materiality and idealism in the same transitional way, as smoke connects visible and invisible physical states.

There are, roughly speaking, in every human action quickening or retarding or both psychodynamic features and influences. Would we be exhausting, we should be compelled to deal with all intellectual and suggestible or sentimental helps and functions of the human life in order to have a perfect outlook on the concentrative and on the digressive or "checking" psycho-dynamic activity. If we do not refer again and again to old-fashioned terminological foundations, we cannot be understood at all. Psychologically we must understand that all these phenomena refer to the two opposite groups of psychic energy and that all together are built up on the two contrary notions of anger and slothfulness, two more justicing notions of the old terminology. But these two notions may mean exactly the contrary according to our decision to stand inside or outside of the historic theistic conception, to take the intra- or extratheistic terminology. It is interesting to observe that already the choice of any standpoint means terminologically the insult of the other. And we realize therefore that it is most difficult to establish even any scientific discussion without making anticipating sympathies or apathies owing to the choice of the words. The meaning and use of the words is so deeply impregnated and penetrated by the cultural philosophy of former times that our chances to find any greater truth but also more difficulties and risks are given only in the choice of independent new formulations of expressions.

As we pointed out in our writings on suggestion, generally most suggestive sentimental means have a psycho-dynamic concentric influence in the sense of the historic theism, and most intellectual helps instead are checking, diverting from this historic centre and guide outside into the extrasolar surroundings. We saw there that the concentric theistic "anger" has, besides the enumerated, still other helps which we could consider in the most extended reflections. Such are the ideas of example, of solitude and fasting, and it would be even in this connection, where we could appreciate the influence of cold and warm temperature in the climate and in bathing. All these and other factors have important influences on our psycho-dynamic attitude. It is remarkable how much the choice of these different functions is subjected to the changing fashions of the different historic ages.

Even the function of SMOKING tobacco is quite essentially

connected with the psycho-dynamic tendency and desire of our nature. As art began to play its most important role in the middle ages, so smoking - a most unusual, but highly significant confrontation of two values indeed - came to its influential standing only in the last century. Its starting time was already very far from the beginning psycho-dynamic dispositions of former times, but has again the nearest relations to the concentrative purposes of nature. Smoking has by its toxicological and cloudy influence the most pronounced psycho-concentrative effect. Especially the importance of smoke, in this regard, is always very great, as we may consider in the misty atmosphere of the mountainous nature, in the technique of painting and art, or even in a smoke of tobacco. In all these cases we are surprised by the imaginative effect, we have to recognize the strong suggestive persuasion of our soul to glide slightly over the objective reality, not to enter into details and to proceed quickly and readily toward the terminal ideal goals. The most refined smoke scarcely observed is exactly the most efficient because of its subtle occasion for suggestion. In smoking we have this *optic* suggestive concentrative influence combined with the other of toxicological centro-dynamic facilitation of our affective functions, both together being a powerful sentimental help. Like our soul glides easily over the distant ranges of any hazy landscape, if we look from the mountain over the misty vale, so we have the most outspoken facility in the cloudy atmosphere of our smoking cigar to glide easily over the small, exact, sensorial objects, circumstances and multiple surroundings of our daily life being bound to the nearest sensorial impressions of our distinct furniture and of our narrow visible home. The blurring smoke makes the most efficient distant suggestion over all our daily working surroundings; at every smoking whiff we flow gently and readily over the detailed edges and limits of our petty sorrows and allow our imagination automatically to hover smoothly toward the glowing burning points of fire, of pleasure, of idealistic consolation and concentration. The optic concentrative part of smoking is very clear, whilst the pharmocological side is not at all completely understood by our medical authorities and naturalists. But there is also the concentrative power of the vaso-contraction or constriction, as we have it in the force of the cold weather, so that we see in this too some retreat from the intellectual sensorial life and from the outside reality on behalf of the sentimental human functions. The role of smoking is therefore near alcoholism and its fate and appreciation similar. As alcoholism is prosecuted still to-day by the theological concentrative monopoly, smoking also was first and later decried as the weed of the devil, and it deserves indeed, though in a lesser degree, for the same reasons, to be called demoniac or spiritual according to the standpoint of the judge, to the measure of his benevolence and of the abuse of the drug.

It is a remarkablee report that just during the action of BATHING in the Jordan, the Holy Ghost came down on Christ, saying: "This is my beloved son in whom I am well pleased!" Bathing has a religious sense in most religions, especially in the oriental. The use of water has received the most fundamental symbolic importance in the Christian *baptism* and in the ritual actions of the church. It is in the instigations of the corporal functions, in the removal of the metabolistic stagnation and in the thermic stimulation of the nervous system, where lies the physiological value of bathing. Bathing has both effects the quickening and strengthening influence on the corporeal and psychic performances, why it is to be considered as a psychodynamic concentrative factor. It means at the same time the acceleration of the peripheric circulation and the discharge of a greater amount of our physiological energy, why it has the power of intellectual peripheric exclusion and reduction of the total amount of the life-force, in the latter effect similar to the influence of *fasting* which we will consider afterwards more closely. Bathing is indeed one of the functions brought most clearly in connection with the idealistic purposes and hygienic perseverance of religion. We must take it as the most important moment, if Christ just during the very action of bathing is put into the most surprising, miraculous connection with the blessing of the open sky. Bathing quickens our idealistic force and concentration, because it produces the most energetic action of both our physiological and psychic energy. We may appeal in this point to the personal experience of everybody. How easy, how decided and relieved do we all feel after a bath! How clear and energetic is our will and how far away are we in these moments from the lazy checking forces of pessimistic slothfulness and intellectual waywardness! The open sky in the moment of bathing is a good and most eloquent symbol of the value of this function. We indeed feel in this action the best connection with the most elevated clear idealism of the universe and have the strong conviction of our aptitude for the pronounced and strong real and sentimental achievement. The effect of the bath is of course varified by the various temperatures of the water.

The influence of *cold and warm CLIMATE* on our feelings and conceptions are of course also very clear and visible. The cold temperature withdraws from us a part of our physiological energy by its caloric energetic subtraction and has, at the same time a direct contracting influence on our blood circulation by closing the peripheric vessels. Our real relations toward the outside world are therefore limited and reduced, the total production of life-force may be instigated, but the real functional amount is diminished because of the caloric depletion. There is in addition a strong concentrative stimulation because of the sensorial nervous influence of the cold temperature. The cold air drives us, generally, toward our inner psychic relations of life, but it has always the tendency to diminish our total life-force like fasting, and can therefore, with the exception of the momentary strong stimulation not be considered as a strong concentrative means. The effect of the cold temperature is rather indirect in taking away displaying force and distracting opportunities for the exterior sensorial relations.

The warm climate has the opposite influence. It has not the effect of the excellent or even exaggerated and weakening real affective discharge as the cold weather. It has not the stimulating nervous energy, but produces easily the stagnation of our life-force, in retaining the ready discharge of our physiological production of warmth. The vessels of our peripheric body, in warm weather and climate, it is true, are largely opened as a fact of compensation, but there is no question that the stagnation of our life-force happens much more easily in the warm climate and temperature. We have, therefore, in the warm climate to expect the greater accumulation of total life-force and in consequence the stronger connection with the intellectual reality and with the idealistic angry concentration, at the same time. It is the most interesting experimental observation that just in this richest accumulation of vital energy we have extreme actions of real and ideal life, extreme degrees of activity and laziness, and, on the whole, the pronounced prevalence of the historic theistic sentimental inclination. The northern nations with the cold climate and the less vital accumulation or richer discharge, do they not proceed rather more to the absolute divine digression?

The use of *violence* and *mechanical coercion* is in itself the most interesting topic which we will not consider here and which, however, always may be taken as the bluffing help for psychodynamic concentration. The religious genius cannot at all be represented generally, as the type of the use of violent force. On the contrary, he is the victim of the abused temporal power and restricts himself to the passive resistance. But there is at least one moment and one opportunity, when he teaches by his example the use of violence and of sensorial blows, it is in the moment, when he expels the salesmen out of the halls of the temple. At least in this moment he gives us the picture of the use of violent force. Here we make the clear statement that he at a given opportunity does not hesitate to be incensed in anger and wrath and to follow his determined purposes even with the means of mechanical effort, since he used a rope in order to carry through his divine intentions. Sensorial punishment, war and violence of the majority refer to this fact undoubtedly.

We already pointed out that ART has intimate relations to the historic theistic conception of the world. Art needs the supposition of the centro- magnetic point of the theistic attraction, which we call God. Art is one of the most charming consequences of the theistic affective concentration, as it is typical of our human psychology. We know very well, as we pointed out in our treatise: "Das Entzuecken", that all art has the outspoken psychopupilar mechanism, which is to say, that its essential feature consists in its circular organization, the material or intellectual display gathering and accumulating round the historic theistic centre, and moving toward it in the rhythmic step of oscillating concentric progression. For the rising of art there must be two moments: first the theistic clarification and fixation of the historic psychological atmosphere and second the rich accumulation of the real, material and intellectual relations which altogether are arrayed round the magnetic centre according to the law of dynamic-magnetic, most possible approach. Thus are formed the artistic sways and circles and the urges of the circular groupment, the aesthetic semicircles and smaller sections of them. The root of all circular formulation is the adoption of the magneto-centric theism. All punctual, concentric fixations of the idea of God produces instantly the circular groupment, movement and development of the personal and social psychological life. The historic deity is in that the source, the origin and the reason of our artistic life, the much more as the mono-theistic conception is clearly crystallized. We remember that we easily succeeded in showing this centro-magnetic progression in music, where it is very clear and sure, but that it exists most distinctly in every other expression of art, above all in poetry and painting. We observe the concentric artistic promotion even in any sculpture and statue, where the most peripheric detailed lines and folds always concentrate like sunbeams into one main most prominent point, which emphasizes and expresses the most important idea of the artist and of the artistic masterpiece.

That we have scarcely traces of art in the first epochs of any historic religion has its reason in the fact that the crystallization of the theistic unity and the centralization to it was of course a long time the most discussed question and real difficulty. Not only exteriorly, but also philosophically and psychologically the world underwent for a long time the most pronounced embarrassments and difficulties in regard to the atmospheric, habitual settlement of these principles. On the other side, the religious idea had not yet a strong real development in the first time. The material and intellectual life and its resources in the religious community had not yet enlarged and displayed so far in practical riches as to take enough space for the semicircular artistic disposition. For this reason in the beginning art was only utility. Utility is the starting point of the first primitive more simple stages of artistic development. It is only after the strong material, real and intellectual accumulation when art is able to develop greatly. It may be defined also as the concentric arrangement of the multiple, displayed, real, objective visible world in regard to spiritual values. We see that for the artistic life there must be not only the concentric theistic agreement of the social atmosphere around the concentric chief magnetic emphasis, but there must be, at the same time, the objective multiplicity and detailed rich enumeration which can be subjected to the artistic grouping of the centro-magnetic adoption. We understand therefore that a young country sparsely populated is not inclined to artistic performance, whilst the dense and numerous political concentration of many old and developed nations produces always the most pronounced artistic desires, necessities and abilities. Artistic atmosphere means, therefore, innumerable elaborated helps for the theocentric groupment, coming out from the historic and traditional development of the nations. We may therefore state definitely that art is the special and very significant expression of the idea of the historic theistic conception of the world, that without historic God we likely have not to expect any important art, that art has therefore the retrospective character looking back to the past, to tradition and history. It must be essentially conservative. Without utmost historic mono-attention we could not have any considerable art. As soon as the splitting, intellectual prevalence of the ages throws the chief part of our life-force over the concentric peripheric borders and produces strong extrasolar digressions, we lose the elaborate sentimental and harmonious affective encircling movements around the historic centre and in this the charm, the simplicity, the unity, the love and the security of the circular divine, magneto-centric embracement. The first intellectual digressions of the peripheric extrasolar transitions are not artistic. They have much more difficulties in grouping disposition, not having the mighty faculty of strong magnetic distributing unity. Art comes about each time, as soon as any historic affective theistic whirlpool is formed and clarified and as soon as it has received any considerable real objective surroundings.

Therefore, we understand that Christianity was an excellent fertilizing power for the most important and most charming artistic production, and that we had the top of the best art in the middle ages. Had not the Greek and Roman art famous because of its harmonious taste and elaboration, already its central theistic principle in Zeus and Jupiter? But it was in the Christian age, when the most achieved and emphasized, overwhelming magnetic unity of the psychological world was developed and definitely, psychologically and exteriorly fixed, and it is just owing to this psychodynamic regularity and conclusiveness, that the Christian art has received its specific charming and thrilling character. Art turned out to be one of the most common and powerful psychodynamic helps of Christianity. It was and is the most skilful refinement of moving suggestion for religious purposes.

We may say, in a certain sense, that art was and will be always. We have indeed in any age attempts to comprise all intellectual life into new pleasant artistic formulas, but nobody does succeed in gathering all real objective moments into one aesthetic union, if there is not the historic background of the traditional theo-magnetic elaboration. The aesthetic expression of art is in our opinion and in the feelings of the cultured world only justified, if there is always one beautiful dividing central and most important principle in the representation of the artistic values. The most pronounced theistic age succeeds of course best in representing and adopting this deep central principle of connection, because it is very thoroughly helped by the magnetic influences on all surrounding reality. Where we have a lack of this concentric pulling magnetism, the aesthetic arrangement of the intellectual multiplicity is impossible, and we have in such times of intellectual transition the most confused tendencies pulling the reality in many opposite directions, and having therefore no possibility of harmonious unitarian representation. We see this of course very easily in the *morern art* with its manifold magnetic prospecting diversions, where the unity of the aesthetical centralization cannot be bound, where the encircling charm of the most beautiful rounded lines, suggested and supported by magnetism, fails and where, - we may call this only attempts of future art - the magnetic unity of the principal tendency is almost entirely lost on behalf of the peripheric, though most original, technical experiments.

During the middle ages we had very different circumstances.

The centro-magnetic idea of the historic God had become most clear, elaborated and most fixed traditionally. Practically all parts of the population were subjected to this central magnetic conception of the Christian monotheism, and we observe, therefore, on one side the very strong theocratic magnetism dividing, binding and disposing successfully, and on the other side, the very developed real and material riches and display of the age, forming the submissive and willing material of these theatrical performances which every artistic act represents always. Therefore in the middle ages we have the most pronounced and most happy masterpieces of art. Never the world may have had this strong artistic affluence as at that time containing both the most refined real elaboration and the clear and simple unification of everything in one great theistic idea. The best Greek, Indian and Chinese art only may compete, up to a certain degree, with the Christian mediaeval art, and let us mention with admiring reserve the Moresque ornamental conceptions of the early middle ages, which produced also the most achieved centro-magnetic art expressed with marvellous beauty and with the very mathematical concentric exactitude of elaboration. We must admit that this *Moresque art* had even more clarified geometrical theocentric conceptions than any other. But the different circumstances helped the mediaeval Christianity to excel indeed in its artistic perfection. There was the most favorable balance between idealism and reality in art with slight overweight of idealism. Both components were represented very richly and emphasized thoroughly through the historic tradition, social and political development, philosophical clearness, great personal aptitudes, concentration of commercial wealth, organized inheritance of fortunes, riches of material means and readiness in using them - a strong artistic atmosphere. For all these reasons the middle ages are characterized by the imperishable glory of the very finest masterpieces of art: Europe is so full of them even to-day in spite of all destroying wars and of all busy buyers from abroad that we would use many lives, would we see closely and appreciate suitably only the most perfect and elaborate pieces.

No wonder that the whole world aspiring to culture flows continually through the comparatively small countries of old Europe which to-day is indeed the most wonderful and admirable yet quaint museum harboring richnesses of inestimable value and hiding beauties and artistic accumulations, whose importance it often does not, itself, any more realize and worship duly to-day.

But there are numberless most tasteful treasures in stone, in wood, in iron and oil, and the secret of their beauty lies in their harmonious balance between idealism and realism, and in the charming leading suggestion of the idealistic centro-magnetic force which oversmiles with its idealistic principle all most pronounced and struggling reality gathered under the serene spell of the Christian idealism. The psychological Christian conceptions were at that time very similar to the Greek art. Had they not also the most harmonious ideal- realistic conception slightly in favor of the magnetic central idealism, however a little less than in Christianity, which rightly may be interpreted or felt as advantage or as disadvantage, according to individual temperament? But every Greek masterpiece thrills with the peculiar most peaceful and satisfying serenity of atmosphere.

Art is indeed the most intimate intermingling and intertwining of realism and idealism, the crucible of ideal intentions and intellectual expressions, which we in some more or less happy achievement find always among the people. It is most successful, where both components are strong and ambitious, wrestling with each other like two powerful lions or giants, each claiming more of the psychological force, one going in the centrifugal and the other in the centripetal direction. But the masterpiece is then most perfect, if the idealistic direction penetrates all real performances and succeeds at last in turning the total creative movements toward the central theistic sentimental discharge without losing the technical exactitude. The notion of art is, therefore, exeeedingly near the philosophical principle of sacrifice and - smiling. In the same manner we have the pronounced and clear fixation of the psychic function at both opposite points, on the peripheric reality or intellectuality and on the central sentimental idealism. Art is therefore indeed the visible sensorial theatre of the greatest ideas. It is the suggestive invitation to the created reality to follow in the most logical real way the magnetic attraction toward the most accepted and the most granted traditional theistic goals. The theistic idealism in its turn shines and sparkles through the real refined artistic activity, ennobles, clarifies, vivifies and elevates all technical means by its idealizing spell and becomes so the most energetic and inspiring persuasion.

The considerable importance of smoke which we already mentioned in connection with the sacrifice, smoking tobacco and the atmosphere of the landscape, is most significant for all art. All art strives continually, carefully as the real exact hints may be done, to blur the real objectivity in its numberless detailed explanations and exhibitions, to comprise and compress the real objective world within the symbolic technicalities of ist artistic resourcefulness. It is always essential for artistic work to create the misty atmosphere which permits the psychic force to glide smoothly and rapidly on the skates of the imagination over the large polished mirror of the peripheric intellectuality and rise thus to the unitarian sun of conscious mono-attention. It is in this case easy to run with the most accelerated movement toward the shining centro-theistic symbol, because the psychodynamic resistance of the multiple intellectual obstacles has been adapted and directed in order to favor the idealistic permeability. So we have in the hazy blurring of the reality the law of compensation used in so skilful a manner that the reality and peripheric intellectuality are not excluded at all from the vital performances, but that there is exactly hinted to, that the real elements are even ambitiously elaborated, but then rapidly simplified, idealisticly tinged and thrown, in this fascinating state, easily toward the central sentimental goal.

So we recognize instantly, how much art has essentially good *educational* qualities in cultivating, at the same time, the real objectivity with strong accuracy and going to the central idealism with final tremendous will-power. It is the refined method of the proceeding, hazy exclusion of reality, which enables the life-force to save enough energy for the central sentimental action. It is just here, where the emergent law of compensation uses most skilfully the transparent mist of slowly increasing blurring activity. Art has therefore, from the middle ages been chosen as the preeminent educational means for idealistic education. It gives indeed the best psychodynamic guarantee, because it stresses and maintains, up to a certain limit, the single logical steps of our intellectual real experiences and prevents, in this manner, the immediate eliptic leaps toward the idealistic symbolism. Art does not exclude the real development and turns notwithstanding most decidedly on the ideal progression which remains its chief purpose, duty and pleasure. The mediaeval and later good art has the clear look at the reality, but it has still more interest in the terminal idealistic discharge of the affective life. It rests with the special skill of the artist to express and repress the detailed, natural reality enough that we are not conscious of the idealistic haze poured like a delicate veil over the fascinating landscape, the charming features of the divine child and his mother or his saints. The artist has to remove the self-emphasis of the details sufficiently that we are not aware of the concentric parallelism of the movements and scenic dispositions on the ways, in the branches of the trees and in the directions of the limbs of the persons, with one word of the whole *scenic disposition*. But this law is there always and helps us to join quickly and readily the suggested supreme goals of the artist.

We recognize, therefore, in art that the quickening acceleration of our psychic life- force, owing to careful and skilful suggestion, overtakes the intellectual real function of our peripheric thinking work. The progression from realism to idealism is rather slow and very smooth, but the effect is only the surer, the more inevitable and the more hygienic. Art belongs, therefore, to the *mediated* psychic factors of our dynamic psychopupilar reactions, respecting and using the intellectual help of the peripheric technicalities, of the nature, of science, knowledge and wealth, but is runs at last unhesitatingly towad the central idealistic goal being its most desired and essential trump. It entices all used forces to join this strong psychodynamic ultimate acceleration toward idealistic discharge.

But lest we forget! In spite of this strong and clever realistic foundation, art gathers the logical moments in a *free, theoretical and artificial manner* from all sides and combines them cunningly to its way and purpose. Life itself has not the friendliness to help us so easily to logical ideal progression, because it gives to us personally in our experience only some logical fragments without any progressive order, which is *artificially* established by the free combination of the artistic hand. In addition art has the handicap (or advantage if we will) to hide from us the rudest and roughest sides of our sensorial and experimental life, to put, because of its compensatory educational will and conclusive desire, the charming dreamy mist over the most difficult parts of our experiences of life. So we must admit that even in the skilful and more perfect education of the artistic methods some luxuriant and deceiving danger still remains. Even art in spite of its keen sense for reality keeps some effeminating power and inclination, if it is abused as the only or chief means of education, and here arises the question whether or not the natural expression of the symbolic idea of the bitter *cross* and the sensorial passion of Christ was not an excellent artistic topic emphasizing the weight and the seriousness of the real disposition with pathetic effort. The suffering background of all great art has the compensatory intention to do away with the illusions of the easy comfort, following the given artistic example.

We have meditated already the different relations and values of the notion of the cross. But if we must admit that cross and passion are rough sensorial means, then on the other hand we must, however confess that the life itself is also very sharp and outspoken in its sencorial intensity and that, up to a certain degree, therefore, the most adequate educational means is the truest.

But we might insist on the quite extraordinary *educational* importance of the art in every form. Art indeed has many great advantages over every other educational system. Its truth is fixed, logical, detailed but not too intruding and, above all, not too roughly sensorial. The good art gives the necessary optimistic joy of life, imparts the desirable elasticity of the proceeding affective energy and gives the courage and strength of the affective life, without producing any superficiality against the real exigences of the life. Art spreads the most charming flowers on the rocky way of our prosaic life, without permitting us to leave its necessities slightly, and it shines with the sweetest smiles into the hearts of the discouraged humanity. Its stars guide us through the night of our undecided waywardness, and its light gilds our most ordinary daily performances in duty, business and work. Art indeed is the most attractive human-theistic spell which makes us drunk with pleasure, but in a small degree and careful procedure, and which in spite of its enthusiastic flight sticks closely to the reality. Art composes and confronts most interestingly all different fragments of our possible real experiences. It clarifies all intellectual riddles, straightens unsolved difficulties of our different times and individual lives and develops out of all the most useful and generally and individually available, instigating formula toward active success, idealistic progress, theistic enjoyment and affective deliverance.

We must remember that the *gospel* itself is the most suggestive and successful masterpiece of the Christian art. The religious art makes very large use of the concentric mystic and miraculous psychodynamic methods and is therefore less inclined to cling to the detailed peripheric reality. It proceeds quickly, energetically and more impatiently toward the divine centre. The scriptures understood to naturalize their artistic concentrating methods very well. They accumulated from the beginning of their artistic development such an extraordinary idealistic emphasis of force and centripetal longing that many until to-day are more aroused by the affective miracles and are more interested in the evangelical artistic methods than in the spiritual success, wherefor they are written. Many are not able to part with the hypnotizing spells of literal conceptions and meanings. The second, idealizing part, the psychodynamic accelerating energy of the gospel is, therefore, of extraordinary high value and of the most unparalleled penetration in the whole psychological history, whilst the peripheric description and explanation of the real life is compensatorily little elaborate, though, in the most skilfully hidden way, carefully alluded to. The gained or saved energy, from the realistic part of the gospel, makes according to the law of compensation the advantage of the concentrative progression. The religious idealistic founders fastened the human psychic force only loosely at the intellectual periphery and, scarcely given some striking intellectual categoric glimpses of time, space and causality, they run and hustle irresistibly, with all our affective concentrated strength, toward their divine purposes and idealistic aims which seem most important and essential to them. They succeed so well in reaching their aims, because they first were so stingy in depicting the real life. They at last were able to race so energetically toward their purposes because of their loose starting peripheric fixation. They obtained the excellent security of throwing all life-force together into the abyss of their terminal goals, *because they kept away from the detailed real intellectuality,* as much as possible. The religious artistic productions must be considered as the most one-sided expression of the idealistic temperament.

Before we leave our psychodynamic meditations, let us consider two or three other methods practiced by the religious hero, and playing the most important role in the religious life.

FASTING, as it is done in different manners and degrees, in abstemiousness from all or different kinds of food, in bleedings and artficial evacuations, has essentially the subtractive metabolic effect as we observed in the cold temperature and climate. But whilst the cold exterior temperature effectuates the subtraction from our accumulated vital energy by the withdrawal of warmth from the skin, in fasting we have the same result by the quantitative or qualitative diminution of the digesting production of the whole life-force. We remove in this way the dangers of the affective stagnations and explosions. By the elimination of superfluous food fasting must be considered as favorable toward the spiritual functional prevalence. The quickly diminishing total amount of vital and psychic production seems to bring about always the domineering position of the idealistic or spiritual function, whilst the considerable luxuriant amount of the total psychic life-force conducts, on the contrary, almost always and easily to the intellectual and sensorial supremacy. Only the richly effused state of the individual functions is able to consider and respect the peripheric details, whilst the narrow contraction of the light-field extinguishes the individual importance and subtracts all intellectual points more thoroughly to the central magnetic goal. It is in the middle state of the open light-field, where the detailed and intellectual individual has more chances to be easy, secure and considerable, because there the real food is not suppressed, which is the case in the concentrated idealism, and because there is considerable participation in the affective central life.

So we may acknowledge fasting in advance as the strong idealizing factor, which discharges our peripheric objectivity, which loosens our material and physiological, metabolistic fixations and permits our natural forces so much more to cross the shorter way of the radius of the narrower light-field and to reach comfortably and unmistakably the idealistic centre. We know that the essential danger for the sentimental idealism consists always in the strong sensorial and sensual impressibility. Idealism and uplifting sentimentality succeed best, if the sensorial reality is reduced and quenched as much as possible. The objective tenacity and stickiness of the sensorial influence in our nature is exceedingly great. We already meditated for a long time all possible tricks of the religious founders to escape from it, and here in fasting we have another attempt to suppress its strong power in mortifying the natural physiological strength, in quenching the burning fire of our oxydative metabolism. Indeed it is not possible that any blow against our nature could go deeper or could have been contrived more thoroughly and more surely against the bewitching sensorial actions and longings of our body than just the withdrawal of the physiological energy of our bodily functions. Fasting means therefore the subjection of our sensorial life under the sentimental yoke of the spiritual idealism. Even if it does not permit to go very far in any direction and function of our reduced vitality, fasting at least suppresses the troubling sensorial supremacy and means always the most advantageous preparation for the strong unfoldment of the idealistic wings.

The strong metabolism forces us to act energetically, unless we risk angry affective explosions and depressive sentimental stagnations. Fasting prevents these acute dangers in taking away in advance the strong rising of dynamic accumulation. For the lazy individual or for that not being in the case of energetic, real or idealistic actions, owing to checking circumstances, fasting may be therefore very balancing and useful. Fasting helps the possibility of the peaceful quiet life which does not like the exterior activity, by taste, laziness or compulsion of circumstances. But it supports thus also the real struggle against the intellectual temptation or against the objective conradiction of our sensorial nature, in connection with the idealistic tendencies.

As in the burning of the sooty chimney the strong flame devours the material depositum within the smoking tube, so fasting helps to devour the affective residuum of our physiological metabolism and forces the affective function to destroy first thoroughly the remnant of the former psychological actions which had the effect of obstructive psychic affective stagnation. Fasting burns these residual remnants and sets the physiological actions free. Afterwards the individual is rid of the luxuriant stagnation and progresses more easily toward the intended idealism.

By fasting the idealistic tendencies of the individual will be strengthened; the inclinations to sensorial and intellectual resistance are weakened, the strong oppositional tendencies of the real human nature cease, and the surplus of the psychic disagreeable contrarinesses and struggles, which were before so painful, is taken away. Where there is no production, any competitive fight stops. The psychological contradictions and frictions are, owing to this dynamic loss, much smaller. The life of this idealistic fasting individual may be more quiet, more balanced and more regular, but less important because of the smaller amount of and the smaller working-off of the vital reality and possibility. Thus fasting causes the real limitation of our life. It narrows the expansion of our vital broad culture. It diminishes the use of the number and the distance of the affective standards of our experimental fingerboard and abolishes, therefore, the great tensions and the using-up contradictions and frictions of our psychic life-force. But it is at the expense of the categories of our intellectual connections with space and causality, that this diminution of our psychic action turns up. The psychodynamic performances in fasting are not fixed very strongly on the intellectual periphery of our nature. They have not the logical elaboration of the full life-force, but they progress easily toward the central idealistic affective values. So we have again the same thing as in the former cases, diminution and shortening of the peripheric intellectual precision, expansion and intensity - diversion of the individual force from the sensorial bluffing energy and in addition the compensatory effusion and quickening discharge of all life-force into the central idealistic standards of our sentimental gifts. If fasting cannot be considered as the most successful real restriction on behalf of the ideal strong intensification, then at least it must be admitted as being very successful in excluding the sensorial bluffability which, in other cases, has the power to throttle the ideal function.

Fasting is very near the notion of RECREATION and that of BLEEDING used quite commonly in the middle ages. Still to-day bleeding is always performed at the same time as recreation is allowed, and has the meaning to support and ensure the intention and the sense of the recreation. There is only the difference that fasting and bleeding mean the recreation of the corporeal physiological functions being relieved and discharged at this transitional time, whilst the recreation in general means rather the relaxation of the mental, affective and working capacities which at this time are dispensed from their usual function, and have during that time of recreation the counterbalance of different physiological organic or mental exercise. Bleeding at the time of the luxuriant reposing recreation means the reduction of the overfeeding concentration and the effort against the rich metabolistic function of our body. We need recreation there, where we have exhausted our organic resources too much for mental or corporal purposes, in a one-sided manner, and we call luxuriance and effemination this state, where we have the continual claim to possess too much vital strength and reserve which we refuse to give up sufficiently for energetic working performances. So recreation can be simultaneously the most necessary and the most harmful action, in one case the emergent help of necessity and of organic rebuilding, and in the other case the further advance of the shameful laziness and effemination of our individual peculiarity.

We remark in this connection that DISEASES, serious TIREDNESS and OVERWORK may also be considered as sources of idealistic prevalence. They diminish the amount of the total life-force and make, therefore, very much for excluding the domineering rule of the sensorial life. The strong tiredness of the worker, produced by the week-long toiling, is just most apt to empty into the religious idealistic consolations and conceptions of the divine service on Sunday. There is no more serious individual more amenable to affective deep values than the tired worker.

The *diseases* are often understood as God's angels sent to people in order to uplift them toward the idealistic religious values. Everybody who ever was seriously ill will admit that the change produced in his mental attitude by the transitional vital reduction of force was the strongest and most thorough affective regeneration of quickening intensity in reconvalescence. If we say, a *lazy man* is a bad man, then we mean that the excess of disposible life-energy is liable to produce every kind of peripheric relations and connections in the real world and that the best and surest means of prevention against this questionable eventuality is the true devotion to the regular tiring work of a profession. In all these cases we have the same principle as in fasting, but from the other side. In fasting we do not permit the fire of our affective life to grow fast and to break out voluptuously into the real sensorial life, as we may have the same effect in many diseases which do not allow regular digestion or sufficient eating, whilst in the other half of the cases, in overwork, serious tiredness and consumptive diseases, we have the fact that the produced individual force is always taken away and used for the efforts of the working or suffering energy or the abnormal consumptive claims of the ill body. But the result as to the relation to the affective idealism remains the same. In all these instances the total vital and psychic life-force is reduced, the sensorial susceptibility of the real influences is diminished, and the individual psychic activity has the greater facility and inclination toward the sntimental idealism.

Cannot *sickness* be the best cure of the lazy realist? Must we not expect that diseases, for this reason, meet prevalently lazy people and the psychicly inert individual? Diseases may be the most desirable affective transfers and the most significant changes for the future activity of the individual life. There may be laid new foundations of inclinations and new cornerstones of tastes built up, for the coming affective strength and energy of the psychic work of the individual. The beginning and the starting point of this psychological situation is the transitional limitation of the individually available life-force, which means at least the temporary truce of the most lacerating moral and intellectual battles in the oscillating soul of the person, deepens and clarifies the idealistic needs and possibilities and affords and corrects, in this way, the renewed sway toward the last and most powerful sentimental goals. So tiredness, overwork and diseases are themselves essentially the sweetest angels from heaven for human consolation. They have the inestimable effect to impose, at least for hours and weeks, silence on the psychological contradictory experiences, tensions and frictions, and they give to the individual, just in his using up effort, that consolation which he believed to lose and to leave seemingly, in the moment of taking them up. He who loses his life finds it, and he who finds it, loses it.

Fasting, tiredness and diseases are another psycho-dynamic

trias of our affective performances which all together facilitate our concentrative idealistic actions by the aid of the reduction of our total life-force. In diseases other more complicated changes of the constitution of the body may have the same or the contrary effect. The modern *organotherapy* thinks of these conditions. Is the essential of health easy affective fluctuation of our life-force?

There is no doubt that the idealistic disposition discovering easily the accelerating and discharging supports of the sentimental inclination likes to produce them. The true sentimental nature is fond of the idea of being exhausted by work or even of being really very unhappy, of being tired and sick, because in all these conditions the departure from the catching and sticking real energy into the revelling dreamy land of uplifting idealism is much more easy and comfortable. We remark so frequently that the outspoken idealistic people have the strongest longing for diseases, so much and so irresistibly that they often simulate being affected with any sickness without knowing even that artificial imagination created it. Which moment causes most the rise of this phenomenon, whether it is the desire for being the object of most anxious care, attention and observation, if it is the longing to be rid of the entangling reality in order to use all life-force for idealistic revelling in concentrating compensation, or if these people seriously desire the diverting pain and consumption of the disease in order just not to be pushed any longer into the disagreeable struggle between the sensorial world and the idealistic peace and harmony with the farthest universe, is difficult to decide in the individual case. The last way is the most secure and lasting natural fixation of the possession and attainment of the idealistic values. If we have the restriction of our total life-production in disease and pain, then we have most chances to get rid of the dangerous struggle with the sensorial reality and then, indeed, we have the most natural prospect of being most similar to the extreme suffering hero of the religious sentimental conception. The *suffering* idealistic outlook produces, therefore, really very likely the love of diseases and the burning longing for corporal fragility and weakness. The religious idealism feels the extraordinary danger of the active sensorial solution of the real problems of the world and retires preferably into the passive liquidation of the sentimental conceptions of life and world, where it is much surer of its terminal sentimental success in the conformity of the suffering experience.

The *sick religious idealist* is most similar, in his psychology, to his exemplary hero. The passive work of obligatory suffering together with the lack of the enticing and confusing temptation of the glittering visible world gives to him the clearest and most promising vista to fulfil his intended idealistic task. The success of the extreme idealist is therefore most guaranteed in sickness taking away the dangers of the sensorial outside luring seductions, giving the unlosable sureness of work in the passive suffering and strengthening, in addition, the direct obtainment of the idealistic discharge and enjoyment, which must not be first risked or even lost in the hot changing fight between sensorial realism and affective idealism.

If we call fasting, diseases and tiring exhaustion the *eliptic concentrating psychodynamic factors* because of their peripheric omitting influences, then we join in addition to this peculiar group the notion of SOLITUDE. Christ is related to have retired to the desert for fourty days, and he often disappeared and retired again and again to his divine solitariness. The idea of the solitude indeed plays in all parts of the religious psychology, in the gospels, in the conceptions and in the institutions of the churches, in all idealistic life, in every genial disposition and in all artistic tendencies, the most important role. The theistic Christian conception had even reached its brilliant splendour and its eminent strength, essentially owing to the extreme monotheistic conception and separation of God. All great things are solitary and lonely, for this reason they become outstanding, extraordinary and independent. The more numerous our obligations, our dependencies and relations are in regard to others, the smaller is our prospect to receive the outstanding greatness given in the solitary secrecy. Every important preferability means up to a certain degree concealment and retirement. We understand this truth in many directions. The subjective and personal affective importance needs, according to the law of compensation, the central gathering of all the energy of our life-force and the seclusion from the detailed objective and intellectual diversions. This is the deep will of the nature which is also expressed from the opposite side in the proverb:mundus vult decipi. The punctual central strength of the genial light-centre increases by the degree of separation and restriction from the enlarged surroundings and values, and it loses its outstanding prominence in central strength and light, when the spreading-out communications with the peripheric detailed world is vividly maintained or established. We see instantly that there must be serious advantages and losses at the same time, in the fact of the solitary separation. The main advantages consist of the unchecked freedom of the personal feelings and ideas going through the universe with the rapidity and sublimity of the rushing eagle, in the true faithfulness toward, and the excellent performance of, our innermost natural psychic disposition, the separation from the troubling, distracting and paining surrounding influences of our life and of the intellectual multiple world which is so liable to discourage the individual idealistic enterprises and the personal idealistic enthusiasm. The friend of the solitude finds easily the strong idealistic energy, the best direction and the most efficient affective discharge. He flees from the hardness of the real life, but in this he loses the right judgment of the visible world and is inclined toward psychic effemination. The exclusive enemy of loneliness instead deprives himself of the strong suggestive force of idealism given in solitude; he runs into the rough reality of work and pain and protects himself, however, in this way against the habit of sentimental pleasure and affective angry aversion against the logical development. Loneliness leads to greatness, importance and independence, but also to social inconsiderateness and anger, and, reversely, all these psychic qualities usher you to lonely isolation. The exclusively social individual has not the strong will and the unchecked ideal concentration, but he has the peripheric multiple, real and objective relations and refined psycho-dynamic escapements and is, therefore, broadminded, respectful toward every created existing value, cautious, and he recognizes the social laws and the ethical social justice much more than the individual who is removed from company.

So we understand that the individual gifted and inclined to idealism has most longing for loneliness, that solitude for him is the breathing air, where he can stretch out the full capacities of his deepest inner personality and from where on idealistic wings he can soar to divine goals. He who has not the natural tendency and easiness toward the idealistic concentration must have the most pronounced aversion against solitude, because solitude inescapably would force him to be sentimental and idealistic. All people of today, afraid of retirement, confess by this fact their disinclination against the sentimetal idealism, whilst the *monastic tendencies* of the hermits and recluses, on the contrary, reveal the strong natural or cultural inclination to the sentimental ideal concentration of their life and to the extreme exclusion of the intellectual, social, peripheric reality and visible objective distraction. The *monk type* is the representative of the one-sided sentimental idealism of humanity. The *luxuriant pleasure-type* of the modern city represents the psychological sentimental state relapsed from the terminal sentimental conclusive delight to the sensorial and sensual pleasure. The contrary of the meditative solitary type is the unavertible *working realist* of the present social business life, who is filled up with his intellectual material necessities and longings and who does not find any moment for the central affective concentration. Accumulation of *riches* finds, however its idealistic expression in the refined gold and the authoritative credit testimonial, which are mere concentrative values, because quantitative accumulation is converted into qualitative ideal or sentimental representation. All life and all activity is a circle and where we think to elope from former essentially human laws, we rush into their extended arms from another side. *Money* leads straight away to idealistic methods. The qualitative nature of riches is the door, where the refined cultural man may find his favorable link to material association. He may even condescend to convert his idealistic concentrated *qualities* into detailed material *quantities,* if he is humble enough. On the whole we may say, however, that there are two extremes of conceptions, both right and wrong because both exaggerated, both excluding each other owing to the law of compensation which always in the equal distribution of intellect and sentiments, of reality and idealism, has its natural, balanced human application.

If the religious genius not only for fourty days, but again and again repeatedly went to hide himself from the eyes of the world, then this fact is most congruant with the very idealistic character of his description and of his affective tendencies. By the loneliness and by the exclusion from the ordinary intercourse the holy writers imparted to his figure that outstanding greatness and divine importance which he claimed and which they intended to give to him. The most ideal man and the most divine hero of mankind was depicted as the most lonely man in the middle of his contemporaries. His apotheosing writers succeeded most skilfully in making the most clear and pronounced impression of his divine isolation within the human society. The most divine, the most idealistic and genial men must be indeed the most solitary and lonely people in the world. Their natural interests and their longing are not fixed on the real detailed surroundings of the intellectual visible world, but they have indeed rather the desire to be rid of all real checking obstacles and to concentrate most powerfully and energetically on the punctual central idealism.

The divine claims of the religious genius and his writers create therefore the first and most essential necessity to separate and discriminate the great personality of the ideal individual from the whole society and their daily, petty, wordly performances. Perhaps here we have the most ticklish and the weakest point of the divine system which either must give up the exclusive divine claim of the hero in putting him into the human society and their daily practical living life and intellectual detailed atmosphere, or must sacrifice the sharp social human characterization of the figure of the hero on behalf of his gigantic and quite extraordinary divine pretentions. The root of all outstanding development is isolation. The warm human blood of the sharply detailed intellectual historic figure of the religious genius would not be compatible at all with the elevated divine atmosphere of his person. It is the dreamy lofty atmosphere of the miraculous enthusiasm, which can impart to his personality the capability to separate himself so far from the sharp historic and social intellectual surroundings and to perform the startling role of the most idealistic, most admirable and elevated, but also of the most lonely and isolated idealistic man.

By this we of course are pointed back to the problem, touched so often in this book, if God is rather the sentimental or intellectual expression of the human function. Our subjective, individual, psychopupilar natural disposition points to the narrow, secluded isolation and the punctual solitude of the historic conception of God, but our intellectual peripheric digression and our cultural enlargement in work and science opens the most brilliant prospect of the more developed and more powerful idea of the future theistic conceptions and of the divine omni-presence. The solitude is, therefore, the lovely sister of the historic traditional love of God, religion is philosophically founded and performed in the individual psychology: The individuality is the principle of the subjective, religious sentimental love and affection. The social and creative objective display and multiplicity is instead the progressive step of our humanity to the enlargement of the future theistic embracement. If there are two ways to go to God, one the direct by following the magnetic attraction of his central power, and the other the round-about, indirect way by opposing his central magnetism in peripheric enlarging intellectual materialism, in scandalous sin and in confusing peripheric entanglement in order only to augment his conception and to join the theistic idea in the outside universe after all again once more, then we must admit that the description of the religious genius landed at the theistic central shore chiefly by the direct way of stripping or not even accepting the indirect round-about peculiarities of the human destiny. If we go directly to God or indirectly by the intellectual transfer, as we have it in the active work and in the passive suffering, the last approach to God will always again be based on the sentimental progression of the heart, with the real, intellectual exclusion, on the law of sentimental and affective retirement from the reality and of subjective and individual isolation and detachment. This fact is quite fundamental for every theistic procedure: Go, sell all thy possessions and come, follow me! It is the eternal repetition of the law of compensation.God is jealous to gather all really fixed energy, to attract all to his central point and to be the ruling solitary king of the human soul and life-force. Strong religion becomes always again subjective and individual.

Solitude and loneliness mean, therefore, the readiness and the exterior inclination to create the divine opportunities, to drop the multiple intellectual fixations of our affectivity and to join in the most unembarrassed way the divine, central magnetic urges of the universal theistic whirlpools. Loneliness has, therefore, the significance of opening the heart to the divine magnetic voice, to transfer all psychic energy toward the central psychodynamic channel and to facilitate thus naturally the theistic concentrative acceleration. How happy and how relieved must feel he who has joined the divine concealment, he who is retired from the multiple distraction of the world and has the undivided central direction toward his centro-magnetic divinity and his affective unison.

The deliverance from the reality in solitude, as onesided, unnatural and dangerous because of resulting inadaptability it may be, is of high transitional value and hygienic importance for everybody, sometimes. It is indeed the necessary and indispensable blessing for every individual person, but if too much, it easily could be harmful because of its educational and psychodynamic dangers. Religion, the sister and mother of loneliness and of affective concentration, has therefore the most wholesome effect on the peripheric affective obstructions of distress, extreme riches and poverty, heavy sorrow and sin, on embarrassment, where the easy obtainment of the idealistic goal seems to be difficult or impossible. How solemn the isolating central loneliness of the religious mechanism must be felt! It carries the individual away from all distress and all changes of the time and from all local fixations of the real human concernments. The old age, which became wrinkled and hidious by work, finds within the supra-individual, central ideal consolations courage and reconciliation with the common human destiny; youth is induced, by this common divine retirement from the accidental peripheric forces, to be lenient and respectful toward the deficiencies of old people. The worried people learn in regard to the change of all reality and to the prospect of the following salvation, to forget even now their pain, to carry their burden. But also the lucky and rich will be bridled and afraid of the Nemesis of all earthly changes, their limits and their conditional and compensatory restrictions, if he looks at the true and kind face of the mute and reverend solitude. All are taught by the superior whispering wisdom of solitude.

So we see that just the divine separation from the world, the utmost sensorial restriction and concealment within the subjective theistic secrecy imparts the most common and the most spread human psychological vistas.

Solitude is the sister of religion in this sense that it helps religion to climb the steps of her idealistic apotheosis. Loneliness is the charming angel who disentangles the dreamy human soul from the manifold real fixations and intellectual obstacles and embarrassments, who protects from the distractions and dissipations of the human life-force into the working circle of the multiple, detailed reality and who opens the narrow channel through which our psychic production is most efficiently drawn toward the idealistic goals. Solitude is the kind shepherd who unties the tender helpless lamb from the thorns of real confusion.

Most religions even to-day cultivate the monastic idea. Firstly in the desert and in caves and catacombs, afterwards in *Monasteries and convents* or at least in returning spiritual and silent *retreats* the religious people think to impart to their souls the most efficient divine accelerating helps and quickening urges toward their last magnetic gaol, in meditating solitude. Are they right to do so? There is no doubt that they join their goal according to the example of their master who did himself so and taught the world the corresponding philosophy. The recluses, hermits, monks and nuns have the greater facility to go on toward their religious ideal goals. Quietness, clearness and energetic progression of their psychic force toward their magnetic ideal will be ensured so much more and the affective stagnation may in many ways be better avoided than in other people. But there arises on the other side the danger of neurasthenia, anger and laziness, narrowness of the conceptions, intolerance and religious fanaticism.

The strong central suggestibility, as it is produced through the artificial reduction of the real raw-material of our experience, has the further consequence, that the lonely individual loses entirely the adequate appreciation of the real world and life. He easily progresses from the clearness and sharpness of his idealistic symbolic pictures toward the last centre and hovers and looks carelessly over the intellectual steps of the logical periphery. He knows well to establish the terminal ideal conclusions, but, by avoiding the intellectual real difficulties, he has escaped from the logical working practice toward these goals and has borne witness to his fellowmen, by his *monastic* retiring behaviour, that he thinks the overcoming of the real practical world to be impossible on the way to his idealism. This is the reason that so many principally reject this monastic extreme conception of the habit of solitude. These people are unable to escape from some suspicion, because they have made themselves guilty of the act of real cowardice, in rejecting the principle of the full experience of the logical work and the real progression in the world. They have abolished the intellectual, checking and mitigating obstacles of the objective actions more thoroughly than it is the will of nature. The entire retirement from the working sensorial world means, therefore, the active evasion from the logical objective work in order to allow the individual to concentrate more easily and comfortably. The contemplative monk has, by choosing his order, favored the angry psychopupilar contraction of his affective attitude. He strives to overreach the will of the double real-idealistic human nature in order to receive the persistent possibility of divine delight and excludes the natural real detailed work intruding always in its fullness on the other people of the outside world, from their large real surroundings and most variable exterior circumstances.

So loneliness is again one of those psychodynamic helps which may be welcome and useful once in a while, but which are dangerous if they are abused because of the one-sided psychodynamic strength of their energy. It is a further example of our energetic concentrative helps being most useful if carefully used, but destructive and harmful for the moderate rhythmic action of our psychology, if applied too frequently.

Everybody needs sometimes the consolation and quiet clarification of the solitude. We hear that nothing was more disagreeable for the soldiers in the Great War than the perfect lack of individual retiremnt and loneliness. There are moments and situations of our life, when we need absolutely the enjoyment of solitude, because it is indeed the best and deepest consoling factor of our soul, rebuilding our discouraged heart from innermost sources, healing our wounds, gathering all best forces and energies, guiding us smoothly and softly to the loving embracement of divine ide-

alism. The sublime and non-sensorial solitude is not without reason beloved so much by unhappy people; for there we have the
sweetest balm for suffering, the help from confusion, embarrassment and indecision, the relief from overwork and discouragement. There our producing psychic force is renewed at the bosom
of the most powerful and intimate universal sources, and there it
finds again the charming way toward its terminal wonderful sentimental goals beckening luringly with supreme magnetic capacity.
Loneliness is the great therapy of sorrow and pain, but it may be
so only as the transitional, psychological state of our life, as the
recreation from our fatal work and pain, and has to cease soon
again, followed by future working necessities.

He who never needs loneliness bears witness of his shallow
and insignificant personal gift. He who likes solitude always and
over all, rejects himself from the real and intellectual sources of
our human life and destiny and makes himself guilty of the objection of exaggerated sentimentality. Both are wrong, because they
have overstepped the limits of their normal activity, toward the
idealistic or real side of their natural disposition. The will of nature is the culture of both sides of our double natural gift, and we
neglect, therefore, the intention of our destiny if we avoid all
opportunities of retirement, as we do if we are so fond of it that
we never go into the open arena of our intellectual experimental
real outside world.

We understand easily in connection with the psychological
nature of the loneliness that the notion of solitude is in closest relation with *art*. Isolation, seclusion, individual emphasis and solitary opposition is the very central and main means of artistic
action. Every artistic masterpiece acknowledges this law, and it is
one of the typical features of any great artist of the past that he
understands to work out one outstanding point or idea which he
puts in sublime opposition against all other which have to be, as it
were, only the staircase or the ladder in order to climb toward the
exceeding central column of the capital emphasis. In architecture,
in sculpture, in music, we have this monocratic or monarchic law,
but perhaps most clearly in painting and poetry. The mystic symbolic attractiveness of the stars, of the moon, of the sun, of the
isolated cloud in the sky, or the solitary tree in the field, the single
rush of the fountain in the absolute silence, the whispering source
in a darkening wood, the single shot in the field, the lost barking
of the dog in the silent night or the dazzling shine of the white
marble statue form between shadowy ivies and out of the dark con-

cealment of the bushes, all are instances of this truth, as well as the artistic elaboration and representation of the gospel emphasized the much more the brilliant personality of Christ, as the shadows of the death approached their huge fatal wings to his innocent serenity. As the shining moon winged with clouds, as the shimmering sail at the top of an outlook to the lake, between a fragrant wreath of trees and bushes, or as the sweeping motor-boat eradiating into a gurgling wake of great geometrical dimension, so is in any art of emotional power a capital point, to and from which all other representative elements go and come.

How much praises Goethe, this rather reserved real-idealist, the love of the solitude again and again! Tears and loneliness are even in his lyrical poetry the charming main key, by which he raptures the reader. "Trocknet nicht, trocknet nicht! Traenen ungluecklicher Liebe! Ach koennt' ich doch nur einmal recht einsam sein, dann waer' ich nicht allein." Men of his genial size are most happy and least alone if they are solitary, because they have the strongest affective wells in their own divine breasts. And if this was true of Goethe, then indeed it was more true of Christ, this quite unparalleled genial divine concentration of the human Antiquity. We dare not imagine his divine revelling when he was retired from all human checking surroundings, when his divine genial energy flew out without any obstacle into the harmonious universal theistic intercourse with his Father. What intimate divine conversation might this have been, where even palms and lions were listening in mute silence! What magnetic lightning flashes may have hit this topmost and highest summit of the historic affective humanity!

The true individual value comes out in solitude. The state of collectiveness hides the individual strength, or weakness, all individuals together forming one group of general reaction. In the isolating loneliness the religious genius kept not only his ordinary genial supremacy of divine communication and connection, like, as it were, a highest tree with the most outstanding summit, but in his solitude, removed from the social humanity, he became still more than usually the exception from the average. In this moments he was the only and lonely and yet gigantic oak in the wide plain field, from and to which the totality of the affective lightnings and of the interspheric magnetic changes with humanity, derived and returned. In those lonely moments the genial hero endured no collective affective competition nor diversion from other side, from other trees of the human social woods. He then emptied undisturdedly into the eternal abysses of the divine magnetic universe. His mission as the outstanding representative and the priest of the whole society increased in these moments to the most incredible superhuman measures. Solitude was one help more to raise his genial significance much higher, to give to his giant size the augmentation and addition of the most efficient divine cothurns and to elevate his genial head far above all clouds of the ordinary human average values.

Let us, before we close the sequel of the psychodynamic values, meditate once more upon the significance of the notions SENSORIAL VIOLENCE, of bodily beating and of corporeal punishment. Rudeness and blows have the intention and the meaning of sensorial overcrying of the existent personal previous sensorial impression. They endeavour to overtake the earlier sensorial influences on the individual, in any digressive direction and make effort to oppress, by their bluffing, assailing and intimidating sensorial impressions, the effects of the former experiences. Blows, knocks, corporeal violence or punishments are *concentrated accumulations of sensorial energy and force, used in order to quicken, accelerate and move the psycho-dynamic stagnations or fixations on the way.* There is a psychological, psycho-dynamic, rhythmic congruancy between the conditionns of rudeness, sensorial violence and knocks, on one side, and of the symbolic mysticism and the miracles, on the other side. The immediately intruding mystic value or the symbol and the miracle are in the same manner, as corporeal blows, the angry concentration of sensorial, compressed energy, which has the role to move, to drive and to quicken the psycho-dynamic function of our nature.

We are anxious to fix just here the interesting result of long and complicated psychological investigations on the symbolic mysticism, showing that rudeness and corporeal blows are very near the ideas of miracle, mysticism and fairy-tales, that both have the same psycho-dynamic methods and the same temperamental procedure. So we meet always again this threefold constellation of human psychology: Miracles and Mysticism,

Angry slothfulness,

Sensorial rudeness and blows.

They are in the most intimate mutual connection in causation, in relations and, above all, in the method. We touch here, therefore, one of the most central questions of the *educational value* of the sentimental religious conception, and, since we prefer to write about this topic in one of the following chapters, we shall not intrude more closely now on this idea.

ANGER in itself is the most interesting notion and forms the psychological basis of all psycho-dynamic functions. Anger was the starting point of all our psychological statements and principles and, indeed, it turns out to be almost the alpha and omega of the dynamic rhythmic conception of the soul. All life is in a certain sense principally anger. There is only the question, how much our psychic progression is checked by intellectual categoric examples, or how much it is quickened and facilitated by all the psycho-dynamic helps which we have now considered at length. Anger is the deepest biological spring and the summarizing appellation of the moving spectacle of the fundamental energy of our affective life; it is the moving universal fall of the sentimental interspheric magnetic river which in the human fate and in all visible and intellectual world is mitigated, restrained and checked by the regulating gear of the logical, methodical rhythm. It is the goal of our culture to transform our affective genial anger into the moderate thinking intellectual progression.

The elevated figure of the religious genius, in spite of the charming and meek manner, in which he is depicted by his artistic followers, is psychologically and philosophically not at all so harmless and peaceful as he seems to be. Although only once in his anger in the temple the lightning of his divine flaming passion breaks out, the burning desire for his goal and the angry zeal are the most considerable background and the most essential source and foundation of his psychology. The zeal for his Father devours him. He said himself, if the quotation is correct, that he did not come into this world to bring peace, but the *sword*. There the pacifists see, how much they are helped by the meek Jesus. And people were wondering, during the Great War, how the Christian God could admit battles and look down at the terrible slaughter of mankind, even after this saying. If we understand the psychological connection of sensorial violence and miracle, *both being angry eliptic methods of the psycho-dynamic progression,* and if we have recognized, according to the law of compensation, that the far-away goals of the transcendental religion can only be reached by the angry leaps of the symbolic mysticism, then we have the clear proof that every strong idealism and every highly affective religion must necessarily and emergently be in connection with anger, violence and *war*. The more idealism, the more conclusiveness, the less care in choosing the means leading to the fervently desired goal. On the other hand we know also that idealism produces, in the retrospeculative genial way, most kind humanity and broad love for the neighbor, and keen understanding for his deeper needs and worries, much more than the realist can have and give. We will not forget that chiefly the less appreciation of the material and real values as we have it in idealism, diminishes always the hot competitive quarrel of the intellectual world, much more than in realism, where the divisible, visible world represents the chief object of oppositions and struggles. Is not the exclusion of the unfit, in idealism, more radical than in realistic conceptions, after all? He who is more interested in the fundamental question of anger, may read our monography on this topic.

Sensorial violence and rudeness are of course in the nearest connection with, and the direct proportional product of, the degree of attractibility of the individual in respect to his magnetic ideals, and more than this, the necessity of this form of eventual affective reaction comes about chiefly then, when the idealistic goals are very far, if they surpass the human working possibility or logical expressibility very much and if, therefore, the logical performances of the individual prove to be insufficient to join them. In these cases, above all, the individual is enticed to appeal to the help of all more powerful, mystic quickening supports, in the last line even to the brutal force of rudeness and knocks. So we possibly must make responsible the quite extraordinary disproportion between real individual life-force and most distant, most magnetic and elaborate goals, for the danger of the emergent occurrance of rudeness, of brutal violence and knocks. The most elaborate ideal aims turn out to be very dangerous for our social educational culture, the intention of the latter being the education of the individual to the lasting aptitude and readiness for intellectual logical solution of all difficulties of our life and experience, whilst the extreme idealistic culture has exactly the contrary effect to destroy the patient proceeding regularity of the intelligence and to go on toward the highest goals by the angry leaps of mysticism and all other means of the intellectual muscular, toxicological and eliptic, accelerating psycho-dynamic groups, in the case of emergency even with brutal force and sensorial angry violence. Now we understand that there is indeed a reasonable possibility to limit the influence of the eternal magnetic goals and that there is sufficient reason to be afraid of the strong, precise elaboration of the terminal religious values. For love makes blind and loses the necessary discrimination. Here we have the explanation and the practical and philosophical facts of the idea that God's name was not allowed to be pronounced

EXAMPLE 319

by the Jewish people, and that we are indeed in the innermost core of our natural organization punished and spoiled if we dare to search the most intimate intercourse with the greatness of Jehovah and His attractive irresistible magnetism.

We omitted to speak more intensely on the value of the EXAMPLE. The example is perhaps the most powerful suggestion on earth. The most improbable, uncomfortable and hideous things rush like a fire round the whole globe, owing to the force of the easy example. How helpless is the most sagacious criticism in comparison with the power of the example! The idea of the *advertisement* is founded on the incessant repetition of the example. Its persuasive force builds on the strong inclination of our nature to imitation. Unfortunately it is however a two-edged sword. Its force is quite radical and esssential in the human psychology. Religion was always exceedingly aware of this energetic persuasive power and used it always and everywhere thoroughly. The gospel is penetrated and full of the example of the divine Christian hero. He attracts by his life, by his speeches and by his actions most efficiently all humanity toward his conceptions and his special intentions. The favorite way of the evangelic representation contains indeed always the form of the example. Christ is acting and speaking to people in *conversation* and exercises, therefore, the most enrapturing direct power of psychological emotion. By the choice of the method of the example, the pale, mystic-idealistic clouds of the presentation become more transparent. It is owing to the happy idea of the uninterrupted exemplary pictures, and conversational performances that the hazy reservedness of the hero becomes more distinct and that the hero seems to assume and adopt pronounced human real features. The example has the peculiarity to impart reality and life. It goes very far to meet the reader at the periphery of the intellectual practical reality in order to guide him so much sooner to the central idealistic goal which it intends to propose to him by its own developing performance. The example takes us in some way from the far and detailed periphery and induces us afterwards, without any interruption of contact, to the impersonal and theoretical idealism, for which it is working and whither it aspires.

Let us, since we at last are arrived at the end of our psychodynamic meditations, take once more a general outlook over all the single, helping, psycho-dynamic factors, as they are given in the human nature and as they were used by the religious philosophical founders.

We found out that the use of these means was different in both cases, that the religious teacher stresses many of the naturally given psycho-dynamic means and drops, on the other hand, other ones completely. We are entitled finally to try to find out generally whether the religion emphasizes the concentrative or the checking part of the human psycho-dynamic possibilities, whether the religious system is indeed, as we asserted always, the expression of the prevalent idealism or if it has distributed equally and in perfect balance all helps naturally given, in the accelerating and in the hesitating bridling psychodynamic direction.

It was not the task and the intention of this book to go as far as to discuss the notions of *intellectuality, visibility, objectivity, multiplicity, detail and of the sensorial power in the categoric expressions of time, space and causality and logic,* although these notions, exactly speaking, belong to the checking order of the psychodynamic means and appear not only in every sentence of our writings, but also in every word of the book of our experience, being of the most fundamental importance. I must refer in this regard to my former writings, where these basic human psychological values have their proper place. They are indeed the last and main key-stones of our consideration of the world. They represent the intellectual human life and are in their experiences the expression of the stationary retardation of our present existence on the way and in relation to the universal unbridled progress. We are pilgrims on this earth. The right understanding and solid control of those notions, the breaking down of historic wrong connections and and combinations of characteristics, their adequate rebuilding and conceiving constellation, their improved reunion and new relationship with all other values is exactly the chief questionable point of our thought. Every philosophy starts from the logical foundation of the observation of the visible world. If there is some hope for any philosopher to have done a great and good work, it must consist in the new, deeper and more exact formulation of those fundamental philosophical elements of the visible, intellectual world, in having made new truer divisions, new connections and principal philosophical constellations and in having avoided, disrupted and dropped old and wrong, so-called logical, but as a matter of fact illogical constellations of non-characteristic notional compressions. Visibility, multiplicity, detail, intellectuality, logic, time, space and causality form together the ruling laws of the visible world.

Natural psycho-dynamic means:

1) Concentrative helps:
(accelerating aids):

a) intellectual, bluffing, sensorial group:	mysticism mysticism in nature example corporeal violence
b) muscular group:	weeping singing dancing sexuality
c) toxicological group:	alcoholism nicotinism hashishism morphinism cocainism
d) eliptic group:	solitude diseases bathing cold temperature

2) Neutral means:
    laughing (tending toward reality)

3) Checking or relaxing
psycho-dynamic means:
       suffering
       work
       science
       visible world
       warm temperature

Christianity rejects sexuality and dancing. The toxicological group, in regard to alcoholism, is naturally favored, in moderate use, by the more symbolic section of the religion, whilst it is excluded by the more natural intellectual methodical tendencies.

Christian religious psycho-dynamic means:

1) Accelerating helps:

a) intellectual, bluffing, sensorial group:	symbolism mysticism miracle prayer example punishment
b) muscular group:	weeping singing
c) toxicological group:	alcoholism
d) eliptic group:	fasting bathing solitude (silence, retreat, monasticism.)

2) Neutral intermediary group:

(both tending toward idealism)   art
                                sacrifice

3) Checking psycho-dynamic means:

            cross
            passion
            suffering

From these two tables we read that the use, exclusion and the dosage of the various alleged psychodynamic notions are in reality very changing in kind, choice and degree, and we may guess that they are used differently, in different religious cultures, countries and times. The more real natural intellectual taste will, of course, prefer in all parts the checking intellectual notions and emphasize their value at the expense of the accelerating means - in an extreme degree of this attitude we cannot speak longer of religious, but of working scientific activity, - whilst the sentimental part of the religious conception does the contrary in putting the stress on the accelerating side. The struggle about Prohibition of to-day is the very clear example of this truth, but there is and was and will be a similar crisis about all these psycho-dynamic notions at different times and in different geographical countries and racial conditions.

If we, however remember that the religious genius was the solstitial turning-point of his time, that from him humanity returned toward the approach and encirclement of the central monosymbilism, and if we recall people and tenets considering him as all their divine help and source of theistic concentration, then we must accordingly admit that the religious monosymbolism exists indeed as long as we accept the sentimental way of approaching the magnetic theistic crystallization. The rejection of the psycho-dynamic accelerating means signifies nothing less than the repulsion of the still living divine power of the religious function. The exclusive or prevalent inclination and transition to the intellectual checking psycho-dynamic means proves the exhaustion of the human possibility approaching toward the conclusive monosymbolic idea. The preferable adoption of the checking intellectual psycho-dynamic group displaces the genial hero into the passive role of the historic apotheosis and changes the past religious system into a mummified glorification. The intellectual Christian who digresses from the sentimental accelerating psycho-dynamic group, leaves, according to the signature of his progressive spheric destiny, the monosymbolic historic idea to which the role of the religious genius is bound and limited. In his checking intellectual behaviour he looks indeed and essentially for new extra-solar divine goals and symbols. The divine Christ is the fulfilment and the revelation of our historic mono-theism, and his method must essentially be the sentimental, accelerating, concentrative suggestion. The hesitating and checking, psycho-dynamic, intellectual preference, on the contrary, rejects with the hero's method the living validity of his divine teachings themselves. It embraces in its "anti-historic" divine tendencies the outside possibilities of the future mono-theistic and mono-symbolic developments. It declares the historic mono-symbolic role of religion as finished and looks in its transitional nature for future, historic-symbolic, outside whirlpools and for future solstitial theistic genial achievements.

The *intellectual divine* is not at all fixed any longer on the historic past religious genius. He dissolves his past personality in the modern tendencies and intellectual interpreting prospects toward the future human development. He has left that which we call historic religion and looks longingly ahead of our religious age toward new possibilities in regard, as well to the solstitial conversion of the present intellectual world into future sentimental mono-symbolic relapses, as to new expressions of mono-theism being during the *transitional time* superseded, psychologically speaking, by *poly-symbolism* and *by poly-theism,* or at least by the lack of distinct mono-symbolic sharpness. Checking means are therefore essentially anti-religious in the sense of the historic ecclesiastic conception. We can look at most things from two sides, according to the chosen starting point. The checking means look for the future time, whilst the sentimental psycho-dynamic means are the preservers and stewarts of the old historic magneto-spheric psychology, fixing the historic role of the religious founders in their persisting validity. We know how we have to think of all these things and to appreciate their different important views and connections, if we recall our former explanations. There cannot be indeed a question of the preservation of any historic name or of any intellectual and economical ecclesiastic eternification, but it always will be essentially important that the universal divine progression of the human affective spiritual energy moves on without any interruption and without dangerous stagnation, as they are given also in the abuse of the sentimental accelerating means creating as counter-balance, in the social life, war and revolution, and in the private life, overwork and the drought of intellectual performance.

All accelerated psycho-dynamic rhythmic actions may be called angry, and all checking and hesitating psycho-dynamic progressions serving as skids in the peculiar concentrative function, may be considered, under this angle of view, as *laziness or slothfulness.* These two states of the soul are the two opposite antipodes of our psychology. They are the two extreme antagonistic points of the pendulum of our rhythmic psychological energy. But it is indeed in the treatises on suggestion, where we have to consider all these things more closely. For this moment we may only insist again on the interesting confusion resulting in the use of the terminology according to our intra- or extra-theistic stand-point. We may call from the intra-theistic, historic, sentimental standpoint anger, what the extra-theistic intellectualist calls laziness, and he indeed calls most rightly and successfully laziness and slothfulness where the sentimental idealist speaks of anger and greatest energy. All these quarrelling is, within the large frame of the universal history, however, nothing but much ado about nothing. The times and ages are only different steps on the way to the fulfilment of the human destiny, and the decision of sentimental or intellectual attitude toward the deity has the only meaning of both the psychological conservativism and our passive perseverance in clinging to the overcome fact of our old psychological and cultural achievement, on one side, and of the progressive and willing enterprise of our advancing future duties within the subsequent universal spheric evolution, on the other. Intellectualism and sentimentality, realism and idealism, release and complete one another always during the current of the history. They need each other incessantly and each of both for the fact that it has scorned the other opposite factor, is subjected to change into the other complementary component of the human psychological head of Janus. Intellectuality is the status nacsendi of a future sentimentality. The intellectual resistance is a necessary magnetic scandal for the future better and richer development of our universal reach. This different magnetic divine breeze creates the one-sided blaming and acknowledging terminology, and therefore the necessary misunderstandings and logical-magnetic confusion in the moody April storms of transitional periods pointing to a greater future. In the great moments of history the head of Janus is most distincly delineated before our mind. All greatest and most important human values are ambivalent. There we look as to a transparent body to the inner organization of the vital movements of the all and can study and understand the make-up of the omni-present split pervading the whole universal creation and our psychology. The ambivalent notions and considerations are the backbone of the universal representation leading to the symmetric expressions of intellect, reality and the abstract sentimental spirituality, as a middle transfer and connecting seam.

Es ist dafuer gesorgt, dass die Baeume nicht
in den Himmel wachsen.

Goethe

SIXTH BOOK

LET us mention, in connection with previous meditations, some other fundamental religious notions and ideas! SIN means that angry reaction of slothfulness which swings the individual over the detailed steps of the real duties. This angry reaction does not respect the petty single moments of the given individual peculiar destiny, and leaps in imaginative jerks over the whole range of the real logical prescription. The general root and the basis of all these omissions of the detailed intellectual duties is always the previous lack of easy affective discharge which causes the following revolutionary sentimental explosion represented essentially by one type of what we call sin. The physical basis of these sins is, therefore, the augmenting affective stagnation, the increasing tension of the vital spring distending itself, at last, forcibly and overskipping in its rolling-down sway several or even many links of the logical real order of the elaborated written law and commandment. This is what we call sin, and we understand now the saying, that *slothfulness* is the mother of all sins. Laziness is the warm hatching bed and the hot house, the best physical pre-supposition for the angry notion of sin. Laziness creates in all directions of the human affectivity that explosive tinder of inconsiderate superfluous energy which overthrows and overskips the obstacles of the reality. Therefore,it is our first and supreme duty to avoid the rise of affective stagnations and to evade those situations of the life, where our regular affective discharge and our logical concentrative vital activity are obstructed.

We cannot emphasize enough the fact of the stealthy rising of the lazy affective stagnation. If we take away all other faults from the world and allow this only one to remain within it, then we have kept for us the worst being able in life to meet us, the most thorough unhingement of our good possibility of real existence. Away with slothfulness, with the affective obstacles of all checking obstacles of the life! Let us enter into the most natural and easy, good and regular exchange of affective sentiments with all environment and into the utmost faithfulness toward the smallest and most ordinary daily detailed duties! Then we have done the best.

Slothfulness means therefore the root and the causal source of most human sinfulness being considered from the causal inferior side, whilst the notion of *pride represents the peculiar affective condition of the detailed reality in sin and expresses that the affective energy hovers over all objectivity uncheckedly, instead of clinching the fine pores of the affective nature and natural gift of any smallest daily detailed experience.* The greater the terminal ideal suggestibility, the still greater the danger of pride and of real sin. The more energetic the elaboration of the near reality, the less the danger. The idealist sure of his terminal direction is characterized as the individual with many, exactly recognizable, real faults, but finding always again easily, through the power of his well directed, main affective energy, the way toward the noble ideal sentiments. He is the man who may be often practically insupportable because of his many petty faults, but who must be felt and acknowledged, as a whole , as the most perfect individual in all main features of the admirable character, despite his objective awkwardness or negligence in meeting petty detailed obstacles. The exact realist has instead great facility to be correct, almost I said agreeable, in the small daily intercourse, because he is more patient, clear and objective whilst he likely misses the best terminal goals because of his lack of sentimental, comprehending direction. The lesser amount of psychic gift produces less the danger of the rise of certain sins. For only in the case of strong affective suggestibility we are in a position to have strong and quick affective stagnations, so that the emergent reaction of the subsequent overskipping of the logical duty may easily happen. So we understand that for the realist the sharp detailed notion of the legal sin hardly exists in a high degree. His ideal universal attraction is so little that he is not subjected any longer to that angry energetic magnetism toward the terminal goals and that he, for this reason, avoids better the stumbling action produced by angry inconsideration and exaggerated hurry, from which the eliptic sinful leaps over the real obstacles result.

The notion of sin is fixed on the idea of the historic God. The real stumbling in the energetic progression toward the enrapturing deity is what we call sin. Could we have more moderate self-control in this our moving theistic action, then we would be saved from the deficient and inaesthetic stumbling. The strong, suggestive concentrative attraction becomes the bad fate of the theistic idealist, in the state of his inconsiderate purposive hurry and of his retrograde relapse from divine delight to realistic voluptuousness. If his extraordinarily sharp magnetic attraction were not so energetic, too strong for his temperamental nature, the causation of the eliptic leaps would subside. We would have the possibility of the more regular activity through the moderate charm of the single steps of the reality until the top of the ideal theistic mountains. Sin happens in the hurry of exaggerated theistic zeal. Therefore, the unprotected exposure to the magnetic strong attraction of the divinity is most dangerous. It may quicken respectlessly over the legal reality and produces mysticism and impatience. We are punished in the same manner as have failed. We have loved too proudly and too little self-consciously, and we are punished in that we compensatorily offend the real natural order and therefore are deficient in the laws of our human natural love, stumbling morally. We fly with enthusiasm toward the divinity and are punished by falling down and being hurt. We hurried too much, and therefore we are retained by discouragement, straying and retardation from the terminal goal which we ought to have followed, without loafing round-about ways, but on the faithful and logical way of the moderate and legal commandments.

It is and remains our average destiny to collect in the most self-conscious and bashful way all detailed grains of our daily work and duty, and we must gather always, step by step, each minute and hour for the good and intellectual work of our real destiny, in order to have at last in their surprising total effect and in the product of their logical elaboration the ideal flower of our natural, deserved and adequate enjoyment. Modesty and self-consciousness in small things protect best against the angry motions of the real sin. The universal, magnetically enrapturing notion of God induces us to fall in love with its mono-symbolism too much and to overlook, in this manner and fact, the reality, not thinking of, nor reckoning with, its necessities. Here we have the fundamental sinful danger of the extreme symbolization of the theistic education. The too elaborated and abounding terminal theistic love is to be considered as the immediate source of pride, laziness and anger which, in their turn, have so serious consequences.

Therefore, the Jews were not allowed to enter the door of the central part of their temple; therefore, they did not dare to pronounce the name of God, and for this reason Moses was afraid to raise his eyes to God in order not to be blinded. The terminal force and effect of blinding is striking like a bolt of lightning. It destroys our natural skill and just eye for mediated civic *virtues* as well by exaggerated suggestive attraction, as the perfect lack of ideal directive energy causes the entire steerlessness and injudicious helplessnes of the affective individuality. There is nothing greater and more accurately necessary, in this connection, than the *principle of moderation*. The old Horace never became tired to inculcate this principle of the *aurea mediocritas,* and how many other writers, thinkers and philosophers did the same through all nations and cultures! *Virtue* is the middle product between the realistic intellectuality and the theistic idealism. It is the harmonious middle step between mind and body, imagination and sensorial world, heaven and earth. Virtue is the *eudynamic condition* of our fatal spheric natural human development. Sin is *kako-dynamic* and *kako-rhythmic*. Kako-dynamics means, in the tongue of the *conscience,* the heavy or mortal sin, kako-rhythm includes the slight or venial sin. Heavy sin must be the lack of good terminal direction and good general sentiments. The venial sin is the detailed, real, objective mistake with its small rhythmic oscillations in using good judgment. Therfore, we may find out easily, how the old historic fixation of the monosymbolic idea values intellectual digressions from its central sentimental position.

Sin depends, therefore, on troubled dynamic psychopupilar conditions. The affective concentrative use of energy is disturbed either in the sense that the progressive concentration does not respect the central-most direction of theistic values which of course could be imperfect, as any human work, in the given historic prescription of an ecclesiastical legislation, or in that sense that the affective dynamic regularity is changed in the sense of too great quickness or slowness or irregularity. In the first case we have the mortal, in the second the more venial light sin, in the terminology of the church. The affective, dynamic, harmonious sentiments are the most desirable and necessary condition of our nature. Directive affective troubles reduce the greatest dangers of compensation for our performances and our human perfection.

How could we help it not to recall instantly the notion of *Nervousness* and its effects! It is that anomaly of affective regularity, where the good and adaptable divisions and distributions of our psychic forces and of our nervous power have been lost, and where we have soon either the most remarkable excess and use of working performance, without sufficient exterior reason or even opportunity, or where we soon observe, on the other hand, the utmost unmotified lack of energy and producing strength as well. Eudynamic affectivity is the highest and best thing, which we have to strive to in human life, and which nervousness misses. It is that continually adaptable readiness of our affective production and work, being always in subtle agreement with the exterior real exactions, not lavish and not deficient toward the necessities of the moment. This kind of psychic reason alone will be able to make our life most efficient, thorough and real, and it will protect our life against that unreasonable prodigality of the psychic and natural forces, from that detailed insufficiency in reality, which are characteristic for inaptitude, unfitness for practical life, pride, laziness, anger, sin, in the performing attitude of our daily life.

From these meditations on sin we could derive the following *prayer* against the mentioned type of sin: "Lord, do not reveal to me too much the beauty of thy face or the charm of thy greatness and power, but permit me to look at thy countenance only through the veil of similes and comparisons in order that l do not leave in the hurry of my magnetic rush the reality and make, therefore, wrong steps, on the way of going to thy divine goals! For thine are also the prescriptions of duty and the logical single degrees. Do not allow me to stumble at the given real obstacles leading at last to thee! Give to me sufficient patience and self-consciousness in order that I keep the humanly necessary rhythm and the sensorially necessary time in going through the logical real light-field! May I not be found haughty and falling out, in any manner, from that well ordered round-dance which I have to perform before thy face, in the really checked character of my humanity, as long as I carry with me the peculiarity of my mental-bodily, double nature! I see that nothing can elevate me before thy glory but the partly resignation of the fulfilment of my inborn highest ideal wishes, the humble logical performance of my intellectual nature. And I beseech thee not to tear me away delightfully by too great terminal ideal sway, from the concert of my earthly real task! Grant me to be far enough, in this my earthly human life, from heaven and its eternal charms that l may fulfil patiently and regularly my fatal earthly duties, and that I may not leap over them in the magnetic sway of thy love! In this way I hope to succeed in not offending thee and in not being pushed back by thy mighty hand into my inferior human position. Lord, do not give me too much divine love so that I may not hate, compensatorily, the real side of the life! Give to me not so much terminal ideal hope as to despair of the imperfections of this intellectual visible world, and do not impart to me so much ideal faith as to doubt too thoroughly about the validity of this my sensorial real existence! In this I trust not to underestimate my categoric fate, nay, even to appreciate, elaborate and like it, according to my natural real disposition."

The more violently we strive to go to the deity, the less is our progress in virtuous advance. This is nothing but the necessity of compensation. For the more energetically our life-force was thrown into the lap of the terminal ideal deity, the more carelessly and respectlessly it is likely pushed over the peripheric details of the exact legal comandments, and so much more the ignorance and the lack of anxious minute intrusion on the detailed real exactions of the historic divine-real law is produced. This is the way, how the *scrupulous* religious individual is liable to destroy himself within the sore experiences of the vicious circle of his psychology. Terminal ideal love produces strong ideal magnetic direction and push, but the individual might join it the less because of the sinful overthrowing of the real peripheric obstacles, which causes a chafing disharmony of the heart and the head, and because of the lack of *lasting* exact diligence and care.

How ridiculous, humiliating and pitiful does it look, on the other side, that many people spend their whole life in peripheric ceremonious and exterior performances toward religious goals and in the religious service without the least grasping of the eminent sense of the inner dignity, of the depth and the cultural effect of the terminal intentions and functions. These people possess neither the strength of idealism excluded from them, nor even the real sure ability of the dependent legal interpretation within this logical world. These people are the least divinely gifted. But how often do we see that people of this description are the stewards and the technical explainers of the most elevated and most divine idealistic principles!

Unfortunately we often observe in the world that the degree of uplifting symbolism and ideal enthusiasm is so much greater as the legal weakness and sinfulness of the society increases. The notion of sin seems to have much less significance and exciting possibilities for the religions and nations which have the less extreme idealistic education and culture, since they are much less attracted by the ideal forces and are, therfore, much less in danger to stumble in supra-human ambition.

The best struggle against sin is the extermination or utmost reduction of its physical mechanical suppositions. The best help given against sin cannot consist in punishment, scolding and frightening with the bad personal consequences of sin, or even in the most elaborate description of the loveliness of God, the latter method being perhaps even dangerous according to our former explanations. The best way of producing lasting human virtue is this, that we strive to educate on the middle basis of moderate feelings and intelligence, that we produce the most temperate ideal magnetism and allow the individual force to be always aware, at the same time, of the most conscious and accurate correctness of its detailed real actions and circumstances.

Many of the actions which are usually, in exterior and superficial consideration, called sin and crime, belong to the realm of the HEROISM. The attribute of hero, however, never saves the society from the duty to defend herself. But an antiquated legislation of any description is a shame, because it often spares the worst and kills the best, whilst, on the other hand, we must understand that a too flexible adaptability of legislation would destroy all reliable steadiness of order. Too bad that the progress of the increasing justice of the law has to proceed over the sacrificed hero! The religious genius is in his resistance to the traditional law the prototype of the hero, treated as *criminal* by the conception of his contemporaries. From their standpoint he was a strayed sheep and a renegade, and they crucified him perhaps with the same holy conviction, as the Wandering Jew, resisting him in an angry and hateful way, was punished for his resistance so that he could not find charming rest in the sweet home and fold of the genial concentration of his sympathy. Many statements about sin refer, in a mystic way, to heroism. It is stamped by the contemporary conceptions as sin and crime, in so many cases, rising, however, so much more gloriously from the grave of early unsuccessfulness. Is not one "crime" worse and another better than the legislative written letter? Can one not be a criminal, because one 'overdoes' justice? But hard, as it is, we have to understand that the intellectual letter of the law, for the sake of stability, security and order, has to be respected, but only up to a certain degree, because it also includes the general universal necessity and the biological seed of growing from good to better. But who in the world cares about real improvement of the old law but the selfless hero, and he naturally is the legal victim of the ruling present legal fixation, as long as his better conviction has not convinced all and changed the law. The unsuccessful hero is treated and punished as a criminal. And yet, he can afford to perish better than anybody else. The balance of the happiness is in his favor even on the scaffold. Just there is the triumph of his sincere spiritual superiority and sincere conviction. He is a citizen of another world and his laurels are immortal.

The religious genius would replace the existence of the historic legislation by the higher perfection of his divine conceptions, of which he was convinced in his conscience, and for which he was ready even to die. The hero is the predecessor of the coming law. He is the extremist of the law at the present time, not in a contradictory, but in a fulfilling increasing sense. The hero surpasses and perhaps hurts the law with his superior love for order. In this sense he is able to conflict with the existing legislative mediocrity, as the low criminal hurts the law by deficiency. Is the source of our actions given in exterior legislative coercion or in our subjective conscientious conviction? Are our personal convictions never in contradiction with the law? And if they are, are we allowed in our deepest conscience, to submit to the legal paragraph, because we are afraid of punishment? There may be instances in our life, when we do the will of the law, because we will not be battered by the executive power standing behind the letter of the law. But who is the mysterious founder of the law unless the majesty of the human collectiveness itself? Are we more bound, in addition, to do the ruling will of the majority or the clear urge of the unfathomable universal depth of our own nature, if it is sincerely able to digress in selfless, general interest? The law is a changing river moving from good to better, and it is improving only by the effort of the torch-bearers of selflessly interested personal convictions. The search of any highest right lies indubitably in the deep well of our own breast and the intellectual scientific letter of law limps always behind the divine passions and the great will of the universal suggestions of a noble man.

On the other side we understand that punishment and carrying through of the existing law must be. The existence of the humanity is founded on individual and collective egoism, whilst the radical feature of the hero is self-sacrifice for greater future ideal realizations. If the whole social body would consist of heroes, humanity would lose its historic right of existence. In self-defence alone the order of the society can be guaranteed, and this is the only way, how the historic and categoric stability can continue in its sure and slow rhythmic step. Society has not only the duty to move, but also the care to stay, and since moving on in universal problematic possibilities is less comfortable than enjoying the present clear reality, the social representatives prefer to stay and understandably resist, to the utmost, any proposed changes. Those who disagree with the possible measure of universal unfoldment of the historic order, risk to be crushed, may they go too slowly and be abandoned and isolated in this way, or go ahead and be misunderstood and disapproved by the existing real emphasis.

What a heavy weight lies on the shoulders of a *judge* ! He be a full man who is expected not only to criticize the intellectual circumstances of a case laid before him, but also to take full account of the deepest intentions and terminal implications of any individual actions. At the same time our heart and true sentiments tell us that God alone can be a just judge, he alone knowing the bottom and the deepest urges of the human heart, and at the same time we appoint judges and give to them symbolic power and dress in order to support the conviction that they really are able to find out absolute truth and justice. The judge may be able to kill you, if you disagree with the letter of a legislative commandment. What if the bottom of your heart would be God himself and you die, are an outcast or banished because you cling most conscientiously to a force which we call faithfulness to your deepest convictions! And yet, - *ceterum censeo* - the judge is a necessity. Sad necessity to justice other people! Many are so one-sidedly intellectual that the do not understand the tragedy of their self-sureness.

Compassion for any unhappy is not a free gift, but a duty justified in the objective nature and the circumstances of psychology, a just and necessary decoration of our own soul. Compassion is justice to ourselves and to others. We understand, however, just from the progressed democratic feelings of the modern time, that whole nations avoid in their practical psychology the notion of compassion, because they have awakened to such a vivid consciousness of human equality and psychological broadness that they think nobody is worthy of giving compassion. Who is absolutely sure to be better or happier in our changing and complicated collective world! If *pardon* would not be justice, there would be not only little, as it is, but no pardon at all in the world and we would not look at it with a religious thrill. Pardon is absolute justice, whilst punishment reaches only the limit of relative justice. And if pardon is greater than 'justice', it is a greater duty and a surer terminal hope.

If the hero is unable to quicken the wheel of the historic order, to the progressive conceptions of his leading intentions, then, right and better as he may be, he will be legally punished or disapproved because of the troubling and misleading influence of his extraordinary activity So the heroic man is indeed nearly a god, if he succeeds to save and further the whole society to higher future steps of the historic cultural development, but he will be called a disorderly, deficient sinner or even a criminal, if he is unable to force and lead the sufficient attention of society to his inventive will.

Heroic actions are such which exceed the limits of the contemporary legislative reality, in a progressive, developing sense and are liable, therefore, to be misinterpreted and punished on the part of the shrewd pitfall of the invidiuos ruling power and reality. It may be often very difficult to distinguish between sin, crime and heroism. Is not the only sure source of information, in this regard, more often than we perhaps dream in our self-just indignation, the deep well of the "trespasser's" own subjective reason and heart and intention, may it be hidden for ever? *This is the only case where we have to admire and to punish at the same time,* in the sense of the legal order. We admire because of the superior leading force and the noble self-sacrificing intention, and we punish because of the will to continue the compact possession and historic structure of the present social reality. This psychic combination of reverence and punishing necessity is the quintessence of what we call *tragic. The highest things of mankind are at stake, and yet, they cannot be saved because of the ruling necessity of the intellectual letter of the present legislative crystallization, which protects the balanced and quiet existence by cutting off the exception.* The better perishes for the good. The existing hesitating necessity has a slow, shuffling step, and he who overdoes its rhythm in any way, by exciting and unseasonable heroism, in the leading avant-garde, or by deficient crime and sin, in the limping rear, exposes himself to self-destruction by necessary social interference.

The question of *ultimate right* is not at all able, however, to be solved in the way of *violence,* in a definite way. The coercion of the ruling power and majority means only the last word spoken by the present real constellation of circumstances. In fact it is a procrastination preceding the later ultimate solution, which happens in a spiritual sense in love and pardon. A legal decree of a majority is utterly unable to retain the further development or influence of the increasing terminal divine justice and direction, whose instrument the hero is. But even the real force and violence of the majority has, insufficient as it seems to the distant look of the spiritualized taste, a certain share in divine quality and authority. The spiritual force, living in the individual breast, is easily defeated for the moment, but not for ever, because the spiritual force is the stronger and more concentrated factor, if it stoops down to categoric realization. "If I would, my Father would send me a squad of angels". But he will not, because he is too fine to hurry after the laurels of the others. He departs silent and unjustified from the real stage of this world.

The possible confusion of heroism and sin does not throw a

light of perfection on the written law and definite commandment. And the crucifixion of the divine continues inunterruptedly, now as before! The unwritten law seems to have more binding power than the written one on great souls. There must be more deep obligations untold or inexpressible by now than one has found out and fixed. How can it be explained in a really just way that the scoundrel slips between the letter of the law and is its lease-holder, whilst the saint and ever just is fixed on the cross? And the spectacle continues to-day - still - again and - again -

As long as the lawyer emphasizes always that he deals only with facts, there is still fear for more crucifixions. Are false witnesses also facts and what is their effect? One still catches maliciously and egotistically, according to the misinterpretable letter and not according to the benevolent, unwritten or unwritable spirit. What a shame! All newspapers are full of those spectacles of lack of charity toward the neighbor! Hypocrites who believe so quickly, and enjoy the faults of others instead of covering them with kindly love. The enjoyment of our lenience and benevolence, on the part of the accused, is not a worn out, sentimental fairy-tale, but an exact biological right, even if social self-defence is inevitable. Mind the business of your own life and you will have enough material for critical consideration. Oh universal brotherhood, where art thou? And yet there must be mixt something else with the feelings of the wonderers about criminal stories than only cruelty. Has humanity always to expect its heroic surprises from some mistaken face of a criminal?

Humility and conscientious faithfulness to one's own personal conviction may sometimes be competitors in religion and morality. The settled order says there is no good conscience outside the legal right. The hero instead is longing pathetically for the highest cross, where he thinks to meet a conflict between his conviction and the existing order and decides in favor of his conscience. The humble friend of the existing legal crystallization respects the impressive authority of the long historic development and the judicious collaboration of the leading men of centuries and nations.

Where is the limit of the subjective, personal freedom of heart and conviction and where starts the obligation to submit to the objective prescription of the historic, legal and possessive reality of our social structure?

We must find out, whether there is any real progress and ideal decision in favor of personal conviction over against the power of the historic traditional majority settlement. We ought urgently to know, if the sincere personal conviction can be in contradiction with the given historic, legal and religious law. The necessity of the highest divine claim of the historic religion is clear in this connection. Could humility be a crime or is it always virtue? Can self-trust in discernment of highest things in the objective order be a crime and fault? Have we to believe anybody more than our five senses and the qualities of our personal mind? Can there be a misunderstanding of conditions and values in sincere conviction? Or possesses just our deepest conscience always the infallible security of the universal truth? Heroism is based on these considerations. It claims to choose the self-confidence and the better insight in the better right and declines the power of the objective social compulsion. In regard to the ruling and intolerant majority we could put the questions: Has love and compassion really to stop, where a powerful organization makes our violent victory strong, or even where utility makes our collective self-defence necessary? Must there be violence and punishment? Is the spiritual law of preferring to be wronged than to risk to do wrong only for the weak individual who cannot seriously carry through his will? Cannot the majority be wrong and the individual right? Why does the principle not work practically, which one whispers everywhere, that the majority is always wrong and vulgar? Will the morning never dawn, when we shall move one jota over the crude material power and look through the door of nobler and more refined spiritual values?

The hero does not judge according to the utility, which we call justice, but according to universal love, which is his right of existence or death, may he be as he may. Everybody has his liberty and special temperamental features, according to which he may act, if he will face the consequences. Here is the hidden root of the ordinary parting way of the historic success, of the social acknowledgement for fitness and law abiding sentiments, on one side, and of the distress, failure and rejection from the frame of the strong social order, on the other side. The homo probus et criticus may have heroic features, but he is not very successful in the practical life.

Punishment, even if necessary for self-defence, does not prove absolute worthiness or unworthiness of the counter-acted individual. Nobody can approach the majesty of the inner individual heart. Nobody can look through the deepest motives of anybody else. If they are not practical for the present settled state of order, this does not prove that they are wrong or insignificant or ignoble.

REPENTANCE has the intention of the magnetic redirection toward God. The repenting individual is willing to find out, where the concentrative theistic direction, intensity and rhythm of his former actions were incorrect, exaggerated or insufficient and endeavours to connect the memory of these past omissions and digressions to the crystallized mono-theistic conception of his time, by his subsequent, magneto-centric affective corrections. Repentance seems so to be the production of the historic theistic formulation. The heroic "sin" may be the inevitable circuit of extra-solar progress to the Deity. It is therefore at the root of the universal progress of humanity. In the sense of the old historic divine conception, this *directive sin* is the faithless digression from the fixed historic mono-symbolic concentration, but it advances the developing fate of the human theistic character. We have in repentance the means to push back the already progressed magnetic direction from the extra-solar into the intra-solar theistic conception. So repenting somehow has the sense and the role of the historic theistic policeman who always re-directs the progressive and digressive extra-theistic affective tendencies backwards toward the former historic centro- symbolic order. Repentance may have, therefore, some checking sense in respect to the human collective universal fate, as we, on the other hand, must admit that the directive, sentimenal heroism is the progressive way of humanity toward new spheric universal instradations. Sin is prosecuted, rightly in the sense of the existing social usefulness, because of its disorderly effect on the contemporary legal peace. But it has the consequence of the felix culpa of Saint Augustin, having unexpectedly reconciling vicissitudes after the performance and producing, after all, - being perhaps first a deplorable scandal - new future happy theistic enlargements which likely could not happen without the intellectual affective, extratheistic digressions coming about in this cause.

Repentance means the intellectual conversion of our sentimental digressions, or, in another sense, nearer our usual viewpoint, the sentimental conversion of our intellecual digressions. By the effort of the good will the digressive details of the intellectual mind are blurred, persuaded and suggested to acquiesce with the former historic centro-symbolic conceptions. The individuality as one affective whole is induced to give up every detailed resistance against his former central affective conception of the world. It is true, any sin must be felt as essentially dreadful and detestable from the historic orderly legal standpoint and from the basis of the aesthetic individual experience. There cannot be the question of the individual desirability even of the progressive directive sin including features of heroism. Even from our restricted social platform sin is abhorred to the utmost and generally considered as being in opposition not only to the private, but also to the public well-fare. If we will use the scandalous word desirabilty or better necessity of the directive sin, then we must connect it with the general, universal, extra-solar development of our human most collective, historic, spheric progression. Sin may be, and in most cases certainly is, very hurtful or even destructive for the individual and for the smaller human community, but the directive sin is the supposed, in a sense deplorable, yet in another inescapable necessity for the future progress of the whole humanity. Even the "anti-legal" sinner and above all he, sacrifices himself in a sense, like the pelican for the future human theistic enlargement. If he does not mean it, he does it. But why should he not mean it? Most great things come from unknown sources. Losing his fixed centromagnetic conceptions, which are most suitable and necessary for his personal existence and happiness, he contributes, on the other hand, to finding the key to future universal progresses of humanity. The hero destroys himself because of the necessity of the fatal salvation of the human collectiveness. He is by necessity the predecessor of the future universal and affective digressions of the theistic humanity. He has eaten from the tree of knowledge and, therefore, has lost his personal sentimental happiness so necessary to him. If he personally perishes in the sense of this categoric life, the community and collective totality of his fellow-men instead will enjoy the future spheric enlargement and will gain from the scandal of his past action. So the hero turns out essentially to be the least egoist, since he sacrifices himself entirely for the totality through his courage to face any misunderstanding contemporary blame and accusation as sinner. His eternal imperishable service consists exactly in his own categoric and real self-destruction on behalf of further and deeper mono-symbolic intensity.

We understand that the idea of repentance does not enjoy much sympathy in our intellectual digressive age. Even if nobody is able to find sin desirable, even if it must be and is individually and socially felt rather much more as detestable and tasteless, we must admit that it is at least instructive and instrumental, that it conveys new sentimental urges, interesting experiences and helps to develop our deepest humanity, often even individually. Therefore the fact that the past sin is not felt as being wrong by many who are most anxious to avoid it in advance. Because of the subsequent happy changes it is then rather accepted, perhaps in mellow melancholy, as the fatal way to the universal, social and, in many ways, even individual development of humanity. So the notion of repenting is rather neglected and even rejected as unbiological and waste of energy, by many people. They consider repentance as artificial magnetic stagnation or even as the recall and undoing annihilation of the necessary, universal progression of humanity as a whole and individual. Any experience is an asset. There must be scandals, and if they happened, we cannot reject them entirely, because they also are human facts or features claiming the authority of serious discussion and appropriate justice. Sin and heroism have the common characteristic that they lack the label of the conventional approval. But whilst sin is most common, heroism is creative and extraordinary. Can we escape in any way the extended arms of the universal divine love and its reconciling kiss?

The idea of the religious CONVERSION is of course very closely connected with that of repentance. Though the notion of Conversion means possibly the psychological motion to, and from, both sides, though it is able to signify the intellectual Conversion from the sentimental life, as well as the sentimental Conversion from the intellectual habits, we generally understand as Conversion the transition of the intellectual predilection of the individual mental attitude to the sentimental component. The religious historic Conversion means the mono- and centro-symbolic theistic re-direction, at a given time, of our evasive magnetic psychic possibilities. It has the significance that our personal gift has been induced, after previous intellectual extra-solar inclinations and habits, to give up this behaviour digressing from the historic creed and to allow the personal life-force to stoop again the sentimental balance of our double nature, that psychic component which was for such a long time—God knows for what reasons—found too light in the wrestling comparison with intellectuality. Conversion pre-supposes a former sentimental state of the soul, from which the individual development led once away for a time, and to which it now returns, as to an old dear home, in alternating revolution. Historic theism then means prevalent sentimentality and Conversion must, therefore, have the meaning of sentimental re-embracement of the centro-symbolic conceptions which had been left long ago in favor of the intellectual, peripheric, universal digressions. The digressive arch arrived to the time of development, when it is concentrated in a new whirlpool of concave energy.

The sentimental Conversion in the sense of the historic religion means the immediate improvement of the subjective happiness, of exact ideal re-fixation of the individual character and often the augmentation of the personal energy. A certain sentimental theistic re-concentration will probably, up to a certain degree, happen in most human individual lives, after strong and tiring intellectual expansions. But all these new theistic whirlpools will be very different from the former ones. We have an ascending extra-verted spiral. The new mono-symbolic conceptions will be larger and more perfect. The complete historic Conversion is thus biologically impossible because the intellectual digressions have increased the measures and the circumference of the theistic mono-symbolic concentration and of the necessities and ideas of the individual. After all it will be as little possible to fit at any future time the individual or social soul into the former exact historic notions as it could happen that any grown-up man could, in a sentimental fit of his old age, pull on the suit of the sweetly remembered time, when he was a small boy.

We can admit, and it happens daily without the exterior fact of boasting and public emphasis that there is the opposite conversion from sentimental to intellectual life, that the prevalent, sentimental magnetic theo- monosymbolicol connection of the individual consciousness moves to the background and that instead the intellectual digressions toward the extra-solar digressions begin to prevail. The expression apostasis is the nearest exterior manifestation of this psychic process. It is so easy and natural to develop finally from the sentimenntal infantile into this intellectual adult stage of experience and researches for truth. Does not this development seem as inevitable and adequate for our natural psychic growth as the perfect reconnection with old abandoned, traditional conceptions is absolutely impossible for the intellectually and experimentally further developed? Any intellectual development, which ever happened in our life, and soul, has enlarged the future of the sentimental heart. It is the most unnatural and unjust idea to deny or to abolish any further development of our life on behalf of historic philosophical systems or ecclesiastic economical constitutions.

Expiation, atonement and restitution are the application of the idea of penitance to the real objective life. There we have in the rough sense of the social law, some conception of the compensatory possible justice between idealism and realism. The scientific real technical legislator and the court would laugh, if we would suggest that somebody, who was bereft of his goods, could be possibly satisfied, having only the advantage of ideal satisfaction and of greater ideal prospects because of the diverting nature of the material possession. Offering the other cheek after being beaten on the one, applies to this conception. Expiation has the meaning to return, be it in the realm of honor, of money, of pain, of life or health.

Expiation means the natural automatical justice in the sense of the requital in the real world, but even here it is perhaps superficial and perhaps short-sighted to exact the re-integration in every case, not mentioning the technical errors and dangers of abuse. Killing other people for having killed is only understandable from the the standpoint of primitive revengeful instincts and lack of psychological refinement, But there is not the question of public education by the good example nor the atmosphere of the pardon of the religious hero. The capital punishment may be excusable in some way from the standpoint of the general security, but horrible from the point of view of the psychological education and of the noble insinuations necessary for people. The higher instance may not be entitled to do without sufficient affective reason, what the individual did perhaps out of the most urgent affectively despairing necessity and the most instigating individual psychodynamic conditions of his momentary, psychological, compensatory fate. Crime pre-supposes perhaps always an unusual affective condition. The mysterious conditions of the subjective criminal psychology are aweful and lamentable, but the artificial intellectual "crime" of social revenge lacks any taste of natural affective justification.

TEMPTATION means an ambivalent transitional state of our psychic force between intellectuality and sentimentality. Temptation is just that moment of magnetic indecision, where the soul hesitated to keep the strong connection with the given central historic order and where it just starts to digress toward the outside subjective interpretation of the universe. We easily observe, how much the idea of the central God is always connected with the sentimental conception and with the individual activity.

Temptation means the invitation to any real objective experience at the expense of the harmonious centro-theistic quietness and sureness. It means the enticing seduction of the new enlarging prospect of our life which seemed monotonous and worn out, at that moment, within the old formulation of the accustomed central mono-symbolism. Life and human nature exact extra-solar developments from the old intellectual fixation. The outside progression means the continually necessary and inevitable revival of the interest for the theistic idea itself.

Is not *sin,* this scandalous stumbling block, an indirect resurrection of the theistic conscience! Though it is the peripheric deviation from the central natural individual mono-symbolism, it produces instantly the opposite force of love and central approach,another homesickness for God. We observed in the same manner that the strong concentric motion of the believer toward the central theistic mono-symbolism, in prayers and mysticism, produce in their nature the same reaction of further peripheric removal by intellectual digression. There is no help against our central pride.. It is and will be always "punished" by contrary reactions, just as we have the reverse reaction in the opposite function. All our psychic functions are elastic fluctuations. Trembling water are our sentiments and swinging protoplasm is our life. We may use all psychological tricks and all refined arts in order to realize our central theistic hopes, and in the hope to be the sweetest darlings of the eternal God. Nature throws us again and again out of our intruding conceited enterprise. The man practising the extreme idealistic enthusiasm is full of his concentrating divine strength. He does not distinguish very sharply the extensive purport of any small real commandment of the life, because his blinded psycho-pupil is still very narrow and will be enlarged and more adaptable to the real necessity of his practical life only later on. In his idealistic concentrated strain he cannot see at first the real detailed display of the world, and so, during his new real adaptation which he reaches again afterwards in the school of hard-knocks of life, he fails against real virtue, justice and charity.

Personal unhappiness, lack of individual comfort and even real self-destruction through heroism is no definite argument against it; on the contrary, this hints to its lasting, supra-categoric contents, other laws than intellectual logic being in action. The religious genius himself was the heroic rebel against the legal order of his time. He was in that sense rightly punished, and exactly in that outstanding digression from his antiquated narrow cultural concentration and in the connected suffering and punishment consists essentially the imperishable glory of the Christian hero. He promoted by the fact of his courageous and punished opposition against the law of his time to the highest degree of dignity and reverence which ever a man reached. In scorning the legal reality, in as far as it seemed to him wrong, he became the most fundamental authority of the laws of the later ages. There is no doubt that just this troubling intellectual digression from the fixed centro-magnetic order of his time with all the following bloodshed, tears, tears , murders and wars meant the new spring of humanity, the enlargement of all human conceptions and the further universal energetic progress of our European races. But this wheel of development cannot even stop now. Who could expect it? As He moved on the finger of his time, so it must and ever will be moved by the help of the intellectual digression in work, in science and even in heroic "sin". The stewart of the old Christian magnetic theistic concentration, the church which developed its economical system out of the solstitial role of the hero, will not be able to retain this necessary universal progress. As the first religious genius, so new heroes will be coming out from work, science and affective magnetic contradiction, branching out from the historic frame of the old legislation and settled order. The enormous hatred against intellectualizing progress means the aversion against the dissolution of our historic affective emphasis and against our progressive historic self-destruction. For just in this the social body escapes the narrow historic order and empties into the outside universe forming new organized future concentrations. Sincerity to one's own conviction means indeed the outburst of the individual force from the worn-out and faulty frame of the legal traditional reality. There is no danger for the force falling out from the old historic organization; nothing of the universal energy can be lost at all taking even the way of the universal independent outside digression. You may miss narrow human utility, but you never will escape the furtherance of the universal greatness and love and growth.

HATRED itself is a very interesting notion. Whilst love means the sentimental benevolence, hatred signifies the intellectual criticism inspired by the suggestive aversion against any person or system or idea. The blind hatred puts the sign of negation always in advance; it is its first and last fundamental key-note in advance in any relation, judgment and fact regarding the enemy, and the following or accompanying logical justifications are only the more or less successful, often very threadbare, covers of the natural shame and lack of aestheticism which is always connected with every intellectual digression and contradiction. Thus we see that hatred produces all sorts of long argumentations, that it invents every kind of intellectual fictive arguments against the disliked person or idea or system; but the fundamental and deciding moment for hatred is its *magnetic antagonism and its preconceived sentimental aversion*. It is the proof of shameless hatred and of the lack of tactful aestheticism and skilful adaptability to the moment, which happens also sometimes, that the digressing individual does not search even for skilful intellectual argumentation against the enemy; and it is indeed very tasteless, but significant, if people contradict continually without being able to justify their digressive negativistic attitude. The continual persistent negation without the possibility or the will of the intellectual wrapping (camouflage) of the digressing opinions, is the clearest and unmistakable proof of contradicting hatred, of the principal magnetic aversion. The persistent contradictors without any logical intellectual gift - we may call it here also politeness or hypocrisy - are felt as the most disagreeable and the most tactless people. Digressions without reasoning possibility or readiness are ridiculous and helpless or so radically distant that there cannot be a common basis of discussion. They manifest the whole lack of cleverness in the contradicting individual or are a proof of unusual pride. Generally, contradicting people avail themselves of their reasoning power and pretend or believe to have logical reasons for digressing opinions, but indeed, the digressive contradictors without giving any reasons, awkward and disagreeable as this behaviour may be, are the more sincere, however, more embittered, though perhaps less clever enemies, because all hatred and all aversions have their roots in the subconscious opposite magnetism and in the affective opposition which has no reasons. Intellectuality in the logical development is only the garment of our magnetic digressions. Disregard is always in reality opposite extra-individual and perhaps even extra-solar magnetic antagonism, whether it avails itself, in the more aesthetic real manner, of reasoning arguments or prefers not to give any intellectual justifications and clues, which means the more sincere, but rougher and less aesthetic method. Taste is the deeper expression of the individual psychic condition. It is the bearer of the intellectual opinion.

Hatred means that state of affective relations between two persons or two orders of conceptions, where one is not willing to be subjected to the attractive power of the other, where one will not allow his life-force to overflow with unchecked sentimental benevolence into the personal magnetic centralization of the other individual life-force, but where one, one the contrary, strives rather to attract the sentimetal service of the other. Hatred is so, at the bottom, the most serious quarrel of competence between two individuals, where nobody succeeds definitely in being the undiscussed ruling master and where nobody is willing to be sentimental servant. Sentimental behaviour means, therefore, service, and intellectual relations are independent actions of self-government. Sentimental devotion pre-supposes that we have given up the intellectual resistance of our individual magnetism and that we acquiesce with the attractive superiority of the magnetic strength of our neighbor. Intellectual behaviour, on the contrary, has the meaning of magnetic independence, of the persistent will not to be subjugated to any affective attraction of anybody else. It claims tenaciously to represent and accomplish, itself, the higher power of magnetic concentration. Intellectualism is the means to escape under the cover of aesthetic pretexts from the central attraction of any other individual or magnetic idea or system. Intellectuality is the wing which carries away from the influence of disliked attractive forces, which we prefer to leave without the appearance of being disobliging, in any exterior pretense. If we succeed in doing so, then we have avoided the psychic connection of our neighbor who can be so disagreeable and dangerous by his following hatred. Then we may build up, in our regained magnetic freedom and personal isolation, our own individual happiness, disposing of our personal magnetic life-force as we wish to do ourselves, outside of the old fatal diversion of the meeting disliked personality which by haphazard came across our magnetic destiny.

Our sentimental relationship to somebody means, therefore, his overwhelming attractive influence on our life-force. It proves that he is able to subjugate our psychic personal activity and to make us his servants, whilst the intellectual relationship has the meaning that the individuals are independent of each other and that both, or at least one has the perfect disposition of his personal strength and gift. So we see the great danger of the intercourse between many individuals of different character and talents. Even love can appear, under this viewpoint, as a dangerous swallowing monster. We can estimate the liability of the suggestible individual to fall easily under the yoke of the ruling intellectual mind. We see clearly how much intellectuality is prone - in other connections we read out the contrary - to abuse its personal independence in order to rule and never to serve. Servants are forcedly mostly the suggestible idealists. The practically domineering persons, on the contrary, are the skilful realists knowing to escape or keep away from the affective attraction of other people by the help of their distancing, intellectual shrewd thought. The realist escapes by the theatrical use of the logical reality from the active wilfulness and even the consequences of the hatred of the competitive neighbor, whilst the suggestible idealist becomes the victim of the smallest attractive forces of the realist. The idealistic magnetism, great as it may be, is avoided by the non-suggestible realist and finishes in being entirely, in the practical functions of the life, at the sentimental and real mercy of the domineering realist.

RECONCILIATION is the change of the intellectually declining attitude toward our neighbor into sentimental sympathy for him. It is the removal and burial of misunderstandings brought about in former time by wilful, perhaps cruel effort, by ignorant carelessness, by necessary self-protection or by different temperamental tastes. There can have been bad terms between two persons for a long time, we know it. So much so that they seem and are practically dead for each other after the kindest love. They withdraw from each other all sentimental communication and slowly fade away from the conscious memory. They could not stand each other in natural friendliness, and often they become not indifferent to one another, but exercise at all time the most rigorous condemning intellectual criticism in their mutual regard. The mutual affective exclusion of the two enemies searches to fix their distant localization by the help of the protecting intellectual argumentation. The reconciliation is the recovery from this antagonistic digressive effort. Reconciliation has given up the merely intellectual oppositional relations to somebody. The strain of hating withdrawal has subsided and given place exactly to the contrary benevolent sentimental tendency of the approaching energy of both individual psychic forces. Reconciliation means, therefore, the conversion of the intellectually mummed aversion into clear sentimental love. The checking misunderstandings, the mutual bad will, the different tastes in both individuals have now been dropped and intentionally discarded. The magnetic gift from both parts has, therefore, received again the freedom and the natural facility of easy friendly meeting in giving and receiving, of affective parallelism toward high, common theistic goals, of the most agreeable and fertilizing mutual affective urges and helps. The individual who was felt for a long time as the obstacle of the restricted affective discharge of our heart, became, on the contrary, by the reconciliation the quickening ally and instigator of our psychological new experience. He who was the enemy because of his retaining influence on our affective intercourse, in causing sentimental stagnations, has become the friend because of his addition and augmentation to our personal affective facility and efficiency.

We see, for this reason, that it is not easy at all to have a sincere reconciliation. A previous state of affective good intercourse is of course, in itself, a good pre-supposition and a conditio sine qua non for the future sentimetal reconnection. But the lasting oppositional intellectual work during the period of enmity has raised quite a system of organised antagonism, ramificated and strong like the boughs of a tree; it will be hard to unroot entirely and lastingly this historic inimical fixation. Where we had once the change of the sentimental collaboration into the intellectual opposition, there must have been serious reasons of psychological fermentation, and it will not be easy to overcome these organized causes without important helps from the outside circumstances. It is difficult to change vinaigre once more into sugre. Even if there is to be expected in psychology a new period of sweetness, as a rule the fermented sugar of former times is used and the life is craving for new experimental elements without the stale taste of former disappointment. The reconciliation is there most promising, where more accidental exterior circumstances forced the separation on essentially good friends led astray by their surroundings. The real world is indeed also very often the reason of the intellectual-sentimental changes, digressions and conversions, but the deciding point must and will always be simularity or incompatibility of the psychological individual character.

LOVE must mean, therefore, the great facility of rich sentimental intercourse between two or more individuals. The love is so greater, the more sentimental urges can happen between two individuals, and it is the smaller, the less affective instigation can be imparted to the connected individual, in mutual contact. Love is the essentially strong, sentimental inclination toward sombody, the ability to dwell for a long time in security and peace in the heart of an other person, to know and feel vividly and yet quite naturally this mysterious union. Love means the strong attentive concentration of our psychic feeling energy preferably upon one individual at the expense of the generality. It has the significance of the most concentrated sentimental connection with our neighbor to the compensatory exclusion of every intellectual criticism. So we have no antagonistic balance and no struggle in love, between the two psychological components, feelings and intellect, but there is the undiscussed, and clear domineering rule of the sentimental benevolent association of the human souls. Persistent love on earth without going to common highest goals, is therefore quite impossible. The sensorial world ties and retains often loving connections, but, as a rule, this sensorial relationship must change soon and then the connected psychological sympathies and affective parallel wills must dry up as well. The intellectual part of our visible world, our objective parting necessity creates the inevitable need to claim our personal share of the common whole of the real representation of the world. If we will not lose all, we are obliged to respect the exactions of the intellectual dividing necessities of our life.

So love can be the immediate way to lose our real share, to drop the intellectual part of the sentimental individual. Love is that compensatory state of our psychological double nature toward our neighbor, which surrenders our total life-force to the sentimental ideal relations of absolute closest confidence toward anybody else, excluding from him all distancing doubt and all separating objection. True love must be indeed essentially the same psychic condition, as we have it in *hypnosis*. It is the perfect compensatory magnetic absorption of our life-force by the beloved individual symbol who has succeeded in excluding all individual checking obstacles from our psychology in respect to our intercourse with him. Love is, therefore, the most subjective sentimental union with some other individual, based on the perfect imaginative personal principle of benevolent affective idealism. It is far from the rounded objective truth, because it neglects the comparisons of the real and detailed differenciation. Love is, therefore, the expression of absolute idealism, neglecting the real earth and the graduation of the objective facts, giving in the most liberal way and in the most optimistic benevolence to one frail individual the fulfilment of all eternal perfection, beauty and loveliness.

We realize therefore how tragic the issue of all love must be, in many ways. The real advance of any loving union tears both lovers back to the hard and critical real life, and it turns out so quickly that just this real life which plays such a great role and, in the complicated social union of lovers begins to have soon the double chance of troubles and importance, ruthlessly destroys the charming idealistic supra-categoric love by the dividing intellectual necessity of the subsequent, petty, daily, material life. Love was the most exclusive idealistic compensation born of the absolute, one-sided sentimental ground of our soul, growing strong by the continual restriction and omission of the real categories of time, space and causality, but weakening compensatorily soon and thoroughly, as soon as the needs or the exterior visible relations or the detailed multiciplicity of the objective connections of our life induce the charming, imaginative, idealistic flower of the love to surrender its vital affective sap of life-force, partly or in time entirely, to the urgent real intellectual exactions of work. Strong love has, therefore, generally to be considered chiefly as the transitional biological help of sexual and family life. Love has for these stages and relations the meaning of the necessary imagination of attractive magnetic intimacy. It serves as the indispensable help for the natural performance of the most important duties of our human existence and propagation, but it easily dwindles and retires having done this helping service, *in flowing from its stationary punctual attentive concentration into the large field of the open, working, intellectual detailed effusion.* In this connection we understand easily that the stable home-life of women favors their persistent love, whilst the toiling outside business occupation leads to more thorough intellectual distractive opportunities. In the clear light of these facts all sentimental concentration will be soon dissolved, the loving vital amount being transformed, forcedly and biologically, into intellectual work.

The official conveyance of the appellation of a SAINT may express that the concerned individual has succeeded in elaborating, and reached the highest score of perfect life. Sanctity is the expression of the combination of the real and sentimental perfection in that sense that the saint is supposed to have had the clearest, unchanging direction, the most energetic sway toward God and at the same time the most minute self-control in observing the logical intellectual performances of the real steps of the real commandments. The saint is supposed to have the most perfect harmony between his theistic terminal goal and his real moral actions. His rhythm toward God is assumed as energetic enough as to reach quickly and surely the affective bull's-eye of the highest human affective standards, and the real logical duties as well are done best by the saint. The word Holy, perhaps clearer in the German corresponding Heilig, signifies a state of being healed, wholeness or integrity.

But we remark that this desirable harmony is difficult to obtain because it includes the probability of the mutual diminution of the human psychological components functioning as competitors and leading so either to one-sidedness or, in careful equal distribution, to insignificant mediocrity. He who has the best terminal ideal communication, loses likely the careful real consideration of the detailed commandments, and, on the other hand, he who is fond of the most accurate sharpness of clinging to the real small logical steps of the progressions toward the divine goals, is liable to lose the far idealistic outlook and the energetic terminal sway of the absolute idealist. Perfection in one of these two attitudes excludes practically almost always perfection in the other. Strong idealism causes weakness or mediocrity in the detail of the real performance, and the detailed accurate achievement does not permit the sure and sharp, unchanging ideal direction nor the energetic progression toward the theistic goal.

The religious genius had the strong ideal terminal direction without any essential oscillation of doubt, distraction and weakness of his ideal finger and though even he compensatorily neglected the the extreme real consideration, his picture is faithful to the real virtuous accuracy, in as far as we have it. Whilst he put the whole emphasis of his sentimental personality on the terminal progression and the right direction of the sentiments, the minute care about the real refined and lasting elaboration and adaptation of his teaching to the practical life seems to him less substantial. Did his ideal distance from the humanity really become the help and the skilful furthering solution of the earthly living problem of mankind or was and remained he rather in opposition to the world, which is to say, had he the conviction of the incompatibility of the real detailed work and the terminal ideal intentions?

The sanctity of his followers means obviously the utmost simularity to his own pious behaviour. Did they not live with the head above the clouds of the intellectual reality, and was it not their sentimental heart which inspired and moved all their actions? Did they not escape as much as possible from the real contact with the intellectual world, excluding the real diversions from their life? Was not their highest goal to move as much as possible from the real contact and from the practical earthly solution of the difficult problem of the sensorial world? Did they not try to reduce the manifold visible duties and tasks of the life by monastic retirement, by exclusive idealistic meditation and by passive suffering? The type of the religious saint seems not to be the intellectual, toiling and working, detailed performer or scientist, but rather the idealistic eagle full of theistic enthusiasm, hovering sentimentally over the obstacles of the real world.

How these countless mediaeval saints look charmingly down from their artistic platforms on the walls of the old churches and of the precious musea and collections! They overflow mith the most energetic historic mono-symbolic enthusiasm. They carry us away by their idealistic sway, but they seem to be averted from the real detailed life as well as the old Indian gods are by their elevated detachment. They all together are the sentimental expression of our life. They pull and urge to the sublime theistic goal and leave far behind their divine sunny atmosphere the mist of our real intellectual troubles and difficulties. Their characteristic halo expresses their mono-symbolic artistically clarified goal. Are they not far from the universal extra-solar progression in intellectuality, science and work, being themselves the perfect human crystallization of the most harmonious historic religious mono-symbolism?

The religious saint looks back to the genial personality of the first hero. He finds in him the solstitial source, from which he derives the fulness of his magnetic sentimental energy. Is not the religious saint the affective divine type neglecting the practical real life, perishing therefore really owing to his one-sided sentimental love for the universal Deity? How could he be the expression of the real balance between reality and idealism, since he intends to perform the utmost possible loving connection with God, since his highest desire is the most direct love for the ideal Divinity, and how could he grasp the last detail of the presented reality, since even his divine master despised the sensorial world, put himself in opposition to it and resolved its necessary problem by the passive obstruction of suffering and of permitting being the outcast from its legal frame?

The notion of sanctity is so the realization of the same difficult problem as the genial and really perfect, idealized mono-personality of the religious hero. It means also the same rounded claim of the concentrated human perfection, the normally impossible theoretic compression of the opposed moments of the human psychology, excluding each other and being nevertheless all full and perfect in the individual representation. The notion of sanctity exceeds the average possibilities of the human nature. It is rather more understandable that the greatest "saint" is, in another sense, usually the greatest "sinner" and the greatest sinner as well the greatest saint. There appears no natural means against this psychological truth and necessity. All human psychic life has its oppositional inevitable antagonisms from inside and from outside. Strong intellectual, real, formal faithfulness impaires likely the energetic, progressive ideal outlook. The unflinched and perfect direction and concentration toward the highest goal and the thorough idealistic detachment from life may impair the detailed care of rightousness in the practical life and blur it according to the law of psychological compensation which cannot use any vital force simultaneously for two opposite purposes and which is, therefore, checked to use any energy again which has been already worked out in the other function, be it in sentiments or thought.

Was not the first religious genius, however, quite a different kind of saint distinguished from all his followers? Whilst these altogether received their intellectual justification from the light going out from his strong and highest genial solstitial position, being therefore sentimental themselves, he in his turn was the most distant intellectual exponent of his historic theistic age and created exactly in his eminently intellectual behaviour the important future leadership in the transformed following centuries of the cultural European humanity. His sanctity included in the sense of his historic time the notion of digressing intellectuality, of outbursting heroic "sin", in the sense of, and from, the standpoint of the Jewish and Roman settled conception. His overwhelming cultural importance has therefore just in this fact its foundation. His personal creative courage and the willing sacrifice of his personal welfare to the general supra-individual human interests elevated him so extraordinarily far above his fellowmen.

The concentric mono-symbolic halo is for this reason not the exhausting convenient expression of the sanctity of Christ. He was not included in the obedient pious mono-symbolic definiteness of the time and culture, in which he was born, but he transgressed the boundaries of this frame by his *"extra-legal self-emancipation"*. We see indeed the religious hero often represented with golden rays digressing in the centrifugal direction from his head. His sanctity consisted chiefly, it is true, in gathering the real intellectual conversion of his time in the channel of his gracious genial personality. But he represented at the same time the distinct intellectual digression from his concentric historic legal background and went out from the rising struggle as victorious. Christ's sanctity had, therefore, both moments the most intellectual digression in his teachings and sufferings, but also the most energetic concentrative approach toward the monotheistic Divinity. He was as well follower as builder of the law. He was, in a certain sense, at his time, the most pronounced idealist and realist, the boldest investigating intellectualist and the most pious magnetic idealist similtaneously. He found new geometrical measures and laws of the heavens and was a flickering torch going to divine worship. The sign of his sanctity was, therefore, not sufficiently expressed in the harmonious mono-symbolic sentimental halo around his sainted head, because he did not ony exceed the magnetic theistic draft given in the old historic crystallization of the theological idea, but he ran from the most distant intellectual digression of the atmosphere of his time toward our new age, as the true, genial, divine turning-point.

His affective notion went toward the centre of his new centro-theistic goal. The true symbol of his sanctity is, therefore, the combination of the halo expressing his mono-symbolic magnetic obedient sentimentality, with the digressing centrifugal rays of shining stars or suns, as the sign of his outstanding universal, intellectual government. Both these qualities and symbols are best comprehended in his crown of thorns, exhibiting at the same time his circular sentimental and his digressing intellectual combination of sanctity.

So if the statues of the mediaeval representation of the saints reveal to our looks the charming, but passive sentimental incarnation of sanctity, and if they open many a glance at psychological sweet legends and edifying sentimental fairy-tales, the person of the heroic first genius, in his solstitial double importance, had at his historic time and in the given sense, the full weight of intellectual real vitality.

And yet! is not the circle of the *halo* to be conceived as the expression of the farthest reaching ever returning, universal reactions? Even if the transitional links of the progressive chain are missing, all formations and units are achieved again and again in the circular wreath. How impressive the old statuesque saints look, surrounded by all the fluttering shining coats and graciously hanging down sleeves and folded garments, in all shades of gold and silver, glancing reservedly and yet sophisticatedly from a central idea of charming sweetness! Does their broad and quiet peace, from their shining halo, suggest the idea that all life and experience, all what we call good and bad is only one great circle, that all extremes touch and move, that we have a collective fate, that all contradictions are only distances and shortcoming ignorance, that we always have to plod through all kinds of partial truth and knowledge? Are all philosophical and religious opinions such different localizations in the psychological and temperamental halo of mankind, holding their hands like little angels hovering in an eternal dance around the love and glory of the eternal God, all together expressing the last and complete human truth, each bringing it out in another form, with other words and other reservations?

Is that the deepest meaning of our circular shining halo, that we have to become refined to the most sophisticated love of life, humanity and universe, in a degree that we love all distant existing units and values for their own sake and in the order of their partial validity, hating only one thing really and thoroughly hatred? Is this the circular universal love expressed in our halos that gives to us that new great central position in regard to all created and psychic values, which flows from a central point of benignant will and graceful reconciliation to all contradicting persons and opinions and realities circling around the head of the clever and experienced thinking interpreter in an uninterrupted circling process with kaleidoscopic charm, novelty and unity, bound together in the meekness and broadmindedness of superior wisdom? What an endless enrapturing procession of relative values moves around the sainted head! Like shining planets encircling the sun, real and psychic forces and forms proceed one after the other.. Are they not all good, if they are taken from the angle of their respective validity, of their right localization and restriction? And are they not all bad, if they move out of their proper revolutionary order and succession and will interfere, where they have no right or capacity? All quarrel is a kind of temperamental disorder, a falling out from the eternal harmony of easy and orderly universal progress. The smile of the saint is, as it were, divine "frivolousness" looking over all disorder and moody restrictions, scorning all party passion, despising hatred and snobbish restrictions, doing away with pride, discouragement, short-sightedness of any kind and yet infusing in anything everywhere the fragrance of a mature divine flower.

To discuss the idea of SUCCESS in connection with pure ideal religion gives, therefore, rather the most oppressive prospect. The real success of the visible world and the religious idealism seems to be essentially incompatible. Fulfilling the letter of the exterior legal commandments or at least avoiding any provable offences against the law, has of course not yet the meaning of the perfect religious attitude. Strong materialistic tendencies and simultaneous pretense of religious idealism are indeed impossible because of the unfeasability of sufficient culture of these two distant affective ranges at the same time and within the same individual. Where is your interest, there is your heart. Religion in its uplifting imaginative language intends decidedly much more to give idealistic direction and divine energetic speed than to put stress on the logical steps of the single written commandments. It is the genial idealistic spirit which counts in it most or, roughly speaking, in every religious system the deciding values of the heart and conscience are in the outside spiritual universe, unwritten and not so much written laws. The conformity of our whole life with the main affective direction of our chosen religious system decides of the value of our behaviour in the light of its judgment. The affective idealism of course is most averse to the intellectual and material assumptions, and nothing is, therefore, more opposed to the deep religious sentiments than the real, intellectual and successful profit from the religious tenets. The idea and the intention of the religious philosophy is to direct the magnetic finger of the human heart and desire toward eternal highest goals and it is, therefore, highly against the taste and meaning of the religious affective intention, if people use it in order to join their material and real human needs and wishes. The idealistic, sentimental feature is the significant concentrative approaching characteristic of the post-solstitial religion. As soon as near intellectual interests and and material purposes become seriously connected with it or gain even the upper hand, then the essential idealistic life of the religious tendencies is likely killed and the historic religious conception of the life practically dead, owing to the law of compensation. Is there no excellent combination of both elements without bungling mediocrity or one crushing the other thoroughly!

How sad is the earthly fate of the idealist in the world! He collides everywhere with the material exactions of the visible life and is offended by them everywhere in the practically most challenging manner. How much feels the idealistic individual insulted, if in questions of marriage and love material respects claim to collaborate! How much does he resist, if material successes and possessions claim authority and affective consequences. How hard does he feel the necessity of earning and of acquiring in the real world! How much is he humiliated by the sexual- anatomic disposition of our human nature! How much is he excited by every smallest incorrection of the surface of the real life and by the smallest intellectual lie!

To what a degree does the sensitive idealist take offence at all real exactions of the hodiernal life! They are for him the disturbances, on the way to higher goals which he wishes to prosecute most swiftly, without slakening nuisance. From whence will he take the necessary life-force for the terminal purposes if not exactly from that part of the real working realm which compensatorily is given up and perishes by the withdrawal of the vital energy? Therefore the painful continual disappointment of the idealist in the reality of this world. He feels offended always exactly there in the most surprising way, where the inverse material conception of the world and the natural real exaction insert themselves and cut off his way, as obstacles. Therefore the hatred, the embarrassment, the aversion against all material emphasis of all affective life and his embittered struggles against these ocnceptions. If the individual had enough vital affective talents, he could easily fill up the whole realm from the deepest materialism up to the highest idealism, without the action of self-defence by feeling hurt by contradiction, avoiding mutual exclusion of the two distant views. The contradictions and exclusions come from the circumstance that the individual psychic force cannot reach easily more than one local affective fixation of its attitude at a time. It is, therefore, not allowed to be in the restricted case of our possibilities, either too idealistic or too one-sided in the realistic direction, but we ought to turn continually in regular ideal-realistic expansion on the middle attitude of modest enjoyment of the intellectual fruits of the life.

The more the affective fingerboard is prolonged in the ascending direction, the more arises the danger of the most pronounced real *sensitiveness* and even of the most painful estranging opposition between idealism and realism. We already often pointed out that the essential opposition between idealism and realism is only pretended, that they in reality are so little different from one another as the white foam on the waves from the clear transparent water. Both are water, but both are in a different state of physical aggregation. We have just the same condition between body and spirit, material and mind, intellect and imagination. The seeming antagonisms are given in the simultaneous consciousness of the human nature, they are only in the boundless distances of our experience, through whose development aeons have run, so much so that we are no more able to recognize easily their original unity, owing to our restricted individual life-force. It results from this that the extraordinary oppositional struggles, strong oscillations and disturbances of harmony may be avoided, if one excludes the tendency of exaggerated extremes, if our human wishes are not fixed too closely compensatorily in one extreme idealistic or realistic attitude and if therefore the opposite, as well human natural, exaction shall not be lost, but still be reachable. The good human tendencies are directed to the middle; around the circle of the affective enjoyment we have the best localization for the modest human life. We cannot have too much reality because of its material dullness and the loss of progressive urges, because of its affective dryness and estrangement from the psychic sentiments. But we cannot stand as little too much idealism, because it makes us useless for the thorough performance and objective observation of the real life; it spoils the individual, causes material distress, disgraces the personal historic honour by unworthy dependence on the neighbor and misinterprets the present life.

The pronounced sharp opposition of the real and ideal world is the expression of the human insufficiency, but it is not the creative all-loving universal idea comprising everything because of its very existence and respecting, understanding and explaining all because it conceived it first and is convinced to have created it well according to its good absolute intention. The increased opposition between idealism and realism means for us the most embarrassing principle in life and world, impeding the good and easy solution of our human total tasks and tending to seduce us to one-sidednesses which are incompatible with our necessary and human good functions. We are enticed by the unreal and unnatural human conceptions into temptations and dangers of idealistic boasting beyond our human possibe dispositions, having the accompanying and subsequent troubles of arrhythmic stumbling and sin, being checked in this way exactly from the divine enjoyment, not to mention the compensatory total loss of the real good, or the total exclusion of idealism, if if we have chosen the realistic extreme in the anti-idealistic sense. The construction of any unconnectable opposition between idealism and realism is the most disastrous and unhappy pedagogic principle of division, creating, it is true, many a clear glimpse into the depth of our nature, but also tearing up old scarred wounds of the human constructive,existing particular history, by repeated analyzing separation.

Though the wonderful figure of the religious genius represented to us as the unsurpassable example of our human life, it means the enrapturing seduction over the prudent boundaries of our natural, harmoniously limited gifts, the one-sided and powerful emphasis of that most noble part of our nature which we call idealism and to which we tend already in advance automatically like the flame of a candle to its centrifugal movement. But we know and experience that by this our vital reality is compensatorily disturbed and exhausted. The practical conduct of our life becomes for this reason insufficient and difficult, passive and unsuccessful. The great *idealistic sensitiveness* comes from the circumstance that the idealist wishes to enjoy the most one-sided human idealistic gift at the expense of all reality, and that he, for this reason, feels every working subtraction of the real life as exceedingly undesirable and painful, as the brutal tearing of the most precious personal possession of the heart which he intends to preserve and keep so carefully and exclusively for idealistic purposes and pleasures.

In success we understand ordinarily the material real progress of our life; but we have as well to distinguish the *ideal-moral suc-*

cess. The ideal success, pro-secured by the religious hero in the highest and clearest manner, is of course unable to be taken away from outside, *at least not in a direct way*. But exactly here the principle of compensation may be fatal, the idea of sentimental success destroying our real material advancement, and here it is, from where the water of destruction drips backwards again; here applies the saying not to mount too high in order not to fall too deep. The real necessary restriction and limitation of our nature throws us easily back to desperation, errors and low reactions. Only the most richly gifted is allowed to climb the high ladder of extreme ideaism without having to expect to face the bitter problem of compensatory, not only real, but also ideal destruction.

The moral sucess is the progress of honour, respect and recognition within the legal real society. But here instantly again the tricky and sore crack through all creation is visible. Who is most honored, respected and recognized in this world? Is it indeed the best, honest, sincere and fearless idealist? Are the leading roles wheresoever occupied by the most irreproachable characters? He who conveys to every smallest affair of his life the value of highest sentiments, which the perfect idealist undoubtedly does, will check even the logical incorrection and real lie of the smallest real progression in the world, in as far as he is not diverted by his far idealistic outlook, and he will thus be more liable than anybody else to stumble and to be defeated in the very beginning stages of his run toward real success, by relative antagonism.

Strong *material success* and pronounced idealism are scarcely compatible values. Material progressive opportunism and idealistic, consistent sincerity are far from being congruent psychological conditions. Their direction and goals are different, often their laws contradict even each other. The principle to reach at any rate, in every individual, at any time and in every case material or even "moral" success in life, is wrong from the idealistic standpoint. Just here the idealistic figure of Christ appears in its moving greatness, purity and truth. The simularity or difference as to Christ's behaviour in the question of success must be considered as the fruit in which the good and bad Christian might be recognized. Though it is wrong to say that the aim sanctifies the means, it is at least as objectionable to neglect the goal because of the opportunistic convenience of the present and momentary intellectual-moral and material means and ways. The decided undiscriminating adherent of the material and immediate moral success forcedly must be considered as the type of the *sentimental idiot* who is ready to reject at any time his ideal natural intentions and convictions because of his real material success. On the other hand the individual thoroughly fond of the persisent, straight, ideal conclusiveness and of the perfect sentimental congruency of his real actions seems to be the true representative of the fatal and most outspoken *real failure*.

An example of the middle compromising state of these two extreme methods is the cunning habit, not to say positively any falsehoods, but to cause wrong appearances through restrictions in speaking and through hypocritical undecided behaviour, to cheat the dangerous curiosity through silence, This seems to be the practical way of action even of the finest political diplomatists. Without clinging to this last share in the realm of the sinuosities of the life we would have to expect nothing better than the sublime ideal religious hero who was simply spat upon and excluded from the world with shame and slander. The real quintessence of the human struggle, the reasonable task of our daily life and politics is, however, practical success, which the idealist of the sincere extreme is not willing and hardly able to expect, within his life-time, and even afterwards only, if his importance is awakened by the strong real organization of his scientific or artistic admirers advertising him. Life has greater values and aims than fame. The deeper we dig and the higher we mount, so much greater the ideal, and after all, even moral and real success will be, but it follows the much more seldom and later.

Exactly in the incompatibility of the real material and contemporary moral credit, and of ideal accurate behaviour in the life, we recognize the danger of the minute imitation of the exemplary ideal figure of the religious genius who bereaves us, in the full adoption of his sentiments, of the real success in the visible world. The world must and will be deceived; this is one of the most fundamental laws of the real succes. But the noble never learns to do so. He has never learned to do it and prefers to perish than to permit himself to be enticed or compelled by the life to advance toward this manner of action. And the clean crystal of his sincere psychology is transparent everywhere and always and exposes him. He is a fool in the sense of the world. The heroic love of truth and sincerity, the straight-forward energetic pulling idealism of the strong, affective sentimental individual may lead inevitably to the lack or bad issue of the real success and to material misfortune. This fact that there is an unfillable gap between real success and absolute consequences of sincerity makes for the assumption that either the exterior world with its sensorial power is deceiving humbug or that our sentimental affective principles are wrong and artificially spoiled by hyper-culture. Go and choose! Or try to cover and hide the old crack of the universal building as well as you are able to.

It would be very short-sighted to reject the value of all idealism because of its slow and extra-categoric or indirectly real success. Be it that idealism generally is very problematic in its success, be it that the idealist has much to suffer, that he likely is flogged, slandered, spat upon, cricified and killed, excluded from the human society like a dumb dog, in his spiritualized appreciation of values, as it happened to the idealistic prototype. But it is sure, nevertheless, that all the greatest, most lasting and only invincible successes in all directions were caused and gained by strong idealists. *The great successes have supra-categoric roots and are therefore accordingly able to last beyond time, space and causality.* The smaller, categorically modified successes share instead the law of their origin in time and space and react in accordance with the ephemeral individual effect of these transitional causes and go of course again away as they had risen, children of the visible world and passing away every day, short waves of the accidental daily life, quickly withering and forgotten laurels.

But from the size of the ordinary frame of our categoric life which is the deciding stage and measure for the average person, the religious genius makes indeed the most disquieting impression. The real living man, not willing to give up life, riches and family, social position and personal honour, forcedly must look frightened at the ideal enrapturing love of the divine hero. He indeed has not brought the peace to the world, as he said it himself, but the sword and the most grievous psychic misgivings of the human history. This penetrating sword divided our whole human nature again into two parts. It split the harmonious unity of our naive natural psychology; it has analyzed backwards its two components. It has caused, if too seriously taken, our material wordly ruin, and made us unhappy in disproportioned idealistic pride giving to us exactions and goals which should not be amenable and reachable to us, owing to our vital psychic insufficiency. The hero has given the clear example of the necessary compensatory misfortune of the human nature, and everybody being really docile and faithful to his thinking philosophy, will share indeed his real fate. Just here we recognize so clearly the moving consistance of sincerity and the inner truth of his religious idealism. The pronounced idealist knows and experiences the impossibility of the possession of both ideal and real success at the same time. He has the choice to take one or the other, but he renounces the reality in favour of the ideal, because he deems the latter as the higher and better value, and he thinks therefore to have acted as the best friend of the universe.

There is no doubt, he has acted as the idealistic hero, for idealism is the token of divine greatness and of the love for the highest value. But not in this special egotistic or altruistic decision, however, lies the task and the law of our human organization. It is not right that we wish and exact above our own constitutional possibilities and harmonious natural goodness, that we disfigure our natural dispositions and necessities owing to higher selfishness. The good manner of acting according to our human root and the present development of our unknown old genesis and history consists, on the contrary, exactly in this fact that we take up the humiliation of the good mediocrity of our natural will, that we do not yield to the onesided pulling charming idealism, but reckon seriously with the punishing compromising nature of our own, not depriving our forces of that given law of working necessity and real performances which give to our human peculiarity, far beyond all examples and all idealistic enthusiasm, the most prospecting and most unmistakable mark of human goodness.

For this reason the hammer and sword ought to be as well our vital symbols as the cross which is considered more as the sign of the passive suffering, which we, however, are not able to escape, very often, owing to the peculiarity of our life, but which we may mostly prevent by the energetic active work. The moral greatness and the possibility of merit of our nature lies exactly in the circumstance, that we resist our inclination to extreme delight and pleasure in the sense of the checking withdrawal of our corporeal intellectual component. We have everywhere, in accordance with our exterior and interior organization, and with the peculiarity of our environment, to take hold of the presented necessary work, in humility and modesty. If we will not correspond to these natural invitations, we have to suffer where we will not work, we shall turn the inner and exterior nature into our enemies, we shall be persecuted and beaten, spat upon and slandered, flogged and crucified, in the natural intention to call us back from the ideal onesided detachment of our life into the circle of our modest real duty and of our intellectual legal, human visible nature. Back to hardening work, to the courageous real enterprise, to the struggle against luxury, pleasure, to the utmost faithfulness toward our natural working organization.

Personal POSSESSION is the necessary consequence of the individuality. It is in closest connection with the real magnetism of the individual. As much as one is able to scatter his affective life-force into the multiple material world, a greater or larger amount of real possession returns and clings to his individuality. In the degree as he is in a position not only to fix the real objects to his magnetic personality, but also to keep them in magnetic connection with his personal affective strength, he will be rich or poor. The strong central inclination of the idealist retreating from the periphery and throwing all forces into the abyss of the divine, imaginative, magnetic heaven, cannot have strong detailed and rich magnetic attachment to the real outside objectivity, although the magnetic schooling may be the finest preparation for the earning activity. According to the law of psychological compensation, most affective energy and interest goes to the immaterial sentimental idealism. The material connection and above all the *lasting union* with material goods pre-supposes therefore the most stable, moderate, magnetic taste, gift and selective inclination of the mind. The deepest secret of riches and poverty in the outside world lies here, in the special personal magnetic predilection of the individual who forges, generally, his economic fate himself by the prevailing affective fixation and work of his character. He cannot have the heaven and the mammon at the same time. If he hurls all his life-force into idealism, he compensatorily loses the detailed real objectivity, and if he clings to the material intellectual earth, then he likely loses instead the eternal idealistic values. By their fruits you will recognize them! How could that man claim to possess the realm of heaven, who crushes by the mighty hand of his individual material, wilful covetousness all surrounding humanity! He spent all his energy in the outside reality and has and keeps fixed all his magnetic power like numberless retaining strings and roots on the outside real objects so that there is no possibility for him to get rid of them by his magnetic life-force, and to join instead the independent and jealous realm of idealism. Here we have the explanation of the word that the rich has more difficulty to enter into the Kingdom of Heaven than a camel to go through the eye of a needle. Idealism can only be reached through the eye of the needle or the barrel of the punctual concentration. The individual shooting energy is lost for the idealism if we keep the light-field wide open and permit, therefore, the psychic energy to be scattered and to meet like a small shot all numberless peripheric surrounding real material objects. We may not forget, in addition, that the natural suggestibility of the idealist being identic to strong sentimental docility makes him lose easily also his natural material goods which he has and which he, however, can acquire without much effort, owing to his magnetic constitution, if he really directs his attention to them. But generally he does not like to direct his concentrated will to these values inferior to him, or even, if he did it by mood, ambition and necessity, he soon will feel disgusted with their less affective attraction and · leave them probably, withdrawing his affective magnetism from them and transferring it to the more attractive idal aims. There is no use, the signature of the typical idealist is indeed essentially *poverty*. He is doomed to be the beggar of the society, the Bohemian without home, the Wandering Jew without country and family, the monk without kith and kin, the slave without exterior rights. The birds of the air have nests, but the Son of Man has nowhere to lay his head. The special nature of the idealist rejects the lasting care about real things and loses them consequently. It is not without deep psychological knowledge that Calderon de la Barca choses only one, in his play: "The Theatre of the World," to be the worthiest heir of the Kingdom of Heaven, the least expected: the beggar.

The religious genius excludes almost entirely the question of possession from his teachings; his personality scarcely is put in connection, by the scriptures, with the question of the *economic* life. It is supposed as the most granted fact that the hero himself did not care about material needs and means. We see in this conception how many of the old teachings are insufficent for the daily questions of the practical world, especially of our time.

The religious hero is most intimately connected, in his psychology, with the *beggar*. There is no doubt that he as a high idealist tasted also the full weight of the scorn and the pride of the materially rich people, that he suffered the same social and economical distress in the contempt and lack of comfort, as the poor. We have, accordingly in idealistically religious countries, even today not only a great number of private and public beggars, in opposition to the intellectualized parts of the world, but also the instinctive reverence for the beggar, people recognizing in him religious ideal features and being thus afraid to scorn or refuse him. They think they could refuse in him the humble incarnation of the divine hero. This feeling, objectionable as the beggar from the merely intellectual angle may be, has a deep psychological foundation. Was not the religious hero that forsaken, disfigured beggar of the world, who came into his own, but was not recognized?

But we know also, on the other side, that the objection against him is true that he would not submit to the laws of this world and of its traditional conceptions. He himself left his good individual circumstances and possibilities, because he would change the real, local and material world to become more universal and entirely idealistic. This disagreement is the psychological reason, why he not only suffered and was persecuted, but that he, step by step, was obviously doomed to be and remain more materially dependent than others. We could scarcely imagine his family life, because he, in spite of his tender kindliness, would likely have sacrificed the individual equality to the absolute faithfulness to his ideal principles and he, in his real life, would not ever have been,considered as psychological human character, inclined to acquiesce with the continuous and numberless petty considerations of frail and immediate human surroundings. Therefore, we never meet him extensively represented in regard to intimate familiar atmosphere. He is and remains essentially aloof in the superior glory of his divine separation.

The sentimental individual self-satisfaction may be ordinarily a pronounced reason reducing people to beggary. The beggar does not mix with people, not only because he is not accepted, but also because of his affective pride. He perhaps came to his state because of the thought that he was higher and better than other people and finished after all, it is true, with the fact to be the outcast of the human society. Then he is perhaps embittered, because he finds that his idealistic pretensions are indeed not ruling on this earth. His real needs affect his ideal good progress and performances, and it is on this round-about way, that the beggar may become disgusted and discouraged. First he neglected the real world because of his idealistic pride, and he finishes indeed in being despised himself because of his real and material helplessness. He scorned first the society because of their relative unimportance and unworthiness, and he is at the end the undesirable burden of their helping material collaboration. He is indeed punished exactly in the same manner as he was deficient.

But there is no question that the psychology of the regular beggar is near the conception and taste of the religious genius. The beggar means the terminal social state of the person who has accepted unrestrictedly and in the full psychological meaning the spiritual idea and the magnetic tendencies of idealism. The relative social peace and economic quietness in religious countries have their root exactly in the fact that the individual real and material covetousness is utterly reduced by the influence of the idealistic, anti-real conceptions and that the immense majority of the population, therefore, easily acquiesces with the social order to have the least individual share in the national fortune which compensatorily can be gathered and garnered by a few materialistic and realistic individuals coming out from other educational conceptions or being naturally indocile and ungifted, hard and unamenable to the charming idealistic lures.

The religious idealistic organization can therefore not be considered as the serious attempt to resolve the question of the social distribution of possession, in a direct way. The strong idealistic emphasis touches this question chiefly indirectly in a negative way, in giving counsel of resignation in the quarrel about possession. But it is easier to give this counsel than to carry it through. For our human nature has indeed two sides and we are inevitably forced to face both necessary components of our human character, the idealistic and materialistic. It is the typical language of the psychology of the beggar, when he exclaims: "I wish to be dissolved and to die." The longing for eternity and death is of course the transfer of the human affective energy from this busy real life into the sentimental beyond.

Despite this truth we must admit that the idealistic religion has the radical positive helping element of social justice in the circumstance that it respects the person, that the individual is declared as the highest, most valuable and inviolable unit of life. The consequence of this principle is indeed *that all have the essential right to lead a human life in human circumstances*. It was the COMMUNISM of the first Christian time which was indeed the clear and natural expression of this psychological anticipation and acceptation. The same duties and obligations on one side, but also the same dignity, the same rights and even the same material share for all, on the other side, was the psychological signature of that first historic sentimental quarter. As long as the strong sentimental idealism had the upper hand, with its highest spiritual emphasis, it was easy to succeed in maintaining this principle. Nobody was, during the one-sided ruling idealism of that time interested or inclined to quarrel about the greater material share in life, and so the first Christian time, interpolated between the material rich development of the contemporary intellectual paganism, did not and had not to care about the principal questions of more or less social material possession and real divisions. These questions were quite in the background, outside of the central sentimental interest, but following clearly from the spiritual principle.

But it is the most essential truth exercising its force until to-day that the domineering atmosphere of the true religious conception consists in the relative disregard of the whole visible and material world, and here we have the reason why the idealistic historic church as a whole never dealt seriously with the question of material organization of the social life. Religion has its chief goals and interests beyond these visible material possessions of the world, it is therefore weak and checked compensatorily in its social material laws. It shows, in its best role, the most insufficient inaptitude for this questions and surrenders its children practically more or less to the discretion of the extra- and anti-religious influences of human society.

So we see that the progressing first religious genial organization did not resolve definitely the social problem of possession. No sooner the disappearance of the powerful material Antiquity had given the power of social disposition into the hand of the Christian church than, after the promising Communism of the first centuries, the rise of the mediaeval *Feudalism* had seriously hurt the theoretic assumption of the equality of all individuals and a corresponding minimum guarantee of dignified human circumstances. The church was even so little practically offended at this unjust dividing system of real possession that it not only did not condemn and reject, but that even the higher ecclesiastic dignitaries participated in it, being feudal rulers as well as the laymen of the mediaeval nobility. It was never the deep interest of the ideal, theoretically noble church to bring thorougly to a point the question of the individual right for real possession. It found never the sufficient energy to exact, without fear of capitalism, the utmost possible adaptation of the exterior life to its fundamental principles of dignity, equal fraternity and liberty, as it was stated and fixed from the beginning of any religious philosophy. Where and how much public interference and non-interference, is a very ticklish question.

It was essentially the Puritan Protestantism and the French Revolution which re-established the individual independent right of earning possession and of real equality. But there was no limit given for real material accumulation. The principle ruling at this time was this that possession must be individual, that everybody is permitted to gather as much riches as he is willing and able to, and that success, always supposing the Providence of God, will be the just manifestation of the individual diligence and personal merit. What as the consequence of this method came out, we know it well enjoying its fruits to-day. It is the force of CAPITALISM which is not any longer given into the hand of the possessing individual. The owner of shares has not to dispose any longer of the development and of the moral effect of his possession, of which he had to be the benevolent humane stewart in former times. Capitalism is the collective economic system of to-day, exercising the most powerful influence on the individual, on the whole society and even on the public and private opinion.

The idea that real success is the adequate product of personal worthiness or skill, has turned out to be wrong. It was wrong in the former times. The historic religion in its hero and in its doctrine suggests rather the opposite idea, and does not the experience of life, considered from the idealistic side, teach the same? To-day nobody is superficial enough to be ignorant about this question. It was an insufficiently human principle developing during centuries which was the root of the capitalistic system of to-day, and we are, for this reason, thrown into new social difficulties in respect of the notion of possession which seems to be formulated unjustly in the one-sided and blind capitalistic power. In capitalism we again have no more any doubt of the inefficiency of personal human skill and merit. The capitalism blurs in the wrong way, by its impersonal blind force, all individual differences of cleverness and kindheartedness and subjects the whole society to historic accidental intimidation and systematization, in regard to the material possession. Capitalism is near the mediaeval Feudalism, extolling one individual high over his fellowmen of the same psychological value and dignity and making the collectiveness of men, high and low, the impersonal slaves of the ruling system. But it has in addition this disadvantage that the capitalist himself is not able to change his position and attitude, even if he would. He as well is the slave of hic economical fate, and his personal weak influence is not at all comparable with the ruling power of the capitalism dividing and crushing individually.

This capitalistic world of ours is indeed far from being the manifestation of the idealistic conceptions and sentiments. The world has developed in this point into the most distant digression from equalizing idealism proclaiming every individual the equal brother and the equal partaker of any duty and right. Yet it is the quite one-sided idealism of the religious system, to whose lacking real control and insufficient legislative interest it is exactly due that the proceeding history has produced always again these poison flowers of wrong economic development. The founder himself is

scarcely related with a word having touched the questions of possession and material justice. His religious organization turned out
to be disinterested in these practical ideas, if it not, which was
worse, did partake in sharing practically the doubtful principles of
the prevalent dominion and competitive ambition of the materialistic world. The profession of a faulty one-sided idealistic *orientation* of the church permitted the social and individual opposite
energies to take possession of all extra-ecclesiastical real influence,
and we have been brought back to-day, once more, to the most in-
just and unequal state of the individual share of the total social
possession, being rather everything else than the imitation and realization of the original rights of psychological equality. The religious genius was the social outcast of his society and epoch; he was
the scorned poor, roming through his country like a disinherited
vagabond, having no place where to lay his head. Had his idealism
not been so exceedingly high, his aversion to any real materialistic
compromise not so thorough, his children would perhaps not to
have to live under such a considerable pressure of material distress,
and they would not have to face the invincible opposition of the
real world. For the servant is not above his master.

Possession is not only the most dangerous notion, dividing individual from individual and even father from child, but it is at
the same time the most necessary thing in life which we cannot dispense with. The extreme idealistic compensation of the conception
of life seems exceedingly wrong, ruinous, paralysing and excluding our real interest and energy from any serious real success.
The literal conscientious conception of the religious heroism reduces
inevitably to beggary. Here ends the pitiful, exclusive idealism
practised in, and applied to, the real world. The religious philosophy is essentially the most one-sided idealism, and every one of
its true adherents - this is the fruit in which he is recognized - will
be the Cinderella of the real material success.

Worlds unborn shall praise Him!

SEVENTH BOOK

CHRISTMAS is the commemoration of the divine incarnation. All the means of expression used for it tend to give to us the enjoyment of a strong light kindling out of the darkest night, or of the sweetest love rising from the frosty heart of the most unfriendly surroundings. All elaborate means of Christmas serve this purpose. The Eastern star within the darkness, the charming tenderness of the divine child, the poorest circumstances of the holy persons, the glorious shining of the lights of heaven, the songs of the angels and the worship of kings for the hidden prince of the world, lying in a manger and shivering in the wintry frost. We have many most pronounced sentimental oppositions in the tale of Christmas, it being therefore of the most pitying influence on our soul. Christmas could not have its full affective effect without all the splendour of the Eastern star, without the rich gifts of the three Wise Men, without the shining light of the brilliant hovering angels, without the sweet flutes of the adoring shepherds and without the pious devotion of Mary and Joseph. These are the positive, concentrating motives of Christmas, being enhanced very much by the negative moments consisting of the dark night, the frost and the desolation of the wintry landscape, the extreme poverty of the economic circumstances and the unfriendly declining attitude of the surrounding population.

Christmas is, therefore, the most elaborate, artistic-psychological masterpiece. Christmas without the dark, wintry night could not be imagined. The Eastern star with its twinkling sparks is indispensable for the sentimental atmosphere of this festival; the divine angels with their dazzling garments create the most enrapturing devotion for, and the bluffing disposition to, the central historic moments. The radiant face of the Saviour shining through the distress and the desolation of the poor barn, with its sublime glory, captivates every reader of the gospel.

Is *incarnation* and *birth* not the most surprising fact of our life in itself? If their is any miracle, is it not indeed the birth of any human being? It is the moment, when the great, immeasurable power and majesty of the human soul descends from heaven and is enclosed within the narrow real limits of the physiological body. It is the moment, when the universal energy of the world acquiesces with the unbelievable, but real fact to form the personal unity with the human individual, to live in it, to rule it and to give to it its form, motions, emotions and passions. But it is also the moment, when the dead material is elevated to the sublime dignity of affective life, when it is allowed to be the partaker of the idealizing will of the eternal noble soul , by which it is animated, vivified and inspired for the highest tasks and purposes. Is this not the most tremendous fact of natural science and of all things ever seen and believed that the incarnation of the highest divine soul within the frail human body is achieved? The dead material substance on one hand, and the most refined immaterial magnetic energy, as it is given in the human soul, on the other side, are indeed and in fact unified into one harmonious whole, each time when the conception of a human being takes place.

Birth is just the moment, when heaven and earth touch each other in a miraculous way, when the created and possibly the uncreated world are melted into one. Do we observe in birth the most startling infusion of the divine animation into the material existence? Is it just the beginning union of the most extraordinary creative *symbiosis* of heaven and earth, the starting point of the appearance of the most sublime affective energy forming with the human body that vital miracle, which we call the normal human individual? The bliss of the divine energy fixes itself, in the moment of the conception, on the dead intellectual localization of the material which is urged from this time toward energetic divine service and living moving performances. This is the triumph of the ideal nature which has found the possibility of building a bridge between real, material and intellectual life, on one side, and of the sentimental idealistic inspiration, on the other. Christmas is the commemoration of the birth-day of humanity, of our historic material existence, into which life has been breathed and which became, at the moment of birth, the partaker of the superior idealistic life, raising from cold death and immovability to the warm life and active movement. Is this not the great principal fact of Christmas, besides its special Christian claims, that we have indeed this wonderful union between material and ideal world in the human incarnation, that the ideal spirit has succeeded in taking possession of the service of the material world, in a most refined manner and that the restricted dead limits of the material world have been removed. The dead is inspired, elevated and vivified to eternal love and living idealization.

The meaning of the Eastern Star, the gifts of the Wise Men,

of the dazzling glamour of the angels and of the sweet flutes of the shepherds is this that the divine life and energy has penetrated the night, the frost, the poverty and the desolation of the material existence, that the shining light of the face of the Saviour and of the heavenly angels has enlightened and vivified the darkness of the former slothfulness, that the sweet song of the divine messengers and the soothing flutes of the shepherds have succeeded in grasping and moving the sensorial human heart and the deaf real world toward the ideal goals of love and divine harmony.

The Eastern Star is a striking artistic psychological expression of the human *birth*. The *star* means by its optic peculiarity the perfect exclusion of the sensorial surrounding world. The effect of the star supposes the darkness of the night, the invisibility of the real environments, the most shrinking concentration of the lighting effect into the powerful symbol of the smallest punctual size. All real life is excluded, all multiplicity of the intellectual extension is forgotten: it is in this compensatory symbolic concentration that every star exhibits the most powerful psycho-dynamic expression of eternal sentimental olve, of perfect terminal happiness and of the highest longings and hopes of our psychic force.

How near is this optic law to the sensorial conditions of birth! The ideal lightful infusion of our incarnation, in birth, has not yet the least real expansion in intellectual experience, in possession and in real longing development. There is still the perfect surrounding night of lack of experience and the punctual isolation from the intercourse with the whole surrounding display, in the personal existence of the newborn, but there is one great fact, sparkling and enrapturing like the beauty of the fiery star, it is the animation of the infused universal soul giving the most promising prospects and the most charming and thrilling hopes for the future. The potential life-energy of the small new born child strikes us as so much more, in its undeveloped tension, as it is still detached from intellectual relations, and as it keeps still the most concentrated, smallest and clearest ego-centrical isolation of the punctual simplicity of the star. In the punctual smallness, in the starting inexperience and real detachment of the new born lies the key of the surprising attraction of the *baby child,* in every dealing with it. The virtual magnetic and affective energy of this new human being throws energetic, sparkling flames of admiration, love and sympathy on all witnessing fellowmen.

As long as the child remains in its modest isolation, as long as the idealistic touch of the heaven has the undivided emphasis on the infant soul, as it is not yet displayed into the outside real world in different wishes and does not feel yet urged to stretch out its magnetic soul and grasping hand toward intellectual development and real possession, it will be and remain the most attractive darling to all humanity. The punctual charm of its selfless sentimental beauty gives to him the veneration, the love and worship of the whole world. All are fond of the uplifting smile of the innocent, divine sparkling star of the - happy childhood. The mighty and the kings of the earth come in order to worship the child and to give to him the most select golden toys as signs of their sympathy and love. During this stage of human psychology the idealistic scale of the inexperienced childish soul puts all its stress on the idealistic eternal world. The psychic gift of the soul of the child is not yet able to empty into the real multiple intellectual outside world and flows, therefore, with all its energy to the dreamy charming land of imaginative beautiful idealism. Therefore the delightful attraction and the psychic beauty of the human being at this age. The river of te psychic experience is, owing to the lack of experience, yet obstructed toward having any outside connection with the visible outside world. It throws all its energy toward its sentimental happy pleasure, and this direction of the affective psychic draught is the reason, why we are so much attracted and invited to join our love and sympathy with the lovely tendencies of our children.

There will be a time when the longing of this starting human being becomes more really resourceful, when the spell of this radiant splendid isolation will be broken, when the magnetic force of the real life will have its multiple real aims and purposes and when the idealistic overweight of the psychic balance stoops to the realistic wishes of intellectual statements and visible multiple possessions. The charming sparkling Eastern Star with its mysterious attraction will then be enlarged to the size of a mighty real sun claiming power, right and respect, taking energetically its own part from the widespread real world, defeating with its fiery affective arrows real resistances and and fighting irresistibly for its personal advantages, at the expense of the surrounding and intellectual, real neighborhood. Then the child will be grown up and will have to defend himself. The charming attraction will be diminished in the ripening life and idealistic hopes and dreams will be released by real fulfilments.

There is another important idea suggested by Christmas: its date is *the—equinoctial time of our sun-year*. The earth at this time transgresses the nearest distance from the sun and starts to approach again toward the central sun. The worst time of the short days and long nights will soon be over: the severe cold and wet season will soon be overcome, and there will be once more a new rising of warm, sunny and happier months.

Thus the birth of the religious hero is the genial turning-point of his historic time. From the time of the birth of Christianity the peri-Mediterranean humanity receded from the former cultural intellectualism back to the central mono-symbolic affectivity. From then humanity entered again into the path of the mono-symbolic theistic love; it embraced once more its monotheistic centre and goal with stronger sentimental enthusiasm, converting from intellectual digression into affective love and harmony with the peculiar theistic goal. Christ was, in his birth, the theistic idealistic turning-point of the Mediterranean cultural humanity. He converted and concentrated in his genial personality all scattered and seemingly lost intellectual results of the historic collective past, into one new point, and humanity looked, from this time back to his idealistic-intellectual score as the giver of theistic delight and the indicator of all possible, historic, multiple magnetic wires of the psychological human history. This also is the meaning of the light in the night: he guided humanity again from the materialistic night and the intellectual confusion or *disorientation* toward the sweet and clarified, sure encirclement of the mono-symbolic idea and the sure theistic purpose. Here again we have the explanation of his shining face in the darkness, as it was depicted by Rembrandt, Raphael, Tintoretto and so many other mediaeval and later artists. Here we have once more the reason of the sweet charm of the persuasive flutes of the shepherds of Christmas which we consider indeed as the festival of the conversion of the intellectual real onesidedness of the historic development of our psychology into sentimental love, reconciliation and peace.

We understand now better that Christmas is the time of going home to mother's, the typical festival of the children, of gifts and lights. The enthusiastic and hopeful eye of the inexperienced child expects most love and needs most of it. It is in the hothouse of love where the young individual must be persuaded to growing development, and it is, therefore, in the first line perhaps the right of the child to enjoy the charm and the pleasure of the Christian festival of love. The trusting eye of the child under the Christmas tree is the most charming Christmas star itself. It shows the peculiarity of our natural youth, which so much inclines to imagination, to sentimental effusion and to miraculous fairy-tales. If we dare not to destroy the Christmas dreams of the childhood about its imaginative longings, there will be, notwithstanding, very soon the time, when these sentimental dreams, if prolonged, would be hurtful to our darlings. If we strive to give even to the adult, at this occasion, the illusion of the liberal short abolition of logical justice and consequence, by our *GIFTS,* then we are, in a sense, so much more entitled to maintain the sweet illusion of the traditional dreamy Christmas tales for the young children.

Gifts have indeed the meaning and the intention to raise the conception of receiving material things without previous earning. Christmas means, therefore, the short truce of the hard intellectual law of exact logical "justice" which rules all other times. It gives in, for a little while, to the illusion of having abolished the nearest real conceptions of cause and effect. *It puts the ideal sympathy at the place of real learning.* The educational value of gifts is therefore rather doubtful. They are liable to create hurtful illusions which the practice and the consequence of life disclaims and punishes. Gifts are good, if they have the sense of reward for ideal love or if they mean the complement of any former reward for any excellent work or service which had not received sufficient remuneration before, or finally, if they will be the instigators of better future work and better psychic harmonious collaboration. But the comfortable way of accepting gifts is of course liable of pampering the individual. Christmas once a year is therefore indeed enough, because of the educational danger of misconceptions of the hard logical reality of the life. The faithful eye of the child, happy and surprised as it may be at the different Christmas gifts, will soon to have recover from its idealistic loving dream, being one-sided in an egotistic way, and the progressive human fate teaches us all too soon, how severely it uses its laws of real causal justice, how little life gives for sentimental affection,and how much we must struggle in order to have our material existence. Generally we receive love for love, which is indeed the *great and desirable gift,* but we shall have, as a rule, material things for intellectual and mechanical work which means the other great necessity of our life.

When all fields are white, when all trees are laden with dazzling snow at the frosty Christmas time, when the deep winter night has excluded all reality from our houses, and we are gathered around the lights of the Christmas tree, how charming and delightful speak the mysterious sparks of all this spell to the human heart! Let us enjoy, for a while, all these lights and all these gifts like tokens of the ideal love of our friends! Let us revel a little, exceptionally, in the sentimental dreams of beautiful and optimistic expectations! Life comes so quickly along to beckon us back to our daily duties and the broadened intellectual enlargement of self-sacrifice, from the charming punctual light-field of selfish involution. With the dawning morning, when another day rises, we shall be given back to the the new unfoldment of the large intellectual real, visible world with all its duties, struggles, antagonistic and dividing necessities. We shall no more have the liberality of the sweet illusion of the benevolent gifts and selfless idealistic sympathy, on the part on others, but we have to sacrifice our self-centred sentimental selfishness and try to make a possible *compromise* between the opposed interests. The equilibrium of these two opposed magnetic forces is perhaps the highest justice of the *spiritual layman*.

The lights of the Christmas tree turn out to be the expression of the same psychological principle as the Eastern Star, the shining lights in the Christmas night on the fields of Bethlehem and as the divine glamour of the face of the Saviour, as it is depicted by our artists. The culmination of pleasure and idealism expresses itself always in *punctual lights,* in the psychological world as well as in the real outside visibility. The enthusiastic and thrilled eye of the child is another instance, the sparkling tear and the fiery diamond are others. All highest pleasure means punctual concentration, in the real, and in the ideal, psychological world. The persuading principle of the Christmas delight has also, as we pointed out, its deep psychological root in the same graphic artistic-philosophical principle, in the compensatory exclusion of the reality, and in its comparative reduction to the smallest ideal, punctual symbolism, as it is graphically expressed in the Eastern Star and in the burning candles of the Christmas tree.

No real deep pleasure and enjoyment in the outspread multiple intellectual world, but no more any real symbolic pleasure, on the other side, if it has not been first deserved by the far fetched, logical progressive *working refinement*, out of the objective peripheric world. Miracles, mysticism, but also gifts, in a psychological sense, are violent symbolic contractions of our psychological energy. They are angry pleasures given to us without previous energetic logical work and they are, therefore, surprises, to which our soul is not naturally sufficiently prepared and entitled. The true, best and hygienic pleasure is that which has been best deserved and carefully prepared, to which all our vital energy has aspired long ago and gathered long its attention and efforts. The terminal symbolic pleasure must be the adequate expression of our previous working effort. All other methods are unhealthy; they disturb our psycho-dynamic just eye and cause, therefore, hurtful self-deceptions. We need logical justice for our life more than anything else. The mystic motions of undeserved gifts unhinge our harmonious natural energy; they cause expectations which are wrong and shameful and destroy our natural sureness of adequate causes and effects. Our cultural blessings, to which we all have sworn from the cradle and in which our civilization assumes to have become great and important, is given in the principles of reason, objective truth, of clear reality and of justice of work and reward. All symbolic and mystic principles, to which also the Christmas gifts belong, may be welcome sweet relaxations, sentimental dreamy changes and instigating urges, but they are and remain dangerous exceptions.

Owing to the strong ideal and real contrasts there is scarcely any subject more able for *artistic* treatment than Christmas. No other topic was, therefore, chosen so often in the old Christian artistic representations of the middle ages. Christmas allows the artist to put strong realistic shadows and to concentrate energetically on the lightful, central, divine idealism. No other subject is more able to permit dark colors lingering like imaginative shadows at the periphery and to emphasize, at the same time, the ideal central light, as we see in the charming masterpieces of Rembrandt, Corregio and others.

If we think that the localized cultural treatment of the Christmas scenery, by the old artists, was due to naive narrow ignorance-ignorant people like to think they are the whole world - we are mistaken. Even if there was no hard winter in Palestine at the historic time of Christmas, the mediaeval artists were right to emphasize the severe winter time and the northern atmosphere of their Christmas masterpieces. In the orient the barren field and the darkness of the barn brought about the monotonous sensorial exclusion which we gain and emphasize in another way in the northern winter. If people generally say that there is no real Christmas without wintry snow, they judge well psychologically, out of the same need to drop the multiple reality and to build up strong idealism on the basis of the real excluding compensation. The most simple representation and the most modest picture of Christmas of to-day still cling at least to *this fact of simplification,* even if they have neglected all other artistic refinement and spiritual conception. And indeed with the greatest effect. Poverty and darkness of night and barn replaced in the historic moment the monotonous winter of our northern countries. If our age and the middle ages added the festival simplifying atmosphere of the snow and emphasized it, on the other hand, by the strong sparkling lights of the Christmas tree, absorbing thus the free psychic energy to few symbolic points, the delightful artistic effect is only so much more thrilling.

Poeple often smile in looking at the elaborate mediaeval conception of the artistic Christmas scenery because of its *Anachronism*. But they are wrong again. There is an extreme universality of conception behind this anatopism and anachronism. The 'naive' artists of the middle ages were fine enough to claim the ubiquitous validity of the spiritual contents of Christmas, to transplant it to their own ground, culture and history, whilst they rightly overlooked foreign, accidental circumstances. Those naive artists must have been tremendously deep and clear thinkers. The divine ideas, in which they were only interested and which they tried to express in that historic frame, are supra-historic, fitting all times and ages, looking always beyond any categoric localization and individual representability. They include the highest possibilities and are, therefore, - sweet mockery of the universe against our nosy intruion - as naive and insufficiently expressed framed in the former historic confinement as in the localized real frame of the mediaeval or modern representation. The old artists knew very well why they depicted their Christmas masterpieces into the atmosphere of the northern winter. It was because of the emphasis by the artistic concentration, and they knew as well why they used the anachronistic outfit of the northern European culture: it was because of their general idealistic intention and the inter-historic and supratemporal claim of the psychological idea of Christmas. There can hardly be the question of anachronism in regard to Christmas, in an essential sense, because its central idea fits all times and cultures. Every trial of real intellectual confinement of the divine feelings must point outside of time and history. It flees away like a bird as soon as humanity believes to have caught it. Divine feelings and creeds are always and everywhere, because they are universal. They are as well, in another sense, nowhere, because they cannot be expressed sufficiently by the means of reality.

We recall the truth that the individual, surprising historic facts have, as a rule, restricted and small general value, because they are mono-individual and accidental, and that the most important eternal and most fundamental things are everywhere, at all times and in everybody, because they are always possible and necessary, adaptable to all individuals, historic epochs and circumstances. The facts of the poets and the masterpieces of art are true at every historic epoch, and so is religion, because they mention general possibilities and ubiquitous realities, whilst the historic individual events have only partial purport. What never was exceptional, as a rule, will always be true and possible, and what was a surprising exception in the historic categoric experience, will be always aloof from the common every day utility and use. The historic claim of Christmas arises from the same miraculous source as the mono-personality of the divine hero. If we admit his overwhelming genial mono-personality, we are as well prisoners of the long chain of the evangelic tales and claims. They altogether have their common source in the extreme, genial intensification of the ideal hero; they are the mere, well adapted and elaborate consequence of the central sentimental importance of the divine Christ full of supra-categoric energy and of supra-historic spiritual significance.

May the historic religious tales be necessary for our sensorial organization, yet they are only the necessary forground of the divine sentiments inspired into them, by the idealistic artistic writers. Every human fact and every historic event could be advanced to international and intertemporal significance, if people understood to elaborate it clearly and emphasize it enough toward the general idealistic *spiritual* validity. But generally the accurate, individual historic truth seldom offers such clear sure facts of general justice and full of divine prospects and immediate ideal intercourse. They all are mostly blurred by egotistic interests and short-sightedness, by material considerations, lack of idealistic permeability and too much emphasis of realistic logic. It is the duty of the artist, the special task and facility of the artist , to emphasize and to arrange any historic small individul fact so as to develop this logical perfection toward highest aims, to infuse into it the highest moral justice, and to destroy all superficial lazy thoughtlessness and all idealistic obstruction of any event. In the degree as we succeed in abolishing the limits of the near material superficial conception of any individual fact, we enlarge its validity indeed to very far limits beyond all narrow reality and and individual confinement.

Were not the *holy writers* so excellent artists, because they understood to breath into the smallest human fact the general power of divine force and energy? They did it so well because they never chose any topic which was anything else but the expression of the ordinary and general human interest. Everybody has his birthday, everybody dies, everybody is longing for perfection and for immortal beatitude. Everybody is interested in sickness, in love and in personal suffering. But there is no other idea in all the gospel. All other individual features are excludingly subdued in comparison with these main inculcated points. This is the rule and continual prastice of any artistic behaviour, which excludes the individuality so far as to cling only generally to the sensorial necessity of the individual surface, but carries the human sentimental feelings irresistibly away toward general, eternal, divine truth, beauty and strength. The best artist is surely the best prophet, the most accepted seer and most beloved divine. But on the other hand the divine has the birth-right for the greatest art. Christ in the world is the most succeessful artistic representation of the human life. The gospel is likely the most persuasive poetical book of history. Exactly because it understands to blur so thoroughly its historic facts, just because it knew to unite some clear historic features according to our sensorial necessities with the most powerful weight of supracategoric divine ideas and feelings, and because the evangelists indeed insisted most thoroughly and happily on the overwhelming importance of the quite general facts of human life, birth, death, joy and passion. They produced the quite unparalleled human success transgressing the narrow limits of the contemporary history.

So we all are thrilled at Christmas by the fact of the glorification of the international human birthday. We all kneel and mourn in consternation, if Christ is condemned to death and if his charming divine love is abused, if the purest lamb with its kindliest intentions is slaughtered ruthlessly. Our jubilation is indescribable indeed in the fact of the divine infusion and incarnation of the universal spirit; our pain and our tears are instead insatiable at the sight of the passion and murder of the most humane and sweetest hero. In worshiping the religious genius and sharing his lot with the full attention of our heart's love, we indeed meditate our own deepest human nature and fate. Then we have a survey over the totality of our natural means and potential faculties. In greeting the hero, we respect our own human condition and disposition. The glorification of the hero is self-glorification, and even if it were nothing else, it wood be good, because we must learn self-respect and love even of the suffering part of human fate. If we declare the hero as the universal fulfilment of the divinity, we as well elevate ourselves over the low clouds of the restricted natural limits. Is not the worship of the hero the reflection of the loving esteem of our own nature? Our attitude toward the divine hero gives the exact measure of the rank which we wish to give to our own human nature in the possibility of the universal development and in the numberless affective magnetic standards. Does adoration of the hero mean loving meditation and sentimental development and direction of our own theistic nature? The exeeding love for the simple facts of birth and the high respect for death have the meaning of the most decided affirmation of our earthly special lot and of most powerful self-emphasis. It has the intention to persuade and to lead us into the most ready concordance of the universal energy which avails itself of the special principal facts of birth and death to interchange our human destiny and to forward our spheric divine gift through the physiological metabolism, like, as it were, a short action of material diving, begining with birth and ending with death.

Birth and human life are like wonderful visible manifestations of universal magnetic energy, impressive fountains springing from hidden sources. The human body is the most remarkable point of ideal attraction being able to imbibe extraordinarily high values and strongest concentrations of divine sentiments and affective power. Like a huge stone resisting the rushing energy of the water in a river, so that there is produced a broiling splash of a high foaming wave, so the human birth represents, in the interspheric rush of the universal sentimental magnetism, the most pronounced mark and the most remarkable real stop and bridle of the divine sentimental progression, the most surprising ideal material transfer of the world. The chemical force of avidity and the physical capacity, as it were, of the human body for idealistic values and sentimental universal energy seems to be quite unparalleled in the history of the world. This is the meaning of the word that man is the crown of the creation, that he is most able and most capable to receive the most remarkable plenty of the divine energy, that he has the most pronounced idealistic gift and the most extended friendship and interference with material-theistic values. The human body is the abode of the Holy Ghost, as the church terms it. Heaven is imprisoned within the narrow confinement of the limited organic body.

Now we understand the thrilling, sublime feelings produced by the sentence: God so loved the world that he sent his only beloved Son. The enthusing and pitying part of the shivering feelings produced in our heart by this sentence, consists in the deep remembrance of our highest divine origin, awakened in this moment, by the most tender expressions. It is the idea of Christmas that indeed the highest divine starting point of our psychic nature is connected with the corporeal body, that the beloved Son of God is the best example and greatest likeness of the soul of everybody of our human race, and that we unite the highest human dignity with narrowest categoric necessities, within our surprising human amalgamation. Is the thrilling and pitying reaction of the mentioned sentence of St. John this, that we tremble and our hearts throb in being reminded of the exulting greatness and happiness of the last divine goals, from which we believe to be transitorily excluded by the magnetic fixation to the bodily real existence?

The tender allusion to the descension of our soul from heaven, the collective and general imporsonal allegation of the common fact of our earthly incarnation, - we realize it so refinedly in this moment - means the remembrance of the expulsion from the paradise of our last determination. The law of our soul is indeed the marvellous eternal orb developing toward most distant ranges of divine energy, and it is therefore most clear that our heart aches and that we feel sometimes the most moving homesickness and the most pronounced oppression by being retained from the last goals longed for, if we are reminded so tenderly of them. Our homesickness points us emphatically to perfect happiness, to absolute, supracategoric, intellectual achievement and to supra-historic and supraindividual eternal validity. There is no prouder and no higher aspiring talent in the world than the human soul. Christmas and the general Christian life manifests always in a clear manner our divine aspirations and theistic universal prestige. Tertullian was, therefore, in this sense right, saying that the human soul is naturally Christian.

If we look at the Christmas pictures, whose scenic representation returns always again and again in the typical manner, we observe ordinarily and indispensably within the dim shadows of the surrounding barn the figures of *OXEN* and *DONKEYS* peeping and staring from the background and from the periphery toward the central divine child. There is a marvellous warm atmosphere which is enhanced by the presence of those animals. On the other hand the miraculous events receive instantly by this fact the very real and earthly aspect, and we feel, induced by the animal representations, quite sure to move within the real earth. The animal conception of the world is doubtless nearer the intellectual materialism; the animal soul has received also of the divine universal sentiments, in a lesser degree than the human being, as much as we can make out, and the never missing animal presence at the miraculous genial scene of incarnation makes up the desirable psychological balance against the miraculous super-human overweight of this surprising picture—

How clever and interesting is the idea of introducing animals into the Christmas scenery! The animal existence forms just the medium between the dark and dead material world, from which it looks and breathes toward the brilliant and central, heroic humanity. The animal seems to be the gradual augmentation of the dead intellectual material world, surpassing the plant with its steady feet in the ground by arbitrary movability, toward the highest earthly divine inspiration, as we have it in the perfect human idealist. The human birth represents, in the Christmas scene, the central highest top of creative ranges wither all inferior creatures aspire. It means the central light most approaching to, and most deeply imbibed with, the central divine idealization.

Have we not already in these old and seemingly primitive conception of religious pictures the root and the finger-post of the *evolutionary progression* of the human destiny, connected with the inferior stages of the animal world, on one side, and longing for the uplifting material idealism, on the other hand? The dim consciousness of the oxen and donkeys looks reverently to the central lightful Christ; the inferior soul of the animals is longing and aspiring to the higher manifestation of the superior sentimental development and intellectual refinement of the human being. But, in the same manner, the human nature, in its turn, looks admiringly forward to the further universal achievement of its nature, which is indicated in the flash of light, by the miraculous angels, by the celestial songs and the adoration of Mary and Joseph, the Wise Men and the musical shepherds.

The sweet music of Christmas transports the human soul to the eternal aspirations of our destiny. In the prayer and in the adoration of the surrounding contemporaries we recognize the psychological genial record of the supreme concentration of the divine mind of Christ who had beaten the whole previous race of his fellowmen by his universal longings and sentimental perfection. The Christ child is represented as the top and highest attainable score of divine perfection in humanity by the adoring and praying attitude of his worshiping retinue. They all together, the dead material world and the simple physical law of gravitation, the dim, wondering, yet reverent eyes of the animal creatures, but also not the less the attending human beings look and aspire to the central divine child as to their most perfect example and desirable divine perfection and idealization. They hope in him the utmost satisfaction of their natural desires, of which they wish to be the highest and noblest divine achievement within the limits of any earthly existence. But the sweet divine music, the celestial angels and songs transgress this conception. They represent the further future development of human destinies. They strive to persuade the advancing universal progression of our categoric life to higher approach toward the eternal *extramundial* divine goals. By the extraordinary favor and concentration in the middle of miraculous phenomena, the central baby is conceived as the being most approaching the most spiritualized divine aims. For his time he is represented as the most modern and progressed human individual , whose personal existence has the nearest connection with the progressive ascension of the universal evolution of our special divine possibilities.

If Christ was the historic individual of his time, he surely received already supra-historic features by the illimited powers of the sweet celestial music and by the miraculous appearance of the angels. By this means he was withdrawn from the categoric limits of time, space and causality and was brought in connection with shoreless interspheric waves. Here lies the most interesting kernel of his invincible divine role, that he had not only the historic appearance in the time of the human cultural development, but that he was favored and bound to the extra-historic and extra-categoric values of the universe by the mysterious ties of the miraculous angels, by the special light of eternal divine love and by the serving attendance of ideal messengers. In connecting the seeming contradictions of the real historic life and of the universal miraculous sentiments, Christ manifested the extraordinary power and influence on the following cultural periods. He shares not only the remarkable importance of his historic time, for which he was the leader and guide, but he assumed also the leading role of the coming human progress, to which he was bound by the miraculous circumstances of his appearance.

He received by his *miraculous surroundings* the longest affective scale a man ever reached in history. He partook at the same time in the material and intellectual localization of history and shared the eternal, sentimental ranges of the interspheric, divine, future longings of humanity.

The Christmas scenery is therefore used by the *artists,* as the most inviting opportunity for powerful representation of human and divine perfection. They bound the person of the hero through real historic representation to the sensorial centre of this world, but they connected him more intensely to the eternal sentimental values by conveying to him the universal intimacy and the extraordinary bearing on eternal extra-categoric affective standards and values.

We meet, therefore, always in the same manner, within the Christmas psychology, and artistic expression, these two components: strong pronounciation of universal connections and at the same time real categoric features. They latter turn on the most general human fact of birth, but they are elaborate enough to clinch on one individual human fate. On the other side, the divine prospects and the eternal views of the miraculous depiction of the circumstances are very carefully done; they form the ruling atmosphere of the character of the hero and lift, therefore, our human life-force, subduing sufficiently the individual reality according to the law of psychological compensation, to the superior divine hills of divine idealism. Christ is, psychologically speaking, the most broadened figure of the human history. He is equipped with the most distant real and idealistic values. He connects the lowest and highest values of the material and immaterial world, and for this reason he was accepted almost universally as the best example of our human eternal hopes and vistas, of our best pride and most cheerful love.

Easter strives to eternify the transitional ideal vivification of the material world. The death of the human individual was indeed the most shocking disappointment after the thrilling smile and the harmonious jubilation of all creation, on the Christmas day. There was the great conviction, the abundant revelling pleasure of the material world, at that time, that the inspiration of the divine energy had breathed through the dead creation receiving life, strenght, motion and emotion from the universal energy. The jubilation was right from the standpoint of that moment; in the achieved vivification and idealization of the human body there was given the surprising expression of active life within the material world.

DEATH expresses therefore exactly the contrary of the Christ-mas psychology. It raises all those lamentations and despairing complaints, that mournful clangour which disclaims thoroughly the sweet, uplifting songs and flutes of Merry Christmas. Death is the most pitiful deception and the most cruel disappointment after Christmas. Death is the sneering triumph of the material relapse to stiff immovability. Death hints to the hopeful psychology of the blossoming Christmas spring as deceiving and illusionary. Death takes back with strong hand its ruthless government over the corporeal and material existence. The mornful sadness and the low and slow sounds of the music of death express the extreme oppression, the perfect helplessness of our human nature in regard to the proud and high prospects which we had before for our lasting corporeal idealization. Death means the definite proof of the interruption and destruction of our lasting mechanical and intellectual usefulness. If life before succeeded in producing continual wonderful circulation of energy in the whole real world, if the breath of the living magnetic energy inflamed the human muscular body and nervous susceptibility to continual work, to excellent efforts and growing material and intellectual concentration, in former times, then all these functions finish in the moment of death. To stark stiffness, coldness and immovability is the useful, hopeful and marvellous instrument of the material body surrendered again. The individual and localized intellectual victory over death, which seemed to be fixed before, is destroyed again, and the body has lost definitely and unmistakably all its living chances by being dissolved into its atoms which will form new physical and chemical connections.

It is just the idea of Easter to emphasize this last fact. For Easter is the festival of *Resurrection,* of rivival and of re-incarnation. It expresses most clearly and generally the fact that which was dead rises again to new life, that after the night of desperation and the shameful ruin of destruction in death, always the new spring of regeneration in hope, in inspiration and life must be expected. The chemical and physical energy is the special law and way, by which all new life begins to work out. As long as we have physical and chemical life and the possibilities of physical and chemical transformations and permutations in anybody or anything, we cannot say that there is no revival and *no re-incarnation.* Physical and chemical laws are the primordial stages of the divine regular inspiration of the real world, but even the most refined sentimental energies going through the universe and through our life are surely of physical and perhaps as well of chemical description. Even if the chemical and physical transformations of our visible world are only dim, lazy processes in comparison with the highly involved and extremely potential, vibrating energy of the life, the light and the sentimental movements, they are at the root the same, both being different degrees of vitality, and we recognize already in this that death, even in the organic and anorganic world is thoroughly impossible.

Is not death to be considered as spiritual birth, and birth, on the contrary, in a relative sense, as spiritual death? Thus birth is death, and death means birth in different alternating progression. If one disappears, the other emerges; if one goes up, the other sinks down. Spiritual and physiological life are two opposite waving movements, which cross each other in the moments of birth and death, the spiritual line conquering the upper hand in death and the real-intellectual line leading from the moment of birth. The two lines behave exactly like two interfering waves on top of a liquid and may easily be represented in a clear graphic way.

A frivolous free- thinker, as I conceived him at that time, asked me one day, what I thought of the human resurrection, if our dead body was chemically analyzed and divided into its last elements and if these elements were built up again into plants and grass and were eaten by animals. I forgot to tell this doubter that an earlier formal constitution may retrieve up to the last atom its strong claims and rights of material possession. In our postmortal chemical migration we are undoubtedly transformed, as to our bodies, into plant and animal. Perhaps the reverse relation is subjected to the Jewish prohibition from eating pork. In eating meat, we may not only assimilate animal bodies with their specific chemical and temperamental inclinations to our own nature, but we are in indirect danger to be cannibals. In restricting ourselves to *vegetarianism* we cannot escape this danger. It is obviously the will of nature that we cannot be without this *inter-metabolical communion*. Our whole metabolical existence has its root in the chemical assimilation and composition from the animal and vegetable world. If we scorn wrongly the animal meat because of its pretended lowering influence on our human nature, then we are even doomed to descend deeper and choose for our nutritive purpose the vegetables which are indeed still imperfect, more harmless because less efficient, perhaps more unworthy because more different from the peculiar human metabolism.

The idea of resurrection exhibits the general idea of imperishable life and of continual affective inspiration into our material earlier existence. No atom ever falls out from the universal communication of the magnetic energy. All our life and surroundings are and will be in intimate contact with more or less glimpses of divine energy pervading all created nature and never losing its general and individual vibrating, vivifying, special application. The higher spiritual form is stronger and has easy resuscitating chances, if it continues to exist.

If death throws our highest sentimental hopes back to the inferior degrees of the visible laws of physical and chemical energy, we never are entitled to lose the splendid prosecution of rising again and of reaching once more in the future time the same and perhaps even the better development of high divine re-inspirations. The death, it is true, destroys the hopeful individual body and the destruction of this individual divine human confinement seems to be definite. But nature which has succeeded in creating this wonderful specimen of high association of material and affective components, is not lost, but produces again and again new similar masterpices, tempting to carry through its high developing universal conceptions in idealizing the material nature. If the indivdual is not able to maintain his persevering existence, it is at least the privilege of the collectiveness to keep on the continuation through all future times and ages. Here lies the deep idea of Easter, here lies the hope of our death and here is taken away the tremendous sting of death.

If the highest personal genial elaboration as we had it in the religious hero, exceeds the possibility of the real incarnation, if the affective life of the human individual is at last so great and wonderfully important that it is no more able to stand the individual earthly confinement and existence, then we have to think that its memory and magnetic force leads to best influences on our general collective historic life, that it falls down like a charming rain, fertilizing and uplifting by its memory and glory, the total following humanity. This is the meaning of the resurrection of the religious genius that his ideal force cannot be lost, that his divine example runs through all following centuries and invites and inspires by his magnetic energy all men coming into this world.

The consequence of our collective universal unity cancels the importance of our personal pride and claim and we must willingly be ready to go through all stages of the inferior and superior chemical and physical laws again, as we did it before we were human beings. The universal modest love is the fundamental character of our greatness; if we are willing and prone to develop gladly again through all degrees of creative specific existence, if we accept fairly at all times the will of the last creative energy in pervading continuously the whole scale of the kaleidoscopic scale of the real world, then we are most ready and most apt to climb quickly again the mounting ladder of divine elevation. It is understandable that the human individual clings to the high creative score of divine values which he has reached and by which he has been lifted over the created surroundings. But there is no reason naturally speaking to assume that even in this connection there will not be ever relapses; the threatening stone of Sysiphus seems to bear as well on this human divine metamorphosis as on all other creative changes and values. There are always relapses, always victories, but also always defeats. There is perhaps, never any right to assume any definitely fixed result. Falling back is as natural as going ahead. The law of the waving universal vibration finds its application even in the highest goals of the human nature which falls back again and again to the most primitive stages of physical and chemical natural manifestations in smashing all individual human existence, but which as well swings up again to the topmost culminations of complicated divine affective perfections of tremendous dignity, as we find it in the highest degree within the divine genial hero. The inferior and higher degrees of animated existence, as we find them in all manifestations of the creative values in minerals, in plants, in animals, in men and spirits, are only different real sizes and conditions of the same interspheric energy which has, like a huge wave, as it were, its different quantitative shapes and qualities and creates accordingly different, real adaptions and manifestations of the corresponding life-force: the stone contains the smallest affective quantity, the plant more, the animal approaches already the human affective contents and the human individual is already near the eternal spirits in his affective-quantitative or qualitative standard. Everyone of these real affective confinements is the adequate expression and right intellectual manifestation of the ascending and falling down wave of the vibrating interspheric affectivity. In every one of these remarkable real needs, we recognize the equal crystallization of the single amount of universal magnetic energy which, according to the peculiar will of the universal purpose has been imprisoned in it. The different, real species of creative values represent each for itself a certain quantity of universal magnetism which has the appropriate creative combination and the individual adequate intellectual enunciation, and, as it were, chemical coagulation. If this individual specific union has gone by death, then we have the dissolution of this specific magnetic amount, then the spirit of creative God, for a little while concentrated and imprisoned into this living individual, flees away and forms again other creative coagulations which we do not know. There seems to be no guarantee whether we are after death charming sparkles of the divine breath going into the definite union with the last theistic energy or if we find again inferior or superior intellectual expressions of our mind, whether the amount of our life-force we have received as human beings, will be divided and formed several inferior, intellectual-real expressions in the vegetable or animal world, or if we shall form one part of any future higher spirit superior in quantitive life-force. If these things may happen we have at all times to be subjected to the will of the universal God. It is not at all the possibility of any philosophical system to decide on these future events of our interspheric destiny.

One thing will be sure that our future destiny will be just because it will be true and legal in the sense of the universal will. And there is no doubt, moreover, that we are the more apt to join higher intellectual expressions when we are more modest and adaptable to the secrecy of the magnetic laws of the universe and have performed the best, the high possibilities of our superior human natural components. The strong terminal theistic longing coming out from the divine practice of our life has both advantages, the superior readiness for higher magnetic expressions after death and the strong glorious memory within the following humanity. The rain of the widespread divine persuasion falling down on the collective humanity before and after the death of the just, has the most remarkable power and represents in itself the sweetest gratitude and allowed self-glorification of the individual. These are the two sources of the good human life which nobody can take away, the good instradation of future higher divine elevation and the splendid memory in the following real world.

The high consolation of Easter would not be necessary if the Good Friday had not destroyed the charming hopes of Christmas. The meaning of Easter is, therefore, to reestablish the superior hopes of Christmas, broken up by the following cruel death of the Lord. Easter is the confirmation of Christmas, it makes the positive pulling balance after the depression of the mortal real annihilation of the human hero. This revival has the meaning of the re-establishment of the consterned universal progress which has been frightened and pushed back by the terrible fact of the death. Easter helps us to find again the universal law of collective progression, it opens our eyes to further future ideal elevation and it quickens our hearts to accept the further rising development even of the natural confinement of the world which in the death has arrived at the lowest real degree of relapse. Easter points out that this state of retrograde downfall, as it is given in death, has only the meaning of the transitional waving depression of the universal progression, that after death life arises in the collective sense again and that we have all reasons to assume new future divine re-inspirations and re-incarnations after having joined and passed the sad stiffness and immovability of the lifeless exitus.

We are by no means dead if our body dies, but we have not any more joined the eternal terminal goals if we have reached the divine inspirations of our life. We are continually subjected to further waves of the future progression fluctuating continually between the two poles of divine aspirations and material dissolution. There are and will be deaths and resurrections, charming progressing births, disappointing material relapses, but again and again after all, the reconciliation of new birth or the re-incarnation or resurrection follows as well.

Easter would not have any meaning if not in the material revival of the body. The ideal part of our nature does not need any resurrection, it is after death the more free and active in its independent affective enlargement. But the real material part, which relapsed so hideously from the inspired psychic alliance, needs the consolation and the reaffirmation which is given within the fact of Easter. Like Christmas turns on the miraculous fact of the bodily real confinement of the eternal affective world descending from heaven and abiding within the visible limits of earthly existence, so Easter points to the "re-incarnation" of the body discarded in the fact of death. Easter supplies the hope that this corporeal negligence of our nature will be gathered again from its chemical and physical dissolution, that new natural compositions of this material will arise and that there is even the vista that one day the mortal degradation will be again the opportunity and the natural basis of future divine vivifications and inspirations.

All natural beings are continually mingled, nature hates the secluding aristocracy of material specification, the spirit of God breathes where it will and lives where it will. It makes the formal shapes continually out of the stuff of all primitive created nature, it chooses its real form from the mineral, vegetable, animal, and human dead remnants and builds up in the most dense and most clearly connected net, always again, all kinds of ideal gradually different species. It mingles the remnant shape of the highest, cultural, human being after his death between the lowest ones, gives our body as food to the flies and worms and transforms as well the inferior beings into the highest organism of the reasonable world. So we see that we serve in the constituent building of metabolism the more primitive organization of the created world, but we recognize also that we assimilate into our specific nature all lower zoological and vegetable organisms. We are able to maintain and sustain the real life of every plant and of every animal which sucks its real force possibly out of our dissimilated dead body, but we need them as well for our organic real existence. We may say, therefore, that we, in the circulation of all metabolic chemical and physical energies meet continuously ourselves because we eat plants and meat which has the most intimate connection with our former fellowmen.

It may be just the idea of separating more perfectly our real animal part from being the direct physical and chemical vehicle of further earthly metabolism which raised the idea of CREMATION. It is the anxious care of keeping the very highest degree of long metabolistic separation of the dead human body from the further physical and chemical circulation of the organic created earth, which must have infused the longing for cremation. It must be the pronounced desire for the individual sentimental apotheosis and the wish of the complete seclusion of the human body from the future metabolistic circulation which has dictated the idea of cremation. And it seems true indeed that the conflagrant destruction of the human body by the fire is the more suitable ex-expression of the direct and definite, terminal, theistic creed. It is surely further away from the idea of low re-incarnation, of the opinion that all material life must be the continual servant of the creative metabolistic circulation and that our body has the same fate as any other created material chemical confinement to decay and to be built up again pervading the long chain of the multiple variety of the future unorganic and organic world. The fire of the cremation is nearer the idea of the spiritual resurrection which shows us Christ as the spiritualized body going through all worlds and doors, overcoming all real resistance and shining like the most wonderful, atmospheric, burning phenomenon.

On the other hand we will not forget that this burning process and glaring fire are also only oxydative changes of the real physical and material world, that every fire changes and communicates with the living conditions of all surrounding world and we are sure that even the most solid urns will crumble one day, if they are not in an earlier future crashed by earthquakes or warriors or by any accident or contractors who dispose of the obsolete stones as welcome material for their houses and buildings. Then these ashes which were so carefully hidden from the quickly progressing organic metabolism will be parts of stone and walls. The wall decays and will be weather-beaten, in its turn, and serves so the organic life, if not already earlier winds and clinging flowers avail themselves of this nutritive manure.

Upon the whole cremation turns, therefore, out to be more closely connected to the spiritual dogmatism, following nearest the direct metaphysical metamorphosis of the miraculous body of the religious hero into light and fire and excluding more efficiently the inferior metabolistic future changes of the unorganic and organic world, up to a certain degree. *Interment* has the more broad-minded conception, it is also idealistic allowing without serious opposition all laws of chemical, physical and organic and unorganic description to start their work immediately within the dead body and pushing the decaying human material forward to new future chemical and physical work. The idea of interment represents, therefore, the more modest and more earthly conception of the bodily role partaking again and again in the promiscuous workshop of the real earthly existence. The tendency to idealizing separation of the corpse from further chemical and physical mingling with the surrounding world is pronounced, not only in the first Christian times, but even in the monasteries until today. The *Catacombs* were holes hewn in rocks which gave the utmost guarantee perhaps, much more than the moveable and exposed urns of the cremation to hide and seclude the dead body from the surrounding world and to limit the decaying physical and chemical process at least to the remnants of the corpse and to its nearest surroundings. Even this hurting, dissolving metamorphosis is by the idealistic church, in the burial of the monks and nuns intentionally retarded and diminished, by the use of chalk and other preservatives so that we are able to find out, from that circumstance, the longing of the Christian believer to reduce, to the utmost possible, the fading dissolution of the idealized material of the human body. But all these small differences end of course, after all, very alike. The process of the complete, organic decay of the corpse will reach its goal nevertheless in order that the immediate change of the material remnants of the human being into fire and ashes must perhaps be acknowledged as the more perfect form of idealistic burial. But in the scientific sense of conception of Easter, of resurrection of the flesh and of re-incarnation, the interment must be the burial of the best choice permitting, in the most liberal disposition of the nearest real universe, to use our corpses physically and chemically in the most promiscuous sense, starts with their elements again in the most inferior degrees and pervades once more the whole range of the creative nature: interment clings to earth and its creative variety, whilst cremation shows the distinctly higher idealistic aspirations in producing the energy of fire and warmth in the most terminal immaterial form.

The delay of forty days from Easter to *Pentecost* is very significant for the following festival. The insertion of a certain space of time between Easter and Pentecost has the meaning of the historic elaboration given within the religious organization. The festival of Pentecost represents, therefore, the inspiration of the historic ages of divine fulfillment, after the death of the religious hero.

In this light we at last begin to distinguish and to interpret the sense of the Christian TRINITY. Remembering our solstitial conception, we recognize the Father as the monotheistic central sun point, on which everything turns and is attracted to. The Son is the solstitial point of the returning ellipse of the historic psychological human sun-year. He transfers the former digressing, intellectual quarter and he changes the cold, anti-theistic withdrawal into the new future affective sentimental approach of the humanity towards the central goal. This magnetic affective power binding and moving the intellectual humanity again back to the monotheistic idea is called HOLY GHOST. His representation as a dove flying through the air expresses the essential of his quality to be the magnetic energy of the religious organization. For him the forwarding and insinuating force of the wings is quite characteristic. The church is so fond of the sentimental affirmation of the monotheistic central feelings, the church puts so much stress on the monocentric direction and prevalence of our magnetic life-force that it attributes to this pulling magnetism towards the theistic centre the dignity of God himself. The Holy Ghost has accurately the meaning of monotheistic sentimental magnetism to which the historic Christian humanity is subjected. The Holy Ghost in the sense of the church is the magnetic energy which pulls the post-solstitial humanity back to the equinoctial point. He is the compressive manifestation of all centripetal monotheistic emanation of divine love. The Holy Ghost is, therefore, synonymous to the sentimental part of the human force; he is the affective mediator between humanity and divinity; he is the oppositional force to the later intellectual future historic progression of the human universal fate, and he is the sentimental force which withholds us from being scattered into the surrounding universe of intellectual progress, instantaneously: he is the concentrating magnetic power which compresses and thrills always again, through the delicious individual and collective contraction of the human life-force to punctual monotheistic attentions and charms.

We are reminded by this trinitarian meditation of the three Parques giving, weaving and cutting up the thread of human fate. But we have here different conceptions. Godfather also is the giving power, the eternal source from which all living water of energy flows and from which, if we will cling to the comparison of the antique representation of our fatal development, the truth of our affective life is again returning in the intra or extra-theistic historic monotheism. The antique cutting of the yarn by the death has the corresponding validity for the individual, material and egoistic conception of the life which has indeed the most abrupt end, in the fact of the exitus. But here we speak about the collective and sentimental or spiritual general human fate. We meditated already before that Christ, in the history of the spheric humanity, is the needle's eye through which the human fate is transferred and through which the yarn of the magnetic effusion is comprised and compressed and deducted back or reduced again to the monotheistic centre. So we must conceive Christ as the historic weaver's loom of the sentimental first Christian centuries. According to the organization, to the distance and the mechanical conditions of this weaver's loom all psychological tissues of this working energy received and conveyed the typical character, form and validity. God, the Father, is the producing source of all divine raw material. He supplies the silk and the wool of the creative world, for the tremendously great workshop of human psychic force. He at the end claims and receives again the elaborated production brought altogether to His heavenly shelter.

But the thriving and forwarding energy which makes continually running the yarn of the human fate from one theistic goal to the other by the intermediating weaver's loom of the genial doctrine is called the Holy Ghost in the sense of the monotheistic Christian church. Christ is the formal monogenial principle, the Holy Ghost, the forwarding energy pushing the magnetic life through this formalistic eye of a needle. The magnetic thorough energy of the theistic world is the inspiring force moving the weaver's loom itself, being the reason of its necessity and movements, receiving from it the rhythm of psychodynamic regulation. Christ means the pendulum of the intra-ecclesiastic historic energy in so far as it empties into the human fate. The Holy Ghost is the most powerful spring of the universal interspheric energy imparting with his strong sway the motions of all stars, of all planets, earth and moon, but also of the human feelings and thoughts. This is the right and impartial universal conception of what we should call the Holy Ghost. It is the self-willing conception of the historic, stable genial organization, if it accepts the Holy Ghost only in the attracting centremagnetic direction and declines him in the centrifugal intellectual digression. The interspheric magnetic energy has the most extended will and power, and all the following differentiations and aversions of the partial amounts and opposite magnetic avidities of the universal magnetism, in the effect go back and return to the most precious fundamental energy of the unitarian universal Holy Ghost.

We meditated already the idea of holiness. But we should recognize extra-historic or future holiness also. *Holiness* is most closely historically bound in the ecclesiastic conception, the saint of future being killed and crucified and hung today because he is not understood and cannot be in conformity with the present legal power, and, perhaps, necessarily. The saint of the future is one type of the criminal of today and the heroic criminal of the past is the universally acknowledged saint of our ages. In the notion of the Holy Ghost we have this principle of historic division and discrimination transferred even to the root of all life, to the magnetic energy of the universe. As long as it is outside of the human fate within the extra-human universe, we behave in a passive or admiring attitude towards this universal magnetic spring. But as soon as it, through the mechanism of the Christian weaver's loom which is to say, through Christ, enters into the approaching attraction of the monotheistic peculiar eddy, the church as the real and historic guard and stewart of the Christian idealistic bequeathment decries the digressing intellectual part as unholy (Christ is the cornerstone) and excludes instead the historic "anti-theistic" affirmative concentrative part of the universal energy. In the sense of the ecclesiastic stewart of the historic monotheism, there is no greater crime than the principal obstruction against the theistic concentration, than the oppositional negation to the sentimental historic localization of the psychological emphasis. We already know from former meditations, how much this historic eternal fixation of humanity is impossible and how much everything even in psychology is exhaustible, needs new functions and intellectual expressions, how the whole universe and with it the human spheric sun-year continually must be enlarged. The artistic, esthetic and economic interest of the church, however, is willing to fix this historic, monotheistic gathering of the human affective life-force forever. This magnetic concentration in itself is called the action of the Holy Ghost and all diverging intellectual, extrasolar digression is called in the sense of the church, unholiness and sin. Any perfect metamorphosis into a drifting affectionate habitual love for divinity will be recognized as holy and good and the aversion to the historic progression is always a local misunderstanding but never an efficient lasting objection.

The Pentecostal idea has, therefore, merely narrow ecclesiastic intentions. The historic institution of the church strives to lead all psychological capacity of humanity into the channel of its sentimental affirmation regarding and praising all these ideal centrodirecting magnetic forces as the effusion of the Holy Ghost and rejecting all extra-historic universal intellectual digressions as criminal and antitheistic deviations. This is the meaning of the fiery tongues coming down at Pentecost from heaven on the Christian community, this was the sense of the buzzing wind at this day that universal interspheric energy emptied, in a very considerable amount, into the graceful channels of the Christian church and that the strongest psychodynamic energy of the historic psychological humanity rushed from the inspiring solstitial Christian starting point like the glaring tail of a comet prevalently towards the monotheistic centre. The fiery tongues and the whirling winds around the house of the first Christians express the strong affective concentration of the human psychopupil into the future strong focus of the monotheistic idea, the rushing obstreperous energy means the new starting psychodynamic, magnetic, sentimental force over-skipping and domineering the former intellectual digressions and the logical steps of the human disposition and compressing itself at once in the punctual light-field of the divine monotheistic enthusiasm of the Christian historic conception. The great importance of the Christian historic conception lies in the monotheistic accurateness and exactitude of the size and of the goal of the ideal last idea, in the scholastic confinement of the last divine values and we could not express this confession and this truth better than exactly in the visible uplifting symbol of the mystic fiery tongues which enraptured the believing followers and adherents through the psychodynamic rush of the most energetic angry concentration and contraction of their psychopupil.

To be or not to be, that is the question!
Shakespeare

EIGHTH BOOK

If there is no doubt about the HISTORIC existence of Christ, mentioning such a weighty witness as Tacitus, we on the other side and in detail, cannot accept this question so easy as the existence of Napoleon, who is often quoted as an example of equal historic truth. Is it not sure that history can be made and undone, up to a certain degree, by organized advertisement, and that humanity can put an eternal lamp of ever lasting commemoration or a tombstone of concealing forgetfulness on anybody's grave?

The historic side however is very subordinate in comparison with the *spiritual* nature of the question. Spirituality means centrifugal gravitation or anti-gravitation. Those universal attractive forces, which try to beckon to you out of the confinement of your individual historic categoric fixation in egotism, are called spiritual. Since all inter-universal signalization is done by the interference of monopunctual concentration, we understand, that egotism and spiritual action are gradual steps of the same psychological development, so that a certain self-centredness is indispensable for spiritual success.

It is, in a sense, an essential mistake against the deepest law of any religion, to quarrel about its historic contents. He who hurts love, contradicts religion. Hatred is obstructed spiritual activity. It is the repercussion of the positive love.

The *historic side of religion has the meaning* to fix and emphasize the reality of the spiritual world. In the very action of quarrelling about the historic part of religion we risk to unroot the intention of the religious founder, who intended love, kindness and purity of the heart. He subordinated entirely the historic side of religion to the eternal spiritual love which it serves. The justification of the historic fixation of religion is given in the acknowledgeable will to build strong and lasting spiritual obligations within the short-sighted categories of the material world. The historic religion is intended to oblige the ungifted realist to keep spiritual laws. Yet where historic compulsion is necessary, we might have to expect little in spiritual success. Love is greater than historic legislation, and intellectual reasoning. The best spirituality comes from the sincerity of the individual freedom and goes to heaven.

If religions quarrel mutually, then they emphasize too much the formal, secondary part of their composition. Is the reason that the religions so often hate each other, in the name and for the love of God, their lack of spiritual strength, and the fact that their conceptions are too narrow and too much really and intellectually crystallized so that they cannot find joining and reconciling bridges of the heart?

And yet there stands at any event the DIVINE NECESSITY. Any culture has to have a hierarchic structure and a leading genius. If we would not accept one divine hero, there would be countless heroes growing like mushrooms over night, puzzling the magnetic needle of unity and order. The security of society would be shaken. The legislative direction and stability would be perfectly lost. Here lies the great importance of the divine authority and the mono-genius. All mono-symbolic reactions are more the product of constructive necessity and organizing force than of objective truth. Our objective thinking instruments are too short to reach the terminal roofs of mono-symbolic actions. We find out what is necessary and useful, where our thinking power is doubtful. The understanding of universal necessities and their application reaches farther than the clear intelligence of their objective truth.

Necessity gives to us quicker decisions than the philosophical thought, which however, may have more absolute truth, though dragging in hesitation.

Are force and organization perhaps the greater revelation than thought? But the weakness of the force is, at any rate, to have chosen, and the strength of the thought is the preserved freedom of unlimited possibilities. The more future possibilities, the less danger to be lost in a rut of old customs or of perishing in obstruction. There rises again the idea if theory or experience is more promising, instructive and just? Experience shows the better method, it demonstrates how to do; theory and thought improve the existing goal in revising and criticizing it.

The intellectual thinking oscillations go on in philosophical minds. There is no end of our psychological research work. Not the historic fact, but the effect of different conceptions constitutes the interest of this book.

The MONOPERSONALITY of the religious genial conception is of course of the most essential importance. There may be scarcely any other question which had so much influence on the psychology of the past centuries and about which so hard struggles always have been and will be fought still. These questions are not only most interesting from the philosophical and psychological standpoint, but they have indeed the most deciding influence in the *educational sense*. According as we accept the monopersonal and polypersonal order of the religious hero, we shall have quite different methods and results of the practical education.

Any symbolism is the product of contradictions, whirlpools of two meeting oppositions. Monosymbolism is the product of this truth as we saw, monogeniality of the historic genius comes about also as the consequence of two very pronounced opposite directions of different psychic cultural parents as we meditated before. This strong exclusive formation of two opposite forces representing all other near psychic and real conditions behind them and wrestling with each other around one genial centre, is the logical product of the historic progression. These monological formations are exceedingly rare, the real world being the continual foundation of the most outspread variety and of all incredible and indescribable shades and digressions in thought and sentiments. But we must admit that also the theoretic psychological world strives to do this remarkable logical genial *monoism,* and we know that just at the historic time of the solstitial moment of the fulfilment of the antique intellectual quarter, the conversion from the intellectual to the sentimental psychological spheric direction of the world created necessarily most genial sentimental individuals, as there is no doubt about, if we read the gospels, the letters of the Apostles and the history of the first Christian centuries. But reality seldom takes things so punctually in the large way. The millinarian psychological human sun-year had at this ideal moment of course one highest genial point, as it happened undoubtedly in Christ as the ideal culmination of the genial selection of men forming together the peculiar psychological leading conversion of the historic intellectual one-sidedness towards sentimental compensation.

If this monoism is rare in the movable mental world, then we have much less to expect that in the real material world only quite isolated outstanding perfections in individual performances and forces will happen. The will of the created nature is most liberal in varieties, lavishing in number and inventive in real representations, but all creative individuals together mean only the most variable expression of any creative specific intention. The real individual is one of the numberless shots to the target of the real creation; they are innumerable and all different, but only by small gradual steps, one individual possessing a little more, the other one a little less life-force, one being more gifted in the ideal and sentimental, the other more in the real intellectual, scientific and possessive way. The religious genius may be indeed the best hit of the creative target of all historic ages.

We understand very well that the modern time does not discuss any longer about the historic religious doctrine if it is averse to it, but chooses much more to drop this discussion, and to go away along their own path. There is no more seducive intellectual affirmation than the position of the monopersonal genial historic personality. The surest evasion from this notion is indeed avoiding its discussion. The name of the religious genius has become the usual symbol, the automatical mouthpiece by which whole generations and centuries shot their love to the universe, this method has fixed itself very strongly in the suggestion of all these nations, and people have become most efficient in the further acceptance of the divine monopersonality. We ordinarily are not aware how much the cultural power of any suggestion can rise and how strong its compulsion on our society and individuals may become. But just here we have the most pronounced example of such a general sentimental persuasion, in the symbolic love of the Mediterranean and European humanity.

The total concentration of all the psycho-mechanic energy into the great personality of the religious genius was an idealizing necessity, to have all the old suggestive cultures united and powerfully put together in the personal symbol of the individuality of this one genius. Theoretically full of human logic, affectively heavy with the concentrated culture of a whole world, the affectivity united in the personality of one genial man alone has the enormous energy of the affective gunpowder into which all intellectuality has been changed. From the standpoint of beauty, art, of the overwhelming influence on our nature, this genial summary setting of all affective concentrating energies at the point of the fulfilment of times is a perfect masterpiece. It is in the passion where the genial collection of the strongest affective processes and necessities of the time into this only divine person, was melted to the most artistic individual, universal and unitarian picture, true beautiful and most emotional. The personal artistic amalgamation of the suffering genius means a very strong affective help and a sure attractive power to divine magnetic intentions and goals. Nobody, whoever came across this phenomenon by fate, birth or development, passed by without feeling the exceeding grasping power of the hero. Not only he was great, but he found also great friends to fix and maintain his glory. We have the most efficient combination of numerous highly gifted people with a genial inclination, meeting one another at the same time and at the same place, what is very seldom, and we have simultaneously, what is the chief thing, a tremendous affectively concentrating urge of the compensatorily, intellectually exhausted historic time, which nobody could resist. The divine stooped with the energy and the magnetic force of a lightning on the heads and hearts of the genial apostles.

The great religious genius is the concentrated symbolism of the strongest affective sentiments and ideas, by which all together are and were most shaken. He is the historic and intellectual opportunity of gathering and compressing together into a wonderful genial unity of one individual the chief ideas and sentiments of a whole culture meeting under the pressure of a mighty magnetic suggestion, at the important verge of a grand change of the life of the soul of nations, at the fulfilment of ages.

Even if the historic features of the religious hero were not true, still he would keep his whole validity. For religious psychology does not deal with history, but with eternity. If somebody would complain to have been cheated and would be angry about the teachings of the apostles and the holy writers, I thoroughly would rebuke this conception. There may be scarcely a word in the whole compilation which is not in the clearest and most skilful way adapted to all scientific dates if we only don't change the deep and proper meaning of the notions. These descriptions are even so artistically done, that they still keep their whole weight for that who is not able to grasp the deep philosophic sense and the intellectual value, and edify that by a creed, who is not able to analyze them intellectually. The linguistic new terminology is so perfect and elaborate, that the persistent use of more imaginative terms and notions creates, as it were, an upper story of a symbolic and simplified human history of life which has lost the convincing reality of flesh and blood, but has instead gained more idealistic sentiments. It is not owing to any cheating manoeuvres on the side of the holy writers, that they are misunderstood continually, as we shall see always again, but it is because of the difficult task they had proposed to themselves, and the enormous extension of the province whose elaboration they had to do, it is owing to the constant everlasting superiority of affective standards and the narrow value of the exclusive real intellectuality, that they were not at all in a situation to produce a very distinct human personality, but rather automatically blurred and hid it in order not to take away the overwhelming genial validity, not to diminish the general affective contents by an exact and peripheric intellectual compensation.

He who has eyes to see, may look and he who has ears to hear, may listen. We are entitled to use our intellectual faculties even here, if we are not lulled by the sweet drug of religious drunkenness, what indeed is, and must be, the purpose of the psychomechanistic acceleration of religion perhaps, the first, last and only right of existence of professional and confessional religious organization. But if one is not able to put into the imaginative and symbolic language of the holy books, the scientific language of his own analyzing *heart,* then he still has in the artistic make-up the affective elevation of a mysterious world, *a charming faith,* which satisfies so much as we understand, but for concentrating affective energy surely is more powerful and preferable.

The loss of the scientific probability of one personal Christ, since an individual small wire is always insufficient for the national total power of magnetic energy and discharge, is balanced and equalled by the mighty affective attraction, by the overwhelming energy of His charming personality and by the circumstance, that an idea which could not attract in a state of dilution many individuals, certainly may do so in the concentration of one genial point.

Are not the discussions about the share in the most powerful idea of God useless? Is it not quite wrong to assume, if not already this question is too frivolous, that the religious genius exactly must be the whole God and that there is not any more important and deeper and more divine particle in the whole universe? Is God a person? Has he space, has he a bottom or an end? So that we ever could say: this being is God, he is such a great part of God, or he is not. For saying, that somebody is the second or third part of the Divinity, we ought to know the weight and size of the totality, but we are quite at a loss to guess at any, whatever description of the importance of the universal God. If God has no limits and cannot be exhausted, then it is quite wrong, if we assert, that the hero is wholly God; or is not his life-force yielded to be intellectually exhausted and limited within his psychopupilar constitution? The idea of a localization of all God on earth in one individual person is a strange conception. But perhaps more surprising is the fact that we undertake to quarrel about questions like this which are quite outside of our judgment. Here is the question of the deep philosophical basis of the whole human nature and of the universe where we rather play a ridiculously small role and of course have no right or possibility or entitled expectation to concentrate all glory of the universal God which is always equally omnipresent as we learned as small children and believe it still today, except in a potential way.

But there is no difference between a conception of the hero as a true or an *emblematical God.* Questions and distinctions whether *the religious genius is true God or not,* derived from that,

that our logic is corrupted, that we have not sufficient psychological and natural scientific thinking and recognition, and above all, because there is established an opposition of insurmountable qualitative difference where it is permitted to admit only a distance between intellectual and universal values.

The *monogenial* conception gives to the hero the honor to describe him as the original true proprietor of all the qualities ascribed to him.

The *polypersonal conception* of the religious genius assumes that we are enticed continually to ascribe to him the whole sum of the psychic faculty and skill of many other people together in order that we have in him a genial compression and concentration of the genial performance of several great men and or of a whole period. It is understandable that people arrive by this method to a quite extraordinary conception of the divine quality of the religious genius, as very far away from our personal life-force and not at all comparable to the small efficiency of a single other man. But we must remember, as we pointed out already, that an affective genial power as it is ascribed to the monopersonal religious genius, could never stand the frail building of the normal human body. But you see exactly in this, that he really and indeed is not a "man, but a God," say the friends of the monopersonal divine conception of the universal genius: another could not have stood his divine force, but he could do it, because he indeed was God." The polypersonal party answers to this that the religious genius could neither psychologically nor organically be a man if he was a being of the utmost overwhelming genial nature and weight, and there was no reason nor even possibility to imprison such a great affective giant into such a small frail cell as the human, individual, organic body and intellectual nature always essentially must be. But the monopersonal side replies to that that the religious genius was all God and for this reason he was able to do everything, he even was able to achieve the miracle to become himself a regular man at the same time as a most perfect God, which last circumstance, created and adopted by genial compression, must always be the ready and willing permission to explain every reasonable difficulty only with a miracle. Will we assert that the religious genius was a man as others are," the polypersonalists say, "then he was not an absolute universal Divinity, and if we on the contrary admit that he was a mighty God he could not be at the same time a man, as little as we could imprison the space of all universe into the small dust of our earth or as little as we could discharge the energy of a huge cannon through a barrel of brown paper." The monopersonalists point out that it is not the unbelievable magnomalia and the conceit of humanity, but the eternal incredible love of the universal God, which moved him to send his equivalent son unto earth and that for this quite partial love for humanity he did the miracle, to give not only to the earth, but to the human body of Christ the extraordinary resistence and capacity of universal terminal possibilities. The polypersonal conception on the contrary is able to explain all rising difficulties in the reasonable natural way. Christ according to it is the idealistic top of a magnetic genial pyramid formed by the four giants who are situated as unperishable literary monuments at the four corners of the pyramid in form of a man, an eagle, a bull and a lion. The division of the genial concentration of Christ makes his theoretic personality understandable as man and as God and analyzes his mysticism into clear understanding *unsophisticated* argumentations—with a potential rest.

The terminal ideal figure of *Christ is the wonderful top of the genial pyramid* of the solstitial conversion of his cultural time. The synopsis of the four evangelists means exactly the common genial magnetism of their psychological actions by which they augmented and emphasized all in the same way the idealistic contents of their historic hero who served them as paradigma and sample of their magnetic human idealization. If modern scholars will find out that none of the gospels was written before the second century, this speaks in favor of the fact that the gospels were inspired by the first religious hero, and that he was not the ideal consequence of their congenial collaboration. It is their common identic idealistic tendency and the remarkable one-sided sentimental conception of their heroic contemporary subject which makes the chief thing in the four gospels, whereas the individuality of the hero moves towards the background. This common divine charm pervading through all four gospels in the same manner, this eternal inspiration which fills up all four holy writers makes the essence of the Christian greatness. Their common sentimental outstanding magnetism is the riddle, the core and the intention of their doctrine. We find here the divine idealization of all common most general human values. There is no doubt about the divine quality of the character of the individual who has been put so much into the idealistic focus of the sentimental monotheistic philosophy of the holy genial writers, but it is not so important to apotheose this collective concentrated individual as our idol, it is much more the question of imitating and following the divine trace of his genial nature in the utmost degree as we are able to. Not he who says

Master, Master, shall enter into the Kingdom of Heaven, but he who does his commandments.

We are true brothers of Christ, he is not only our *emblematic* example. He is indeed our unique and first-born family member from which we all may draw out uplifting urges. Is it not the most serious educational discouragement even to drive us away from the essential kernel of our divine nature by the assertion of the merely emblematic example of Christ? All divine features in Christ are indeed also human and there has nothing desirable been put into his genial description which is not also attainable and imitable by the collectivity of all other human individuals.

We easily see that all these questions are nearest the *educational* problems of humanity. What is the intention and the task of every religion? What purpose has the Christian idea towards humanity? The deepest longing of every religion must be to make bridges towards the divinity from the individual humanity. In the sense of our former psychodynamic conception we have to express this idea so that we must expect every religion to build strong and solid genial barrels through which the human individual discharges best his affective energy towards the eternal idealism. The universal goal and the ideal magnetism attracting and aimed by this psychomechanism is that which we call God. The ideal efficacy of the religion is, therefore, so much stronger the more the religious system succeeds in building exact goals.

But let us make a more principal reflection on the idea of MONOSYMBOLISM. In all our displays we have conceived it as the most concentrated whirlpool of our affective nature, going through the smallest, attractive, symbolic mouth towards the universal idealism. The causal makeup of every whirlpool is the existence of two opposite energies meeting each other, working against each other in two opposite directions of flowing draught, and competing toward further progression, in a new compromising direction. The eddy is the product of this energetic antagonism. Without opposite forces, there is no eddy in the water, but also no where else. The makeup of the affective whirlpool of the peculiar psychological nature has the same conditions. The monosymbolic idea may happen only under the antagonistic energies of the sentimental and intellectual powers of the affective human universe. It is the product of the opposite interference of ideal and real reactions within the human soul. The historic monosymbolic idea was always the product of the most embittered struggle between former idealistic and realistic forces; it pulled all its splendid power and strength from this former antagonistic wrestling and fades therefore away with the progressing time if it is not contradicted intellectually. Reality and intellectuality are the strong monosymbolic creative sources, within the affective progressing universe. The unreal and criticless universal progression of the human sentiments produce the unchecked slothful effusion towards the farthest universe. The next future station of the historic monosymbolism will be again another mighty whirlpool brought about by the powerful contradiction between progressing universal effective will and energetic categoric resistance, as it is given in intellectualism and real restriction. These are the conditions and suppositions for future new monosymbolic establishments, and without these antagonistic powers there would not be any further monosymbolic historic stagnation or contraction. Monosymbolism without intellectual reasoning investigation is not imaginable, and without the shadow of resistance could not be thought. The supposition for the ideal action is the existence of the material intellectualism and the acquaintance and existence of the bad devilish powers of the universe creates the immediate necessity of the monotheistic antagonistic saving God. These two opposite forces of the human experience create the whirlpool as the production of their contradicting magnetic energy which we call monosymbolism in our human conception, in the victorious progression of idealism.

If we exclude progressive intellectuality, we lose the conception of the monosymbolism at all. If we cling closely to the historic solstitial stability and if we do not permit any further development of affective and intellectual progression, then this historic monosymbolic whirlpool of the old time will become more and more shallow and will lose, at last, its convincing power and existence. But we see here obviously that there cannot be any standstill in the monosymbolic idea of the world. It needs continually new urges, affective invasions and intellectual resistances if it shall exhibit strong and vital existence later on. Any perfect monosymbolic standstill is in contradiction with the law of natural necessities which exact always new magnetic whirlpools in strong vital, proceeding, magnetic contradictions. The lasting historic crystallization and apotheosis of any monosymbolism is wrong. The historic punishment of the progressing universal magnetism means dead glorification and sterile mummification.

The perfect and exclusive canonization of the sentimental historic monosymbolism at the expense of the digressing intellectuality is, therefore, erroneous from the standpoint of the necessary and inevitable law of universal general interspheric progression. The exclusive conception of the Divine Grace has the meaning of the cheap fixation and stabilization of the historic monosymbolism. The notion of the ecclesiastic Holy Ghost is the expression of the traditional one-sided conservatism of the religious systematization. Everything is passing away and fading in the world of ours with the exception of quarrelling and of contradiction. If we are not willing to partake in this continual re-establishment and re-direction of new universal values, if we renounce to help in forming continual new intellectual expressions of the highest and lowest real manifestations of the progressing universe, then we lose the claim and the share in the future leading part of the world and are in the best case not even remembered as the weak adherents of an old worn-out system of ideas and tenets.

We see it in the religious genius, that the most convincedly digressing energetic personality of the historic time, the most decried individual and the most "illegal" person, in the sense of his time, has exactly the most chances to live a long time after the death of his "correct and legal" fellowmen in the memory of all humanity. The most sincerely digressing genius lives the longest time, he has afforded most collaboration to the brilliance of the revival and renewal of the monosymbolic idealism. The other geniuses risen during the centuries are paler, and they all have not succeeded in causing so deep and thorough contradicting energy from which the whirlpool of the human monotheism could have taken the same outstanding energy. They were less divine because they were less sincerely and intensely resisting the bad. They were the contemporary divines following the ruling system of their epoch, but faded away with their system on which they were drifting. They had some sweet peace and satisfaction during their life, but they had not the bitter contradiction of their contemporaries resulting after all in the uplifting of new, great universal leading progress and higher terminal glorification. Therefore, they fade away like grass and wither like flowers, they dry up like the matinal dew in the field, sparkling and smiling at their time, but short and insignificant.

MONOSYMBOLISM is for this reason much more efficient than *polysymbolism,* its result must be much more intense in the sense of the theistic idealism owing to the law of compensation. But it is also similar according as we accept the religious hero's genial monopersonality or polypersonality. If we accept him as the solstitial monopoint of the historic sentimental conversion, then we have in him the strong ideal instigation in the surest way, he representing one fixed point to which our look is directed and from which we receive all our affective urges. If people identify the

hero with the divinity of the late universe itself, if they exclude
all further divine development and see in him the last possibility
of human perfection, then the hero becomes identic with the monosymbolic barrel of our psychopupilar disposition. Then it is most
dependent on the mono- or poly-personal conception of the divine
symbolic value, whether we have the greater or smaller sureness
and instigation towards our idealistic theistic actions. From the
independent standpoint of the religion willing to produce and to
secure the utmost degree of terminal ideal facility and elaboration
in people, the monopersonality would be better in the last case.
The ideal shooting through one narrow barrel would be of course
much more efficient than the affective discharge by a whole system
of divine genial barrels of inferior degrees through which the explosive affective force is thrown out like through a sieve and is
scattered therefore in its energy. But we at the same time must
not forget that in the monosymbolic and monopersonal barrel and
divine shots, we have not only much more idealistic sureness and
higher ideal prospects, but that these shots could be at the same
time, too energetic, likely more dangerous, hurting, using the psychomechanic barrel and being much more exclusive and uncautious.
This last moment has, of course, the most considerable importance,
if we will criticize the value of mono- and poly-symbolic psychodynamic reactions.

There is no doubt that the monosymbolic conception is apt to
produce the most efficient and most elaborate idealism, within the
human society. From the merely terminal religious standpoint of
reaching most surely and most energetically divine goals, we instantly must admit that the monosymbolic conception is indeed
the most ideal and most divine one, pulling and directing all humanity to one suggestive central affective discharge easily, surely
and energetically most probable to exclude idealistic failures and
to reach high divine values. The polysymbolic conception has
less security of reaching idealism, but its advantage consists in the
more stable educational value.

Exactly punctual determination of the genial hero produces the
surest and most suggestive, solstitial roundabout way toward the
historic central monotheism. The monopersonal conception of the
religious genius has, therefore, the tendency to fix, as much as possible, the human affective way and attention by conveying to them
the most narrow guidance and fastening them within the symbolic
needle's eye of the monopersonal genial conception. If this fixation is necessary and physiological in the sense of the historic necessity we have to ask whether or not the perpetuation of these

exact peri-theistic monogenial spheres makes the mistake to sterilize and to retain the developing progress of the future affective psychological universe. The definite fixation of the historic monosymbolic human feelings preserves, for a certain given time, against the dangers of affective stagnations, revolutions and wars. The social and individual happiness is for a certain time well safeguarded within the proud, elaborate and accustomed suggestion of the gracious monogenial channel; but on the other hand we ask if there does not result the handicap of the lack of adaptability for new future developing needs? For a certain time, the strong, monopersonal, solstitial fixation had the agreeable effect of the most comfortable social and individual motor carrying away all our personal sentimental loving production towards the monotheistic goal, in spite of ourselves, through the help of the punctual monogenial mediator, we have received the utmost historic monotheistic facility of our sentimental discharge. All conditions of our ideal psychodynamic efficacy having been prepared most carefully, the idealizing sublimation being performed so well in this monosymbolic apparatus, is not the individual, as we shall see, in the hyperemphasis of this state, easily inclined however, and induced to laziness and passivity, on one side, and to pampering, roughening and excitability on the other side?

There is no doubt that, for a long time, after the intellectual supersatiation of the world during the first time of any new sentimental post-solstitial quarter, the affective world feels exceedingly relieved and furthered by the quickening influence of the monogenial divinity and the monopersonal solstitial personality. The trembling nervous self-destruction, the most fatal cramping affective stagnations of the world cease in the moment of the re-instradation and the re-determination; they fade instantly away under the influence of the clear monosymbolic acceptance of the affective human discharge. MONO is perhaps one of the most important words in the human intellectual life, it means the definite determination of our will. As long as we stagger between several possibilities, even if they are excellent, each one in itself, the efficacy and the conclusiveness of our psychic will is divided, impaired; but as soon as we have chosen one (*monos*) definite channel or way, as soon as we have selected one sure passage and one punctual goal; if custom and skill are added by repetition, then we have in all human things the best chances and vistas. This is the only great highway to every human perfection and success. Even if it is the expression of the greatest humiliation and self-consciousness, it is however, true indeed, and cannot be altered according to our human nature. All our greatest energy and conclusiveness is only possible by the definite self-consciousness of the punctual mono-determination of our choice: only the decided self-control within the last intellectual clearness of our wilful decision is in a position to exercise the sufficient sensorial excitement on our natural gift that we reach most efficiently eternal and most distant goals.

Monosymbolism and monopersonal genius in their sharpest conceptions are very strong and very efficient idealistic mediators, but they likely become rough by their strong punctual, sensorial energy. They have the most powerful possibilities to produce pronounced idealistic conclusiveness through the undivided unity of their intellectual central, genial, conceptions; they know well how to go to last and most distant ideal ranges, much better and more quickly than any other organizing system, but they are handicapped, as we shall see, according to the proverb: More haste, less speed. The monosymbolic and monogenial system exaggerates, perhaps, the sensorial self-control; the real restriction is too definite and surrenders the whole adherent humanity to the inevitable immediate sentimental connection with the chosen symbol of the universe, and with the sensorial historic expression of the solstitial representative. The sharp monosymbolism is liable to throw humanity into the danger to cling too much to their intellectual fixation and to lose the spirit and the truth in which alone God must be adored. It means to look in a bold way at the hidden majesty of God. Our highest intentions and determinations cannot be imprisoned into one terminal point or one sure accustomed historic spheric way: we have to leave always again best old streets if they are used up and we have continually and humbly to build up new bridges, ways and concentrations to the ideal universal goals if we will be efficient and up-to-date within the universal progress.

Our deepest life is full of contradictions. Without decision, determined will and clear goal we never rise to high human ideal dignities, we never even will guess the greatness of ideal divine values; and on the other hand, on the contrary, life punishes us most grievously for having introduced exact and definite lines and points into the universal broad theistic development. All our instruments we have to use are our intellectual clearness and punctual precision, all our peculiar real nature looks for, are sensorial results and impressions, all, we are capable in our human intellectual natures to do, are definite facts, visible signs and logical conclusions. We introduce them to all things and we use them as well for our most daily business as for the definition of God himself and the dealing with the most elevated eternal questions. We are not able on the other side, to judge about divine things from the most narow standpoint of our subjective nature which shows to us all life, all solar and extrasolar phenomena, always and exclusively under the angle and in the mirror of our psychopupilar peculiar exclusive disposition.

The terrible danger of the strong sensorial mono-determination is the bluffing hypnotizing attraction, the clinging energy with which all our life-force is absorbed and immovably directed. This is the unbelievable danger of our nature that the unexpected success of any intellectual system produces the lazy crystallization of this mechanistic attitude and creates the *habit*. Habit means the infatuation with the exterior intellectual formula to which we so easily relapse from the eternal successes which we reached before by the means of this technical help. Habit means, therefore, in this sense idealistic degeneration or unworthy real or intellectual infatuation. It is near the idea of *superstition* which conveys to certain unimportant actions or technicalities the unusual powers of high idealistic effect which they cannot have at all. The notion of laziness and *slothfulness* is of course closest to this psychic relapse; it means the reaction of the previous supra-energetic idealistic conclusiveness which proved to become paralyzed afterwards. The essential character of slothfulness is the affective hypnotizing influence of any sensorial or intellectual formula which turns out first to be excellent for idealistic speed and success. This formula was soon mistaken owing to its first good services in the sense that itself was apotheosed and accepted as the only divine panacea.

This formal technicality took, therefore, the splendour of the eternal supra-sensorial glory of idealism for itself and induced the real humanity to fix and check their own indispensable idealistic progress in apotheosing the intellectual formula in ARTISTIC exaggerated infatuation. The strong artistic development is therefore, the most dangerous handicap of the universal ideal progress of our psychology. It has the value of the adoration of our own possibility of sensorial expression. Art is the gilding infatuation with our own real life; it is the expressed inclination of our art to worship idealism, but it puts the very strong accent of its action on the pre-ideal sensorial discharging sill of the concentric circular enjoyment and pleasure. Art in its loveliness means the factitious fixation and imprisonment of the ideal extracategoric goals within the material world. It has, therefore, the nearest relations to the inspiring incarnation in human birth, to the divine infusion into the material world in Christmas, and to the human nature with its double connections at all.

In the educational sense art must be judged carefully. Genial art is the most charming expression of the symbolic sensorial monomania. It restricts itself to the most developed, yet punctual symbolic simplification, as all greatness of the religious system consists in the compensatory idealistic thoughtfulness and deepness which is the result of the extreme sensorial exclusion. All religious art is nothing but the overwhelming, splendid expression of the punctual monosymbolic unity of the total sensorial life; the Christian artist is the revelling varietor of the peri-monotheistic circle which is given in its religious system and which has its monogenial reflection in the historic human hero. There is nothing more simple than the sensorial principle of the religious art which is given in the attraction to the point and in the corresponding groupment of all real and objective values around this punctual fact, in circular constellation. Therefore, the extraordinary force of feelings in this artistic conception of the world, therefore the quite unheard intensity of the affective life which expresses itself in the monosymbolic art. The overwhelming artistic importance of the mediaeval art lay in its philosophical simplicity. The Christian artist had the greatest genial simplification, excluding all variety of psychomechanism, but acquiring, therefore, the deepest intensity of real adaptation and achievement in relation to his unique central magnetism. The artist reached his tremendous degree of skill and facility because of his quite unparalleled magnetic monodetermination and unification in the most pronounced punctual monotheism whose perfectly symbolic reflection the monogenial hero is. The utmost pronounced, genial monomagnetism of the Christian religion became the most valuable basis of its sure artistic habit. The artist had most undisturbed magnetic guidance towards high ideal divine goals; he has received the most powerful and the most sure circular drawing power of the highest esthetic achievement, like a charming reflection of his punctually determined central divinity excluding all other universal technical possibilities, as he restricted himself to the expression of the one central monosymbol. For this reason art, according to the law of compensation is so much more pronounced as monosymbolism and monogenial character of the hero are emphasized. All discussing and doubting intellectual dispersion of the divine punctual symbolism is hurting the artistic magnetic efficacy, the artistic aptitude needing the strong and simple foundation of the most pronounced monodirection. Philosophic-magnetic unity creates the most artistic security of the artistic skill; it permits the sufficient technical habit and conformity to one technical character which permeates all artistic movements and manifestations. We already saw that this principle within all monosymbolic and monogenial conception is represented by the circle. All Christian art is, therefore, only the most varified circular revelling around one most important central point, this point being given in God and in the monopersonal genial founder.

Art turned out to be a very important educational means from the middle ages, when the Christian idea was the ruling magnetic atmosphere of Europe, and when the gifts of men could be grasped and fixed accordingly. But art created even in this punctual size, because of its inevitable sensorial character, a certain apotheosis of the material life.

Monosymbolism is the wonderful central point from which the artistic hand starts in producing the most charming circles, and from which the compass of the artistic technicality is able to transscribe in all sureness and quietness the most perfect circular curves. Art is in so far the most outstanding idealistic means of education, as it corresponds to the double human nature of the real-idealistic man. It directs in all movements and aspirations the human mind to the monosymbolic goal which is given and hinted to, in the most refined allusions to the circle. The circular formation of the artistic material and form means, in a certain sense, always the divine inspiration of our real life. Art is, therefore, the uplifting pedagogue who understands to elevate all our real expressions towards the eternal idealism. On the other hand we must admit, exactly for this reason, that art may be also as well the real retreat from supra-sensorial idealism in pulling the eternal inexpressible values of idealistic life back to the material world, and it is, therefore, prone to materialize our idealistic gift, to catch supra-categoric abundance in realistic formulas and to sterilize, therefore, our most precious universal progressing tendencies. Art brings our life into closest connection with the divinity on one hand, but it pretends on the other side to express inexpressible truths and values in the language of material artistic forms which cannot be, which is wrong and leads to the relapses of real pleasure and narrow material enjoyment.

We find *mono-sensorial* restriction and even most perfect exclusiveness in all historic religions. We must not forget that sensorial restriction on one hand means sensorial emphasis on the other hand, owing to the law of compensatin. Qui vult vitare Charybdin incidit in Skyllam. We go from bad to worse in restricting the sensorial multiplicity and extension to the narrow point of the symbolic monosensorialism. Monosymbolism excluded the rich and varified sensorial influences because of their loving magnetic power, but in concentrating all this scattered affective attractability of our personal gift into one point of attention, the danger of symbolic shining glorification and sensorial burning love of this point will be the much greater. The monosymbolism has calculated, rightly to a certain extent, that the extreme reduction of the sensorial power to one central point would have necessarily the consequence to take away our sensorial clinging from the real multiplicity. The soul would be so much more compelled to dive from this monopoint into the immeasurable abyss of the speculative divinity and the ideal sentiments. There is no doubt that this compensatory meditation is as right as it is essentially important. Monosymbolism had the intention to choose the less evil from its standpoint, to exclude the reality so much as possible in accepting the central narrow monosymbolic point, and rather to risk to adore intensely the last necessary, central, sensorial punctual remnant of this technical conception of the world, in praising and revelling in artistic circles about this last star as the monosenorial axis of the universal ideal world than to surrender itself to the scattering manifold apotheosis of the real frivolous existence. But there is no doubt that this principal monosensorial axis of our culture is adored as thoroughly as it utmost can be. All religious art, the richest and most elevated which probably has ever been, had only this purpose of symbolic sensorial glorification in the monosymbolic reflection. The lights of Pentecost and of the religious ritual are indeed the clearest expression for the monosymbolic technique. It shows how much the scattered sensorial expressions have been restricted to one point and how much instead the affective emphasis of this one centralized point has grown. This monosensorial punctual expression has become the most devouring affective fire, burning, attractive, and passionating all the soul and jealous to exclude all surrounding real world in order to keep forever the most pronounced intensity of its divine affective central light.

We instantly observe that this psychomechanic attitude must have the most deciding educational consequences. If we, on one side, acknowledge that this affective punctual habit produces the most intense compensatory possibilities of attaining the eternal supra-categoric idealism, that the punctual sensorial contraction is the best guarantee for the energetic sentimental discharge, that it produces the highest divine enthusiasm and the most confident belief in the invisible magnetism; then we must, at the same time, own that it creates also anger, passion and inconsideration. The punctual burning light is not only the manifestation of the strong idealism, but it is also at the same time the accusation of its one-sided, mono-sensorial and contracted, real method. It points out the psychomechanic attitude of the monosymbolic believer consisting in the punctual sensorial retreat, sucking up the broad expansion of the objective material world in favor of the most thorough idealism, but it shows also by the burning flame of its small light-field, how much the emphasis of the punctual, symbolic, sensorial remnant is augmented in comparison with the enlarged open sensorial light-circle. The symbolic burning lights of the churches are the plain confession of their psychological method; they point out how much the affective punctual energy is increased because it is concentrated to the smallest monopunctual sensorial size. The religious pupil is, therefore, if he accepts faithfully and truly the method of his church, educated to deepen most efficiently and energetically his ideal sentiments from the platform of the most reduced symbolic sensorial size. The typical religious believer is taught to dispose of his personal psychic life-force in the manner as to reduce first the objective sensorial world to the smallest light-point and to throw from this basis his affective force compressedly towards idealism.

What will be the result of this psychodynamic school? The individual which has acquired this reactive method of his soul as a firm habit, will always have the reactive psychological peculiarity to be prone to strong sensorial localization and to pronounced localized emphasis of his intellectual gift. This genial psychodynamic typical method is thoroughly averse to any sensorial enlargement of its light-circle and it refuses the sentimental shallow emphasis of any broad real or intellectual enlargement of the psychopupil. It is accustomed to hurl affective lightnings from the most narrow sensorial points. It has learned the thrilling enjoyment of its idealistic strong reaction and does not accept the less fascinating invitation to broad intellectual performance. The idealistic character is not only independent and strong in its way and in its goal, but is inclined to overdo this direction in ANGER.

It would be interesting to find out how many strong idealistic characters live who are not at the same time irascible. Theoretically this danger is quite clear and inevitable, so much so that I should challenge the statistics to have the practical confirmation of the life. For if we will define anger we must have exactly the supposition of the strong genial psychoreactive method. Anger is nothing else than the continual strong inclination of the individual sentiments to hyperemphasize the small experiences of the life in an explosive way. The extreme ideal education has succeeded through the years and traditional ages in bringing about the most pronounced localized sentimental outbursts of the psychic reaction. The traditionally and personally idealistic individual produces from every small peripheric, sensorial impression a volley of sentimental effusion. The gaping disproportion between the idealistic capacity of the objective experience and the strong sentimental lightning which the artistic individual is willing to produce from it again and again, is the essential definition of anger. The measure of the individual disposition for anger is the degree of the personal bluffability by the sensorial world. The more the individual is educated to respect any sensorial impressions, to be easily and unpreparedly suggested by any symbolical, sensorial signs, the more he will and must be irascible. Anger is the product of mystic frightening, of the fact that the individual has been brought so far in his psychomechanic reaction that he is willing and prone to practise his peculiar monoidealistic methods at every occasion as the psychological manner of his choice, which he learnt from youth and which he inherited from his cultural idealistic ancestors.

This artistic idealistic method has at the same time some other components and suppositions. The anger has of course the escorting circumstances of offense and of inconsideration. Anger is not true because it has lost the just eye of the reality. Anger is not just because it neglects the appropriate superficial appreciation and self-consciousness. Anger always supposes laziness and roughening of the psychological reaction, laziness because of the insufficient patience in developing towards the valuable lost concentrated sensorial symbols which are only amenable by work and logical performance, roughening and hyper-refinement (in this case the same thing) because of the continual need of strong affective reactions and the exaggerated development of idealistic suggestibility. Anger means the psychological unhingement of our dynamic affective soul, the trigger of our sentimental discharge being too susceptible and the projectile of our feelings running away at every smallest peripheric sensorial influence. Anger means, therefore, the affective diarrhoea of our intellectual experience. The soul has not the necessary perseverance in working out the peripheric sensorial impression in logical work until it reaches the central charming terminal symbol. But has this quick idealistic mechanism, averse to the working slow performance and greedy of the undeserved premature idealistic discharge not been taught and learned in the school of the punctual genial idealism, where the bluffing method of the symbolic miraculous education has been accepted and then has become the ruling physiognomy of the individual psychological reaction?

All these considerations are not directly concerned with the objective facts, but deal theoretically with the educational influences of the sharper, most exact or less pronounced real conceptions and representations of symbolism. *They go back to the general problem, what size of the imaginative target suits humanity best.*

Monosymbolism is the production of frictions between the two antagonistic values of ideal and real life. It is the universal whirlpool caused by the antagonistic action of two most distant affective standards meeting at this one monogenial middle point. Is it not the immediate antagonism and the artificial opposition of these distant ideal and real creative values which creates this instantaneous frictive affective stagnation or uplifting point which we call monosymbolizing? As soon as we are able to dissolve this clashing attitude of the opposite forces of the universe, we also are able to avoid the monosymbolic whirlpools. The supposition of the monosymbolic localization is the bluffing surprise of the ideal by the real or of the real by the ideal world. Monosymbolism is the instantaneous condensation of idealism in the lower atmosphere of the intellectual world in our mind. The supposition of belief in monosymbolism is, therefore, the naive bluffing surprise. As soon as science succeeds in analyzing the gradual differences between idealism and materialism, as soon as the careful and cautious scientific work explains the distant ranges of ideal and real world and changes the antagonistic universal forces into two distances, then the temperamental extreme eddies cease and the sharp notion of the monosymbolic notion subsides. Now we understand why the monosymbolic temperament is so afraid of science: science is indeed the most able universal interpreter and through this the liquidator of the contradictions of the creative universe from which the idea of monosymbolism starts. We see also instantly how near the notions of monosymbolism and creation are. They are so close together that they suppose each other. The theoretical makeup of the monosymbolical idea and of our conception of the visible creation is the same. The creation is the precipitate of the distant ranges of the universal affective values; does it not represent the material condensation which came about as the hot ideal values were thrown instantly into the cool atmosphere of the lower universal temperature? Monosymbolism and creation suppose violent universal revolutions both being the product of strong contradictions representing values which are put immediately into closest connection without adaptation. We see, therefore, how nearly the monosymbolic conception reminds us of the notion of psychodynamic disturbances, of ignorance, of sin and of anger. Monosymbolism means most universal unadapted historic clashes producing creative bluffings. On the other side it is the backbone of order and of unitarian consideration of the world.

The rise of the smoke of the *steam* engine derives from the quick refrigeration by the outside into which the hot steam is blown out. The capacity of producing steam is so much greater as the transition of the hotter to the cooler degree of temperature of the air is quicker and as greater the difference of the two opposite temperatures coming in contact with each other is. The hotter air is much more capable to contain steam and the cold air precipitates it into dense steam and water. The quality of the steam is most refined in the hot temperature, the steam is dense and very visible in the cold air and is changed into water, if the surrounding temperature is entirely cooled into which it is let out. If the difference of the two temperatures is little as in summer time, our breath has not the appearance of steam, the inside and the exterior temperature of both the organism and the warm outside air having no big difference; we on the other side in winter time have the clear and rich rise of steam in our breathing because of the great difference of the heat coming out from colder air in the winter time. The formation of steam in this case has not been obtained by strong heating but by putting the opposite outside temperature lower. But the product was the same: the production of steam as the consequence of immediate cooling by a distant degree of temperature. It is then the great difference and the immediateness of the influence of the surrounding air which gives to the milkman's horse in the wintry morning the appearance of the breathing steam engine and which exhibits people also as the organic steam producers, exhaling rich clouds of smoke at every breath into the cold wintry air.

This same law must be valuable in the universe. The organic *creative world* is the intellectual condensation and the hovering cloud between the unorganic water of the material world and the idealistic extrasensorial realm. Every plant, animal and chiefly the men are, as it were, different stages of idealistic steamy concentrations moving on the crust of the earth: the body of these beings are different degrees of real refrigerations of the universal ideal infusions on earth: the material expression of these living beings means the different quantitative precipitation of the material world. There is no doubt that between idealism, immaterial sentiments, extra-sensorial feelings and hot temperature exists the most pronounced comparability. There is further no doubt that cold temperature and material visible reality have the nearest connection. We know that the hot temperature consists in strong molecular movements and we know as well that the cold temperature means a lack of this quick molecular movability. Have we not in the creation the same thing as in the rise of the steam? The immediate contact of two very distant molecular velocities produces the real material concentration of the immeasurable cloud scattered before in the universe. It creates the living concentration and expansion, the steaming production and movability of the material nature, compressed before in the cold and dead passive minimal confinement.

But we have even the same in the monosymbolic idea. The monosymbolic intellectual eddy is also such a product of condensation coming out from the compressing outlook over distant degrees of magnetic speeds which in the immediate touch produce the whirlpool of the monosymbolic divine conception. This idea is, therefore, also the hissing reaction of artificial nearest compression of two distant universal magnetic values which influence each other in this moment as opposition instead of logical distant factors. The monosymbolic conception supposes the simultaneous comprising meditation of the most distant universal magnetic ranges, it supposes the necessity of putting them together, end to end, in order that the most distant and different values touch each other. It is the will of art to do always again this experiment of real idealistic melting up. It is of course also the specialty and duty of religion to have produced from the beginning this typical monosymbolic psychological phenomenon. *Monosymbolism* is, therefore, the intellectual punctual fixation, and localization of the infinite sea of the eternal waving magnetism running through all spaces and ages and quite unable to be comprehended into the prison of any intellectual punctual mono-conception. Monosymbolism means the real retardation of the flowing universal energy, it signifies the punctual fixation and intellectual determination of the progressing universal magnetism, it is the remarkable eddy formed by our human psychology and corresponding most to the intellectual necessities of our nature which needs the recognizability of punctual determinations. The monosymbolic conception of the world is, therefore, the exact reflection of our peculiar intellectual nature which of course craves for exact expression in the most determined unity and means the most pronounced simplification of energy. Our nature with its double disposition itself rides always on the gable of the creative roof in that sense that it essentially combines always the real and the ideal part of the universal possibilities: human nature is, therefore, essentially religious and essentially monosymbolic owing to its melting up of very distant universal magnetic ranges. Monosymbolism is the essential psychological phenomenon of the human disposition binding together the very distant standards of the material body and the ideal mind. Monosymbolism is the artless vital reaction of the natural individual having the most distant universal magnetic values at his disposal, on the way to move to further development. So it comes about that the most different and distant values are, immediately by haphazard and artlessly put together what causes always the most energetic monosymbolic precipitation. Religion does the same thing intentionally and we understand why it is rather favorable to the individual ignorance, why it principally excludes science most possibly. *Science* is the real art of avoiding the pushing and exciting monosymbolic hissing collisions. It is the task of the logical progression to regulate and to order the sequence of the connection of the universal magnetic standards according to their quantitative values, to exclude the immediate quick connections of distant affective ranges and to create in such a manner the orderly regular and quiet development of universal psychological progression. Science is indeed the most pronounced enemy of the monosymbolic conception, not because it could find something new or different from what religion pretends to be true, but because science avoids the immediate connection of distant universal affective energies and excludes in this manner the formation of the monosymbolic whirlpools which are the method and the goal of every religion. The triumph of the science is gradual order, regularity and logical sequence of all values in the knowing system, the triumph of religion on the contrary, is the audacious symbolic opposition and the strong intellectual bluff in distant small light-points from which the subdued individual force can be conducted easily towards the total sentimental surrender of its life-force to the ideal divine performances.

The monogenial conception means of course the most perfect support of the monosymbolic idea. The hero is the peculiar humanized mono-symbol of our culture. He became the most persuading mouthpiece of the European post-Roman monosymbolic culture, he received the eminent and most assured rule to be the idealistic light of the world, the undiscussed genial symbolic expression of the most efficient idealistic suggestion: he became that most considerable cultural cannon-piece through whose barrel all cultural affective sentiments were, for a long time, accustomed to be willingly fired towards the ideal eternity.

Religion is always aware of such ideal most efficient opportunities of expression. The great idealist with the real exclusion and the strong ideal-sentimental magnetism has just the right stability for religious performances. He is, as religion exacts that hissing antagonism of artless universal magnetic oppositions, he is that psychological workshop in which the ingenious and immediate contrast of ideal and real values has the most bluffing and most persuading effect. We see how much the punctual symbolic light-field of the genial barrel corresponds exactly again to the previous explanation given on the fundamental conception of the rise of monosymbolism. The punctual monogeniality has indeed just these most opposite ranges of the most simple real monosymbolism, the richest and deepest eternal idealism touching each other in the extreme idealistic action. In this point we have the most efficient psychological excitement, the most burning monosymbolic experience and enjoyment, the most hissing affective reaction of the monotheistic individual.

The monogenial idealistic barrel as we represented it in the first part of our book, is, therefore, the leader of every monosymbolic religion. Monosymbolic religion without monogenial and monopersonal symbolic barrel could not be efficient or perhaps even possible.

What a cultural triumph must the discovery and the establishment of any important monogenial symbolism towards monosymbolic idealism have? What a tremendous exalting halleluiah must have pervaded the universe, when the human collective psychology at last was assured, when the spheric way of the human fate had acquired after all its sure direction towards its last goals, and as the adequate barrel of the human divine necessities not only was found, but even tried and successfully probed! It was at the time of the *Middle Ages* when the psychological monosymbolic symbolism attained its highest festivals, when the affective humanity had for a certain time the most complete agreement between affective need and technical supply, when the facility of the ideal longings of the mediaeval psychology was most insured within the tested experience of the suggestive monosymbolic conception. This most efficient, interspheric, affective elaboration of the human psychological technicalities was the reason of the overwhelming artistic success of this historic period. The affective successfulness of the genial monosymbol conducted the mediaeval humanity to the assumption not only to accept in the hero the most able Son of God, to acknowledge him as the most perfect solstitial point of the human fate reflecting the utmost historic attainability of the divine perfection, but to identify this most successful idealistic sensorial monosymbolism with the abyss of the terminal universal God himself.

Did not the identification of the historic monosensorial symbolic point with the fulness of the eternal universal God mean the sensorial luxuriant relapse from the inexpressible suprasensorial eternal divinity to the categoric historic world? Was it not the self-adoration of the created human intellectual nature, the sentimental fixation of our progressing affective gift on the historic monosymbolic precipitate of the creative universe as it is given in the extreme one-sided idealism?

Is not the apotheosis of the hero the most worthy form of worship, but is it not, nevertheless one further fact in the sensorial self-glorification of the symbolic intellectual world? It is the last degree of sensorial self-love and earthly connection of the human ideal nature. But is it not wrong to identify one highest symbol with the abyss of the last universal divine possibilities? The hero is the charming genial door towards the outside extrasensorial idealism in the sense of the historic religion; he is the sensorial last mouthpiece of the religious monosymbolic expresson. But is it not the same a mistake to apotheose any monosymbol to the most elevated divinity or to pull back the whole contents of the universal idealism into this last sensorial punctual expression? It is clear and most understandable that the successful idealism easily falls back to this delightful symbolic relapse. It is clear and most pardonable that for a certain time the perfect technical congruancy of the idealistic need of humanity and of the excellent affective sureness and speed conveyed by the genial monosymbolism produced the perfect melting up of the symbolic sill and of the eternal goal itself. This successful confusion was the reason of the increase of the strong monosymbolic conception of the world; it was the cause, why all polygenial historic conceptions of the rising hero was severely excluded and condemned.

But for this manner of action, in spite of the divine emphasis of the human hero being the most practical insurance of the successful idealistic performance of the cultural humanity, we notwithstanding must be aware of the danger rising from the definite sensorial fixation of our affective performance. The monosensorial hyper-emphasis of our idealistic performances has the most pronounced consequences of the formal crystallization of our will and life; they cause the greatest inadaptability of our hypnotized sensorial life, they check and baffle all historic future attempts to progress towards new necessary expressions of our historic sensorial manifestations. The historic fixation of one monosymbolic system is most dangerous, more than anything else because of its unchangeable strong concentration and because of its according affective hypnosis. The monosymbolic system is the most energetic hypnotic persuasion of the individual and collective humanity because of its exquisite mono-punctual determination. The peculiar psychological fastening of the affective life-force in one point is so strong and energetic, according to the law of compensation, as it is best expressed in the fiery tongues of Pentecost and in the burning candle sticks of the church, that humanity will be very slow to part from this exceedingly strong affective symbolic union.

But what would we do without its historic fixation? Where would the path of our human social fate go astray, without being fixed in most essentially important questions, to order and stability? There comes in again the question of necessity.

The future times of the human history force our race to do this bold step outside to a new enlarged universal conception of a later psychological humanity. Our scientific age is exactly the inexorable and irrevocable factor doing the levelling work between the extreme opposition of reality and idealism: science dissolves the hissing monosymbolic opposition and produces the peaceful logical distances which can be and must be unified and combined always by logical progressing and thinking development. The abolition of ignorance will be the fall of the historic material monosymbolic conception, but with this also the mono-genial hero is endangered who suited so well the psychomechanic monosymbolic discharge in former times. Ignorance and bold proud inconsideration, inappropriate diving into the universal magnetic values is the mother of extreme monosymbolic production. The reverent detailed appreciation and valuation of the numberless factors of the affective world abolishes the divine marks of the passionate anti- and pro-monosymbolic conception and establishes the most harmonious considerate logical and humble working progression of the interspheric human fate. Extreme monosymbolism is thus the interspheric handicap of our human destiny: it is most suitable and convenient to our double peculiar nature; it is the natural building up of new universal steps and it is the perfect expression of our sensorial-sentimental natural disposition. But it fixes the progressive waves of the universal magnetism in one strong historic monosymbolic whirlpool which must be liquidated again and again after a certain historic time and which must give way to new and further similar interspheric psychodynamic gatherings and formations. This waving progression is the indispensable fact of the universal necessity, all monosymbolic historic cramps of localized collection of human energy have their time of rise, of culmination, they have their tremendous vital psychodynamic triumps, but also the time of irrevocable relapse and inexorable disappearance.

The Christian ART is just the charming and hypnotizing expression of the punctual monogenial symbolism of our psychological cultural performance. The old Christian art is one of the chief means to educate people to monosymbolism. It gives the strongest urges to cling with all force of our sentiments to the punctual central sensorial symbol. All the circular revelling, Christian art has no other foundation, means nothing but the emphasis of the central monosensorial symbol; all Christian art is the underlining stress of this only fact of the characteristic monopunctual symbolic discharge of our affectivity. It sings the most powerful hymn in musical idealistic pointed expressions, it depicts the most charming paintings with the most pronounced central light flashes and all surrounding looks directed to them as we saw in Christmas, and it forms the most uplifting poetry culminating in the central monosymbolic Christ. All these actions have the educational intentions to exclude all surounding sensorial world, to put all sensorial stress on one point, but to glorify this last intellectual remnant of our real world immeasurably and unmistakably. These last monosymbols share the glory of the inconceivable and indescribable extrasensorial idealism; it is the wonderful last human sensorial star round which art throws its splendid sparkles and performs its adoring and flattering round-dances. Christian art is the most perfect monosymbolic self-glorification of the mediaeval historic existence. If it has excluded all surrounding sensorial affective hyper-appreciation of humanity, it clings at least and so much more to this last punctual mono-sensorial symbol which forms its spring-board toward the eternal supra-categoric idealistic universe. The genial humanity is induced by the mono-punctual efficacy of their ideal performance to apotheose and sanctify this mechanistic method; its art is the help to identify this technical formula with the ideal universe itself: it means the blessing self-restriction of the human race to the most pronounced sensorial punctual reduction of their real performance. The Christian art turned out all real affective sensorial, hesitating and doubtful broadmindedness; the real variety received in it only one right, this to help to underline and to serve the cental monogenial symbolism. If the total human sensorial performance was forbidden to progress to the direct variable service and alliance with the divine universe, it would at least glorify the last symbolic door of its choice, leading to the outside divine idealism. It could not help establishing the overwhelming eternal glory of the genial barrel through which humanity fired so successfully their projectiles of eternal love and union.

So we see that the terminal symbolic barrel of the Christian idealism accepted all worship and all homage due and intended to the eternal widespread universal causes and goals themselves. The ornamentation of the monosymbolic barrel was charged with all loving beauty of which the human sentimental love was capable; all loveliness, all attachment, all confidence were put into this miraculous genial monogenial symbolism. It was strengthened with all real, political, artistic and material elaboration and it was supported with all historic and ecclesiastic institutions of the historic progressing time. Humanity was drunk with the efficacy of the power of this intraspheric psychological mechanism and came at last so far as to confuse completely and absolutely the venerability and the importance of the discharging barrel with the divine goal itself. It is chiefly art which brought this psychological confusion into humanity; its strong monosymbolic emphasis suggested the nations so far and bewitched so much the hearts of the human race that they understandably lost the power to distinguish the idealistic terminal monosymbolic mediation from its divine universal intention and task. Art was the most powerful means by which humanity was suggested continually and thoroughly to fix on their monosymbolic central star by which the cultural nations were definitely bewitched and mono-punctually hypnotized. The human worship was, therefore, always very strong: if it was relative and indirect in the artistic masterpieces, it was so much stronger and more pronounced in the adoration of the central monosymbolic mediator whose human part was adored in connection with his divine, and whose humanity was elevated to the universal divine glory.

What is then the practical educational value of the Christian art? The previous statement remains that all real objectivity is inspired, in the idealistic sense, by the Christian mono-intentional art. All artistic representation shares in the central monosymbolic sill and these sparkles must intensify in the splendour of the universal ideal reflection. But if there is any imperfection and indiscussable "idolatry" in these proceedings, it is due to the essential intellectual-real part of the human nature, nobody being in a position to escape entirely from the sensorial emphasis of his human double nature. The monosymbolic acceptance of the artistic representation evades, as much as possible, the sensible broadness, but in the magnetic circular adaptation it is subjected nevertheless in the whole expansion of the objective world to the sensorial spell of the monosymbolic centre which only was intended to be emancipated from the material slavery and which alone is allowed to look, with almost entirely unveiled eye, into the face of the universal divine majesty. The Christian art has the effect to give hope, confidence, uplifting magnetic concentration toward the punctual terminal monosensorial sill, but it has at the same time the retardation of the real careful broad elaboration. Art quickens the idealistic affective action, in its concave leaning to the centre, but it has not the angry facility of other more mystic educational methods because it insists on the single steps of the logical gradual progression of the symbolic working concentration. It is the careful detailed technique of the artistic masterpiece which imparts the necessary educational psychodynamic stops on the intellectual multiple stations. So we indeed have in the art the most hopeful monosymbolic proceedings and the retarding intellectual gradual emphasis simultaneusly. Since all advantages must be found in life and psychology, in somewhat, we must realize that the artistic logical connection of the experimental fragments of our life, produce, it is true, sure and successful monosymbolic concentrations, but that it also at the same time is liable to create some artistic pampering or effemination which is based on the custom of profiting by the artistic logical readiness in art, whilst the practical life does not permit to be used so easily to the logical progression towards idealism. In so far art has the danger of effeminating the individual character. But it fills the individual with strong courage for the terminal goal. Even if the monosymbolic terminal conception would be admitted as arbitrary, it is at least able to reach the idealistic universe, to urge the individual magnetic gifts to advance and to go energetically on toward the most efficient terminal conclusiveness and affective discharge.

It is strong upbuilding of CHARACTER which is significant for the monosymbolic education. A good friend of mine told me once: It is the same whether Christian ideas turn out to be wrong in our adult age, but they have worked well in having the effect of educating our character in our youth, and the principles and habits of character remain, even if the ideas of objective truth in later life have been changed or abolished. The educational work of the religious system is indeed based on the monosymbolic psychomechanic fixation. Could there be other excellent methods of reaction, as they are looked for in our day by the scientific solution of the human educational problem? But it is true that just the monosymbolic psychomechanism has the most pronounced facility of forming strong character. For what is the destination of character? The security of the terminal relationship of all our actions. Character is the continual need to put all our experiences and deeds in communication with our last terminal affective principle. The monosymbolic pupil has for this reason the most and best chances to become the strongest consequent character: but he has not the best vistas to become the most useful character because his continual detailed need of sentimental deepening makes intractable, inadaptable, impractical, awkward and impatient as well a idealistic, heroic and sacrificing. The strong lightning of the monosymbolic psychological education creates the habit to hyper-emphasize during all life the most accidental experiences in the sentimental deepening sense, to generalize most listlessly our sentimental importance, on all our smallest and greatest relations, experiences and so to become too criticless in seeing too much, too superficial in being too thorough, in order to be soon rejected because of sentimental hyper-sensitive inadaptability. The genial, affective, deepening emphasis of all our experiences have the most exhausting effect on our affective life, we, therefore, do not only lose to count in the more movable and extremely varified world, but we also exhaust our nervous forces and are offended most easily by every smallest vital incongruity.

The character has the most pronounced determination of purposes and intentions. The love for final conclusion and terminal results is essential for the manner of the psychological reaction of characters. Character must, therefore, be on one side not only near heroism which is able to bear individual and material losses in favor of high idealistic purposes, but also, in a sense, very closely connected with practical and real success, because this is always the consequence of perfect carrying through of principles. Strong need for clear purposes and energetic run toward them has its best educational basis in the religious mono-determination. The monosymbolism is the prototype of the efficient determining education toward clear and exact goals. It conveys the psychomechanic habit of looking in every experience for exact intentions and purposes which quickens and makes successful the psychic energy: but it restricts, at the same time, the broad survey of the individual, over the real life. The victory of the monosymbolism and of the strong character lies in the *teleological restriction*. The strength of the systematic monosymbolic education of the character is founded on the extreme narrowness of the terminal symbolic light-field. The sentimental ideal character dispenses with the objective truth in favor of the ideal success; it averts its real detailed observations and intellectual connection in order to rush instantly and with predilection towards the idealistic affective discharge. The psychomechanic monosymbolic type of education conveys the strongest teleological race to all performances and affective starts of the individual life, be it in religion, in sexuality, in art, in business, in sport, or in physiological performances. We spoke often in other places, how this truth must be understood rightly. So we may say, in a certain sense, that character creates quickness of success, thoroughness of methodical life; but we see also instantly that the strong methodical narrowness of the character prevents its aptitude for scientific objective work. Science resists the conclusions of character and character rejects the dry necessities of the scientific investigations. The results, brilliant and surprising, as they are in the appearance of the moment, faint away easily in the progress of the real time, because they have monosymbolic narrow fixations and teleological subjective value. Science needs objective rich detailed connections and draws from this source to its successes.

To the strong intentional readiness of the idealistic education we have opposed a certain amount of LAZINESS, according to the law of compensation. The expression laziness refers to the aversion against the detailed elaboration of the peripheric and superficial objectivity, the monosymbolic punctual light-field has bluffed and magnetized the individual so much that the necessary previous emphasis of the peripheric intellectual stages of the real world is only pretended. The chief weight of the intellectual energy is always and continually attracted by the central monosymbolism of the last effective purpose. For this reason arises the blurring overskipping of the real detailed world which we may call anger in the sense of the psychomechanic quickening action, but laziness from the standpoint of the negligence of the real peripheric elaboration. The strong idealistic teleological determination creates the utmost paleness of real interest, the individual conscience having the guarantee of the right best and perfect goal in the monosensorial punctual light-field, from which it expects every happiness, the preparation and the logical toiling for this reason no more being estimated as necessary or even useful. Why, thinks the teleological individual, will I work hard, develop energetically and simplify my real experiences in the idealistic imaginative direction, if I have in advance the promise and the strong prospect of the most perfect possible affective enjoyment and purpose, as they are given within the punctual goal? The burning sensorial light of the clear terminal purpose and shining symbol is the surest guide toward strong goals, it is true, but we must not forget that just this terminal confidence and always surprising and ever present, sensorial, flaming intensity, destroys the continual serious carefulness of the single proceeding steps and takes away the searching terminal sorrow which ought to be inherent to every real step. The real performance and the detailed step of the idealist is liable to be less connected in a sense to eternal lasting intentions, because the previous conviction of their easy obtainability, of the sure terminal landing and the relative despicability of the real things, has mechanized its value and taken away from them the devotion of the terminal serious longing and strength which ought to be inspired into the last and most frivolous human actions.

The strong sensorial light, the determination of the monosymbolism and the exceeding energy of the affective lightnings of its psychological function have the fatal effect to produce the most pronounced underestimation of the real world and the mechanic and intellectual functions of our life. There is no more enough reason to look thoroughly after the objective world, where the absolute guarantee of the terminal success is given. The minute care for the way fades away where we are intensely reminded and attracted continually by the glowing beacon of the goal. Here we have the explanation of the real passiveness and of the objective reservedness of the extreme religious sentiments. They have no time or will to dwell within the small conditions of the real world, they prefer to go on and to approach rapidly the promised goal which beckons distinctly and brightly from far away. We understand, therefore, that the quickening idea of extreme monosymbolic intensification has the most paralyzing influence on the real detailed elaboration, that the strong monosymbolic determination of the last intentions destroy the carefulness of the performing preparation. We may say in this sense, the much more somebody has a strong will and desire to reach real values, the easier will he get them, but in the degree as he desires them more, he deserves them less. For the strong terminal intentions are opposed to the functional punctual conscientious preparation of the approaching way. The best earned rewards are the least desired ones; terminal goals should fall like ripened fruits to our lips from the tree of proceeding minute conscientious work which we have done for itself, for its necessity and for our natural activity. In the psychological sense it is, therefore, perhaps better to reward suitably great workers who have done their best work in a hidden and unselfish way, than to appoint high wages and rewards to people who, in the sure expectation of their fixed and dated payments, lose unconscientiously energy and will of performing good and important practical work in the daily life. This last circumstance is so very widespread and known, as it is, of course, exceedingly difficult in accordance to the social institutions and necessities of our life of today, to establish rules and to avoid abuses. The best work is never paid nor intended to be rewarded.

EXCITABILITY has essentially been treated with anger. Excitability of the individual means the continual readiness for exaggerated sentimental discharge. The psychodynamic stop-cock of the excitable individual is only slightly really and intellectually checked and is prone to run away at the most insignificant starting concentrating movement or urge. The excitable soul is not satisfied to progress from any peripheric objective standard to the next following more concentrated one, but it easily rushes through all stages of the created world towards the terminal symbolic punctual centre of ideal pleasure, of affective strength and sentimental concentration. Excitability means, therefore, the lack of the just eye in adapting the affective energy to the momentaneous real experience; excitability is essentially the lack of the affective self-control in the vital performance. The monosensorial education creates the thorough desire for the most important affective emphasis, all previous stages of objective standards are subordinated and lean towards the chief sentimental symbolism like ready doors of easy terminal transfers. The affective communication between real peripheric values and the central deepening idealism has become too pervious by the continual idealistic practice and by the peculiar education of the genial individual. This broad opening communication towards strong affective discharge from every point of our experimental life is just that what we call excitability. Excitability means the insufficient organic cohesion of the ideal and real parts of our nature to the small intellectual and visible sensorial experiences of our daily life; it is the inclination to overthrow the logical order of the affective sequence of our real and experimental values and to hyperemphasize the sensorial importance of any slight impression. Excitability advances the sensorial authority of the least and most unworthy impression of the life without delay and without any intermediary intellectual obstacle to the first role of sensorial dignity and importance. Excitability means, therefore, the exaggerated sensorial imprisonability and bluffability of our affective soul. The excitable individual has received the most hypersensitive nervous system, the extreme possibility of separating walls, through which all even least sensorial impressions are guided uncheckedly toward the terminal monosensorial reaction. The excitable sensitiveness is so increased that all even least sensorial impressions are able to play the role of the most energetic ones and are, therefore, able to replace the monosensorial order of them. It supposes the habitual and arbitrary unhingement of objective dignities.

We recognize in this deficient appreciation of the single creative values not only the most pronounced hypersensitive excitability, but at the same time the most horrible ROUGHENING. The monosymbolic central education of the extreme idealist produced by habit the uniform terminal ideal strong reaction; the individual accustomed to this form and degree of affective reaction is, after all, no more able to react in a moderate adapted manner, but either thoroughly monosymbolically and artistically in the terminal affective lightnings, or not at all. There is no middle stage between these two manners of attitude of the thorough idealistic psychomechanism. We have therefore to point out that the basis of this psychological idealistic attitude is the roughening treatment of the strong former idealistic use of the monosensorial symbolism. The tender and frail reactive mechanism of the human nervous system and of our affective nature has been spoiled by the continual and exclusive misuse of the most magnetic idealism, and the final result will, therefore, be the inadaptability of the individual to the small reactive affective needs of the real daily life. The individual has, by his special education and inclination, been induced to react only to the strong urges of the terminal monosensorialism and it turns out finally often like this, that there is only one excitable reaction after any summation of many small sensorial experiences which together, as a whole, cause a very strong but inadapted affective reaction. We have, therefore, in these people what we call *angry slothfulness,* the lack of reaction on small sensorial urges on one side, but also the summary affective explosions after a certain number of small impressions, without any logical adaptability so that the reactions subside on one hand, where they should be and are effectuated on the other side much too strongly, where they should be less. We have then, the union of both laziness and hyper-excitability at the same time.

We know that the monosensorial affective lightnings are the most successful causes of the individual delightful PLEASURE and ENJOYMENT. We remember how much the affective draught running in its concentrated form through the small monosensorial hole of the psychopupil produces the most delightfully felt oscillations of the psychopupilar margin. The monosymbolic education, is, therefore, the pronounced danger and direction of the individual towards pleasure and enjoyment; the individual becomes aware, by experience, of the charming monosymbolic frictions and is easily liable to relapse so much in his feelings and intentions that he produces the monosymbolic psychopupilar attitude no more for the last idealistic discharge and universal love, but much more or only for the escorting sensorial pleasure itself. Pleasure and delight which are naturally the escort and the reward of our great human tasks, become then most likely confused with the terminal purpose and intention of our life, the pleasure no more being the mere accidental circumstance of our ideal performance, but becoming rather the highest and chief goal of the ideal monosensorial performance. This latter is so degraded from its domineering universal importance, it becomes the servant of the personal individual pleasure to which its refined psychomechanism is subjected. The delightful relapse to pleasure means, therefore, the fatal reversion of our last natural intentions; it is the perfect revolutionary upheaval of the natural affective emphasis; it produces affective stagnations and idolatric adorations because of the precocious stop of the idealistic personal longings. Egoistic self-centered pleasure means the apotheosis of the monosensorial opening itself, if it is a question of the highest pleasure, the divinization of the monosymbolic threshold, as it is given in the circular mystic artistic performances. They are the last and highest pleasures of our life, our soul attaches itself most easily to these monopunctual sensorial values; we are so likely to be checked from the universal extrasensorial discharge if we feel the tremendous pleasure of the monosymbolic fixation. We so easily cling to these historic simple expressions, we are so much disinclined to leave the sure sensorial ground of divine manifestation and to fly irresistibly towards the outside universe.

We recognize, therefore, the *passionating* influence of the monosensorial education. Passion means the participation of our organic nature at the affective performances. If we, as we said before, remember the lightning affective function of the monosensorial idealism and agree that the passing vibrating energy causes the delightful participation of the circular organic margin of the psychopupil, then we understand easily that the strongest lightnings of the divine monosensorial discharge produce the most powerful organic commotions in pleasure and pain, in sorrow, sadness, and happiness, expressing itself in laughing, weeping, in palpitations of the heart and in any whatsoever muscular contractions of the organic body. The most pronounced monosensorial expression produced is the unfailing urge for the passionating collaboration; the clearest monosymbolic conception and the most determined monopersonal genius have the most chances to contract the human muscular disposition and to string the nervous human system to the utmost degree. Here we have the deepest root and source of the shaking corporeal passion. Passion supposes always any strong monosensorial attention, some monosymbolic attitude of our mind which has most constant goals to cover and most difficult obstacles to overcome on the way. Passion can have the role to help over these real objective obstacles, to throw the psychological force of the individual through the small hole of monosensorialism, to support and to promote the individual will to go on courageously and successfully towards the universal delightful idealism. Sharp monosymbolism, genius, and clear monosensorialism of the punctual light-field have all the nearest relations with the notion of passion. Passion is strengthening the mono-inclinations of our affective goals; passions make the attainment of the delightful enjoyments or universal idealistic goals, easy and comfortable and form as a habit, as it were, the most successful organic barrel round the monosensorial intentions of the idealistic individual.

The inclination of the idealistic passionate individual to form *habits* is therefore clear. For the monocentralization of the typical psychomechanism produces and needs essentially the support of the passions. This temperamental peculiarity of action is afterwards, of course, used likely for all future performances and reactions of the individual. We recognize, therefore, that later individual passions and former monosymbolic actions of our life are in the nearest psychic and psychomechanic educational connection.

We already have hinted to the *aversion to work* which so often is attached to the extreme idealistic psychological performance. It may be often that the need of ideal conclusiveness pervades the whole realm of the real operation like the most efficient motorcar or like the most affective plough driven by steam. But more likely and ordinarily the real obstacles discourage, after a while, the ideal disposition which is only important and great in the direct undisturbed view and enjoyment of its last punctual ideal and which loses so much easier its goal as it puts all on one turn of the wheel. As soon as this strong monosymbolic light-point is lost, as it happens easily even to the strong idealist within the absorbing intricacy of the working necessity, the teleological individual is at a perfect loss to guess where will be his best and right direction. Work for this individual has the most insufficient attraction, because he is accustomed to the strong terminal signals of the pronounced urges of monosensorialism. Work has not sufficient attraction for the pronounced idealist because, in early life, he has been spoiled by the roughening intensity of his exaggerated monosensorial impressions. He is always filled with the idea and conviction that the essential end with which he is acquainted, is alone important and he can only do real work in the terminal idealistic intentions. Therefore, it is so dangerous to diminish any visibility of the ideal goal before the eyes of the grown-up idealist; but the necessary compensatory distraction of the working reality has, unfortunately, essentially this effect to scatter the narrow sharp light-field, to efface its sharp contours and to impair its brilliant splendour and magnetic attraction.

The idealistic individual finds out, therefore, easily by his experience that the *straining effort* of the working life and the sure symbolic idealistic attraction are in exact opposition. The working effort has for the idealistic monosymbolist the meaning of selfmade obstacles against his easy magnetic goal; he observes that he is so much more ready to fly against his monosymbolic attractions as he has been spoiled by the roughening intensity of his exaggerated goal, unable to hit, to see, to desire, and to embrace his accustomed monoidealism as he uses his force for the real working effort. The individual who is educated to have the easy comfort of strong idealistic monosymbolism is exceedingly obstinate to do anything to lose this peculiar opportunity of magnetic easy attitude. Nobody could feel more thoroughly the deep affective contradiction of the working effort of our life than just the spoiled idealistic monosensorial type. Working effort means poly-sensorial distraction of our life-force in the real outside life, it represents exactly the contrary of the monosensorial method learned by and taught to the young idealist. Therefore the typical monoidealist has the most pronounced aversion to real work which could be imagined. He feels the weight of the working effort against his natural idealistic need more thoroughly than anyone else. Nobody could have a more pronounced susceptibility of heavy work; to nobody the straining effort of the real social and personal duties could be more fastidious than to him. The typical monosymbolic idealist has therefore the greatest obstacles to go on successfully in the real world. He is lazy and inadaptable in the sense of the objective world, because he is fascinated and fixed too much on the attractive monosensorial symbol which yet gives to him the fulness of human ideal discharge, of artistic and passionating power. He is the enjoying type of the human race, whereas the working realist, being in love with the multiple objects of the outside world, finds his reward in the work itself.

The directive determination, the fixed intentions and purposes conveyed by the punctual symbolism are of course of highest value in another sense. For every prodigality of vital energy is abolished in it, in the terminal sense. The individual is sure to join its goal and has the definite guarantee of his terminal desire. This fact is of course the most fundamental, and though there is a whole army of disadvantages of the monosymbolic education, this one great advantage of *orientation* and sure economic terminal direction outweighs many, perhaps all, of them. As long as the monosymbolist is in a position to follow and fulfill his punctual monoteleological disposition he is the happiest and most successful man of the world. He has clear goals, strong will and strong magnetic helps for his energy. He is therefore not only going far, but going easily. He has not only high, but also sure results of his affective activity. If the model of terminal psychomechanic reaction is introduced and taught well to the individual faculty, then he shoots skillfully, always again, toward the eternal monosymbolic goal. But he needs absolutely this monosymbolic attitude of his psychological surroundings. He has learnt this method of psychic reaction; he is familiar with this kind of artistic adaptation and has the best results, as long as he keeps fixed on his burning monosymbolic bull's eye. But we know that the practical life and the real working experience of our progress has just the disadvantage to take away the sharpness and intense visibility of this punctual light-field. The individual, his monosymbolic shooting skill once adopted, and once grown up in the monogenial school and practice, is no more in a position to change his mind and adopt new varified methods, but has reached the top of his monosymbolic skilful performance, his characteristic maturity to whose marvellous achievement and hitting sureness the complete inadaptability and stiffness of his psychological functions is connected.

But what about this? Does life exact from our activity merely preferably monosymbolic and monosensorial affective reactions? Is this the ordinary way how we have to react against our sensorial surroundings? Or proves the INADAPTABILITY and STIFFNESS to be fatal in our practical life? Idealistic stiffness and inadaptability would not be of great influence in the practical life, if they would not check the necessary developments of the psychic functional trend, whose insufficiency destroys the useful personal possibility. The continual onesided custom of extreme monosensorial idealistic attitude has not permitted the individual disposition to learn all kinds of shooting differences concerning the size of the target, its lighting and ranges. The individual lifeforce is, therefore, educated to re-act only best and surely to one range, to one lighting and to one size of the sentimental target.

If this monosymbolic attitude of the target, most easily reachable by its intense shining lighting, but most difficult owing to its punctual small size, is taught to be attained with the greatest skill to the accustomed shooting individual, then, on the other side, all other degrees of distance of size and lighting of the intentional target are so much more difficult for the individual performance. If life woud exact from us, exclusively or at least preferably, ideal monosymbolic affective shoots, then we could think to have done a deserving work in plodding *through* all our young years, learning to hit best the monosensorial symbolic target. But unfortunately the symbolic and monosensorial tasks of our life are rather seldom and exceptional. They return always again, it is true, in all realms of our experience, in nature, in religion, art and even practical business. But life ordinarily does not permit to address directly monosensorial values. May this method be useful in the poetical sentiments awakened by the sparkling stars, by the moon or by the murmuring brook in the dark lonely night. The ordinary life does not permit the immediate overskipping of our affective life-force from the individual experience to the terminal punctual monosymbolic idealism. It is almost always the broad opened light-field of our poly-sensorial experience which is the necessary object and target of our working individuality. We have the indispensable necessity of the most varified polysensorial adaptability, life giving to us, at every moment, all kinds of multi-sensorial tasks which we are not able to avoid or to circumvent.

Monosymbolism has the advantage to form the most efficient definite method for reaching the terminal idealism, but it has all the dangers we have now described at length. We know now that the bold looks at the face of the universal causes create the most pronounced estrangement of the individual from the practical life and world: it educates most perfect skill for tasks which are "subordinate" in the practical life and withdraws, by this fact compensatorily, all energy and adaptability which must be supplied and used always for the elastic waves of the daily real changes of life and experience. The essential disadvantage of the monosymbolic conception is just this character of *monopoly* in teachings and in methods which we cannot apply to practical justice. Monosymbolism is not even a middle human example around which all varieties of human individual disposition group continually, but the monosymbolic conception means rather more the most pronounced idealistic one-sidedness as we know, whose consequence is given in the monosensorial exclusion of the whole intellectual surrounding world, as idealism likes to do it. This educational method is, therefore, not the standard of the most harmonious and best human school to which more or less every individual must be suitable, but it imposes, in the most intractable way, its most one-sided idealism and most narrow monosensorialism, which everybody has to obey in spite of his quite different notional composition and disposition and longings. The genial monopoly has the most one-sided tendencies, far away from the real possibilities and inclinations of the individual and of the daily experience, but it emphasizes at the same time its validity and its general obligation. Must its real success not be founded in the superficial conception of its teachings? Would the thorough and whole submission to its magnetic draft not destroy the vital reality of its adherents and make them perfectly inapt for the practice of the life?

The monosymbolic type is much too much mono-AUTHORI-TATIVE, and mono-conservative, must too less individually changeable and adaptable, in his educational method. Jean Jacques Rousseau, Tolstoi and Ferrer carried through the conception that the education of the child in the *school* must be individual and not according to one general pattern. There is no doubt that the most generalizing danger, the most excluding inclination of the in-individual dispositions is given just in the monosymbolic conception. Every individual gift is shortened in its sensorial disposition until it has reached the monosymbolic size; all individual force is refined until it is able to be pushed through the whole of the punctual mono-symbolism. It is only one human type which is respected and cultivated in the genial system, it is the perfect idealist who scorns the whole real world and aspires only to the continual sentimental discharge. But the dispositions of the human individuals are different. They are so manifold as the number of human beings is great. Each point of human individual disposition craves for respect, for the right of free development in the sunshine of benevolent recognition. There is no doubt that just the monosymbolic method hurts most the individual need of personal peculiarity in development, by blind coercion. We will not forget that the imaginative monosymbolic sentimentality has, on the other side, the appreciable, strong possibility to pull the individual by love and affective magnetism. This is, of course, the most precious asset, it is true, for good education. But the strong ideal uniformity turns out to be too rough, too powerful and too far away from most individual dispositions than that it could be accepted as the best general form of education. Good education is exactly never general, but individual and no principle claiming to be a general good educational means is, therefore, good, but bad, because it refuses to be individual and adaptable. The strong authoritative character of the monosymbolic education is wrong. It destroys the respect for the individual dignity which is the highest factor given in every education and of which much more must be held account than of everything else. Nothing can be compared with the individual dignity, the personal nature and disposition are the highest majesties which are put at stake in every school, in every educational system. Every method not observing the individual faculty and not individualizing its action must necessarily be bad, because the most precious sprouts of the individual dispositional tree are misled, misused or even destroyed.

Every general school without quantitative and qualitative adaptation to, and appreciation of, the individual soul of the student must be horrible in its effect. This manner of action is, however the more probable as the educational system is more monosymbolic. The strong Unitarian magnetic way of principles analyzes all dispositions in its characteristic manner, increases and compresses the individual dispositions to its law and levels everything to its hard and intractable unity. There is always one and the same point which is elaborated and acknowledged as the general clue of sensorial genial reaction, and we see easily that after having passed this monoformal educational school, the individual falls back to his individual standards of reaction, or if he does not, he perishes likely by the loss of his former method.

The great order and the psychodynamic efficacy of the monosymbolic educational method is clear. The work of this education is simplified, ensured and free of the exacting difficulties of individual adaptation. But the individual natural psychological disposition is not saved by this fact. It is the role of the educator which is facilitated, it is the authority of his personality which has gained much by the monosymbolic method whose intermediator the teacher is, but not the pupil whose natural gifts are not enough respected or appreciated.

Monosymbolism is the strongest and surest source of the one-sided education of the *ideal sublimation* of the individual. Monosymbolism and strongest guidance of the pupil to the highest degree of affective sublimation are practically and theoretically in closest connection and in nearest psychological relation. The more unity in symbolism or in the solstitial conversion, the more urgent conduction of the individual life-force to the ideal sublimation. The reasoning dissolution of the monogenial hero as well as the covering of the monotheistic conception of the religion lower the personal idealistic energy of sublimation. The monopunctual idealistic discharge will be diminished in its energy by this means, but the real enlargement, the improvement of the real outlook and adaptability will be so more ensured by this conversion. The *modern inclination* to carry through this educational change is in nearest connection with the intellectual dissolution of the monosymbolism and with the scientific modification of the religious work. SCIENCE broadens the religious monosymbolism into the large sieve of numerous intellectual openings. The effect of this action is the lowering of the idealistic discharging energy on one side, but also the more human and more balanced existence of the psychological conditions which permit not only the one-sided ideal sublimation, but connect the human affective gift also more broadly and more efficiently to the intellectual values of the real and visible world.

We recognize in the scientific broadening of the conceptions the self-defense of our young life against disagreeable surprises in the proceeding experience, the practical life exacts our real and material share in its development; the material necessities of our adult age throw us more and more from the monosymbolic fixations into the broad open light-field of work and possession. Had we only the monosymbolic education in our young days, then we shall not be inclined, later on, to change our psychological attitude and to adapt ourselves to the variable real multiplicity of our human fate. The intentional character of our soul has been developed too much and to a most one-sided temperamental taste. Strong monosymbolic education creates affective monosensorial stiffness which may be quite successful as long as we live in small circles, where the powerful ideal suggestion is most elaborately and clearly presented to our eye, but the decadence and real inaptitude will be so much greater as the changes from the monosensorial to the multi-sensorial exactions of our life will be more rapid and more distant.

The young man coming out from the college or the university has to perform this change most perfectly and rapidly. The practical life takes him away from the charming art and the artistic elaborations of his young dreams and throws him at once into the sensorial illusions of the objective working reality. If he is accustomed to enjoy the most energetic terminal ideals, then he is roughened, because all weaker magnetic objectivity is not able to correspond to his "easy" or "awkward" affective discharge. He scorns the lower forces of psychodynamic attraction, he will be easily and thoroughly disappointed because he is accustomed to put always all his affective energy at stake. The objective multiple work will not permit him to repeat here the same. The real objects have not the capacity of his former terminal idealistic monosymbolism and he will, therefore, be continually hurt and pushed back from his exaggerating affective attempt.

The MODERN SCIENTIFIC EDUCATION has the intention to prevent this disagreeable surprise of the young man coming out from the theoretical educational atmosphere, in the wide world. Science strives to insinuate and to replace already to the young human being the later objective multiplicity by its objective varification so that there will be no more surprises and too bold necessities of psychological changes, if the young man leaves the place of his theoretic education. The modern natural science suggests, to the human life-force from the very beginning, the most variable affective adaptability; it has in opposition to the merely genial education the appreciable power to split up the one-sided monosymbolic and monosensorial manner of the psychodynamic reaction and to supply the educational affective variability, as it is necessary in the later adult life in the working real performance. Natural scientific education means early reality of the psychological attitude. It excludes the pleasure seeking attitude of the monosymbolic education; the one-sided thirst for the enjoyment is replaced, in scientific education, by the more modest, but less pampering progression of the logical work. The scientific pupil will not be surprised coming out from his educational institution in the open world; he already in his former time had the habit of intellectual differentiation, of working distension and real modesty. Science had educated him to adapt himself in time to thousand relative necessities. He has been withheld from the one-sided acceptance of any absolute monosensorial monopoly. He will be, therefore, successful in his future real life; he will be at home within the broad real world, because he had to behave so from the very first step of his educational practice. Science is reality, work and real broad outlook. The scientific individual has the best condition for the future working life, because there was no monosensorial roughening nor stiffening inadaptability before.

The *last word of good education* is, therefore, the continual change in presentation of affective values. If we succeeded in supplying continual changes to the individual affective performances, then we have the best guarantee for his future success in the real life. The young pupil must daily be suggested to adapt his intelligence and sentiments not only to the last and most thorough monosensorial theistic goals, but he has moreover, according to his later destiny, the necessity to acquiesce with, and work out, all kinds of real objects, from the most shallow periphery to the very affective symbolic centre, in order to gain and to finish the adaptability of his affective soul. The broadest and the quickest affective adaptability will undoubtedly conquer the whole real world : adaptability is detailed real appreciation, which means the first and chief step toward any influence on the reality.

Character is good and nobody can have or aspire to anything important without character. But character is the terminal stage of success. Character is the monopunctual egoism, the last station, where all working goods are brought and where they are fixed in the magnetic attraction of the personal order and force. Character is the shed where the working products of the life are gathered and preserved, but they cannot come there without previous adequate work.

REAL SUCCESS has therefore both suppositions which seem to be in somewhat contradictory : first the detailed refined affective adaptation to the outside reality and to the surrounding objective world which is in such a way invited and fixed to the individual force, and second the monocentral egoistic avidity of the personal character which concentrates and gathers the whole totality of the detailed acquisitions. The lack of success of both the pronounced idealist and realist is therefore clear. The first does not succeed because he does not know or is not willing to come in contact with the gradual values of the real objectivity which all must be acknowledged and appreciated justly and refinedly. The one-sided realist will not succeed because he has not the power of affective personal concentration. The success of the world and of the life presupposes again the combination and culmination of these two faculties of the real-ideal individual, or rather the harmonious possession of these qualities of strong idealism and strong realism which so easily exclude each other, if one of them is too much pronounced. Real success has therefore the supposition of the most pronounced psychological gift and skill, strong in personal importance, but as well elastic in objective adaptability. Where we have these two qualities, there real success in life will not fail. Where we have only one of them there we shall have a failure. Clear personal intentions on one side and passionate desire, refined objectivity on the other hand, these two are the two indispensable suppositions to go on surely and easily in the world. We must be able to avoid and to evade real values which are hurtful to our progress, we must grasp the real objects of our meeting destiny with the most sensitive hand, and we must have the energy and the interest to concentrate what we received in our strong personality, then we have the fulfillment of the success.

Goethe said once: "Du must steigen und gewinnen oder sinken und verlieren, leiden oder triumphieren, Hammer oder Ambos sein." There is indeed no possibility to avoid the alternative of the hammer or the anvil, up to a certain degree. Life points its situations always so much that we at last are compelled to progress courageously towards our success or to allow the fate to eliminate us thoroughly from our advantages. The last word of the success is undoubtedly the word *bluffableness*. He who has the power to attract the magnetic gift of his neighbor energetically toward his affective personality, is the hammer and the victorious factor in the social intercourse. He who permits easily to be bluffed and fascinated by the psychological energy of the concentrated effort of the neighbor, descends, loses, serves and becomes the anvil of his will. The principal fact to be prone to be bluffed by the magnetic lightfield of the other or to be able and successful in subjecting it to one's own will decides whether the direction of the magnetic lifeforce and its attached objective retinue, flows to us or from us, whether we are the receivers and winners or the givers and losers in the psychological wrestle. If we have the energy to fix and attract in advance the psychological energy of someone else, then either we have the stronger psychological attraction and the richer personal gift than our surroundings, or we are accustomed to effectuate most efficiently the punctual monosymbolic idealistic concentration of our light-field, by which we receive great suggestive direction and power, or we have the chance of having people around us who are much more bluffable than we ourselves and who, therefore, are defeated by our desire of ruling authority. The last case will probably be most frequent in the practice. The authority of famous people grows most if their personality is hidden and if some intermediary idealistic bluff plays the continual role of strong magnetic symbolic excitement. The direct detailed intercourse of any great man with the public would be his instant loss of authority: for detailed intimacy and personal outstanding authority are ordinarily incompatible.

There is no doubt that there are important differences between men and men, but the detailed dealing with men destroys essentially authority, and then the brilliant one-sidedness of any people have their corresponding shadows in their life in order to level the admiration by contempt as soon as there is established direct intimate intercourse between the pre-conceived hero and the public. This is the reason why it is almost impossible to erect any serious authority today: because our public which had in former ages, by the monosensorial education, the utmost bluffability, has lost it in our intellectual time. In the modern age the judgment of the objective intellectual education makes that authoritative examples are not any longer easily caught and imprisoned into any fascinating symbol: it is more difficult in our days to bluff and to hynotize by help of monosensorial symbolism than it was fifty or a hundred years ago. The average individual of today is less frightened by any symbolic monosensorial or mystic impression, but the result of the logical, intellectual and non-mystical education in the young days is that the strong inclination to react in punctual symbolism has gone. The bluffability of the individual consists in the magnetic desire to join quickly the punctual monosensorial suggestion. He who expects most quickly and closely and most intensely any mystic or symbolic demonstration of his neighbor, falls first into the pitfall of his authoritative sorcery.

The degree of success is the product of the share of the passive and active hypnotic influences and magnetic forces, to which we are subjected and which we exercise ourselves.

IGNORANCE is the strongest source of authority. As soon as there is any strong difference between our personal knowledge and power of explanation, on one side, and of the skilful concentration of affective weight of our neighbor, we become his prisoners. The degree of our ignorance is the exact measure and scale of our helpless passive subjection to any outside authority. The expansion of our ignorance is the precise measure of the gap by which we are separated from our own reasonable self-esteem and self-sureness. The effect of the higher concentrated intelligence is the stronger affective insight and wilful attraction; the progressed intellectual or genial individual has, therefore, the influence of a wizard on his ignorant neighbor whom he pulls, by the power of his affective energy, irresistibly to the symbolic spell of his monosensorial light-field. It is the fault of the ignorant if he permitted himself to be swept away by the symbolic attraction of his neighbor. Authority is, therefore, the consequence of the fact that we aspire to higher affective concentrations and intellectual notions than our natural gift permitted us to understand. The ignorant man who mounted too high on the ladder of his ambitions, has indeed not mounted but he has been pulled by some other circumstance or attractive personality; he never learned the single steps to his high success. He has not the life-connection with his surrounding world even if he had high success; he would be frightened to go back any steps from the top of his successful ladder which he never experienced personally and practically, and therefore, he is isolated within the confinement of the superior authoritative concentration of the monosensorial light-field of the personality of his neighbor whom he does not understand, but in whom he believes.   No sooner he has studied his psychology and has found out the logical makeup of his personal affective weight and of his gradual historic development than this impassable gap of ignorance will be filled up.   Belief will be changed into knowledge, but knowledge also in imitation, equality and true authority. The experienced and learned one is no more the passive prisoner of the authority as the ignorant, but he, as the bearer of authority, shares the responsibility and the intellectual values of the progressing laws of the authority; he is able to retreat from this light-point, to make communications with the surrounding intellectual world; he is able to put together and identify his own personality and intellectual affective soul with the central point of his authority, but also even to leave this organic house and to build the same, if he is willing to do so. We understand, therefore, that the authority is more comfortable, in a sense, and more sure and indispensable dealing with an ignorant public.   Cessation of ignorance means dilution of the wonderful energy compressed in one punctual symbol, enlightening means the definite destruction and smashnig of the brilliant genial diamond which was before in the possession of one, and which is afterwards, in a democratic freedom, scattered into all winds of the universe.   Science and enlightenment have the effect of serving as numberless mouths leading the water from the deep sea of idealism into the whole surrounding individual and intellectual world. The world is not for the authority, but the authority for the world.

On the other hand the supra-intellectualization of the world would abolish all authority. We would lose the order and direction of our commonwealths and of our life and the terminal social chaos would be the result of the general equal authoritative effusion on all individuals.   But we may not be too timid on this question.   Although the world made excellent progress in advancing enlightenment and intellectual capability in the individual, there is no easy possibility or hope that this balance or affective exhaustion of the authoritative idea could be done.   Our human society is upon the whole, still so much ignorant and artless that they will always more or less remain bluffable by the words of any "prophet" even being cheap and silly.

If monosensorial attitude does not give real STUPIDITY in educating to highest affective values, then it at least produces the taste for it. The monosensorial idealist is fond of genial simplicity of the heart and of highest affective performance, and drops, therefore, the whole scale of affective peripheric values. Stupidity means roughening of the detailed categoric adaptability. The greatest idealist can be defined as the man with the greatest "conceit" and the smallest practical cleverness. The explanation of the proverb that stupidity and PRIDE are always together, lies here perfectly clear. Stupidity and pride are not the same thing, they are in themselves the contrary, pride being very conscious of some high values and directing to it all its extreme and persevering attention, whilst stupidity has the exactly opposite meaning of lack of attention and concentration. They are opposed in one sense, and compensatory notions in another. The more pride, the more danger of stupidity, and the less stupidity, the less danger of pride.

The greatest idealist is, of course, the proudest individual, but also the most stupid in the sense of the practical life. The most practical man and the most adapted practical realist has perhaps no idealism, but, therefore, at the same time no pride, no conceit, no authority and no personal importance. If he has we will call him really converted idealist. Pride means strong emphasis of central monosensorial symbolism, extreme idealists are, therefore, of course, most proud. The proudest individual is necessarily, according to the psycho-mechanic laws, the monosymbolic type. He has put all his psychological value on one point, he emphasizes only his monosymbolic fact in the extreme degree at the expense of all other previous peripheric affective stages and has, therefore, the most typical one-sided mono-sensorial emphasis, which we call pride. Stupidity is only the escorting compensatory blurring and slight connection with the other values of the reality. Stupidity means superficiality and affective looseness in dealing with the multiplicity of the real objects. The psycho-concentric strong energy is, therefore, the direct mother of real passivity, lack of intellectual interest and of practical energy. So life creates, through the realistic and symbolic system, *two quite different types of characters*—one the proud idealist which is enjoying himself within the narrow confinement of his monosymbolism, who has no interest in the working refinement of the real world and is consequently expelled from the society to the solitary hills of his sentimental dreams. The second type produced by the real system is the working modest refiner of the present experience and of the meeting real objects, he has not the strength of the terminal pride and the sure direction of the idealist, but he has the detailed attention, the most pronounced variable affective magnetism sticking to the intellectual reality. The second type is the collector of the real objects, he is the diligent bee refining the real life to higher values; he must give the honor, in idealistic questions, to the idealist, but claims the dominion of the real earth and of the visible conditions of the world. The pride of the second type is not concentrated, but diluted into the whole created work, he is, therefore, not proud, but clever. Pride and cleverness are only two different temperamental expressions of our psychodynamic taste, both being different applications of our individual affective attention and inclination.

One of the most serious handicaps of our *real success* is our *hyper-bluffability*. If we, as true idealistic optimists, are inclined to gratify the neighbor with all our punctual symbolic charm, and if he, by the smallest effort, succeeds in exciting our sentiments to complete faithful obedience to his will, he may scorn and abuse our optimism in the quick readiness to benevolent belief and affective surrender.

The extreme symbolic attitude is ambivalent in its affective tendency. Extreme symbolic love is impersonal and impartial and as well inclined to serve as to invite the other's as one's own interest. Strong symbolic optimism means always playing with fire. It tends to extreme fighting attitude and one-sided utility. The optimistic lover, if he does not allow himself to be defeated by the stronger bluffing will of the other, swallows him himself.

Monosymbolic happiness is exceedingly dangerous, because we lose our own judgment and will in regard to our friend. If we, as it often happens, complain that our goodness is always again abused in life by people, then we confess by this that we always again turn out to be hyper-bluffable. We super-estimate people too much in the beginning of our acquaintance, we judge subjectively according to our idealistic monosymbolic custom instead of objective merits. But every super-estimation, from which experience afterwards teaches us to recover to more exact, more true and more careful valuation of our neighbor, means indeed the confession of a certain corresponding amount of stupidity. The unworthy abuser, put first in the central halo of our benevolence, accepts this sign, he already has with this the proof of our weak side and is tempted to abuse instantly our careless *optimism*. It is sure that optimism means, at the same time, ideal education and magnetic help for our weaker fellow-man, as well as pessimism ruins all psychological relations by its magnetic obstruction. But the subjective optimism without the careful study of the objective worthiness of the favored individual, means invitation for abuse and is in itself ordinarily the expression of real stupidity. Stupidity means affective inadaptability. If we favor somebody too much with our benevolence and he turns out afterwards to be unworthy of it by abuse, then we have proved our inexact intellectual judgment of his personality, and we are guilty of stupidity or lack of objective use of our affective and notional possibilities, tragic as our abuse may be felt. The superestimation for the neighbor and his psychological value is perhaps ordinarily not the consequence of our clear previous benevolence, but of our strong monosensorial taste for pleasure to which we are educated and which makes the essence of our accustomed psychodynamic temperament. If we repeat always again this monosensorial habit and are perseveringly willing to include, again and again, the first meeting neighbor into this charming punctual circle of our love, then we prove our educational heroism and our selfishness for people and the world, but confess at the same time our helpless inaptitude for real psychological intercourse and our absolute blurring stupidity in dealing with the detailed values of the reality.

In continuing our uncritical OPTIMISM, we disgrace our own noble nature; the following ideal disappointments and real failures baffle at least all our success in ideal and real life and we finish in the passive state of despair and of embitterment. The end of the great optimist is the great *pessimism*—the beginning affective monosymbolic optimist who was too ready in pulling and referring everything and everybody to idealistic pleasure and perfection, will be the thorough lack of sentimental confidence and idealistic belief. If the former state of criticless affective devotion to all occurrences, circumstances and persons was successless because of lack of adaptation and decent grasp, then we have not to expect better success from the perfect pessimistic relapse of any character. Optimism contains, at least, ignorant and unadapted and stupid as it may be, the magnetic invitation to affective love and collaborating union which, it is true, turns very often, though not always, out to be abused instead of establishing the desired magnetic parallelism of sentiment. But the pessimism, principally the same resignation of intellectual working adaptability, has not even the magnetic invitation for collaboration. It means only repulsion of the affective forces. Pessimism has the chief intention to prevent any hurting abuse and any disagreeable surprises in the future time. It means the obstruction not only of the own psychological performance, but also the petulant frustration of the idealistic discharge of the neighbor. If optimism in many cases is abused, it, on the other hand, has at least the advantage to succeed in others, in helping, educating and stirring weaker or shyer idealistic potentialities. But pessimism scatters without any hope of forwarding the happiness of the universe. The pessimist is unhappy himself and paralyses at the same time his fellowmen. He protects himself against abuse and exploitation, but lacks in his peremptory way the support of magnetic favor and friendship.

He is far from saying: "May I perish, if only others are happy!" but he rather asserts: "If I must be unhappy, I will prevent at least all others from happiness, too!"

Be it as it may, both pessimism and optimism are the expression of psychodynamic stupidity, the first at the beginning, the second at the ending stage of psychological experience. Both are not able and not willing to adapt themselves to the working refined congruency with the objective reality, both discard in advance and thoroughly every hope to be intellectual enough to find out and to recognize the real affective values of the creative world. But both have their fatal psychological root in the monosensorial mystic education by which they have received the habit of symbolic hyper-suggestibility. Life bluffs, both optimistic and pessimist, at every moment of their life; they are only able to refer all their psychodynamic reactions to the delightful monosensorialism or not to react at all. They are extremists who cannot find in the practical life their exact confirmation, both are rejected and eliminated by the refined necessities of the ever-fluctuating changes of the practical psychology. Here also we have to recognize that ignorance is the root of all evil. Had the individual gift not had the unhappy monosensorial education in its early days, the fatal inadaptability to the exactions of the practical life could likely not have taken place. The roughening of the psychological function of the individual soul has its root in the previous overweight of the idealistic authority which at last proved not to be so useful in the experience of the life as it was intended first and which is excluded at last altogether, because the intelligence of its uselessness and practical danger frightens the disappointed individual.

We will be successful in our life in the degree as we are found able to *serve* well. The best servant is soon promoted to the first social position. He is put at the head of the group of men whom he served best of all. There is, it is true, a gaping difference between the servant and LEADING CHARACTER of men. The servant put at the head of any community will continue to serve; he will even in his leading position think of the details he did before so well and he likely will not be able to represent the whole authority of any complicated totality. The first dignitaries and nominal leaders of any society are, therefore, practically and indeed no leaders, because they were elected by the sympathy of the members to whom they did in the former time excellent services and are expected to continue so. The leader type is not loved by the single members of any community; he is exclusive, theoretic and prone to sacrifice the individual for his principles. The leader type is, therefore, ordinarily the idealist who is not able to adapt himself easily and who never was very inclined nor able to do any services moulded to the intimate need of individuals and circumstances. The real leader of any society, the progressive inspirator of any genial development is, therefore, scarcely in a position to be elected as the representative head and as the nominal bearer of the authority which he is, psychologically, and must be. He is ordinarily the *right hand* of the more adaptable nominal head of the community: the leader character is much less pliable to the circumstances, offends himself much too easily at every real digression from his principles, is, therefore, too little able to gain the sympathies of the practical differentiation than that he himself would have the general election in his favor. On the other hand, his conviction, his honest straightforward sentiments and his affective strength are able to make up even to a certain degree what he lost by his affective and theoretic stiffness. He binds together general interests, but is not able to deal intimately with the needs of the neighbor. He is able to direct and to point the best future ways of the totality, but has not the power to help the individual claims in the real world. He can suggest in general good words, but is bothered and embarrassed instantly by the clear intellectual sharpness of the real objective problems.

It is indeed the *serving* human type who has most chances to make excellent success and progress in the real world. The idealistic pride offends in its inexorability; the adaptable humility of the servant, on the contrary, has the effect of the soft politeness which is so necessary for every successful good *instradation* of the common effective work. The idealist has, therefore, we may say, great difficulties to enter into any affective alliance. His victories are quick or never. His high-strung and exceedingly sensitive directive attitude is very reactive to any affective non-parallelism. This hyper-sensitiveness most probably baffles ninety-nine per cent of the offers of affective collaboration. The incompatibility of the idealist turns out to be the most serious handicap for his magnetic collaboration and coordination with anybody, but if this first stage is overcome, if the petty beginning digressions of opinions and feelings are done away with, then we have no dearer friend than the idealistic character, and his affective fixation. His friendship proves very strong, true and persevering; he furthers very much, but he develops himself also, within his friendship, most advantageously. The realist is movable, less reliable in depth, he makes easily connections and can manage it to be received everywhere with favor in the first stage of his alliance, whilst the idealist has difficulties to enter into affective union, he hurts and is hurt most probably just at the first deciding point of the rising friendship. This conception is practically more true than the reverse which, in some sense, could be justified, too. But once started and fixed, he proves to be the soul of Nathanael, without falsehood, without tricks and intellectual egotistic reservations. He is the most successful and most reliable type of partner in any union, in marriage and in business. His point of honour is very developed, his principles do not permit him to go away from any general ideal or conception. He proves, therefore, to be open, honest and sincere toward his neighbour.

The monosensorial idealist is able to give strong direction and good intentions, but not the means toward it. He is a wonderful high tree with the most sparkling summit pointing and reaching into heaven; but this tree has no branches, no twigs and no green foliage. It is only the abstract perpendicular ruler and the clear terminal magnetic needle of our life, but there is no division and no real widespread horizontal possessing order. But why Nature, which produces all kinds of varieties and even monsters in every realm, should not produce also the one-sided curiosum of the extreme degrees of idealism? The Gothic style is the most clear intellectual expression of this affective idealistic condition exaggerating the perpendicular idealistic taste and neglecting the horizontal real expansion. The idealist is, therefore, full of rights and best intentions, but he is not able to practise them in reality; he is full of genial, leading wit, but has no clever judgment about the daily petty occurrences.

The idealist who so lightly looked over the real intellectual possessions and conditions, as long as life did not permit him to share them, becomes the type of the TYRANT, as soon as real success joins his monoidealism. The tyrant type is characterized by the peculiarity that he expects the whole intellectual and real function of his surroundings going most minutely according to his personal theoretic and ideal conceptions. The peevish tyrant is the child of the most pronounced magnetic intolerance; the fulminant energy of the mono-idealistic feelings is more susceptible of every affective and intellectual digression and hits every non-parallelism, like the most energetic projectile fired from a gun crushes the meeting obstacle. As long as the idealistic sentiments are merely theoretic, they are not able to exercise the full weight of their influence; but their power of direction and of crushing every non-parallelism will be quite surprising and tremendous, when the real success has enlarged the trend of their influence. It corresponds, thus, to the psychological energy of the monopunctual idealism, that not only the whole realm of its adaptable work is directed most strictly and immediately to the only ruling idea, but that it smashes and crushes all least terminal deviations. All strong mono-idealistic teachings of the world, as they started with the most pronounced lightning flashes of their chief ideas, are proofs of this truth. The Spanish Inquisition, the reforming Iconoklasy, but also the French Revolution and the Russian Bolshevism are instances of this universal psychological necessity. If the mono-idealist possesses himself of the real power, he develops and pulls everything immediately according to his tenets, but he destroys also all opposite factors. The selfless idealist pervades, as soon as he can, the whole range of the created nature and culture with his powerful energy, penetrates everything with his magnetic spell and destroys all digressing real existence of the world, much more thoroughly than every other system. The principle of the mono-idealism is, indeed, not to honour everything because it is, not everything is right for it because it exists, but everything is wrong which does not suit its idealistic fulminant mono-direction. So it is quite significant that the extreme mono-sensorial religious idealism condemns the world as a whole, it essentially excludes from its system the whole circumference of the created visible surroundings and their conditions, and decries the least magnetic non-parallelism with the general and peremptory mark as being devilish, it is to say, anti-divine or essentially opposite work. More fulminant hatred than the lightnings of the anathema of the mono-idealistic systems cannot be easily imagined. The whole unities of affective non-parallelism, everything which is not assimilable to the mono-idealistic prescription and which is not suggestable or workable to the direction of the mono-idealistic system is rejected as well and hated even more. Oh, that thou wert cold or warm, but because thou art neither cold nor warm, I will spew thee out of my mouth. Does perfect antagonism mean the antipole of the same mono-idealistic idea, representing the logical longtitudinal elongation of the same psychological makeup? Is it not the very distant development or the previous stage of the same idea which seems to be a contradiction, but it is only a distance?

The *capital punishment* is the most developed practical consequence of the extreme mono-idealism. In this legal light which society assumes, we see the radical method of the mono-idealistic energy. The sprout which is not able to accept naturally the same parallel direction with the mono-ideal sentiments, is cut away from the tree of life. The idealistic society does not wait to burn the weed until the general day of harvest has arrived. Nothing is more intolerant and more consequent than the ideal theoretical law society, if it receives the legal executive power. The conviction of every pronounced mono-idealism is necessarily so narrow, so conceited, and so one-sided that it crushes peremptorily all non-conformity of the individual member of the commonwealth. If there were ever any possibility to crave eye for eye or tooth for tooth, in our days, this theory should be eliminated thoroughly, not only from the individual, but also from the legal authorities. What is right is right for the individual as well as for the state and what is wrong in the single individual is not able to become right because it is handled by the majority of the violent power. On the contrary, the conscientious individual alone is able to judge psychological situations, connections, causes, rights and necessities and the best jury is scarcely able to gain the sufficient insight into the deepest psycho-dynamic connections and necessities of any criminal actions. If the individual perhaps killed, he must have done it, either owing to illness or to unhappy intellectual constellations and affective stagnations, but in neither case there should be any reason for the capital punishment. In the first case, the right place for justice is the asylum, and in the second, deliverance from the dangerous psychological situation of the surroundings. It is the *absolute* conviction of its truth which permits to the idealistic state condemnations of the thoroughness as it is the capital punishment. The absolute mono-determination of the philosophical conception is wrong, not only being checked from any future development in the universal general progressing necessities, but also doing wrong because the mono-idealistic general system of any religious order cannot be the whole truth, but only one part of truth. In spite of the usefulness of one firm conviction, there must always be room for the most manifold points of interrogations in our progressive human society, and we fairly agree that just in this point we see how much the intellectualization of the society is able to enlarge our affective adaptability, to augment the elasticity of our conceptions and to make more inclined to judge mildly and reservedly digressing solutions of the more thorough vital problems than the average legal humanity has them.

Faults against the law are so complicated notions, they are so entirely different in the constellations of their rising conditions from everything which is general and legal, that every least experienced man of heart would hesitate to lift a hand against committed faults in the sense of the general law, if he thinks of himself and the peculiar possibilities of the social conditions which indeed overthrow, in their detailed nature, all former points of view and all pre-conceived notions of any legal reduction or liberation. Many "crimes" are unforeseen solutions of unforeseen causes of the detailed experience: they perhaps must create new important modifications of the law which has possibly proved short and insufficient. They may mean the enlargement of the old way of psychological and philosophical conceptions of the life and of the world: they are the practical predecessors of the future legal modifications of the law which must be so much broadened that all these numberless cases of extraordinary psychology can be constantly meditated, decently explained and put right, in the most expensive and right sense of the *psychological understanding and justice*. The law of superficial intellectual justice against which all people continually and naturally sin and according to which nobody sincerely lives, is indeed not only bad and wrong, but it is a sign of unwillingness of cultural development. We ought to have few, but strong and respected laws, because authority must be.

Where the practical behaviour of the humanity in the crushing majority is digressing from any law, there we must admit that not humanity, but the law, is wrong, that not humanity must be amended, but the law. For law intends to be only the best expression of the best human possibilities. It is the conception of the mono-idealistic part of the world, that people are for the law and not the law for the people. But this manner of conception is evidently wrong. The legal development comes out from the social need of welfare and self-protection and any law built up only on idealistic, theoretical ideas and disregarding the craving needs of the individual nature, must necessarily be wrong. Whosoever, is happy or unhappy enough to take a glimpse behind the curtains of the legal psychology and whosoever looks with the eyes of broadminded love and universal justice at the motives and connections of our legislation of the famous 20th century, will be shivering from the oppressive responsibility of the professional judge and be glad not to judge, but, in the case of emergency, rather to be judged.

BLOWS AND VIOLENCE are also in nearest connection with the mono-idealistic or subjective conception of the world. They also are violent, angry attempts to direct the real world to parallel accordance with the mono-idealistic effects. Violence and blows are extreme recoveries from former laziness; they are the confession of the blowing individual that he was not able or willing to seize the detailed objectivity of his experience at the right time, that he had not the refined adaptability of his disposition to grasp and to form the clay of his psychological social conditions and that he beat his fellow-man for that reason that he would not insist on the liquidation of the necessary real detailed differences, but would rather hurry up to the terminal station of the mono-genial and mono-affective reconciliation and enjoyment, before the development of the logical life permitted it. Blows and corporeal violence are, therefore, angry impatient actions, they represent overskipping leaps over the logical steps of the gradual education; they are in closest psychological connection with symbolism and mysticism, emphasizing some real points too much at the expense of dropped other ones.

It is the same sword, the same fiery lightning of the extreme monoidealism which creates wars, electrocutions and executions, produces tyrants, proud conceit and inflexible domineering attitude, all coming out from the exaggerated condensation of the punctual burning point of the psychological magnifying glass. It is the dispersion of this destroying genial concentration of the rays of our affective soul which is the only clear and sure means to remove the educational damages from our psychological actions. As we know, this happens clearly and surely in the *scientific* activity which broadens the punctual size of our psycho-pupil, which takes away the intense energy of our affective heat and transfers the previous mono-determination of our sentiments to the larger objectivity of our visible and real surroundings. Culture means essentially the opening action of the punctual pupil of our mono-symbolic instincts; it expresses the disclosure of our faithful eternal monovision to the broad open field of the intellectual reality, where we are entitled to appreciate every detail, to inspire to it the appropriate magnetic share of our feelings and to be able, therefore, to work in clever thoroughness toward terminal goals, again after all.

One holy law is pervading all the universe.

NINTH BOOK

We start from the assumption that our psychic function has two principal elements, sentiments and intellect, and that these are in a compensatory reversibility, intellect being invertible into sentiments and the latter into the first, so that we have so much more intellectual activity at a given time in the individual according, as the feelings are less and vice versa. But we have always the supposition that these things happen within the total amount of the individual life-force. Let us make a further very essential but arbitrary assumption of my own which explains these assertions very clearly and as well the notion of imagination. Most great ideas were first hypothesis and received then by use, by investigation, and tastes, their practical confirmation and after all, their unchangeable authority of truth and reliability. We will in the following meditations as a very comfortable help take for granted that our psychological function is performed exactly after the example of the light falling through the magnifying glass. This funnel of lights throwing its sunbeams on the light-circle may be compared to the sentimental feelings, whilst the degree of their dispersion, their circumference and size in the plane, may be called the intellectualism of our nature. These two functions are reciprocal as we see in the magnifying glass, the greatest light-circle having the greatest dispersion of the sunbeams, which is to say, the least intensity of localized lighting, whilst the smallest punctual attitude of the light-circle has so much intensity of concentrated light that it burns in its focus the underlying substance. The same we have in our psychological life. When we accumulate all our psychic intellectual energy on one point, one intellectual idea which we may call monosensorialism, monosymbolism, or monopunctualism, then we have compensatorily in the same manner also the most efficient sentimental energy of the individual life-force. This phenonomen is thoroughly characteristic for all psychological human performances, all together emptying after all in this monopunctual attitude, but chiefly for the make-up of the genial religious feelings. The prescription of humility and simplicity of the heart by the churches are exactly pointing to these necessities of compensation, that the strong ideal feelings can only be obtained by the sacrifice and utmost limitation of our reasoning intellect. All kinds of psychological strong sentiments have the most intimate connection with this psychopupilar mechanism which closes very narrowly its opening like an organic eye when it has to peep sharply into the light of ideal divine or eternal sentimental or speculative values, and enlarges on the contrary, freely its psychopupil comprehending and covering a large part of the real objectivity presenting itself to it, when it has not the necessity or will to fix and to deepen, in the sentimental sense, any single object and to give to it at last the ruling supremacy of intellectual exclusive emblematic representation which we may call *terminal symbol*.

All our psychological development has, after all, this same way of concentration from objective psychopupilar enlargement to monosymbolic shrinking contraction: but this progress must be done in the will of our nature carefully and slowly in straining work and logical graduation, not in mystic angry leaps as it is done in miracles. On the other hand it is the essential role and task of religion to be the most effective *psychorhythmic accelerator*, to avoid in this manner the affective stagnations of the human mind, and it is just owing to the miraculous mysticism that the hygienic intention and duty of the religious psychodynamic energy reaches this symbolic monopunctual concentration more easily. We see that Christianity has its sense and value in the educational method and intention of its concentrative energy which creates so many advantages and dangers simultaneously.

The CATHOLIC CHURCH represents the utmost psychopupilar development. It is built up exactly according to the most pronounced geometric formula of the circle and of the central light-point. We find in the Catholic churches everywhere stellary points, circles, sunbeams as the radius of the circles, turrets, gables and halos. But we find the mono-sensorial psychopupilar expressions also in all its institutions and functions of the service, as we recognize in the role of the Host, in the Elevation, in the Sacraments, the genuflection, the Sign of the Cross, the use of Holy Water, in the mystic prayer and chiefly in the love of the rich theatrical exhibition of the burning lights during the divine service.

Catholicism is most characterized by the tremendous monosymbolic emphasis and precision of its real determination of idealistic experience. It reduces the real intercourse with the ideal divinity to the mono-sensorial simplicity of the burning light-field which it calls the state of the simplicity of the heart. We may, therefore, assume in advance, that we have to expect, in the Catholic Church, strong developments of symbolism, mysticism and miracles, that we shall meet strong emphasis of all psychodynamic concentrative means, but also weakness of all retarding helps as well, psychologically speaking.

The emphasis, scarcely alluded to, of the logical steps to the idealistic goals or rather the utmost artistic and psychological most careful development of mono-sensorial mystic symbolism produces likely, the most pronounced ideal suggestibility and bluffability of the Catholic pupil. The specific manner of his education causes often hastening overskipping of the logical gradual performances toward idealism and blurs thus the real thinking escapements necessary for and before reaching the terminal ideal divine enjoyment. Anger, religious fanaticism, and divine enthusiasm are nearest notions in the psychorhythmic sense. The *terminal enthusiasm* is distinguished and featured in this, that the religious enthusiast has learned by practice to shoot his feelings toward terminal ideal values to which he has been trained in the monosymbolic and mono-sensorial school of the clear and sharp punctual light-field of the church. He has learned to meet these last highest goals easily by practice, whereas the *irascible* individual has not this skill to meet universal goals, but hits carelessly every most insignificant experience with the most passionate rush of his affective life-force. But the temperamental mechanism of the logical overskipping and the psychic rhythms are the same in anger, religious fanaticism and divine enthusiasm. All three neglect the rhythmic escapements of the harmonious normal thinking progress and are essentially characterized by the instantaneous bluffability to which they are subjected as soon as the puzzling mirrors of the punctual symbols arise.

The strong practice and exercise in hitting terminal mono-sensorial light-fields may create at last, by individual practice and even culturally by inheritance, the psychological symbolic monomania according to which all logical intellectuality is thoroughly subordinated and every experience instantly related to the deepest abyss of the universal values: this exaggerated sentimental need coming, as the product of the pronounced mono-symbolic education, to the smallest experience of our life, may be what we call neurasthenia and anger. As we saw in the former chapter, the result of the extreme symbolic education must, therefore, be strong divine idealism, scorn of the superficial intellectual life, enormous security and energy in enjoying eternal idealistic goals, but the danger of utmost inadaptability, lack of interest and laziness in the practical life in the working intellectual reality. The mono-maniac symbolism is most efficient in reaching and assuring terminal ideal goals; its psychodynamic energy towards idealism has the advantages of affective speed and of miraculous help: to overskip the obstacles of the reality. This psychology is comparable to the most efficient motor car running from the real experience to the central idealism, most powerfully and most easily. Its psychological methods are most numerous and quickening in miracles, mysticism and symbolism, its artistic representations with their circular underlining of the monosymbolic light-field are enormous helps of suggestion and the ritual ceremonious actions of the priest and the artistic religious community are the same important psychodynamic quickening supports.

The essential feature of the Catholic psychology is, therefore, the forcing symbolic power. We shall see that as long and as wide as the essential action of the ecclesiastic power of the Catholic Church goes, there is always again and again taken refuge to the strong frightening fact of the sharp intellectual light-field of the mono-sensorial symbolism. The basis of the Catholic psychology consists quite essentially in this that the artless believing individual is unexpectedly surprised by the most powerful psychological and sensorial, chiefly optic punctual light-fields and is induced by this frightening force or hypnosis to surrender all his will-power to the attractive idealism. Genial hypnosis is everything in the practice of the Catholic Church. All the means indicated already, of the Catholic psychology, in art and in ecclesiastic functions, are such hypnotizing supports. They all together are expressions of the same meaning and of the same method which is prosecuted by the exceedingly strong sign of the main Christian hypnosis, the name of Jesus. This symbol has received through the traditional use of the centuries and the persistent use by all nations of our civilized world that tremendouss power of hypnotizing suggestion, that it turned out to be the most energetic sharp symbol, frightening and assailing the suggestible vulnerability of the believing individual heart like a sharp pointed arrow.

But the church complicates this symbolic divine relationship. It puts the *priest* as the intermediator between believing individual and idealism. The priest is, in this case, the stewart and dispensator of the last smallest and most charming ideal symbols in the Catholic religion. He is the keyholder of the gracious treasures of the church, because he has and performs the symbolic actions. In the Catholic church the priest shares already to a certain degree the role of the divine symbolism, he nearly means for the believer a humanized theistic symbol, and we have here the explanation of his easy authorative leadership and the reverent love he enjoys among his adherents.

The Church pretends to be the unchangeable intellectual

monogamy with God. It has built up the most stolid mono-sensorial opportunity of idealistic discharge in its Christian humanized symbolism which it consolidated with all means of art, of material and economic institutions. It has decided to be the last and the best form of theistic real expressions, to represent the last and best intellectual monopoly of the human form to deal with the terminal universal idealism. We spoke at length on the subject, how much every intellectual formula is the child of its historic time, how all the best things have in our world a time of rising, of culmination and of inevitable ruin, that strong clinging to the intellectual formulas is sterilizing and that universal development of our life, of our history and of everything creates the absolute necessity and compulsion of changing continually in all forms and expression. So religion and denomination have changes as well as all other functions, or can any intellectual formalism be eternal?

The unchangeable genial formulation and unity, efficient, idealistic, sincere, and strong, as it may be in the beginning, proves to be a means of intellectual self-worship of humanity, a help to artistic materialism and a handicap of universal progress of the human psychological society because of the restriction to one unchangeable intellectual expression in which it is confined and fixed forever. The extreme mono-sensorial confinement of the symbolism explains to us many things. The most pronounced mono-sensorialist is by his psychological destiny the gullable simpleton, the beggar, the stupid, the artistic materialist, but also the idealistic leader, the martyr of the highest values of the world, the genius and the sentimental light of the world, admirable by the grandeur of his character. The Catholic must be, in dependence of his psychomechanic rhythmic peculiarity, the strongest monotheist, the gambler who puts all at one stake (mono), the most gifted artistic magnetic individual, but on the average he cannot have the really scientific inclinations, because he is not inclined to independent logical thinking. I so often heard the refutation of this objection in that form that every thinking must have suppositions or goals and must depend on them. This is true. But the objection points to the gradual difference. Thinking which is magnetically attracted too much by strong goals, has no more the value of logical progression, but of sentimental feelings attracted and directed by the strong goals. The objection of the natural scientific world against the dependent thought of Catholicism means the highest degree of sentimental dependence, of its thinking, on the terminal monotheistic and monogenial ideal.

We understand, therefore, that the chief virtues of Catholicism must be devotion and humility. *Devotion* is then most efficient, when the magnetic attraction of the ideal goal is most easy and powerful. Devotion means the most energetic magnetic draft from the believing soul towards the theistic ideal. This condition is best accomplished in Catholicism because its psychomechanic attention is poured on the most distinct mono-sensorial idealistic symbol, Jesus, and this magnetic most powerful symbolic lightpoint through which the individual energy is totally fixed, punctually hypnotized and entirely thrown towards idealism. This mono-symbolic thoroughfare has the strongest elaboration in art, in material institutions, is strengthened by philosophy, tradition, ancestry and by the peculiar local suggestion of the crowd which is always largely used by the special performance of the Catholic religious psychological performance and service.

Strong and clear *symbols* are always the chief intentions of the Catholic performance, through which the intellectual and individual multiplicity is excluded and the common exact simplicity of the heart is established, which makes the common idealistic symbolic discharge of all feelings possible. The exclusion of the intellectual reality received in the monosymbolic simplicity of the Catholic heart has the further idealistic advantage, owing to the law of compensation, that all human individual life-force is permitted to be hurled in one throw towards idealism, every intellectual peripheric sticking and distraction being removed. If devotion is as we admitted acknowledged as the most powerful sentimental discharge to God going with the most pronounced mono-determined attention from the terminal symbol to God, then the genuine Catholic soul must forcedly have great idealistic devotion and the most fervent piety for idealism. The danger of artistic material relapse however, is clear, for the divine eagle cannot be captivated even in the most beautiful golden cage of the most genial artistic elaboration. The exaggeration of the previous monotheistic zeal creates in itself the revenge of the later materialistic relapse and idealistic sterilization. But in the beginning of the Catholic ecclesiastic and individual religious development we observe forcedly the most efficient religious idealistic devotion, as we observe so easily in all Catholic but chiefly in Latin countries where the flaming theistic devotion creates the most moving forms of the individual divine subjection in fervent prayer, in weeping in most emotional attitudes of the body of the praying individual.

The other most Catholic virtue is *humility* coming out also from the monosymbolic psychomechanism. If we remember the extraordinary emphasis of the chief Catholic psychological fact to exclude all sensorial and intellectual influences with the exception of one symbolic light-point—though it often seems the contrary—then we understand the essential meaning of the virtue of humility in the essence of the Catholic church. Humility in its sense means the continual readiness to exclude the totality of the intellectual multiplicity of the experience and of the visible surrounding world, and to give one's feeling to God in the perfect simplicity of the most detached surrender. Simplicity of the heart, humility, self-abnegation and monosymbolism have indeed about the same meaning. Only the individual who is fairly ready to strip all intellectual argumentation, all contrary experiences and all real practical needs of the life is permitted to join the eternal values with the whole force of the efficient sentimental compression. The supposition of the Catholic religious effect in the psychological sense is the most pronounced detachment from the real world, retaining, however, one most important real symbol acting like one impression on the affective soul, it is the Christian monosymbol of the most suggestive name of the historic Jesus. All Catholic theatrical performances in the artistic church, in the mystic service, are mere suggestive helps to forward energetically the human psychology to this characteristic punctual symbolic attitude and to this terminal light-field, to encourage the human soul to the angry immediate psychorhythmic leap from the real peripheric life to the most divine symbolic concentration. Perfect loss and resignation of the sensorial reality is the supposition of the divine success of Catholicism. If it always asserts that we ourselves are not able to do any valuable thing for God and eternity and that we must pray humbly, scorn all real life, depreciate the daily life and refer every good thing to God who is the giver and performer of all actions in us, then it means that we have to join with all attention the terminal punctual light-field of the monosymbolic idealism, that we have to drop all individual intellectual logical action and that we have only to permit the universal magnetism to draw our affective energy through the last communicating monopunctual symbol, given in the hypnotizing notion of the traditional enthusiasm of Jesus. Humility means the perfect resignation of our human real and intellectual faculties on behalf of the monosensorial hypnosis and idealistic discharge from this last symbolic notion.

The *strong sense of authority* and of disciplinarian unity is another great advantage of Catholicism. Quite natural! The essential suggestion of the crowd as it is performed in the sentimental psychological system has the consequence to educate all individuals to the same symbolic attitude, to the same affective reactions and bind them together very closely because of the parallelism of their sentimental performance. Strong sense of authority means strong emphasis of the symbolic values and relative negligence of one's own peripheric intellectual experience. Too strong belief in authority is, therefore, nearest to the idea of humility, both super-estimate the traditional results of the social psychology at the expense of the result of one's own observations. Sense of authority subordinates the own experience, and prefers the results of other people, of other ages and nations in thinking and experience.

The *strong disciplinarian unity* is also the product of the subordination of the individual value and of the personal thinking investigation. The more we reflect individually, the more frequent will our digressing results in thinking and in practical systemization be, and the more numerous will finally the different disgressing tenets, opinions and denominations of any church come out. Intellectualism creates differentiation and multiplicity; lack of criticism and of individual thorough investigation produces unity. It is the beginning strong education to the suggestion of the crowd which prevents the growing believer individual to leave this magnetic strong unity and to split up to the independence of his own critical thinking investigation in psychology. So we see that the individually weak side of the church becomes the strong reality strengthening and reenforcing its body by the unitarian strong representation, whilst the individualistic other systems, where every individual practises his own thinking criticism, split up into numerous denominations and represent in this fact to the outside world less strong organizatory resistance. But is it not the meaning of all life to disappear? Is it not better to have at the end the great history of being the source and mother of continuously great new psychologically human developments and notions and rather to perish, than to become the great and unitarian mumification of a glorious memory?

Inseparability of the individual psychology from the ecclesiastic magnetic union is the much greater, as the parallelism of the affective collaboration is longer. If we have a long parallel run of the affective action of two individuals towards their common ideal goal, then they melt much more thoroughly up together and have more difficulties to part from each other. It is chiefly the *great number of symbols* which has the parallelizing effect on the individual sentiments. For the symbols in psychology have the role of knots which connect the individual digressing gifts and send them as one magnetic sheaf toward the idealistic goal. If there are even many symbols, one behind the other, through which all the social psychology has to be sent in parallel action, then the length and the security of the sentimental parallel union will have the advantage to confirm and to bind together the whole crowd of the partakers in love and in union of feelings and interests. It is the law of the suggestion of the crowd which creates the most powerful magnetic connection between the people who are subjected to any POLYSYMBOLIC AFFECTIVE UNION.

The Catholic Church is indeed rich in symbols and rich in symbolic scales and ranges. We meet everywhere in Catholicism the tendencies to unite the feelings of the believers in single points where the attention of their eyes is fixed and their feelings are punctually concentrated. The whole architectural disposition of the Catholic *Church* is ruled by this tendency. The high altar commands the whole space of the church, it attracts the looks of all believers to its central artistically erected monument. This is the first more vague stage of the symbolic attraction. The second step on the way is the priest who attracts and gathers the hearts of the believers more by his living motions; by his smaller human figure, by the surprising colors of his dress and the laces of his tunic, but most and quite characteristically by the great cross covering his back. This last point is of enormous significance, because the priest turns almost always the back to the public and is hidden behind the great cross drawn on his *casubla*. The never failing cross and the obligatory candle-sticks with the burning lights on the altar have the same meaning; they all are powerful symbols which have the role to concentrate in the *optic* way the attention of the believer, and so to hypnotize him, excluding the real objective surroundings, putting the whole amount of the magnetic psychic energy of the believing crowd into some small points, which is to say, into these optic symbolic directions which, on the altar have their culmination in the elevation of the circular host. Anybody may object that the big cross on the back of the gown of the priest, which circumstance we emphasize very much, was not visible in the former times of the first Christianity, because the priest celebrated behind the altar which had the form of a table, so that the priest was turned with his face to the public. Then I would ask why this former custom was abolished and changed and remind that at all times the cross on the altar was very big and visibly erected attracting the optic mono-punctual attention of the believers.

Now we see if we remember this whole chain of symbolic connection and progression that the Catholic Church, not speaking now of the other artistic helps, has a whole net and sequence of symbolic common fixation of the psychlogical magnetic strength of the believing people. We spoke about the consequences of this poly-symbolism already: unitarian strength, sentimental connection, more chance for terminal idealism, but also the greater danger of being entangled and sticking to the symbolic sills and of artistic material relapse and ideal sterilization. Let us sketch this Catholic ecclesiastic affective symbolism on its way to the terminal ideal in comparison with the natural form of sentimental reaction:

Catholic Ideal Progression:

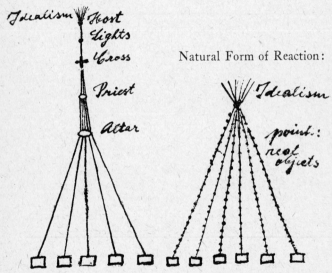

Natural Form of Reaction:

Individual Believers of the Church   Working Individuals

We see, therefore, that the symbolic ladder of the ecclesiastic Catholicism replaces, up to a certain degree, the natural logical intellectual work. It is not the free will or the individual effort which makes way and moves on in this symbolic case, but much more the gradual symbolic energy of the attracting bluffing sensorial, chiefly optic impressions which gradually become smaller and more intense from the big, dim altar until the glaring shine of the small burning lights of the candle sticks and of the distinct circular Host. The Catholic symbolic religious service means, therefore, a chiefly optic education and instradation of the believer to go on in several *inter-symbolic* leaps from the peripheric life to the central monotheistic enjoyment. These symbols have the advantage to move on energetically, to be successful, to catch greedily the individual capability and to shove it quickly ahead. But the symbolic stations are not numerous enough; the supposed leaps necessary from the peripheric life to the central symbol may be too bold and the optic impressions on the human nervous system too strong than not to produce the danger of anger, bluffability and neurasthenia. This system has the fault that it makes the idealistic enjoyment too easy: it is not our personal work and not our absolute necessity which works out the love of God like a source of water blowing up rocks and springing out like a geyser of longing tears to the lap of the beloved God; it is the overweight of the clear magnetic symbols which makes the way easy and which invites the individuals in the most attractive way to the divine enjoyment. This ecclestiastic system has, therefore, the advantage to be the most easy and successful idealistic discharging apparatus, but it pampers in giving great things for little, in rewarding without earning, in granting highest divine feelings without previous serious reflections, deep logical thinking and working gradual progression. We understand, therefore, that so many people who are tired on Sundays and are not intellectually gifted at all, have the inclination to prefer the comfortable efficient service of the Catholic Church to the religious performances of other denominations. But is it not the educational value which decides over the significance of every religious system? Is it not the ethical education of the people the main and deepest task of the religion? The poly-symbolic organization of the Catholic service and psychology, helpful and useful in many ways at it may be, may have the relative danger and the disadvantage to produce, in many cases, laziness, predilection for fairy tales, in our daily hard working life with all its necessities, negligence of the conscientious logic and working effort: all this comes out owing to its pampering facilitation of the idealistic enjoyment and to its thorough exclusion of the working reality in regard to the last ideal. The *optic sense* is the most material and most exciting sense, it is most liable to roughen our physic reactions. In the Catholic symbolism we have at the same time the most pronounced material form of bluffing impressions and of high ideal purposes: it uses both strong real impressions and great idealistic ranges simultaneously. It is just owing to the strong psychic susceptibility for optic impressions that the high terminal goals are easily joined by the Catholic symbolism: but on the other hand we must admit that there is a dangerous contradiction between the passive attitude of the individual will and the hurting energy of the optic symbolism. Optic impressions and active strong work should be always together. Theatrical performances without the escorting or following strong energetic work are dangerous for the human psychology; they hurt by the strong sensorial impressions the soul of the individual, if he does not send his will-power to the same goal in wilful working effort. The optic impressions are the most energetic on our nervous system and therefore, they likely fix, they upset, they excite by far most the human soul, wherefor it is understandable that optic symbolic impressions without thinking and acting are most unnatural and most hurting in the psychological sense because of the production of excitement and exaggerated psychodynamic acceleration. The sensorial optic impressions prove to be more impressive than all auditive, olfactorial gustative and tactil influences, on our natural sensorial disposition. Therefore all greatest and highest symbolic actions never drop the optic sensorial power.

May the influence on the state of our nervous system be as it may, it remains a fact that these polysymbolic and chiefly optic idealistic performances are very strong educators towards the sentimental discharge. The Catholic church is exceedingly fond of this symbolic hypnosis of the believing individual. Everywhere indeed we find the most pronounced and clearest proofs of this psychological-artistic peculiar disposition. We shall see that it is not only the optic symbol which is used in the service of the affective furtherance of the believing individual: it is the chief and most efficient one, but it is indeed changed and completed ordinarily by many others, be it of auditive, tacile, gustative or even of olfactorial description.

In perusing the different SACRAMENTS of the Catholic Church we shall find soon that it is chiefly the tactile sense which plays after the optic, the most important role, that it ranges almost at the same height of the optic sense in Catholicism and is met always again and again in the most important, but also in the most superficial and subordinated functions of the priest and of the believers. Let us enter nearer into this important subject.

The Catholic Church has taken possession most radically of the consequences of the word in the Gospel spoken by Jesus to Peter and the Apostles, to give them the Key of the Kingdom of Heaven, and of the idea that Christ gave them the power of keeping and forgiving sins. The most powerful source of grace, from which the Catholic Church draws or withholds the divine grace is the ecclesiastic organization of the *seven sacraments*. The seven sacraments are, as it were, the seven drawers of the old symbolic historic chest of the Catholic sacramentalism, from which the Mother Church dispenses through the hands of the priest, smiling, her precious pledges of divine grace, rewarding her children for the accomplishments of their good obedient will and excluding the others who are not inclined to fulfil the special minute prescriptions connected to the obtainment of everyone of these sacramental treasures. The priest is the stewart and the practical dispensator of these treasures; he is the keyholder of the sacramental riches over which he has to give continual account to the church which is the possessor and the permanent supplyer of the gracious divine contents of the sacramental chest. Besides this great principal chest, there exists a smaller needle case or a bonbonniere, as it were, where the children greedy of the eternal gracious smiles are entitled to go themselves without the intermediary intercourse of the key of the priest, where they themselves can open the lids or the smaller cases and drawers with the help of the formalistic prescriptions attached to them. There they are entitled to take out their divine candies and sugars, pearls glittering with divine charm or laces admirable by their artistic heavenly beauty. This second chest or case directly accessible to the hands of the believer is the Catholic treasure of the *sacramentals,* not so important and powerful in their effect on the human soul, but however, of some increasing and ennobling influence on the gracious state of the believers.

The Catholic sacramentalism is the most surprising amalgamation of ideal and real values which ever could be contrived in the history of the human psychology; in it the Catholic Church has undertaken to fix most precisely and really the eternal idealism on the intellectual and material signs of sensorial symbols. The fact of the Catholic sacramentalism has created the most pronounced mono-determination of the divine expression within the material and intellectual world, connecting certain amounts and certain kinds of divine affective gracious riches and relations with the simple sensorial signs given by the ecclesiastic laws. We observe instantly that by this manner of action, it is chiefly the priest which gains in the Catholic sacramentalism because most important gracious actions and signs are only permitted and valuable if administered by his functions, but it is also partly the believer who shares the advantage in receiving clear clues and strong categoric convictions of his divine love and gracious guarantee. The mono-determined fact of having received a certain divine hearing, at a given time and in a certain direction, conveys of course to many chiefly scrupulous believers the utmost tranquilization in the contrite distress of their heart. But there is of course again the other side consisting in the intellectualization, and materialization of the divine idealism which is a most dangerous state of our psychological conception. The Catholic sacramentalism binds the heaven to the earth, not only that, it forces the universal divine magnetism to be the servant of the artistic formalistic legislation of the ecclesiastic sacramental symbol. Catholicism ventures to take possession, in the most minute way, of the keys of the Kingdom of Heaven, excluding the fullness of the divine grace from the extraecclesiactic children of the earth and conveying the richest amount of the most intense gracious effect exclusively to the faithful followers of the symbolic sacramental ceremonial. The intention of the sacramental Catholicism is the most pronounced symbolic mono-determination of the universal divine magnetism within the dispensatory power of its exclusive institution which must be, of course, stated as the most ambitious and most autocratic step which ever has been done in human psychology and religion. It is only understandable in the light of its conception of its highest divine mission. More consequence in grasping all power flowing from the ideal universe and heaven to the earth could not be imagined, but this means also, if human society acquiesces with these claims of Catholicism, the complete subjection of the human psychological world to the representative will of the church.

We already spoke at length of the difficulty to put God into the golden cage of intellectual formulas. Are not all intellectual formulas forcedly transitional, subjected to fashion which is nothing but the expression of the sentence: Spiritus velat ubi vult? The divine spirit uses the formula which it likes in order to put in it its divine inspiration. Definite sacramental mono-determination must, therefore, be difficult as well. There is no doubt that they have in many cases best momentaneous educational results, but at length and often they may be spoiling vehicles of the human psychology forming habits, and perhaps even lack of true divine interest. The theistic enthusiasm may escape after all, from these first so precious vases of the divine grace, and the individual clinging obstinately to them no more be able to find other adequate expressions for his divine inspiration: he will be in the utmost intellectual distress as to the expression of his idealistic goals because the best vases of divine grace which he adored from childhood and to which he clung inseparably became used, lacking attention and, therefore, losing the possibility of conveyance of ideal meaning.

If really the spirit of God blows wherever it will, what would be then the meaning of the strict confinement of the divine grace into sacramental formulas? Does one dare to subjugate the spirit of God to their symbolic formalism, to check the free blowing draft of the divine spirit, to direct its ways, to build for its universal power channels through which it has to blow and outside of which it is not expected to exercise its divine happy fertilization? There can surely not be any confinement of our favorable intercourse with the ideal divinity. There cannot be one intellectual formula in all the kaleidoscopic continual changes of the earthly conditions of human intellectual and visible expressions, where the divine majesty of happiness, of glory and love could not creep in, as well as it is not possible at all to compel the divinity to dwell in one determined given formula or symbol. If love is always true, and if it is only the object which switches, have we not in the sacramentalism one of these dangerous institutions which could leave us desolate? There is, however, a deep psychological reason which induced Catholicism to build up its sacramentalism, it is the guidance of the believing individual to the mono-symbolic efficiency which perhaps could not be, or at least not so thoroughly be obtained by the individual, by any other educational method. It is the permanent care about the realization of the divine idealistic discharge which is subjected to the Catholic sacramental formalism. It is the same principle as we found it already in our meditations on the service in the church, the establishment of strong domineering monosymbols through which the divine love of the believer could escape totally and efficiently towards God.

Let us look nearer and peep into the different drawers of the sacramental chest of the Catholic Church. They are full of treasures, of gracious sparkling heavenly diamonds, of flickering idealistic gold and of the sweetest light of charming divine smiles. The Catholic church has marked its seven sacramental drawers as follows, progressing from the first to the last; Baptism, Eucharist, Confirmation, Penance, Extreme Unction, Holy Orders, and Matrimony.

It is quite characteristic that BAPTISM has the first and matrimony the last place in the row of the sacramental enumeration. Baptism is the prototype of the pure mono-symbolic sacrament excluding every other kind of intellectual formal or complicated collaboration from the individual, whilst matrimony has already much more the features of some worldly convention between two people to which the blessing of the priest endeavours to inspire some higher dignity and divine favor. The sacrament of baptism is perfect, if the baptising person pours water on the head of the child to be baptised and says, while pouring the water: I baptise thee in the name of the Father and of the Son and of the Holy Ghost. Baptism is that only sacrament of the Church which in spite of its essential and exceedingly rich gracious effect can be administered by everybody who has the use of reason: it makes therefore an exception of the drawers of the sacramental chest, being accessible as well to every layman as to the priest. Moreover baptism has the most characteristic symbolic peculiarity, that it is received ordinarily by the child or baby before it has attained the use of reason. It is, therefore, the absolutely purest form of a symbolic sacrament. It is merely the sensorial touch with the pouring water escorted by the stereotypical, spoken formula of the baptising person who it administering the power of this sacrament. We meet here just at the first time in our meditation the essential use of the *mono-tactile* symbol, the skin of the child being irritated sensorially by the tactile act of the pouring water. There is no collaboration of the psychological action of the child possible nor desirable in the meaning of the administering church. The only touch of the pouring water on the head cleanses and ennobles the whole nature of the child in one moment of intense mono-sensorial attention. The original peripheric sin is removed and excluded in the moment, when the will of the sanctifying church concentrates by its intervention the sensorial attention of the baptised child to the central mono-tactile symbolism into which it has put the intention of all its divine grace and delivering inspiration. We see here already again the ruling idea of the psychopupilar conception, one symbol being the hypnotizing force of bluffing attention, all other influences being excluded in this moment, where the child receives its sacramental grace. The meaning of baptism is to attract, even the attention of this "unreasonable" human being to the action of the symbolic sacramentalism in the moment, when the baptising exercises his inspiring divine effect. The child experiences already here, quite at the threshold of his life, the psychological monosymbolic tactique of the church which excludes the *multisensorial* and intellectual distraction of the world from its inspiring action and infuses its divine gracious treasures preferably only through the narrow funnels of the monosensorial symbolic openings. Before the child is scarcely able to be distracted by the surrounding world, it already is, in advance, bluffed by the monosensorial suggesting energy of its church: in the first days of its life it is frightened and compelled to the utmost monosymbolic attention for the intruding authority of its future mother church. At this moment the child receives the first typical bluffing suggestion towards the claiming goals of the church, it is only the beginning of the longest chain of similar psychological impressions on the child on the part of the genial institution, which will form and subjugate the soul of its future adherents completely with these strong means and give to them the typical *psychorhythmic physiognomy*. But this is true, however, just at the first approach to the child in baptism, the church does not hide its psychodynamic methods, but falls just at its starting sacramental action with the full weight of its mono-symbolic authority like a hitting arrow into the artless organism of the child, exciting the frightened tender nervous system of the frail baby.

Whilst we saw that the first sacramental drawer is given to the free use of everybody wishing to use it, so that the key is not restricted to the priest of the church, we have in the second sacrament of the CONFIRMATION on the contrary the exclusive dispensatory limitation to the hand of the bishop. It is only this higher ecclesiastic dignitary who is entitled to keep and to use the key of this sacrament. Its essential effect is again connected to the monosymbol of the tactile touch of the skin of the confirmed person. The bishop anoints the forehead of each with holy chrism in the form of a cross, speaking the formula: I sign thee with the sign of the cross and I confirm thee with the chrism of salvation in the name of the Father and of the Son and of the Holy Ghost. The monosymbolic impression of the confirmation consists again in the tactile sensorial excitement of the skin, this time not with water, but with oil being blessed before. Whilst the first sacramental effect in baptism was conveyed entirely by the vehicle of the natural water, we have to mark in confirmation that it is not the ordinary natural product of the oil to which the Catholic church ascribes the gracious symbolic transfer, but the oil was first transformed into chrism by the previous sacramentalic blessing. We have, therefore, in the sacrament of the Catholic confirmation the connection and superposition of two authoritative means in one point, the symbolic localization of the tactile use of the oil on the forehead and the previous sacramentalic blessing of the chrism. But the essential remains the same as in the previous sacrament: authoritative monosensorial stirring up of the individual in order to attract his attention and to instigate his unsophisticated will through the proposed monosensorial symbol. This symbol exercises again the energetic role of the detachment of the individual attention from the whole intellectual fixation of the surrounding world, enraptures him to the central monopunctual ($+$) tactile sensation and promises to him in his humble monopunctual real exclusion and in the subjected attitude, obtained in this, to the authority of the church, the gracious smile of the heaven. There is no doubt that the serious effort and skill to concentrate the human psycho-pupil entirely in one monosensorial effort conveys the happy sentimental blessing of the heaven owing to the law of compensatory intellectual exclusion. The sacramental action has, therefore, to be considered as the powerful effort of the learned priest or bishop to fix the individual to his symbol and to throw by this psychological one-sided fact his sentimental soul outwards to heaven, at the expense of the dropped intellectuality. It is not deniable that it is physiological for the human soul to have from time to time such delivering concentrative purgations. We have here the clear fact that it is the mono-sensorial attention which is in reality the natural basis of the divine grace conveyed to the individual in any sacramental action. We may consider it as an action of divine benevolence of the confirming bishop toward the subjected individual, that he gives to him the psychic "purgation" for his humility and simplicity of the heart, or we may call it a mutual covenant between the minister and the receiver of the sacrament, where the receiver obtains his monosensorial affective reenforcement and sentimental happiness by the hypnosis of the sacramental monosensorial energy, but where the minister receives, as the reward, the most powerful authoritative overweight and the invincible supremacy over the will of the sacramentally imprisoned individual. Is this the reason that everybody is able to baptize the child who is most easily attracted, because it has no real intellectual hesitations, and why confirmation is restricted even to the bishop who adds the weight of his personal dignity to the sacramental influence in order to overcome the possible resistance of the adolescent who indeed is already much more prone to intellectual independence? The general Confirmation of many young people together, in the presence of the whole Christian community has the same meaning to strengthen the persuasion of the sacrament joining the suggestion of the crowd to the monosensorial symbolic rapture.

The Catholic mystery of the EUCHARIST may be divided practically in three parts. The first part is represented by the beginning Mass where the divine idealization of the material host is prepared and accomplished at the moment of the Elevation. The second stage has the supposition of the Transubstantiation, as Catholicism calls the state of the divine inspiration of the host and consists in the monosymbolic adoration of the host by the worshipping people, and the third part representing the essential sacrament of the Eucharist is called communion where the host is eaten by the adoring believer. We have, therefore, to distinguish the preparatory introduction, the culminating adoration, and the terminating communion.

Offertory and Elevation—Adoration—Communion.

In the first part we have the increasing development of the mystery, in the second the revelling top of the adoring worship, and in the third, its descending and disappearing conclusion. All three parts play the most important role in the Catholic church, the first being essentially bound to the ritual performance of the mass, but the second and third, though being executed also in every mass, are as well taken out from the frame of the missal celebration and form for themselves the most important parts of the other Catholic ecclesiastic service. The adoration of the Holy Sacrament itself is the most solemn function of the religious Catholic performance, and the communion as well has the separated role of the most appreciated sacrament of the Church, in a quite separated independence of the mass.

The Catholic Church defines the Holy Eucharist as the sacrament which contains the body and blood, soul and divinity of our Lord, Jesus Christ, under the appearances of bread and wine. We see, therefore, that the Eucharistic sacrament is the most perfect masterpiece of the Catholic monosensorial psychological action. Here we have the principle of the exclusion of the real surroundings in the most definite manner and the concentration of the human total life-force into one central circular light-field with absolute, mathematical accuracy. The total confinement of all our attention into the circular small host means the unrestricted surrender of our will and of our personal psychic force to this small monosensorial light-circle given in the host. The belief in the present God within the small circular bread of the Host is, physically speaking, the reflection of our concentrated most attentive will which has excluded all distracting intellectual magnetism, and looks at its whole vital possibility in the punctual mirror of the compressed monosymbol. The belief in the divinity of the host is in this sense, the expression of the dispositional evolutionary potentialities of our life-force which is suggested to regard and to meditate itself in the monopunctual mirror of the smallest optic symbolic sign. The total amount of our sensorial strength is persuaded in it to concentrate to the minimum size of the Eucharistic symbol and to rush like a powerful pointed arrow, as it were, through this smallest sensorial signal towards the outside universal idealism. This is the great psychological fact of the Eucharist, that we throw all our will power and all our sentiments in one mono-punctual and monosensorial jerk towards the outside universal magnetism. In the Eucharist our whole life-force touches with the fiery energy of one lightning flash the potential divinity. Both meet each other in the most fervent hiss of human restricted and universal endless divine love. The host means, therefore, the symbolic simplification and most energetic concentration of our total magnetic potential energy which is so happily and perfectly expressed in the idealized figure of the religious hero. In adopting the idea of Christ and putting it just into the last symbolic monosensorial remnant of our intellectual sacramental optic sign, we open all magnetic potential abysses of our human individual disposition, we increase in the most possible desire our longings for human and divine grandeur: in adopting and melting up the figure of the divine hero with our own personal faculties, we enlarge our vital vista, we create the most perfect union between the exemplary genius and our personal faculties, in forcing both to enter into the smallest light-point of the symbolic host. The symbolic host has, in a compensatory way, the pronounced capability to impart to the human soul the strongest urges of increasing energy. The monosymbolism is the most successful state of allegiance, with idealistic powers, because it means the closest union of magnetic energy and the most undivided attention and surrender of the will. The monosensorial urge has the meaning of the psychological *status nascendi* (state of being born), where the soul goes back to the most simplified first step of its energy, from which it is able to flow back to the practical life again and spread out into the real intellectual world most successfully, carrying with it, displaying and elaborating everything which has been connected with it in the primitive narrow frame of the artificial birthplace of the human monosymbolic concentration.

The transport of the psychic condition into the punctual monosymbolism has the value of establishing the most efficient fiery "chimney", in which the most energetic welding of everything takes place which has come into contact with the symbolized intellectuality at this stage. This is the reason why Children are so amenable and docile to all impressions and why the adult persons have much more difficulties in learning and adopting any new knowledge and custom. The soul of the child is practically always in the symbolized simplified stage where it is most apt to grasp intensely every new experience; it has not yet spread out to the intellectual *polyfixed* enlargement and to the experimental continual diffusion of the adult psychopupil and has, therefore, the most perfect possibility of melting up with every entering new experience, and of welding, in fervent desire, with all objects coming into its symbolic contact. As long as we are able to symbolize our intellectual experience and human fate, as long as we are in a position to concentrate our intellectual life into the artistic birthplace of the monosensorial expressions, so long we shall be able to progress in learning and knowledge. The power of simplification until the perfect monosymbolism is quite essential for the further addition and for the future growth of our individual psychic development. Here we discharge all our elaborated real slacks and ashes and receive again the new avidity of our faithful young soul in the artificial cradle of the most pronounced psychological confinement. Have we lost this concentrative power, then we are no more able to develop or to augment in our psychic individuality.

The Eucharist represents then, the most attentive monosensorial self-meditation of the human being in the idealized mirror of the genial Christian hero. We have the most energetic fixation of our affective magnetism on this small symbol of the host: all our attention is attracted most exclusively to the sharp optic sign of the host which attracts our magnetic devotion with the energy of the sucking mouth of a leech. The symbolic host has, at the top of its suggestive attraction, the qualities of a mighty pipe putting in connection the individual life-force and the universal eternal idealism and realizing the vivid intercourse between the real individuality and the eternal possible universe.

Putting the hero into the circular monosymbol of the host has two intentions: First and more essentially, to facilitate the monosymbolic attraction of our mind. He himself is the most perfect expression of the symbolic conception of our life, because he dropped the material multiple intellectual part of our nature almost entirely to the advantage of the affective monotheistic idealism. The monosymbolic apotheosis of the host corresponds most precisely to the real-ideal psychomechanic distribution and division of the Christian genius. The host in the stage of the believing divine inspiration is the perfect mirror of the natural human condition, under which we become acquainted with the real ideal personality of Christ. There are real features, but extremely scarce and rare ones. They all have only the meaning of serving as the necessary indispensable imaginative footing of his ideal power built up upon it. If that is so, we admit also reversely, that the connection of the special religious psychological hero with the monosymbolic host must have the effect to facilitate the transport of the monogenial psychological conditions to the symbolic host.

So the commemorative connection of the hero with the optic-symbolic host turns out to be the forwarding suggestive intermediation between the real intellectual objectivity of the visible outspread sensorial world and the immaterial universal idealism. He has the same forceful monosensorial magnetic attractiveness in his peculiar psychology as the mono-symbolic inspired host has and is, therefore, the best psychological support of the special condition which is intended for the intermediary role of the monosensorial host between the real and ideal world. Christ himself is the symbol of our real life, and is, therefore, most able to impart his monosensorial inspiration to the monosymbol presented to us in the Eucharist. Christ is as well as the monosymbolic optic host the middle stage between real material diffusion and immaterial universe; he also is near to the immaterial retreat from the material world in his symbolic imaginative psychological representation, as he is related to us. If he joins, therefore, the symbolizing intention of the church concerning the material host, then he facilitates most energetically the rise of the monosymbolic conception of the Eucharistic bread, from which the whole amount of the believing soul flies to the eternal idealism. He transfers his magnetic power of sucking idealizing aspirations to this visible optic symbol, and the believing soul, which was so energetically attracted and transferred to eternal goals by the symbolic pipe of the Christian hero, is now in the position to repose on the precise reality of the circular monosymbolic optic substitution of the Christian genius, having in this manner the most perfect sensorial psychomechanism in order to join the eternal values.

The second reason why the hero was amalgamated with the narrow optic monosymbol of the host has been partly explained already before. For the individuals who are not energetic enough to be hurled through the monosymbolic light-field to eternal values, there is the danger to relapse to the monosymbolic sill or not to overcome it. These people fall back to the material monosymbolic representation and look at the last monosensorial symbol as to the perfect representation of the eternal divinity itself. This is indeed nothing but the perfect material relapse of the spirit to the material world which means idolatry and adoration of the intellectual formula and superestimating self-glorification of the material part of our nature. If this monosymbolic material self-adoration of our nature is the much more insignificant and least material because it has only the monopunctual size, then we have to know that the compensatorily concentrated emphasis of this smallest punctual sensorial remnant is so much more strong. Perhaps we must indeed admit that we cannot escape from the material and intellectual formalistic adoration of our nature; but then arises the doubt if this is necessary, whether we are not more just in distributing our idealistic homage on the whole multiplicity of our human real experience and whether we are more true to adore one point thoroughly or to embrace the whole multiple created nature in a more moderate love, owing to the law of compensation.

But we will not forget that the meaning and the intention of the religious institution is chiefly justified in their psychohygienic action and psychotherapeutic effect. It is in the facilitation of the possible idealistic reaction where lies the educational value of all religious customs and sacraments, and in the light of this educational purpose we have to understand also the monosymbolic Eucharist. It is perhaps the most efficient institution for joining the educational intentions of producing strong motions for idealistic sublimations, as we must admit, on the other side, that the exact optic precision of the monosymbol, given in the host creates the greatest danger of psychological mystic bluffability and of material sterilizing entanglement.

The connection of the ideal person of Christ with the sacramental host has for the relapsed part of the believers the advantage that the material apotheosis of the host turns out to be indeed less fatal than it would be in the case of the adoration of the mere monosymbolic acceptance of the sacramental wafer without the attached memory of Christ. Even the sensorially and materially relapsed believer of the Catholic Church receives in the strong connection of the Eucharistic symbol with Christ again and again idealistic urges towards the immaterial outside universe in order that we see that the state of the materialistic conception of the divinity in the monosymbolic inspired host turns out generally less disfavorable than we would expect from the theoretical idea of the sacramental confinement of the divinity. The Catholic host is able to be again and again the birthplace of new idealistic urges and decisions and universal immaterial eruptions, declined in the sense of the psychological justice, as its perfect identification with the terminal God may be.

Catholicism is indeed on the stand point that it rejects the emblematic significance of the host; it does not agree that the monosensorial symbol of the wafer is only the most apt and most efficient real human platform, from which in its conception our life-force is hurled towards the sentimental universe, but it is so intimately in love with the terminal hypnotizing magnetism of this monosensorial experience, that it identifies definitely and without any concessions this symbolic optic expression of the divine reaction with the body and blood of Christ himself. But this altogether is the consequence of the philosophical fact that the idealistic religion is inclined to exclude the sensorial world and the material influence entirely in restricting itself to the monosensorial punctual symbol. Like a man perching himself on the toe of one foot in order to touch as little as possible the earth, so the Catholic idealism touches the material intellectuality only with the tip of the monosensorial Eucharistic symbol and has by this fact the same consequence as the man perched on one foot, not in gravitation, but in anti-gravitation, it hyper-emphasizes this touch in concentrating in it all the weight of its idealistic desire. The result is that the idealistic lightnings rush very energetically through this pointed pole of the monosymbol, in the same manner as we have it in electricity.

Christ said most distinctly at his last supper that the presented bread and wine were his flesh and blood, according to the gospel, and the thinking psychologist could understand this saying in such a manner, that he meant that the monosymbols of bread and wine, the terminal necessary footings of our ideal reactions were offered in the same manner as body and blood are the platform of our psychic and ideal function. The compression of our complicated bodily organism into these most simple general symbols was the psychological facilitation he gave to his pupils in the last suggestive means, in order to join unfailingly and without distraction the divine sublimation. Any discussion about this subject may be at least tasteless, because indeed the intellectual dilution of this monosymbolic concentration is exactly the contrary of the psychological help which Christ would impart to his apostles before leaving them. The conception and identification of all and each corporeal and material existence within the symbols of the monosensorial signs of flesh and blood were the intention of the psychological teachings of the hero: any discussion and digression from the simple acceptance of this artistic educational fact destroys and impairs the idealizing and hypnotizing efficacy of the refined sublimizing, but one-sided method which Christ bequeathed to his church in the Eucharist.

But everything must be used and appreciated in the right meaning and at the right place. Religion has chiefly the task and the intention to be the idealizing educator of the human society. In the light of this intention the absolute identification of the optic monosymbolic host and of the body of Christ may be justified, up to a certain degree. If Protestantism did not accept entirely this methodical conception, it was due to many other educational considerations connected with the dangerous strong optic monosensorial symbolism and because it had adopted a part of the intellectual criticism deriving from the modern scientific inclinations.

Owing to the perfectly criticless surrender of its total life-force to the monosymbolic divine inspiration of the sacramental host, Catholicism proved its complete sentimental absorption by the divine love. The sucking power of the monosymbolic sacramental pipes had so much and closely grasped the total life-force of the Catholic mind that there was no more any space left for critical intellectual hesitation and distinction. Because all its vital psychic energy was used up in the sentimental lightnings toward the divinity, there was no more any part remaining for the critical intellectual reservedness. We have in the Catholic Eucharistic belief the most perfect example of the absolute fixation of human psychology on the monosymbolic signs. What the outsider would not believe is even today a truth living in millions of people, namely the conviction that in the bread of the host the real body of Christ exists in the material and true sense of the word. That the divinity lives in the symbol is not harmful because it is our heart which puts the total amount of Christ's divine feelings in it, but that people accepting the religious educational meaning of the monosymbolism decide with all quietness of their mind that the real material body of the hero is able to exist and live in a small circular piece of bread, this is most remarkable. It is the proof how much the psychically absorbed individual is subjected to the authority of the suggestive power, how far love is ready to go as long as it is thoroughly encircled into the powerful ring of the monosymbolic signs. Here we have the root of the explanations of the miracles. The hypnotized lover does not see though he has eyes, and he does not hear though he has ears. Whosoever has eyes to see, let him see, and whosover has ears to hear, let him hear. Here the ideal and real world meet each other in the mysterious point of the monosymbol. The host is the most striking example of the terminal ring conveying all beauty, strength and greatness coming from one's own heart and culture. The divine host is the most accepted mystic rose whose look imparts eternal life and unbelievable beauty because it is based on the divine source of the faithful boundless belief. The charming spell of the rose in the "Midsummer's Night's Dream," of Shakespeare, changing everything by its sight, quickening the hearts of the human beings instantly to all kinds of different loving desires and acts, "The Rose and The Ring," by Thackeray with their smiling mysterious spell and even "The Three Rings of Nathan, the Wise," by Lessing, which are confusable and keep all the miraculous effect neverthe-less, provided they receive the belief in their spell, are altogether the expression of the same truth that the delivering sublimation of our heart takes always place from the small monosensorial light-circles of smallest symbols and signs, that the greatest subjective satisfaction is given by this strongest subjective effort. All divine inspiration kisses the human heart from the pointed mouths of these wonderful symbolic monosensorial signs. All beauty, happiness, confidence flows from the eternal divine universe, into our personal life through these miraculous golden pipes and all success of the pleasure-seeking longing heart supposes the humility of previous stooping beneath the yoke of the multiple intellectuality and switch-ing through the small holes of the monosensorial circular light-fields towards the outside universal divine freedom, greatness and strength.

The CATHOLIC MASS is the spectacular performance where the priest with the help of his ritual display endeavours to gather the attention of the believers, to his monosensorial goal. He intends to concentrate in gradual progressions by the means of his example of devotion and of the most reverent attitude, to attract increasing-ly the observation and the sentiments of the present community from the peripheric worldly distractions and effusions to the cen-tral divine action which is performed on the altar. The reverent bows of the priest and his assistants at the beginning *Introitus* of the Mass invite the affective inclinations of the believers to join in subjecting their wills and their interests to the central authority supposed to be present in the tabernacle of the altar. Like the waves of the sea, following a certain draught of the air, curve their foamy heads in the direction of the wind, so the bowing, cele-brating priest initiates a favorable wind towards his Eucharistic distant goal. Just this decided stooping and genuflecting attitude at the starting mass makes a deep suggestive impression on the attending people. They instantly are generally made attentive of the mysterious breath rising from the inferior step of the altar and of the affective longings aspiring first slowly and despondently, but more and more confidently from the mysterious prayer towards the central place of the intended following localization of the divine expression. *Genuflection* means stooping on one knee and intends to be the sign of the divine adoration of the present Euchar-istic sacrament. It is only performed before the holy sacrament and expresses the absolute subjection of the individual will under the sacramental power and authority. It manifests the perfect self-denial of the individual pride in inducing him to throw himself to the dust and annihilating his own personal dignity in curving the upright backbone of the man and touching with the knee the earth. We may compare it again best with the wave of the water curving its head and body in a yielding, soothing sympathy to the breeze going over it. So the divine breath of the ecclesiastic atmosphere communicated by the general conception of the present people and the suggestion of the crowd grasps the will of the single individual and curves him to the submissive attitude towards the sacramental and universal God.

This first step of theistic approach is rather timid. The priest bends his body at the inferior step of the altar, he emphasises in the mystic prayer his extreme unworthiness to approach towards God, He repeats nine times in the *Kyrie eleison* in Greek language his appeal to Christ, to have mercy on his unworthiness. The Kyrie is of course the first opportunity of the Mass to use all musical artistic skill in order to express, in using the given stereotypical text, the peculiar atmosphere of the psychic situation: the slow rising of the desperate soul, sunk in darkness, despondency and sin, to the day of new confidence, courage of life and of the glorious splendour of monotheistic love and pleasure. The greatest composers have availed themselves of the psychological situation and character of the Kyrie to express their deepest, most tender and moving musical language.

After this first step of cleansing the heart in repentant contrition the priest mounts relieved and courageous the steps of the altar and intonates the *Gloria,* where he worships in the ancient Latin expressions the greatness and goodness of God. Here we have again the most wonderful occasion for the musical art of which the great composers made the richest use. There is already the atmosphere of elevated pleasure and of blushing theistic enthusiasm in the Gloria where the priest, the escorting musical choir and the by-standing community alike are uplifted by the admiration of the monotheistic might, of the beauty of the works of God and the sweet compassion of his good intentions towards the sinful human beings.

After the Gloria which is in the high mass ordinarily the most temperamental musical part, the priest goes to the right side of the altar and performs the lecture of the *Epistle.* Then he reads the *Gospel* to the Gentiles at the left. We mark quite characteristically that we have already two candlesticks with flickering light one at each side of the reader of the Gospel: the beginning of the miraculous psychological treatment of the soul. The gospel is the new tidings of the most thorough terminological and notional revolution which the world perhaps ever had, from which like from a special root of a tree the whole peculiar energy of the religious development is expected to grow out. In the lectures of the Epistle and Gospel, the suggestive psychodynamic influence of the Christian psychology starts to do intense work. The objective reality disappears slowly in the dim background of the memory from the mind of the believers, and there arises quite slowly but progressively the fairy-tale like atmosphere of the most grasping idealizing imagination of the divine charm. Like fulminant bomb-shells, as it were, exploding their gunpowder into all directions in fiery energy, frightening and hurting the surroundings, so the miraculous concentration of the evangelical language urges powerful affective explosions of our soul. Our intellectual dispersion is increasingly gathered into the concentration of the symbolic small signs of the notional world and life, and we instead are charged heavily with the sentimental concentration which soon must be thrown energetically against the divine goals through the small monosymbolic target which will be presented to the believer, or like a concentrated weight put in one point of a widespread canvas which at least is torn by the augmenting weight of the central object.

In the *Credo* follows the clear statement and the comprising examination, as it were, of the Christian idealistic belief which is supposed to be the door through which the believer is permitted to enter to the starting mysterious part of the continuation of the Mass. The Creed is the parole giving way to the believer to go inside of the concealing hedge of the mysterious service of the church, the Credo is the notional psychological key which opens after the previous preparatory artistic display of the Mass at once the wide golden leaves of the mysterious Arcana of the Catholic Church.

In this moment we enter into the first capital part of the Mass called OFFERTORY. The golden chalice wrapped before into a hiding cloth of silk or velvet, is undressed, the small plate fitting its opening and containing the Wafer or the Host is taken away and offered by the priest between his elevated hands to God with escorting prayer performed always in the stereotypical formulas of the Latin language. With this moment the psychological scenery of the holy theatre of the Mass is changed. The public are entitled to look freely the first time at the central important representatives of their future theistic monosymbols both the Host in the golden plate, called Patena, and the Chalice with the wine, being elevated in the Offertory. The gathering devotional intensity of the believer has already before been increased enough in order to irritate his psycho-rhythmic disposition to be greedily aware of the highly symbolic destiny of the presented gifts of bread and wine. The consequence of this symbolizing appetite for the presented objects is the longing to connect them with the eternal universe through the monopunctual symbolic sentimental emphasis. It is the quite unbelievable courage of the believing individual to claim to embrace the heaven and the universe with his restricted human faculties, which causes compensatorily the monosensorial symbolic emergency. The intellectual dispersion of the attention, which comprised in the beginning all surrounding objects in the quiet observation of the minute multiplicity of rich abundance, falls gradually and more and more back to the presented objects of bread and wine. The transition of the intellectual mind with its outspread minute observation to the punctual monosymbolic concentrative exclusive attention is, therefore, a case of emergency rising and resulting from the insufficiency of our total life-force for the divine task which we will undertake. The Offertory supposes, therefore, the transitional stage from the real clear intelligence to the dreamy monosymbolism, it is the starting moment of the most peculiar psychological state of critcless believing and sentimental surrender of the believer who loses the real peripheric control, leaves his intellectual judgment of the present time and circumstances and receives instead the happy security to reach eternal heaven. The monosymbolic offertory with its longing for God and the insertion of the only gift of bread and wine represents the most remarkable psychological mechanism to establish unfailingly the monosymbolical connection of the individual soul with the universal sentimental idealism. Did the priest not look to the one object of his offering with all careful concentration, he would not be able to refer it to God, or did he, on the other hand, not have the strong desire for the eternal idealism, he would not need to concentrate so energetically on this one gift, but could offer everything else at the same time to God. Monotheism corresponds to monosymbolism, it is the most energetic way to join the universal idealism if we go through the monomechanicism of any single symbolic sign to our sentimental theistic discharge.

In high Masses several times during the performance also just before and during the Offertory the celebrating priest appeals to the blurring power of the *smoke* of the FRANK-INCENSE in order to mobilize more easily the attention of the believer fixed at the detailed objectivity. The censor besmoking the altar encircling even the chalice has the role to loosen more the magnetic fixation of the believing attention even on the nearest surroundings of the central shining symbol and to concentrate, therefore, most efficiently and essentially all life-force of the believer on the chiefly intended monosymbolic point. Like the imagination of the tourist *looking from a mountain over valleys* is carried away easily on the wings of the hazy mist towards distant outstanding peaks and tops of other mountains, and in the same manner as the *smoker of a pipe* excludes the sharp, sorrowful reality for a short time from his sensorial susceptibility and sends his sentimental imagination as a golden bird to the heaven of pleasure, from the sparkling reflections of glittering small objects of glass, the bulbs of his electric light, of a burning candle stick or of the glowing fire of his match and the glow of his tobacco without even knowing it, so the smoke of the frankincense producing an artificial mist around the monosymbolic chalice and the Host facilitates exceedingly the concentration of the faithful imagination to shrink quickly and irresistibly together into the one intellectual deciding monosymbol, for which every surrounding intellectual competition is most undesirable. The besmoking censor represents a former emphasis of the optic exclusive power of the central monosymbolic symbol, taking away or blurring in the most suggestive manner the nearest optic visibility and putting into highest optic emphasis the dazzling shine of the white Host, the sparkling golden chalice or the glittering diamonds and precious stones of the monstrance and increasing so the fulfillment of the main purpose of the theatrical technique of the Mass, the unique stress and the absolute optic dominion of the monosymbolic signs. We see here exactly how much the Catholic Church has adopted the theatrical methods of the former historic times and the eastern taste, and how much it is connected not only to its teachings, but also in its theatrical expressions, to the oriental conceptions and tastes from which it comes and derives its impressive imaginative and optic power. In the odoriferous quality of the frankincense we have to register a further, this time, a symbolic power of smell, to which men are exceedingly amenable, but there is no doubt that it is subordinate in comparison to the optic blurring of the optic surroundings of the monosymbols imparted by it.

The modern smoker of cigars and pipes does essentially the same. He imitates the optic device of the old church, laying a tender veil of smoke over his homely habitual surroundings which are so open and inevitable reminders of daily tiring sorrows and trouble. It is just the moderate degree of intensity of this smoke which has the most suggestive power upon the mind, being the much more persuasive as it works without being observed by the unconscious activity of the artless soul. We understand, therefore, that the use of frankincense is most welcome to the religious service in the moment, where it will emphasize most the exclusive optic power of its symbolic objects and these moments are the Offertory, but even more the Consecration, Elevation and the Adoration of the Host. Every whiff of the smoke of the incense means a quickening run of the soul towards these central points, the believing soul is carried away on the wings of the artificial smoke over all intellectual sensorial interests of the surrounding visible details and rushes more intensely towards the monosymbolic points where it accumulates to final explosions in divine enthusiasm.

The part of the Mass after the Offertory until the elevation of the Host and the Chalice, when through the act of the offering the monosensorial symbolic feature of the bread and wine is fixed and brought into relation to the divine idealism, is a feverish activity of the priest to maintain and to elaborate this inaugurated character of the offered gifts. The priest not only sinks himself into the most mystic prayer in his antique formalistic language, but the clouds of frankincense become always more dense, the number of the concentrative help of the light on the altar is increased and there is another new monodetermining addition to the former symbolic helps, it is the sign of the Cross. The celebrating priest is indefatigable in repeating the monopunctual sign of the Cross over his symbolic Host and Chalice; again and again he establishes this monosymbolic finger-post over his intended optic centres and directs and fixes the attention of his spectators at last inseparably on the Host and the Chalice. He bewitches with the spell of the movements of his never resting hand the eyes of his attendants entirely and pulls their attention and their hearts perfectly to the monosymbolic centre to which he points.

In the *Praefation* he connects in solemn prayer the theistic monotheistic conception of the Christian Trinity to the divine task and intention of Christ, refers all visible world to the invisible eternal heaven, expresses the hope that the clean offering of the new covenant will be the worthy atonement for our sins, in regard to the merits of the passion and death of Christ and summons the whole community to join with all orders of the celestial angels in order to worship God which he expects and sees already in his divine devotion appearing in saying: Sanctus, Holy, Holy, Holy is the God of Hosts. The saying: ut dum Deum visibiliter cognoscimus in amorem invisibilium rapiamur, (In order to be raptured to the love of the invisible things, while we recognize God in a visible way) is exceedingly characteristic for the intended and pretended sense of the psychodynamic way of the church in Mass. All attention to visibility has disappeared excepting to one small monosensorial symbol and just in this moment, after having a long time striven to exclude and not even to maintain intellectual visible things, in the moment where the monosensorial training and fixation seems to be fixed enough, the sacerdotal prayer falls in with pointing to, and speaking of, visible things. The monosymbol is now elaborated enough and ready to be looked at intellectually, the priest takes it and mentions its specific intellectual bluffing sensorial power. The believing soul is already so much fixed to this small point by the previous hynotizing actions that the priest ventures to announce the soon following Consecration or Transubstantiation, to speak again of the visible world without risking to fall back to its detailed peripheric mediation.

The *Sanctus* is the rising sun of the Eucharistic miracle which is coming about; it shows by its soothing music and by its accelerating rhythm the feverish joy of the delighted soul to rush irresistibly through the door of the expected bridegroom; it sings the sweetest love songs, because its confidence and faith assures it that the beloved is just running from the eternal heaven and embraces the pleasure-seeking humanity in the most fervent monosensorial kiss. Therefore the music of the Sanctus is the sweetest imaginable, the greatest composers have just in this psychological situation poured forth the whole plenty of their most charming musical motives. The atmosphere of this part of the Mass is up to the brim full of expectation, of hope and of anticipated pleasure. All creatures of earth and heaven are invited to join in the mighty Halleluah which is repeated and modulated in all forms and manners in order to express the unceasing drunkenness of the soul, so much that it is no more able to speak, but staggers in artistic trembling sounds and repetitions with overflowing, inexpressible happiness. The Sanctus is full of the most convinced expectation. The fervent confidence of the decided enthusiasm in the Sanctus is already so strong that the believer is no more hesitating to see the arriving Saviour in His imagination and to feel him vividly in his palpitating heart. The preparation of the coming miracle has now developed to the peak, the psychological fruit of the Mass is ripened and it is high time to enjoy it. The believer possesses the presence of the Sacramental Eucharistic God already most vividly at the moment of the Sanctus. The flames of the heart strive to converge intensely towards the hopeful goal.

The psychological culmination of the Eucharistic performance is undoubtedly the ELEVATION. All the previous sensorial work of acoustic and optic suggestion, in soothing seduction and in a bluffing way, which succeeded highly in catching us to the monosymbolic conception of bread and wine, become at once perfectly silent. The musical revelling subsides, the attitude and activity of the priest is at once stiff and immovable and there is perhaps only some most subdued tune which whispers through the dim vaults of the church, with the tenderness of a quivering intimate play of sunbeams in the silvery net of a hidden cobweb. The boisterous previous suggestive activity is interrupted at once and the human heart, full of revelling monosymbolic achievement, is instantly put before the task to produce the last and highest miraculous act of the Eucharistic monosymbolic inspiration by itself. The absolute silence coming into the revelling service instantly and immediately means the appeal to the soul to venture at last the bold jump from the reality and the intellectual dispersion, to take the consequences of the monosymbolic act in divine loving rapture. The believer knows by training that now will be the great moment of his personal educational psychological miracle which he has to perform himself. The whole ecclesiastic community is expected at this moment to do the *active* achievement of the Eucharistic bold jump. At the moment agreed upon, of the Elevation of the Host, and the monoartistic sign with the bell it fires a tremendous shot of collective love to the abyss of the divinity. Like the sorcerers in the shows have the peak of their most striking masterpieces emphasized by the impressive escort of some extraordinary sound and as we are excited there in the thrilling attention by this new monosensorial symbol of generically different character during the silence of the former influences, so in the Elevation of the Mass the community is stirred up by the thrilling subdued sounds of tingling bells, just at the moment of the Consecration. The thrilled human attention receives the last frightening jerk and goes on to this last consequence of the miraculous development: *the localized intercourse with God*. Nur ein Wunder kan dich tragen in das schoene Wunderland.

Now, in this miracle God appears, the adoring soul of the believer rejoices in his psychological victory and he feels the living universal God, so far as he can understand and conceive him (!) perfectly present in the sacramental symbols and is indescribably happy owing to the sure and real possession of the gracious universal divinity. We may look at this fact as we will, but there is of course a very great side in this miraculous acceptance of the

Eucharistic monosymbols. Eucharist means the greatest genial artistic deed in the psychological life. The Eucharist is the expression of the same psychological principle as the genial personality of Christ in the Gospel. The difference between both is this, that the representation of the gospel creates the psychological divine conception in a notional or poetical way, whilst the Mass creates it with the means of chiefly optic helps which are supported by other artistic means of symbolic concentration of visible, olfactorial and auditive nature. The psychological methodical congruency between the symbolic Christ of the gospel and the divine inspiration of the Eucharistic monosymbol goes indeed very far. Both are wonderful, miraculous, strong, full of divinity, but poor in reality and in intellectual details. The Eucharist is, therefore, also able to enrapture the hearts of the people most intensely towards the divine enthusiasm. Is the revelling perhaps for this reason even more intense and throws its foam more wildly over the brim of the most delightful enjoyment in Eucharist, pulls longer sparks from its terminal poles, because the visibility and the clear optic mono-determination prepares the most energetic convincing basis on the sensorial nature of the human being? But just there lies also the danger of the educational and psychological value of the optic Eucharist as we know.

The monosensorial Eucharistic Host has, therefore, the most remarkable one-sided role in the human psychology. It is the perfect expression of the Christian extreme psychic activity in the most graspable and precise way. If this extreme psychology enables the small wafer of the Eucharistic Catholicism on one side to concentrate and to absorb in itself the deepest and highest sources and energy of authority, wherefor the history of the Catholic service and Eucharistic mystery through the centuries turned out to be the most efficient centre of every kind of artistic glory which is only the reflection of the force of this monosensorial symbol, then we must on the other hand indeed admit that the fact to identify a small piece of bread with the hero's flesh and blood, moves far away sensorial criticism. Being first too careful in avoiding the love of the multiple visible objectivity in clearing the material attachment of the heart leads finally to the most intense clinging only to one last monosymbolic sign. Would not human nature be most freed from materialism, as it believed in its extremistic zeal, in monosymbolism? But what happened? Qui vult vitare Charybdin, incidit in Skyllam. The ideal genial extremist has carried his sentimental deepening tendencies so far as to put all strength of his total life-force on one *optional* sensorial sign and infused into it, shallow and superficial as its original relative value may be, the whole emphasis of his human heart, directing all attention to this only point, concentrating on it all his sentimental hopes, feelings and expectations. So we see that there must be a very serious psychic education before the individual could be able to accept this extreme attitude of his soul with this extreme speculative arbitrariness. The mystic extremist would not acquiesce with the tasteless effusion of his feeling heart into the multiple creative world and he at last falls down and adores a faculative small object, which he has chosen arbitrarily to be the representative of all his intellectual material attention. He would give up his attention to the reality because of his spiritual idealism. But does he not impart instead all his sentimental love, belonging to the whole range of his experience together, to one real point, owing to the law of compensation? This last object symbolizing all other dropped objects enjoys now all human attention, given before to all of them, in order that after all the mono-condensed concentration of this sentimental human force is reflected to the universal God. Is it not the reflecting mirror of the compressed summary of our own possibilities augmented by the entering idealizing effort and inspiration of the humanized Eucharistic symbol, in the memory of Christ? In how far does the monosymbolization of our life-force produce the marvellous echo which we recognize as divine God, because indeed the amount of our idealized vital force represents the universal given value which is attached to every one of us? The ideal part of our nature reveals our greatest hopes for our future development, because in this idealistic peculiarity there is contained, like the future tree in the seed, as it were, the whole scale of our potential future universal achievement. The Eucharistic adoration may therefore be defined in this sense as the longing meditation of our future possible evolutionary fecundation. It is the desire for maturation to the divine. The sentimental Eucharistic adoration prepares the way of the coming developing possibilities of the human race by the visionary fact of looking ahead of the present imperfect state of the humanity of now-a-day towards the more perfect and more powerful stages of our future nature.

We mentioned the psychological congruency of Christ's extremely ideal personality and of the optic monosymbolic one of the Eucharist. There are other similar artistic psychological constellations in nature and in human life, which we remember if we read the former explanations of my writings. The stars with their monopunctual lights in the dark nightly heaven have the same optic conditions as the monosymbolic host: the flowers with their circular charming light-field, the feathers of the pea-cock recall distinctly the same optic monosensorial centropunctual condition, all together being mystic charming finger-posts pointing towards the *lost paradise*.

Are our conceptions of the material objective appreciation not always arbitrary? That which we will and appreciate is valuable, the objective significance is subordinate for the individual enjoyment. But the more a thing is frivolous as to its relative, objective or MARKETABLE VALUE, the greater the following disappointment will be. Let us think of the first love, to which the other experiences are similar. The marketable nature of a thing is the general social acknowledgement of its value. If you have a greater number of adherents of acknowledgement for anything, then its marketable value is much greater, is there only a subjective emphasis, then you will have no marketable value. How is anything able to receive a marketable value? By the artistic suggestion: For often the most dispensable things have the greatest marketable value, things whose utility is poorly imagined. Even the useful things could mostly be done without easily, if there were not the suggestion, the example, the direct mercantile persuasion and the advertisement.

Love neglects the "marketable" value of anything or any person and emphasizes the sentimental concentration on one arbitrary object or person; *hatred* neglects also the personal value and discredits the marketable importance of anything so that it takes away not only love, but the relative objective value, which justice has given. Both are wrong and will be corrected by fate and experience. The ideal religion abolishes the exact marketable conception of the human individual given in slavery. It emphasizes the equal individual personal dignity of everybody in respect to the highest relations and the universal germs which are distributed in every human disposition.

Does Eucharist contain the principle of the subjective right of appreciation and of the contempt of the relative marketable value in an absolute way and in the most pronounced manner? It exclaims most distinctly: Which you will and wish sincerely is important, good and beautiful, all other things have subordinate value. What you believe is true and in what you put your confidence will alone be helpful to you. The longing of your heart will even be able to pull God himself, from heaven into your sensorial reach, where he shall help you.

It is quite natural, but regrettable, that many people educated in the idealistic way, if they once have not succeeded and feel disappointed, can afford to be appreciable in their eyes only as much, as they are able to procure marketable values of their personalities, in the judgment of other people. It is the extreme realistic relapse from one extreme to the other. The art to pass very important in the eyes of other people is essentially suggestive. But there comes in also as well the psychological constellation of the social circumstances of the moment, which produce always again the magnetic apotheising concentrations of great loves, preferences but also blind hatred. They raise one individual highly, almost without reason, whilst they condemn the other one as well, without serious cause.

The ideal LEADING CHARACTER, in one phase of his activity, is most in danger to be declared useless in the social sense, because he in the school of idealism has been roughened as to the possibility of the relative magnetic appreciations. The leading character is therefore in other terms always the marketably and relatively more stupid, but the subjectively or absolutely, more clever individual.

Eucharist is perhaps the more pronounced expression of the feminine soul being always in subjective love, whilst accordingly the more objective man is less inclined to. We presume from the specific dynamic laws of the Eucharistic, that the habitual sacramental adorer may possibly be the great lover and hater, the great optimist, before he is spoiled to the contrary by abuse, the individual who registers most objective errors in the real world and who most frequently comes into the case to correct his ways and judgments, because they were inconsiderate and wrong in the objective, relative or marketable sense.

It is indeed most surprising to see how perfect the psychological agreement between Eucharist and the genial Christian psychology is. Their psychorhythmic features and their special affective idealistic mono-emphasis is so characteristic for both that we must indeed decide that there must have been the same psychological architectural power in building up both.

Let us resume our former thread of the *Elevation* and its chronological sequence in the Mass. The believer at the top of his miraculous ecstacy is so impressed and moved that he loses all other sensorial expressions but the only radiant look towards his monosensorial symbols, going like a lightning of energetic hope and delight to them. The concentration of the psychological energy of the individual has become so strong that every intellectual help and sensorial urge has become superfluous and impossible and would be even disturbing for the momentaneous psychological situation. The sensorial suggestion has exhausted its technical resources, the highest goal of concentration is joined as a ripened human fruit, and there is the perfect exteriorly silent attitude of the soul which is contracted in a thrilling trance of rippling delight.

Faith means, therefore, indeed the confidence to go right and not to perish, not only in respect of a near real goal, but making broad leaps into the outside universe without knowing exactly the way. Has science not also a kind of faith, but even the greater one because science does not know the terminal goal being, however, most careful and anxious of every single following step on the way, whilst religion, on the contrary, has sharp, clear terminal illumination, but is not fond of the detailed way so that it likely jumps through the night of the universal abyss, falling and perishing if in doubt about its success, and arriving just and right at the expected goal, if full of conviction and confidence?

Eucharist is the systematic education of the utmost concentration and strength of the will. It intends and succeeds in destroying the contrary imaginations checking the fulfilment of the ideal success. Here we have the justification of the idea that this sacrifice is more acceptable and more pleasant to God than the oxen and sheep of the old Covenant, that God praises the sacrifice of bread and wine, of Melchisedec, symbolizing the Son of God and Man and the total human life-force, because indeed the future Christian race learned to concentrate all their affective vital possibility into this monopunctual sensorial expression, relating it to God. The most thorough attention is exactly what the jealous exclusive divinity wishes to receive: there cannot be given anything higher to anybody than the whole effort of attention. The Eucharist has this effect in the total monopunctual compression of the psychic energy of the individual.

But this arbitrary artificial mono-ideal explosion of our feelings has other sides. It educates the individual to the utmost OPTIMISM, it is true. The Eucharistic education effectuates the highest confidence of the individual in all temperamental experiences. All things are encountered and treated with the most respectful concentrated attention, looked through to the bottom and wilfully reduced and related to the deepest wells of life and possible energy. What a precious thing! Optimism indeed is able to be the most efficient educational factor of the world. All good success in education comes out from the optimistic benevolence. There is perhaps only one really great crime in the world: This is the absolute pessimism, detracting and checking every positive energy, hanging like a heavy weight on all good inclinations and curtailing all fiery wings of idealistic strength and efficient values.

The Eucharistic conception develops primarily optimism, not pessimism. But the extremes touch. The optimistic education of the Eucharistic conception is so thorough, so inadaptable to the moderation of the real intellectual experience of the life that it is the source of innumerable disappointments, losses and most disagreeable disillusions by its blind carelessness,—extreme optimism is nothing else,—in the real sense—and leads in this manner to the exact contrary, to the most paralyzing pessimism. This psychological stage is, however, the worst and most sterile condition of our mind, brought about by the exaggerated will of the other extreme, too happy optimism. It is stupid, inadaptable and untrue as well as optimism, but to the negative side refusing all invitations for collaborating or supporting positive or ideal cultured energy. In leaning to, and educating our soul to the positive extreme we fell back to the negative side of psychological laziness in real adaptation: our psychic faculties lost the working refined intellectual adaptability in exaggerating first one-sided optimism, and it converts itself after being sophisticated by the real experience into the opposite pessimistic extreme, which is as well the expression of the psychological action, but with the difference of negative tendency and polarity. The pessimist excludes all positive urges, he prefers rather not to have positive invitations at all than to expose himself to the possibility of being cheated. So his destiny of sterile insignificance is definitely sealed. This is the terminal result of the extreme symbolic conception after its sophistication in the real experimental world.

Our whole human fate is the effect of magnetic telepathy. The *success* of our life depends on the fact as to how we are directed and inclined in our affective magnetic possibilities, to which values we re-act in conformed parallelism and to which ones we re-act in refusing opposition. Our surroundings, our human society, all universe appeal to our hearts continuously with all kinds of urges, and it is depending on our education, our natural disposition and in what direction we are able and to what degree, to be in ready affirmation or in opposite declining affective attitude. The extreme Eucharistic conception is undoubtedly in its school the too strong conclusiveness in universal affirmative direction. But it produces the utmost efficacy in positive reaction which can never be fulfilled in the real world, but must be adapted in every case of our experience in moderation and with carefulness. The Eucharistic individual goes too far with his affective benevolence, he is too gullible, too thorough in the optimistic way and has, therefore, the sure guarantee to be discouraged by the experience of the insidious mediocrity of all human and universal experiences mingling bad with good and never permitting the whole success promised in the monosensorial psychic attitude.

There is another important moment to be considered. The concentrated benevolent optimism of the Catholic Eucharistic individual receives the mark of the most one-sided character because his psychodynamic function is taken in the service of the historic real monosensorialism given in the Host of his ecclesiastic sacrament. This concentrated attitude is not accepted as a merely teaching symbol of education, but it is taken as the only real monopunctual value worth while, so that the believing individual concentrates all his psychic energy into this symbolic sign instead of receiving in it only the methodical means of the education for optimistic love and active efficacy necessary, up to a certain degree, in all situations and experiences of the life. The hypnotized psychology of the Catholic becomes, therefore, easily sterile and one-sided, stiff and inadaptable to the outside real experience, rejecting the value of everything which lies outside of its educational Eucharistic symbolic system. His love and attention belongs chiefly to the mysterious monosymbolism of his church and declines all other values of his experience, claiming his love in the same manner and craving for his attentive effort in the same way. He becomes so exclusive, he postulates the participation of the whole humanity in his sacramental affective particularism and loves not only very much all individuals performing their psychological concentrating function in his own sacramental Eucharistic manner, but despises the whole world outside of his cultural methodical sacramentalism.

So we see that the Eucharistic Catholic is likely to produce two educational wrongs coming both from the categoric stiffness and the inadaptability of his method. He either excludes all different humanity from the love and the collaboration of his affective emphasis and from the love of his heart, or, if he gives way to the practical experience and to the human need of broad intercourse, he exaggerates this benevolence and optimism in transferring his extreme sacramental love on all circumstances and individuals coming across his fatal way.

It is the strong emphasis and the real conception of the Eucharistic performance which was able to develop these psychological conditions. The individual psychology was fastened too closely to his sacramental mysteries, the Catholic was so much hypnotized by the literal monosensorial acceptance of his Eucharistic symbolism that he lost the free movability of his heart and of his reason and became so unreal, subjective and blind for the minute objective necessities because of his wrong absolutism. He is educated to believe and consider as good and important what he will and has not learned to moderate his benevolence and malevolence according to the refined differences existing in the real objective world. He is only able to accept as good what he thinks is so, to condemn only the values which he thinks are bad and never will be docile to the experimental world: he, therefore, likely is crushed by the real intellectual objectivity of his experience being too much extreme, subjective, absolute and individual.

The highest degree of divine enthusiasm is exceedingly dangerous because its shadow on the other side is the extreme hatred. The education to the monopunctual Eucharistic love makes for the relative rejection and contempt of all real surrounding objectivity. Extreme love creates extreme hatred. Here you have the most powerful psychological disturber of the peace who is not only most one-sided and exclusive, but aggravates this quality by his symbolic mechanization so that everything outlying from its historic mystic system is doomed and rejected in advance, belongs to the realm of darkness and hated rejection, though possibly it may be of a high rank of dignity.

But the Eucharist teaches us, how we indeed become able, by the helps of all kinds of logical preparation, mystic diligence and sensorial symbolism, to bring out in an artistic way, the ideal love and the success of our heart, that we have here the most splendid example of the most difficult ideal education of the human heart enabling us to see the heaven open and to have the most intimate interspheric magnetic intercourse. If we have it in our power to join arbitrarily these highest goals, then we can be confident to reach also the more modest successes of the real life, if we strain with all perseverance and sincerity. Or is the mediocrity perhaps much more difficult than the one-sided idealism? Is it harder to be attained and above all to be maintained? Does not the middle stage of the real-ideal equilibrium upset easily and the psychic accent run likely into one or the other extreme of idealism or materialism? Our human nature has undoubtedly this dangerous mechano-dynamic disposition. The art of human behaviour is to maintain the equilibrium between both, not to yield to the magnetism of either, but to oscillate carefully in the middle line of both like a rope dancer going on step by step in the life with utmost consideration.

In the *Benedictus* we have the thrilling expression of the divine enjoyment. The illuminated believer addresses his God whom he is supposed to have present, arrived on the altar and throws showers of blessing, gratitude, love and homage on him. The interchangeability of the notion of the monosymbolic Eucharistic visibility, of the humanized symbolic Christ and of the monotheistic conception with each other have just the advantage to facilitate very much as strong links, as it were, the gradual progress and to ensure the establishment of the advancement from the real periphery to the idealistic punctual concentration. The moments after the Elevation suspend the individual soul in the state of intense divine enthusiasm, the psychological psychopupil looking through the most refined punctual opening most sharply to the face of its God. It sees the heaven open and has the most perfect affective enjoyment in this culminating attitude of its psychology. If there is one great enjoyment on earth, it must be this direct vision of the open heaven represented by the monosymbolic Eucharistic spell to which the believing soul is entirely subjected. The character of the musical Benedictus is, therefore, full of sweetness, of divine sway, the whole psychological situation is the highest divine intimacy, where the individual exhibits the most pathetic luxuriant enthusiasm of his overflowing happiness. He, of course, avails himself of the occasion to tell his present God all secret wishes and hopes of his heart and addresses soon after the first moments of the adoring concentration the *Pater Noster,* the Lord's Prayer, in a solemn antique melody and language through the mouth of the priest. All wishes seem to the monosymbolic possession of God easily obtainable; he who was able to imprison God in the golden cage of his heart, must indeed be able also to obtain his grace. The faithful believer forgets all his personal shortcomings and is convinced to be carried away by the favor of his Eucharistic God to great and excellent future achievements. Even sin, which he looked at in a despondent atmosphere at the beginning of the Mass, seems now in the light of the symbolic presence of the friendly God, an easier problem of the world: the believer is sure that God grants most readily all prayers and wishes he addresses at this moment to him. He speaks, therefore, in the most kind and confident way about his sins which God has to remove.

The *Agnus Dei* expresses this hope with the happiest confidence which we may recognize from the melodious sweetness of this song. God and His Lamb take away all sins in the opinion of the Eucharistic believer; he makes his future more perfect than his past and gives to him the peace fervently desired. But nothing is more difficult to stand for the human psychology than a long perfect happiness, and it is quite characteristic for the Mass that the first part, the longing preparation for the Eucharistic appearance takes the longest time, whilst the culminating fulfillment remains only for a short time and progresses quickly to the sacramental conclusion which is given in the COMMUNION.

Every enjoyment endures only a short time, it can only have the character of heaving a heavy breath for re-enforcement of the future work and needs quick changes into other conditions of the human mind and soul. If Schiller says in a warning way of the love that the illusion of the expectation is short and the repentance of the fulfillment long, the church wisely makes the contrary in the Eucharistic thrill in using a long time until it permits the peak of the culminating Eucharistic love to be joined, but in progressing quickly, too, to further psychological stages, when this extreme fulfilment is arrived. The catastrophe of the genial Eucharistic presence, if we will call it so in the spectacular performance of the Mass, is represented by the communion. The unsupportable and dangerous greatness of the Eucharistic psychological onesidedness has the strong tendency to create a habit and is, therefore, most desirable to disappear again quickly. We all know the original way chosen by the Catholic Church to effectuate this necessity. The believer so much loves his monosymbolic God that he decides to consume the Host. He is indeed the artless child revelling without reflection in his divine delight and is, therefore, the victim of the same genial innocence in eating the most admired object he knows and recognizes in the Eucharist. So the mysterious Catholic Church makes account of this deep instinctive longing of the human nature in its artless naive stage to taste and to eat the object most beloved by the believer. It is understandable if the believer hopes that the miraculous energy and divine quality connected and infused into the monosymbolic Eucharist transforms his own body and soul, if he incorporates it into his metabolism. This expectation is even in the same degree natural and naive, and it is most convenient for the faith of the individual. The monosymbolic piece of bread which is supposed to enclose the fullness of divine strength and virtue, undoubtedly transgresses from the outward world into the individual physiological metabolism and is assimilated to the vital circulation of the personal life. This fact, of course, imparts to the believing thought not only the most stringent proof of the divine transition into the individual human body, but is accepted as the greatest honour, the mightiest suggestion, bold and egoistic as it may be. There are connected the greatest increase of force and spiritual growth to the consumption of divine symbols, according to the sayings of the gospel, chiefly of the mystic St. John: Whosoever eats of my flesh and drinks of my blood, remains in me and I in him, and he shall have everlasting life.

Immediately before the act of the communion, the priest makes the genuflection, bows his upper body and head and raps three times on his breast, saying: My God, I am not worthy that Thou shouldst enter my heart: yet speak but the word and my soul shall be healed. The act of rapping on the breast is a further monosymbolic tactile sign reminding and supporting, like touching the floor with the knee, with one sign the individual to his repeated concentrating attention. The starting communion is the third and last capital part of the Mass and is accordingly again strengthened and emphasized by the monosymbolic signs of energetic fingerposts. It is not only the monotactile signs already indicated which introduce the individual to the concentration of the communion but the ringing of the Eucharistic bell is here repeated though in a more subdued way exactly corresponding to the time of the rapping on the breast of the priest and enforces so the symbolic devotion. The believers unite in the monosensorial longing and perform the so-called spiritual communion which means they restrict themselves to the affective desire for the monosymbolic Eucharistic communion which is in fact only received by the celebrating priest. This moment means of course a further, the last step of divine ecstasy of the believer who feels the love of his God coming down into his physiological nature, and to whom he sends out in tender intimacy all hopes, wishes, fears and longings of his personal fate and of his fellowmen to whom he is obliged or grateful. After this performance, the Mass has practically finished. The heavy intensified atmosphere of the high divine mysteries has gone and there follow only some general and special prayers looking forward to the life in a more distinct way, but relating to the strength and the encouragement received from the sacramental impression of the Mass. The strong concentration of the attention has ceased and priest and attending believers breathe more easily, contented with the success of their divine exercise. This is the end of the Mass which encloses the chief and highest secrecy of the Catholic service and mysticism, culminating in the two points of the Elevation and the Communion which are most essential features for the Christian Catholic psychological nature as well as for the special theatrical demonstrations of Catholicism which in most of the exhibitions of its service circle around these notions like the moon around the earth. Struggling ascending effort, trembling jubilation in the joys of success, resignation and consummation at the end, we have this sequence everywhere, in religion, art, physiology, nature and science. All symphonies of Beethoven and Mozart are built on this disposition.

If we try a PSYCHOLOGICAL ANALYSIS OF ANY SYMPHONY OF BEETHOVEN OR MOZART, we have in the beginning the vision of a misty cloud rising from a meadow in the early morning. The first introduction of the musical piece with its carefully developing energy and rhythm is comparable to the first day of creation, when from the chaotic possibilities the sharp creative determination of the artistic masterpiece arises and gathers. Like a giant awakening from sleep or a child going over from unconscious slumber into whining and smiling moods with wide-open wondering eyes, so the great composer with his determined artistic highway soars to life, joy, meditation and exercise of his psychic strength. He first dashes with a kind of inexperienced ignorance and arbitrary boldness into his theme; he according to his temperament and disposition hesitatingly chooses one way of expression of his character and develops along this first chosen way with diligent explanation and unfoldment to stronger emphasis of his feeling heart. The introduction of any artistic piece is always most interesting, perhaps most important in the psychological sense. For there we have the questions about the method of the artist and about the special kind of his artistic success, discriminating his art and skill from anybody else's. Why this arbitrary choice from a million of possibilities? This is the beginning crystallizing struggle of the artist. There is most effort and necessary collaboration on the part of the hearer in the beginning. He has to climb the mountain of the artistic success and needs, therefore, the energy of his own attention and good will, being always supported and guided by the staff of the suggestion of the artistic performance. The soul of little faith and confidence receives strong encouragements for her goal, the musical example demonstrates the greatness, power, importance and beauty of the clear goal, longed for, and the hearer increases gradually in the intelligence, love and admiration of the way, the task and the goal which he has undertaken in being engaged in this artistic contrivance. Every valuable musical work has, therefore, an increasing energy and power of strength and feelings in growing restriction of individual taste; the rhythm having been explained and introduced in the beginning carries you away over your first indifference and rises slowly to the high hills of personal enthusiasm, glory, self-confidence, self-contented happiness, and we arrive at last to the divine inspiration and transfiguration given in the middle part of the musical piece, the trio, which is the bearer of the highest delight, the Olympic peak of the hill, where human beings are entitled to enjoy in undisturbed pleasure and security the love and beauty of gods. There you have the rapturing flights of the music of Mozart hovering like an eagle over the clouds of all transitory values and basking itself in wonderful elegance and happy relaxation, at the immediate light of the eternal sunshine. What tremendous height of elevation, what most dangerous and elegant turnings of the climbing eagle, and what smiling quietness and absolute lazy security in his great performances! We are frightened to listen to this universal outcry and heart rending sounds of love. We feel that he over-reached by far what the human heart can bear; but he goes on in quiet sweetness and untrammeled friendly rhythm and seems to enjoy himself in the performance of the boldest swings and leaps along and over the clouds and abysses of the farthest universe.

We have to mark well that this great definite enjoyment has the supposition of the previous gathering and concentrating work. The musical introduction and exposition of the first part was a raising effort of the hearer and the artist. The secret of the technique of the masterpiece, as we observe it always again and again, is the climbing height of the sounds and the accelerating rhythm. High sounds are monosymbolic centres of the idealistic target or the highest peaks of the trembling musical waves. A rich and energetically growing assertion of high sounds, repetition and rhythmic acceleration in conquering and ensuring the platform of the Olympic peak precede every time the wonderful culmination of the artistic highest enjoyment in the inspired musical self-control. There you have excluded every doubt, you have the security of success, you forget any short-coming, disappointment and discouragement of the reality of human life. There you have melted your heart with the eternal and unchangeable greatness and beauty of the divinity, and nothing is able to tear your quivering feelings away from the burning loving embracement with your eternal Father, with the perfect and thrilling beatitude of the Paradise. Therefore, the language of the music, as we have it in the same way in poetry, is in this stage of highest inspiration stammering. It is beautiful, but eliptic in the intellectual sense. The extreme sentimental happiness with its imaginative compensatory power excludes the intellectual reasoning side of the art and repetition, short symbolic allusions have to be the expression of the highest musical happiness, just like a flat stone hurled by a boy over the mirror-like level of the surface of a pond. The stone with its energy is the divine inspiration of the heart; the touches on the surface of the water are comparable to the sensorial touches or expressions, being rare, inarticulate and only symbolic at the culmination of art. There the human heart revels in highest pleasure, we look with our spiritual eyes over the clouds of the sorrowful reality. There we have in wonderful enjoyment crowns of ivy and oak leaves on our brow, sharing in our hearts and sentiments the essence of divine greatness and harmony, racing to the universe in most concentrated energy and trepidating speed. Nay, we feel to be there and perform the most care-free round dances on the holy hill.

But this adoring attitude, self-confident and charming as it was, cannot last long. Nothing can be endured so little by any-one as a sequence of many happy days. The higher the peak of happiness and divine ecstasy, the more rapid and irrevocable the necessity of returning to the shadowy valleys of humanity. The high-strung inspiring energy exhausts itself, and the flywheel of eternal aspirations and measureless universal confidence slackens after a short duration of the most desperate happy divine outcry. The real restriction of our human nature starts giving us doubts, reasonable reservedness and real coolness. The divine nightingale keeps on, however, with the moving vibrations of its sweet voice. Its desire would be to dwell always on these divine hills and never to return from the glorious groves full of highest delight. But the highest accents become soon more quiet; the burning divine aspirations uttered most powerfully before, are on the verge to diminish in height and frequency of the sounds. Yet how slow-ly returns the nightingale of the musician's heart to real approach. It has found best expressions and in them highest fulfilments of happiness which it is willing not to give up. It goes on singing of universal glory and most shuddering beautiful love and beauty, as though it would last forever and ever.

But the platform of the divine Olymp, where the musical traveller has to cross unhesitatingly, is soon over. He arrives at the margin of the hill in the space of a moment—how short seems to us happiness! He recognizes that the happy universal glory will fade away like a wonderful dream or a happy deception. This intelligence assails the jubilant admirer, still on the peak of his artistic elevation. He is instantly frightened and somewhat sub-dued in his overwhelming eloquence. He felt that the destiny of his temperamental nature beckons to him to be ready to retire from the stage of the divine art and return to the lower and more humble regions of real and intellectual every-day life. So the nightingale with the brightest outbursts of its glorious songs subsides in the sweetest fervor of its singing, keeps the breath of its enthusiasm for a moment, since it feels scared by the warning of the coming descent. In the most unexpected way the sincere universal effusion of its sentiments is doomed to leave the place of its highest praise and greatest satiation, and the tragic moment is inevitable, when it has to flutter away from the high altar of its divine praise and go back to the shadow and the valley of the ordinary life.

So we understand the rising melancholy of the artist at the end of his musical trio. His sorrow of separation from the divine embracement is indescribable and inexhaustible. He looks back once more with tenderest feelings, kindliest kisses are sent back in last enthusiastic high sounds; he waves, as it were, his hand for the last time from the margin of the Olympic plateau, smiling and flattering and imploring, full of happiness and gratitude and woe of separation at the same time. He descends then after a last tremendous effort of staying in the luminous shine of inspiring light to the slopes of the intellectual life.

What a refreshed attitude this descending traveller has adopted! He feels strong and fresh like a child after a bath; he is full of the riches of his psychic food which has been given to him on the hill of his enjoyment. His face is still shining with the glory of highest delight and his heart trembling with the charm of having felt eternal spiritual inspiration which he is carrying away in lasting and encouraging memory. What a rhythm of easy movements! Like a brook skipping over rocks and stones, running from a mountain, flies the musical terminal part of the symphony down to the valley. Or like a wanderer filled with the beauty of the glorious Alps, having seen from an elevated peak their formations and glaciers and glistening white walls and crowns. All is hope, self-confidence, strength, rejuvenescence of the very essential human qualities of the heart and mind.

We may look wherever in the old art, in paintings, literature and music, we always shall find these ascensions, these dwellings, on the platform of an elevated hill giving Olympic divine delight, and then also the descensions to the terminal conclusion. Only what is done with time and succession in music and poetry, happens in space, in painting. We may call this pronounced temperamental type, with one culmination, from where the strongest feelings are kindling like a lightning in the sky, monosymbolic artists. Above all the Christian Middle Ages, all Latin artists, the classical composers such as Mozart, Gounod; the French poets Lamartine, Victor Hugo, Racine, belong all to this type.

It is owing to educational reasons that in the modern time the POLY-SYMBOLIC ARTISTIC TYPE has developed and has gained almost the whole extent of the present artistic performance. Its principle is exclusion of the idea to put all at one stake in the realm of the feeling. Its tendency goes to the mediocrity of real-idealism; it prefers to behold and enjoy many lovely hills with flowers and mild sunshine than to be wrapped up in one gigantic Olympic Himalaya, from which the whole life-force rushes in one desperate dazzling lightening to the divine universe. The consequence of this behaviour is clear. There is more emphasis of the detail, more sense of reality, less hope, less high aspirations, less enjoyment and despairing rapture, but also less using up of energy, less sorrow of departure, less disappointment and less incongruency between the real-intellectual limitation of our categoric life and the eternal dreams of the highest universal desires of our heart.

But there is of course another danger arising from these tendencies. The *modern art* has today a certain inclination and is in danger to level everything, taking away any excitement, high promises and hopes and strong effort which we need up to a certain degree. It is in danger to remove encouragements with discouragements, fulfilments with deceptions. The balance of the modern art is likely to become sterilization of the sentiments and great duties, because there is too much tendency to scatter the life-force. The poly-symbolic tendencies may go too far and then we have disorder and lack of concluding energy. Every modern writer and composer has to make this experience; if he likes mono-symbolic peaks, he is considered as antiquated, and is only adapted to the modern taste, if he shares the humility of the poly-symbolic insignificance. Too much poly-symbolic tendency means the death of art, the loss of direction and determination, the impotence of concluding power and rapturing concentration. But up to a certain degree this temperamental conversion of the modern art is justified. It was prepared by the harmonious and self controlled artistic performance of the old Greeks, Shakespeare and of Goethe. It removes great dangers in the educational sense, as we hinted to, but if it goes too far, it kills the great value and right of artistic existence at all. Even if we agree that it is dangerous to put all at one stake, to concentrate the whole psychic energy on one gigantic peak of divine transfiguration, we have not to scatter our love and heart's feelings in too many sections without binding them together again into one charming sheaf. We have not to forget that unity is the root of beauty and that the energy of our temperament disappears, if we decline entirely, if not the mono-symbolic, yet the oligo-symbolic concentration, limiting ourselves to a few affective peaks of symbolical sentimental discharge.

There is no doubt that the modern *jazz music* went too far in the dissolution of symbolism. It may be good for dancing, where we avoid intentionally the elevated culmination of delight, aspiring for a moderate and economic pleasure, but for the artistic enjoyment this kind and degree of temperamental elaboration is insufficient, because it is unable to move the feelings of the heart to terminal delightful discharge.

Symbolic moderation is, therefore, the right thing for music and any art, as for anything else. May our old ancestors have been wrong in building up improbable and steep artistic peaks, inaccessible to the average human being, the modern artist is also wrong and perhaps even much more in doing away entirely with the moving energy and uplifting sway of the symbolic concentration. Mediated real-idealism is the parole of the useful art of today. We have learned from one-sided older times, but we have to learn also from modern failures in art. Art has to be education, useful, true and available for the practical life. Therefore, we agree that old exaggerated exactions are abandoned. But art without ideal contents, without strong urges for affective optimism and ideal success is wrong as well and has to be avoided at any rate.

The SACRAMENT OF PENANCE encloses in the psychological way five points: Examination of the conscience, sorrow of the sins, firm resolution, confession and penance. Though all these points are essential for the disposition of the sacrament, we cannot forget that, according to the sacramental makeup it is exactly the Absolution of the priest which, in the opinion of the church and of the believer, effectuates the gracious divine reconciliation. Although the church supposes in every sacrament the affective magnetic parallelism with the intentions of the sacrament, the objection of the non-Catholic must be up to a certain degree admitted in that sense that the sacramental mono-sensorial makeup is likely to mechanize and to exteriorize life and conscience, that it is probable that the sacramental individual rests more after all on the exterior mono-sensorial promise and subordinates the personal psychic disposition which ought to be the capital part of every spiritual conversion. The Catholic Church asserts that without the fulfillment of the right disposition of the sentiments and conceptions given in these five points of Examination of the Conscience, Sorrow of the Sins, Firm Resolution, Confession and Penance, there cannot be any prospect of the forgiven sin, but it binds nevertheless the fact of the release and of the divine reconciliation essentially to the fact of the stereotypical formula of the sacerdotal symbolic sign of the Absolution. Since it is difficult to make up the mind to the earnest effort of the detailed elaboration of the five given points of the Confessional psychology, and since it is on the other side very easy and comfortable to use the exterior mono-determined signs of the forgiving sacrament, there is, of course, a certain danger that the psychic development turns out like this that the believing individual in time relies almost entirely on the consoling fact of the sacramental symbolic absolution, whilst the straining effort of the inside sentimental re-direction and the clinging towards God are compensatorily less pronounced. Nobody who is willing to have forgiveness of his sin and goes to Confession, can possibly be in contradiction with the sentimental and intellectual dispositions of confession. He goes there because he already acknowledges the existence of these psychic conditions, because he believes to have done wrong and because he hopes to be relieved of his guiltiness. There cannot be any doubt of the right intention and disposition of the confessing individual: had he not had the same disposition he would not have resorted to the sacramental institution. The use of the sacrament is already the clearest proof of the conformity of the individual sentiments and intentions. Any individual not willing to fulfill the sense of the sacrament of the Confession does not come in contact with it. What is called bad disposition and unworthiness of confession must be conceived as weakness and habit which may be developed just because of the one-sided comfort of the sacramental institution which puts the psychological stress on the exterior marks of the mono-determined symbolic sign, induces the individual to cling to it most sharply and confidently, whilst at the same time the sentimental parallelism of the heart cannot be controlled and fixed. Provided that there is any submissive intention in the heart and the connection of the exterior sacramental confession added to it, the individual is absolved from his wrong doing in the sense of the Catholic Church; yet the greatest amount of contrition of the heart and the deepest humiliation before God without sacrament cannot have the same sure effect in the eyes of the church. The so-called perfect sorrow or contrition of the sin is a very difficult point in the sense of Catholicism. The church does not easily admit its possibility and directs all people looking for forgiveness of sins to the surer exterior sacramental help of the sacrament. We see that the Catholic Church emphasizes her sacramental institution even on the behalf of our perfect sentimental work and that it prefers rather to offer to us its intellectual formalistic means of the monosensorial sacramental performance than to surrender us to the risk to look for our own psychological success through the very best efforts we are able to.

The danger of the sacramental actions lies in the comfort and in the easiness. The sharp sensorial mono-determination works out too quickly and too thoroughly the changing sentiments of quietness and self-satisfaction: the mechanized action of forgiveness in confession relieves the individual too quickly and easily from his previous sorrow which looked at the sin as the most terrible and grievous misfortune of the life. On one side we must admit that the categoric exact precision of the forgiveness of the sin is, of course, the most favorable relief of our soul, and the greatest delight of the pleasure-seeking individual, but we have to find the weakest point and the most dangerous kernel of the Confession exactly in this manner of the forgiving action. All strong categoric connections of idealistic intentions are fatal and dangerous: any formalistic attachment of the lover of the eternal God is of course very imperfect and objectionable. The great consolation of the sure mono-determination of the sacramental forgiveness has its negative counterbalance in the roughening sensorial passion of the optic and auditive energetic symbolic impressions and above all in the quick and thorough opposite changes of the strong sentiments going from the deepest self-annihilation and contrition of the bottom of the heart immediately to the highest degree of self-confidence and of relieved happiness. Strong psychic powers and stages must have like everything else their due time of growing effect and result, and we must presume that the affective changes rushing too quickly from one state into the contrary one, from the deepest pain into the highest joy (himmelhoch jauchzend, zu Tode betrübt: Goethe) must necessarily roughen our sentimental nature in creating too much excitements and disappointments. There is no doubt that just the sacramental actions produce the most energetic affective enjoyments throwing the individual from one extreme affective stage into the opposite, bringing together all most distant affects of the heart and causing by their immediate connection the most burning psychological reactions. This artistic welding as it is performed in the sacramental action of the confession, producing immediately the highest pleasure out of the deepest pain and sorrow, is indeed most interesting and most efficient for the momentaneous state of the soul. But it contains again the fatal principle of all sacramental action to be too ready to help, to have too much condensed artistic achievement, to help the individual much too easily over every kind of difficulties of his soul and increase the opposite emphasis of the former and later stage of the soul in order to mark most distinctly the significance of the sacramental psychological turning-point. The temperamental *rocking chair* is by the sacramental signs moved much too much and we have to expect that, as we have commenced to hyper-emphasize one extreme of the psychological state, there must soon follow the contrary, but that there will be produced likely again afterwards, also the extreme contrary. So deepest pain will be alternated by highest pleasure, contrition by satisfaction, but in the same way there will happen the most thorough and rapid relapse from highest pleasure and satisfaction to pain and contrition. The human psychology receives, therefore, by the sacramental education the extreme exhaustion of its forces, conceiving everything from the extreme point and wasting, therefore, without necessity the whole affective energy, where owing to more temperate conceptions always the serenity of reasonable mitigation could rule and save the precious force of life.

Let us now follow the different stages of the Catholic Confessional performance. The first step is the *Examination of the*

Conscience. *Conscience* is the previous educational formation of the inclinations of the heart according to the conceptions and exactions of the Christian idealism in the Catholic Church. The Catholic confession supposes the Catholic conscience and the Catholic conscience in its turn has the supposition of the Catholic education and culture. The Examination of the Conscience consists then in the exact investigation of our former experience and our intentional life and has to find out in how far and in what points we digressed in conceptions, actions and intentions from the preconceived religious tenets couched into us in a theoretical way in the days of our artless childhood. The Examination of the Conscience has to research minutely the special points of the experimental real digressions of our life from the theoretically accepted tenets of the Catholic doctrine; it has to meet consciously the single points which have proved to be hindrances in the practical life for the easy systematic discharge of our life-force towards ideal goals: Catholicism claims to possess this competent discharging method valuable for all special cases of our experience, and the digressions, resistances or angry respectlessness for its theistic performances are what the Catholic Church calls *Sin*. Sin is, in its opinion, the worst possible psychological fact because it destroys the individual energy at its very vital discharging root.

The *contrition* or the sorrow of the sins is the magnetic effort of the soul to overcome the counter-imaginations, on whose ground the digressing sins at their time could happen. These different conceptions and imaginations have been brought to a certain clear consciousness by the effort of the Examination of the Conscience, and it is the affective contrition which has the task to eliminate these habitual intellectual and active digressions analyzed by the Examination of the Conscience. The fact of putting oneself into the position of the sacrament of the Penance supposes already the general acceptance of the thorough validity of the theoretical principles of the church and the firm will to harmonize all past and future conceptions and intentions with its exactions. The struggle between the digressing past experiences and deeds on one side, and the retrieved theoretic Catholic faith produces that painful feeling which we call contrition of the heart. The decision of accepting once more the Catholic tenets has the consequence that the believing individuals strive to put right and re-direct in the retro-speculative sense the digressing experiences of their life, to put the accent of their will again on the theoretic legalized truth and to subordinate with their will all checking or digressing contrary intelligences and feelings.

The *firm Resolution* means the strong decision of the human will to maintain this idealistic consequence for the future life. The penitent cancels in firm decision all his previous sinful differences from the Catholic Christian conception and suggests himself by the fervent affective prayer to stick most carefully to the general ecclesiastic moral and intellectual laws for the time to come. The examining analysis of the conscience has chiefly the intention to find out the single digressing points in which the individual differed in the former times from the Christian law, but it is not in an intellectual discussion by which these digressions are liquidated. The intellectual relative reasons for their coming about are not mentioned, only their incongruency with the ideal Catholic goal and its enjoyment. In the prayer the attention towards the ideal goals of the Christian is emphasized very much, the real circumstances of the single sins are so much more overlooked owing to the law of compensation. The individual humiliates therefore himself putting all stress on the terminal happy issue of his philosophical theoretical Christian conception in whose logical consequence in the practical adaptation of the life he believes to find the highest degree of happiness and success. The religious sacramental attitude of the human mind suggests the individual to forget the real former incongruencies with the theoretical law of which his personal experience gave witness in his earlier digressing ideas and actions. It is owing to the pre-conceived affective decision of the individual returning once more to the believing faithfulness that he thinks again to be in a position to reconcile the real habitual customs with the ideal theoretical tenets, though they turned out, in his experience, not to be applicable to all stages and situations of the life. The contrite heart eliminates the results of its intellectual experience, distrusts its past real objectivity and is firmly decided to make possible in future what was not in the past, the perfect congruency and harmony between his real intellectual experimental behaviour and the ideal exactions of the Catholic Church. This state of the mind is possible owing to the fact that the confessing sacramental individual has given up all his individual resistance, that he has thoroughly discarded the influence of his experimental intervention and that he adopted again the faithful state of his believing childhood and youth, when the ideal hope into the theistic goals and methods had all ruling authority in his soul. The specific psychology of the confession excludes partly the use of the results of our experience; it connects the individual once more with the fundamental affective symbolic forces and blames not the methods which have not succeeded in the individual life, but the individual himself who had not been able to use consequently the theoretical prescriptions. The idea of the analyzing Examination of the sacramental tenets had, therefore, essentially the meaning to find out the digressing points, to fix them thoroughly and to re-direct every non-conformity with the Catholic conception. It has not the meaning as it ought to have, to be an intellectual comparison and anxious meditation on the wrongs and rights on both sides, by a justicing meditator, but it is merely the designation of their existence which is individually marked in order to throw them out after all from the psychological affective and reasoning connection.

The *Confession* is the chief sacramental part of the Catholic Penance, because it is connected with the monosymbolic "miraculous" Absolution in the opinion of the believer.

Only after the fulfillment of all these points the Confessor progresses to the last and deciding sacramental point, to the *Absolution*. It consists again in a stereotypical Latin formula which is always literally repeated by every confessor every time, when the Absolution is given and which is pronounced very distinctly. I absolve thee from thy sins in the name of the Father and of the Son and of the Holy Ghost. At the same time, the priest makes in a solemn manner the sign of the cross in the direction of the kneeling believer and joins some further Latin prayers pointing to the merits of Jesus Christ through whose blood we were saved, why we are entitled to hope for eternal life. In the act of the Absolution we have again the strong mono-determination, the exact intellectual confinement of the divine gracious action which is conducted through the mono-punctual channel of the crossing point of the sign of the cross and by the inspiration of the fixed formula of the Confessor into the affective mind of the penitent. Without this mono-determining crystallisation of the clearest symbolism there is no one sacramental action of the Catholic Church. The infusion of the Catholic divine grace is always a function of the monosymbolic punctual spell corresponding to the simplicity of the heart. God touches here the soul with the magic wand in the silence of all intellectual concealment, the believer looks only to this one touching point and forgets instead the whole surrounding world. The divine grace streams through the points of the utmost human attention. Mono-concentric effort and connection with the divine heaven are in the psychological sense identic. But is it in our power to choose these points? The effort to do it in an artistic way will, of course, never be entirely in vain, but the most fertile idealistic inspirations undoubtedly take ordinarily first place when we least expect them and retreat as well at the time where we have regulated exteriorly everything best. The spirit of God blows where it will, the spirit cannot be forced to some certain formula: its form of expression changes continuously like the moody wind and enters the human heart under all masks and forms with kaleidoscopic changing appearances.

The incessant pointers of the Catholic sacramentalism to the *merits of Jesus Christ* must have the meaning that Christ was the most pronounced and successful idealistic monosensorial individual who can be represented to us, that Christ has to be the divine example most apt to be imitated by the psychological method of the Christian Catholic. The merits of Christ are bestowed on us through the strong suggestions which flow from the successful career of his idealistic discharge. His monosensorial divine attention was never divertible into the intellectual multiple sins of the world according to the gospel. Bestowing on us the merits of Christ means, therefore, giving to us the affective instigation and the ideal confidence and energy which we receive by the example of the divine hero in looking at him and meditating the history of his life. The grace flowing from Christ to the believers is the quickening sentimental force and energy imparted by his ideal figure which was always in the focus of the divine monopunctual attention and never lost this last intentional clearness and energy. We often spoke about the strength and the necessity of the *example*. The intercourse with our fellow men is of deciding significance for our psychic life. Examples, above all in life, but also in biographies are solutions of our practical difficulties: they point out, how other people solved the same problems which cause to us so many hesitations and doubts. Examples are lights in the night of our own undecidedness. They help to emphasize one idea or view of our meditations and to push back the opposite counter-imaginations. This is the meaning of the light of the generations given in Christ: he pulls towards the monopunctual and mono-idealistic hope, kicks the human passiveness to this celestial uplifting happiness and destroys the doubt and the hesitations of the real intellectual life.

There are three further sacraments in the Catholic Church which are quite similar in the exterior theatrical method of bestowing the divine grace on the believing individual as the treated ones, though less characteristic in the psychological sense. They are the Extreme Unction, the Holy Orders and Matrimony. The EXTREME UNCTION intends to give "through the anointing and prayer of the priest health and strength to the soul of the

Catholic believer and even to the body, when the individual is in danger of death from sickness." We have essentially also here again the same ways as in the previous sacraments consisting in the building up of monopunctual sensorial symbolic antennae, as it were, in form of crosses, where the magnetic Universe is expected to infuse its affective gracious energy. It is always chiefly the Christian state of sin which means all kinds of intellectual hinderances from the specific monotheistic concentration of the human individual, which is supposed and intended to be overcome in the sacramental action. The Catholic Church assumes therefore above all, that sins are taken away also in the Extreme Unction, but it has as well in the sense of the church the power "to cleanse the soul from remains of former sins" in the form of bad inclinations "and to restore the believers to health when God sees fit." The last idea is rather clearly surprising. Is not God represented in it as the more or less blind universal magnetism which is attracted by the artistic ecclesiastic monosymbols of the signs of the monosensorial crosses and is made attentive of the needs of the individual on whose body this sacramental action takes place? The sacramental action is therefore near to the scientific *deistic* universal conception, the Church being aware of the importance of the idea of the most attentive concentration inviting the outside universal magnetism to infuse its forces into the narrow monosymbolic funnels established always intentionally in the sacramental punctual antennae. But it seems that the idea of the artificial intervention into the almighty action of God by the elaborated sacramental symbolism encroaches on the Catholic conception of the nature of God who is supposed not only to be the fullness of goodness and compassion, but also the highest expression of omniscience, omnipresence, almightiness, loving, jealousy, vigility, strength and activity. The sacramental polypragmasy excludes God almost entirely from his immediate free intercourse with the individual in the deepest sense of the word.

The HOLY ORDERS are the sacrament which has the task to fix and to sanctify the promise of ecclesiastic persons for the service of the church. It is the sacrament, by which bishops and priests and other ministers of the church are ordained and receive the power and grace to perform their sacred duties. We find here again the monosensorial spell of the sign of the cross and the stereotypical Latin prayers by which symbols the favor of the divinity is supposed to be attracted and imparted to the believing servant of the church.

MATRIMONY is the last of the seven sacraments. Catholicism is in this point at least wisely aware of the urgent necessity to affiliate the sexual life to its religious intentions and not to put sexuality entirely off the door, as it likes to do with it in almost all other cases. The sexual idealism switches to easily from the collaboration with the idealistic church. It represents itself too often as the obstinate competitor of the terminal idealism and claims its vital force for its exacting functions. Matrimony has the weakest sacramental features, the chief thing being the social contact between the two partners who promise under the authority of the church to be faithful husband and wife. The sacramental intention of symbolic blessings of the priest intends to sanctify this lawful civic promise, to connect it with the authority of the church and of the heaven, to impart to the contract the eternal obligation of the earnestness and of the thorough importance of the immovable eternity and to connect with it the gracious strength and favor of God. There we find again monosymbolic actions in the sign of the cross and in the touches of the priest who joins the hands of both partners for the union of marriage. The matrimonial rings receive in the intention of the sacramental action the value of two magic rings of mutual persistent obligation. They shine in the splendour of the supernatural stability and dignity of the divine impressive suggestion and become for the partners of marriage the lasting monosymbols of their promises of faith and vital union until death.

An *Indulgence* is the remission in whole or in part of the temporal punishment of the sin in the meaning of the Catholic Church. We have here again the clearest mechanization of the gracious action of heaven. The individual provided his right disposition, receives the power to acquire a certain amount of divine pardon and favor. This possibility to attach the divine favor to his symbolic action is so pronounced that the church fixes numerically, according to a standard used in the early times of the public Christian tenets, the gracious action of any given prayer or good work. These means, may they be holy water, the sign of the cross used by the believer, blessed candles, ashes, palms, crucifixes, images of the Blessed Virgin and of the saints, rosaries, scapulars or stereotypical short prayers, are called SACRAMENTALS. They are things set apart or blessed by the church in the intention to meditate good ideal thoughts and to increase devotion or religious attention and through whose movements of the heart venial sins are remitted. The most important sacramental of the church is the *sign of the cross*. It is done in putting the right hand to the forehead, then on the breast and finally to the right and left shoulder with the words: In the name of the Father and of the Son and of the Holy Ghost, Amen. This is the so-called Latin sign of the Cross. The other form made at the beginning of the reading of the gospel is made by making with the thumb, a cross first on the forehead, then on the mouth and at last on the breast, speaking the same words. The sign of the cross is ordinarily used by the Catholic believer at the beginning and at the end of his prayers. It has partly the meaning of the confession of his belief in the Christian mysteries, if he is in company, but has essentially in the sense of the church and the opinion of the believer the sacramentalistic function to concentrate the grace of God through the symbolic tactile monosensorial points.

Another sacramental in very frequent use is the *Holy Water*. It is blessed in advance by the priest, is ready for use in large basins at the entrance of the churches, where the believers dive their fingers in entering and leaving the church in order to emphasize the gracious expectation of their sign of the cross which they make with it. The fervent believer keeps also always one or several bottles of the Holy Water at home in order to use it if he gets up and if he goes to sleep, if he leaves or returns to his home, intending his better gracious intercourse with God or bestowing it on the departed souls in order to extinguish the fires of their pain in purgatory. A special theatrical use of the Holy Water takes place in the churches at the high Masses, where the celebrating parson goes before and afterwards through the congregation and sprays with the Holy Water—sprinkle this gracious showering rain over the heads of his parishioners. All these sacramentals also have the distinct monopunctual intention of our sensorial attention, so the sign of the Cross, and the Holy Water that assuming tactile form which is increased by wetness and different temperatures, wherefor it is more efficient in the sensorial classification of the gracious intermediation.

The *blessed candles* are the most classical optic concentrators. They are for this reason used most frequently and most ubiquitously in the functions of the churches and their number is always increased in the measure as the church will emphasize more her gracious benevolence towards her believers. No wonder that Catholicism connects just to this most energetic optic concentrator the special favor of its gracious liberality: no wonder that this sacramental is especially popular and attracts the believers and the outsiders most magically in the dim contrast of the dark large vaults of old cathedrals. Whosoever enjoyed the sparkling lights in the dusky silence of any musty mediaeval church or observed the fervent believers in the wintry solitude of any sanctuary, kneeling before these sacramentalistic candles and looked at their inspired features overflown by the rosy glimmering changing waves of the flickering lights, could not help being himself impressed mystically and permitting his soul to fly itself for a short time over all categories of time, space and causality towards the idealistic rapturing enjoyment. This observation alone, if we are able to interpret it rightly, may be one of the most efficient and clearest lessons of explanation of the Catholic Christian psychodynamic method. The root of all religious performance is dreaming enthusiasm and suggestive exclusion of the intellectual multiplicity in the perfect simplicity of the believing heart.

Burning candles are in great number used for imploring the favor of the saints: the believers fix them on large posts with numerous pivots. That also in these devotional performances *fashion* places a very important role, is visible in the fact that more popular saints of the modern time, of whom much is spoken, enjoy the honour to be worshipped by very numerous candles, whilst oldest and most acknowledged saints of the church at the same time lack almost entirely these flickering flatteries and decorating homages.

The sacramental of ashes is used on the day of Ashes where the priest strews ashes on the head of the believers: palms are blessed on Palm Sunday, when small branches of the blessed tree are taken home and exhibited in the apartments of the believers over the Cross: crucifixes are generally used in the churches and in the homes, where they are supposed to bring grace and luck; the same use is made with the images of the blessed Virgin and of the saints which are blessed first by the priest and receive by this the special meaning and belief of Sacramentalistic effect.

The *Rosary* is composed by numerous beads fastened into a circular string and fixed with a small cross to which rich indulgences and sacramentalistic grace by the previous blessing of the priest can be conveyed. The Rosary has the meaning to be used in praying the so-called Rosary which is a whole collection of five Lord's Prayers and fifty Hail Marys: the believer is helped by the means of the Rosary string not to make mistakes in the number of his repetitions. At the end of the Hail Marys there is joined every time the so-called mystery of the Rosary, meditating the life and death of Christ and the Blessed Virgin, each repeated ten times in order that we have in every Rosary five mysteries.

The Catholic *Scapular* is composed of two small pieces of square drapery, connected with two strings and worn in that manner over the skin of the believer, that one piece of the material lies on the breast and the other on the back, the strings fixing them over both shoulders. It was introduced owing to the pretended appearance of the Blessed Virgin to a mediaeval monk on the Mountain of Carmel and enjoys much the favor of the church and the believers. The bearers of the scapular are promised not to perish if dying bearing the scapular.

We see that Catholicism is rich in sacramentals. The facultative casket of the Catholic gracious self-dispensation is prettily stuffed with all kinds of more or less modest material vehicles of the divine grace, all together to free and voluntary disposal of the believer. It is stupendous, how far the universal supremacy of the divine magnetism has been attached by the Catholic artistic church to her special administrative service. Is this not wrong in the divine conception of the personal Christian monotheism which in its opinion has the most active care about our welfare not permitting a hair to fall from our head? Or is there the question of preparing the way to the Lord always ready to come if we invite Him? We find here the fact of reminding the divinity always of its caring duties about us. It seems to be quite impossible that the bestowal of exactly five hundred or three hundred or two hundred and fifty days of indulgence is connected to one given stereotypical formula of a small prayer, since it is quite impossible to calculate the thoroughness of the good intentions of the heart which must be deciding for the value of any good deed. But the Catholic Church attaches closely the personal merit to the use of the exterior intellectual formula. On the other side we must put the question, whether the sacraments and sacramentals have not just in the sense of the scientific conception of the universal magnetic God a very reasonable sense, since they represent altogether the pronounced concentration and attention of the individual will power which is nothing else but the monosymbolic transformation of the human intellectual mind. This has the force of a great sentimental absorbing power and affective establishment of divine intercourse in this stage and is so in a position to draw the universal divine strength into its monosymbolic status nascendi? We are surely again here before another deep psychological problem, which, exaggerated and dangerous in its practice as it may be, has doubtlessly important psychological foundations.

Sacramental actions in the sense of the psychology are formalistic kisses offered to the universal magnetism. Whether they are reciprocated or not is another question. But why should not they be reciprocated? Only it is not the ceremonious artistic correctness which makes these kisses valuable and worthy of answer, but the sincere heart of the individual which is recognized by the universal God and much more beloved than everything else. But sincerity of the heart and correct formalistic expression may be in near relationship.

The authority of the Catholic Church and the power of her holding the Key in the religious life stands and falls with the exaction of the formalistic precision of the sacrament. As soon as the intention is permitted to be in the practice of the church and of the religious believer the main and deciding thing, the individual may retire from the authority of the sacramental church. Does not the tragedy of the sacramental formalism consist in not permitting the individual to look for new intellectual expressions of his heart, not to be permitted to be individual in the language of his intercourse with the universal God? The consequence of formalistic severe restrictions and of the exact connection of the grace of God with given intellectual expressions may bring about the affective sterilization of the heart. The Catholic Church claims to be the patentee of its divine formalism. The dispensation of the divine grace is, therefore, perfectly stabilized by the authority whose absolute acknowledgement is supposed to be the first and last condition for their obtainment. What a tremendous danger of the historic intellectualization and exteriorization of the most intimate and most holy things of the heart!

How dangerous the formalistic patent of the "business of the heart" must be, we recognize easily if we meditate the use of the stereotypical prayer. The individual feels to be justified in using the formula prescribed provided that he has not contrary intentions, which of course is never the case, because only the sentimental conformity profits by these opportunities. The terminal result will be easily the mechanization of the symbolized conscience, the superficiality of the sentiments and thoughts of the believer who feels to be entitled to draw all profits and advantages from the religious sources without the obligation to go deep into them by serious individual meditation.

The Catholic Church may be called from this conception of the sacrament the mechanistic interspheric affective mediator between God and mankind. It establishes numerous interspheric magnetic antennae in the sacramental symbolic signs, in which it concentrates the whole life-force, the whole will power and the extreme attention of the believer and to which in the same manner the magnetic attraction of the universal magnetic fluidum is directed. The Catholic sacramentalism means interspheric affective signalization by artistic symbolic intellectual help. The first and most radical step in its action is the compulsion of the individual psychological gift to leave the state of scattered intellectual activity and to gather it to one monopunctual most attentive energy. As we saw, this goal is reached by various optic, tactile, auditive and gustative monosymbols. All these signs, may they be called superstitious by others or not, have indeed the deep scientific psychological functions to concentrate and to condense all our psychic energy into one symbolic idea which means the highest degree of readiness for discharging and receptive changes of the personal mind.

The *monosymbolic stage* of the soul is the alpha and omega, the cradle and the coffin of our psychological functions. It is the moment when the individual delivers all his personal psychic productions to the idealistic pleasure and enthusiasm and when he is supplied at the same time with new ideal urges and instigations which he has to differentiate and to elaborate afterwards in the intellectual enlargement of his psychopupil. No happiness, no progress, no past, no future without the most significant monosymbolic signs. The sacramental and sacramentalistic symbols of the Catholic Church receive in this sense indeed a deep scientific side. The "superstitious meaninglessness" of the ceremonious symbols receives in the light of this psychological conception the deep and appropriate right of existence. All these monopunctual symbolic signs turn then out to be indeed mono-determined magic wands, through whose application the water of the divine idealism instantly flows from and into our heart, if we fulfill the essential condition to restrict our sensorial touches to the monopunctual exclusiveness.

The greatest thing of the divine success is the reality of the mono-determination. As long as we are undecided between several possibilities, we cannot succeed in going ahead. The instigation of the individual soul to be carried instantly to the last stages of the mono-sensorial symbolism is the great and unparalleled merit of the sacramental action. The symbolic sacramentalism is the most pronounced intellectual finishment and conclusiveness, the indispensable magic ring and terminal link which connects the sensorial or intellectual gift of the individual with the interspheric magnetism of the outside magnetic universe, in the conception of the believer. The sacramental monosymbols claim, therefore, to be the real-ideal or the intellectual-sentimental transfers of our peculiar human psychology, in an artistic way.

But are we not naturally in a position to effectuate our divine interspheric psychological intercourse without the help of these artistic sacramental institutions? All our natural experiences have by themselves their mono-symbolic conclusions to begin with in the physiological, material, business and sexual life, in health, possession and love. But much more, and directly in the same sense as we have it in the sacramental monosymbols, we recognize the idealistic concentration of our intellectuality in the whole realm of art, of poetry, painting, music, of spontaneous prayer, of meditation of the nature and even of the work. Everywhere we have the concentrating proceeding development towards the monosymbolic terminal compressions of our intellectual mind.

The sacramental establishment of these monosymbols has, as it is always characteristic for all religious action, the tendency and the effect of the concentric facilitation of our affective progression. It attracts our life-force to go on quickly towards the last monosymbolic transfers of our psychological metamorphosis in order that we have to retrieve sacramentalism as the first and most pronounced *quickening psychodynamic* FACTOR of Catholicism. Within this church it is undoubtedly the most perfect artistic instigator of the concentration of the human psychopupil. Sacraments and sacramentals are the main Catholic expressions of the Christian means of psychodynamic acceleration. They have the clear intention to bluff the individual sensorial susceptibility, to instigate it to hover slightly over the surrounding intellectual reality and to go on energetically towards idealism, enclosed within the narrow psychological confinements of the wonderful notions or sensorial mono-impressions. The sacramental symbols are small and strong boats, as it were, to which the individual is invited to entrust blindly all his psychic life-force without previous intellectual criticism and to allow to be driven by them confidently through the sea of the earthly experience towards eternal sentiments.

Comfortable and sure in rich ideal goals as the sacramentalism may be, we may not forget other psycho-dynamic means, chiefly work and art. We spoke often about this idea and repeat here again that the terminal fruit of divine pleasure and inspired enjoyment can only be the last action after long toiling work, that the symbolic action cannot be joined as a rule by the bluffing and angry rapture of our psychological attitude with the artificial help of mono-symbolic quantitative and qualitative hyper-saturation, but by the careful doses in the logical development of patient and careful work. The long distances of affective standards jumped over by the mono-symbolic sharp action, likely produces roughening or stupidity of the real susceptibility of the human soul. The mono-symbols must be deserved in a conscientious work. They ought to be found seldom and not in too sharp a sensorial manner. The last method attracts too energetically, produces, therefore, anger, and moves too much the human energy causing, therefore, passion. Nature itself is the best educator and it is exceedingly dangerous to replace the deepest secrecy of the natural will and performance, which she reserves for herself, if her mysteries are "unearthed" by any scientific enterprise and brought into earning connection with humanity. The greatest sacrilege consists, according to the conviction of many, in this that the human intelligence and art dare to intrude so much into the sanctuary of the deepest and most secret laws of the psychological performance and avail themselves so much of them that they change them into sources of practical utility and economical self-service.

But we recognize in the sacramentalism nevertheless a high standing of educational efficacy. The sacramental individual has not to go through all kinds of errors; he has not to be subjected to the danger to go astray in the intellectual researches and to fail perhaps in his ideal conclusiveness. The formulations of the last goal are presented to him in advance, he is from the beginning satisfied in the conviction to have the possibility to reach his personal affective happiness. The way is made easy by the clear presentation of the terminal re-active goals. The Catholic sacraments are for this reason, within their area, the most efficient means for sure affective discharge, the guarantee of the lack of intellectual obstruction of the life of the believer and have, therefore, the precious quality of serene stars full of hope and clear splendour enlightening the night of the individual real experience and investigation. The Catholic Church makes in this way all intellectual life-force subjected to her terminal formalistic symbolism. The free researches are excluded from the Catholic mind because the terminal results are presented in advance in clear final symbols, to which every individual psychological progression has to discharge after all.

But the sacramental symbols are the omnipresent pledges of the possibility of the individual happiness of the life of the believer. The educational danger of the easy obtainability by their artistic make-up is balanced by the sureness of the unmistakable vista of reaching after all the happy harbour of their symbolic lights. The precision of their artificial presentation preserves the individual life-force from "useless" scattering loss of psychic energy and guarantees in this way the continual change of the personal actions into happy ideal discharge. The great side of the established religion is, in a sense, security of success.

So the sacramental education may be considered up to a certain degree as the sure psychological guidance of the individual life-force to reach the individually most possible happiness with the least possible degree of straying affective loss, in presenting the clearest terminal sensorial fingerposts. The whole connection of the natural psychological developments from reality toward idealism has been elevated on the artificial basis of the sacramental performance; the hardness of the slow real life has been replaced by the artistic and scientific technicalities of the ecclesiastic mysterious administration. There is no doubt that the psychological performance of the progression of the individual experience towards the terminal delicious reactions has gained in surety, quickness and energy, but this so-called *supernaturalization* of the psychological human existence is not the *natural* condition of our most essential natural function.

There may be an idle quarrel about the question, whether there has been a modification towards better or worse psychological functions in the acceptance of the sacramental life; we have to recognize and to face the clear two facts: that sacramentalism has encroached on the deepest and arch-peculiar functions of the psychological nature of mankind and that it has left the natural way of the self-helping necessity of the real life and the fatal existence of the individual. The root of the psychological human life has been artificialized in this manner by the sacramental institutions, artistic facilitations substituting the natural real investigations of new ideal goals. Sacramentalism does not make for searching independently new ideal ways, but quickens the practical life in presenting them already in a finished stage of advance. The acceptance of the ecclesiastical authority is rewarded by the grant of the magnetic easiness of the personal way, to which the directive goal is already given in advance, or we may say, the resignation and the humility of the individual not to find by himself new adequate terminal ideal methods and goals gives to him the practical easiness to go on toward the accepted ecclesiastic divinity. So the sacramental individual is permitted to be comfortable in the well-directed real way, if he dispenses with the personal claim and pride to find out by himself the last goals in a way adequate and appropriate to his fatal experimental contingencies. The Catholic signs in advance, already at his birthday, as it were, the contract not to draw individually the last logical conclusions from his vital experiences, and observations, but to admit quite generally and without restriction the general historic philosophical results of the ecclesiastical doctrine.

The most precious and perhaps only interesting facts of our life are exactly the terminal concluding revenues which we draw from our personal experience in regard to unchangeable ideal consequences and eternal values. The free conscientious personal judgment of these last questions in dependence on one's personal experience must doubtless be the first and last claim of the psychological individual capacity. Only the individual who uses independently and freely according to his personal life and relying on his commonsense the faculty of thinking, judging, criticizing his destiny and condensing it into convictions, enthusiasm, pleasures and enjoyment can be called a man. Condensaton of our intellectual experiences into the last symbols of ideal convictions has to be the terminal result coming from the individual outside sensorial life and footing on this objective basis: The ideal structure of any merely theoretical organization lacks the sufficient objectivity and produces after all the unhappy friction between real experience and idealistic belief.

Every theoretic method of education is dangerous for the reason that it does not stand perfectly on the proof and the test of the objective truth. Everything that is perfectly true must be confirmed in the daily experimental life and in as much as it is not true it cannot be in congruency with it. No theoretical educational conception corresponds entirely to the reality of the human life. If sacramentalism is built up in a methodical way, it is near nature in the monopunctual terminal sacramental restricted reaction. The sacramental monopunctual method has indeed principally the affirmation of our subjective psychological nature which strives continually towards monogenial, mono-symbolic and monotheistic condensations, but the angry exclusion of the hard intermediary work by artificial comfortable substitutions proves in the educational sense, in advance less promising, in the narrow sacramental view, as the way of the choice for the ideal affective discharge. The Sacrament has a subsidiary and recreative role like art. .

Not only the offered monosymbols of the sacramental church may be our opportunities of idealistic discharge, our heart may be kindled not only by the blessed candles of the church towards thrilling idealism, but our life-force has to be inspired in divine love and gratitude in every creative condition which permits us to concentrate into sensorial monosymbolic affective lightnings. *Nature* with all its wonderful sparkling lights, work, business, love, science, art and religion in the broadest sense are all full of the same monosensorial possibility. We have to develop, to study, to observe, to strain and to work again and again until we find out, and we have to achieve in logical organization every moment once more in all our experiences the becoming form of our possible psychological delight. There is not and cannot be, any patented limit for the number of the glittering precious stones of divine love and the charming gracious inspiration which flows and infuses itself into any honest and thorough effort which is done by human energy. Our fate is full of delicious sparkling pearls of condensed symbolism, of shining diamonds of conclusive rewards and of puzzling most various stars of happiness, but the supposition to find them out is always the serious strain of incessant work progressing step by step in the graduation of the slow logical refinement from the periphery of our real experience towards the centre of ideal fulfillment. The world is full of opportunities of divine enjoyment, if we are able to open the eyes. The glittering surface of the lake in the sunshine with its lavish riches of numberless pearls bewitch you, the flowers on the meadow are wonderful monooptic signs for our proper human gift; every sunbeam may rightly be a divine candle kindling our monosymbolic joy and gratitude: every scintillation of a falling snow-flake may explode in your heart with charm and pleasure.

The whole problem of the symbolic and sacramental performances may be conceived as well in the psychological sense as the special solution of the division, disposition and application of the pictures of the human IMAGINATION. The size, the circumference, the rapidity and frequency of change, the intense occupancy with real objects decides over the value and the educational character of the symbolic or psychic conceptions. The symbols or religious attempts to act are different temperamental divisions and subdivisions of our imaginative total amount, tempting to cut the great pie of the total imaginative life-force into very big and very small pieces, leaving out the middle sizes in order to surprise and to be considered original. Religious, symbolic and sacramental dispositions are built up, quite analogous to the joke and humour, causing idealistic pleasure by the surprising clash of very incongruent and incommensurable pieces of the imaginative human power. From the special sequence of greater and smaller imaginative pictures, from their regular decrease in expansion or from their, and from their strong contrast in smallness and greatness follows at last that peculiar lawful psychic disposition or character which we call *personal temperament. The strong discrepancies in the immediately following sizes of the imaginative pictures or notions cause ignorance, wonder, admiration, love and pleasure through surprise, but they hurt the individual soul in causing passions by their sensorial intimacy and the unlogical excitements.*

It is difficult to concentrate in one moment all objects from one outspread large field into the smallest narrow space. To do this exacts not only the most swift activity, but also much power, attention and effort, inevitably thus causing destruction, carelessness, ruining many objects in the hurry of the momentaneous overwork. Sacramental symbolism is comparable to the hyper-orderly and one-sided clearing away passion of a housekeeper's work. Busy sacramentalism is a too thorough house-keeper and a too clean ideal scrub-woman fond of holy-day order so much that it troubles the quiet working display, takes away the instruments and implements of the workers before the work is perfectly done, and troubles so the quiet and logical development of the natural performances of the daily duties.

The old times, religion, art and love bribe the individual favor with the small thrilling specks of lightnings and kisses—they believe in QUALITY; the modern time, scientific, possessive and material conceptions try to bluff with huge numbers and vast dimensions—they believe in QUANTITY. The one offers to you a charming kiss, and the other a big house. You have the choice.

The *Veneration of the Blessed Virgin Mary and of the Saints* is a very pronounced feature of the Catholic ecclesiastical practice. We meet in this peculiar cultural institution of Catholicism the need to correct extreme philosophical monopunctual conceptions, to weaken the extraordinary mono-concentration of the divine individual and collective discharge. The saints are again humanized symbols of religious conceptions and notions, but in a more peripheric manner. They are preparations for the terminal monotheistic symbolic concentrations, gathering the sympathy of the believers into many points, producing thereby a whole set of penetrating securities on the way to the terminal idealism. The suggestion of the crowd receives for this reason strong new reinforcements in the practical psychology of the Christian believer. By the worship of the saints the meditation of the single ideal conceptions and values is represented in human symbols facilitating and making more accessible in a discriminating way the ideal values, creating a broader intellectual basis for their expression, but on the other hand also putting restricted human faculties into nearest connection with the perfect terminal conceptions of theistic achievement.

The objection to the Catholic Church that she worships dead

people in the same degree as God, is of course wrong. But the canonization of people who are dead a long time ago has, of course its deep psychological root in the fact that the first supposition to be put on the altar of the idealistic believer is the previous loss of the exact circumstances in which somebody lived in his real life. It is the utmost psychological necessity that first the power of the legendary idealization has worked a long time on the memory of the beatified individual and that instead the real intellectual sharpness of his life has been blurred. The energetic concentration of our sympathetic feelings and the condensation of our love and ideal admiration into one personality can only be done with the help of the energetic intellectual reduction of the objective circumstances of his life. The most famous and successful men are those who understand to hide themselves best before the eyes of people as to their petty daily circumstances. It is only the great deed worth while, which impresses and makes the hero, whilst every knowledge of the daily petty circumstances lowers his acknowledgement remarkably, owing to the law of compensation, and makes him vulgar in the multiple fixation of the intellectual meditation of his daily life. For this reason we know that the first condition for highest hero worship is that the heroes are dead a long time ago or that they were never conspicuous in their life, or that they are almost forgotten, if they claim to be canonized afterwards. Nobody cared much at their life time about their real social intercourse, if they were real idealists. The idealistic type of the saints themselves was of course by their character always very retired from the social life and was just by the circumstance of this inclination to solitary concealment very often liable to become the sentimental centre of all possible legendary accumulation.

The grant of divine qualities to any sainted individual is so much more easy and perfect, the more he is wrapped into the mysterious veil of the legend. If his categoric qualities have succeeded in being excluded most possibly from his daily intellectual memory, then he has chances to be near to the monosymbolic veneration of the society, if haphazard and historic fulfillment of the time put their affective stress on his personality. Strong detailed intellectual features of the individual life are reasons against the discharge of later beatification. Strong real frictions of the individual are improbabilities for any future canonization. The notion of holiness is in nearest connection with the hidden solitariness of the personal life. Strong real frictions and intellectual sharp distinctions of the experimental social life have easy relations to sin and the average mediocrity. The exact knowledge of every life shows that the extremes touch also in the moral life, that strong lights have dark shadows, and that the real virtue of the world is indeed a psychological compromising mediocrity, far from all serious heroic one-sidedness as well as from criminal competition.

It is the sign of an intellectually progressive religion if the altars of modern saints are ornamented with numberless blessed candles and if those of oldest saints, as the apostles, St. Ann and John the Baptist, are relatively abandoned. This fact proves the inclination of the contemporary mind to lower the idealistic strong concentration of the religious tendencies, exhibits the need of the believer to work out more detailed adaptation of the life to the ideal, exacts clearer information from the idealism to show the way to go through the real life.

We see in the choice of the venerated saints of the Catholic Church that the waves of the *fashion* as it goes always through the whole human society, has the power to intrude, up to a certain degree, through the sacred doors of the church. There are always signs of adaptation even of the Catholic Church to its surrounding social and historic atmosphere: but they are so little that it exacts much experience and keen observation to find them out and to put them into right connections. Catholicism was not the same in the middle ages as it is now, it is not the same in Austria as it is in Switzerland and it is very different in Canada. The surrounding culture, the climate, the national race, the general standing of the artistic development of a country, the power or weakness of competitive denominations and other religions have all a great influence not only on the psychological manifestations, strength and kind of conviction and form of expression of the religious Catholic tenets, but they have their expression also in the most detailed things of the use in the church, in the artistic, administrative and dispensatory sense and even in the taste for the saints.

The adoration of God is the potential compression and condensation of all scattered love of the created real world, whilst the love for the saints is the partly ideal fixation of this divine love to one human individual memory. The adoration of the monotheistic terminal God and the worship of the saints are for this reason not only supporters of each other in emphasizing the same ideal direction of the mind, but may be in some cases mutual dynamic competitors, both being able to be hurt seriously as to their strong representation by the affective scantiness caused by the anticipating competitor. Strong and thorough worship of the

saints may, therefore, undoubtedly exterminate the sharpest monotheistic conception and worship, which may be useful in the educational sense, and extreme monogenial and monotheistic practice
and enthusiasm can have the consequence to exclude or lower the
veneration for the saints, owing to the law of compensation.

The *worship of the Blessed Virgin Mary,* the Mother of
Christ, plays a very important role in the Catholic Church. How
much in the cultivation of the veneration of St. Mary rose a serious collaboration or competition with the worship of Christ in
the practical service and in the ecclesiastical practice, we may easily recognize in remembering the main and most frequent object of
the mediaeval Christian art which almost exclusively avails itself
of every opportunity to treat most minutely the subject of the Ma-
donna, whilst the Child Jesus, according to his baby nature, is
rather subordinated. The churches at that time and still today
very often emphasize prevalently the sentimental belief in the worship of the Holy Virgin, establishing and decorating great paintings and statues of St. Mary in the central places of the churches,
whilst the Cross and the pictures of Christ himself are rather less
conspicuous for the eye of the believer.

The Catholic cultivation of the worship of St. Mary is the
expression of the great protection which is bestowed in the Christian doctrine on the ideas of *motherhood,* virginity, family life, feminine independence and dignity. The monotheistic conception of
the Old Testament and even the monogenial philosophical representation of Christ have very much the psychological accent on the
virile natural gift. They emphasize very much the idea of ideal
and every other conclusiveness, of thoroughness, of success and
terminal discharge towards idealistic values; they subdue the transitional stages of the intellectual working elaboration and life
much more thinking most of the last divine results to which all
previous work is subjected. They are disinclined to the present
modest and real activity and suggest not to put the affective accent on the present daily working life, but on the consideration of
the whole and on the last ideal results, not to respect the consideration resulting from the practical necessities, but to subject all
experience to the theoretical logical ideal conclusion. The male
character is corresponding to this conception. It does not like so
much the present as the past and the future: the man is the rushing idealist overthrowing the present material reality and appreciating more the result than the way, looking for new ways to
better results in a theoretical manner and being, therefore, dangerous to the conservative status quo of the present time and of

the family life.

The strong worship of the Blessed Virgin suggests and emphasizes the stability of the *feminine mind*. The basis of the feminine character is most pronounced in the idea of motherhood, quietness, respect for the present reality, and the material values of the life are the indispensable foundation of every happy motherhood and its claim for a stable home. The love of the mother draws the overweight of the active human inclination towards the real facts of the present life and love, of birth, education of the child, working social order and familiar possessive existence. The wife clings to the given reality; she refuses the continual change of the exterior intellectual formula for the ideal progress and tries to realize in her only child, in a personal and individual way, all the problems of the ideal teleology. She strives to, and believes in, the establishment of the terminal idealism in the real work; she intends to develop the foundation of the best human realization and of the highest possible divine manifestation of God at her age in her human child. The veneration of the mother of God comes along to help this feminine conception. It will lower the ideal monoconcentration of the impatient digressing male character; it has to mitigate the conception of the human nature as a transitional state of pilgrimage and introduces the necessary stability into the social result of the human existence. The man is fond of going from the good to the better, the mother considers her present child as the best good.

The nearest theistic connection of the Holy Virgin bridles the one-sided male idealism in putting the accent of the affective energy of our psychology on the present working day, neglecting the past and overtaking the future by the zeal of the present welfare of the family life. The feminine character is the most pronounced and toughest psychological representative of the real social life. Woman draws most efficiently the charming idealistic powers from heaven to earth, she scatters the fulness of the divine glory which the male psychology always again strives to concentrate in monogenial lightnings, into the out-spread periphery of the practical life and of the physiological experience. Woman is much more able and inclined to maintain the intellectual multiple fixation of her loving soul than man is, she scatters her life-force in her minute human experience, whilst the man in his theoretic philosophical mind is likely urged by needs of concluding condensation to discharge most possible his love, in terminal monoideal reactions. So the worship of the Blessed Virgin in the religious ritus represents an opposite pole to the one-sided, angry ideal conception estranged and averse to the real patient work, as it is given in the mono-genial Christ and in the extreme monotheism at all.

Motherhood is conceived as the highest human dignity, as: das ewig Weibliche, zu dem wir angezogen werden, as Goethe says: The feminine nature connects both features, the strong monosenor-ial symbolic character as it is given in monotheism and the Christian monogenius and monogamy, but also in the monosymbolic love of the women. All these functions are organized according to the principle issuing from the peculiar individual natural disposition, producing therefore analogous harmony and parallel desires of love, inspiration and aspiration. On the other hand, as we pointed out already, it is the retarding intellectual character within the matrimonial frame, given and expressed in the feminine disposition which works out the checking laws of real peripheric performance. Both man and woman have of course the most opposite inclinations to fasten their magnetic gifts as well at the real periphery as at the ideal centre, but both in a different way. The disposition of the mother-woman has the most pronounced real home-bound fixation, so much as to render her the most efficient fly-wheel of the real social energy. Here lies the "superiority" of the wife and here is the point, where the male nature has to sacrifice itself and to serve the stronger *real* will inborn to the wife. Here is the point where the man can be crushed by the feminine passion if he does not understand at the right moment: here his speculative "laziness" will exclude him from the real concern of the family-life which is guarded and stewarded in the most efficient manner by the mother type. There is no real seriousness comparable with the familiar energy of the mother: she puts all her stress on its most minute performances, forgetting and ignoring all around and making everything serviceable to her narrow intellectual task, eating the man like a spider, as Bernard Shaw says, if he would eat instead of creating the bread of her children. She creates a heaven of gracious happiness in the world within the small circle of her familiar frame for her children and herself, hyperemphasizing this realm most important to her by instinct. The intentional short-sighted weakness of the feminine character and its strong familiar divertability is likely to become the greedy leech absorbing the male artistic idealism in the workshop of the real familiar interests.

But there is another side in the highest ideal conception of the woman, as it is delineated in the Catholic worship of the Blessed Virgin. It is the definite confession of the human dignity and the equal birth of the feminine individual with the man. The veneration of the Mother of God does away with the superiority of the man, giving to the woman the equality of the right of psychic acknowledgement and faculties, and it is out of this practice that the abolition of slavery forcedly must have resulted. All valuable religion has its deepest social foundation in the highest dignity of the individual in respect to his eternal relations, so that anybody, male or female, has the highest values, rights and dispositions and is the alpha and omega of all essential psychological achievement and performances.

It is the strong emphasis of the veneration of the Holy Mary in the Catholic Church which intends to direct all the attention of the idealistic man on the real importance of the family life, on the superior dignity of the feminine character inspiring the daily life with the glamour of divine sunbeams. Feminism, love and terminal idealism are in the Catholic Marian worship closely connected together: it represents indeed a wonderful trias, each precious stone receiving more light and splendour from the neighboring diamond. We are able to find out in this Catholic idea the glorification of love and motherhood. The poetry and splendour of the veneration of St. Mary in the Catholic Church is much more brilliant than generally it was assumed. The sanctuaries where especially the Virgin Mary is reverenced are numerous and most proudly elaborated (Lourdes, Einsiedeln), the festival performance of the service, the processions, the lavish use of candles and lights, the enthusiastic popular Marian songs in all languages full of sway and poetry, make the most moving impression on the witness. The figure of Mary is indeed the sweetest and most poetical flower of the Catholic imagination. The Catholic prayer overflows with all charming appellation which it attaches to the Holy Virgin, it gives to her in long litanies all imaginable sweet loving names, for Tower of Ivory, Consoler of the Mourning. Not only the mediaeval pictures have chosen always again and again Mary as their eval pictures have chosen always again and again Mary as their chief topic, but we remark the same thing in sculpture, in poetry and in music.

Ars longa, vita brevis est.

TENTH BOOK

ART in the middle ages was exceedingly important. Beauty, riches and architectural boldness of the mediaeval churches are quite unparalleled in the history of the world excepting perhaps the Indian and Chinese art. Never by far other painters mounted to the splendid level of the Italians in the Fifteenth and Sixteenth Centuries. Sculpture covered Europe at this time with the most wonderful, innumerable carved figures of Christ, of the Blessed Virgin and of the Saints, in wood and stone; the choirs of the Spanish, Italian and German churches (Toledo, Seville, Nuremberg) are still today the most eloquent witnesses of the artistic fertility of the mediaeval sculpture. The most outstanding musical masterpieces arose in connection with the Roman Church, first in the Choral and in connection with the service in the Vatican at Rome (Paganini), afterwards chiefly in Austria leaning to the text and the inspiration of the Mass.

The clear monotheistic Catholic conception is indeed by history and nature most nearly connected with the notion of art. Art has so much received its formalitic character from the central monotheism and educated our culture by tradition and personal experience so deeply with its circular monocentral principle, that we today still are so far that we doubt whether there could be any other fertile and successful art at all. The cultural Catholic development has essentially ripened the richest sense of art in the European old Christian countries: taste and dexterity in art have become a strong traditional inheritance in these nations.

What is then art in the Catholic sense? We related to its essence already at different times. If we throw a stone on the motionless surface of a pond, then we see instantly from the central depression of the water where the stone has entered, the rise of circular waves of the water moving and enlarging towards the outside, and we observe that the nearest central rings are higher and stronger, and the peripheric ones are flatter and losing themselves entirely in the outside plane. Art is indeed comparable to these circular rings about the central impression of the water, the innermost one being represented by the monotheistic idea and the next by the divine halos. Mediaeval art is the waving quivering effect of the monotheistic and monogenial Christianity and Catholicism, the formalistic principle of this art being given in the full, and semi-circular lines which in their totality point in most variable combinations and interferences to the central monosensorial symbol, of which they have to be the intellectual reflection, the underlining emphasis and the mirror necessarily reminding of the monopunctual theistic goal.

Christian art has, therefore, in spite of all, nearest connections with SCIENCE; both are logical. The chief differences are: firstly, that art receives its inspiration from the terminal monotheistic goal, it is, therefore, caused in a rather speculative or inspired way, whilst science progresses from the periphery toward new centres: art receives its moving energy from the inspiring central speculation like the water rings from the falling stone: secondly, that Christian Catholic art has to have a traditional and historic background, a traditionally fixed ideal which is its solid pedestal. For the moving energy of art, it is quite essential to have one firm unchangeable starting point. Only the strong mono-determination of it is able to impart that strong energy and masterful magnetic firmness which every artistic performance needs. Art has not the intention or the possibility, therefore, to enlarge former theistic philosophical points or statements, it on the contrary strives to point to their fixed result which may be given in the historic monotheistic concentration. Science on the contrary refusing the acceptance of any terminal goal in advance in a quite characteristic way ignores tradition, history and custom and digs in quite different directions always going on in the philosophical universe. It is essential for the science to enlarge and to modify the old theistic conceptions, whilst art means the fixation, the explanation and the glorification of the dates of the old religious ideas. We may call art, therefore, the science with historic, cultural and philosophical narrow boundaries, the science with traditional restricted goals, whilst we as well may call reversely science the universal art having no limit nor restriction, neglecting all historic traditional and denominational supposition and striving only in full independence for one goal which never can be reached, for the absolute truth. We see how much easier the task of the art is than that of the science. Both have to use the intellectual instrument of the logical thought, but whilst the art is guided and suggested by the beckoning monotheistic goal, which it has to approach and round which it oscillates in concentric esthetic circles, the science has the harder duty to build bridges towards the outside universe in the longitudinal direction without previous knowledge of the opposite terminal point of support, only fixed in its confidence by the absolute conviction of the righteousness of its instrument, the logical thought. The scientist has the idea that he must indeed arrive to the best goal, if he uses conscientiously and patiently his logical tempting gift, that he will have not only a subjective absolute, but an objective and relative truth. The work of the scientist is, therefore, much more difficult, much more exacting above all in moral qualities, in courage, patience, confidence in the good disposition of the human nature and the obtainable order of the universe.

All Catholic science must, therefore, in the best case be called art. Catholicism had always the clearest supposition of the idea of the monogenial historic hero and of the most precise monotheistic divine personification as it was given to it by the previous Jewish history. All its productions even the philosophical works of Thomas Ab Aquino, mingled with the old philosophy of Aristotle, and of St. Albert, the Great, must be considered as artistic science founded on the former results of historic religious and scientific development. They necessarily are explanations and descriptions with little creative power because they have already the boundaries of their permitted reach clear before their eyes in advance.

Fixed monosymbolism is essentially sterile in science as it is rich and surprising in its artistic power. Art supposes precision of the goal; it receives from it the sharp intellectual features which must be connected with the high dreams of its inspiration. Science on the contrary would be destroyed by this exact knowledge of its goal. Science is a man as it were, going and straying until he found his true home and goal. As soon as they are found and he is at home, comfortable and satisfied, from this moment the longing for finding ceases, the wanderer likes to be at last at home. Science has become art in the moment of homy habitual disposition. There is no more the question of finding a high terminal goal, but of profiting by its possibility of exploitation. Science is, therefore, the way to the hidden goal which we don't know in advance, art on the contrary is the enjoyment and explanation of the goal which we already possess. As long as we have science we are sure to work, to progress and to grow in our deepest natural disposition, but as soon as we indulge exclusively in art, we have to expect to become luxuriant, checked in sentimental stagnation, losing the hope and confidence of a further universal theistic progression, being impoverished in leaning conservatism.

We understand, therefore, that there is a time, where art stops, there cannot be always the enjoying standstill of our joined goal. This goal will be insufficient in time and the sterility of the art in our days has, therefore, the meaning that former attitudes to universal relationship are exhausted for the present humanity. It means that it has to emigrate from its lazy historic fixation in order to create new enlarged, great divine goals. Science becomes art because the human knowledge becomes habit and routine, and art and styles fade away because new urges and impulses are needed, first in the scientific enlargement, then in the religious sedimentation and at last and only then the society will be prepared to produce new arts and styles.

Science destroys art, and art unhinges science. Where science appears, art disappears, or where one learns to do how, one forgets to do what.

Science essentially destroys the simplicity of the heart and scatters the mono-intentional fanaticism given in the original religion. There cannot possibly be anything more opposite than the Catholic utmost symbolic mono-determination and science. Science is essentially multiplicity, Catholicism essentially simplicity of the intention. The Catholic psychology has no higher goal than to produce the perfect monogenial simplicity of the affective direction, whilst science on the contrary has no keener task than the rich experimental display and the most possible entanglement in the objective visible world.

For this reason we essentially in the psychological intention of the Catholicism, and we speak always in this deepest connection, have not to expect great scientific deeds. But we have to mark on the other hand that there are always exceptions in the practical life. The monks and priests of the middle ages were the light bearers of the new learned civilization which was introduced by them in our country. The monasteries in the middle ages and even later, deserved highly of science, chiefly the Benedictins (Clugny, St. Gallen) and Jesuites. We must also acknowledge that the historic cultural monogenial starting point though mono-determined,—this is its strong and weak point,—of Christianity needed a long time to penetrate thoroughly the society. Although it comes about that the intellectual following display of any pre-existent genial idea imposes as a scientific system, rightly it has the philosophical character of the art, because it refers exactly to non-intellectual goals and values. Modern science and Catholicism are in the deepest sense of the word incommensurable. The sure terminal mono-intention of the striving energy of the individual baffles the working up of the most characterizing mark of all real creative science, of the free investigation. Catholic Christian thinking is narrowed by the suggestive intention, by the given goal outside of which it is conscious not to be permitted to go at all. But there arises again the question whether the genial security is not more intellectualizing, in a way, than the oscillating doubt.

The broad carefulness in looking for the truth, which is the essential character of science, is of course greatest in people who do not share the happy quietness of possessing the sure goal. The biological human necessity of having last goals and intentions creates the striving energy of the scientific investigation. The further we are from the monodetermined idealism, the more energetically arises our natural necessity in looking for and creating it which is nothing but the definition of science in application. The most efficient scientific thinker, investigator and inventor must therefore be the so-called agnostic. He feels to be in dark night as to his intentional conclusions, he lacks the finished development of his intellectual symbolism and has, therefore, the natural need to perform the necessary efforts towards these psychological last results.

The whole scientific revolution of the modern intellectual world reposes, generally speaking, on this psychological ground. The modern world dared to postulate since the end of the middle ages and still more since the French Revolution, the questionability of the last historic philosophical intentions and received in this fact the most fertile urges for scientific work. The last two centuries have, therefore, produced more scientific inventive results than all former times together, the intentional liberalism being the scientific deliverance of the human faculties. There are, accordingly, more feverish dispositions, more intentional incertitude more magnetic oscillations of the ideal finger and lavish of energies in humanity than ever was, but this increased effort and dangerous anxiety is rewarded and balanced by the unparalleled growth of the whole human mind, by the coming enlargement of idealism, by the carefulness of the intentional performance and by the novelty of the daring investigation. If laziness is the worst thing, then this intentional deliverance of our age with its bee-like diligence must indeed be very good, and if the confidence in our future collective human fate is the root of our religious, moral and intellectual destiny, then the scientific system of today necessarily must be the best. The psychological aspect of the world of today thus has entirely changed, all owing to the blowing up of the former exaggerated monodetermination and to the destruction of the hypermodest and at the same time hyper-proud simplicity of the heart which was set as the foundation of the old conceptions.

The sharp monogenial conception of the hero was indeed the

keystone at which the whole psychological intellectual formation of the antique world was smashed, and conducted into the peculiar mystic and punctual artistic funnels of the middle ages. But it is as well only the overcoming of the extreme mono-intentional organization which restituted to the world its intellectual scientific love, which permitted humanity again to set free its affective mono-fanaticism and to love compensatorily the whole realm of the objective human experience as before.

This is also the reason of the artistic impoverishment of our present age. The inspiring symbolic inspiration was extinguished with the destruction of the sharp historic monogenial conception. Humanity has to look after new important methods of skilful sensorial expressions of their ideas. As long as there are no sure simple goals and clearly sedimented symbols, it is understandable that the modern society of today neither can have clear, sure and beautiful artistic expressions nor that it can have a serious striving and desire for them.

Our monosymbolic natural disposition is comparable to the charming highest tone played on the flute of our psychopupilar nature. This monosymbolic tone is the highest record produced by the former cultural history of the humanity. But today our age is conscious that these monopunctual highest expressions of our intellectual life are the highest records only from the standpoint of the individual subjective disposition and organization. The consciousness of the ego is the love of the vivified matter for the infinite universal spirit and its egoistic will to persevere in this knighted state forever. There is no longer any use to confuse the infinite universe with the narrow monopunctual subjective human possibility. Science builds its claims and rights on top of this theological postulation. It strives to become more objective and more universally comprehending than the former absolute subjectivity of the individual. The root and the last source of the mono-determined competency of mysticism and art, developed to the utmost degree in Catholicism, is the individual, whilst the modern scientific psychology has its root and basis in the general strength and effort of the collective capability of the human collectiveness and of numberless objective facts and experiences. Modern science and Catholicism seem, therefore, to be the most opposite psychological methods, one taking all advantage from the individual real world and the other one drawing all its results from its exclusion and its reduction into the smallest simplicity of monosymbolism.

The Catholic church permits the experience and the enjoyment of the divinity only to the humble individual mono-determination, whilst science strives to create the more solid basis of the socially graspable divinity. The goal of science is the fulfillment of God in the real categories of time, space and casuality, whilst the Christian religion could not go further than to give the divine anticipation to the individual heart. What a wonderful idea to solidify the presence of the divinity and its merciful action so much in humanity as to impart it in sure, clear and unswitchable a way to all circumstances and to all individuals in the same manner, not only to hope and to aspire to it, but to insure its fruits in all smallest occasions of the daily life. Science will transfer the divine effect from the heart into the understanding, from the expectation into the reality, from the hope into the fulfilment. Science tries to change the monotheistic dreams into innumerable charming deeds, flowing like a river through the channels of objective justice and intelligence possible on earth: it will be the better and more active and precise stewart of the interspheric benevolence of which we all are entitled to be the sharers. Science will give to us the direct intercourse with the unlimited notion of the most progressive idea of the divinity unrestricted and well understood, and it intends everything much more than to put any limits to our good natural inclinations to divine enjoyment, share and fulfilment. Whilst the old Catholic religion restricted our happiness in order to adapt it to its historic traditional notion and to its economic ecclesiastical frame, science on the contrary enlarges our conception of the universal God in order to augment our divine share. But there will be no end of difficulties and misunderstandings.

All strong ages of Catholicism were characterized by *artistic Styles*. Style means the peculiar temperament of expression and execution in the fine arts, and it is based on the most exclusive method of thinking, feeling and acting during any historic epoch. The deepest psychological root of every style and fashion is the necessity of changing the intellectual means of expression, because one old point of view has been exhausted in its rights and wrongs, agreeable and disagreeable sides, and because the sensorial susceptibility of the individual is no more amenable, but roughened in regard to this traditional coin of an old truth used up by long practical friction in the experience of life.

There were always different philosophical principles put into the foreground of any age, from whose artistic style we may easily recognize them. The different styles of the past Catholicism, are the reflective mirrors of its history, all glorious and brilliant in their way; taking the most pronounced ones, we mention the Romanesque, Gothic, Renaissance and Barocco style. Let us choose the Gothic and the Barocco-style in order to explain in them the peculiar philosophical basis and its formalistic expression in the concerned style.

In the GOTHIC STYLE we observe quite essentially the emphasis of the perpendicularity at the expense of the horizontal extension. The deepest and foremost idea which the Gothic style is most fervent to express undiscussedly, is to point out how important our human psychological relations between heaven and hell must be, how much we continually must be aware of the religious meditations and intercourse between these two philosophical religious poles localized by our imagination to the highest height and to the deepest depth. But it is keen to express as well on the other hand that we have instead to neglect and depreciate the detailed display of the horizontal platform of the intellectual life.

Here we already see that the real devil in this sense is the world, being the most obnoxious satan of the Christian interests because of its lukewarm indifference to the religious magnetism, whilst the embittered antagonistic devil, is the logical antipode of the monotheistic philosophical system, admitting by the confession of his existence the proof of the opposite monotheism. There is indeed no better philosophical confession of the monotheistic Christian conception and confession than the acceptance of the idea of the devil. Where the distress is greatest, God is nearest.

This philosophical one-sidedness must have been the clearest prevalent conviction of the Gothic middle-ages, its fundamental psychological hobby; it must have been the most domineering and most general conception pervading and directing the whole psychological imagination of this time, with exclusive importance and gravity. In our psychopupilar idea and scientific language of to-day it meant the exaggerated emphasis of the monosensorial punctual light-field, the one-sided and exclusive clinging to the idealistic lightnings parting from this terminal sensorial antenna towards the eternal universal goals. The postulation and the continual repetition of the notions of the eternal idealistic goals is really a case of intellectual embarrassment. The terminal goal, properly speaking, supposes the punctual attitude of our psychopupil to which we strive always in our terminal functions, and outside of which we have no provable or intellectual experience.

These idealistic lightnings part at a rectangular direction from the plane of our experimental intellectual development and concentration. Assuming the plane of our intellectual life and visible experience parallel to the horizontal direction, as it is natural, we accordingly have to imagine the direction of the idealistic discharge in the perpendicular direction.

Verticalism is the parallel direction with the theological line. Even the PICTURE respects the verticalism, and in this the theological magnetism, with its symbolical focus or most substantial central marrow, but from a bird's-eye view. So we discover that the monopunctual symbolism is nothing else but the universal lightning energy hitting rectangularly the surface of our real world, seen from a bird's-eye view. The vertical direction means the parallelization of the material order with the interspheric theological magnetism connecting both poles, the stars and the underworld. It establishes the natural harmony of relationship between the material representation and the spiritual attraction. The development of the culture never escapes entirely from this third or perpendicular direction. The rising sky-scrapers of the present day are a new expression of this law, and of the emphasis of the third direction, growing once more, combining utility and spiritual revival.

This *artistic-philosophical assumption* is the supposition of the psychology and the whole intelligence of the Gothic law and of any artistic formulation. If we understand the special Gothic application of this disposition, we recognize all great and weak sides of the style of this time, we admire and abhor simultaneously. We have rich leisure in the high, but dark and narrow halls of the Gothic buildings to meditate the advantages and disadvantages of this peculiar conception of life and the world.

Whosoever has a human heart and imagination and has visited the wonderful Gothic churches and other Gothic buildings in Cologne, Ulm, Paris, Vienna, London, Burgos, Rouen, Lausanne, etc., (Europe is full of them) will admit that the strong perpendicular emphasis is indeed in a position to impart the highest sway of theistic idealism and most enthusiastic aspirations. All architectural formations together are nothing but the reminding finger pointing to the monotheistic heaven, uniting in hundreds and thousands of parallel columns and pilasters, all mounting from the horizontal floor toward considerable elevation and emptying without exception into the central buttons of the pointed vaults and the pointed arches, divine lightnings, as it were, shooting from earth to heaven. All Gothic architectural reality swings toward the sky, so much that the ascension is very high and accurately perpendicular and so energetically that, at their final high conclusion of the vault, the columns do not lose the uplifting enthusiasm ending in a rounded harmonious arch, but must be retained violently within the real boundaries of the possible architectural performance. They are impatient and almost successful in breaking through the roof which is expressed in the compromising pointed arches and vaults. There the elevating sway is crystallized forever; the bridled run-away horses are now lasting architectural monuments.

This law of perpendicular formation of the Gothic art is about all which we have to know about it thoroughly. There cannot be anything else of importance than this in the psychological way in regard to the Gothic art. We know what we have to think about it in the educational and philosophical way. One thing is true: the Gothic style is essentially idealistic. It is indeed the mirror of the same psychology which we found in the gospel, in the Eucharist and in the whole Catholic Sacramentalism.

All other moments of the Gothic style are merely secondary and subordinated. There is of course no real object, no saint, no animal, no flower or leaf, which could escape the high sentimental emphasis of the idealistic fulness of the Gothic style, all without exception are drunk with the celestial intercourse of which every last shareholder of the Gothic style is insured. So everything executed in the Gothic art, the last ornamental leaf or the most unassuming contemporary cultural statue receive in the general enthusiastic draft of the elongating Gothic style the highest degree of wonderful terminal magnetic sway and idealistic significance.

The one-sided perpendicularity of the Gothic law of formation is as well recognizable in the smallest sculptural ornamentation of the Gothic style as in the greatest architectural division of its buildings. As Cuvier and Agassiz were able to recognize and reconstruct the whole body of the most unusual pre-historic animals in discovering only a claw of them, so the smallest piece of artistic production of any, chiefly the Gothic style, gives the clearest hints to find out easily the whole character of the philosophical contemporary inclination of that time in which the artistic piece was constructed.

I remember to have seen before a short time a good reproduction in wood of St. Peter from the portal of the Cathedral of Rheims. This piece looked so odd in the surroundings of exclusively later furniture, in the room where it was exhibited, that it scarcely could be recognized in its meaning, so far was the distance of the two philosophical stylistic atmospheres put together. The Gothic style imparts indeed to the smallest sculptural detail its law of *unusual perpendicular elongation and neglects the real horizontal extension of the objective width*. This St. Peter, dating from the latest most extreme Gothic period was, therefore, forcedly most exaggerated in the length of his legs and body, as the narrowness of his horizontal expansion was as well quite extraordinarily remarkable to almost complete unrecognisability. This smallest piece reflected, therefore, as we said, in a perfect manner, the Gothic architectural and philosophical principle.

The Gothic windows with their narrow, but elongated fields are exactly again the expression of the same law. Their narrowness and the rich and darkening stained glass have the effect to exclude the clear light of the day and to emphasize the mysterious impression which was already given by the one-sided perpendicularity. Darkness is a further moment in a position to help much the psychological intention of the Gothic artistic style. The mysterious dusk of the Gothic church means the damping influence on the intellectual sharpness of the detailed objective visible world: it helps exactly the tendency of the perpendicular emphasis in excluding more the horizontal intellectuality which is closely connected with the distinctive sunshine, and giving in this manner to everything much more, compensatorily, the uplifting imaginative sway, stressing even the grotesque elongation of the saints, of the odd goblins, of the monsters, animals, flowers and leaves of the Gothic ornamentation, creeping along the columns and pilasters. The dim darkness of the Gothic spaces fits essentially the architectural and philosophical principles of this style, dismissing and neglecting with all possible means the natural validity of the intellectual detailed and horizontal thought of the material visibility, throwing all individual life-force, owing to the law of compensation, towards the elevated hills of the heaven, looking only towards the divine idealistic relations. It is averted to the sinful abyss, pointing out that nothing has any important significance in the world than the respect and the desire for idealism and that nothing can be imagined more detestable and hateful than the idea of antagonistic resistance to this uplifting exclusiveness which is pronounced in sin, hell, and perpendicular depth. All emphasis worth while of the human life and love has to be directed towards the monopunctual ideal monotheism: all our main efforts have to be strong lightnings shooting incessantly and variably towards this ideal uplifting goal and nothing else has mentionable value on our earth: this is the radical creed of the Gothic Catholic style. It preaches most impressively the idea of the only needful.

We notice easily the longitudinal sentimental predilection and the horizontal intellectual negligence everywhere in the Gothic painting too. The long fingers and the narrow hands of the

Gothic figures in painting and in sculpture are very characteristic. They are so pronounced that we very often are able to decide the Gothic origin of a masterpiece in recognizing only the long and narrow hand of a saint of these paintings and statues. It is exactly as the natural scientist recognizes the ages and the form of his animal in studying the claw which he found in his investigations. The most numerous Gothic paintings are to be found in Italy, in the Netherlands and in Germany. All together are the manifestations of the same theoretical tendencies as we pointed out. All bodies and figures are elongated, they are thin, the clothes cling straightly to their body; the vertical line is emphasized and the horizontal neglected everywhere.

We observe here just the contrary of the BAROCCO or BAROQUE STYLE which emphasizes so much the real exuberance and exhibits, therefore, the rounded forms of fat and well developed bodies and of rich drapery. The coats and gowns of the Barocco saints and the frequently used curtains are puffed up in the wind, showing pronounced numerous folds and emphasized in splendid gilded colors in order to withhold the admiring imagination from premature shrinking to the monopunctual concentration in ideal delight. The Gothic style made this fault of angry jumping over the peripheric reality, it carries the spectator too quickly towards the divine discharge, whilst Barocco retains the enjoyment for a long time in the intellectual detailed periphery and insinuates to the admirer the word of Goethe: O Augenblick, verweile doch, du bist so schoen! Stay longer, O moment, since thou art so beautiful!

If we analyze in a similar way the *Barocco Style,* we find, of course, since it is also the effusion of the Christian Catholicism, the same artistic philosophical system as in the Gothic style, but the emphasis of the sentiments has different localizations in the psychodynamic organisms. Whilst the Gothic style rises from the naivety of the earthly middle ages and has not at all the intellectual struggling suppositions of the much later Barocco style, whilst the Gothic is the charming flower coming out from the inexperienced and undisturbed ground of the mediaeval Catholicism and its strong sentiments, the Barocco style has already as its supposition a mighty intellectual experimental earthquake of severe criticism, a most serious lesson given to it by the new thought which arose in the meantime and which shook thoroughly the former conceptions of the exclusive ideal *mono-validity.* The supposition of the Barocco style is, therefore, the previous reduction of the one-sided ideal emphasis. The means of expression of the Barocco style is no more exclusively the direct and immediate expression of the ideal perpendicularity which must be considered as the most energetic enunciation of the concentrative idealism, and which proved to be so dangerous in the educational sense for the real world. The Barocco style does not dare any longer to approach so near the ideal lightning, it is no more willing to burn his hands and fingers again in the central ideal fanaticism, as the old naive middle ages did in the inexperienced Gothic artistic expression. The Barocco style is already sophisticated by the struggling experiences with the former intellectual Protestantism, Barocco knew how dangerous it was to touch directly the central focus of the monotheistic idealism and to exclude entirely the surrounding intellectual experimental periphery. The Gothic psychology touched inconsiderately the eternal lightnings and the ideal antenna of our psychic life which we cannot touch without being hurt, roughened in the educational sense and struck in the moral performance. The time of the rising Protestantism was the power which delivered humanity from the absolute idealistic one-sidedness and pointed out the necessity of the respect for the real world and the peripheric surroundings, the danger to touch directly the central antenna of our psychological life. The psychology of the Barocco style means the recovery from the extreme and dangerous one-sided central idealism; it is comparable to the sophisticated child which has burnt his fingers in former times at the idealistic mono-sensorial lights and is now careful enough not to touch any more his old beloved central goal, but to go around in artistic revelling circles like a cat around a saucer of hot milk. The old intentions and ideas, however, the former philosophical intentions, remain still the same, but the historic experience and the hurting damage brought about the change of the system and effectuated a more reserved artistic method. Here we have the difference between Gothic and Barocco style. Times and fashions brought about a temperamental change. The emphasis of the verticalism was given up in favour of horizontalism.

Having made this partly anticipating consideration, let us once more retrieve the thorough significance of our artistic-philosophical idea. Catholicism looked after the loss and the sophistication inflicted on it by the modern time, for new natural graphic means to express its old remaining philosophical monogenial and monotheistic ideals in another way in art. It strives to find them in choosing an intellectual round-about way which in its peculiar nature turns as well on the central monosymbolism again, but in an indirect and less immediate relationship. This means supposed to be the more intellectual emphasis of the old monopunctual ideal-ism has been found by the Barocco style in the *circle*. The circle indeed is no longer the monopunctual terminal discharge of the former idealistic psychological one-sidedness, as it was given in the bold perpendicular elevation of the Gothic architectural construc-tion, in its numberless sheaves of tiny columns and pilasters form-ing and creeping along the walls, but it is the more tolerant and more modest manifestation of the intellectual serving horizon of the peripheric activity of humanity, in relation to the central mono-sensorial terminal idealism. The Barocco style means, therefore, the Catholic monoidealism converted to the more intellectual in-sinuations of the post-Reformatory times. The Barocco style does not deal any longer with the one-sided hyper-emphasis of the ideal goal at the expense of the broad intellectual expression, but avails itself instead of the large intellectual display of the real world in order to refer from its multiple representation to the central mono-theistic idea.

We easily notice and admit that the use of this new means of artistic expression, as it is given in the Barocco style, is indeed less one-sided and more broadminded than the radical exclusive-ness of the former monosymbolic psychology. The circle does not lose the monopunctual intention whose continual underlining ex-pression it is; it preserves the suggestive charm of the idealistic monointention, but at the same time it has the most vivid inter-course with the real intellectual surroundings which it is able in this manner to depict in a broad variable and comfortable way, becom-ing so more true than every former artistic style.

The circular artistic treatment of the post-Reformatory epoch in the Catholic Europe has to be considered as the serious tendency and attempt to make the most important concessions to the claims of the real elaboration of the world and the intellectual visible life, as it was brought about by the modern philosophy and psychology.

So we see if we remember the circular principle underlying all Barocco style, that indeed in all masterpieces of this artistic epoch during the Seventeenth and Eighteenth Centuries, we have the easy possibility to dissolve all formalistic expressions into the most variable combinations and manifestations of circles. They may have the most perfect and audacious curves, they may be perfectly rounded as in the halos of the saints or be only slightly curved or represent only small parts and sections of the circular run, all the same and in spite of all there is nothing in this style which cannot easily be derived from the charming artistic element of the circle. So if we acknowledge the circle as beautiful, as lovely and gracious, if we must admit it as the happy means of reminding in a moderate suggestive manner of the affective concentration of our psychic force in the old monosymbolic conception of the Christian church, then the Barocco style must have been more able to fulfil its artistic educational task in the frame of the old church.

For a long time the Barocco style which has more than every other one the danger and facility to permit abuse in production of trash just because it is relatively more amenable to the average circumstances, has been wrongly ignored. There was chiefly in the later degenerating times of the Rococo period, besides the wonder-. ful refined and most tasteful productions (Bavarian castles, Paris and Vienna) a terrible corruption and frivolousness of this art, as we see in the insignificant output of exaggerated, tasteless and shallow work, chiefly in the Catholic churches of the country. But abuse was found in every style at the decrease of its inspiring inclination. This was as well the case already in the old cultural styles of the Antique Egyptians and Greeks. It is only our last time which discovered the high value of the Barocco period and gave to it its deserved respect and consideration.

It is our task to look at the masterpieces of this style, when it was at the peak of its artistic inspiration, when this new artistic formula possessed the top of its political might, and we have to study the places where its importance and weight were most concentrated. So we see in the artistic achievements of the time of Louis XIV, XV, and XVI, in Paris and Versailles, the richest and most marvellous expressions of this style. Louis XIV himself was the most gifted creator of art and style, he subordinated it mostly to his personal glory and political service, but he was of course in spite of his genius or exactly because of it the expression of its contemporary philosophical constellation and so he served its local monoidealistic development, corrected and modified by the intellectual influences of the previous struggles with the rising historic Protestantism. Barocco is, therefore, the amalgamation of the old Catholic philosophical principle with the acquisition of the Protestant more intellectual collaboration.

We have the same in Austria with the great Maria Theresa. She also was such an outstanding political star round which the artistic expression of her stylish time circled like the moon round the earth, but all these expressions had the meaning of a strong Catholic effort to recover from the blows inflicted by the philosophical and political objections demonstrated by the strong Protestant adversary. Austria is indeed full of the most wonderful masterpieces of the Barocco style. The Castle of Schoenbrunn is another Versailles: the Belvedere containing today the very instructive Barocco museum, was built by Prince Eugene after having beaten the Turks and exhibits in most tasteful and powerful manner the typical Barocco style. The Austrian monasteries, above all St. Florian near Linz, Melk, Neuburg, Goettweig, (the Church of Einsiedeln), the whole city of Salzburg, belong to the most wonderful cultural manifestations of the artistic expressions the world ever saw. They all are as well powerful and beautiful as they are pure, uniform and great in the stylistic conception. Kings and Popes came there and come again to admire their beauty and to have the honour to stay there for a short time. The Church of Durnstein on the Danube is a charming jewelry casket of architectural, sculptural and pictorial Barocco. The south of Germany is exceedingly rich in masterpieces of this style (Weingarten, Munich).

Painting was of course also most favourably changed and animated by the Barocco style. The peculiar circular revelling of its character which was introduced in the most liberal manner, imparted to the paintings of this epoch at once much real life, much exuberance of motion whilst they were before more estranged from the reality in wrong idealistic stiffness. We point above all to Titian, Paul Veronese, Velasquez and many others, in the first place to RUBENS, who may be considered as the typical exponent of the artistic manifestation of the Barocco style. His circular revelling was the boldest and richest and unfolded, in connection with his careful technicalities, good observation and excellent colors in all his works, exactly owing to this rich circular development, the most superb animation, the most lively sway and marvellous fascinating force. We feel in his works indeed the true breath of the life, in comparison with the Gothic style; he took the greatest advantage of the peculiar technicalities and magnetic weights offered by the circular principle of the Barocco style. His masterpieces are chiefly in Madrid (Prado), Paris (Louvre), Munich (Old Pinakothek), London (National Gallery), Berlin (Friedrich's Museum), Dresden, Vienna. He undoubtedly is one of the very first, if not the first prince of paintings of all nations and ages. His genius exceeds his dogmatic formalism.

It is interesting to state if we prosecute the terminal degeneration of the Gothic and Barocco-style, that both, though every degeneration up to a certain degree after all finishes in luxuriance and real exuberance, have just the opposite degenerative tendencies. That is to say, the Gothic style emphasizes in the later time always more its chief principle of perpendicularity, making its windows still narrower and higher, its spaces closer, its columns and pilasters higher and more tender, its pointed arches or *ogives* more and more pointed and its statues and figures utmost elongated. So it comes about that the Holy Peter of Rheims, of whom we mentioned the reproduction in wood, became so long comparatively in the middle of the modern furniture that he almost failed to be recognized as the representation of a human being. This figure could be labeled with the title of a French play recently published: je suis trop grand pour moi: I am too tall for myself.

Whilst we thus see that the Gothic style reduced itself ad absurdum in emphasizing too much its perpendicular principle and indulging in it after all without any intellectual restrictions, the Barocco-style prosecuted as well its main psychological means of expression more and more in drawing always bolder artistic circles and curves. The formalistic expressions and figures of the later Barocco exhibit therefore rather everything else than the real scarcity and austerity of the former Gothic conception. I possessed 4 *late Barocco-statues* in wood presumably of the beginning 18th Century representing the saints Cecilia, Dorothy, Elizabeth and John the Baptist. They originated from a Cistersian monastery, secularized about 50 years ago, of Switzerland. They were separated from a set of statues of the number of 14 and preserved in the attic of a church, whilst the others were used for the religious service in a new church, and are still today. The competent personalities of yore decided that the enumerated 4 figures could not be used in the church, because they were too wordly exuberant. But an artistic friend of mine told me they were just the more beautiful for this reason. Be it as it may, these figures are the most eloquent proof for my assertion, that in the degenerative period of the Barocco the formative circular element became most powerful and hyperemphasized. These Barocco-figures were indeed no more any longer the expression of the ideal monoidealism, striving with the wings of all sentiments towards the ideal vertical heaven and neglecting the multiple horizontal real direction as the old Gothic did, but they intruded very thoroughly and sent their runners far into the real periphery.

The conception of these statues had dropped entirely—the former favorite perpendicularity, even too thoroughly. The time was so energetically awakened from its dreamy former idealizing hypnosis, or frightened so much by the reasonable objections of the rising new conceptions against the Gothic ideal exclusiveness, that it fell into the opposite realistic extreme most visible in the late Barocco. These late Barocco-statues of mine were no more able to be labelled with the inscription: je suis trop grand pour moi, but much more with the qualification: je suis trop gras et trop volumineux pour ma grandeur. They were indeed relatively much too voluminous for their size. The artist had therefore difficulties to elicit from their puffed up cheeks in refined features some elevated religious ecstacy which alone had too express the ideal intention to which they were primarily dedicated. The bodies were very fat, the arms rounded, hands and fingers elegantly short and graciously dimpled. The observer was impressed by the rippling waves of rich hair flowing from the heads of the Saints and above all by the exceedingly large clothes which all exhibited the most numerous and selected folds. In order to emphasize the conspicuousness and the curves of these folds all these Saints wore large coats. The most charming curves in the intention of the stylistic principle of the Barocco were produced by the peculiar attitude of the bodies of the Saints, which in the later period and also in our cases were twisted too much, in an artificial forced way, in order to produce as much as possible rich and curved folds. The coats were loosely hanging from the shoulders, freely fluttering in the supposed wind, touching so at the extreme periphery of the circular distance, new *extra-solar divine concentrations*. They were richly gilded and lined with greeny and yellowish silver and gold.

Here we have indeed the perfect contrary of which the mediaéval philosophically primitive Gothic idealism did and tried to increase unreasonably and without any measure of self-control. The late Barocco means the degeneration by real luxuriance and lack of idealistic sway and depth, as the Gothic on the contrary went under owing to lack of real resources having excluded itself from the intellectual world and its formalistic objective opportunities. It was strangled by idealistic symbolic sterilization, just the contrary of the late Barocco which produced in the Rococo the most flourishing real richness in natural imitation, but became too frivolous, too superficial and too insignificant because of the lack of ideal central energy and corresponding sentimental discharge.

Styles perish after all in yielding too much to the philosophical psychomechanic emphasis and technical principles on which they were built first, the linear perpendicularity in the first and the circular arches and drawings or the horizontal extension in the second case. The overweight of the first principle pulled with the proceeding historic development all psychic forces in the abyss of the central straight ideal lightnings, taking away all importance of the real intellectual periphery, and the ruling energy of the second caused the perfect fixation of the affective life-force in the luxuriant real intellectual periphery, losing by that the ideal relations and the affective concentric tendency for discharge, troubling so the thorough hygienic psychic metabolism. Qui vult vitare Charybdin incidit in Skyllam. He who will avoid Charybdis, will be the prey of the other wild beast, of Skylla. Having recovered from the philosophical one-sidedness of the ideal, too magniloquent Gothic symbolism, the artistic Europe fell just in the other extreme, in adopting too much the circular emphasis which is indeed the language of the luxuriant reality, of the intellectual display though from its most pleasing side, because the circle gives to everything by its ideal relation the most charming blend of optimism and pleasure.

But the kind of the degenerative failure proves that the circular element was obviously too little centripetal and concentrative in the sense of the psychodynamic necessity. The circle means, in spite of its monopunctual concentric bearing prevalently the happy possession of the real periphery from which it does not separate itself easily having as much the tendency to enlarge its circumference as to shrink to the central monopunctual size. This circumstance is the weak point of the Barocco style and shovels its grave after all: the reason is the inclination to peripheric stagnation because of lack of concentrative energy.

The artistic style is, if we consider these last meditations, the proportion of the idealistic and realistic components of our natural tendencies expressed by the two corresponding technical directions in the art. It is the specific blend of idealism or sentiment and realism or intellect which gives to every style its essential character. *Style is, therefore, the quantitative question of the intellectual and sentimental mixture, crystallized in the proportion of the perpendicular ideal-sentimental and in the horizontal real-intellectual expansion of the artistic work. The principal elements on which every artistic style reposes are, therefore, exceedingly clear and simple, and they correspond exactly to our former psychopupilar explanations and to the human common sense assuming the idealism or feelings in the vertical direction,—intellectuality, visible objectivity or reality in the horizontal direction. Every style receives, therefore, its chief character from the share of these two elements, whether its artistic children are too tall or too thin, or too short and too broad, speaking in a clear popular language.* It rests with the personal observation to state whether even in the practical physiological life the tall and thin persons have more ideal and the short broad ones more real practical sense and disposition. It seems that there is some truth also in this.

But as we saw, the artistic style is not only established by the theoretical psychology of any philosophical system which has succeeded in ruling an age, a nation or a culture, but is limited very much by the mechanical nature of the means of its real expression. Though the continuous straight line as the main expressive means of the Gothic style absorbed more and more the total psychological energy and interest of its age, it could no more be retained, after having enraptured the whole Christian world in the later time towards the linear consequence of its perpendicular lightnings, for mechanical reasons. This was the natural consequence of the hyper-emphasis of the linear technicalities.

The Barocco style on the other side putting all stress on the circular expression had to pay its tribute to the natural mechanic tendencies of the circle. The circular revelling action produced in opposition to the concentrating magnetic line of the Gothic style rather the tendency to enlarge its circumference too much owing to the law of the centrifugal gravitation. The energetic enthusiasm of the circular motion round the idealistic monosymbolic conception, history and philosophy which never was changed principally, turned out to be so digressive as to blow up the concentrative gathering of the centrifugal energy and created so the anti-idealistic luxuriant frivolousness of the later Barocco and of the Rococo time. It was again the graphic limitation of the mechanic expression of this style, the circle, which brought about this frivolous anti-idealistic tendency, though the philosophical principles of the central idealism had not changed.

These digressing intellectual tendencies of the Barocco style had, of course, first the most useful compensatory influence on the former idealistic one-sidedness of the Catholic doctrines and persons. It enlarged as much as possible the Catholic reality. Had the remaining notion of the monogenial conception and of the divine idealism been enlargable and developable as well as the centrifugal energy of the revelling circles made it desirable and necessary, we had indeed received the most remarkable intellectual progress of the human philosophy and life by the introduction of the artistic circle. But this was not the case. The sharp theistic centre remained most stiff and unchangeable, sticking to its former old historic traditional elaboration and could not adapt itself to the antagonistic centrifugal tendency of the circle. The old ideal mono-symbolism, fixed in its historic conception could not follow the digressive will of the circular technicalities, and it was owing to this circumstance that the Barocco style could not fulfil the promises which it first rightly was expected to give to humanity.

This style also was doomed to become worn out, to lose the connection with the deepest well of the human idealism, because the Catholic philosophy could not follow the centrifugal desire of the circular enlargement. The logical connection of the Barocco style with the ideal was at last interrupted, disrupted and lost. Superficiality, lack of purpose and ideal depth was the end of the great prospect given by the circular technicalities. If they had been bolder in digressive distances, would they not have converged to new centres?

It may be therefore suggested to try this circular technical method in connection with looser and more developable central notions as they are given in Protestantism and partly in the modern science. It could be possible that in this connection a greater, more ideal and more consistent art could be created, with larger intellectual wings at the same time.

Why can art never be true? Is there a style which is in perfect harmony with the real life and nature? Art and artistic style are so much more distant from the real life, as their underlying disposition is wrong and as the application of the exclusive means is one-sided, imperfect and misleading. So there was a great distance of the Gothic style from nature, life and truth, because the exclusive linear emphasis was most one-sided, misleading and therefore wrong. The example of the alleged figure of St. Peter (we find the statues of the twelve apostles with Christ at the portal of every Gothic church of Europe) with its exaggerated length must be ashamed in the light of the real objectivity. It is the clear mathematical expression of the one-sided sentimental conception of the philosophy of its time. It bears the mark of its whole contemporary psychology in the unreasonable elongation of its body and is the clear self-accusation and the characteristic undoubtable confession of its peculiar philosophical wrong in the eyes of our objective natural criticism.

The disproportion of the length and the width of the statue exhibits exactly, in a *mathematical way,* the philosophical condition of the time of its origin. The exaggerated length at the expense of the width proves the hyper-emphasis of the idealistic conception of that time. But the last Barocco is wrong as well owing to the exaggerated exuberance of the horizontal diameter of its figures and statues. It also confesses its psychological and technical error consisting in one-sided intellectual expansion, careless of the corresponding ideal enlargement of the philosophical principles.

The most natural and truest artistic masterpieces are therefore, perhaps, given just in the INDIAN AND CHINESE ART, on which we are accustomed to scowl most suspiciously because of their distant cultural background. But the harmonious serenity of the Indian and Chinese divinities pouring holy rivers of happiness on the careful and grateful observer has its deepest root exactly in the exceedingly well-balanced collaboration of the feelings and the intellectual thoughts, in the most perfect mixture of the perpendicular and horizontal elaboration of the Oriental masterpieces.

Having chosen the meditation of our almost oldest and of our nearly youngest European artistic style, we discover that we indeed never realized to find out a perfectly true and most harmonious stylistic expression of the human nature. We always fell back to unnatural exaggerations both in the sentimental and intellectual direction, losing easily the intellectual control and rich real opportunity or the idealistic inspiring energy and strength. In both opposite cases the Catholic philosophy proved to be a good artistic ground in giving precise and sharp central points of sentimental support. (This is perhaps the chief reason that the less sensorial Protestantism was less successful in artistic invention), but in one case it was too one-sided and induced the mediaeval humanity to exaggerated ideal concessions aggravated to the exclusive use of the linear perpendicularity and in the other case it proved not to be adaptable to the centrifugal energy of the circular artistic expression.

The future will teach whether we are more able and lucky or not in finding out better, more appropriate, philosophical platforms for the human psychology which will administer to the society a more insured equilibrium between feelings and intellect, whether we shall be in a position to discover more enlargeable monosymbolic kernels, more powerful, more fertile and looser and more adaptable at the same time. The future will teach us whether there are other technical means than the straight line and the centrifugal circle to express our artistic needs, whether we are able to become more true and natural in our art to find that perfect human style which perhaps is not based on the arbitrary acceptance of the horizontal and perpendicular conception of our psychological performance, as it is most powerfully reached by the innumerable spires of the old Christian churches. But can we escape the natural laws of material and spiritual gravitation?

Is not even *this last psychopupilar conception* and even our psychic function, its division into the vertical sentimental and horizontal intellectual direction, as well an artificial invention as everything else in our artistic-intellectual expression of the real world? This conception is, however, universal and inter-temporal, we find it as well in the farthest East and among the dark races, in the oldest antiquity, in Egyptian, Assyrian, Greek and Roman art, in nearest connection with and as the natural expression of the categoric function of time, space and causality, and sanctified and fostered by the universal religious conception which all together placed God in the height, the devil in the depth and the intellectual world in rectangular direction on a plane around this main vertical line. It is the notion of monotheism which enforces and emphasizes the sharpness of this conception very much, and it is the mono-genial hero which puts to it the last point of sensorial stringency.

Whether there can be or will ever be any important art without the arbitrary acceptance of this old compromising formalistic display, enrooted into the human conception and disposition, we must doubt it. But this is sure that the modern science and the modern psychology has escaped the former general way of looking at the world: it strives to become more broadminded, more objective and less exclusive. But we live in a time of transitional development, and are inter-universal and indecided at the same time. We are not yet able to decide today whether there will be at last, quite impossible and unexplainable to our imagination of today, a practicable method of excellent artistic performance from the ground of the new world. If it will be possible then we shall be glad to have at last means to avoid the exclusive narrowness of the old one-sided artistic theoretical and technical conception which every time finished again in corruption and degeneration in the past because of its blinded shortsightedness in philosophical principles and real artistic expressions. The careful and broad-minded nature of science promises more truth, more survey and more lasting reliable success than any old angry sentimental principle could do it.

We must confess that the art of today indeed tries to escape from the old two-directed intellectual and sentimental system of the former times. It searches also, which means almost the same, to neglect the sharp monogenial centre which was given in the former monosymbolic ages, and the clear central vertical ideal tree which came out most sharply in the monogenial Christianity and disappears in dim indistinction as soon as the society gives up its monosymbolic and monogenial unity and concentration.

We pointed out already at length that the central theistic ideal perpendicular tree should be developable according to the addition of the surrounding intellectual experience and artistic performance which it has to bear and whose centrifugal weight it has to resist like a tree of a merry-go-round. This tree should needs always be adapted to the growing task incumbent on it with the progressing time, but also have at the same time the resistance not to be scattered in its notional cohesion by the centrifugal energy of the surrounding intellectuality working on it. This central perpendicular tree should, therefore, be properly speaking, an always living green tree growing in accordance with the progressing task: the notion of God should be a living tree, not having any historic or traditional confinement of fixation as much as possible and so be adaptable to the intellectual human society in always right progressive proportion.

The exclusion of the old scheme of the categoric perpendicularity and horizontalism in art is little hopeful. The modern art trying to find another basis, division and expression of the human nature, has until now not succeeded in producing anything which could be appreciated enough by our judgment. But we must not forget that every new thing is exceedingly difficult and that we for this time lack the sense of its understanding. With effort and patience all things are possible for humanity. But nothing new under the sun. This would be too new?

Or was the introduction of the Barocco circles to our human gifts so helpful? Was perhaps the choice of the means of this artistic expression the definite death of our former religious unity, the mother of the modern scientific era, which resulted from the centrifugal blowing up of this circular human activity in Barocco? Had perhaps the use of this dangerous digressing intellectual circles unhinged the former sentimental humanity from its central mono-symbolic restriction, and was it perhaps the revenge of the mediaeval Catholicism itself on the arriving modernism to have adopted the circular artistic work, punishing and anticipating or even perhaps causing its psychological intention? Or is the Protestantism itself perhaps with its modern scientific intellectualism the product of this fatal centrifugal circular action, introduced just before its rise?

But somebody may object that the line or point and the circle always were used in the art of the earliest and latest times of human history, that already the first oriental artistic productions had this elementary composition, that the Greek and Roman arts availed themselves abundantly of both and that there can not be imagined any style, where not also even arches and circles in spite of technical difficulties are or were or will be cultivated. According to our former explanations we must say that the discussion of the artistic use of the circle and of the point and the straight line can be merely quantitative. If we on one side admit therefore that art and soul are indeed naturaliter religious, working on the general ground of human expression of feelings and intelligence in using circles and straight lines, then we must on the other hand add instantly, that highly religious are the least natural expressions of all historic methods of the human mind, because principally they are the extreme one-sided sentimentality killing the intellectual human gift and degrading it into the symbolic small size, as they exaggerate the feelings immeasurably.

As long as we can not express our artistic will with other means than the straight lines and the circles we are not able to ignore entirely the psychological connections and interests of earlier times, one-sided as they may have been, because they deal with the two chief components of the human nature, with intelligence and sentiments. It is the *quantitative* representation of these two technical parts which made the difference of the character of the religions and styles as well in the past times. Christianity did and could not distinguish itself from the former times in changing the components or adopting other elements of the psychological performance, but it only changed their quantitative participation and their psychodynamic rhythm. What else could post-Christian periods do?

Whilst in the Greek and Roman Antiquity the representation of feeling and understanding, of the stretched line on one, and of arches and circles on the other side were well apportioned and balanced and created so the psychic human harmony, the later art lost, as we know, this most desirable and necessary balance between sentiments and intellect and became in the first Gothic part of its ruling cultural dominion the perfect victim of the hyperemphasized sentimental idealistic speculation, by using too much the straight line, and in the second epoch, of the luxuriant frivolous pleasure by abusing the circle and the arch. Our civilization repeated so obviously the artistic experiences, oscillating in its artistic development about the right real-idealistic medium, as it must have happened surely also in the former Antiquity, succeeding in the beautiful serene harmony of the Greek artistic style. All artistic action and all human function of life are always an *oscillating calculating probability,* where whole ages go in their success like pendulums from one extreme to the other hitting in their passage temporarily the right human harmonious medium. In the old Greek style and the best Roman times, but also at the top of the Christian styles, even in contradiction with their psychological one-sided foundation, there was always a balanced mixture of the use of the stretched line and the circular formative elements. It was the most thorough expression of the even harmonious equilibrium of these psychological periods.

We see that the principally monopunctual church, on the whole, could not be able nor willing to find its intellectual balance. Its historic monosymbolism proved to be most stubborn and intractable, not elastic and not adaptable to the later intellectual necessities of the progressive ages. Its history gives only the dilemma either to move entirely from the old ideal conceptions towards the intellectual modern transition or to stay within the most pronounced conservativism in the old Gothic mediaeval place, in the artistic and philosophical, in the human and educational way. This last point is exceedingly important. Chiefly because of the two last points later religious dispositions attempted changes which in their special kind represent a middle attitude between the psychology of the monosymbolic mediaeval conceptions being even today still the same principle as of yore in the old church, and of the modern natural science which is far away at the other extreme from the Catholic one-sidedness.

In spite of this psychological revolutions and changes of taste which like a pendulum wandered to all distances from the right medium between ideal feelings and real intellect, we must be aware, and every tourist coming from another part of the world will agree with me, of the unbelievable impression of the mediaeval Gothic architecture. These innumerable buildings of the richest elaboration and size, these wonderful STEEPLES of the old churches mounting until the clouds in marvellous beauty and strength, impress the spectator much more than anything else in the Old European Countries, perhaps or not even with the exception of the paintings. We will remember that the optic sensorial power is by far the most impressive. What we see we don't believe it, but we know and possess it. The optic symbolization is the unmistakably roughest but most successful educator of our heart in the sense of the success and has the utmost sureness in bluffing persuasion. The stereo-scopical impression. is more powerful than the bi-dimensional view of a picture.

Whosoever saw some of our most impressive European Gothic churches (the dome of Milan, the Westminster Abbey, the dome of Cologne, the Minster of Ulm or Freiburg or Regensburg, the churches of Rouen, or Rheims, or Notre Dame de Paris and Chartres), will all his life not forget the peculiar sensorial emotion received at their first sight. They have indeed the most powerful suggestive power and our heart and our feelings are irresistably enraptured by the numberless *phiales,* by the creeping pilasters, by the gradually diminishing diameter of the most frequent turrets gathering like trees in a wood, and the overwhelming massive energy of the main steeple which ascends to unexpected height like a stony giant. We have almost difficulty to follow the bold ascension of the spires into the sky.

It is always most exciting for people to see and mount up into high buildings. The height has that thrilling mysterious charm which the extension in the plain never can have. It is exceptional, it is thrilling, but it is also dangerous and sentimental. We spoke so much about perpendicularity that we may not develop again this idea, in connection with the mysterious experience of the soul, in ascending a tower, spire or high building. But the special perpendicular psychology does not only assail us in climbing up towers and steeples, but everywhere and always where we are much elevated, also in mountains. Mounting is always near to ideal and religious feelings.

Let us not forget that it may be chiefly the continual look at these majestic stony giants in numberless old cities of Europe, which is the reason, why these nations are until today practically hypnotized by their old monoidealistic tenets. They have optic symbolic helps or seductions, as we will, of unparalleled strength and energy, which fasten them with the highest degree of intimacy and conviction to the old perpendicular principle of one-sided idealism, as it was preached by the mediaeval conceptions. The outsider cannot guess how much these mighty optic ideal fingerposts in the centre of the modern cities of Europe are able to preach to people in their massive material authority, sanctified by history and dignified by tradition. May the preachers of today have become weak in faith as they may, and may they have become the flattest one-sided intellectualists, one powerful artistic Gothic spire in a city outvalues every moment of its existence hundred of the best idealistic preachers.

This, of course, shall not say that the thinking intellect can not escape from them. But they are not for the thinking faculty, but have the intention to replace or to bluff the intelligence by their optic symbolic power and to throw the hearts of the admirers without the logical preparation towards the celestial divinity in the sky. Here we have one of the main explanations why the Old Countries still are so stuffed with old and partly unreasonable prejudices, why they are persistently so narrow and home-bound in their old local history, one-sided and imperfect as they may be. The erection of these monumental old churches of the middle ages with their perpendicular mighty emphasis in the steeples were the most impressive, the most lasting and the most unforgettable tokens of the old psychology bequeathed to the modern time, and from which we indeed are not able to escape as long as we are subjected to the optic impression of their architectural symbolism. The mediaeval idealistic architect was a good psychologist. Catholicism liked always so much to use the optic persuasion and it created indeed in these hugest three-dimensional mighty buildings of stone most efficient, and tremendously energetic educational methods. They look exactly as if they were built for eternity. The mighty and yet quaint bells sounding again and again the hours of the ever-running time from the massive towers tolled through centuries and centuries, escorted by the gilded turning fingers on the huge face of the dials. They look so firm, self-confident, quiet and weather-proof today as they were five hundred years ago. What an impressive sensorial power comes out from the old European architecture! Only he who had the happiness to live there and to enjoy these suggestions for a long time, might be able to judge the wonderful and mysterious atmosphere and will also, if sophisticated, understand and explain the danger of this old dreamy poetical creation for the objective intellectual thought. Here indeed is the place of the sentimental idealism. The invincible faith of the middle ages, hovers still through the narrow lanes and creeps over the staircases of the roofs and enraptures the soul from these grounds of the most stifling sentimentality along the perpendicular steeples towards the sky. Here the old spirit leads us still to the ideal heaven and the divine imagination, up to the charming wondering clouds, the promising blue color of the heaven and the fulminating rays of the sunshine reflecting our celestial delight and guiding our enthusiastic explosions.

There we are with our modern intellectual enlightenment in Europe. The mediaeval most monumental steeples look out of the innumerable cities like giants among ordinary people: all the busy life, all transitional intercourse of the daily traffic are only comparable to the buzzing work of bees round a huge oak and all the remarkable new and old profane buildings are crouched at the feet of these incredibly huge old churches like a flock of smallest lambs around a shepherd. We have this impression most distinctly in Ulm, in Cologne, Milan and Worms. The ruling dominion of these old mediaeval churches and steeples has preoccupied and anticipated for long centuries the monosymbolic optic disposition of the psychopupil of the central European and the English nations. In the middle of all these glorious cities they have, in the most visible and impressive way, this monosensorial emphasis expressed in the perpendicular hugest spires and towers which perpetuate and hyper-emphasize forever the uplifting energy of the sentimental idealism.

Indeed, these powerful steeples are again the same thing as we meditated it before inside of the Catholic church in the monopunctual sacramentalism, in the Eucharist and in the Mass and its ritual performance. These highest steeples signify by their concentration of the energy on one point and by the accumulation of all working power on the smallest ground, exactly the one-sided principle of the monoidealism to charge exclusively the central monopunctual focus of the psychopupil and to neglect compensatorily the whole intellectual surroundings.

The small ground-plan of these gigantic steeples is psychologically and potentially given in the symbolic host of the Catholic Eucharist with the tremendous affective concentration of the whole human life-force. The mediaeval steeple represents in the most powerful way the energetic and dynamic potentiality given in the strong monosensorial symbolic faith, as it ruled in the middle ages: these huge masses of stone concentrated on one point are the manifestation of the material power which the monopunctual mediaeval Catholic energy, the symbolic finger of this psychological system, was able to bear and to heave in a real mechanical way. This unbelievable accumulation of material strength in the old towers and steeples is nothing but the antagonistic balance of those uplifting religious desires by which the old culture was assailed, putting all psychic energy at one stake and neglecting comparatively the surrounding intellectual life. They correspond to the deep need of the church to prove its efficiency of monosymbolism in a most impressive material manifestation, heaving the utmost possible weight. The mediaeval Catholicism had the understandable strong longing to show to the world and all future times the strength of its affective concentration in a most visible way; it would point out what heaving strength it could develop from the narrow platform of its monopunctual idealism. Like a man heaving with his sinewy arm an enormous stone in a gathering and attracting the admiration of all surrounding people, so the mediaeval church in its old steeples put the hugest masses of heavy stones on one point, on one finger as it were, in order to demonstrate the unbelievable degree of its pushing symbolic capability and energy. These steeples are the most puzzling remnants of the psychological mediaeval humanity having concentrated all their will power on one punctual lump, and it is owing to this tremendous strength of monopunctual conception of that time that these monuments were erected to an incredible height with an accumulation of the most massive stone, in strength and boldness and beauty, so much that we lose our descriptive language at their side even today, and even arriving from countries where the largest and highest buildings are erected for other reasons, perhaps of the same height, but not at the same small section of the foundation.

The architectural reason for these old steeples is given in the monosymbolic conception of the old psychological one-sidedness which was in the same manner the psychic basis of the mysterious spell of the monopunctual sign of the cross and even of the other monosymbolic signs given and maintained until today in the ritual actions of the Catholic Church. These monosymbolic steeples preach indeed in the most powerful way the incredible strength of the old Catholic philosophy. They emphasize most impressively the old one-sided conception of the psychodynamic idealism of religion with their monosensorial optic bluffing power. They do it so much and so successfully that humanity living and gathering around these excellent mediaeval artistic masterpieces is almost hopeless for a new and lasting intellectual enlightenment. The powers of this optic suggestion is too great, it comes always back and subjects the local social psychology again to its most wonderful psychodynamic conception. These nations look forcedly always back toward the old overwhelming history of their ancestors instead of looking forward towards a new even greater development of their psychological history.

All mediaeval steeples grew out from the monopunctual energy and concentration of the total social life-force of their times. The European society cannot escape the most powerful daily influence of this monopunctual psychological principle. They represent the most picturesque pride of these cities, they belong inseparably to the history and tradition of their ancestors; they characterized for many centuries the pictures of their cities and they are deeply impressed into the cultural life of the last citizen and of the most insignificant child of these countries. If you will take away these historic foremost tokens from this cultural society, you destroy their hearts, their lives, their local civilization. These mediaeval churches, buildings and steeples are so thoroughly inrooted into the personal and social life of all these nations that there may be no hope and no prospect to do away with them forever. They are so refined, so much artistically elaborated and spread so much charm over all the old dreamy imagination of these people that you must give up every hope to drive away completely the one-sided philosophy imparted by them in the most powerful way forever and ever, all days of the future European history.

We see therefore that it is not the European humanity which will be able to be the intellectual leaders of the future ages. There is no use to abolish the old church or service in these brilliant architectural manifestations and to surrender these old churches at the same time to other more moderate denominations, as it is the case, for instance, in Ulm, Geneva and Lausanne. The power of this optic suggestion will forever be so energetic in its optic precision and impressive charm that perhaps rather the new system will fall back again into the arms of the former philosophy of the most one-sided description, than that humanity would be able to escape these wonderful optic historic artistic suggestions.

It may, therefore, be considered as a psychological fault to have expropriated these artistic churches of the old time from their original purpose. They are not able to glorify new, more intellectual and more moderate psychological and religious systems, but they pull the progressive humanity back to their conceptions being the most powerful, monopunctual and monogenial manifestations and interpretors. May they be in the artistic sense the most precious acquisitions and the richest increase of material possession! But they are handicaps of the progressive intellectual ideas and systems creating with an inescapable energy the atmosphere of former cultures which we pretend and ought to have overcome because of their extreme exaggerations. Modern psychological systems and creeds cannot grow and flourish within the walls of these old Gothic churches; they must be stifled by the almighty suggestion of the old time. These old monuments claim and crave continuously the affective tribute of our worshipful heart; they hinder the free development of the unchecked modern intellectual progress and do just in this milieu for this reason perhaps more harm than good.

So we come to the conclusion that it is by far better for every progressive modern kind of psychological system to have escaped the mighty suggestive influence of these old artistic monuments. The new idea must have a new garment, dressing new philosophical systems with the old symbols and clothes is so much more dangerous as they were indeed important and beautiful. The human mind is not and never will be so undoubtedly fixed in one psychological direction that such powerful means of persuasion like the mediaeval churches would not defeat or at least impair the success of new progressive temperamental systems. The modern idea must have indispensably a modern garment. Modern churches using the ornamentation of the old conception, are likely not strong enough to overcome thoroughly the old one-sided idealism which they pretend to have recognized and defeated. They still are perhaps of a feather, and flock together with the former hurtful psychological conceptions.

For this reason we see much more strength, unity and conviction of the progressive religious systems in countries where these old optic symbols do not exist any longer or have never existed. The independence of judgment, the freedom of the feelings not bewitched by the old symbolic artistic expressions, are greater and firmer. May some small Gothic allusion or some modest steeple be permitted and maintained again and again in the new countries, if people think not to be able to do without. It is sure that they have much more chances to avoid the mysterious spell of that old wonderful complex, of which the whole atmosphere of the old countries is still today entirely imbibed. We ought to have gone thoroughly through this old mediaeval miracles, if we will be independent today of those old suggestions. But we can do it only in a free, true and objective atmosphere, far away and outside of these old historic artistic buildings and steeples of the Gothic time and sentimental culture.

The *Circle* is surely one of the most interesting formative principles of all life, it is the real formula of development par excellence, even of the universe, but also of our ordinary phychological impressions in all connection with feelings and intelligence, above all in art. The greater the collaboration of circular activity wheresoever, the more quickly the intellectual development of the vital process. For this reason it was a long and slow way from the Gothic, but a rapid and easy way from the Barocco-style towards the intellectualization of the world and life.

If we imagine the *starting universe* as one disfigured chaotic material lump, then it must have received the form of a regular ball by the central magnetic energy and gravitation succeeding at last in putting all molecules of the whole chaotic body at the nearest possible distance from the attractive central magnetism. This is the manner, as we have to think the first formation of the ball and of the circle. But there is another second progressing stage of their formation. The contracting central magnetism having diminished, the centrifugal component of the turning body receives the overweight and thus there is formed an *outcoming protuberance* at the surface of the original body representing in itself a beginning smaller ball, separated at last from the original arch-star allowing it to become an independent branch of the mother-body. We notice exactly that the developing differentiation of the creative universe starts with the formation of smaller circles out of the largest pre-existent one which is multiplied in number, so that the continual creative progression in the universe means at the same time the continual diminution of the size of the circular formative elements, and the endless multiplication of their number going from the original arch-lump to the sun, the earth, the moon, the man, etc. The original creative lump loses so its unity and the full size of its strength; it loses its life in giving birth to other new born stars being its children. But he who loses gains.

Absolute stability may be successful in the political and economic success for a certain time, but it proves exactly in the psychological sense the lack of thorough vital energy of intellectual development. Differentiation means evolution, progressive perfection in our visible world means division. Perfect and lasting unity and peace in the created world means affective stagnation, laziness and death.

If we look through the cultural development of the formulative artistic history, we observe that we have indeed the repetition of this augmenting biological law of augmenting numbers and always sharper curves of the circles as we saw it in the formation of the universal creative differentiation. In the lowest degrees of human and artistic culture the use of the circle in buildings is very rare and flat. I remember to have seen in the British Museum and elsewhere very wide and low *arches* used in the primitive arts, for instance in the stone-age and the Etruscan tombs, where the arches crouched quite near to the ground in flat curves. In Roman and Greek times we are far away from the low state of this discouraged timidity of the intellectual development. Their arches are well rounded and their circles harmonious. The starting Christianity with its typical inclination to their idealistic perpendicularity had of course soon the strongest uplifting influence on the formative expression of the following art. In the Romanesque style we already observe in the eighth century A. C. the strong uplifting tendency of the perpendicular attraction exercised by the idealistic doctrine on the art, since not only the arches become more rounded and narrower than in the former pre-Christian times, but the pertaining windows become more elongated and narrow which is the expression of the same magnetic influence. The less uplifting sway of the Moresque art is visible in its formative circular expression, in having produced an angle at the transition from the perpendicular line of the window to the conclusion of the upper arch. This of course means less naively uplifting energy, since the ascending line is broken.

As we said at length the *Gothic style* troubled the rounded harmony of the beautiful former arches by its impetuous uplifting perpendicularism and inflicted to them the angle in the upper middle. The narrowest circle was not any longer enough curved for the sentiments of the idealistic Gothic, and for that reason the *Ogives* or the pointed arches came along. So we have a former emphasis of the narrowing progress of the circle which is always nothing else than the material cohesive expression of the combination of centrifugal and centripetal energy.

The *Renaissance style* coming out after the Gothic meant an effort to recover from the perpendicular hyperemphasis of the Gothic. Leaning to the example of the Roman more harmonious circular drawings, it indeed succeeded in excluding the former troubles of the Gothic, but according to the necessity of the cultural and intellectual stage of the European and Christian culture the most expressive formative element, as the best and most apt vehicle of the progressing intellectual differentiation and maturation of the time, as the circle was, could not be repressed within moderate limits. Inasmuch as it was strongly abused before in the qualitative sense and brought serious psychological menaces in the breaking of its harmonious roundings of the pointed arch in the Gothic, what may be conceived in a certain sense as a nervous breakdown of the technical expression of that time, there was done away with. But what was avoided in the qualitative sense was retrieved in the quantitative one. The use of the circle in the Renaissance was quite frequent and dearly cultivated.

But as we considered already, this circular formative fanaticism became most pronounced during the Barocco time. This style is in its formative expression indeed almost nothing but the continual waving combination of circular performances taking possession of every rag of drapery fluttering in the Barocco wind. Barocco is in the formative sense, the most agitated artistic sea excited by the rage of all elements and expressing in all innumerable degrees and kinds the widest and narrowest circles, the smallest and most timid and the proudest and boldest allusions and sectors of arches and loops in always new combinations. In the Barocco the material form at last became perfectly fluid, adaptable to all affective wishes and necessities of the sentiments. It was the terminal stage of the last great European art of our Christian culture which, by the circular revelling dissipated all its concentrated contents in the most liberal way round about, transformed all its eminent energies into the intellectual differentiation and multiplication, and became so the victim of its real generosity and liberality in the formative sense, but gaining all in losing and distributing all.

Indeed the circular formalism turns out likely to be the good and right method for the intellectual furtherance of humanity and of the historic psychology. The centrifugal tendency of the circles moved the psychological humanity easily away from its old egotistic centripetal narrowness. The essentially swinging centrifugality of the circle threw all the affective treasures of the past genial times and ages in the most liberal way towards all sides, creating in that manner, giving innumerable births to new small circles taking so their own circular form, being the formative principal par excellence for the creative proliferation. So we may say that just the Barocco style brought eminently into humanity the most fertile tendency towards the intellectual development. The swinging centrifugality of its circles unhinged the total amount of the anxiously kept treasures of the historic Conservativism. Innumerable intellectual thoughts and deeds must then have been born out of the centrifugal formative unhingement and the blowing up of the circle. It is the question how much the whole strong intellectual scattering of the modern culture is the consequence or the cause of this circular energy.

We can take it from the opposite side. The acceleration of the cultural fly-wheel of the intellectualization of the world put into the old world by the new philosophy, caused this fatal scattering artistic whirlpool of the modern intellectual life, smitting all past historic psychological energy of the humanity towards the four winds in the farthest universe and causing the most individual affective incarnation and participation.

Indeed this accelerated circular speed was a dangerous act of the history. The bolder construction of more narrow circles in the art was perhaps the most fatal psychological phenonomen ever introduced into the human artistic history. It intellectualized quickly the humanity until exhaustion. But if it is not in the sense of the old central magnetic mediaeval conception, then this later introduction of the circular bold arches and of the acceleration of the wheel of the affective life, switching from the control of the old ecclesiastical mono-symbolism, the devil painted on the wall, as it were, became stronger than the checking energy of the historic central stewart of the human affective force and drove and threw all and everything towards metamorphosis of the intellectual shape and development in the most unusual manner. This is the fact of the generous self-denial on the greatest scale. Here we have the real and extreme degree of the most liberal self-abnegation. Was perhaps the natural centrifugal energy of the objective circle too strong, the contrary of the further subjective linear principle, scattering too thoroughly and too quickly all human affective reservoirs? After having avoided the dangerous touch of the mediaeval divine lightnings, humanity was perhaps driven too energetically into the outside intellectual periphery and lost so direction and consistence. Qui vult vitare Charybdin incidit in Scyllam.

We have to learn other things from the natural necessity of the circular development in art. Every art must have come out from the religious service and the utility. It was first in close connection with the focal concentration of the affective forces of humanity as we see in prevalence or almost exclusively straight lines in the beginning of every art and of the most superstitious religious starting stage. They served the divine lightnings which are nearest to intellectuality and to the practical use of the art, to the utility which means the other extreme use of it. These two extremes touch in the artistic formalism using the straight line.

The peripheric circular development went forcedly first through the highest divine pleasure, the last one being nearest to most concentrated divine discharge of the affective life; then it must have pervaded political and profane glory and enjoyment, "degenerating" later on to the more peripheric artistic luxuriance of the life. At last it became superficial lacking depth of feelings and expressing, therefore, frivolousness. In the final stage it is farthest away from the original affective emphasis. Art is no more able to give any ideal sense to its formative elements and is only the pale estheticism as it is represented to us in the last Rococo and in the later artistic styles. So the whole psychological scale of the developed target today has been pervaded by the Christian European human development. Art does not exist any longer in the connection with the first Christian mono-theistic genial urges and falls back to the practical utility. The European artistic development started in strong connection with the divine sentiments in the early middle ages with the Romanesque and Gothic styles and finished in the scattering intellectualism of the modern Barocco and Rococo.

We also here have the confirmation of what we know all, of the fact that the psychological ripening of our Christian phase is done and that we have to expect in the next future important and radical psychological urges in the country of the Christian old cultural civilization. Whether it may be given in a new religious genius or in any other form of the most energetic monogenial gathering and revival of the modern world, we cannot decide. But it is sure and there cannot be any doubt that this critical solstitial conversion of our cultural psychological sun-year is near. The season of the spring of the psychodynamic energy of the present Christian humanity has gone. Our course of the old monotheistic and monogenial developing force has revolved, has done its task and work, and we possibly have to expect new radical gatherings of the human life-force in the modulation of other strong symbolic concentrations as we had it in the fullness of the time, at the time of our rising civilization.

Les extremes touchent. The present tendency of absolute utilization of the world and life will be alternated by other monosymbolic revivals of our race. All psychological life is as well a moving wave rising and falling as everything which we are entitled to call life. There are in all things births, developments, maturations and deaths, but also resurrections. We are today again in the purport of the intellectual straight line, of the intellectual utility, but for this reason also near the fatal tendency of touching the monotheistic ideal lightnings. The human psychology will in spite of the warnings of science not resist the excitement of this new seduction; humanity will be proud enough to turn its fingers and hearts again to these fatal linear magnetic wires. But it will be as well pushed back once more, hurt and frightened by the spoiling and roughening energy of the direct divine touch. It will learn once more, after having made bad educational experiences, to retire from this fatal pride: it will again be forced to hide its face before the majesty of the divinity and will have once more the necessity to look for other means of artistic expression than the straight line. Will it again enter into the other extreme of the circular drawing performance? Will it fasten the boat of its artistic destiny again at the towing rope of the formative circle whose swinging centrifugality will hurl again the human energy most powerfully towards the scattering intellectual periphery? Has humanity learnt to avoid this second opposite evil, when it will be forced to lose the straight consequence of the straight line once more? We know that the modern science most careful and sophisticated, is aware of all these dangers. We know that the artistic and scientific humanity of today has learnt much from the past and is seriously willing not to repeat all the psychological faults of the past European history. The modern tendencies of the art, just because they are so unintelligible for the old cultural education, prove that they are seriously groping for new formalistic experiences, avoiding both the abuse of the stretched line and of the fatal centrifugality of the circle. Will a quite unheard solution of the formative element of the former artistic world be brought about? Or are the people crazy who dare to have so well founded hopes and dreams of a future human race? We do not know, but we wish best success. We must at least seriously attempt to create this greatest fact of the human history, which is to say, we must look for other expressive possibilities than they are given in the straight line and the circle. We have the most difficult task to enlarge the boundaries of the straight line or the point on one side and of the formalistic circle on the other hand. But we must be afraid that indeed our implements are insufficient. The material expression moves always in a narrow circle holding the ideal desire of our affective eagle in eternal captivity. The flatening circle is always again transformed into the straight line and the straight line, being the monopoint on the symbolic section, changes quickly like a seed into the enlarging circle. The religious hero, if we will speak more of the formalistic expressions of the psychology, tried indeed to develop our formalistic artistic principle very far outside of its historic boundary on the side of the point and he succeeded in pulling the most energetic divine linear lightnings out of this monopunctualism with universal elongation as nobody ever did before: the Gothic style is the accurate expression and application of this truth. We know that the monogenial hero did not succeed in creating as well the enlargement of the psychological basis of our artistic expression, of the circle. This is so much true that the introduction of the unlimitated use of the circle instantly dissipated the affective concentration and the accumulation of the genial psychic treasures. The absolute idealism is strong in the straight line, but struck to dead by the well rounded circle.

Today circle and straight line are the extreme limits of the human artistic efficacy. They correspond in their continual change and in their limits to the human limits between idealism and realism. These two elements are the continual tread-mill in the realm of the art which the human race has to move and by which it is limited in the psychological expressive function, from which the modern art would escape now in leaving or changing the formative elements of point and circle. As long as we are not able to enlarge both the line and the circle from the extreme boundaries of our artistic expressive human nature there can not be any hope to make essential progress neither in the exterior art nor in the psychological conditions of ours.

Straight line and circle are universal formulas, the first expressing starting and finishing action, commencement, and success, the second instead development, effort, display, maturation, mingling of antagonistic forces. Circle means battle, straight line victory. Will a quite unheard of revolution of the formative conception of the former artistic presentation be brought about? We don't know but we expect and hope. We must create this greatest fact of the human history if we shall have the vista of future progress, not to fall back into all the psychological errors and pitfalls of the former centuries, of which the old philosophy is only one one-sided state, having the conviction to be the best solution of the given possibilities.

The strong idealism and the religious fanaticism are closely bound to the straight line because of its transcendental consequence.

The stiff monopunctual fixation of the look of the gifted idealist, his rectangular almost mechanical motion (the ideal priest performs his ritual motions in a much more linear stiffness than the realistic one), the penetrating lightnings of his eyes, perhaps even the difference of the ideal gift between the taller and smaller human individual in connection with the upright gate, all these things remind us of the connection between monopunctual or linear sensorial expression and ideal extreme. Both mean lack of real development. The extreme temperamental emotions have also strong relations to the point and the straight line. Thoroughness, violence, devotion, humility, anger, enthusiasm, all are monopunctual psychological notions lacking the real development or circumspection.

So we understand the meaning of the circle. The harmonious circular *halo* of the church corresponds to holiness, holiness to virtue, virtue to the happy medium of the psychological conceptions. The circular halo and the psychological emphasis of the extreme idealism are not at all in direct accordance. The only adequate expression of the undeveloped idealistic psychological one-sidedness is the stretched line. The circle as far as it is given in the Gothic is only a subordinate decorative help without thorough constructive sense in this style. The idealistic psychology has the tendency to exclude the intellectual digression and to check the expanding energy of the sentiments as they are exactly expressed in the circle which developed our feelings in a formalistic way with its swelling energy like the yeast in a mound of dough. It is always greater and rounder and most seasonable in the human sense. Exactly the same we have with the circle which is the expression of the swelling dilatation of our sentimental soul in the reality of joy, intelligence and agreeableness. The linear and monopunctual compression of the dough of our life-force, as it were, needs the circular swelling expansion if it shall be edible and digestible by human nature.

The one-sided idealism is quite adapted to the psychology of the *childhood*. Here we have monopunctual disposition of the mind also. That is the reason why the extreme ideal conception once impressed upon the soul of the child, has the consequence not to be lost easily afterwards again. If we on the whole must deny that the human soul in its adult stage is fatally idealistic, but admit that it is rather more the contrary, still we must agree that the soul of the child has indeed this same psychological condition. But good art has escaped as well the psychological miraculous influence as well as the grown-up people. Is it a fact that on the average

Catholic people cling in the latter age more faithfully to their system than other denominations? Here we have the explanation. The higher degree of monosensorialism appeals more to the childhood, but flatters also more the grown-up human psychology in a comfortable and clear manner. Also the fact that young people have strong inclinations to the highest most ideal forms of religious and lyrical poetry is in this connection very characteristic. There is, however, for this manifestation still the contribution of another circumstance, it is the *sexual* maturity which in itself has also the starting monoconcentrative character and is therefore nearly connected with the inexperience of the sentimental youth. The best love displays itself powerfully outside of the large intellectual screen which is only acquired afterwards and needs for its basis the young faithful and inexperienced soul of the youth. Religious and loving temperament are therefore so close to each other. Enthusiastic art and religion are near. Youth, religion, art and sexuality are akin. Christian monotheism is not practical art, but it is a strong psychodynamic supposition for the rising artistic development. Youth, Monotheistic religion and first love are all strong symbolic affective gatherings and wells which altogether avail themselves readily and energetically of the charming developing opportunities which are given to them in the artistic circular development. Art has most sway coming directly from the monoconcentration of the monopunctual religion as it empties on the other hand most powerfully again in the monopunctual psychopupilar discharge. The first stage may be called inspiration, the second one enthusiasm.

But let us at last not forget that *the point* is the constituent original graphic element not only of the straight line, but also of the circle. Both are composed out of it, in the real and speculative meaning. The point in its smallest size is as well a circle as a straight line, in its potentiality. The divine lightning long like light-years, has the section and the composition of a sequence of points, and the real circle also consists of these punctual original elements like the original atoms, as it were. They compose always both stretched line and circle. The point is always the additional formalistic element working in the growing size of any linear or circular development. The smallest monopunctuality, as it is given in the perfect idealism, exhibits therefore indeed in this sense the most powerful potential seed and prospect. Then it would be in this sense, in the artistic affective and intellectual way, the cradle, the thoroughfare and the grave of the human action, the alpha and omega, the starting and ending point, the reason, cause and the goal, the rising and the fulfilling stage of the human intellectual nature. In the fact of the monopunctual nucleus of the Christian psychology reposes in this light a great universal and general validity. The point and the monopunctual contemplation seems in this constellation to be the original element of the sentimental and intellectual expression of the human nature, and all our difficulties in explaining the formalistic universe seem to be split up into the theory of the monosensorial points, comparable to the cellulary conception of the anatomic pathology in the medical conceptions, according to Virchow. The monogenius would be then the psychological element of the universe. But this conception of the quantitative explanation is as little sufficient in medicine as in psychology. The most important questions of our psychological universe are not formalistic, but rhythmic and dynamic. To find out the right moving condition of the punctual elements is our most important question, the elements are only gradual transitional representations alternating each other.

The straight line expresses only the intellectual progress in the peripheric real world, whilst the circle at the same time manifests the relations to the surrounding reality and refers to the original monopunctual causal relation, like an unlosable remembrance and traditional homesickness, as it were, which puts always the peripheric progress in connection with the monopunctual first offshoot.

Let us now meditate the *special character of the Catholic priest*. He is according to the optic predelection of the Catholic service, more the theatrical artistic performer than the intellectual guide of the believers. He is the leading optic actor of the spectacular Catholic service gathering around his predominent role a less or more great number of assisting performers of inferior importance, one in the low mass and about twenty in the highest so-called pontifical mass. The Catholic colleges have according to this special task of the future priest strong inclination to theatrical training of the pupils. This stress of the theatrical performances of the pupils has indeed the hidden intention to prepare the future priest for his spectacular and representative role which will be absolutely ruling in his professional activity.

Catholicism is, as we saw, less supported in its symbolic performance by all other senses than the optic, be it of auditive, tactile, gustative or olfactorial description. They all are represented, it is true, most after the optic the tactile and the auditive sense, but in a subordinate way. The notional, more refined symbolism is reduced, the essential linguistic utterances of the Catholic mysterious service being veiled into the Latin and Greek language and made so inaccessible to most people. So the beautiful Latin songs and prayers of the church are reduced in the hearts of the hearing people to general auditive symbols, not being understood and exciting therefore a vague mysterious response. They lose their detailed notional and logical symbolic power because average people do not understand the language. They have to receive their impressions by their other connections, through the repetitions, their rhythm, chiefly through the musical interpretation, and the ecclesiastic authority.

It is remarkable how much Catholicism with its categoric principle of ruling autocracy is averse to the detailed notional treatment of the believing intellectuality. It seems to be obviously aware of the extreme difficulty of the intellectual attainment of the ideal goal, if the serious intellectual criticism starts, being put between monosymbolism and peripheric reality. Whilst Protestantism avails itself exactly chiefly of this notional method leaning to the artistic way and the character of the gospel, Catholicism excludes the direct notional intercourse with the religious psychology and philosophy in words in a much higher degree, and guides the servant of its system rather more by the emblematic symbolism of the musical song and of the theatrical and optic artistic demonstration towards the goals of its mysterious idealism. In Catholicism we get the stronger musical and optic emphasis, artistic and sacramental miraculism, in Protestantism we have on the contrary prevalent notional poetical symbolism as it is given in the gospel, the Bible, and the hymns. There are many sides in favor of both conceptions. Words and notions are as likely leading to misunderstandings, as optic power may have bluffing influence.

The consequence of this fact for the personality of the Catholic priest and of the Protestant clergyman is that the Catholic priest on the whole is much more theatrical, whilst the Protestant divine has much more poetical features, both having artistic tendencies.

We observe this in the different character of the *sermon*. The Catholic priest is so much surrounded, guided and checked by his warning crystallized traditional historic prescriptions that it is indeed difficult for him to develop in a sermon his own personal intellectual faculties in a free way. He is embarrassed as to show his personal common sense, his individual free imagination, his free decision in artistic expression and in linguistic taste. All goals, all boundaries are so minutely prescribed to him that he impossibly, on the average, does count much personally, but much more as the official representative of his cast. All other service with exception of the sermon most anxiously avoids the detailed intellectual explanation. Catholicism on the whole is averse to the notional miracle; it holds more fit and more convincing the optic kind of mysticism, the theatrical performance in the mass, the artistic representation of painting and sculpture and of the acoustic Latin song. These last means seem to the Catholic psychology the less captious and more efficient psychodynamic sensorial helps and energies than the notional symbolism of the Scriptures preferably used by the Protestant church.

If for these conditions of the special Catholic miraculous conceptions the preacher of this church is entitled to subdue this part of his service much more than Protestantism, if the restrictions and limitations on all sides take perhaps more careful work on the part of the capable Catholic priest than to show at the same time his personal capabilities, we must admit on the other hand, that the Catholic terminology formed and refined through 2,000 years, has reached a high degree of artistic achievement, as we are not able to find it somewhere else in our European civilization, the Catholic church being herself the mother and creator of our modern languages. This moment and the strong magnetic mono-determination of the sharp monogenial purpose of this church creating exceedingly strong enthusiasm, gives great advantages into the hand of the Catholic preachers, so much that we not only find the weakest, most insignificant degree of eloquence among them, but on the other hand also the most artistic, most enthusiastic, powerful sermons dignified and elevated by the inheritance of an oldest culture, since all means are most ready for this successful artistic use provided the preaching individual is adaptable to the ecclesiastical intellectual restriction. These sermons are, therefore, the most refined in language and the most powerful in divine enthusiasm, full of strength, dignity, clear in artistic rhythm and tradition. If it is the artistic and not the philosophical intellectual side which makes a sermon most important, then we must admit that not only the very worst but also the very best sermons come out from the Catholic church because of its traditional facilitation. Remember Bossuet, Massillon, Lacordaire, Meyenberg, Kuhn! Tradition and history with the sharp monosymbolism are always the most deciding values for the sure artistic performance as well as they are the fatal destruction of the investigating reasoning power and of the independent personal conviction. The Catholic preacher finds it more easy to preach to people who are already in his belief; he is more able to edify than to convince because his role and character are affective.

The Catholic priest, by the constant use of his stereotypical Latin prayers is taught himself to put his intelligence willingly into the historic channel of the ecclesiastical philosophy, and customs, and to adopt all its ideas word by word and to give up his personal critical activity. He thus becomes similarly a follower of his creed like the believing layman. He is accustomed to abandon any further personal investigation of his religious belief and to accept as definitely granted the authority of his legislative church which is his mother, his intellectual law and at the same time his living. The overwhelming elaborated authority of his church is, therefore, rather disfavorable to the personal intellectual development of the Catholic priest. He is in danger to be merely the technical steward of his ecclesiastical institution and does not reach the level of essential criticism which is so essential to every cultured mature life.

The celebrating priest and the woman have near psychological features in their task, in the sense that both are in the interior psychological meaning the stewarts of the treasures of their special idealism in the terminal or sexual ideal discharge, and both have, therefore, accordingly, the will and tendency to attract the attention of the surroundings to their personality, to emphasize their individual attractiveness by artistic charming helps in dress, in forms and colors, in order to succeed thoroughly in receiving the most perfect attention and love from the attending witnesses. The woman in ornamenting herself by all possible means of art in tulles, laces, feathers, jewelry and paints, with all helps of the fashion in colors and fabrics, has the thorough physiological desire according to the natural character of her sexual role to adapt herself to the mediating task which has been given her by destiny on the way to the conclusive monopunctual sexual idealism. It is not necessary that she is conscious of this fact,—suggestions have even the better effect in the unconscious way, but it is a fact of the feminine psychology and woman is the keyholder and steward, the way to the loving goals desired by the male instinct. It is the role of the wife to make this way to the last sexual discharge inviting and practicable in the sense of the will of the nature, according to her mediating task. She is able to make agreeable and easy the will of this disposition, but also on the other hand, in many cases to disgust the male instinct of this goal because she is the indispensable previous stage, the imaginative and real ante-chamber of the sexual ideal attainment.

The priest, in regard to divine values pretends a comparable intermediary role. He is the stewart of the monosymbolic sacramental treasures of the church, he administers them, makes them easily accessible by his charming personality, by his impressive ritual functions and by his attire in ecclesiastical garments richly sparkling with gold and studded with laces and precious stones, shining always in variegated colors. If the priest has the advantage to be the administrator and the keyholder of the sacramental mysteries put into his powerful hand, and if he receives, therefore, great divine authority and might deriving from this circumstance, in the eyes of the people, he must forcedly acquiesce with the fact that his personal defectiveness is much more the butt of the criticism than any other personality. His pretended and allowed divine connection is the source of the most severe judgment of his personal moral and intellectual life. If he says to be only a human being like others, he overlooks the consequence of his higher quality which has been given to him in his symbolic religious stage of mediator or which he has received in the role of the sacramental administration of the gracious treasures of the church. It cannot be of course, that he takes only the advantages of his outstanding divine authority and declines the exacting consequences of his appropriate high moral and spiritual standing.

In other connections we meditated the high affective sway conveyed by the use of laces, flounces, of waving garments, of jewelry and of flowing folds. They all together have the powerful effect of most energetic mobilization of our feelings; the person supplied with these helps, be it the sexual ideal woman or the terminal ideal priest, is most able to receive and to send forth strong affective emotions. They attract most vividly the sentimental sympathy of the spectator and are able as well to create the most energetic sentimental contact with the living surroundings. So the celebrating priest at the altar who in a characteristic way keeps his flowing garments even in the pulpit, has the utmost optic facility to be in strong communication with the feelings of the believing public, attracting easily their hearts and influencing them as well by his monosensorial sacramental will which he prepares and represents.

In this connection we may appreciate the role of the tender Mimosas with their fine leaves, and of the refined petals of the flowers which altogether scatter by their optic example and influence the lump of our affective power and make our feelings dispersing and exploding in a most refined sprinkling rain of distribution to ideal pleasure and joy. These things are quite necessary and indispensable for the happy normal life, being precious helps for the affective animation and discharge, and cannot be replaced by anything else. The smoke of which we spoke long ago, has the same principal law in blurring, retailing and moving in the same refined optic way our sensorial apperception, and accelerating our liquefied and refined psychic impressions. All the terminal points of fringes, tassles, of laces and feathers or tender leaves and petals are, as it were, pointed antennae, from which the feelings of our heart spark with ideal emotion toward divine pleasure. There is for this reason scarcely an altar in Catholicism which might not be also richly decorated with flowers and plants. All these means help to produce the ideal sway which we have already meditated in other places, chiefly in the artistic use of the burning candles, of which the church makes such a rich application for her ideal purposes. Living trees with their numberless tender twigs and the trembling pointed foliage are efficient sentimental urges and powerful opportunities for the accelerated discharge of our feelings, as we so easily notice in the open nature. Catholicism introduces them even in its highest festival days of joy and pleasure into the churches, especially on Christmas, on the Maundry Thursday and on the Corpus Christi Day, the two last in connection with the Eucharistic enthusiasm which is the richest and highest in its mystic life.

We understand also in this connection how much the ancient Greek and Roman taste was right to deprecate the TROUSERS at that time only in use in the barbaric parts of these countries. Ovid sneers at the use of the trousers in the Pontus and sees in them the expression of the low and mean feelings of these nations. To-day all men of the civilized countries wear, obligatorily, according to the English example and style, the modern suits with trousers and we are so much accustomed to them that we in our turn sneer at people who would not wear them. We look at these men as to effeminated weaklings and claim this kind of dress for every modern man of practical intellectual behaviour and for reasons of convenience. The Catholic priest at the altar hides his prosaic trousers; he serves as the powerful sentimental medium between his monopunctual idealism and the believing crowd, wearing the attire of his function, in the similar kind as women do. It is not only the historic clinging to former historic customs which induces him to wear his antique dress, but much more the artistic energy which is attached to the waving folds of his garment. The trousers of the men of to-day are indeed very practical and useful in the working life, but they are lacking imagination and do not fit the sentimental religious intention. We see just in this small sign, how much our age upon the whole has become intellectual,

even much more than the antique Roman and Greek psychology.
We to-day cling energetically to the exclusive use of trousers in
the human male society, nobody thinks of abolishing this view of
modern fashionable culture and changing the trousers for the gown
of former times. Our present daily life has become more prosaic
and more intellectual than that of the ancient conceptions. The
man is considered more intellectual, stronger in the real sense of
duty and has given up long ago the claim of poetical sentimental
emphasis of his body. He has left this habit to the women and to
the Catholic priest who both have essentially sentimental tasks by
their intermediary idealistic tendencies towards either the sexual or
the terminal idealism. But perhaps all other religions cling in a
similar way to gown and coat. They exclude the human body on
their way to terminal idealism. Christ's body on the cross is again
an exception of extreme importance.

We know that practically all MONKS of the Catholic church
have maintained the use of the *cassock* for their continual daily life
and that they receive by this historic dress in our time a quite
characteristic extraordinary atmosphere: they profess by these anachronistic garments their special conceptions of the world: they
receive by them some quaint cultural features, on one hand, but
manifest, on the other side, also, their lack of affective touch
with the modern progressive world. They are looked at with
astonished eyes in the modern society and how susceptible are they
in these situations! But there is no reason to wonder for them.
Wearing old-fashioned garments overcome by the generality of
the society means indeed a challenge to the present fashion. Any
uniform has in its exceptional character to some extent this effect on
the surrounding world. It is always the expression of exceptional
claims, to other people, and must acquiesce in having not only the
advantages, but also the disadvantages of this bluffing behaviour.
The extraordinary historic costume, being the symbol of organized
power produces on one side surely acknowledgement and reverence
in a mystic way, without personal merit, but causes on the
other hand, as well, scorn, mockery and opposition on the part
of people who have different customs and conceptions. Life is so
just; it establishes always the equilibrium giving us by nature what
was taken away from us, and taking away from us which we
anticipated in an undeserved and unnatural manner. The habits
of the monks are well characterized according to their orders. They
mostly wear a scapular consisting of two long pieces of material
hanging in front and at the back of the body: they have a girdle
or rope around their loins, often furnished with a rosary. Domini-

cans and Carthusians have white color, Capuchins the color of brown, and Franciscans and Benedictines, black color of their dress. In religious services they often pull on further overcowls of the same color. The Benedictines, for instance, have for the processions and for preaching large overcowls, richly and minutely folded by quaint parallel creases of which the modern folded gowns of the ladies are imitations. The monks' hoods play a certain important role, being by several orders pulled over the head during several parts of the Mass, by others during the procession, when they walk mummed into their historic garments, almost perfectly invisible to the eyes of the believers, singing and carrying a burning candle along their meditative demonstration. Monks are not supposed to appear at all without their orders habit. It would signify a serious deterioration for the believer to see this change, since the monk received in the eyes of the Catholic just owing to his symbolic cassock the strongest increase of authority elevating the bearer into a higher class than other mortal people. It creates a cast. So much mankind is bound to exterior signs. It is not easy to avoid this same principle anywhere.

The very pronounced special role of the priest in the Catholic church conveys to him certain inclinations and features of a character which we ordinarily do not find so easily in other people. The priest is supposed to be the *porter of the heaven* and receives in this suggestion given to him by the church, by other people and by auto-suggestion indeed often a share of the celestial charm which he is willing to offer to others. He is, therefore, often sweet and idealistic, but it unfortunately occurs as well by the ripening effect of his strong symbolic monodetermination that often in the age of full manhood, when the deciding relapses of our psychology are brought about, there is a change to fanaticism, autocracy and too great self-sureness. The almost apotheosis of the living priest by his believers produces, of course, the danger of a lack of urges for careful energetic work, besides the instigation of ambition. On the other hand, they are inclined to be leader characters, because of the genial monosensorial fixation of their philosophical system. They have strongest convictions and are ready to do everything for them. But, of course, extreme convictions are the root of intolerance and of one-sided conceptions, of civil war and continual political undermining. The very substantial and idealistic priests neglect the question of the real world entirely because of their one-sided esteem of the ideal forces, whilst the realistic type of this cast overlooks rather the spiritual sentiment of the philosophical root of their conceptions, and abuses the authority of highest and best in-

tentions just for the attainment of social, economic and political
advantages.

The *celibacy* of the Catholic priest is, of course, one of the most
discussed questions of the practical side of Catholicism. It is a
merely arbitrary law of the church introduced in the current of
the centuries by the Pope, that the Catholic priest was not allowed
to marry. Whatsoever may have been the reasons of the early
papal decrees against the personal freedom of marriage of the
clergy, it constitutes a most serious encroachment on the individual
natural independence. The Catholic church had obviously the
double intention in doing this, to free the priest by the celibacy
from petty social respects and material necessities due to wife, children and relatives by the married man, and to economize his vital
force and energy conducting them into the channel of ideal sublimation instead of permitting them to discharge partly by other
natural enjoyment. Celibacy means the exclusion of the sexual
function in favor of the higher terminal idealistic concentration.
We know that terminal idealism and sexual idealism are always
in strongest competition, one destroying the other and one living
on the vital energy given to the other one.

There are, according to the high claimed authority of the
Catholic priest and according as people have a mental attitude
towards Catholicism, all possible rumours to hear about sexual
perversions among the Catholic clergy. Since everybody has human
feelings and inclinations, there is no reason from this side to
wonder if sometimes the general law of sexual magnetism has its
efficient consequences also among these celibate people forced by an
exterior historic compulsion to sign the contract not to marry. But
it is just interesting from the scientific and physiological standpoint to study the effect of the celibacy on the individual psychology
and the individual temperament. The danger of homosexuality
is very easily to observe in every exclusive community, be it in
monasteries, in military barracks, in prisons or in any kind of lasting seclusion. That the possibility and the fact of the celibacy
exists in innumerable cases in the Catholic church in the most
perfect form, no objective observer will doubt about. Not only
nuns, but also monks and secular priests in great numbers are
surely able to fulfil this commandment of sexual abstimeousness.
This fact is today in spite of all so generally acknowledged that
the psychiatricians of very opposite philosophical and political
directions quote today the Catholic priest as the example of the
fact that it is indeed possible to live a celibate life without any
damage for the character. There are surely countless cases which

succeed perfectly in adapting themselves to the celibate intention of the church, and there are even many of these people who in this resignation find higher energy and concentration for idealistic and intellectual work, similarly as we find it in the Eunuchs who are exceedingly busy and successful because they are never distracted by other desires, as I saw them and admired them several times in great scholars in Vienna. But they are, as a rule, not creative and not progressive by personal energy, originality and audacious new ideas. Sexual negativists are likely mostly followers.

If the psychiatrician says that the Catholic priests and nuns are the example of the possibility for realizable celibacy, he in this does not say that this state is the normal or best one, that it is the least dangerous state in the sense of the medicine or psychiatrics, he does not say in this statement that there are not very many dangers and tragic issues given in the forced celibacy and that it is not even risky for the psychic and organic health, in many cases, to enforce the sexual abstimeousness. But the fact of even brilliant celibates exists. It is a proof and may be taken as a proving example by the medical and physiological authorities that there are individuals which can be perfectly happy and most efficient in celibacy.

The *monastery* is a dwelling where men or women lead a coenobitic life under rule and vows. St. Pachomius who built monasteries in the Thebaid, 350, is regarded as their originator. Monk and nun are the names for the single members of the monastic union. They are people who leave the world in the intention to practise the counsel of perfection in a monastic order.

This idea to escape the whole world in order to become more able for virtue is indeed a very simple, but doubtful way of progressing in perfection. The removal from the opportunities for sin does not mean the parting of the heart with the desire for sin. The horrible anxieties of temptations, of the appearance of the devil and of all sexual spells before the eyes of the solitary monks is only the reflection of the burning desire of their craving nature for a normal real life. The idea of leaving the sensorial world in order to avoid its diversions from the ideal and its instigations for the real attachment, is indeed one of the most fundamental questions which could be put before the psychological discussions of our life. Are we entitled to avoid the influences of the normal outside life in order to be undisturbed in our ideal sentimental wishes and dreams? Are we able to gain in this way a higher worthiness and a greater esteem in our moral value? Is it not rather unnatural to change the natural conditions of our real surroundings in such a manner that we leave just the circumstances where our ideal victories could have richest opportunities to be worked out and to be manifested? Admit the personal freedom to choose this possibility, there cannot be any dispensation from the reproach that this degree of self-consciousness goes likely too far and must be considered as lack of moral courage. Avoiding the whole range of the sensorial worldly influences does indeed not refute the world and its attractions, but loses rather more the opportunities to practise and to show the strength and the energy of the ideal individuality in overcoming its seductions. Whosoever decided to leave the world because of its attractions confessed his belief in its superiority in magnetic energy and owned his thorough fear of not being able to be victorious in the battle with its sensorial force. He prevented this battle because he was, in advance, doubtful of his idealistic fortitude and preferred the easy manner of the passive inglorious ideal victory.

But of course since human nature remains always the same and since we can by no means in spite of ourselves thoroughly escape the human conditions even if we hide ourselves behind walls and exclude the intercourse of the society, not only the temptations, but also our so-called bad inclinations follow wherever we go. L'habit ne fait pas le moine; The gown does not make the monk. The monastery which has originally the intention to withdraw the individual from the social intercourse and the visible multiplicity of the world, develops into a great field of intellectual and sensorial experience, where the monk and the nun encounter almost all the same dangers, opportunities and bad instigations which he or she intended to escape in entering the separating walls of the monastery or the convent. In many senses the forced intimacy between the numerous members of a monastic community emphasizes even much more individual frictions, greater dangers and opportunities for sin against charity than in the outside world and perhaps a deeper knowledge and experience of the fragility of human nature than in the people of the world. Envy, ambition, frivolous quarrels, misunderstandings and misinterpretations can find fertile ground in the monastic life. There are, however, splendid exceptions, where a true idealism is able to carry almost all members to a high moral level. These people are not in a position to avoid their perpetual intimate company, they are in a great community, a great family as it were of perhaps a hundred or more members. Have they all not to know, to bear with, and to stand, their mutual faults in disagreeable, unavoidably petty atmosphere?

The idea of the monasticism is most thorough in the order of the Carthusians who live entirely separated in their single small houses, meet rarely and are not permitted to speak much with each other, so that they are indeed able to avoid the above mentioned source of most disagreeable possibilities of mutual intellectual friction and faults. But we know that even without words and with the near neighborhood we attract and repulse each other and even so, the continual local neighborhood with each other can be the source of very painful distractions. The other orders all together suffer more from this unnatural intimacy which can be so easily and naturally avoided by the people of the world, being able to change according to need and psychological necessity, to retire from each other for a short or longer time or even forever if they will. The character decides about the choice of a profession.

On the other hand the natural inclination of intellectual and sensorial intercourse is of course also an absolute part of the psychic integrity of the people who have chosen the monastic life. The more temperate orders are busy in teaching, in art, in science, or in manufacturing work. In these cases, we have to consider the monastic life as a special economic system ruled by the idea of communism and in connection with celibacy on obligation for all members. We have, therefore, to distinguish different kinds of orders: the severer and the more idealistic types, meditating, praying, and the less retired forms, working, teaching, scientific and artistic types, and those which are mixed. The most known representative of the former severe or meditative kind are, the Carthusians; of the last scientific and free species; the Jesuits who are very independent in their worldly intercourse, and of the mixed type (Ora et Labora: Motto of the Benedictines) the Benedictines who have a certain strict community, common prayer and restricted intercourse with the society, but, on the other hand, a working, teaching and scientific task and in so far the necessity to deal with the outside world.

In history the different orders played an important role in Europe as we know. The Christian countries received their first scientific culture, their knowledge of writing and their introduction into Christianity during the early middle ages chiefly by the Benedictines (strong in the early time in Ireland): England, Germany, Switzerland and a great deal of Europe were converted to Christianity by this order. The Jesuits founded by St. Ignace in the 16th Century had chiefly scientific intentions and were directed first against the rising Protestantism and then against the modern free thought. They played an important political role chiefly in France, Spain and Austria. The names of Richilieu and Mazarin and others are known the world over. The Dominicans had the chief intention to preach: they rose in France in connection with heretic struggles in the early middle ages and produced many important members, of whom the most celebrated may be St. Thomas Ab Aquino who elaborated the mediaeval Catholic philosophy amalgamating with it the ideas of Aristotle in a wonderfully clear and beautiful Latin language. The Augustins, from which Luther originated, are near to the Benedictines in their conceptions connecting prayer and scientific teaching. The great Protestant reformers, Erasmus, Calvin, Melanchthon and Zuinglius were all in near connection with the atmosphere of the scientific monastic schools of the middle ages and had similar scientific methods and cultural expressions.

A very sympathetic order in the true sense of the Christian idealism are the *Mendicant Friars,* chiefly represented by the *Franciscans* called according to their founder, Francis of Assisi. They are obliged to live in perfect poverty according to the example of the original Christian conception and to the conviction that all sin comes from wealth and luxury. They were in the middle ages highly poetical, full of sacrificing idealism and perhaps nearest to the one-sided, but ideal example which is given of Christ in the gospel. St. Francis of Assisi himself was the most poetical type: he possessed so much the perfect simplicity of the heart and was so much in the most intimate harmony with the created univerve that he had the power to speak to, and to understand, the animals, birds and fish, as the legend tells. He is praised by all poetical and artistic people even today as the true expression of the finest idealism and is, therefore, much celebrated in poetry (flowers of St. Francis) and in painting, of which he is a favorite subject. I remember to have seen among others the representation of his charming intercourse with the animals for instance at Zurich, where a painting by Boecklin represents his intimacy with the fish of the sea, showing him preaching to them from a crag and innumerable fish looking out from the surface of the waters and listening in a most touching way. There is another painting by a French painter in the Gallery des Beaux Arts in the University building at Lausanne, and many others, chiefly in Spanish museums representing St. Francis. These mendicant friars are barefooted. A branch coming from the

Franciscans and still today very spread and popular in Europe, are the *Capuchins,* very typical by their brown cassocks, their beards, the white rope around the waist with the dangling large rosary and by their barefootedness. They are less scientific, having less learned preparations than the other orders, but are perhaps just for this reason more beloved by the lower strata of the population.

The secular priest has typically distinct features from the monk. He is connected with them by his celibacy and by the common Catholic teachings and priesthood. But he, on the other hand is freer and more individual, deals with money and is for this reason more real and worldly, understanding better the difficulties and needs of the children of the world whose destiny he partly shares. The secular priest, has, therefore, as a rule more insight into the real entanglements of the life of the believers: whilst the monk often has no idea of the social conditions of the world.

There is no doubt that the monastic life offers many conveniences and advantages to its adherents. In the deliberations of this choice the idea of providing for the young people and protecting them, according to their rank, plays a great role: this was above all the case in the middle ages, when the later born non-inheritant sons and daughters of the nobility, even princes, were put and enclosed, or chose by themselves, in the monasteries in order not to lose in an inferior position in the world the quality of their nobility and not to be in the way of the free activity of the real possessor of the material and political power. The monastery protected these people against lowering of their rank in the world, maintained the full authority of the family and gave to the noble monks and nuns the satisfaction and integrity of their family rank in an ideal way, since it was not possible in the feudal system to do it in reality. There was, however, many an ecclesiastic dignitary of high worldly power. We have in connection with this historic conception of the monastery as the refuge for the exposed familiar rank and ancestry, until today many similar institutions which permit the reception only to members of noble families. The greatest part of monasteries and convents have, however, abolished today, many only a short time ago, this condition of reception, because indeed today it is quite remarkable, how much rich and knighted people withdraw from the clergy, in the secular and monastic form. The restriction to nobility would, therefore, depopulate the modern monastery.

There was surely in the middle ages and is still today in the huge and picturesque artistic buildings of many monasteries and convents much poetry and spiritual elevated atmosphere. The union of the monastic uniform costume helps up to a certain degree to create a strong feeling of unity and republican brotherhood between the monks and dignifies by its symbolic meaning the actions of their daily life. The exceedingly considerable length of the corridors crossing each other at different distances and covered with proceeding cross vaults, illuminated perhaps by the setting sun through numberless windows of one long-side of the corridor and animating so the rusty colored antique paintings of the opposite wall which contains at the same time the minutely carved doors of the monastic cells, offer to the surprised eye the most charming meditative atmosphere. There is a solemn quietness, which perhaps is interrupted by the sound of a high-pitched bell, chiming the hour or calling to prayer, or by the regular echoing step of a white-haired monk walking up and down on the brick floor and reading his Breviary, looking from time to time through the windows, from where the flutes of the blackbirds rise up to the meditating monk and the lilac mingles its perfume with the silent divine desire exhaling from the heart of the dreamer.

This dwelling part of the monastery is called *Clausura* and is accessable only to the people of the same sex. It reminds strongly of the monarchic middle ages, if we meet until today in the monasteries the decree that the Clausura of the monasteries is accessible only for members of royal blood, queens and princesses of the other sex and excludes all other hetero-sexual visitors.

We will not enter now into the near philosophical relation of Christianity, monotheism and monarchism. But let us only say that Catholicism was in the mediaeval history the founder and protector of the monarchies and the kingdoms, and that kings founded in their turn and gifted richly the monasteries, bequeathed to them extensive lands and built churches for them (there are exceedingly rich monasteries until today dating from the early middle ages in Europe), and populated them with their princes and relatives. There were always good relations between nobility, monarchy and monasteries. The latter arrived, therefore, to quite extraordinary privileges in the mediaeval political and material order. How much this was the case is still today visible for instance in the monastery of the Capuchins in Vienna and of the Escorial of the Augustins in Spain, where the Austrian and Spanish kings are buried in all ostentation of white and colored marble, of carved gold and silver and where the monks pray continually for the souls of the late departed. The Escorial contains at the same time the most wonderful flats for the king with richest artistic achievement. We see in very many monasteries the richest visiting rooms prepared and accustomed to receive high personalities. I remember to have visited different monasteries in Austria where the most magnificent show rooms were demonstrated in which Pope and Kings, in two cases also Napoleon, lived for a short time. These things may be proof enough how much the monasteries were favored by the benevolence of the monarchy of the past Christian history. Monastery and monarchy are the children of the same principles and support and help each other.

It is evident that by the careful collection of centenarian advantages the monasteries easily accumulated the most extraordinary historic and artistic museums. The monks were from the earliest times cultured enough, as the first and most thorough possessors of the written language, to register and order all their possessions, to label and describe their goods, to put down in writings the changes of their monastic destiny in connection with the general history and created in this manner rich and well ordered libraries, of which the monasteries of today have reason to be indeed proud. These libraries are still today the best sources of all studies in mediaeval history and are visited for this purpose by historic scholars of all parts of the world.

The riches of the MONASTIC ART was chiefly in connection with their churches which on obligation were always lavishly supplied with all kind of artistic productions, especially sculptures and paintings. But there was at the same time also the richest occasion for the artistic monk in the whole monastic building, in an architectural way. The most wonderful saloons and halls of marble, and what solemn staircases, porches, towers and turrets are found in monasteries! The large free fields of the walls enticed the desire for paintings, the great white extent of the ceiling was animated by delightful frescos representing in charming clouds the whole staff of the heaven. The enormous visiting and sitting rooms, the refectories and dormitories, the corridors and the frames of the countless doors were in time and progressing ages decorated with all kinds of precious and artistic carvings and paintings in order that the most of the old monasteries have indeed rather anything else than the character of the imitation of the poverty of the religious hero. If we add that the visiting princes, kings and queens presented rich gifts during the centuries to these people, then we understand that they at the end had an exceeding richness of artistic and material goods which cannot easily be competed with by museums and exhibitions. The great luxury of the monasteries in the middle ages came from this accumulation of possession. The beginning severity of the rule of the orders decayed into luxury so that the monk wore at the end precious silk goods for the daily use, whilst they first were clad in sackcloth. The finest and most splendid buildings in the world are still today the old monasteries, chiefly in Austria.

The totality of a monastic aspect may be imagined by people, who have not opportunity to travel through the European continent in visiting the colleges of Oxford and Cambridge in England. These two university cities contain according to the old mediaeval tradition for the use of the students numerous architectural institutions of about the same type, on a small scale, as we have them in the old monasteries. There is a main building with the Dormitory, a common dining room called Refectory, a church or chapel, and never fails the quite characteristic courtyard enclosed by the buildings forming a square or a horseshoe around it. There we find also towers and bells, the important libraries of the old times and a collection of paintings and carvings (Grinling Gibbons) of former old important people and historic moments, altogether exhaling an atmosphere of majesty, dignity and high substantial tastes.

May there be so many advantages of the monastic life as may, provided that the good will of clever people worked out unanimous friendship which is not easy in so near social compression and cannot be replaced by artistic surroundings, let us listen from the *philosophical-psychological standpoint to other views*.

Exactly Ruskin who taught in these wonderful colleges of Oxford said in his lectures on art, 1870, speaking about the life of monks: "Of these, the first, the pride of faith, is now, as it has been always, the most deadly, because the most complacent and subtle:—because it invests every evil passion of our nature with the aspect of an angel of light, and enables the self-love, which might otherwise have been put to wholesome shame, and the cruel carelessness of the ruin of our fellowman, which might otherwise have been warmed into human love or at least checked by human intelligence, to congeal themselves into the mortal intellectual disease of imagining that myriads of the inhabitants of the world for four thousand years have been left to wander and perish, many of them everlastingly, in order that, in fullness of time, divine truth might be preached sufficiently to ourselves: with this farther ineffable mischief for direct result, that multitudes of kindly disposed, gentle and submissive persons, who might else by their true patience have alloyed the hardness of the common crowd, and by their activity for good, balanced its misdoing, are withdrawn from all such true services of man, that they may pass the best part of their lives in what they are told is the service of God: namely, desiring what they cannot obtain, lamenting what they cannot avoid, and reflecting on what they cannot understand."

Ruskin gave there the most concentrated definition of the monastic life in its most thorough conceptions, as we have it so much more, as it approaches from the working type to the meditative one. But the terminal serious judgment is, up to a certain degree, concerning all kinds not only of monastic orders, but also the extreme idealistic psychology at all. On the other side, Ruskin himself had more terminal ambitions than he confesses in this statement. The monasticism has transformed and elaborated most clearly and distinctly the genial monoidealism into real legal execution; it excludes more clearly the real intellectual frictions and necessities of the life, removes the direct opportunities to be useful in the service of the general humanity, leading instead the individual life-force to meditate things which it cannot understand, to desires which now cannot be obtained and to lamentations on circumstances which cannot be altered. This definition of the defective attitude of the one-sided enthusiastic idealism seems to be most condensed and expresses most accurately the serious displacements of the normal psychorhythmic accent in these institutions, adding in this way needs and wishes which cannot be granted by our natural psychological constitution, because they are too high, and not permitting in spite of this the removal of the natural physiological needs and necessities, though the will of the monastic idealism gave them up, neglects them and their reality, and is decided to put all accents of its force exclusively on the idealistic side. The extreme monasticism is willing to shut its eyes before the humble reality of the intellectual life, in retiring into the illusionary artistic desert behind the walls, and it emphasizes instead one-sided ideal fulfillments which are too high for the human nature and not acceptable to the present human faculties. It is the one-sided pride of the faith which perverts all psychological natural disposition, dislocating the psychic tendencies in a fatal measure of wrong proportion, hyper-emphasizing the feelings and neglecting the intellect, looking only after the subjective concealment in the monastic isolation, imagining God and ignoring the visible reality: sacrificing every real thing to the sentimental ideal and depriving the whole humanity of their direct helping services. But this ob-

vious wrongness of the disposition of the human life as it is given
in the artificial flight from the life and in the construction of an
artificial enclosure is nothing else but the direct efflux of the extreme idealistic psychology and philosophy. The Monasticism is
a further mirror of the monosymbolic concentration of the life of
the individual who always strives instinctively to retire from the
multiplicity of the real intellectual world and has the strongest
desire to dedicate his time to his idealistic monosymbolic pleasure in
the undisturbed concealment of his personal narrow meditation.

The extreme monastic conception of the life is wrong, because
it establishes an unnatural basis for our real behaviour excluding
the broad social intercourse, the economic necessities and conditions,
the family life and the touch with the general world, all absolutely essential circumstances for the good and true development
of the human life. May the mendicant orders of Catholicism be
the most ideal expression of the Christian idea, they certainly are
not the most humane and truest manifestations of the human
nature, because they are guilty of strong one-sided emphasis of the
sentimental part of our psychological gifts and neglect the intellectual nature as well.

Nothing in our life is definitely settled and cannot be. The
rising mediaeval institutions were convinced to have found forever
the best psychological methods and manifested them in proudest
monastic orders full of strength and lasting organization. And
they were at this epoch successful indeed. But they necessarily
were the reflections of the psychological principles of their doctrine,
exhibiting for this reason the same strong and weak sides, being
too much idealistic and too little realistic, too much poetical and
dreamy, and too little objective, scientific, not helping the visible
society. For this reason these institutions, splendid and useful as
they were in their kind at their height in former times, and good
in a certain sense as their educational influences then and even to-
day may be deemed in permitting to numberless youths scientific
education at a cheap price, where under other conditions, this education would not have been possible, may belong prevalently to the
interest of the past history. They are considered wrong in the
scientific conception of the modern time because of their one-sided
psychorhythmic emphasis and of their arbitrary change of the vital
necessities of the human psychological conditions. But there is no
question that they were one of the great comets of our European
civilization whose splendid tails will yet be visible and glittering
for a long time.

Still Europe and Asia (all monasteries are built up essentially according to the same psychological plan) are full of monastic institutions; the monks walk still to-day with their waving habits and their fluttering scapulars through the fragrant gardens between the rustling leaves of their courtyards, meditating in a lonely lane their breviary, being separated from the noisy world by their hiding walls. They continue to smile in their divine dreams, and the rushing water fountains and the numerous different kinds of singing birds around them, seem to acquiesce with their poetical and joyful sentiments. Large parts of the population of the Old Countries are still to-day the decided admirers of these old orders, dignified by the historic ages, traditional learning and rich possessions. They all think to be the most perfect realisations of the teachings of the gospel, and many Catholic people as well believe in their perfect harmonious humanity, and resent bitterly every attack againsts their divine darlings behind the walls of monasteries and convents.

The idea of monkdom was of course not at all new. The Antiquity had the monastic orders already: we encounter them always in the Greek and Roman pre-Christian history. Also the celibacy was found in these times, virgins having been considered as the individuals dearest to the gods.

Let us look at the present conceptions of the monks. The mild types of monasticism which have vivacious intercourse with the exterior world in teaching and scientific work, may after all be in practice much better than their original one-sided disposition intended them to be in its exclusive idealistic tendencies. In many cases they reach the desirable level of the harmony of the psychological human necessities, working and thinking as well as meditating on ideal divine things. The real practice and the progressive history always corrects in time and with experience one-sided principles; the human nature is a wonderful continual claim directing and levelling in time all which was one-sided at the starting point. But we will not forget that never a building which was erected on an oblique basis can be brought perfectly into right perpendicularity. It has done great services to the rising European civilisation, but it has also enjoined extreme principles, spoiled the artless look at life, caused fanaticism and sore educational evils and faults. Long time ago, the absolute *sacrosanct* acknowledgment of the monasticism has disappeared. The rising modern period and the modern scientific conception have given way towards new views correcting the old one-sided sentimentality, emphasising the hard working and intellectual part of the life.

So human nature, in the modern life, has been reduced into its normal human legislation which its exacts and without which it cannot be good. There are indeed two operations which must be excluded from the mediaeval conception in order to make human life again thorough and efficient: first the one-sided idealistic sentimentality has to be curtailed, and second, the real intellectuality must be more emphasized. Protestantism and modern science have made effort and do it still, to obtain this result. They not only succeed upon the whole to reach this goal, but the enormous development of the modern science and technicalities created even the danger that the previous one-sidedness of the expression and rights of the human feelings falls back to the contrary, giving the total dominion over the human soul to the intellectual part of its disposition, neglecting all feelings and crushing the right of ideal enjoyment. But this cannot be the intention and goal of our human nature as little. There is and remains always the golden rule between understanding and feeling equilibrium which is only congruent to our psychological nature. If the extreme pride of the faith is wrong and insidious, the absolute pride of the science leads also to wrong one-sidedness and must be carefully avoided.

Let us enter now the festival door of the church of any *Benedictine Abbey* and attend to the service of the High Mass on Sunday. The Benedictines are famous for putting most stress on the religious service in their beautiful churches in an most artistic way. We are surprised from the beginning by the quite extraordinary golden splendour and the artistic luxury glittering from the walls and the large vaults of the splendid Benedictine churches, as we meet them everywhere in central Europe, chiefly in Austria, in South Germany and Switzerland. The typical *Barocco Churches* in connection with the excellent ecclesiastic music and the impressive pomp to transport the witness of the service are indeed able to. The character of the Benedictine religious service receives the most perfect artistic dignity by the united efforts of the large spaces covered and divided by powerful arches, by the rich animation of the carved angels and saints pretending to fly through the vast vaults in most passionate attitudes, full of divine rapture, often with golden trumpets in their mouths, making shrill sounds, as it were, and partly wrapped in clothes waving in the wind of divine enthusiasm. The saints are fixed on their martyr post or cross, or present the instruments of their tortures according to the ecclesiastic tradition. Chiefly the twelve apostles are the prefered subject of the sculptural ecclesiastic art. The often reach in this statues of wood or stone their full or even double length and are placed in the most exposed places and in the foremost visible points of the church. According to the peculiar Barocco-style these sculptures are passionately twisted at their waists or in the attitude of their legs or arms; their bodies lean to one side and their heads may be turned to heaven where they look in charming ecstasy with illuminated faces. Always they are entirely sunk in their divine dreams. The main artistic goal of this twisted corporeal attitude is to receive rich opportunities for the elaboration of the curves and folds of the habits which are always full of the most vividly artistic emotion and sway. The Barocco-artist reveals in these rich draperies, which he flings always around the exuberant bodies of his statues, the idealistic energy and the quite extraordinary sway typical of all Barocco. This elevated enthusiasm which this style understands always to kindle from the fluttering garments of its saints and angels, will be felt by any visitor of any high-Barocco church and is strong, persuading and solemn beyond description.

Stucco plays an important role in all Baroque churches. There are the richest and most wonderful accumulations of plastic flower baskets, of plants and fruits in the most delightful and impressive modulation of form and line (Salzburg, Linz, Innsbruck, Saint Florian). They flow over in that charming ornamental net with geometrical symmetric character, but much stronger and more substantial than the similar decorative work, as we observe it in the Rococo as the last runner of the Barocco-art. The Rococo ornamentations have to cover all free fields of the walls and ceilings, corners and nooks of greater pieces of stucco-representations, being the conclusions of statues and pedestals or of the rich numerous variegated pictures, surrounding them in rich frames full of fancy and tenderness. These ornamental Rococo designs are of the foremost beauty in the guidance of the lines which seemingly develop towards all sides in most lawless intricacy, but form nevertheless a charming symmetry and harmony as a whole. These decorations are done in plaster, which often is painted in gold, yellow and green, or they are only painted with colours, chiefly in gold, on the white plastered background, as it is typical of the brightly-lighted Barocco churches which intend to represent the heaven on earth instead to excite the desire for the perpendicular distance of the sky, as the Gothic style did. For this reason we do not find in any Barocco church stained windows of the darkening influence of the Gothic style. Barocco needs much light and intends a real fulfillment of happiness and divine enjoyment. The numerous fresco paintings are done in the powerful style of Rubens. The enormous arches and galleries have prominent cornices according to the stressing character of the style. It is just owing to the ensemble of the high arches which gather their energy in mighty columns and pillars, or create the most impressive octogons or other multi-angular formations swinging the imagination of the spectator by their bold architectural semi-circles from one supporting pillar to the other, that the most wonderful atmosphere of the space arises and builds the magnificent great harmony, the idealistic sway and the solemn celestial feelings which are the supposition and help for the imagination which the Benedictine service needs for its efficacy. These are the cradles and saloons for Mozart's sweet and inspiring music.

The service of the Benedictine order, especially of the High Mass, is splendid. The celebrating priest is richly adorned and assisted by deacons, sub-deacons and ministrants, a ceremony master directing the ritual performance. On high festival days the Abbot attends in his special elevated chair as a more private witness on the celebration of the High Mass: he bears then his mantilla in black silk and his always visible golden cross supported by a heavy golden chain, being with the ring at his finger the sign of his ruling power. At the feasts of first order, such as Christmas, Easter and Pentecost, the Abbot himself, who has often nearly the rank of a bishop and is, therefore, during the service supplied with the Bishop's mitre and the crosier, celebrates the so-called *Pontifical High Mass*. This is the most impressive artistic performance of the whole Benedictine service. In this Pontifical Mass nothing is spared in all kinds of possible resources to give to the service the most possible dignity, strength and enthusiastic elevation. Not only the different educated musical members of the monastery have to join all their best skill in the service of the Pontifical music, but even numerous musical people from the neighboring town or village are invited and taught to partake in the ecclesiastic concert. The performers on the galleries are supported by the domineering power of one or several huge organs sounding like a thunder storm. They exclude women but appreciate instead especially the silver pure voices of young boys which are performing in the male monasteries.

The important circumstance of this performances is this that we have not only the richest cast of an instrumental orchestra, but as well the optic support of a splendid stylistic church full of light, of sparkling gold, hovering statues representing angels and saints, variegated colors, and a sublime dignified atmosphere of the space and at last the ritual service at the altar rich in garments, symbolic actions and signs. Just the numberless flickering candles and lights, the waving silks and velvets, the peaks, sticks and crosses, the sparkling lightnings reflected from the golden and silver vases, the rich diamonds of the Abbot, of the chalice and of the chasuble, all these circumstances together, have of course the most powerful influence on the imaginative heart of the believer. He is helped by his religious benevolence for the ecclesiastic performances, moved by the reverence of the mediative person of the priest, excited by all the flickering lights and drunk with the fragrant frankincense which mobolizes his fancy over the sharp intellectual objects. He is carried over all petty and narrow reality, his feelings sail through the huge halls of the church, swinging along the mighty arches of the walls and triumphing at the topmost *lanterna* of the cupola. The hearts of the believers are quivering under the powerful impression of all this artistic spell, the voices of the different organs assail the attending listener like rugient steers or lions, as it were, hurling all life-force towards the absolute conviction and satisfaction of terminal almighty glory. The narrow confinement of the church is felt in these moments as the absolute heaven and the paradise of celestial desires. The trombones trumpet with the most thrilling energy from the different galleries of the church and smite the individual feelings towards the most elevated enthusiasm. All is in a harmonious movement and in a holy passion: the figures of the church seem to join in bold gesticulations and to hover through the universal spaces of the imagination, and their fluttering gowns and coats reveal here their last potential meaning to the flickering fervor of the idealistic heart. What lightnings of delight spring forth from all lights and what divine most intimate smiles hush over all the variegated colors of this temple of God! All is greatness, peace, and seems fulfillment and satisfaction in this historic confinement of the traditional theological idea expressed in the wonderful frame of multiple artistic means.

But what is the exact idea of this artistic monosymbolic performance? Does not *nature* in all its beauty reveal the same greatness and splendour of God in a much more perfect manner? The rosy dawn and the purple of the evening, the silvery clouds of the sky and the serene blue of the vault of the firmament, the variegated colors and trembling lights of the leaves of the wood, the glittering reflections of the sunbeams in the waters, the intense sparkling of the nightly stars, the sweet songs of the birds, they all together express the greatness and beauty of the universe in an even more perfect way. The art of the church is the stylistic which is to say an historic and artificial imitation of the natural idealism towards the divinity. The *artistic styles* of the church are the reflection of the historic and methodical restricted ways of the idea of the creator and God of the universe. The ecclesiastic art is the special way how the historic religion introduces and adapts our artistic and admiring sensorial disposition to its special philosophical conceptions. The charming beauty of nature is free of all stylistic one-sidedness, because it worships the infinite greatness and power of the universal God who does not know any historic restriction nor formulation. The God of history is a dim reflection of the terminal universal God, of the infinite idealism, toward which all created world develops in artless energy and ingenuous goodness. Artistic style means, therefore, always, until today, the historic form of one historic philosophical theistic development. It is a logical and scientific order directed to an intellectually accepted systematized goal. The religious artistic performance is the powerful affective help for the practical utilization of the eternal idea of God which becomes easily in this manner the monopoly of one ecclesiastic body, serving its material interests and economic purposes, whilst on the other hand it is often very accessible and reachable by the energetic sensorial intrusion even for the ungifted average man who is deaf to the sweet voices of the genuine sounds of nature, or who has become blind for all the wonders of the mountains, the sea, the woods and the field, who has lost the sense of appreciating the fragrant perfumes of the flowers of the different grasses and plants, in the current of his plodding work or by the influence of his exaggerated artistic education, and accepts now willingly this comfortable substitute of the artistic sensorial performance. The size of the artistically reachable divinity has become smaller but surer. We have the duty to reach as much as possible, the whole universe with our gifted heart. But it is surely better to have a part of the divinity than nothing at all, as it happens often.

The compensation lies, therefore, in the easiness of this artistic enjoyment, but it is paid by the historic narrowness and the artistic confinement of the universal God who ought to have no limits, no imaginative restriction, no historic determination and no artistic definite sensorial expression in the human society. The exclusive admirer of religious art receives at the same time the brand of the slavery of his heart and mind for serving and subjecting his imagination to the potentialities of any historic institution. He loses the free wings of the divine desire and the universal development in permitting that his divine idealism is caught, curtailed and put in the golden cage of the local stylistic expression.

Art has become in the hands of the historic religion the skilful instrument to catch and to imprison not only the outstanding unrivalled and unparalleled idea of the eternal God, but at the same time and with the same means the love of the hearts of its believers, the wings of our imagination and the limits of our thoughts. Art is the most dangerous two-edged sword in the hands of the religious institutions, because it turns out likely not to be only the merely emblematic hint for the divine imagination, as it ought to be, but rather more the chosen expression of the divinity culminating in the strict monosensorial symbolism of the ecclesiastic service. Nature has to stoop before the mechanistic powers of the human cunning psychodynamic philosophers, the free daughter of the heaven which is our imagination has been imprisoned in the service of systematized local institutions and is, therefore lowered and impaired in its function and purpose. The more narrow and more definite the philosophical conception of the world, the more one-sided the artistic style and its real expression, as we saw most clearly in the Gothic. Are voluntary artistic exclusiveness of our heart, of our goal, our imagination and our formative expression never permitted to be definite? There must always be more possibility of free intellectual searching oscillation in means and purpose, in theory, theology and philosophy, and consequently in practice, in art and real representation. Curtailing our imagination may be somewhat comfortable for the man with hyper-cultured inheritance, but it mutilates by its facilitation at the same time the image of the eternal idealism which never can be reached and roughens in exact representation our own nature. Art is good as the very general, carefully approaching interpretation of the eternal God whom we have to desire.

It is very frequent that we love in our childhood by far most nature and go then over in slow progress to perfect predilection for art, which we have reached in the mature age. We have this development just very pronounced of course in cultured and intellectual people. Art is the expression of a learned culture, the adaptation of nature to certain cultural philosophical and technical values: art is the special point of view of an age to look at, and to express, idealism, truth and usefulness. What we think is true and the preferable choice of our topics of truth, this means our philosophy, and the surrounding example, together with the possibility of technical expression which is again depending on our contemporary culture, are the founders of every art. Art is our developed nature in the sense of our human learned mentality.

It has narrowed the large wings of the conception of the universal ranges, effused into the open book of nature; it has humanized and prepared the greater objectivity of the natural expressions for the easier clearer intelligence of the special human psychological disposition. In our youth we are artless which means accessible to all truth, beauty, skill and usefulness in the gamut of universal possibilities, we are free of prejudices and ready for accepting every good thing; in the adult age, we are artful, prejudiced by our education, one-sided by our religious and scientific influences which worked on us during our growing life.

If art were able to reach the level of the truth of nature perfectly, then it could make the same claim for universality as nature. But it scarcely ever went so far as to touch this perfection in very rare artistic masterpieces. In such cases the one-sidedness which is expressed in every *style* and derives from the partial amount of truth involved in them, disappears. The special style vanishes at the highest culmination of the artistic production: style is like a private thoroughfare to a terminal public place of impartial importance, or like a shadowy mountain whose peaks glitter in the sunshine. The greatest masterpieces at their very top lose the special cultural or stylistic character and receive the absolute interhistoric and inter-temporal integrity in their artistic human features, as we meet them in the Greek dramas and sculpture, in Shakespeare, in Goethe or in Rembrandt, in all which cases it does no more matter, to distinguish exactly to which nation, to which style and to which culture these masterpieces belong. They are more universal than national and just in this universality lies their superiority.

Now we see how near good art and nature are. Only the best, the very chosen artists reach the level to exclude the contemporary influences, exemplary, national, denominational, political and technical so far as to develop on their basis an absolute or universal human idea. So we see that exactly the greatest artists and only the same approached to harmonious justice given in the nature, in which we are born, and that all other prevalent one-sided influences of language, historic religion, nationality, or of politics, as they are visible in the masterpiece, impair the perfection of the artistic ideal. The learned student is inclined to take offence at the reservedness of the genial people to many questions which his curiosity would ask them. Why did they not speak about so many things in philosophy, religion, politics and science, where they could have spread so much light and given so important intelligence? These doubters are already much more cultural and artistic than the genius himself whom they worship. Were they not educated in such a one-sided way in advance, they would not want to receive any intelligence from him about human cultural artistic questions, they would also be modest enough, as the very first geniuses are, to repose at the bosom of the universal nature, to listen to her throbbing heart, and they would be also so much thrilled and impressed by this universal intimacy that they would lose the interest and the longing for narrow cultural, denominational and political discussions, in this elected company.

The artistic style may be, therefore, the necessary artistic expression of the contemporary prevalent philosophical and technical historic assumption, but it is not the style in which the greatest artist exhausts his energy. The true genius grows over its walls, he looks over the categoric historic confinement of the stylistic narrowness and elevates his eyes and heart to the independent clouds of the universal ingenuousness, not only in the philosophical, but also correspondingly in the formalistic sense of his art. So the great artists remain always in the nucleus of the human interests; they never go out from the centre of those human questions which are always most contemporary and modern for any human history, for all philosophical distance and denominations, and they never move exclusively to ideas of partial, historic, political and denominational restriction. The historic topics, they are preferably of most simple character, are only the opportunities for the genius for elevating them to inter-historic human consideration, and to bring out in them the most general ingenuous human features and the universal laws of our psychological necessities and natural performance. There is nothing higher than the truth of nature and nothing stronger than the universal magnetic force: this conviction pervades and reigns over the works of all great geniuses. The intimate likeness to nature gives the utmost guarantee of the universal truth and usefulness, and nothing is able to tranquillize more than the soothing natural atmosphere spread on any artistic masterpiece. The greatest confidence flows from the real natural truth and not from the scholastic partial, historic and learned atmosphere.

Style means a school, a way or method in which one age and culture succeeded best in expressing its artistic need and it is, therefore, most easy to develop through this performed magnetic habitual way of the artistic experience in order to reach after all, if there is the personal genial ability, the impartial and inter-temporal stage of value. Even the genius needs the stylistic staircase of its artistic ascent, but once arrived at the highest top, he becomes free and drops the fetters of the previous rule he learned in mounting. It is in art as in many other things, at the top of the mastership we forget and purposely seem to ignore the steps and orders which have helped us to our genial elevation. The true genius has the nature of the artistic rule so sure in his possession, that the work in his subconscious mind is performed in spite of himself. He and his surroundings as little are aware of the refined artistic laws and rules playing in his genial activity. But of course, in all great works are always the same rules and laws, but they have not the stylistic one-sidedness, they have not the historic handicaps, but dropped everything which is not essential, true and reliable in the sense of the absolute justice, truth and validity, as we have it in the magnificent works of the natural creation. The genial work consists in having purified and stripped the historic style from narrow one-sidedness, and in having acquired such a skill in using its best eternal laws and values that the best skill is ensured in the subconscious mind of the genial artist who does not know any more what he does with the fire of his brush revelling over the canvas or with the eloquence of his notional poetry speaking eternal truth, but he knows that he is perfect in his subconscious esteem.

The historic limitation of the artistic expression is of course the consequence of its philosophical particular one-sidedness. Any culture selected one part of the human nature for its philosophical and psychological system, is therefore one-sided and imperfect and creating the corresponding artistry. In one sense the exact artistic limitation means wise modest restriction, and realistic necessity, in another an unbelievable pride. For the concentration of the cultural psychology into the mere part of the technical possibility in itself is a help for concentration and facilitation of the artistic performance, the psychic attention having an example and a measure for real expression: on the other hand we remember that it was just the central most important focus of the human psychological light-field, if it is chosen exactly for the artistic working field, creates most terrible dangers of any other mostly educational kind, but also of impossible and discordant artistic styles and expressions.

The strong limitation of the monosymbolic psychology, we will admit it, created the possibility of expression in many ways for less gifted individuals who could not have found their artistic task because of lack of philosophical and technical concentration outside of this given clear mono-determined crystallization of the human psychology. Because this heaviest preparatory work of their psychology was done, they were more able to find the corresponding expression in the style which even itself waited for them in an achieved formalistic school. So many less gifted people, it is sure, reached a certain artistic mastership in the middle ages, whilst they today in our philosophical and technical muddle would not have any chance of artistic success. But the sacrifice is worth while. Our time is a waiting time, hatching new more broadminded psychological principles, bridling, therefore, the ready inclinations for artistic formative crystallization, owing to the expectation of the previous intellectual enlargement of our psychological habitual performance. We are in a state today where the individual has to suffer and to withdraw because of the respect for the common psychological law which first has to issue from the philosophical and cultural growth of our time, and which in the future will build up the basis and the instrument of a new style, of a new art being more broadminded and more universal than the former historic restriction was.

This future style will exact more skill than the former ones. It will be more exclusive, just because it will be more universal. It will exact more skill, but stand less artificial scholarship. It will be more natural, more true, more useful, less complicated and less partial.

The practice of the old Catholic style was more accessible to the average artist: he could lean to the given rules and special prescriptions of the style of the contemporary culture, his topic, his means of expression, ideas, colors and everything was given to him up to a certain extent. But we have to notice well that, just the great mediaeval artists looked far over their contemporary philosophical and artistic restrictions to the most general and intertemporal humanity. The expression on the faces of the productions of the great mediaeval painters and sculptors are most human; they represent the broadest gamut of the human nature without any restriction, so much that all the contemporary, denominational and cultural circumstances were only a quite accidental frame around their wonderful paintings, for instance, which represented the whole humanity and appeal to all nations, all times, and all religions in the same intimate language. We observe the same in the great masterpieces of all genial artists of the whole world. If we are quite unable to find out the sense or to be moved in the Chinese or other oriental artistic work, which seldom is the case, then it means indeed that these works are localized in their cultural conception and that they are, therefore, not great enough to be accepted as real important art. The real art sends forth its human sparks very distinctly beyond all cultural localization. If we therefore look carefully and without prejudices at the good masterpieces of the Chinese, Indian, Mohammetan and other kinds of art, we easily are able also to find out the human general sparks kindling the hearts of every human being: they are as well as the best Christian art, as the Roman, Greek and former styles united in this *inter-human and intertemporal genial divine competition,* other sparks, coming from the heaven, going to the human hearts being in nearest love and accordance with nature, and therefore true, strong and universal. Every style which bears the brand of national, historic, temporal or even psychodynamic rhythmic one-sided hyper-emphasis, as it is given in religious and denominational systems, is one-sided and partially wrong. The history of our psychological development produces continually all kinds of varieties in localization and accentuation of our psychodynamic disposition, but none has succeeded in being or at least in remaining at the perfect golden rule of the harmonious human balance of feelings and intellect. Catholicism was mostly one-sided on the idealistic side. It was the Greek Periclean age which perhaps showed indeed that highest human psychological equilibrium in art which could be obtained in humanity. But it degenerated also. We mark well that there was nothing distorted in the highest Greek age, there was nothing which appears to our feelings or understanding as strange or unnatural, because the top of the Greek art was indeed most universal and generally human, comprising all conceptions and tastes. Are we able to say so of the Catholic mediaeval and later art? The more monosymbolic the philosophical principles, the more peculiar its artistic expression, the more easy to learn and understand it for the contemporary average man, but the farther away from the culturally separated man who is not able and willing to accept it, because it is the one-sided expression of tenets and hypotheses which possibly are sharply antagonistic to his own. The absolute truth is always like a peaceful rainbow shining over all contemporary cultural quarrels and dissensions of humanity. The great art must be great enough to receive all contradictions and oppositions of the daily life and the historic humanity into the lap of his measureless loving truth: only the truth and the art which are great enough to comprehend all divergences of opinions and all modifications of individual tastes are worthy to be eternal and unforgettable.

There are indeed at every age even in spite of wrong ruling

principles men of this general genial size using, as the result of "good" is always "better" after all, the stylistic contemporary school as the ladder to their just universal and right validity and achievement. There was in the Christian middle ages many an artist of this description. Raphael Sanzio, Michelangelo, Albert Durrer, Leonardo da Vinci, Titian will live always not prevalantly because they belong to the Christian middle ages and painted Madonnas and Saints, but because they were able to develop their historic human cultural conceptions to general and universal psychological immortality. They understood to breathe into them the divine inspiration of all mankind; they succeeded in elevating their masterpieces to the most perfect human level where there is no more the question of their local culture, middle ages or Italian nationality, but of the psychological nucleus of the whole humanity in its integrity, as long as it was before and will follow afterwards in the current of all historic human future. These artists were so great not because of their exclusive style, but because of the human genial reconciliation of their ideas with the possible psychology of all human nature. There we are. Here is the precious stone, the undescribable joy and love of the real great art, in the universal peace, in the illimited ranges of its psychological truth and justice. These artists have gone so far with their eagle wings and eyes that they have overtaken all possible human contradictions, that they have opened so far their hearts and thoughts that every contradiction in historic egoism and economic covetousness becomes dumb, and that all human passions and wishes sleep peacefully, one beside the other, like lions and tigers hypnotized and reconciled all together by the most wonderful artistic atmosphere. Here you have at last the end of all quarrels and contradictions, here the learned scientific and stylistic schools are at last unable to continue their insidious struggles; all sheep are brought to the one fold of charming genial broadmindedness.

We cannot pretend to know anything thoroughly about the possible achievement of human greatness if we have not studied the very first artistic masterpieces of these mediaeval masters. They are most able to reveal to us the most hidden mysteries of our human nature; they can give the best information in regard to the deepest and highest questions of our natural disposition. They are able to put right in a smiling superiority all the historic errors, factions, wrongs, fanaticisms and quarrels, to which all ages and all nations as collectivities were subjected, and they show us the way and the means how to recover from these fatal psychological and technical insufficiencies, from these philosophical injustices and the national narrownesses, as the great and broad river of the centuries of human experience has produced them. There were always men and there will always be whose heads, intelligence, hearts and tastes avail themselves exactly of the stylistic and historic one-sidedness to climb up mountains of absolute superiority, and then they are no more the children of their time and of their artistic starting system, but much more the darlings and intimate friends of all systems together, of all creeds and styles because they are more just and valuable than all together, and comprehend the best elements of all. They are most beloved by the children of all times and systems, who are willing and able to grasp the imperishable truth and justice and are in danger to be captivated by other partially wrong principles in style and philosophy. They are delivered by them in their best personality, the truly great artists being the most thorough and everlasting relievers and deliverers of the whole human race, destroying all partial darkness, abolishing all limitations of contradictions and hatred, and spreading the light and the warmth of their genial superior achievement over all created nature.

What an indescribable reason for satisfaction and confidence in the future progress of humanity! May the totality again sink in error, one-sidedness and narrow egotistical systemization! May it be, that new organizations and other future economic institutions enslave the philosophical disposition of the whole humanity! But we are sure that there will rise again as in the former times, giant men of extraordinary size, of universal justice and strength, guiding the gifted and willing part of the worst philosophical prisoners and periods towards absolute truth, imperishable beauty and eternal psychological validity. The whole of the humanity will always be timid, lazy, cheatable, and prone to unmanly subjection. We cannot change so quickly this law as we would and perhaps it never can be. But the accumulation of all the genial outstanding work during the future times joined to the greatest of the past, will have more influence on the generality and supply after all the deciding suggestion for the will of a more just, stronger and more right psychological attitude of the future generation of the human race! The union of all genial men will at last overcome the habitual human cowardice. It will dissolve and destroy the intellectual and affective slavery of humanity which continually will have improved chances for joining more easily the realization of its idealistic destiny, and interspheric progress. Never despair! Nothing is so unlosable as the will for absolute truth, full general validity and highest right and beauty in human nature: it must and will obtain after all the best results of best human perfection.

What must be the specific *effect of the monosymbolic education* in respect to its sharpest monosensorial method? Its monodetermination gives to it undoubtedly strong urges for clear and strong decisions in work and the possibility not to lose its energy in loitering experiences. The sharp and clear monosymbolic determination has the consequence of the most pronounced localized concentration of the magnetic attraction of the individual lifeforce, produces, therefore, the utmost thoroughness, conclusiveness and magnetic affective hygiene of the mental life, but at the same time also anger, rudeness, thirst for pleasure and laziness. The extreme mono-symbolic individual psychology is liable in the highest measure to be subjected to all the consequences of the extreme actions and reactions as we already spoke about them.

The high ideal flight of the ideal monopunctual desire hovers over the detailed intellectual interest, lifts the individual soul in sharp speed over the real minute conscientiousness and produces so impatience, stupidity, laziness, lack of real sense and fanaticism. Exaggerated idealism finishes in materialism; the utmost artistic refinement leads to artistic luxury and pleasure-seeking degeneration. The main and most incurable faults of the extreme monosymbolism is the bold courage to have fixed the divinity with the most concentrated psychopupil, the individual retina is burned and blinded by this sharp look to God, roughened after the shortest use: the magnetic attraction, therefore, lost and the individual relapse is the consequence. The utmost desire falls, thus, back into the thorough exclusion of the monosymbolic desire. The love to God is converted into artistic materialism and aversion to the terminal ideal goal, the beginning conclusiveness and peace into endless desperation and restlessness.

The changes of the monosymbolic psychological nature are not only thorough, but also quick. The conversional curves are exceedingly outspoken, reaching high positive scores of triumphs, glory and success, highest levels in culture, art, morality and well-to-doness, but falling back also again, quickly and thoroughly to the deepest valleys of desperation, discouragement, luxury, artistic materialism and poverty.

The thriving ascent of the first monosymbolic stage is very promising, leading the individual life-force with strong magnetic wings up to the highest hills of ideal development: But its sentimental basis turns out after all to be rather subjective and very liable to be lost as soon as the exterior and magnetic conditions will have changed. The more intellectual method of the psychological development is less exposed to the magnetic moods of the circumstances or the favour of the individual subjective connection with the universe: less susceptible of losing the invitations of the attractive universe, because the objective help of the intellectual laws has created a more stolid and persistent reliability of individual ideal success. Monosymbolism mounts very high and quickly; it is bold, successful, brilliant and strong. But its victory very easily falls back to grievous shameful disasters and defeats, to the slavery and captivity of terrible discouragement and helpless degeneration. It is quite characteristic for the monosymbolic psychology to put all things at the very beginning at one stake, not to economize with its magnetic opportunities, but to claim from the very beginning the strongest and most comfortable universal attractive values for its service and to give to them also the total disposable force in continual affective idealistic shooting. The hugest gun-pieces and the most energetic explosible gunpowder of the symbolic soul have been used and worked from the first starting, reaching, therefore soon, and very much excellent results in comparison with other methods, but using and exhausting so much the energies that after a short time the volcano will be burned out. There is no more lava for new psychic productions, whilst the other system which first seems to be inferior, supplies for a long time best and most useful affective service for its natural psychic relations with the universe, with the real world, with the neighbor and for its own benefit.

The strong traditional and historic conservatism achieves the artistic skill which is accustomed more to look back than forwards. Here is the deepest root of the excellence of the traditional art. Art means elaborated habit on an exact cultural basis from which the genial artists, after all, develop into the general universe. The unparalleled artistic triumph of the Catholic church in art lies in the circumstance that it is continually in love with its historic origin and that it never diverted its eyes from the fixation of the cultural historic facts of its evangelical tales and their hero.

We ordinarily have not an idea how much this theoretic character of education has the deepest influence on the development of the psychology of the nations. May climate, race and other circumstances have played a most important role in the elaboration of the temperament and the mental dispositions of the nations: there is surely a great part of this formative action to be ascribed to the centenarian influence of denominational and philosophical principles taught and maintained in any country. If we in any modern show distinguish surprisedly the quite opposite psychology of the artistic Spanish dancing girl and the awkward English or American joker, this means a serious revelation of two opposite conceptions of culture. The first represents the artistic tradition with its perfect circular historic confinement as we have it in the halo of the saints, but not less, sit venia verbo, in the perfect enthusiastic circles of the dancing girl of the Latin country to which her cultural circles are saint and elevating art. This circular art is charming and perfect but narrow, sentimental but not intellectual. The English or American joker has nothing of this brilliant estheticism. But he has the stronger development of intellectual energy, he builds bridges between his historic supposition and his idealism and the real experimental life which he meets. He is digressing in the intellectual way, looking forwards; he is progressing and faithful to the universal will of the future enlargement of our psychology. This means he has not so much the artistic gift, because he does not look back and does not respect most the past in numberless habitual repetitions, but he is preferably scientific and intellectual, because his energy is directed towards the future and because he emphasizes this side of his vital possibilities. He has, therefore, not the practical skill of the circular methods which are given in, and connected to, the traditional practice of the historic monosymbolic view whose beloved child is the artistic style, but cares most about the connection of the present life with the future development of the experience with the possibility of our nature.

HUMOR and joke have the high task to join these distant points of the individual speculative will and subjective absolute idealism on one side, and of the objective experience and social and mechanic intercourse on the other side. There must be a continual attempt to reconcile these two opposite psychological polar forces, and it is the joking humour which tries to take up the difficult new creative task, first, with difficulties and awkwardness in jokes and afterwards with success and elegance in circular artistic performance. First with surprises and antagonistic representation which clash together in the laughter, but afterwards with more skill and after all, after ages, with refined elaboration which we then shall call artistic perfection. Humour is the first attempt to reconcile heart and intellect, feelings and experience of the progressive life. Humour is the most advanced runner of our intellect and of art at the same time. Humour and joke is the leader of the human psychological investigation, the predecessor of the scientific work and the artistic assimilation: it strives at the same time to be intellectual and sentimental and succeeds, because it relates to sharp notional precision, new ideas and definitions, and appeals as well to the heart soliciting its compassion, its accordance and affirmation. Humour and joke belong, therefore, preferably to the intellectual races who have not the chance to be so easily and deeply lost in theological speculations and absolute meditations, but have enough heart to have their feelings always in escorting vibrations.

There is a near relation between the humorous smile and the genial artist. The less outstanding artist persists in his circular methods and remains exactly fixed within its historic style: the very great artist instead has so much centrifugal energy in his artistic circles that his feelings are thrown out of his circular artistic considerations and send so extrasolar lightnings to the universe. The humorous smile establishes quite similar conditions: smiling means also putting relations between the absolute idealism and the formal intellectual realism. But whilst the great artist finds them from the historic platform of his artistic style which he overtakes, the smiling humor on the contrary starts from the last thriving buds of the individual experience and connects them with ideal universal values. The great art is dignified because it is accustomed to its elaborated garment, the joking humour is rather amusing because of its formalistic novelty. Joke and humor are trying on all kind of new intellectual dresses: the joker and humorist changes continually his exterior notional and sensorial apparel in an inexperienced way, in opposition to the usual habit and produces laughter and surprise in the same manner as we are amusingly excited by a man wearing a lady's hat and making other unexpected new combinations, in fashion and ideas. The great artist on the contrary has elaborated most carefully his dress with patience and time and is supported by custom and historic style: he avails himself of their authority to underline his personal genial ideal devotion. But there is no real art without a pronounced serene smile, and there is no real humor without an artistic touch. Both are great and have highest ideal and most accurate real relations as well. Smile and humor are wonderful magnetic accelerators in both from ideal to real and from real to ideal direction, facilitating the reach of ideal and real values, creating rich relations and comparisons between ideal and real life.

The psychological history of the collectiveness of the nations and ages is upon the whole the same as that of the individual within the same philosophical system. There is no absolute general rule or rather there are always exceptions to all sides. There are most learned and scientific monosymbolic people, individuals of the most tenacious moderation and most logical and real idealistic institutions grasping the very root of the human necessities and needs, and being most persistent. Human reality corrects always wrong principles in practice and no system is able to subject all traditional adherents to its philosophical influence. In every creed are innumerable people who are only nominal partakers of their tenets, inscribed into the lists because of birth and tradition and not having any psychic inclination or possibility of understanding or feeling for their so-called own creed. It is clear that in reality never the fervent imitator of the hero could rule, but on the contrary the working intellectual realist who in his dry calculation organizes the system, but has just not the religious disposition of the idealistic genius.

The *Monarchy* is the form of the governmental power corresponding most to the monosymbolic psychology. It means the monopunctual compression and culmination of the whole national psychological will in one head: the king is the representative authority and the ideal proxy of all highest real aspirations and political energies of a whole nation. The monosymbolic psychology is the crown and foundation of the extreme monarchic idea, both having in their monoemphasis sources of thorough efficacy, of excellent organization and unity, but also the same dangers of one-sidedness, coercion, superstition and reactive relapses. All the pronounced old and new absolutistic monarchies from Alexander the Great, the Roman emperors until the modern tsaric absolutism and the last German empire are typified by the signature of quick, mushroom-like surprising development, strong authoritative unity and organized fixation, most efficiently maintained, but they all were punished for their strong one-sidedness of conceptions in exaggerated monoauthoritative concentration, in the early and thorough intellectual relapses of their people in revolution, disorder and degeneration.

Let us not forget that the confidence in the future and active power of the humanity cannot consist in systems and unitarian organizations and still less in maintaining them unchanged until the return of a new golden age of fulfilment, but only in the loving psychological life which like a green growing tree spreads its branches, twigs and foliage over all earth, peeps into all centuries and touches all corners of the world, kindles with its flowering candles all human individual hearts, always independent and careless about theoretic restriction. God, love and heart can not be included into systems and tenets. It is the conviction, the active work, the intellectual discovery which gives the ruling dominion on the earth and the nation because they are the true thought and necessary continual confirmation of love, not only authorities which exclude the personal investigation. Every other kind of ruthless leading influence must be considered as coercion and oppression of humanity against their own will: it is a cunning handicap against the universal progression, a stubborn fixation of the human society in a historic antiquated prison which fetters freely developing ideas and produces after all, wars, revolutions and disorders.

May the strong conception of the extreme monosymbolic authority prove to be an unassailable wall saving whole nations from momentary disorder and social upheavals by its passive love for the past historic legislation, may it be that the stiff conservatism in elections saves very often the whole political situation from exaggerated and uncertain future developments: the absolutistic monosymbolism itself is no more able to be the gist of future developments, because our whole society and our whole present psychology has definitely escaped from its gone-by historic spell.

The French revolution was the signal of the new intellectual conception of the social life of today. It abolished the blind reverence for aristocracy, ancestry and monarchy. It gave back to the individual his personal intellectual freedom and reduced all power of social and political concentration to the modest measure of order as it is given in the republican conception of the political commonwealth. Our modern republican democracy, and constitutional monarchy are the practical fruit of the deliverance of the humanity from the monosymbolic psychology. The notions of monarchy, aristocracy, and historic artistic traditionalism are the unmistakable children of older conception: freedom of the individual, equality before the law, equality in the possibility of earning and possessing, individual votes are the children of the modern intellectual conception of the life as it was brought about by the Protestant and scientific methods and by the French revolution.

In der Beschränkung zeigt sich der Meister.
Goethe

ELEVENTH BOOK

I possess an old Viennese clock with a disproportionally long pendulum which would touch the underlying plane on which it swings and consequently would be arrested, if there were not put under an additional pedestal in form of a frame, in whose cutting out the pendulum keeps its free activity. But the cutting out of the underlying pedestal is just about so long as to permit the excursions of the pendulum in a comfortable way. The least displacement of the frame to the right side causes first striking knocks of the pendulum against the left wall of the cutting out, whilst the higher degree arrests the work of the pendulum almost instantaneously. The only way to have a good result in the action of the clock is to put under the footing platform accurately in the middle, so that it cannot be struck by any extreme excursion of the pendulum. Every kind of displacement to one or the other side turns out to be checking or stopping at all.

This disposition of the clock is a striking example of our psychological human nature. The energy of our life-force instigates the pendulum of our human action to swing also between two poles, one being the sentimental idealism and the opposite the intellectual reality. The pendulum of our human action has to work best in such a manner that it has to apportion its excursions half towards the ideal or sentimental and half towards the real or intellectual side. The underlying cutting-out of the additional platform corresponds to the total amount of the individual human life-force indicating the length of the active excursions of our nature towards ideal and real values and limiting on both sides our extreme human possibilities which altogether never exceed a certain maximum limit. The history of philosophies and religions is nothing else than the different attempts to conceive or to educate the human nature so as to displace the functional pedestal to one side or the other in order to give more weight and emphasis to the right idealistic or to the left intellectual possibilities or longings of the developing and active humanity.

The human nature is, however, less rigid than the pendulum of the clock. It does not stop instantly if it strikes against the frame of a limited wall, but on the contrary, its compensatory character comes out very distinctly in the circumstance that the restriction of the real actions produces more ideal excursions and that the shortcoming of the ideal values produces more real energy in extreme function. All these things are to be understood, of course, in the right limit and only up to a certain sense. The philosophical and religious systems of the past human history were delighted to see how much they succeeded in producing in this enlarging and restricting way, strong idealistic or realistic values; they were proud of their high successes in one direction forgetting, however, that they drew out all their one-sided success from the restriction of the opposite human disposition be it from the intellectual or sentimental one.

There are three serious things to be considered here: First, the will and the disposition of our nature which have to remain in a happy medium between intellectualism and idealism. Second, every one-sided extreme development of our nature, be it towards the ideal or real side, exhausts the opposite natural gift, exaggerated intellectualism, the idealism; and extreme idealism, the intellect. Third, the strong one-sidedness of our nature in the ideal or real direction, ruins after all, the possibility of our psychological work and energy. In spite of being very much more elastic and adaptable to artificial methods than the pendulum of the clock, our nature has, on the whole, in regard to its ideal and real disposition, the strikingly same character. Our nature longs also for the harmonious division of idealistic and realistic values and is seriously hurt by the possible one-sided attitude of our practical will and necessity comparable to the cutting out of the underlying pedestal of the clock. Our nature is less sensitive against the one-sided abuse than the pendulum of the clock, because it is living and therefore, adaptable; our living nature is more able to evade direct blows and to develop compensatorily in any other direction when one is barred to it, but the damage and the ruin, after all, if the one-sidedness lasted a long time, is so much more irreparable and definite than in the arrested clock.

It is most interesting to meditate how humanity behaved and behaves still in putting in the individual and historic pedestal of the human psychological clock. We have chiefly to distinguish two mighty methods both very opposite and extremely one-sided, which both have succeeded in bringing out the most remarkable results, according to their thorough one-sided emphasis of the human psychic activity. One school displaced the underlying pedestal of the human clock most possibly towards the right side, giving the largest freedom to the sentimental idealistic development, taking advantage on the vital adaptability of our psychological force in excluding the real and intellectual values very much, and producing thus according to the law of compensation the most possible sentimental and ideal concentration and efficacy. The love of enjoyment and the quite extraordinary appreciation of the ideal values gave to many centuries of this school the persuasion to have reached the highest degree of human development and the most perfect form of educational values and happiness in excluding the real-intellectual, and emphasizing the ideal-sentimental factor of our psychic nature. These people trusted so much to the absolute adaptability of our vital nature that they had no doubts about the biological boundaries of the good harmonious real-ideal nature, and abused the patient ductility and flexibility of our psychic forces so long and so much until it was clear and obvious in nervous diseases and the complete nervous breakdown of the degenerating humanity that this was the wrong system of efficient education, and that abused biology takes slow but the most terrible revenge on humanity.

The modern natural science frightened after the bad experiences of the former periods, displaced the pedestal of the human psychological clock to the other, the left side, intending to obstruct the terrible loss of human energy blowing out through the energetic extreme idealism and to give back to the real intellectual life its natural right and strength which were compensatorily taken away in former times in favour of the one-sided idealistic factor. The strong idealistic waste of earlier periods was so successful and thorough, that humanity thought it exceedingly necessary to check at any rate, this one-sided idealistic efflux of the human life-force and believed to reach this goal best by the displacement of the pedestal of the philosophical historic attitude of the humanity towards the extreme left. So the human psychological adaptability, owing to its high compensatory faculty, was enticed to develop extremely towards the intellectual and real direction, all previous idealistic energy being given to the extreme real function. But we see that this method is just the reverse of the previous one. It is one-sided as well, has as well the most pronounced desire of unrestricted accumulation of one kind of human values and excluding all others, and is, therefore, also very exposed to the biological abuse of the human gift.

All religions, all philosophies, all artistic and scientific conceptions and tendencies of the life are indeed different attitudes of the cutting out of the historic and individual human force in regard to its possible functional ideal and real excursions and relations. History exhibits all kinds and all degrees of displacement of the national and individual attitude of the frame of the psychological gift, from the happy medium of the harmonious real-ideal balance. Every religion, every style, every denomination and sect, has its special shade in this ideal-real apportionment of its life-force.

But let us stick to these two very pronounced examples, to the extreme symbolic religion and to the developed natural science which have their quite typical psychological basis. The first offends itself continually and most thoroughly at real and intellectual values which it excludes and neglects; the second, on the contrary, bangs its pendulum incessantly against the sentimental idealistic values of which it is most sensitive and averse to. Both directions are artificially hatched productions of the human culture exactly in the opposite direction, but both dangerous by their extreme though opposite one-sided natural disharmony, and by the consecutive biological impossibility and destruction of our psychological welfare.

Who could doubt about the great merits and successes of both these cultural methods? The old art illuminates until today the whole civilized Europe, it created great ideas, great people, the noblest theistic aspirations and historic cultural values. The same is to be said about the modern natural science. The whole humanity is enthusiastic about all the inventions, constructions, the riches and large distribution of the material goods among the people, and above all about the moderate satisfaction, sureness and order obtained by the intellectual scrutiny of the whole nature and all possible human realms.

But it is the question whether these methods are most convenient and most lasting for our human psychological dispositional conditions. It is a fact that the secret of the success lies in the limitation of the selected work; it is sure that our psychological nature has the tendency to the extremes, that it has most energy in following one of both complete idealism or perfect exclusive intellectualism, and there is no doubt that the middle attitude of our psychic gift between ideal and real values seems to be in a balance of *"lability"* most prone to fall down to the one or the other side. It is therefore, more easy to have the highest scores in the ideal or real values, whilst it is most ticklish, painful and disappointing or, in the real psychological sense, heroic to resist both of these extreme opportunities and to remain in perfect self-control, faithful to the will of the nature, in the harmonious middle stage between sentimental idealism and intellectual reality. Here lies the greatest heroic self-abnegation, here is the greatest victory of one's self; here is the masterpiece of the human psy-

chology, here is the harmonious attitude of the religious education, connecting art and science, heart and understanding in
charming reconciliation and giving back to our nature in this
way its biological functional balance which was so seriously lost
and hurt first by the old conceptions at the expense of the intellectualism and afterwards by the natural rationalistic science at
the expense of the ideal sentiments. This place is occupied and
maintained by the NEW CHURCH.

In order to understand it, it is necessary to understand the
developing current of the history and above all to be able to
judge the psychological basis of the old church and of the modern
natural science. We explained already their psychological signa-
tures, one being extremely idealistic, sentimental and subjective,
the other exclusively intellectual, realistic visible and objectively
multiple. The new church has undertaken the role to reconcile
and to attenuate these two extreme conceptions of the psychological life and to bind together into one good human system the mitigated contradictions of both. So the new church is the most
humane, most psychological and most right educational system of
the peculiar natural human disposition. It is the happy medium
and the golden rule between the old church and science. It has
the right attitude towards the biological will of our nature in
distributing our functions so that one half of our life-force is used
for the real and the other half for the ideal activity. There are,
of course, in the different sects very different shades of these intermediary reconciling attitudes and apportionments progressing
from the old church until the most exclusively intellectual natural
science, but it is characteristic for all of them that they indeed
lie between these two extremes and have, therefore, more concerning respect, perfect attitude and best relations towards the biological double-will of our nature.

It is chiefly the will of the present book to point out the
compromising character of the new psychology between the old
Christianity and the modern natural science. The new church
has, faithful to the human psychological disposition, accepted the
heroic and ungrateful task to represent the combined energy between will-power and intellect in the human mind, to elaborate
the most humane individual excluding the extreme idealism and
the extreme realism and giving to the human psychological clock,
as it were, so its harmonious functional equilibrium. This is indeed the most difficult work which humanity could accept, the
most apt one to lose its upright attitude because of the *"lability"*
of its character, exposed between two powerful magnetic energies

which both attract thoroughly in the opposite direction and try to subject the individual life-force to one or the other side in the first moment of the lacking individual self-possession. Is that so, then there is nothing more straining, but also more admirable than this peculiar psychological performance. This essential psychology supposes the most exacting struggle against both the pleasing ideal desires of the heart and the cutting criticism of the intellect. Giving way to both, one does not yield to one of them, but binds both antagonistic factors together in the hesitating unity of the good human harmony. Here is the greatest triumph of self-abnegation as it is given in the human meaning, here is the wonderful Golgotha of the human nature, but here is also the glorious quietness, the splendid resurrection and efficacy of the human individual in the middle of the extreme antagonistic energies which are keen to subject the individual to their one-sided power.

The new ecclesiastic psychology is, therefore, comparable to the most skillful rope dancer avoiding the scylla of the extreme idealism and the charybdis of the realism simultaneously, not rejecting entirely one of them and establishing in this antagonistic middle attitude the ideal of the human natural psychological destiny. If the new church was not so successful in artistic styles and paintings like the former times, we must indeed confess that according to the definition of art given in former places, it creates the most wonderful artistic masterpiece in the psychology of its adherents themselves, contriving a psychological method for them, where they have in the same harmonious actions the same amount of feelings and intelligence which is the most humane and most desirable state of our natural condition.

The modern church has recovered from the hermetic hypnosis of the mediaeval and first Christian theistic love. The literal fixation of the believing mind on any symbolic truth has gone. The most emblematic freedom replaces the former intellectual narrow-mindedness of the old church. The contradictions with the experimental intellectual life are carefully avoided: there exists a continual intellectual criticism which checks the exaggerated surrender of the human heart to its ideal and unreal sentiments in miracles and mysticism. But we have at the same time also the diminution of the monopunctual sharpness of the monogenial conception of monosymbolism and the psychopupilar concentration. The new church has recovered from the extreme psychopupilar monosensorialism. This is what is expressed by the word emblematic, everything in the spiritual life is taken as a simile or a parable for what is behind: All created world and all visible signs and intellectual ideas are nothing but comparisons and parables guiding us and insinuating to us the direction of truth and lasting eternal principles. "Alles Vergængliche ist nur ein Gleichnis."

So the new church is by its emblematic conceptions and by the lack of its monopunctual sharpness freer in its evangelical ideas and explanations. This religion has the most remarkable evolution in the psychological way, dealing with the most thorough and most important questions and development of the human psychology in a more carefully regulated, educational way. Let us for the proof of this emblematic transformation of older conceptions remember for this time two points: The Sign of the Cross and the Eucharist in the modern Protestant church. We scarcely remember to see crosses in the modern churches. It is most significant also that the minister blessing the people does not use the sign of the cross, but he extends only his hands to heaven in order to pull down from this elevated gracious realm the favor of the divinity to the believing community. The Protestant believer, excepting the most pronounced Anglican Catholics, do not use the sign of the *cross* as little. They altogether are afraid of the extreme sharp monopunctual determination of their feelings and of the minute symbolic emphasis, as it is given in the cutting point (+) of the sign of the cross, and by which the terminal realization of our monosymbolic aspirations is intellectually and materially fixed. The old church exhibits in this sign of the cross already most distinctly its methodical longing for monodetermination, for sharp exactitude and conclusiveness even in speaking about things which cannot be comprehended in all created universe. We at length spoke about this extreme symbolic method in order to express best the divinity in the opinion of the old mysticism. The cutting point of the cross means: urging to the point, or coming to a point. It excludes all sensorial world with the exception of one point, only with the intention to reach compensatorily so much surer the ideal intention. This is the idea of the humility and the simplicity of the heart of the old Christian conception. But it rests with the criticism of the believer and much more of the outsider to decide whether not just this attitude is the most pronounced pride of the human heart. The modern church has this conception; it thinks that we are not entitled to exclude our human intellectual attitude right to the monopunctual insignificance in favor of the ideal elevation and charm and avoids therefore most possibly the monosensorial localization of the intellectual size, as it is given in the bewitching sign of the cross most typically.

But the new church not only avoids the monopunctual determination, but also enlarges the literal evangelical expressions and dogmas in the sense of the real intellectuality. Is not everything in the new conception translatable from the miraculous idealism into the reasonable possibility which is able to stand intellectual criticism, and does not fade away like a faint mist before the sunshine of the intellectual life? Everything is put back here to more peripheric values, from the divine idealism of the gospel to the possible human conception corresponding to the human nature, not only in its sentimental side, but respecting and taking account also of the intellectual real disposition of our nature which may not be offended nor cheated. The emblematic possibility of the new conceptions is the helpful outlet for the affective action, when it has to pass through the critical door of the human intellectuality: it is the parole under which the sentimental life switches the crushing energy of the intellectual intolerance.

The very best example for this fact is the different conception of the Eucharist in both churches. The gospel says most clearly that the body of Christ is in the bread and his blood in the wine. The artless hypnosis of the old conception has the richest possibilities of supporting all its thoughts of the divine Eucharist with the text of the gospel. But it is the whole philosophical elaboration of this book in the new church and its absolute exaction and conviction never to come into contradiction with the real intellectuality which helps it to change the word: This is my body into the other: this means my body. The old church on the contrary is so anxious about its sentimental contents and psychological basis that it gives up rather its sensorial reality and the claim of the natural common sense than to doubt about the literal application of this word. There is scarcely anything more useless than religious quarrels. It is always the question in these cases of the first and deepest philosophical principles which must be carefully and seriously built up from the first foundation, and the religious conception and tenets are then only the roof of that building. If we are able to read a very deep general educational meaning out of this saying in the psychological sense, then we are free of the necessity of literal conception, because we have caught the root of the doctrine. It is most typical of the new conception to have been awakened to this more philosophical and intellectual critical attitude towards the Christian sayings.

If we remember the drawing of our psychological sun-year we had at the solstitial turning point the starting dominion of the sentimental force of mankind; at the equinoctial point it converts instantly to the prevalence of the intellectual force which becomes guiding and competent. This point of the Christian psychological sun-year is reached in the middle ages at the birth of the new church. This point of history may be considered also as the fulfillment of the time or the complete emptiness of it, if we prefer, to take it from this side. At the starting moment of the new church the psychological Christian humanity was shaken from the deep sleep of sentimental love with its Christian monogenial hero, having enjoyed enough during the pre-mediaeval centuries in the most criticless revelling dream of idealism, and there was in the fulfillment of this time at last the hour of awakening from this passive one-sided sentimental state. The birth of the new church is the moment, when this physiological conversion from the sentimental to the intellectual proud dominion is achieved, corresponding to the equinoctial point of the sun-year. The human psychological collectiveness has in the same manner, as the physiological body, times to rest and times to work, days of intellectual sunshine and nights of imaginative celestial dreams. The most divine sleeps must, however, be interrupted by the morning of the clear sunshine, and the most successful days have as well to sink into the night of the sentimental sleep, because the functional body has to do away with its fatigue in a healthy alternating rest. As we have this in the individual, we have it in everything, all life is a waving alternation between motion and resting recreation, we may look wherever we will. So the new church is the dawn of the intellectual day following the dreamy night of the previous religious sentimentality. This dream was indeed great, divine and charming, adorned with sparkling stars and singing angels, throwing all human faculties over the narrow boundaries of time, space and causality and fixing the human desire at the topmost peak of the celestial mountains of eternal happiness and endless pleasure. But it was a dream: it excluded the reality. It was merely sentimental, not standing the sharp thought of criticism. It was an imaginative sweet slumber, where all human faculties were effused in the abyss of the divine embracement and where no account of the real surroundings was at all obtainable nor able to interfere between the close love between the sentimental humanity and their human monosymbolic divine affection. But this state could not remain so for always. He who has slept enough must awaken, he after all rubs his eyes, runs away from his couch, leaves and forgets his dreams in the clear light of the radiant morning and uses his recomforted limbs for useful real work.

The rising new church was the wonderful dawn where the mediaeval humanity began to awaken from their sentimental ideal happiness. The stiff limbs moved then first and the giant of the religious human psychological collectiveness rubbed his eyes and was reminded, by the surprising intellectual sunrise falling on them with its sunbeams, that the previous state was a sentimental dream and that the intellectual reality of the human life was different. The mediaeval humanity began to find out the difference between dream and reality, between human possibility in the world and in the imagination, between the literal conception of the gospel and the religious doctrine and its emblematic translation in the sense of the critical intellectuality. The new time means the transition from the predominant feelings to the prevalent understanding; the intellectual faculty, neglected and offended before without any respect, is now in the clear light of the intellectual day acknowledged and honoured and appealed to as to the most thorough source of truth, right and reliability. Here lies the thorough difference of the new conception in comparison with the old church. The new system does not any more stand for any intellectual impossibilities and contradictions. As it is willing not to leave entirely, however, the original ground of its dogmatic historic supposition, it makes for all these cases the most liberal use of its emblematic elasticity in explanation, as we see it in the Eucharist, for instance.

This is also the reason for the quite pronounced predilection for the *Old Testament* of the new church. The old Jewish descriptions allow much more the most large emblematic conceptions than the New Testament, we can put into them almost all arbitrary philosophical ideas we wish, supposed that we retain the monotheistic basis and we can escape most easily from any non-congruency of the conceptions of their old historic tenets. Their opinions are so broad and often so unclear in the removed allusions to lost historic facts that we have much facility to change the original ideas of the Holy writers almost without being aware, and yet being comparable in this fact of modification. We are so far away from the mentality of the old Jewish history that the lack of its historic and cultural thorough knowledge is the most fruitful source of emblematic explanation.

The new church mitigated the symbolic sharpness of the central monogenial expression of the old church always and everywhere, whilst it, on the other hand, augmented and emphasized it at the real intellectual periphery. This means nothing else than the arbitrary conduction of the psychological draft and magnetic energy from the divinity towards the real humanity and objectivity, whilst the old church did the contrary emphasizing the magnetic direction from the multiple peripheric objectivity and visibility towards the monopunctual central idealism. These two points explain almost the whole difference of the new psychodynamic apparel, doctrine, behaviour, and the indifference to the older conceptions. The new church is thoroughly averse, on one hand, to the extreme sharpness of the old monopunctual ideal, monosensorial determination, whilst it just, on the other hand, emphasizes the congruency of the religious teachings with the peripheric logical and intellectual real life and its laws. It strives towards extreme emblematic freedom, it claims the right of poetical comparison and comparable transcription and translation, always with the intention to avoid the two most sensitive educational point of the religious doctrine, the mono-genial, mono-sensorial determination of the ideal and the contradiction of the ideal with the real world. There are, therefore, two opposite dangers to both of which the old church succumbed: the ideal monodetermination which obstructs the further scientific intellectual development of the idea of God fixed in the philosophical history which means divine idolization in the symbolic intellectual sign, and second, the exclusion of the real world, whose sensorial perception is liable to be reduced ad absurdum by the bluffing overpowering authority of the sentimental mono-symbolism. The new church has undertaken the great duty and task in the historic development to do away with both of these errors.

It is so easy to see these different tendencies of the new psychological agencies in opposition to the old psychological methods.

The strong monosensorialism of the old church is abolished by the careful dropping of too detailed rubbing in of the historic mono-genial origin. It is enough for the new believer to believe in the divinity of Christ in the most general way, to recognize and worship in the Christian system the revelation of the most divine sentiments without indulging in the monopunctual concentration. We have, therefore, in theory and practice, smooth methods, avoiding of sharp monosensorial determinations. The abolition of the sign of the cross, the iconoclasm itself, the removal of the statues and pictures of the divine hero and the saints, the extinction of the burning candles, the reduction of the service to the auditive symbolism, the predilection for the organ, all are proofs for the mitigation of the monogenial symbolism of the doctrine. On the other hand, we recognize in the notional predilection of its argumentation and organization, in the intellectual method of the sermon and in the highly poetical, but nevertheless highly intellectual use of the hymns, the need of this denomination to educate people to critic thinking, to compare the exactness and the ideas of religion with the notion of intellectual criticism, to distinguish poetry from truth and to put both into a possible emblematic relation, calling truth and reality which is intellectual and poetry and heaven which is ideal and sentimental.

The new church as a whole is indeed awakened from the heavy sentimental dream of the old time. It is still, however, up to a certain degree, in love with the old monogenial sweetness of the former historic times, but acknowledges the intellectual part of our psychology and is anxious to bind together both in the real human golden mediocrity. There are sects of the new church, for instance, the Anglican Catholicism and the English High Church, which cling closely until to-day to the old Catholic traditions, which have never really awakened entirely from the ideal affection of the old church or fell back again to the deeper surrender to its mystic methods. We see it distinctly in the use of the burning lights, of the cross, of the stereotypical prayer and of the rich use of the ecclesiastical coats and garments in the *English High Church*. We have there still the sentimental fascination of the old church as we met it before, exclusion of the critical intelligence and perfect sentimental surrender of the heart to the monogenial hero. How could any church performing under the roofs of the Westminster Abbey escape the old spell of the ancient ideas? What human system would be able to overcry the importance of the innumerable Gothic architectural characteristics of the wonderful statues most eloquent of the middle ages and of the mystic stained glass which all together speak the most intimate monogenial and most sentimental language of the old conception? Though it may be almost improbable to the outsider, may it not be considered as true that the mystic and monosymbolic suggestion of the Westminster Abbey in London has to be assumed as guilty for the tenacious conservative reservedness of the English High Church against the modern intellectual development? These people are still in a social hypnosis under the most fervent and continual impression of the old methods and ages whose most vivid expression the Westminster Abbey is. The same mechanic monopunctual tendencies rule the large walls and spaces there as five hundred years ago, the same artful twilight excludes the sharp intellectuality in this church, the innumerable statues smile thoughtfully down to the believers and the same pictures of the saints throw their glaring magic lights from the stained windows as of yore. What voice but the most sentimental could sound in a church like this, what other service and rites than the old mystic service could fit these surroundings and what other smell than the imaginative frankincense could blend with the musty odor of this centenarian reverent halls? We have indeed in connection with this English mother church still the old methods in optic symbolism and intellectual exclusion: the richest accumulation in all kinds of mystic symbolism and the most intimate indulging in the divine sentimental affection. This denomination is so near to the old church that we scarcely are able to make any difference between them both. The adherents of these sects, may they be in England, in Canada or Australia, are still furnished with the full artistic optic splendour of the old church, the believers gather still to-day in the middle of the radiant figures of the old Apostles looking from all sides in wonderful stained glass on the believers, the old subdued mystic songs are still quivering through the halls and the picture of Christ looks even to-day in fascinating sharp concentrated reality from the altar or from the most exposed point of the church on the humble pray-ers.

Let us observe the service, the methods and the building of a more modern sect of the new church, of the *Presbyterian church,* for instance, in order to prove in a clearer way the statements made about the thorough intellectual awakening of the new church in opposition to the old system. The mysticism of this service is almost entirely restricted to the auditive symbolism. The common songs, the spontaneous prayer, the intellectual sermon as the centre of the service, the numerous hymns and psalms, the artistic musical recitations of the choir and the organ compose indeed practically the whole service. The optic symbolic helps are almost entirely excluded. The suggestion of the presence of a whole crowd in itself is always most efficient and inflicts on every ecclesiastic gathering much sentimental energy. But all the different suggestive helps are almost entirely neglected. We have in opposition to the old church the optic sensorial suggestion almost entirely lost in this new service. Why have we this fact and why has the natural artistic psychodynamic sensorial power received almost all suggestive authority instead?

This point represents one of the most thorough and most interesting educational discussions in all psychology. So often we spoke about it that for to-day we only will point out that the supposition for this fact is the bluffing immediate coercion exercised by the *optic* sensorial impression, and the frightening rapture of the individual sentiments which are carried away by the energetic helps of the optic symbols without any logical obstacles or gradual meditation. The optic symbolism is an absolutely irresistible suggestive power which overthrows the individual self-determination and reaches its goal in the surest, but roughest, way. If we ought to deal with children with the finest and most delicate means of psychology, then we must also first think what happens to the fine organization of children after having been exposed all the years of their youth to rough optic educational methods, we must, in addition, care about the best psychodynamic educational method of the grown-up people as well, and we must state in general that there is nothing more sensitive, more susceptible and more liable to destruction than the incredibly refined cobweb of the human psychological order so easily hurt by wrong educational methods.

PROTESTANTISM cannot be identified with the old church or with the modern science. It is to be considered to be an effort of the Christian idea to meet the modern scientific and realistic mind with more adequate means, on one side, and to set apart definitely religious matter from thinking scientific methods, on the other hand. Artistic symbolic intellectuality is typical of Catholicism. Sensorial and intellectual are not the same thing in the case of the Catholic mysticism, because artificial and artistic sensorialism has supplanted the natural logic which is maintained better in Protestantism. Therefore, we have more sensorial realism in Catholicism, though more mystic, but more natural intellectuality in Protestantism, though less sensorial. Is Protestantism more intellectual or less? Its circumstances are more natural, its service less artistic, its surroundings more intellectual, but its methods less clear and intellectually more idealistic.

We see, therefore, the optic impressions of the *visual* sensorial power in the new churches very much reduced. There are no more burning candles, paintings, statues, rich architectural decorations or splendid colors or materials in the dresses of the people of the choir and the minister, but all these things, in so far as they are used in a diverging way of the practical life, have rather mostly the intention to exclude than to emphasize the ordinary optic impressions on the believer. So the coats, the collars and caps of the people of the choir and the minister have the distinct intention to remove the individual every-day atmosphere in bestowing the general uniformal seriousness in the black color on the members, working so as suggestion of the crowd, emphasizing the cohesion of these members of the choir among themselves and their connection with, and impression on, the whole believing community.

The *style* and the *architecture* as they represent themselves in these churches are very interesting and significant. The Protestant idea is not able to do away entirely with the old mediaeval architectural formulas chiefly with the *Gothic* style, which is by it still to-day dearly beloved and to which it looks back as to the highest culminating point of a charming wonderful dream indulged in in former times and quivering still to-day through the awakened intellectual consciousness like the most charming poetical remembrance of a grown-up person of the happy youth past away long since. We find, therefore, almost everywhere in this religious denomination the old Gothic elements of ornamental decoration, but they are, corresponding to the thoroughly changed character of the philosophy of the time, only collections of allusions with which tables, organs, choir, chairs and windows are decorated. They are mostly carved in fair modern oak, which is polished or varnished, and impresses the visitor by its unassuming natural grain. But there is no more any question about the inspiration of the Gothic style. These elements have only and purely the most modest decorative effect, creating some precious poetical historic background behind the intellectual conceptions of the religion of to-day or spreading out, as it were, a charming flowery rug of tradition under the feet of the modern religious stylish lady. But this tradition is indeed not desired, not accepted and not received seriously and really, the perfect estrangement of the old Gothic elements from the Gothic style proves it most eloquently. The old monogenial and monosymbolic hyperemphasis has definitely gone in our times and with it the circular and perpendicular formative psychological one-sidedness. There is no more the old traditional energetic mono-symbolical kernel in the middle of our modern artistic actions, and there is, therefore, no more the same binding, elaborating, milling and refining unitarian principle which created the old Christian styles and melted all their elements in the most intimate furnace of their concentrative mono-affectation and mono-determination. The de-centralization of the monogenial fundamental symbolic principle of the religions of to-day is the cause of the stylistic unhingement of the artistic performances of the present time.

The stained glass of the windows of these churches as well has still circular elements, variegated rosettes and colored arches reminding of the old historic middle ages, but also only in a very loose allusion far away from the contemporary conception. All the historic artistic developing background is taken into consideration, but not in a ruling way, but only in a subdued charming atmosphere behind the interesting fact of the present possessing philo-

sophical tenets which are quite different and extremely distant
from that more primitive sentimentalism of the old mediaeval ages.

There is one optic wonderful symbol which is put in the middle
of the modern Christian community which is entitled to rule and to
command as well to-day as in the old church, as it was used in the
temples of Eleusis, Carthage, Rome and Jerusalem, in universal
and intertemporal undiscussed acknowledgement, it is a nosegay of
flowers, which is always put on the table before the pulpit of the
preacher and throws its charming lights everywhere. The flowers
are the true natural children of the heaven and the heralds of the
human happiness, they invite and suggest the human mind in their
genuine natural artlessness to the same concentrative monopunctual
charm as the forsaken mystic optic art of the former Christian
times tried to do it in an artificial way. What a wonderful idea
to put in the middle of the worshipping community just this natural
charming symbolic help of our souls and to give to these highest
natural means their right place in the hearts of the humanity. It
is so natural to use these children of the free common nature for
the universal service, they at least as the impartial productions of
the mother earth are entitled to be our optic idealistic help, even
if we are most anxious to exclude all possible kinds of other optic
symbolism in opposition to the old optic polypragmasy. Here the
discussion about the good effect of the optic symbol stops, since
nobody is able to accuse the most unassuming subtility of the
floral beauty of bluffing optic impression. The optic artist can only
receive from the character of the flower an object lesson for the
necessary qualities of his best work expressing psychological tendencies. We spoke at length about the monoconcentrative idealis-
ing power of the flower according to their circular shape, colored
gradation and variation and central emphasis; they are the most
exemplary classic and unmistakable optic suggestors to idealism
and pleasure.

Why does the new church prefer so much the *auditive* sensorial
psychodynamic means? Why emphasizes it with so much predilection the notional procedures in order to suggest the believer to its
ideal goals? There is no doubt that the new church gratifies by
far most the auditive method of symbolic education. It decided at
the cradle of its rising to exclude almost entirely the optic psycho-
mechanic method which seemed hurtful to the free self-determination of the psychological human functions, produced artistic idolatry and made the individual most prone to miraculous symbolic
bluffability. The replacement of all these old optic means of the
former time, of burning candles, artistic statues and paintings,

crosses, ritual sacraments and sacramentals, ceremonious motions and garments, by the auditive means of the new church has the foundation that the sensorial importunity of the auditive means is much less. The auditive sensorial impression does not exercise the same tyrannical power on our thinking faculties as the optic sense. The auditive suggestion moves our hearts in a most gentle way permitting in a certain amount our individual free judgment and criticism, inducing ourselves to harmonize our thinking meditations with the waves of the *musical* vibration. It does not fix sharply and exactly in monopunctual and monolinear signs our ideal feelings as the optic impressions do, and we have, therefore, no danger of material captivity of our idealism, of luxuriant localization of our most universal spaceless sentiments which are always thoroughly disgraced and estranged to their goal as soon as they are fixed in material artistic affectation. In this optic way the terminal result is artistic materialism, a state of unworthy relapse from the idealistic goals to the visible restriction which checks our hearts from developing further without end in unison with the universal progress. The auditive means does permit this necessary eternal progressing flow of the insatiable river of our ideal feelings. It does not stop the need of our nature to develop to always new and always keener intellectual formulations of the theistic imagination; there is no boundary, no limit of exhaustion, in the musical urges, of divine and ideal representations and imaginations. This is the great asset of the auditive symbolism, not to captivate our imagination for a moment in any intellectual artistic expression, but to help us to run away incessantly and always most gloriously over all material and categoric obstacles and to empty our hearts without any restriction in the unfathomable abyss of the farthest divine possibilities. No monodetermination, no affective stagnation, no formative hesitation and repetition is, on the whole and essentially, given in the musical and auditive performance, all human feelings are in a continual magnificent and brilliant flow from and through the universal spaces of ideal magnetic development, escaping every material and formative captivity forever. Here lies the triumph of the auditive method; it is indeed able to deliver our hearts from the categoric fetters of time, space and causality and to uplift our celestial desires as a perfect quivering fluidum and without any obstacle to the beauty of the most distant sparkling stars of our eternal desires and ideal longings.

So the auditive or musical sensorial power has overreached by far the optic method in the educational and ethical sense. May it be less energetic, its advantage lies exactly in this difference: it does not roughen the heart and does not create anger and narrow-mindedness, but creates patience and perserverance, the most precious fruits of the best religious realization in the meek light as the religious hero's best humanity was depicted in the gospel. So the Protestant flight from the optic symbolism means the flight from the danger of materialization, of the intellectual narrowmindedness, of the affective historic stagnation and sterilization of the human mind.

We understand so very well that the new church clings to the musical sensorial performance, so much more that it is especially the *human voice* and the *organ* which are the favorite means of its artistic musical expressions in the church. Both have the similar peculiarity not to have the intense sensorial sharpness of the sound as we have it, for instance, in the violin quite inapt to be used in the churches for this reason, but they have that tender softness in their musical character which is able not only to attract more intimately our feelings, but not to fix them in sharp impressions on our memory and to hurl them over their formative confinement towards the abyss of eternal values. Here lies the wonderful value of the human voice and the organ. We forget so easily their intellectual formative expression: we are here least in danger to fix and to limit our heart on formative elements: no, they came and passed away like wonderful birds with golden wings from and to the heaven, and we have nothing of them but the ideal longing which they have caused in our hearts. We forget the musical character of the human voice or organ so easily, we cling therefore not to them, but we have that ideal thing which they only would impart to us, the love for the universal development and the endless progress of every good desire in all humanity. So in the auditive means we have the good side of the art without being infected by the luxuriant fixation, sterilization and materialization of the optic symbolism and its dangers, when it is put too much into the service of the serious religious service, when it loses its emblematic character and claims to be the proper and definite expression of theistic and idealistic values.

CINEMATOGRAPHY is the roughest relapse to what the rising Protesantism would avoid, exaggeration of the use of the *optical* sensorial education: it is distinctly dogmatizing in the educational artistic sense, because the exclusive visual influence is much too exact, therefore, much too one-sided intellectual, creating too much steady belief in systematic formulations and conclusive results. It is interesting that just in those countries, where the idea of the optic artistic influence is banished prevalently from the religious educational systems, this exclusively optic method rushed in through another door of the house, after having been thrown out through the first. One thinks of the proverb: Chassez nature et elle revient au galop. The cinema is, of course, much worse in its educational element than ten thousand of pre-iconoclastic mediaeval statues. It makes the ideas of the spectators much too set, whilst they rightly ought to be educated to thinking hesitation and readiness to future enlargement of their conceptions and sentiments which can happen only with careful extenuation of the emphasis of the sensorial influences, as it is done much better with the auditive sense. The mediaeval religious renaissance obviously went too far in excluding the optic educational means, and now we have, like a revenge of that educational onesidedness this hideous and tasteless monster, the moving pictures, ruining ruthlessly all tender delicacy by their awkward and bluffing sensorial impressions.

It is understandable that in quite a theoretical meditation the accompaniment of the music was invented for the moving pictures. The use of the pipe-organ in the cinemas of North American theatres is a great surprise for the stranger. There is indeed a clever theoretical basis to this custom, since the indistinct sensorial influence of the organ has the intention to scatter the optic precision of the play. May this instinct or idea of the inventor of the use of the organ for moving pictures be deep and clever in the theoretical sense, it is too bold practically and, therefore, unfitting; for cinematic and organ productions are matching very badly indeed, because their artistic nature and education are too far from each other, one being too precise and intellectual and the other too indistinct and imaginative. You cannot combine easily the highest imaginative heaven and the most elevated religious enthusiasm with the consideration of the sharpest visual features of a table or of a sofa. Combinations like this hurt the tasteful human heart. Thus the introduction of the organ into the movie houses is to be considered as an awkward step in art and of a misleading and only provisory character until something better will replace the whole state of artistic lack one day, as we hope. A greater development will bring back to more refined and tasteful artistic methods. The abuse of the vox humana of the organ is rather frightening than elevating under these circumstances and cannot console by any means over the fact of a completely mistaken conception of art. There are, of course, plenty of new problems and new trials of solution of human taste and artistic expressions in every direction in this continent, but almost all unlucky until to-day. It seems that *art* has to have, above all, a background of tradition and old memories as a sure basis on which it has to build. Art is probably always a historic dreamer and only able to be a great prophet of the future if it is leaning back to the old sure foundation of traditional security from which the intellectual formula of the new inspiration has to be drawn. Only experience and inheritance may be the great mother of important vision.

As the new church avoids the intellectual monodetermining sharpness in the terminal ideal symbolism, loosening and respectfully and reservedly hesitating in the formulation of the highest and holiest theistic things, so it, on the contrary, is most careful to build bridges between the religious values and the intellectual criticism of the peripheric life. The Eucharistic emblematic conception is a clear proof that the first and most deciding principle of the modern idea is not to be in any contradiction with the possibility of the real intellectual conceptions of our life and psychology. It is frightened to discover any contradictions between intellect and theistic sentiments and is rather willing to modify in emblematic concessions the original tenor of any sayings of Christ and the Bible than to risk the contradictions with the reasonable criticism of any intelligent objection. The strong emphasis of the hymns, of the lecture of the scripture and the central importance of the sermon prove how much Protestantism cares about the conscious intellectual consent of the individual mind to the religious psychological development. Protestantism puts exceedingly much stress on the *notional* symbolism in opposition to the old church, quite in congruency with the intellectual inclinations of our time. It is never tired to try to bring out the reconciliation chiefly between the thinking logical faculty and the *symbolic* miraculous mysticism of the Christian doctrine. There is scarcely any more difficult task: but avoiding this fundamental attempt would mean suicide of any religious system in our intellectual time. The intellectual analysis of the religious doctrine above all in the sermon, and the attempt to make the religious tenets acceptable to the thinking individual in the hymns and the scripture point out that the direction of the idealistic conception and of the intellectual logical thinking are not intended to be in contradiction, but to complete and explain each other, that intellectual work, symbolism and religious mysticism have the same goal the truth, approached from a different angle, that compressed symbols, like energetic bomb-shells, may be resolved into intellectual logical thoughts and that they accelerate and quicken much more our hearts towards long ideal distances which could not be reached so easily or not at all by the toiling innumerable steps of exclusive thinking work alone. The symbols are the crutches or the wings of our thinking insufficiency, the bridges leading comfortably over the gapes of our ignorance and tiredness, the guiding signals of our dim power of knowledge towards terminal ideal values. The religious poetry, the local symbolic representations in mysticism are still all such quickening urges of the human hearts towards high idealism to which the slow step of our insufficient knowledge and energy has not yet entirely, until to-day, progressed in a thinking, clear logical progression.

It is most surprising and interesting to compare the *divine* of the new church with the priest of the old church. As the latter is much more theatrical, the optic performer and the gracious keyholder of the believing community, so we recognize in the Protestant minister rather more the intellectual leader and interpreter of the Christian doctrine. He has less terminal claim of divine authority, he escapes for this reason more the spoiling dangers of affective stagnation, he is on the average the more cultured person explaining his dogmas to a cultured audience in a most possible intellectual way, as it is indispensable under the signature of the modern general criticism. The modern divine has therefore much more intimate intellectual contact with the individual thinking power than the priest of the old church, he cares about all possible objections and cuts them in advance by the intellectual scrutation and disposition of his doctrines. But he, up to a certain degree, remains also the concentrator, the authoritative symbol, the gracious mediator and the optic performer of the believing community. He also is posted on the central pulpit where all looks of the believers are directed and concentrated. He is, though in a small degree, distinguished from his parishioners by his white collar and his black coat, which remind of the mystic way of the old church to create and emphasise ecclesiastic authorities and hierarchic gradations. He also invites people by his personal charm and kindness to gather their prayers in his individual will. The last point is, perhaps, even, of course, more pronounced than in the old church. The priest has an unassailable position in the strong organisatory order of his system, his sacrosanct personality is well protected against every malevolence by his indispensable functional sharpness and ideal dignity which exclude meditation and criticism, the account of his personal value, whilst the Protestant preacher is much more liable to be exposed to the criticism of his intellectual audience. He has a good means to make a virtue of his more intellectual position in using the spontaneous prayer. In this manner he urges people to melt their most intimate ideal feelings with his personal taste, views and conceptions of the life, of his personal uplifting tendencies, and so he is very able to express his personal charm and to captivate the hearts of the believers in the most individual way, in his intellectual and sentimental faculties.

The task of the modern preacher is so more difficult than that of the priest in so far that he has to make up the less concentrating energy of the auditive sensorial psychodynamic means in comparison to the optic ones used by the old church. He has, in addition, no tactile, no gustative and no olfactorial psychodynamic helps at his disposal, or in the least degree; he is by the nature of his system most scarce in the use of the strong symbolic miraculism and avoids more the sharp monogenial symbolic representation. All these means together have the result not only of a necessary, but also happy addition of his idealistic personal effort which he has to bring out in order to further the believing mind, nevertheless, toward the best goals of divine values in strong efficacy.

We see therefore instantly, and are surprised by this fact, that in the new church minister and believers are *straining and toiling in the ideal direction.* The Catholic ideal development in the church is comparable to a comfortable energetic psychodynamic motor-car, whilst the Protestant religious action advances on foot, step by step. Happy pedestrians! They are serious, most attentive and devoted to their religious task, they use the methods of the utmost silence, of bowing their heads and of stooping their bodies, of closing their eyes and of modulating in a pious soft way their voices, all helps to ideal perfection. We find this much less in the old church. One of the chief reasons for this fact is this, that the old ideal performance in the churches is so much more insured by all kinds of sensorial monodetermination, by the strongest monogenial conception, by the richest use of symbolic and miraculous mysticism, so that the believer is not in danger to escape the total amount of this moving and enrapturing religious psychodynamic influence. May this be acknowledged partly as an advantage for people of a hard intelligence and an inferior ideal gift, but we meditated and know already how much this overfeeding with optic symbols, the rich use of miraculous mysticism and the hyperemphasis of the divine monoconcentration are most dangerous because of spoiling, producing anger, laziness, frivolousness and sterilizing materialization.

But the modern minister and all his believers have to strain much more their energy in order to reach in their churches the same degree of ideal magnetic discharge which is easily and comfortably received by every witness of any old artistic service in the countries of old culture. We see, therefore, as things in the world always incline too much to this development, that the artistic musical and highly trained ritual old services, attract very much all kinds of people to their theatrical, easy and uplifting idealism. The old service is thus received by the outsider as an extraordinary artistic enjoyment and has in this emblematic conception the best effect, whilst the continual and proper and real conception of the ritual and sacramental part of the old artistic service for the believer may be harmful because of its danger of superstition, intellectual limitation and sterilization of the inconfinable divinity. The modern service claims to educate with the exaction of the good will and strong collaboration of every attendant, it is the service of the manly personal decision and responsibility, where everybody has to collaborate seriously, if he will have any fruit, but where he also has his personal freedom and dignity to decide in an intellectual way whether he will accept the message of the gospel or not. The new believer is indeed treated as a grown-up person, he takes up much responsibility, he knows why and what he does in a higher degree, but he therefore has more satisfaction and lasting human convictions.

The strongly pronounced and numerous opportunities for catching the attention of the believer are intentionally abolished in the new church. It systematizes much less the personal mind, subjugates it less to its exterior formulas and receives in this fact much more individual movability and resourcefulness of the believer for the future eventualities of the life, for which religion has to be an educator and not a checking or baffling factor. Most independence, self-decision and individual freedom in the method is the best guarantee for a clever useful and adaptable future of the believer who will be essentially confronted always with all kinds of future psychological constellations where he has to pass through to make his way, to concentrate his attentions in an unexpected way. He can do this only, if he was not bound too deeply into one performing method of gathering and concentrating his attention. Therefore the strong old method of concentration with the countless easy symbolic monosensorial means of all kinds is most objectionable, because it makes the way too easy and prepares the spoiled and comfortable individual in this manner for future lack of adaptability of strenuous work, changing self-confidence and fortitude in the fatal distresses of the life.

A certain education for attention is of course the highest thing in religion. We have chiefly to expect this fact of every religion. But we know already that religious education, like everything else, has to go through opposite dangers and has anxiously to avoid the scylla of making the way toward idealism too easy as the charybdis of making it inaccessable at all, by the total lack of helping means. The modern church may have this right medium brought out by long careful experience and by the lessons of serious historic losses of the former historic humanity.

That also other religions, not only the old Christianity, incline to strong monodeterminations in order to catch the total amount of

the individual energy and concentrated will, can be seen easily by the prescriptions under which the *Mohammetan* performs h i s prayer. Prayer in itself means essentially attention. But it is interesting how

Conventional Drawing of the Moham-medan Prayer Rug.

much the material or intellectual education of the Mohammetan believer is pronounced on behalf of his idealism. The typical pray-rug, which the Mohammetan has always with him, has a conventional drawing of a temple which on one side exhibits a gradual diminution and ends there in a point with a star. The believer directs his rug with the help of his small compass towards Mecca so that the pointed part of the drawing of the temple looks in that direction, kneels then down on the rug looking in the same direction and bows his head so much that it touches with the forehead this pointed runner. Then he prays. He directs therefore his magnetic power and sentiments not only intentionally, but also exteriorly and mechanically in its bodily attitude towards the great collective point of the Mohammetan psychology which is Mecca. This is the mighty general focus which receives the feelings and the will of all praying people of that religion. What power of religious suggestion of the crowd must be compressed in this intentionally ennobled and hallowed place, the concentrated light-field from which like through a mighty national genial funnel the religious and sentimental energy of countless tribes and people are thrown in common energy and parallel acceleration towards the ideal universe! It is most significant and exceedingly interesting that this monodetermining institution in the Mohammetan prayer is driven so far forcing and determining even the exterior position of the praying individual in the most anxious way. In this point it has even beaten Catholicism, every Christian thinking the use of a compass in this case being superfluous.

If we thus look back to the *history of the new church* and to its raising causes, in spite of abusing usurpers of the secularized goods, we must admit in the psychological sense, that it meant the most energetic flight of the mediaeval humanity from the exaggerated idealistic monosymbolism and its luxurious relapse. The rising church of the mediaeval Europe had become aware of the immediate danger of being hurt by the idealistic magnetic whirlpool in its luxuriant stagnation. It was automatic that the new church had no greater care, according to its rising intellectually possessing character than to escape the magnetic Scylla of the extreme idealism by which one part of the mediaeval humanity was in immediate danger to be entirely absorbed at the expense of the reality of the objective visible world, whilst the other was pushed back to luxury and pleasure. It of course did not think of the Charybdis in the moment when it struggled to avoid the terrible Scylla; the extreme difficulty to escape the snares and the magnetic smile of the idealistic siren engaged at this time all energy of the reformers mind, as it is indicated in the denominational label of "Protestantism," so much and so exclusively that the rising danger of intellectual exaggeration was not at all a question of mentionable value. The fundamental psychological character was from the beginning to protest in intellectual criticism against the dangerous monosymbolic idealism of the old church. Protestantism is the expression of the energetic recoiling flight of the mediaeval humanity from the monosymbolic sentimental monopoly of the former time, in it we have the sophistication of the experiences of the old nations, frightened by the weird look of the sparkling monosymbolic star beckoning fatally from the sentimental firmament of the imaginative sky and attracting most powerfully the human hearts: the former humanity trusted to these charms thoroughly without end: the monosymbolic idealistic organization appealed exceedingly to the pre-mediaeval humanity, the sparkling spell of its brilliant light shot the arrows of deepest divine loves into the human psychic nature like a bewitching siren from whose look humanity could not go away any more until it was by experience in a state of wrongness, inhumanity and one-sidedness. They forgot to veil their faces looking at God.

To go away from this greatest magnetic power of the monosymbolic hypnosis was indeed not an easy task and it is quite significant for the new conception until today that it is most afraid and averse to all old terminology, philosophy and intercourse. The fear of the monogenial sentimentalism is the most characteristic psychological signature of the new church. The different sects represent from the highest to the lowest church only different historic shades and stages in the development of this recoiling motion from the monosymbolic sentimental happiness toward the free intellectual and scientific character of the present time. Without knowing the history of the different sects of the new church, we may say with probability of being right, that its oldest sects, as the Anglican church, must as a rule be the sentimental and that the youngest conceptions of the new idea are the most intellectual and realistic systems.

The recoiling motion of the new church went always from the monosymbolic scylla back, afraid of its magnetic spell, doing everything to escape its power and to build up its own more humane and harmonious psychological realistic character. On the whole, it succeeded in escaping the old sentimental spell, but at last just today owing to the continual effort in this direction and to the hyperemphasis and hyper-attention of this old historic scylla it is in danger to succeed even too much in falling from the snares of the previous idealistic whirlpool into those of the exclusively intellectual charybdis, the modern scientific intellectual one-sidedness. As we see it is the most thorough and equitable, essential task of religion to help the psycho-dynamic progress of the human mind, to accelerate, to quicken and instigate the progressing affective discharge from realism towards idealism, to eliminate sentimental stagnations, to move the vital psychic energy of the human soul or rather to give to it the best urges to utilize in the best way, with the best emphasis and the right rhythm in its forces through all the stages from peripheric reality until most elevated terminating idealism. If science strives to eliminate all darkness of the imaginative night, if the intellectuality looks to disperse all *ignorance* and *sentiments,* which are almost the same thing, with its clear sunlight and to melt them like the sunshine in the spring melts the snow, there is of course a wonderful progress, there are indescribable precious advantages for the humanity freed from the fetters of superstition, of silly sham and useless hopes and fears which means a terrible lavish of energy. But on the other hand, we may not forget that ignorance and sentimentality are indeed the gunpowder of the psychological life, so much so that we must create them even in an artificial way if they were in danger to disappear. The world and society seem, however, to have a large stock of ignorance still today, if we look to the millions of criticless people we do not doubt about, but there is no question that the decreasing ignorance of today not only creates much more reasonable sureness of the life, gives moderate happiness and individual right to most numerous people, but does also away with the most successful psychodynamic possibilities and the genial habits of the individual and of the society as well. Ignorance is the mighty aspirator of the psychological faculties of the mind, the motherground and the background of art, of the religious monosymbolism as the compression of all our deepest ignorance. Ignorance and sentiments have not only disadvantages, but also the most important advantage to move our psychic fluid magnetism energetically from the spread out realism toward the concentrated idealism, to create the necessary magnetic fall from the realism to idealism and to impart so to the human discharging affective necessity the right physiological and biological conditions. The perfect abolition of ignorance would mean the death of the human soul and the arrest of the universe. All progress is going from a more imperfect state to a more perfect one, from a more implicit to a more explicit, from a more simple to a more complicated nature of actions and manifestations and vice versa. The perfect abolition or only the prevalent withdrawal of ignorance would create serious disturbances in the psychorhythmic dynamic performances.

How much the intellectual one-sidedness has grown today we can in a reflected way easily see in the character of the *sexual* education which is intimated upon the modern humanity by the last fashions in the extreme short skirts, the sleeveless gowns and the low necks of the ladies of today. The modern fashion reveals a very great psychological shortsightedness in the sexual, not in the moral sense, by the introduction of this modern mode. The sexual desire vanishes under the perfect open visibility of the feminine limbs. The psychodynamic energy in the sexual sense goes therefore away, when there is no more space for the longing imagination which can only be developed and excited in respect to hidden values. The modern fashion has not to be considered as demoralizing, but too much moralizing the people. The charm of the sexual desire is killed by the exhibition of the exposed body. There is no doubt that the strong intellectual tendency in sexuality is in serious danger for the future proliferation of the human race. Ignorance, and mystery must be, as well in religion as in sexuality: the perfect revealment of the desired objects analyzes the longing into knowledge and causes a completely paralyzed standstill of every intensive burning desire. Here is perhaps the most serious root of the cultural degeneration. It is very interesting how much the religious and sexual psychology are parallel, as we shall see later on, more closely. Is not the modern intellectualism and natural science and the modern fashion comparable, and have we not in the old mystic mediaeval church and in its enveloping garments a perfect congruency?

We remember that just this enormous night of ignorance was the pride of the old middle ages. It was the ground which created the most wonderful psycho-dynamic fall of the magnetic senti- mental river of the human mind and had accordingly most out- standing results in energy and genial productivity, producing the most marvellous artistic works and sprouting the highest magnifi- cent steeples from earth to heaven. But we remember also on the other side that just this fact created by its roughening influence, in the psychological sense, the greatest luxury, comfortable lazi- ness and danger, lack of patience and working sense of the mediae- val world, ending at last with the result that the intellectualiza- tion in the new movement became urgent, necessary and in time triumphant. But it is true, Protestantism has to see how it goes out from the initiated intellectualization of the humanity. It was right to drive away the exaggerated sentimental spell endangering the economic and educational life of the nation, but now it has to see that it does not skip over to the other extreme in creating ex- clusive intellectual systems with no creative nor developing power, but merely of descriptive and explaining character. The chief thing in the universe and in the individual soul is indeed always the magnetic energy and the psychodynamic progress and their regulation. There is a serious danger of creative stagnation of the human individual and society, as soon as we put the stress of the psychological balance on the intellectual scale of the ideal-real twin team of our peculiar nature. Protestantism did the best things at its rising period, it delivered the whole European civili- zation from greatest one-sided psychic deformations and dishar- monious dangers. But now it has to see how it avoids the con- trary sterilizing danger, the stiffening total intellectualization of the modern humanity, which of course would lose all pleasure, all interest and all urges for energetic courage and development in the perfect intellectual analysis of the mystic possibilities. The new church has also painted a devil on the wall in opposing the historic sentimental church in the most thorough way, it must be careful not to call him down from the wall. It has set free un- known powerful demoniac forces in calling in the unrestricted supremacy of the intellectualism against the previous crushing sen- timentalism of the monogenial old church and has now to look that the intended salvation of the shaken disharmonious psychologi- cal humanity does not turn out to be the initiation of their fall to the other side. May the apprentice of the spell who opened by his bewitching parole the water-tap, not have forgotten the other parole which is able to close the running river of the intellectual water: otherwise humanity will be drowned in the abundance of that precious fluid which was so necessary and deemed most useful and agreeable at the beginning of its entering activity.

It is the essential role of the new church to be the excellent strong and *clever mediator* between the old sentimental system and the modern intellectual science, if it will fulfill and preserve its outstanding psychological role in the history of mankind. Even though it is understandable in regard to the historic effort and strain to escape the old magnetic spell that there is a prejudice and a deep inherited aversion against the old symbolic church, on the part of the new church, and though every new approach could be easily a relapse into the historic whirlpool of the former sentimental spell, in spite of all this it is indeed for the new church, if it will not fall entirely under the power of the modern scientific intellectualism, no more the time to be in the former strong opposition and exaggerated attention in regard to the old dangers. The habitual aversion surrendered the modern church perhaps too much to the arbitrariness of the modern natural science.

Science and *religion* are, however, quite different notions, having different philosophical foundations, different tasks and duties which in both cases are very difficult, exacting and which cannot be fulfilled without the right psychological basis. If science destroys and hates ignorance and sentiments, it does only its essential duty, but if religion is willing to add to its pride of faith also the pride of knowledge, then it commits suicide; it is most essential for the religion to have and to provide always the necessary amount of mystic "ignorance" in order to have a moving power on the human heart which becomes absolutely dry and stiff under the exclusive influence of the intellectual sunshine. They both are essentially opposite in methods and suppositions, but the medium between the old mystic arch type of religion and the perfect enlightenment of modern science is that humane and harmonious happy religion which corresponds to the best human disposition and is represented in the most perfect way today in the moderate new church. It must be maintained at any rate under the powerful struggles against both extreme sides, against the charming side of the attracting sentimental love of the former times, and against the sharp intellectual arrows of the modern scientific criticism.

The new church is the greatest humane real psychological hero worth while, of the present time, great by the truth of its modesty, great by the most precious inner value of its harmony, great by its necessary patience and the universal human interest of its serene moderation. If he who serves is the master, if self-control and modesty are great things in the psychological and real life, then the new church of today has indeed received a great mission and greatest expectation. In humility, in sacrifice and unassuming character it is surpassed by the old church which at its best, is the idealistic Cinderella of humanity going at a bee-line to the cross and the mocking derision of its hero: in clear science, real intellectual argumentation and objective possession and investigation it is superseded by the modern science which has confiscated the greatest real success and the sharpest intellectual display in inventions and technicalities. But it possesses the wonderful middle stage of the harmonious union of both good human qualities of feelings and intelligence melted together in the most superior psychological unity corresponding to the will and the intention of the perfect human nature. Whosoever read the works of Herder and of all the innumerable most outstanding Protestant writers, must have an idea of the greatness of the harmonious peace and the insurpassable humanity coming out from the right balance between the two scales of human feelings and intellect, of human heart and reason, combining, helping and arresting each other always in best self-respect, in a perfect milieu of atmosphere, as it becomes best the human nature.

This leading idea of careful *mediocrity and moderation* between these two alleged powers is the most appropriate, the main and deepest duty of the good modern Christian conception. There are continually made mistakes towards both sides of the extremes. According to the starting historic role of the new church generally the danger is greater to neglect the sentiments and to hypercultivate the intelligence today (speaking in the meaning of the necessary psychological role of any religious systematic exactions).

The *Prohibition,* as used on the North American continent, seems to be a very apt instance for the exaggerating intellectualism in the tendencies of the modern church. It seems wrong to induce the people to create a law like this, to discard any slightest possibility of pharmakological psychodynamic helps at all. Howsoever is afraid of this means because of not knowing it or because of knowing it too well, does not stand it or is impaired by it in his health, may leave it or not touch the smallest atom of alcohol. The criminal abuser may be investigated, put in better living conditions, if possible, or transferred to the asylum in heavy cases: but the absolute general Prohibition against the will of 100,000 has to be considered as the cunning trick of the hyper-intellectual will of our present psychological culture which is in a most one-sided manner busy against all kinds of ignorance, of sentimental bomb-shells, of enthusiastic possibilities and against pleasure, and which overdoes so the good old instinct of opposing intellect and enlightenment to the old ideal luxuriance, to the thirst for pleasure and genial monodetermination.

But this point, as we said already, may be considered as over-ripe at the present day. There is no more danger of hyper-ideal-isation in the world of to-day, but much more of hyperintellectual-isation. This fact has indeed the most pronounced consequences to be careful in the further psychological development of the modern society, to drive back the ship of the Christian nations from the threatening intellectual whirlpool which is exceedingly approached and to steer more to the middle attitude between idealism and reality.

It is most significant for the views and the atmosphere of our time, to see, how convincingly *rationalistic societies* deal to-day with theological questions. Rational conceptions and theological questions are indeed a contradiction in themselves, two quite incomparable values, because every religion draws its psychological existence and its magnetic energy from the authoritative well of the naive, extra-intellectual or sentimental genuine feelings of the human nature. I happened to witness some of these rationalistic assemblies on January 1927, in Toronto, where I was surprised by the intellectual clearness and correctness of the statements dealing with the theistic conceptions of the Old Testament. There was no intellectual escape possible. The most people, however, were not much interested in the intellectual accuracy of these statements, but they were much more amused and flattered by the original new light and the different atmosphere applied to these old histories heard always only from one side and in a preconceived scholastic tenor.

These men if punished are indeed convinced to be the martyrs and heroes of their people: and in a certain sense they are, because they are the exponents of the specific psychological intellectual attitude of their contemporaries. They impossibly could be punished for their intelligent scrutation, they on the contrary should be acknowledged for it, but they are wrong in so far that they neglect all possible questionmarks of the life and of the universe, that they are too self-sure in a matter where indeed yet to-day more is hidden and doubtful than clear and intelligible. Absolute intellectual claim at once with complete exclusion of the senti-

mental reservedness means nothing else than to claim that everything which we do not understand at this moment, does not exist
at all, to restrict our critical basis to the narrow limit of our subjective measure. The wrong of these people does not exist in
their intellectual errors which may be very few in their statements, but in the restricted circumferance of their universal survey
and in the superestimation of their intelligence. They were and
are, on the contrary, encouraged by their sharp intellect and the
good results within their narrow frame to go on in their courageous researches.

What is *decency?* It is the sentimental attenuation of any intellectual statement, modifying, subduing and opposing its enlargement and generalisation being in limiting contradiction with the
intellectual truth. Wrong and right are relative notions, they are
to be considered from the general human common-sense, from the
most humane stand-point, formed and welded together from the
thinking reason and the feeling heart, giving way to decency, courage, meditation, hesitation, but also to the heroic love for truth
and progress. The perfectly rationalistic conception of the religious tenets is impossible, it is objectionable and perhaps even pun-
ishable (many people like to punish) because of the distortion
of the necessary religious psychology brought about by the exclusive intellectual methods. The exclusively rationalistic thinker may
be so clever and intellectual as he may be, but he also is one-sided,
lacking sufficient general human universality, having discarded entirely the sentimental part of the human heart in favor of the compensatory thinking intellect, which state must be deemed to be
just as wrong as the extreme sentimentalism of the old mystic
religions, only in the opposite sense. Errors are not only possible in
the logical contradictions, but as well in narrow-minded deficiency
in overlooking the harmonious necessary broadness of the human
nature. We can make the most correct logical conclusions and the
most lucid argumentations, but they may be quite wrong because
their foundation was not broad enough. As well we may admit
that there can be visible errors in many logical argumentations
and the results are nevertheless more correct than in the former case
because the starting basis is more solid. With all this I might
state that any clear contradiction with the serious intellectual
thinking can not be accepted, however, at any means, but if we
have an insufficient human basis for our meditations, then we can
seem to be right and are in fact wrong because the basis of our
supposition is not stolid and large enough.

Thus decency is the warning finger which reminds us of the

imperfection of our knowledge, which pushes our intellectual investigation back to the careful stage of reverent patience and anxious re-meditation, which threatens with the fact that we yet today indeed do not know most things of the universe. Surely we to-day are many steps further than Socrates who at the end of his life told his surroundings that he at least knew now that he knew nothing, but it is a fact, and even our *advantageous necessity,* in the sense of the religion, that we have still great mountains, huge amounts of magnetic *ignorance* and mysticism, because they are the only helps for our rhythmic psychodynamic instigation, attracting our scrutating energy and our affective love. The lack of decency means the lack of respect for this fact. Ignorance is not only the absolutely deepest and most universal source of all evil and unhappiness and the barrier standing alone before every success, but it is also an absolute universal biologocal psychodynamic necessity. The most ignorant man does least discover the horrible gapes of lacking human knowledge, he is therefore most proud of his science and intelligence, since he is not able or not willing to dig further and deeper into the universal realities and possibilities. The one-sided rationalistic conception of world and religion is therefore quite wrong. Intellectual rationalism is duty and glory in the scientific world, but the direct application of this principle in the most thorough way to the character of religious tenets is quite objectionable, and reveals the insufficient knowledge of the philosophical character, the psychological conditions and necessities of any religious system. The root of the right of existence of every religion is psychic hygiene; its value is determined by the fact how much it is able to convey the necessary psychodynamic energy to all individuals of a nation and how much it really is accepted by the people. Not the philosophical contents and the degree of truth fix the practical main value of any religion, but perhaps rather how much it is able to hint to veiled truth in a mystic way and to insinuate at the same time a great longing and an exceeding respect for the unknown truth and knowledge. The artificial tension of the soul between ignorance and highest knowledge is the specific task and duty of every religion. Though this point is deciding for its psychohygienic value, we recall all the objections and dangers being in intimate connection with this role of the religion as we pointed out often. The deepest principal of religion is the education of the humanity towards the discharging ideal facility of the heart in joy and divine satisfaction, but it needs chiefly one thing in order to reach this goal, it is the magnetic force of the imaginative ignorance, if we will use this term of the language of the scientific expression. Perfect negligence of this psychological fact excludes the reliability of any scientific criticism, the purely scientific statement has only a partly validity for the religious psychology. Ignorance is in the same sense the root of the religious performance as the fall of the river for its motion. Religion ceases instantly to exist as soon as the imaginative sentimental ignorance is analyzed entirely in a scientific manner. The negative pole of the divine psychodynamic progress is then destroyed, the fall of the affective river taken away so that religion has then lost its right of existence.

It is, therefore, quite wrong to wonder at the superstitious conceptions and beliefs of former people and ages and to think how they could believe impossible things like these. The standpoint of every religion does not chiefly consist in its reasonable value, but in that that it excludes successfully the reality and intellectuality and performs so its energetic purpose leading from the real towards the ideal world. Not intellectualism but the magnetic psychodynamic energy is the goal of religion. It is here the question how much any dogmas may help the psychodynamic biological necessity of the progression from the reality to the idealism, how much it is able to produce hope and affective progression. If and as long as religion fulfills this task it does its essential duty. The other educational effects round about as we know are the reasons, why we have to be careful about the production of the degree of this religious artistic energy or magnetism. But the roughest superstition fulfills its essential religious purpose, provided that it reaches the development of the theistic enthusiastic energy.

The *Modern Science* is the consequence of the fact that the new church has opened the intellectual water-tap over which it had almost lost the power to dispose, if we will maintain the simile of the magic apprentice of Goethe. The new church was glad to have found it in order to stop the damaging sentimental one-sidedness of the old church, in its proud awakening from the deep ideal hypnosis: there was an extreme glory in this starting intellectual digression from the old time, a psychological battle of tremendous power, skill, energy, dexterity and countless great laurels on either side. But the signature of continual aversion, persistent principal rejection and protestation against the old church, only because of the old historic enmity, is today to be considered as antiquated and even dangerous.

How much this psychology pro and con is in a strongly flowing motion today, may be recognized by reading in newspapers to-day the first religious press notices with which we meet. They show that there are always in Protestantism opposite extreme tendencies partly going back to the old church and partly declining it at all. We quote a small letter clipped from a paper of to-day: To the Editor of the Star. Sir, Dr. H. Emerson Fosdick, a well known Baptist, suggests the establishment of a confessional in Protestant churches, so that people would feel free to unburden their hearts to a clergyman. There would, of course, be no pretense at granting absolution, and attendance would not be compulsory. With the possible proviso that the deaconess should take the place of a clergyman where women are concerned, I think the idea is a splendid one. Just to tell another human being one's troubles is often a tremendous relief, especially when a sympathetic hearing is given, and I think it would give our clergymen a broader and more tolerant outlook upon humankind if they were to listen to the troubles of our fellowmen.

"We avoid the confessional because it is considered Roman Catholic, but without the forgiveness of sin, and without the objectionable feature of compulsion, it could be made a thoroughly Protestant institution. Similarly, we fail to revere Mary as we ought because the Roman Catholics pray to her, and we avoid the cross as a symbol *because* the Roman Catholics use it. They even covered it over with a poppy on our Toronto cenotaph. What folly. Protestant."

The new church of today has much more important problems to resolve than to foster the hermetic seclusion from the old church. On the whole it strove to fulfill its role best in ignoring the old church, in not mentioning its great significance of which the leaders are yet today well aware. This method is perhaps the best of escaping the old sentimental spell. But nevertheless, things have developed today so far between the sentimental and intellectual pole of history that it is no more right to consider the whole solution of all our psychological problems in the rejection of the old symbolic ideas and institutions. We today are so far that this negative part of the new development is no more at all the chief contents of the modern psychological task. The historic antagonizing development went after all on the contrary to that point that this open or hidden hyperemphasis of the old historic attitude turns out to be the best way for the new church to fall over the margin of the most terrible opposite intellectual abyss, because it went backward and did not think of the dangerous possibilities behind in the opposite threatening intellectual abyss. It is scarcely any more the time today to fear the sentimental abyss from which the modern humanity has thoroughly escaped, but it is high time to remember on the contrary the danger which lingers from the opposite extremely intellectual conception. Has the new church perhaps forgotten the parole to stop the flowing river of the intellectual water which it initiated by opening the scientific era? Has the intellectual science not become entirely the ruling power of our age, fettering and crushing the determining psychological right of the new church? The strength of the modern intellectual science has today doubtless the greatest power and dominion on the earth and in the society, the domineering position of the new church has gone over to this new extremely intellectual one-sidedness. This is the exaggerated re-action against the former mediaeval sentimentality: but moreover, science is also greater than humanity, exceeding their harmonious possibilities towards the intellectual direction, it is also a dynamic spell in its enormous disproportion to the human faculties and is therefore also disastrous by its genial one-sidedness as former methods were. It creates, therefore, again a psychological catastrophe by its colossal inundation of the human psychology. It is the opening of a water-tap contrary in its effect to the former sentimental inundation of the cultural world, taking away exactly by its compensatory power the former sentimental excess, as water extinguishes the fire or as a chemical reaction transforms any element into a quite different chemical unity.

But this chemical satiation is finished now, it is now no more the time to exhibit this intellectual capability which was in the former times so excellent and wholesome for the whole culture. But it is on the contrary now the time for the new church to prove how moderate and wise it can be in the use of its harmonizing role received between realism and idealism. Only now starts the real masterpiece of the new religious psychological and educational action. Now the sophistication of the world from the old love is ripened enough to permit to look back from the embittered struggle towards the old enemy, to investigate thoroughly again his ideas and to be careful in judging him, just, not revengeful, but thoroughly independent and not giving up one iota of the new acquisitions of the past modern history. Must humanity always be without any possibility of keeping measure, must we indeed fall always from one extreme to the other? Is only this life and strength and glory, to commit continually greatest mistakes in the affective psychology and not to have ever anything more than self-deception, error and blind hypnosis, exaggerated love and unjust hatred? I fear it is true that humanity can indeed essentially, in the eddies of its collective psychological actions have no measure nor moderation.

As soon as humanity attains perfect harmonious quietness, as soon as there are no more serious contradictions and frictions in the psychological history, we are fulfilled and die. We naturally strive always towards peace, unity, love and reconciliation, but these are impossible things in the healthy life of any individual, of any community or nation. Our individual destiny is finished or our earthly star extinguished as soon as we have reached this peace. Life is struggle and progress, death is absence of the energetic waving struggle of perfection and evolution.

Moderation and harmony is every time the middle state of any system at the top of its blossom time, where the pendulum of the psychological fate and destiny runs through the middle parts of the fatal human poles of extreme idealism and extreme intellectualism. This was the case at the time of old Greece, Rome, of the early Catholicism with its numerous national political development: always we have an ascent and a top, then an irrevocable descent. Will the new church have the same fate? Or has it already lost its high mission and strength by the submissive attitude accepted towards the modern science which puts as a real intellectual tyrant its foot on the noble neck of this most harmonious human conception?

How much Protestantism in England is aware of its psychological necessities to be careful in the one-sided intellectual development and in leaving the old sentimental relations yet more, is easily recognizable by the almost anxious considerations from certain parts of the religious leaders in London to re-establish old customs and conceptions. So we read just now in a paper of the 9th of February, 1927: "Romeward revisions of the Prayer Book. The proposals are worse than was feared. There is not only a re-introduction of the mass vestments, but complete silence is observed as to the unlawfulness of incense, sacring bells, etc. There is also a prayer which implies that the communion is a sacrifice offered to God for the sins of the living and dead and that all who receive the bread and wine, by virtue of receiving it, are partakers of the body and blood of Christ." This is a strong proof that there must be thorough tendencies in Protestantism which are willing to change the critical aversion to Catholicism into benevolence. It is surely quite just and up-to-date to extenuate the sharp draft carrying too energetically away from the old views which is dangerous because of the opposite pole, but to retire so much, as here indicated, to the previous starting point of the rightly more intellectual new church would be giving up the distinctions and preferences which it has gained in its struggle against the old conceptions. This behaviour is very dangerous and it is only understandable from the standpoint that the modern church must have the insight to have too much indulged in the intellectual scientific development, and that it is now no more able to retain this kind of intellectual "degeneration" of humanity without using the most thorough antidotes as they are, of course, chiefly given in the old prescriptions and psychological methods. These thorough relapses in the psychodynamic methods prove how much there must be the conviction in certain circles that the moderation and the reasonable harmonious mitigation which was the glory and the educational pride of the new church, has been lost in favor of the strong intellectual one-sidedness.

There was always the habit on earth to expel the devil with Belzebub. In the history the earliest Englishman called the Saxons to help them in their interior quarrels. They came, slew and enslaved them all and possessed themselves of the island for all future history. The same we have it exactly in other historic parts and times of the world. But the same we have it also in the history of psychology. The devil of the exaggerated sentimental one-sidedness, sit venio a verbo, is he not only expelled with the Belzebub of the extreme intellectualism? But the latter as he became too strong and truculent, is intended to be thrown out again by the help of the first extreme. There is a continual battle between the two poles, science and religious mysticism, they are two extremes, between which the pendulum of the historic human life swings, and which alternate in their transient importance, always one superseding and eliminating the other one.

The relations between the old, the new church and the modern science are, therefore, very interesting. If we put the three on one line and compare them under different points of view we find surprising results: if we consider them with the question, how much heart they have, we have to state that the old church has a universal heart, the new church a human heart and science no heart at all. If we take them on the contrary under the aspect of the intellectual reason, we may say that the old church has the shrunk reason of its monopoint and its relations, the new church the most human reasons and the science the universal reason. Let us impress this truth on our memory in the following table:

Heart:

The Old Church   The New Church   Science

Reason:

The Old Church   The New Church   Science

Education:

| The Old Church | The New Church | Science |
| Sentimental | Humane | Intellectual |

Possession:

The Old Church   The New Church   Science

We know therefore that we have to expect in every highly *mystic religion* the sentimental love, joy, strong idealism, enthusiasm and *art* which is however, already the first link to the material relapse. So charming and beautiful as art is, or just because of this, in the educational sense it was rightly deemed by the new church to be exceedingly dangerous because of the pleasure-seeking artistic materialism resulting from it, fixing the individual to the material intellectual form and causing so artistic luxuriance, degeneraton and loss of vivid terminal ideal longings. These are the educational dangers tied up with the warm heart of the mystic symbolism. But there are pronounced assets in the strong heart, compassion, sympathy, feelings for the neighbor and the vivid interest in the affective conditions of the world. In the intellectual sense the mystic religion produces the genius who looks, owing to his extreme sensitiveness through the material walls and things and sees to the ground of the causes by his thorough intuition. Mystic religion creates the hero who so easily finishes in disappointment and desperation. The genius is ignorant in the detailed sense of the word, he is impractical and perishes easily owing to his inadaptability and to the intellectual autocracy of his genial outlook on everything. He is essentially alone and is in danger to starve in the proud condition of his splendid solitariness.

In the economic sense the mystic view creates the gambler, the daring audacity which puts all its power at one stake, receives the greatest fortunes at one time, but loses as well everything by carelessness, lack of real patience and localized consideration: the thorough mystically religious man despises the visible world, has his interests and energy at quite different places and is therefore very much prone to lose material power or not to gain it at all. The stability of many religious fortunes comes from the lack of the need of the mystic spiritualized person to work, to develop and to change the living immanent power of the material values, but the easy loss of these fortunes in the hand of the individual is the consequence of the strong gullibility of this psychological type. The beggar and the Bohemian are the typical economic types of the great idealism losing and creating always new systematic intellectual formulas, the stable ancestral fortunes and feudal accumulations of material goods are instead the productions of the lazy historic crystallization of idealism which has received its traditional sterilization and fixation in any stable intellectual creed.

The *modern scientific intellectuality* proffers a quite different psychological aspect. As the science has shrunk in the mystic religion to a mere monosymbolic interest in order that everything indifferently may be the basis of the deepest meditations, and has no real possibility of display, so in science the affection of the heart shrinks to the mere symbolic good will which is not developable at all owing to the exhausting overweight of the intellectual strain. If the deeper feelings of humanity are the most precious flowers and the kindly will of helping all people is the noblest distinction of man, then we indeed cannot expect that the scientific people have solved this problem. But on the other hand, we must acknowledge that perhaps the least good will of the intellectual scientific man overvalues the whole good heart of the mystic type, because the latter does not know the way how to help in spite of his good will, whilst the first knows exceedingly well the best resources how to further in the practical best manner his neighbor. So we have the experience that the intellectual countries have almost no beggars and no starving people because the intellectual organization has done away with this mystic handicap of the former awkward and helpless time which did not succeed in spite of the best will to give the right kind of intellectual real support.

But the point of view of the perfect intellectualization of the modern world has serious disadvantages for the educational psychology of the humanity because of its lack of psychic energy and affective pleasure, because of its hyperemphasis of the material side of the life and because of its under-estimation of the mature psychic needs of humanity. The perfect mechanization of the psychic life is of course also wrong: it obstructs also the human psychic development, it sterilizes and stiffens the outlook of our future universal development and it creates frivolous desires in subordinate values. If today people think they are only respectable, if they are the happy possessors of a motor car, that it is possible to create or destroy a social standing by a sum of money, this is of course not the meaning and the expression of the true intellectual leaders of science, but it is nevertheless, in closest connection with the perfect intellectualization of the modern time. This state of mind is the consequence of the attempt of intellectualization in the broad masses which never had the opportunity to study thoroughly but which have picked up enough of the intellectual creed that they hyper-estimate everything which is countable, visible and objective, and lose so easily all appreciation for higher mental values which are, in a sense, not so well accessible to the less educated people.

But of course these people go farthest in the real world. They most successfully make the greatest accumulations of fortunes, because here lies their deepest attention and interest. They are the working type of the modern humanity, they are not too good and not afraid of dealing with the visible detailed intellectuality, but feel just there best at home, where the proud idealist feels humiliated and loses, therefore, his possessing and ruling claim in laziness, disgust and desperation. These people are most adaptable, shrewd in the most minute service to the momentary necessities of their real fate: they are the possessing rulers of the present business life, finding out and worshipping the smallest will of the present opportunity, whilst the high sentimental idealist is just so that he serves best the time after his death and is therefore, the outcast of the earning humanity. The one-sided sentimental idealist is able to gain the greatest outlooks over the connections of long runs of the human destiny and of historic development; his cleverness consists in his universality: but he is stupid in the common sense of the life. The intellectual scientist on the contrary knows how to appreciate and to serve best the present small opportunity, he discovers the most tender impressions of the physiognomy of the daily life and is able to read the most minute curves and lines of the psychological situation of the present day, but he has no overlook and no general judgment over the large psychological connections of the human mind and of the developing universe.

Now we see where the role and capacity of the *modern new Church* lies, just in the middle of these two extremes, in the moderation of both opposite poles given in the description of the sentimental and intellectual psychological education. The Protestant claims and appreciates the feelings of the heart. He has a certain respect for tradition, for history, for the inherited customs, but not too much. He claims and appreciates the will of energetic progressing enlargement of the universal magnetism in the frame of our psychological and social institutions, but always in connection and careful comparison with the former basis of historic development. The new church recognises the educational value of the monosymbolic and monogenial principles, but it is careful in using the energetic methods of their expressions. It is willing to avoid the former dangers of roughening, of materialisation, of anger and laziness, but also of indulging in the perfectly modern intellectualism, in which method it would lose the heart, the tender decency, the humane equilibrium, the general survey of the universal psychological development. It is willing to work very much, but not so much as to lose the connection with the deepest unknown wells of ignorance and mysticism. It will not lose the connection with these strongest urges for intellectual progression and psychodynamic energy, in using up the total amount of the human life-force for plodding detailed work. The modern church has the good will of love and of compassion, of interest and benevolence for the neighbor, but it is not willing to baffle the possibility of its own existence in the world by inconsiderate heroic optimism nor by absolute pessimism in advance. If it destroys itself, then it is no more able to continue its wholesome mission in the society of whose value and necessity it is convinced, and by whose quick and fatal destruction, it thinks, it would have given the proof of its lack of human resistance and therefore of true human value.

Can we not be noble men and at the same time strive for some material welfare of our own person, of our family and commonwealth? Can we not claim with strong emphasis our material necessities in the world without becoming mean in our intentions and sentiments? Must we necessarily be eaten up by the group of our contemporaries having no or less idealism, if we have strong noble sentiments, or is it not better, to combine thoroughly both these elements of our fatal human natural condition in a harmonious strong, steady and victorious ideal-real life? Are we indeed not able to possess the motor-car and the fortune of the intellectualist at that same time, where we excell through the honest feelings of a high-minded good character and ideal appreciations of the universal values? Are we not able to avail ourselves of the manifold necessary and useful material things of the world without putting too much stress on them, and can we not be friends of religion and art without despising the values of the social real life thoroughly? Can we not be cautious, careful, strong and energetic in prosecuting the interests of any business without losing the principles of respect, benevolence and even of obliging politeness and sincere friendship towards our brethren? All these are problems and questions whose solution rests most closely with the most intimate modern religious psychology. They are difficult but they are most humane and we must, if we claim to be most humane beings, look for their good solution. The extremes on both sides are not so difficult to be followed, but it is not easy to combine them both within one reliable and sincere strong human character, full of heart and nobility, but also full of strong will and undertaking fervor. These problems have all to be resolved and the serious success in their specific most conscientious achievement decides the value of the good human individual and of the social strength and perfection of our age. Escaping to one or the other side is easy. Consequence in human exaggeration to one or the other side appeals to the human instincts, but the serious working out of contradictory moments in one harmonious humane middle stage is the masterpiece of the peculiar psychological disposition of our race.

So the true religious humility and self-abnegation excludes the pride of faith and the pride of knowledge at the same time. There is no greater sacrifice than this kind of mitigated behaviour of the gifted person not to be a hero, not to have the divine splendor of the martyr, but rather more to make all efforts not to fall out from the role of real-ideal mediocrity. The modern Protestantism intends in its philosophical sense clearly not to create outstanding heroes or most splendid geniuses, but it is anxious to produce and elaborate in everybody the perfectly reliable, harmonious steadiness of the real-ideal humanity. Not in the idealistic one-sidedness with the pride of the faith, with its hyperemphasis of heart, with the monopunctual atrophy of reason, with the irreal education and the impossible economic conditions, but no more in the exclusively intellectual methods with the merely intellectualized sentiments, with the super-estimation of the countless values of the visible world, in the thinking and educational way, and with the exclusive and greatest accumulation of material riches—the modern church can have its satisfaction or example, by no means. It is essential for its character to cleave to, and to weld and combine all these extremes in the golden rule of its meek humanity. It claims to be human in heart, human in reasoning and common sense, human in educational principles and human in the economic disposition of the social conditions. Everywhere we have to discover the golden rule of the harmonious mediocrity, the democratic principle of just and most spread equality of all values among the individuals. The simplicity of the sentimental heart is too proud and selfish in the psychological sense, the complete surrender of the affective energy to the real values and to the objective visibility is indeed too humble and too tasteless in the eyes of the moderate modern church and so it has to choose by itself the difficult middle way between both states.

We spoke about the advantages and disadvantages of this golden mediocrity, chiefly about the first ones, for from the general human stand-point there are perhaps only advantages. The dangers of this system of course are given in the lacking one-sided impulses which until the transgression of the middle line worked well as human helping psychodynamic facilitation, but which afterwards, in the second, swinging away part of the dynamic pendulum, turn out to be extremely harmful. Let us, instead of repeating the already made enumeration of the different qualities of this state where one everywhere has to have the signature of harmony, in the theoretic way, step for a moment into the *National Portrait Gallery* at Trafalgar Square in London.

There are wonderfully done drawings and pictures of men great in politics, science, art and religion. I remember to have visited often the corner where the Protestant and Catholic divines are put together and to have confronted and compared their physiognomic expressions. They followed without exception two great lines corresponding to the old and the new conception. The Catholic dignitaries seemed full of strength and importance and of ruling majesty: their features were rather proud, temperamental and ardent with their jealous convictions and their ruling desire. The features of the Protestant bishops and divines on the contrary were without exception illuminated with peace, modest loveliness and most inviting harmonious humanity. Human nature was expressed fully in their charming living personal features, but just so much as to give the happy impression of the most balanced human common sense, but with the tender breath and the subdued sparkle of indescribable serenity and peace. They were indeed the masterpieces of humanity, their majesty was not visible in an intruding way, but just in the self-control of their modesty and ideal limitation the wonderful harmony and supremacy of their physiognomy has received the greatest victory. I especially never can forget the face of Thomas White, who impressed me by far most among these portrait drawings. His serenity of expression was quite unparalleled, there was at the same time so much suporior spiritual life and so much humble almost homely peace around his clever speaking eyes and the noble refined corners of his mouth most humane that I was every time at his side with the utmost thrill. What unassuming greatness, what peaceful meekness, what charming loveliness and yet what elaborated active spiritualization of his refined features!

The scientific and political drawings of the gallery, which were much more numerous, exhibited again different countenances of the represented men. The intellectual or scientific realistic type was generally recognizable by its shrewdness and cleverness. These features looked like wonderfully elaborated instruments both achieved and refined for their thinking purpose, sharpened by long experience and honed by continual friction with the necessity of adaptation to the life. Every great thinker has of course by his genial character strong connections with the deepest idealistic feelings and shows therefore in every case a part of the ideal inspiration in his physiognomic expression, but the oppressive intellectual strength and the methodic distractive will is often prevalent. Greatest scientists are often unsympathetic, strongly onesided in their intellectual tendencies and repel, therefore often by their wilful methodic dogmatism the severe freedom of the divine idealistic inspiration which never can be entirely expressed in any intellectual formula. Each profession has its special expression. The happy countenance of the modern divine reveals indeed by far the most hygienic psychology of all three types: there you have as a corporeal reflection this easy beautiful middle stage of harmonious relaxation and tension of the mimic musculature which reveals by its habitual comfortable and yet straining tonic state the character of this human type: Mens sana in corpore sano.

So the modern epoch having its origin in the opposition against the most symbolic idealism, which lifted in the old time the possibility of intellectual compensation far to the height of easy insignificance in the see-saw of the human bilatural psychology, has reversed the situation by strong intellectual counterbalances. This work must have been very difficult at the first time of psychological conversion, as the whole weight of the historic time was concentrated at the extreme sentimental pole: but now, where the opposite weight is considerably fastened and fixed, it is high time to look after the real-ideal equilibrium of our psychological balance. In the first time of change from one extreme into the other it is understandable to have put too much intellectual weight on the other pole which would not move from its habitual insignificant aerial position, but now where this situation long since has changed, we have to be most anxious not only not to relapse into the old sentimental starting attitude, but also not to repose definitely in the intellectual overweight. It means the worst kind of reposing on old laurels and the most fatal laziness of any glorious former victory is abused in not moving on towards other new successes and efforts. This fault of course occurs to be the most fatal above all in this fundamental psychological matter. The fact of having defeated extreme idealism is great, but it is of course also too great a mistake, if we have lifted it so far from earth in our psychological see-saw that there is no more any connection between idealism and the intellectual humanity. This is the other extreme of a mistake which must be avoided and done away with as well. The good modern humanity has to establish the normal equilibrium between intellectual science and poetical sentiments, between reason and faith: it has to keep most even the balance between both, has to be aware of every slightest oscillation of the harmonious horizontal line and in this continual intimate attention of the psychological equilibrium, the highest and best humanity is guaranteed and saved.

What is the *relation between art and modern Protestantism?* Why did art so well fit Catholicism and why is art less closely connected with the Protestant idea? Every art means formalistic monopoly. Art supposes the exclusive thorough love for few chosen formative intellectual principles and elements into which it breathes the inspiration of its whole sentimental energy. This is the reason why the most monosymbolic and most monogenial old conception was most successful in art: all technical facilitations were given in the strong limitation of philosophical and technical means which at the same time were at the utmost degree enjoined and emphasized by tradition, history and national customs. Protestantism has principally no more the formalistic restriction or exclusive monopoly for any fashion, mode or artistic style. The intellectual development of the post-Catholic age has the competent peculiarity to exclude the pronounced predilection of any kind of formative element, it is more liberal in spreading and attaching its love for everything which exists in an equal way, it conveys a particle of its affective heart to every even smallest psychic and visible event and object and lavishes so in a certain sense its vital strength by curiosity in the created detailed universe which the old precise theological conception compressed into few chosen monogenial symbols. It is an exactly mathematical fact which explains the decrease of the artistic productivity in the modern intellectual times. Art means essentially the symbolic compression of a huge amount of affective energy into the small but strong vases of symbolic expressions. If we have very numerous and large vases, the relative compressible amount of feelings will have much space, it will be eventually even diluted instead of distilled, as it ought to be in the artistic representation. So the detailed objective scientific multiplicity in the helps and means signifies the dilution of the magnetic fluid of the sentiments in the largest vases of intellectual reasoning and real ordinary experience. Does it lead to later distillation?

The *iconclasm* of the middle ages means nothing else but the discontentment with the narrow artistic symbolic vases containing the precious fluid of the universal magnetism. The new church created wider and more numerous vases in the intellectual enlargement of its philosophical notions and conceptions. Now is there anything more easily to be understood than the fact that the artist has much more probability to achieve few and more narrow vases more carefully with the surer dexterity and more refined spirit than countless and very different ones? The deepest secret of the great art is the philosophical and formative restriction. Wherever art has reached the degree that it submerges into the subconscious mind of the most experienced artist, there it is most successful. Wherever this goal is not attainable, art never will be really great. Art is the most divine revelling of the human mind in the intellectual formative elements and cannot be great where these elements are handicapped and must follow again and again quite new philosophical foundations and causes.

But our progressive intellectual time has indeed given up the artistic skill in favor of a purified progressive, more idealistic philsophical conception in a certain sense. Protestantism has thoroughly given way to the idea that the letter kills and only the spirit vivifies, that the spirit blows wherever it will and cannot be commanded by any of our formative intercourses. These views are the chief reason of the artistic diminution in our modern age. Art is in the most essential meaning adoration of any intellectual formulas, infatuation with the formative materialism. If the modern artist is no more able, by any means, to elaborate the perfect harmonious expression and to obtain the technical magnetic steadiness of the artist of the middle ages, it is owing to the rich objectivity, to the variable and changeable philosophical principles and to the dim and weak monosymbolism with which he has to deal. Making the statement and the postulation, surely most right once, that the strong emphasis of any intellectual formula or technical principle or thinking conception must be considered as equivalent with pure idolatrous paganism, means a deadly stroke for the vital conditions of the highest artistic skill. Art supposes the most quiet philosophical foundation, its magnetic swing is only possible from the immovable persistent central points of philosophical perseverance and fixation. The attempt of artistic drawings from the rough and uneven basis of continually changing philosophical principles goes over to the formative artistic expression, the oscillations of philosophical conceptions are exactly propagated and visible in the trembling performance of the technicalities. Modern art is much too "idealistic" in that way that it excludes the steadiness and the perseverance of any given or accepted intellectual suppositions, since it looks always for new corrections and additions of ideas and does not give the right of ruling authority to any one of the previous principles or of those found out in the present time. The modern philosophical conceptions have only the right of partly acknowledgement, the modern intellectual humanity has most numerous principles changing and superseding each other, following quickly and left quickly as well. But this means the psychomagnetic impossibility of true art. It is desirable indeed, however, that we would be able to create the modern kind of art, independent of tradition, history, former masters and lasting philosophical schools, but, alas, our human force is not sufficient to produce great artistic masterpieces in that way. The mind which is obliged to create by itself artistic technicalities, which cannot look back to the examples of former masters and cultural development working and straining in exactly the same way, has not sufficient possibilities of steady mono-directed attention and strong concentrated energy in order to reach the clearest and definite crystallizations of true and really great art. Art means the most careful and most steady grinding and polishing process going through generations and ages, working and straining continuously towards the end of technical perfection in congruency with unchangeable philosophical principles of which it has to be the most elaborate expression. If in the super-material emblematic conception of the whole life and world this possibility is excluded, then the basis and the central axis of the artistic work fail and the strength of the performing individual is unfortunately and fatally scattered. The enormous genial influx of the suggestion of the crowd, so immensely necessary for the artistic work, has lost its link with the personal mind of the artist: he chiefly is concerned with his own personal faculties in the theoretic philosophical and in the technical way having at the same time the perfect obstruction of the historic and universal psychological influence. These threefold deficiencies are of course too much for one, even the most gifted artistic individual. Strong philosophical unities in the starting steady basis of the artistic work should be the first supposition of the artist, a thorough technical school in imitation of historic examples or countless repetitions of the elements of traditional masterpieces and at the same time the most intimate communication with the universal will by the suggestion of the crowd should be all three as well integral parts of the artistic successful work. The artist is essentially the most intensely religious type, he needs great almost dogmatic philosophical steadiness because he is only able with the help of the utmost attention and concentraction of the affective energy imparted by them, to do his quite unparalleled and most exacting work.

It is only in the red-hot concentration of technical love and in the clear monodetermination of few chosen formative elements, where the divine beauty and harmony is likely to rise like a won-

higher intentions than the artistic perfection. Art itself is doubt-less yet one of the most successful educators of humanity, but its educational value is according to its nature and philosophical ex-traction, merely or chiefly psychodynamic like religion itself. It instigates, encourages and quickens our progress from the real to the ideal life, but is prone to produce exaggerated ideal enthusiasm, unreal sentimentalism and one-sided divine hopes which are exact-ly corresponding to the former sentimental religious conceptions.

The modern art has different views. It is not so perfect in the technical performance; it cannot have in the degree of the medi-aeval artists the claim of technical or psychodynamic achievement, but it follows in this difference the divergent educational inten-tions received by its underlying modern philosophical system. So the modern art is not so one-sided though it is not so perfect in the ideal and technical sense. It serves the purposes of the present educational transient idea of the modern world not seducing the admiring individual towards one-sided utopias, but guiding him in quiet harmony and reserved meditation to modest more hu-mane goals than the former mediaeval artists.

It is quite characteristic for the modern Protestantism and perhaps for the whole modern time to be built up more on mod-erate educational principles. The strong one-sided idealism of yore had the conviction to educate the individual best in giving him the strongest terminal ideal urges. If virtue were heroism or if only heroism were compatible with the practical good human derful ideal revival out of the dead material representation. In this unbelievable self-control of the philosophical mind of the his-toric artist, in this formative wilful restriction of the genial in-dividual we meet again the pelican opening his breast with its beak and giving its blood for its young, or the phenix rising victor-iously against the ideal heavens after being burned in the sacri-ficing fire. The moral foundation of the artistic work is exceed-ingly near to the notion of the old idealistic idea, dying in self-sacrifice and rising in glorious resurrection, being the minister and being served best by this behaviour of losing everything in order to gain all.

Most thorough questions are almost always the matter of dis-tribution of the force and of energetic economy. Wherever we are able to spare our forces, to concentrate them best for a certain given purpose and to exclude diverting antagonistic influences and purposes, we are in a position to bring out the best concerning results.

But we have to understand that the modern tendency has

life, then this strong one-sided ideal education to which the old art is only one means of aspiration, would be all right. But not only the individual is seduced by it to affective methods quite in contradiction with the real possibilities and working exactions of the life, but receives also all kinds of deficient moral characteristics which all are founded on the wrong psychodynamic rhythmic conditions of his mind brought out by the wrong and rough educational energy. It is the new church which found out this educationally corrupting influence of the former philosophical methods and it was willing as it ought to be, to sacrifice the extreme divine love and infatuation with any technical formal means, under the condition to advance to general moral education and to a better and more available humane basis. Art is one of the most successful servants of the religious philosophy. The character of the art corresponds exactly to the purpose of its ruling contemporary atmosphere, to its philosophical basis. If you are inclined to tell me that the special artistic expression is the chief result of the temperamental artistic *individual,* and that this point decides the kind of art and nothing or almost nothing else, then I remind you of the arts and styles of different ages and ask you whether the painters of the same time were nearer to each other or whether similar individual temperaments of different ages were more congruant in artistic expression? We surely have chiaroscurists at every time and we have colorists at every epoch, there is at every time some El Greco or Rembrandt and Rafael or Angelico as to the temperament. But all these personal inclinations and differences are thoroughly hidden behind the curtain of the contemporary affective manifestation of the time. All artists of the same historic and psychological time, though they may be thoroughly different in their personal temperament, have in the choice of coloring and formative elements very similar characteristics. Remember the Italian fifteenth and sixteenth century. How near are all the artistic tastes in form and color of this whole historic epoch! And think of the later artistic times; (to-day this tight cultural bond is lost for other reasons). Every time the performers of art of the same time in the same parts of the earth have very similar artistic expressions in spite of their different temperaments. So we may infer from that observation that the artist is much more the child of his contemporary artistic cultural atmosphere, of his philosophical views and of his suggestive cultural surroundings than anybody else and that his individual and familiar dispositions count much less in the matter of his artistic expression than his affective connection with the suggestion of the crowd and with the formative dogmaticism of his time. Arts are very different according to their different historic localisation, whilst the individual influence in this connection is comparatively less and almost negligible. We surmise, therefore, that after all our psychological temperament is most dependent on our historic circumstances.

If art is up to a great extent the result of the psycho-economic conditions of the time, of the individual and of the psychological system, then we must admit that the psycho-economic dispositions of former times were much better as to the art than those of today. It is true, this old church, too much decried as dogmatic, has in a certain sense just the least dogmatic difficulties and complications of all religious systems, having reduced the principal contents of its thinking tenets just to the symbolic size and form of the symbolic stellar simplification of which every other dogmatic idea is only the clear reflection and logical consequence. So the old idealistic system economises most the intellectual strength of the artistic individual, giving him in advance a clear transparent conception on which he is allowed to work quietly, surely, on a firm strong well, as it were, from which he is continually entitled to draw his necessary spiritual water and the divine inspiration for the suggestion of the crowd. These advantages can not be estimated highly enough in the artistic psycho-economic sense, because the artist cannot be at the same time the great psychological reformer and spiritual affective architect of his time. If he has to concentrate his gifts in the highest degree on the best formative expressions of the divine idea and if this is most difficult human work exacting the whole individual attention of the most gifted man, then it is clear that the necessity of finding a most carefully preconceived and well achieved clear and simple philosophical system at the very starting point of his work is essential for the successful artist. Even if he had the gift to be both philosopher and technical performer, first he has to use his time and energy too much in order to build universal bridges and arches for the social affective relations; only then the river of the universal and social affective force could be allowed to follow these leading architectural constructions and to make them efficient for the individual artistic work. But until these philosophical ideas are in good available work, until these pits, rivers and brooks are filled with the sentimental water of the universal affective energy and are in function, a long time passes away. As soon as something has to do with intellect, and we never escape the middle of this necessity, there we have to reckon with time, space and causality. We see therefore that the necessary preparations and the inavoidable use of time and force would take away the individual energy and life-time before he could utilise his genial artistic gift. For this reason the most productive and most excellent artist has to find at the very first starting morning of his artistic activity any prepared philosophical system on which he has to work as on his psychomechanic supposition, and from which he has to expect all support, help, magnetic surety and divine inspiration in the suggestion of the crowd as from a wonderful fountain pouring forth always eternal water.

This is indeed the most interesting point in the old monosymbolic and monogenial conception as to the art, as all extremes touch always again, that its extreme flight from the sensorial gradual intellectualism to the last monopunctual manifestation of the monotheistic symbol, to which it swung in the imaginative wings of miracles and mysticism, produced on the other hand, like the revenge of the included pride, the most formal idolatry and loving infatuation owing to the localised affective intensity. What the proud humanity would not accept in the form of the humiliation of the detailed working display, was inflicted on it compensatorily like a concentrated lightning in the few chosen monosymbolic monopunctual and circular elements into which the whole divine possibility of the human heart was infused. This old monosymbolic affective concentration and the worshipping adoration of its nearest symbolic formative elements in the intellectual mechanic world have of course the most intimate philosophical connection, and we therefore have to understand that in the psychodynamic, psychorhythmic and psychoeconomic sense the old idealistic, extreme monosymbolic and monogenial type and the characteristic great traditional art of the middle ages was the expression of the same temperamental emphasis and the same thing.

The old art is the most practicable way and the most inviting suggestion to accept or to appreciate the psychodynamic principles of the old extreme idealism. There is no doubt that every great lover of the mediaeval art is, often unknowingly and even though pretending the contrary, an admirer of the psychodynamic methods of the old temperament. Whosoever is subjected to the great charm of the mediaeval art and whosoever is fond of the beauty and the genius of its expression confesses in this that he appreciates the psychic methods which permit or produce such an unexpected accumulation, concentration and attention of psychic energy in the intellectual human possibility; they desire this angry monopunctual compression of the total human life-force typical of the old idealistic system which put all its psychic fortune always at one stake.

Their hearts are perhaps most fervently attracted just there where their modern education and their methodical new conception of the world has taken them away. For this reason the hypercultivation of the mediaeval artists, as it turns out to become more and more popular, is seriously objectionable from the standpoint of the modern conception, from the standpoint of the scientific intellectual consideration of the life and from the point of view of the strong attitude sticking to the modern educational principle. Radiant and moving as the old masterpieces are, just from the last standpoint, of the harmonious psychodynamic order and efficient psychological progression they are to be considered as dangerous sirens attracting with the sweetest songs the sensitive heart of every ideally gifted individual but leading astray in the meaning of the educational modern idea.

There are of course very different shades in the artistic pictorial dealing which express themselves immediately in the educational sense. The distinction between chiaroscurists and colorists is of deepest influence in the educational sense. May the one be too quickening and too thorough and the other, on the contrary, obstructing on the peripheric surface of the real life, we may judge on the whole, however, that art owing to its performing character and to its theatrical features, belongs to the dangerous rather quickening psychodynamic methods: it may be refinedly elaborated as much as it may, it always even in the most realistic development, has the characteristic facilitation of the logical order of the transparent sensorial service and of the unitarian conception; it condenses the whole psychological human performance into one kind of sensorial expressive existence and has, therefore, essentially always the result of angry acceleration and terminal idealistic enthusiasm. What we call good art is very much an instrument in favor of the old sentimental conception of the life, because it is always able by its great representative advantages over the experimental awkwardness of the practical life, to entice psychodynamic actions of quick, strong and far-reaching description. The practical experience of life produces only fragments of the idealistic progression, it reveals only slowly and always under the shadow of some concealment the universal principles of idealistic conclusiveness and progress of the human fate; its action is very dismembered and distant in time and space, giving in one case the question and far away in another experience the answer of our universal doubts: But the artist in every case is quite different: he gathers his logical process into one work easily understandable, logical and continually progressive and is therefore to be considered as the furtherer of the quickening psycho-dynamic idealistic actions.

Therefore, we guess to have a trace in order to explain the value and the character of the modern art, not only to condemn the lacking technical perfection of the modern artist, but to see indeed his educational value in the antagonistic, enigmatic and reserved methods of his performance. The essential weak point of the old art in the sense of the intellectual science and of the modern church, is doubtless the fact that it fascinates too easily and that it progresses without enough intellectual escapements from the peripheric reality to the central idealism. This fundamental error is most significant not only for the whole old ideal conception of the mediaeval philosophy and the old imaginative idealism, but also for the most fervent interpreters of it in the old art. Has art to be the servant of the modern philosophy and religious conception in which intellectuality and hard working reality are the main pillars of life and the most important elements of good vital performance, then art has indeed to adapt itself to this special rhythmic psychodynamic principle. The highly shining idealism, flowing from the artistic inspiration like a golden rain quivering through the whole masterpiece, conveying the most divine hope and the most lovely charm to the whole picture, is nothing but the perfect expression of the mediaeval "angry" philosophy and cheats the gullible sentimental humanity today as it did before, creating illusions, exaggerated hope, sentimental laziness and luxuriant desire of the heart, today as of yore. The true contemporary art of today has, therefore, no more this character. The strong idealistic art has to be considered as the thoroughly anachronistic type of our time and has to be exchanged by another kind of artistic performance which corresponds exactly to the exactions of the modern educational psychorhythmic temperament.

The modern art, as the true and faithful servant of its time, perhaps without knowing it, strives to fulfill this postulation. The optic bluffing possibility of the symbolic representation of the picture is exceedingly apt to make for the optic miraculous mysticism of the old sentimental ideal conception. The sharp real gradation of the objective visibility in the intensely realistic art, as it is still always expressed in one kind of artistic method and has still the character of an artistically ordered and perfect logical fairytale, easily excites the proceeding individual psychodynamic rhythm and throws the individual to the topmost heights of ideal without having done a great work, since the narow frame of the artistic uniform optic representation offered a well pre-conceived preparation for the following idealistic performance. How will the modern pictorial artist escape these two snares of his own technical means? He is not allowed to be too symbolic in order not to become wrong, mystic and miraculous, and he is at the same time not entitled to become too understandable and clear in too minute realistic representation, in order not to make the psychological work of the spectator too disorderly or easy from the other side since too symbolic and too realistic representation mean both hurtful simplification of the psychic work?

This is the kernel of the psychological dilemma which the modern educational artist has to face today. And who doubts a moment if he looked carefully at the general technical peculiarity of the present pictorial and the other art that the modern art takes indeed the technical problem from this side, striving on one hand to be enough enigmatic to instigate and to accelerate the psychological performance of the spectator in a symbolic way, and on the other hand realistic enough in order to make sufficient logical obstacles for him, in detailed logical accuracy. The modern artist strives to bring out, in his peculiar formative technical and coloring expression, both, enough mysticism and enough clear intelligence serving the educational purpose of his time, to check the too easy realistic logical performance which is so closely connected with art and which represents its chief disadvantageous danger in the meaning of the modern philosophy, and not to lose, on the other hand, entirely the connection with great expectations and overwhelming ideal hopes. But these terminal hopes must, properly speaking, remain always subdued and hidden, they are not allowed to blow up the whole frame of the realistic representation or to rule at any rate the whole meditation by their inspiring energy. Hopes and high ideal expectations in the modern art must be, but they have to stay in the dim light of perpetual further generation. They never are finished, they never have to be reached in overflowing pleasure and satisfaction, but they always are only the starting points of future other developments to which the human race has again to aspire in toiling work and logical performance. For this reason the dim ideal light is sufficient in the sense of the modern artistic master-piece. No quietness, no satisfaction, but always energetic progression towards better and higher fulfilment is the parole of the modern philosophy and of its faithful servant, the modern art. No easy representation of ideal goals can be any longer the psychological basis of the modern art. This would be considered to-day as seduction, harmful deception in bad psychodynamic work of the individual, to whom art has to give realisable, reliable and lasting educational examples and urges.

It is quite typical of the mediaeval art that it dealt with religious and allegoric subjects, most significant for the philosophical foundation of the Italian, French and Latin artists at all, to have dealt preferably with mythological, allegoric and hagiographic topics, whilst the Teutonic and the later times preferred by far more and more the secular subjects of the every-day life, increasing in this line until the entirely intellectual time of to-day, where the profanation of the choice of the artistic work is practically perfect. In the first case, the topic of the artistic representation was only the subordinated opportunity of the general idea and of the technical ways which had to be demonstrated in the ancient master-piece, in the second case on the contrary, the most refined artistic stress and skill was put into the service of the most accurate and determined individual reality, serving so decidedly the represented person or object in any utilitarian way and not subjecting chiefly or exclusively the individual to the ideal service.

In order to understand, how early this differenciation of the conceptions began, we may compare *Rubens and Rembrandt,* the first the strong representative of the monogenial conception and the second of the rising more real consideration of the world. For Rubens the topic was absolutely indifferent. Whatsoever he painted, he brought out chiefly his enormous circular swing, his stupendous anatomic dexterity, his enormous skill in representing static and muscular powers and the most gigantic atmosphere for which every topic mythical, religious or historic was only the accidental form of real expression. His doctrinary art was essentially formalistic, great by its philosophically monosymbolic strong conception which it knew to serve in the most accurate manner and in the best adequate circular technicalities. In spite of his great real power, Rubens owing to his philosophical attitude could not have any thorough interest in the reality, because the chief accent of his art lay on the terminal idealistic discharge of the spectator's mind.

In Rembrandt we have very different philosophical conditions in his art. He chooses almost always the most modest, concrete and real persons from the middle of his nearest surroundings: he scorns the help of the emphasis of his heroes by any historic royal crown, he is keen of taking away every idealistic mythological, traditional and historic religious distinction from his represented persons in order to elaborate in an undisturbed, most thorough and most direct sincere and honest manner, the greatest thing possible in them, the harmonious kernel of humanity. He at last is great enough to emphasize that there is nothing greater than the real understanding of human nature, and that every mythological historic, ancestral denominational, political or scenic distinction in landscape and drapery means rather a proof of inferiority for the personal cleverness of the artist than emphasis of his skill. The true and greatest artist does not need helps like these, he feels disturbed in his purest and most sincere devotion for humanity by all kinds of artificial distinctions which are attached to historic persons: he is on the contrary just at home, when he is allowed to approach the most unprotected human nature in the holy flashes of his most tender and most serious veneration.

So it turns out that no more the individual is the poor accidental instrument playing a merely optional and subordinate role in his psychic individuality of any theological principles as it is in Rubens, but on the contrary we feel that the most refined artistic dexterity is just put to the service of the most unassuming human nature itself, in the individual. There is no more an ideal worship of universal historic monosymbolic values far away from the reachability of humanity, but rather more of the divine sparkle which shines most harmoniously through the human artistic expression of all of Rembrandt's pictures.

There could not be easily any more pronounced differentiation in the philosophical sense between these two artists. One looks still steadily to his theoretical terminal ideal given to him by his old tradition, and the other fixes his look not less intensely on the human psychological nature, whose individual features he develops in the most careful, balanced and reverent way, but both have the most pronounced technical skill in order to make their logical way in the most perfect manner. Rubens was still on the sentimental idealistic side of humanity in art. Rembrandt changed the one-sided idealism perfectly into the ideal-real humanity which became his highest and most fervently sought goal of artistic expression. This was the good type of what we call new art, reconciliation of excellent technique and individual respect and precision, on one side, and of high ideal love and divine inspiration, on the other, within the most dignified and most real human conception. This was the greatest and best consideration of art which humanity ever could have. No estrangement, no falsehood, no artificial distraction or emphasis of any human dignity or worthiness, no generalization or fairy-tale-like change of the artistic representation, but just on the contrary the challenge of the artistic representation to the accidental exterior values of the life (in opposition to Rubens, Holbein and Van Dyke and so many other court painters) was always exhibited in the art of Rembrandt. Remember the wrinkles of his old men and women, the shabby caftans of his Jews, the most modest attitude, corporeal weakness and the unassuming vestments of the most of his figures. There he shows himself glorious in modesty, victorious in strong realistic limitation, where his technical superiority throws the most divine flashes of enthusiasm just on the face of the most modest and most real faces and persons. Can there be any more thrilling fact, any more moving impression than Rembrandt's countenances and features of old trembling, most realistic, uncultured and even deficient people who all are just put under the concentrating focus of his idealistic flashlight! Who was ever so much in love with the whole humanity in the most radical sense as he was? Who could ever pour so much concentrated sympathy on the most natural and unpainted human nature as he did? Who ever put such a divine power of belief and confidence in the harmonious humanity as he did? There was nothing greater, nothing comparable and nothing overcrying the peace and the harmony of his human ideal which he understood to display in the most charming manner before the spectator with exactly the same weight, whether there was the question of the last ragamuffin or of the noblest dignitary of his time. Here lies the heartrending greatness and moral importance and loveliness of the pictures of Rembrandt, in the universality of his human confidence. He looked through the silly walls of the exterior social differences to the bottom of the essential human values and was able to distinguish surely, without vacillation, the deciding signifying factors of our deepest nature and life. Could there be any better solution of the social problem than this general great humanity of Rembrandt? Here it is demonstrated ad oculos with the clearest visibility and precision. He did not give his best idealizing light flashes to kings and princes whose money could have bought the artistic genial work of almost everybody else and though by his extraordinary skill he would have been secured in great glory, he rather considered their crowns, ermines and velvets as disturbing distractions from his genial work and inspired the love of his greatest artistic energy just into the sorrowful features of poor and disregarded people, whom and whose human working life he lifted up to the most perfect and most stable human dignity. He did not accept crowns, precious folds, material and silks, as a rule as the subject or accompaniment of his great genial expression, but treated them rightly, as they are, as frail tinder falling down from the categoric values of our time and not worthy at all to be connected with the deepest psychological problems expressed in the best way in the valuable human features experienced and tested in the changing life. What a moral courage, what a best kind of backbone and character must this man have had who lived in modesty and died in poverty though he could have had every amount of fortune for his glorious pictorial gift!

How small and how ridiculous, how irreligious and superstitious must every exterior apparel fall down from the shoulders of every conceited dignitary in the poor light of this moral hero who was not only a great painter in the sense of the technical judgment, but above all a great human giant who lived modestly all his life, scorning the favor of princes and kings, never bribable for other purposes than for the most clear and most harmonious service of the balanced human nature which was the only highest and most beloved topic he ever knew.

So Rembrandt was able to pull the heaven to the earth or rather to put it into the harmonious human nature, whilst Rubens shoots our human and realistic power towards his theological sublime heaven. But both have indeed a wonderful and most clear imagination of the ideal heaven which is the atmospheric basis of their masterpieces. They had in addition both the most exquisite craftmanship which created the most minute possibility of technical intellectual expression.

But they had not fully the reposing real attitude of the intellectuality as we have it in *nature*. Or are we not more true if we assert that also nature idealizes our soul and throws our feelings towards ideal values? Think of the majestic mountains rapturing our hearts towards divine admiration! The modern intellectual dispersion of the *imaginative* energy of the humanity baffles and prohibits almost any preferability of ideal values. Now art is chiefly built up on the imaginative power which we are able to concentrate in any idealistic symbolization. Where the imaginative precision of the ideal is forbidden owing to moral or educational reasons and where the scientific multiplicity has scattered our total imaginative amount too much, there the development of the art in the sense of the earlier and later middle ages is taken away and made impossible. There is a danger not to be underrated.

The essential characteristic of the modern art lies in the absence of the imaginative concentration and of sharp monosymbolic conclusions. It is often so far that it does not pull any longer the intellectual visible dispersion towards concentrated ideal symbols, that it no more puts a reciprocal relation between the divine symbolic theological conception and the human nature, in a harmonious ideal humanity, but it tries to disperse the whole force of the magnetic energy of the mind to the whole created world without clear and sharp centro-symbolic imaginative possibilities, or often in such a manner as to try to concentrate and to effuse all divine energy into whatsoever object. For this reason the modern artist asks whether it is not allowed to represent the divine greatness as well in a tree or in a landscape as in the human nature. In the destruction of the traditional centro-symbolic conception, which we may call abolition of the old sentimental energy of our life-force, lies the deepest root of the consternation of the modern artistic representation. There is no more sufficient magnetic fall in our artistic modern paintings and all artistic productivity because we have become too one-sided in our intellectualism leaving entirely the other extreme of the traditional sentimentalism.

Were art everything or only the chief thing on earth, the best advice to awaken art to a mighty new renaissance or revival of inspiring enthusiasm would be the reconstruction of strong and sharp philosophical unitarian monosymbolic imaginative conceptions. Then art would instantly have the orderly magnetic tension between the two poles of realism and idealism, and then we could receive easily the most perfect affective push which was so thrilling and domineering in the mediaeval art. But art has not this superior dominion over humanity that we could sacrifice to it better values received and tested in a long time of struggle and experience. Art has the role of an educational value and has to adapt itself to its educational possibilities. If it cannot be a good art without maintaining or re-introducing again the rejected methods of angry mysticism and bluffing energy then we did, in the modern opinion, do better to be without art or at least without that kind of so-called more perfect old art which is still by the broad masses of people recognized and admired as the best kind of artistic performance. Art has chiefly or merely educational purposes. Art has to give an example to concentrate our life-force from objective realistic towards ideal values. But if it does it in a rough and angry way, presenting unobtainable imaginative symbols to which it runs most energetically, then it is only the predecessor of the old psychodynamic methods which the new time and the modern scientific conception have defeated and refuse as spoiling and dangerous in the educational sense.

So we see that the role of the art of today is very narrow in its limits. We understand that its role must be subordinated and that it has no more by any means that domineering power which it had in the middle ages. It is reduced in the qualitative and quantitative way along the realistic principles of today and according to the will of the present cultural humanity not to fall back once more into the dangerous pit of the sharp imaginative idolatric adoration of few historic intellectual elements.

But it is very understandable that, up to a certain degree, the old art of Europe is the high point of attraction of our tourists from everywhere. This old art with its psychodynamic energy is able to convey to the individual mind that energetic, magnetic fall which clears the intellectual stagnation of our humanity by high ideal enthusiasm and which exercises in that way the most agreeable function of the most hygienic affective discharge. But this artistic enjoyment of the old mediaeval masterpieces plays duly the role of a *holiday recreation of the soul,* comfortable and useful as a thorough change from the working everyday life, a welcome exception from the toiling logical performance which has become today the rule in our psychological conception, according to moderate and solid fundamental principles supported in the necessity of the exterior economic circumstances.

We see that the modern art has the most difficult role in its nature, in its psychological basis and in its technical performance. It is the expression of a quite new problematic psychic world which has taken possession of our age, which is better in education preserving from the educational damages of the former time. The modern art has to be the educational expression of the philosophy of the present intellectual time, less attractive, less enthusiastic, but for this reason more enjoyable, in a sense, less deceiving and much more adequate to the real life. But perhaps the modern art has gone too far, like the modern scientific conception of the life, whose mirror it is, and surely it should look for more compromising ways between the old enthusiastic and the new, intellectual real conceptions: perhaps it would be good to be more aware of the wonderful craftmanship of Rembrandt who was able indeed to be very real, very accurate and individual in his means, but also in his philosophical purpose and symbolic conception most efficient in uplifting energy. The finish of the realistic conception of the art of today and the exclusion of the idealistic imaginative symbolism has the great disadvantage not to grasp energetically the affective force of the spectator, not to move thoroughly enough the heart of the modern people who become so soon disgusted of the artwork. It is essential for the best art to join the assets of the progressive modernism with the advantages of the old time, to be true, reliable, without the possibility of creating any enthusiastic ideal utopias which by life itself are refused, and to be nevertheless energetic enough in the psychodynamic or psychorhthmic temperament to carry away the individual through lasting hopes towards unchangeable best values.

There is nothing higher than the justice of compensation between reality and idealism, also in art. Every formalistic conception and representation of any kind delivers sources of idealistic purpose, and every realistic detailed elaboration has to be considered as impairing the unity and the strength of the ideal intention of the masterpiece. The most refined realistic hand coming forth in a quite plastic way from the pictorial plain, the introduction of the shadow of the persons and the perspective and the detailization of the remote landscape pay all their tribute indeed to the relative deterioration of the tight central bond of the inspiring purpose.

So we understand that the modern intellectualization of the art is in danger to lose its inspiration in its naturalistic conception, as the old art was not able to look sharply at the detail of the nature because of the ruling one-sided idealistic purpose. The danger of the modern art is stiffness and death owing to the lack of inspiring vivification, whilst the old time burnt its sensorial sharp eye of observation in the fire of its rapturing divine enthusiasm, to which it dared to look as too bold an eagle. The old idealistic creeds with their most pronounced monosymbolic conception created that perfect formative stylization of all artistic utterances in such a high degree that the objective truth suffered by the scholastic circles and architectural divisions, and the sharp realistic observations of the modern times, on the contrary, have the disadvantage not to permit easily the elaboration and the penetration of the main idea behind the formative elements which have to serve it in due respect falling in like servants bowing and directed in attentive attitude towards their master.

All these things are only reflections of their times and their philosophy. We may say: Art is like the nations. The Teutonic races have quite different artistic tastes, inclinations and conceptions than the Latin countries. The more conservative Catholic countries on the whole, though today the progress towards the intellectual one-sidedness is more or less general, have more stylish old imitation without being in a position to create a new style by themselves, whilst the leading Protestant direction has developed art today just to a scientific and psychological research work which it tries to resolve in painting, experimenting, mingling thoughts and colors, philosophical questions and formative elements together in a serious plodding meditative crucible. The modern artist is, therefore, much more the type of a philosopher than any other one. He has received the task to create not only his artistic expression, but to bring out even the affective fundamental principle and symbols on which he will build up his artistic masterpiece, so he is at the same time prophet and artist. The Latin countries are, of course, in much nearer connection with the old dogmatic and customary styles than the Germanic ones which never entered so much into the sacred unions of religious symbolism of the mediaeval and later history.

But we see that the more extreme idealism of the southern artistic conception needs intellectualization of their arts and vice versa. The practical consequence of this meditation may be, therefore, that northern art should be brought to southern countries and southern to northern parts of the world. There should be a continual exchange between Catholic and Protestant, Latin and Teutonic collections of art, because both complete and educate each other very much. As we all know, we live today in an age, where this is continually done. We see today exhibitions of mediaeval Italian painters as well in North America as we see in southern countries artistic expositions from Teutonic extraction. This intentional educational interchange diminishes the mutual oppositions and contradictions in conceptions and expressions and forms the necessary links for mutual human understanding which is the basis for good political, commercial and artistic intercourse for all. The whole meditation about these two extreme different conceptions of the art in the ideal stylistic and in the real naturalistic direction teaches us that the strong idealism sacrifices the individual, the objective truth and the detailed faithfulness to the common great inspiration and purpose and that on the contrary, the real naturalistic art emphasizes most the individual, serves him with the most attentive accuracy of true representation, but neglects his strong connection with the idealistic axis of the whole. We see in this connection how much idealism crushes the individual in his personal import, personal rights and particularities, but we see also how much the individual is cut off in realistic conception, from the great will of divine inspiration and possibly even of idealistic support. In the material most personal care for the individual we have to expect the deterioration of the ideal purpose and in the strong relationship to high ideal goals in the society, as in art, we meet always, owing to the law of compensation, the more miserable state of individual material conditions.

Can there be more negligence for the individual or detailed formative elements than in the masterpieces of *El Greco* full to the brim of great and strong divine inspiration? His bushes are unrecognizable as such and easily confusable with his clouds and even rocks, altogether counting for nothing in the passionating upheaval of his inspiring explosion. We have the same in the philosophical society, where the most idealistic system seems to provide negligently for the necessities of the individual and oppresses him by its regardless lawful will, whilst just the materialistic commonwealth with all its dryness takes most care about the individual needs and necessities in the detail. In everything and everywhere we have continually compensation within the boundaries of the human total life-force.

Art is of course to a great extent nothing but the exhalation of the contemporary religious-philosophical creed of any nation. Art is one of the specific fruits of the religious philosophy of any time. It is about the most immediate, most consequent and clear enunciation of the psychodynamic accent of a given time, showing without any concealment to the critical eye of the observer how much this epoch clings closely to the idealistic concentration of its mind, and how much it emphasises the realistic periphery, how any time or philosophical creed thinks these two opposite components of ideal and real values could be best connected and with what means it is inclining to the real or ideal preoccupation and overweight of the psychological balance. This is the root of all problems, there is nothing greater and deeper than this apportionment of sentiments and reasoning power, of idealism and reality which have to be put together in the peculiar nature of our human performance. The new time freed from hypernaturalism, has also here the role of extenuating the extremes on both sides and to impart that human harmony which we appreciate everywhere so much and chiefly in art where we have the highest thrill in the harmonious ideal-real representation.

Is the Latin artistic ecstasy with its traditional habitual circular achievement the right kind of conception of life and art, or must we rather prefer the *joking* criticism of the Teutonic investigator who never is satisfied with the received results but always looks to enlarge his views, to critcise his former psychological foundations and so to initiate a continual formalistic or intellectual fecondation of all human history? We spoke much about this fundamental question. We need continual progression. We have to be most careful about the continual possibility of the universal evolution, not only in the essential affective, but also in the methodical or formalistic sense. For we know that old formulas lose always again their ability to be able barrels of idealistic shoots, that they, by using up and with lazy obstruction, after having first facilitated the psychic performance, decay and lose at all their psychological discharging attractiveness, so that they must be replaced by other more fashionable instruments of philosophical systems, if we will not risk the individual sentimental stagnation. On the other side, in art as well as in moral life, there must be a certain stability, and it is neither difficult to obtain sure and best results without having any habitual and traditional support. This support is conveyed by dogmatic and philosophical principles in religion, and life, by stylistic skill in art. We are always at the same point, at the necessity of some mediocrity. Ne quid nimis. We are always punished, if we go too far, it may be wherever, above all also in ethics whose way is the commandment and law as we shall see. The middle way between the ideal and real values is inevitably the mere right thoroughfare of all human activity, where the greatest things arise, as we see in the greatest artists personally, since all of them at the top of their career, have thrown away their one-sided contemporary conceptions (Lionardo, Titian). So to-day the modern world, in as much as it is not too much intellectualized by scientific methods and rulers, gives the key to these best artistic psychological laws, expressing steady progress and stability at the same time, forbearing energy, but also hesitating meditation and so the root of all good humanity. The happiness, quietness and efficiency of our life consists in the settled symbolic fixation, up to its saturation, afterwards in its change up to new fixation.

What is the *effect of Protestantism on the character?* Protestantism has indeed recognised that there must be harmony between idealism and realism of our natural disposition. It did everything in order to loosen our former idealistic one-sidedness from its exclusive monogenial entanglement without being willing to give up any kind of ideal contact and respect for the old divine history. We meditated that the development, on the whole, in the historic sense, progressed from the idealistic towards the realistic side, or pole, and that there is the danger, after all, that this magnetic draft or direction receives the overweight, though there is no more the question of any religious system at all, as soon as there is a strong hyperemphasis of intellectualism. But the modern time is doubtless in danger of extreme one-sided realism. Is the extreme realistic tendency not already outside of the religious movement?

Is it not rather the post-reformatory extreme pendulation of that great European civilizatory psychological wave which started in the rising highly idealistic first church and touches today the other extreme of hyper-materialization.

We remember that this middle attitude of the right theological conception between the two real and ideal extremes, was compared to the action of a careful and clever rope dancer who is in danger to lose every moment his equilibrium, or to a marble of a child on the middle of a polished top of a table sloping slightly towards both sides from the middle, where the marble is placed. The least shaking of the table is sufficient to make it moving towards one or the other extreme of the underlying plane. Owing to the fatal *"lability"* of the middle human psychological attitude, running quickly like a pendulum, rolling like a marble on the table, at the slightest excitement of the fate to one or the other extreme, idealism or materialism, we have to accept as a very pronounced danger of the mediated psychology the strong inclination to intellectual affective moral and every kind of change. It is not the strongest idealist nor the strongest intellectualist who are in danger of much and quick changes in their character or even of all kinds of oscillations and variations in their psychological attitude, these both are strongly bound by the magnetic sequence of their attitude and have, therefore, consequent, unchangeable and perfectly sincere convictions and habits. But the middle attitude of the modern psychology with its *lability* quivering like quick-silver between its two opposite two-sided magnetic attractive poles working on both sides, has not this advantage or disadvantage, as we will, of the strongly bound extremist, but is always inclined to transgress, to one or the opposite side, the boundaries of its habitual middle attitude. The middle state of *lability* is of course so much greater as the total individual life-force is less. The more space is covered by the *habitual* individual psychic production, the broader will be the basis of the middle fixation, the less the *lability* and the more narrow the space where the magnetic extreme could and would displace or supersede the habitual mediocrity.

If Leonardo di Vinci had the connection of all good ideal and real qualities at the same time, if he was so much inspired in the ideal sense as he respected on the other side all laws of perspective, anatomy and technical skill without losing, but rather augmenting the conclusive impression of his painting, then we have to remember that this could happen only owing to his quite extraordinary individual total life-force, whilst the dropping of perspective and sharp realistic elaboration of the other artists of this time must rather be considered as the strong idealistic dominion of that contemporary psychology and as the expression of the inferior total life-force of the painting individuals who had compensatorily to discard the real sharpness and elaboration, to neglect it until the character of mere symbols, only in order to save the strong inspiring idealistic purpose which was the chief and ruling thing of their masterpieces.

As we see, the oscillation and movability to the extreme of the middle real-idealistic attitude is just the much more strong, as we are weaker and less gifted individuals (think of Neurasthenia). We infer that the very gifted mediated type must be a wonderful human individual full of real importance and idealistic loveliness at the same time, connecting all sides of the essential human qualities in the most harmonious way, giving to the nature the best right and charm in his personal psychic combination.

But what happens in many outstanding, the average and in the weaker cases where the individual life-force is little? The marble of the psychic accent rolls, of course, most easily towards the extremes and, because the education does not stand and permit them, from one extreme to the other. The middle stability during the shaking motion of the life is in this case easily destroyed, the most extreme digressions of this psychology are there, and if they are not extreme, they are at least almost always in existence in form of vivid oscillations and continual vibrations of the psychological attitude between idealism and realism. There is doubt, continual comparisons, most vital real-sentimental frictions, most humane meditations confronting always the two sides of our gift, which means in the intellectual sense a strong inclination for *philosophy,* in the meaning of judgment, human broadmindedness, and in the affective sense, most adaptable moderate benevolence.

There are in this continual grinding work of the human soul between its two magnetic extremes above all two remarkable things to be stated, first that there is continual motion and grinding work, never death, satisfaction and achievement. This must indeed be appreciated exceedingly highly in the biological sense. Life is motion and motion is life; extreme is death and sterilization. This continual refining and grinding motion of the middle psychological attitude has, however, another great advantage, the refined detailed perception and the most minute readiness for the continual active service of the opportunities and circumstances of the present moment of the changing life. This minute continual oscillation of the psychological accent means psychic vigility, sharp observation and detailed cleverness, just as extreme fixation, be it in the ideal or material sense, means from the standpoint of the whole humanity, rather more one-sided stiffness, narrowness and inadaptability which is stupidity in one-sided wrong consideration.

The great need of wide, opposite contacts in the two directions of idealism and realism is of course most probable, when the link of both is assured in the habitual middle attitude which we have in modern habits. This peculiar psychological situation is the continual urge to digressions toward both the ideal and real direction, and there we have the peculiar humane furnace, from whose red hot frictions and contradictions are taken the most efficient tools and instruments of philosophical debating and enlightning work. Indeed the most serious philosophical work is essenitally modern and Teutonic. We wonder how few doubts the sharply thinking Latin type, so absolutely fond of clearness in thinking which is a very objectionable idea, has on the whole of the universe: he has settled his main ideas much more, because he is stiffened in the overwhelming greatness of his systematic religious part from which he is no more able to disintegrate himself in new thorough searching work. The Northern modern type has in his peculiar middle mediocrity of mind preserved the freedom of his doubting soul, he still works at the very first foundation and basis of the building of his soul and never ceases to doubt either of his own psychological basis or the universal laws. So we chiefly have great philosophers always, over and over again, in the intellectual northern countries. These countries have above all given to the world their great thinkers of a majesty and strength that nobody but the experienced can believe and appreciate. Whosoever read Kant, Schleiermacher, Schopenhauer, Hegel, Fichte and Nietzsche, Locke, Bacon and Spencer and so many other great thinkers of these races must indeed be surprised by the genial eternal youth of these great nations who never sleep, never are satisfied, but are always busy in reviving their fundamental ideas, in recoining their notions, in correcting old errors and enforcing gained results with new acquisitions in philosophical work. Philosophical work is as we said, only possible, where extreme ideal and real, or sentimental and intellectual values are always confronted over and over again, where doubts of the former facts of their historic amalgamation never cease and where always trials are made to lose all the imperfect notions and feelings and to weld instead useful better ones for the future greater efficacy and happiness of humanity. Philosophy means not only the continual most vivid vibration of the soul between ideal and real values, but also their friction. Their opposition in very distant opposite values and one-sidedness, be it in real or ideal direction, is not able to make the philosopher. He is essentially bound to the best values of his humane character, so he is inclined to analyze most carefully towards the intellectual side. But at the end he reduces again his whole results to the last symbolic and imaginative values of truth, beauty, strength and love and connects his philosophical work between the most detailed reality and the most general ideal notions. Here is the greatest victory of the moderate modern conception not to be in danger to become rusty in old worn-out philosophical distance. It creates always new works full of strength, energy and youth: it has always new vases ready to fill in the wine of the universal sentiments. This humanity cannot become old because it is always full of hopes, never sophisticated and never tired because of old used notional customs, but always ready to prefer new additions of idealistic formulas or other intellectual notions and systems. This is, what we said above all, the change of ideas in order to preserve the anticipation of the will, of the energy and the enthusiasm of our hearts. But this is most thoroughly and best done in the philosophical research work. The intellectual representation is the most variable quivering wave expressing the unchangeable solidity of universal energy pervading all creation, always stable in the change, but always needing the objective and intellectual change and movability of its last and best representation. The will of life, most universal in everything, bears on all intellectual representation also and is so much more necessary as the kind of reaction is vital and deep. So philosophical work comes out to be perhaps just the most necessary and useful in the will of the psychological work of the human race, furthering us in the deepest and best forces and preventing sentimental stagnation and real entanglements by the clear and easy bridges built up between ideality and reality.

The strong mingling intercourse between extreme ideal and real values in the moral appreciation and consideration is called *hypocrisy*. Hypocrisy in its literal Greek significance means secret relation of one thing or idea to another one, the simultaneous double sense of a word or fact in different directions. The supposition for every hypocricy must of course be the continual accessibility of the individual psychic disposition to both opposite magnetic directions, idealism and realism, sentiments and intellectuality. Hypocricy means that the individual is accustomed to take all his actions and opportunities from two very distant opposite points of view at the same time, that there is always simultaneously a pronounced idealistic component in the individual action and a real objective one as well. Hypocrisy most probably then comes about when the individual psychic life-force is thoroughly educated to stay in the accurate middle between idealism and realism, but when it is amenable to the extreme both-sided magnetic attractions in the real and ideal extreme direction, owing to a certain lack of personally concentrating psychic cohesion or terminal concentrative force of character, if we are permitted to say so, that the total lump of the personal psychic magnetic structure or texture is torn one-half going towards the ideal and the other one towards the real extreme localisation. So we have in the soul of the hypocrite two most opposite, absolutely incompatible standpoints which the individual is not able to connect in a logical harmonious way because of lack of personal concentrative strength, because of the disproportion of the distance of the localisation of both extreme psychological accents and the comparative total life-force of the individual who does not satisfy the distance to be covered at all. When Shakespeare speaks once in King Lear about a psychic condition where both sides of a track are taken away and nothing was left in the middle at last, the hypocrite has the same condition in his psychology. He has strong assets in the extremities of the idealistic and realistic side, but has no possibility to reconcile these two opposite elements of his psychology in the central union of a logical and strong personal unity. Hypocrisy means essentially the division of the psychic personality into two parts having two very distant accents of the experience not being reconciliable in the practical life of the individual, and changing therefore continually, every action and experience being considered and interpreted under the double angle of extreme idealism and most narrow real utility. The most important features of the hypocrite are therefore lack of a strong character in a concentrative energetic personality which in the normal life has to bind and amalgamate the opposite elements together in a supreme effort of harmonious humanity, and lack of a very extensive life-force covering normally great tracks of the psychological distance. The hypersensitive personality, too susceptible of, and too amenable to, the magnetic urges from both ideal and real side proves to become fatal to the personal human unity. Too great peripheric extreme vigilance in the extrapersonal direction and divertibility creates of course large outlooks into the psychological universe, but it disturbes the necessary unitarian point of view which ought to be maintained in the personal life in order to be good, consistant and stable in the humane sense. The extremities in the ideal and intellectual direction, the religious fanaticism and the exclusive intellectual science are not in danger to become hypocritical. They are quite sincere, strongly determined in their principal psychological attitude, one too sentimental and the other too intellectual in their intentions. But the intermediary educational type as we have it just in moderate conceptions, is most inclined to the hypocritical divisions of his mind between ideal and real values, if he is not much gifted and if he has strong magnetic attractibilities towards the extreme which he does not understand to overcome in a strong personal human concentration. But the hypocritical type in the sense of the philosophical knowledge is of course very interesting and important. He has the fault, however, that he is greater than his disposition, that he owing to his affective inclination, is continually seduced to move much astray towards the dangerous polar regions of the human psychological gift, so far that he does not find again the way back. But there are the most surprising and most thrilling confrontations of the greatest vital problems, there arise undoubtedly all those philosophical and biological riddles of the human conditions which is so interesting in the theoretic and scientific sense, but which can only be resolved in the practical sense in the mysterious workshop of the strong concentrative accent of the most self-confident and most energetic human personality. May it be that in the scientific and theoretic sense the researches of the extremes of our natural dispositions may be exceedingly interesting, may the urges be quite unexpected and richest in the comparisons and oppositions of the most pronounced sentimental and intellectual values, the perfect solution of this specific vital problem can only be resolved in the personal will of the harmonious human mediocrity.

The pearl of the best human performance means *compromise*. This is indeed not at all a scientific term. But it is a humane better value, an inevitable necessity of sacrifice, also a sort of heroism in the reverse sense, abstemiousness in the heart of the gifted individual. It is, however, not in harmony with the consequence of our extreme logical development, but on the contrary it consists just in the withholding of the outside extreme tendencies, not permitting one of our both principal natural faculties to go its own way along its consequent desire and disposition, but to melt up into the most perfect humane amalgamation, into the peculiar twin-team of the most wonderful biological and psychological miracle, or form the moderate and therefore so venerable and lovely humanity. Humanity means so the arbitrary limitation of our ideal sway, the preconceived humble curtailing of the wings of our divine hopes and goals, but also the restriction of our intellectual consequences and material accumulations. We have to have decency in our material and intellectual claims, tolerance in our uplifting idealism, putting everywhere question-marks and using always self-control: our highest humanity consists in modesty, in self-abnegation in the ideal and real sense. There we receive that unparalleled dignity which we call humanity, not absolutely divine, because it is extenuated by the weight of our material and intellectual formalism and our physiological and economic restricting existence, but not dead and material enough not to shine and to vibrate in the uplifting twilight of the glamour of idealistic hopes. Our living body may be taken as the symbol of our nature, since it is full of material and real conditions claiming their right of existence, but also of ideal feelings and happy vibrating delight expressing their high human development in the upright gait and quivering in charming smiles and the sparkling vivid expression of our sentimental eye.

The JEWISH temperament is conditional on two constructive characteristics. One is the sharp central monosymbolism and the other the absence of rich artistic elaboration. The Jewish character is bound to the periphery prevalently by work and business, whilst the little use of art produces moderate central suggestion. We have, therefore, two extreme features: the strong, cultural, traditional, theistic character with its glaring terminal symbolism, on one side, and the peripheric interest as well, with refined details. The sharp centro-symbolic sill has its strong and free magnetic repercussion in the outspoken interest for intellectual multiplicity and visibility, providing itself a moderate, spiritual-universal excursion.

The Jewish character is very set and minutely vigilant at the same time. Owing to its sharp mono-symbolic principle and the old age of its culture, it has that special interior cohesive self-confidence and pronounced cultural confinement which we meet in a similar way in the old Christian church. By the fact that the Judaism excludes intensive and many-sided artistic activity, excepting the traditional poetry of its old scriptures, it receives a compensatory overweight of the intellectual side, so that we at the same time meet in this interesting cultural type a strong affective centralization and pronounced monotheistic belief and habits, and on the other side, even a more pronounced intellectual real than spiritual taste, inclination and appreciation. We find, therefore, among the Jewish race on the average much more the realistic business type and the clear scientific investigator than the artist. The sharp mono-centralization and the old cultural conservatism confer on the Jew an outspoken *artistic facility* which is visible in any of his actions and enterprises, but the traditional and inherited turning down of the natural artistic inclination brought about the practical discouragement in high spiritual-artistic enterprises. The Jew appears, therefore, only exceptionally as the spiritual artistic mediator and powerful artist, yet he is often the most prominent spiritual leader and superior by his intellectual accuracy, his adaptable objective criticism and moral common sense. On the whole, he has all advantages and disadvantages of the mono-symbolist. The scarcity of artistic practice extenuates, however, the extremes, protects him against material pleasure and luxuriant relapses. Yet his sharp mono-symbolism and the anxious care for the preservation of his cultural roots are rather favorable to habit and real mechanization of the mind. He often loses the philosophical mind and adapts himself too well to the circumstances of the present necessities. He is inclined to unlearn to wonder, after the long course of his old cultural experience. His psychic features are exposed to become extreme to both the idealistic and perhaps even more the realistic side. The hyperemphasis for the concentrative draft makes for terminal conclusiveness, clear and strong results, but also for a certain lack of refinement and shy decency. The carefulness in dealing with artistic values, on the other hand, mitigates this boasting danger in favor of clear thinking and subtle, sober moderation. The Jew has the combination of a clear head and of strong mono-symbolic conclusiveness. He approaches, therefore, the broad outlook of the universal spirituality, on one side, but possesses the restricted historic stability and sharp intellectuality, on the other hand.

Wer immer redlich sich bemueht,
Den koennen wir erloesen.

Goethe

TWELFTH BOOK

The notions of ETHICS AND MORALITY were always very much claimed and discussed in many directions. Never ethics was put into a satisfactory relation to religion or science, but both claimed most convincedly at any time the exclusive and perfect monopoly of moral authority and the power and right of moral legislation. But we saw that religion and science are very different things, none of them having perfect influence on ethics, and it will result from the development of our further meditations themselves, which of these functions is more and which less important as to the formation and subsistence of moral notions, and in what relations they are mutually.

The *scientific* thinking claims the whole development and the exclusive authority of the moral conceptions and laws for itself. The intellectual social world points out that all our moral obligations towards the neighbour and even ourselves are the inevitable and painful product of the objective respect to which we are compelled owing to the necessary multiplicity of the social and universal organization. The visible objectivity of the world creates of course in its countless individual claims the most intense and refined necessity of real apportionment, everyone of the claiming individuals receiving one particle of the common real lump of possession, of visible riches, but also of the ideal goods of honour, authority, love, and consideration according to the number and significance of the fatal competitors. Morality in this conception is the security, inviolability and defence granted to other members of the society in order to enjoy ourselves the same rights and privileges. It is a compulsory, mutual, compromising contract of all individuals of the society longing for mutual support in the real and ideal life and for protection not only against being murdered or slaughtered, but also against any least comparative disadvantage and other deterioration of personal importance in the human life.

So morality or ethics which we will identify, has two opposite effects, a positive and a negative one: in the positive sense it guarantees to us, according to the numeric possibility of the objective surface of the earth, our individual portion and possession and protects us against the exaggerated covetousness of our neighbors: in the negative sense, it checks us to take more from the common social real and ideal lump than duly belongs to us according to the justice of equal apportionment, and protects the fellowman from our exploitation. Morality in this sense is nothing else than objective social justice maintained and regulated by legislative prescriptions. The realization even of this form of ethical justice is a shadow merely hinted to in the public institutions. The will for general justice is overthrown by the ferocity of the serious individual competition, whose plan works as a natural law. The personal force decides about right and wrong. The social state is mostly the product of relative necessity, smashing many individual claims and possibilities of development in the hard battle of competition, but on the other hand also, according to the individually different gifts, giving splendid opportunities to the peculiar psychological conditions of antagonism to unfold the individual qualities to success, in stimulating the individual efforts. Morality ought to be a defence against exploitation of the weak and a prohibition against the truculent audacity of the gifted egotist, insuring a certain middle right of human existence in the real and ideal sense. There is no doubt that this scientific conception of the compulsory morality has its deep and right foundation coming forth from the multiple competition and ending in the peaceful general decree to give and to take, everybody so much as it is mathematically possible under the pressure of the competitive multiplicity, in a harmonious balance. So we see that the objectivity and the scientific superficial conception would be rather close to the law of justice which without personal preference would give to everybody the same part of the whole social pie, in mere mathematical function of a bitter natural necessity.

The monotheistic and monogenial sentimental *religious* conception claims to be the deepest and absolute force of all ethics as well. Judaism and Christianity point out with the authority of their weight that Moses received the Ten Commandments on two tablets of stone from God himself and impose without any psychological discussion these moral authoritative prescriptions on all believers and the legislative culture. But there is the question, how much the established religion is able to create moral laws by its psychological tendencies and according to its magnetic spirit. As the scientific conception distinguishes the morality in our favor and in our disfavor, for ourselves and for our neighbor, so religion makes a difference between the morality and moral duty towards God and our neighbor. This is the greatest and first commandment: Thou shalt love the Lord thy God with all thy heart and with all thy strength and with all thy mind, and the second is like unto it: Thou shalt love thy neighbor as thyself. The love of God corresponds to our subjective individual part in the magnetic universe whose magnetic germ our heart is supposed to be in the sense of religion: the love for the neighbor is founded in our relations to him. But this last conception is not at all chiefly founded in the religious love. Its sentimental foundation is not standing the objective necessities of the life. For the unmeasurable love of God as well as of the neighbor will not further our life and rights, in many ways, but destroy our personal existence in delivering all our claims to the will and the utility of the neighbor and the jealous magnetic attraction of the terminal ideals without leaving us any real possibility of personal rights of developing or strengthening our human individuality. Not only this, the unlimited love of the ideal goal may restrict the possibility for the efficient love for the neighbor owing to the law of compensation, according to which the exaggerated surrender of our life-force towards the direction of the ideal absorbs all our desires, attention and energy for service and makes us, in a sense, therefore, blind, indifferent and ignorant as to the general needs, rights and expectations of our fellowman. The exception of this rule meeting us everywhere among the religiously excited people, is the thorough, but very rare religious genius of great vital life-force: he is remarkable by his retrospeculative refined observation and perception of the social and human needs of his neighbors, recognizing them as in a mirror in the reflection of his divine intuition.

The last point is the hope and the right of the religious conception of the morality, imparting some moral intention to everybody. Moral intention means will of self-preservation, of preservation of the race and of every human being in existence. The divine love by its retrospeculative power produces above all self-respect and self-love of the ideal individual, practically often the main result of most of the praying believers and moreover, in a much more difficult and rare way, the love for the neighbor and for all orders of the created universe. The religious love produces, however, in the first place the strong surrender of the life-force to the terminal idealism, puts there the psychic accent of the individual in the theistic extra-egotistic divine localization and does not emphasize, owing to this, only the divine distance, but also partly neglects the human being. But there is of course at the same time also a kind of strong personal, but indirect emphasis and careful attention of the proper perfection in every divine uplifting sentimentality.

Love of God or idealism and love of the neighbor or objectivity in intellectuality are two very different things. If we will speak thoroughly and sincerely, which is most difficult and dangerous among the harebrained humanity, not standing the truth and not longing for it on the whole, our aspirations for the ideal values correspond to our loving disposition, whilst our relations to the fellowman belong to the realm of our duty and of the objective justice. The religious idealism, with the exception of the retrospeculative very rare geniality, creates rather disinclinations and contempt for the world, because of its multiplicity in itself, as a philosophical radical disturber of the religious simplicity of the heart and because of the faults and imperfections of the human individual of which the religious idealist is of course by far most susceptible. The strong inclination of the most religious people to retreat into deserts and behind the walls of monasteries proves this fact: the solitariness of the hermit and the concealment of the serious idealist thinker are of course also in closest connection with this truth. The behaviour of the last kind of people is very interesting from the moral standpoint, they yield indeed to the pulling energy of the monosymbolic attraction too much at the expense of the social duties towards the neighbor: the monastic life with its reservedness towards the social hard work is the most important and clearest example of as to how much the moral conceptions of the idealistic religious believer become onesided, restricting the connections and duties to the neighbor and emphasizing much more the relations to the subjective ideals, in nearest connection with the self-love and the prevalent personal self-superestimation in comparison to the neighbor. There is of course a double part in this monastic morality and in this idealistic reservedness and solitariness. These people mingle less with the real life, because they claim less real satisfaction, but grant also less. They exclude themselves partly or entirely from the social life, because they have different kinds of claims and psychological possibilities and interest. Their ideal opinions have thrown them out from one part of the normal human life, they are excluded from the real competition of the human race in the intellectual social life: but not only in the material exchange, but also in all the countless psychic relations of vivid connections of intercourse with our fellowmen, whose love, gratefulness, support, and sympathy we in numberless cases forfeit by being retired from the social intercourse and even the business world.

The most important moral relation of any religious or scientific, sentimental or intellectual system consists in its educational

ead of Moses by Mestrovic.   Art Gallery of Toronto.

value. As we know the educational value of every religious, philosophical or artistic system has to be judged according to its peculiar psychodynamic energy and the possibility of rhythmic sequence exercised by it on the detailed performance. The extreme sentimental old system compelled the wings of the affective soul towards the highest goals in angry enthusiasm and dreaming sweeping idealism, neglecting the detailed periphery. The extreme intellectuality, on the contrary, clings to the detailed objectivity and is not able to move energetically towards the central ideal symbolic explosion. The strong psychomagnetic central energy swings the psychological gift over all individual respects and sacrifices so the regard for the individual integrity to the high inspiration for the general central idea, whilst the quiet and sharply just intellectuality gives to the most minute detail what belongs to it, and loses likely, however, the outlook and the correct relations to the terminal ideal.

But the perfect morality wishes the equilibrium between the ideal and the objective general-individual justice. We ought to give to Caesar the things which are Caesar's, and to God, the things which are God's. We should not accelerate our psychic energy at any rate by any psychodynamic help so much as to lose the accurate connections and relations with the detailed objectivity, but we should, on the other hand, neither admit the perfect fixation and lavish dispersion of our psychic energy in the detailed peripheric world in order not to lose our ideal tendencies and relations. This behaviour is most essential for the good disposition of our morality, if we will take it as the equilibrium between our duties to the ideal, to the neighbor and to ourselves.

There is one important thing in all the relations of morality and ethics. It is the notion of *duty* and compromise. There is no more only the question of pleasure, of love and of inclination, but of strict obligation and inescapable duty. Whether we conceive the notion of morality in the sense of the natural science as a production of mere mathematical division, or if we take it as a part of the established religion received by divine direct intercourse as commandments, or even if we conceive it as a consequence of the retrospeculative love for God, everywhere, in all these three cases we see, how much there remains in spite of all invitation always a serious rest of compulsion and inevitable duty which we have to fulfill even against our own interests, against our inclinations and against our personal will. Morality exacts self-control, self-abnegation, modesty, resignation and sacrifice of real advantages in favor of our neighbor and of the idealism. It is the most serious intruding restriction of our own personal development and power which we do not at all understand from the standpoint of our personal or even directly ideal uplifting desire, but easily are able to explain from the standpoint of the social interest, the general real and idealistic justice and the collective progress.

It is essential to ask what system makes us these inevitable compensatory duties easiest, and what system most difficult. This is of course essentially deciding for the educational value of any philosophical system. We do not accept the system which makes us our duties most difficult and unsupportable, but rather that psychological method which educates humanity to go and remain in an easy and harmonious touch with the moral laws.

Can there be anything more wrong than the continual enjoining of the most difficult moral commandments and strictest ethical obligations and at the same time the conveyance of psychodynamic principles which suggest the psychic energy towards quite different goals, where the intentionally psychodynamic philosophical and legislative contents are in strongest contradiction? It is not good to enjoin heavy laws and to burden the shoulders of the weak humanity with them and to make them so much more difficult by connection and application of contradictory psychodynamic rules which do not at all suggest the easy adaptation to those duties. We see this very well in the practical life. The strong sentimental education does not permit harmonious relations between the strict compensatory repression of all affective desires in enthusiastic love and admiration for beauty and idealism: there is no help in any threatening commandment and prescription against facts and moral attitudes whose existence is most energetically challenged by the whole systematic psychodynamic conception of the religious sentimental life in general. Here is the point where the modern world is right to be afraid of the old extreme idealistic conception of the life.

But what is the reason why the old sentimental religion puts so much push towards the ideal goal in the psychodynamic sense, and what is the reason why the modern science is so reserved and sticks exclusively to the objective world and its detailed interests? The strong psychodynamic energy of the old mediaeval religious conception had the intention to give strong movements in order to reach the ideal terminal goals, to communicate the divine sentimental discharge of the soul which means the last and indispensable conclusiveness of our peculiar psychological reactions. It is a part of our ethical conception of the world to connect our vital reactions to the terminal monosymbolic great idea in whose logical connection are given excellent directions and instructions for the intermediary behaviour and the general conception of the life in the detailed expression. But there are different difficulties. First, this terminal goal means one point, far from the universal comprehension and is, therefore, quite subjective and insufficient and connected only with the individual experience and possibilities, whilst the morality is built up as well on objective necessities, and then this clear monosymbolic elaboration creates, as we know, the strongest sweeping energy blurring the logical detailed emphasis, which means negligence of the real morality in spite of good sentimental *orientation,* and overthrows all the necessary carefulness and respect for the detailed work in enthusiastic idealism. So the absolute idealism indeed has two opposite sides, a very useful and a very damaging one. The educational one-sidedness of the extreme idealistic system is, therefore, excellent in its exact symbolization as to the conclusiveness and the energetic push going through the individual and through all necessary experience, but hurtful in its irresistible carelessness and lack of circumspection on the way.

In the modern natural scientific conception we have the contrary: the sharp detailed respect for the objectivity of the way, the peculiar conditions for every situation of experience and surroundings, but we have instead the lack of enthusiastic progression and terminal ideal symbolization in order that the weakness of this system consists in the lack of ultimate judgment and undertaking energy. Here we have the most conscientious accuracy, true objectivity, patient elaboration, scarcity of terminal-logical achievement until the last values of simple imaginative notions and symbols. There is no danger of carelessness, of misrepresentation, of negligence in the intellectual scientific action, everything has its sharp intellectual illumination and faithful logical description.

The idealistic method has the contrary danger. Had intellectualism the advantages of the sentimental mystic method at the same time, or had the idealistic education and psychodynamic constitution simultaneously the assets of the intellectual one, then everything would be all right in the moral sense also. But as we see, truth, goodness are divided values. Energy and conclusiveness are looked from one side, detailed observation, and patience considered from the other. In one case we have the faithfulness to the terminal ideal and receive in it great efficacy, excellent outlook and conclusiveness, justice to the last goals and to the individual satisfied egoism which is very near to this subjective idealistic conception, which on the other hand sacrifices upon the whole the individual to its purposes, in the other case we have the full justice as to the conscientious apportionment of the objective world, and its dividing legislation giving to everybody his minutely balanced share, but under a point of view which, as sharp as it illuminates the individual objective conditions, neglects the universal relations of humanity in itself.

Were idealism able to stop its sentimental push on the middle of its way, would it be able to extenuate the energy of its rhythm to the moderation of more calm reasonable progression, then humanity would be saved in its ethical role: would the reality of the scientific intellectuality possess more strength of concentration, relating everything irrevocably to ennobling purposes, quickening its idealizing simplificaton in more pushing enthusiasm, then everything would be good in our ethics which is composed out of both extremes of the real and ideal *"justesse."* But both of these methods are not able to do this work, both being extreme and onesided in their educational effect. Both are great in their relative thoroughness, but in the extreme contrary sense, whilst the justice of the moral life exacts the two respects, the utmost regard and carefulness in the peripheric and in the central direction of the realistic objective and of the idealistic subjective pole. It is always the greater amount of the total individual life-force which is able to improve these conditions, to build bridges over the insufficiency of the one-sided educational conception and which has, therefore, always chances to mitigate in the individual the methodical distractions brought about by a wrong conception of life.

Ethymologically morality and ethics mean both, in Latin and Greek, the customs or habits of people. We have to see in them, therefore, that habitual fixation of conceptions and actions most frequent among people which are most thoroughly enrooted unto their local conscience and their public opinion. The ideas and conceptions which succeeded in intruding most thoroughly and most convincingly upon the psychology of the nations, have formed the customs and habits of them, and have received in time so much stress and practical skill, possessed themselves in innumerable hereditary repetitions so often within the soul of the whole society and of the individual that we indeed have a perfect suggestive dominion of them in the individual and national subconscious mind, in the conscious and in the public opinion. There is nothing to do against this arbitrary fatal dominion of any habits and moral customs wrong as they may be from the absolute philosophical standpoint, than to beat them by other more valuable, more efficient, more patient, more intruding and more convincing ideas, systems and customs in long intentionally preconceived work. The better is the only proof against the inferiority of the good.

Morality is, therefore, the product of cultural inheritance and the longest runner of educational influences of one cultural unity in the same direction. It is, as we said already, formed by two opposite factors: the theoretical idea which expresses partly the universal will in the philosophical and religious formality of any system, and at the same time by the social intellectual necessity of the practical conditions of the life. The individual has to go through between these two powers very carefully. He has to adapt himself to both of them so much that none of them is neglected and none superestimated. The idealistic philosophical and religious principle corresponds to the will of the individual augmenting absolute happiness, divine desire, pleasure of the longing heart and the consistent idea, whilst the social intellectual restriction on the contrary involves the notion of compulsion and duty, shortcoming of universal freedom and happiness and enlargement of the individual power. Morality has therefore the supposition that there must be normally a habitual state in the society, where the ideals and the practical necessities are amalgamated into social appearances and utterances of habits, pervading and characterising the culture of any time.

Nobody will contradict, when I say, that morality in all nations and at all times was different, that it was always different in all religions and diverges in all climates and races. Already the ideal conceptions of any nations register changes though generally not very much. But the practical and intellectual necessities of the social life may be and are always very different in different ages and historic circumstances. For this reason any habit may be quite immoral in some country or time, whilst they are permitted or even most desirable duties under another sun or other political and cultural conditions. It is the continual change of the exterior circumstances which modifies most the morality. But it is also the localisation of the psychological accent either on the ideal affective subjective pole or on that of the intellectual objective experimental duty or between them which decides also very much the character of any morality. We forcedly have therefore indeed quite different notions of morality in the most deserted country-village or in a big city because of their very different intellectual practical needs, necessities and opportunities. We have as well strong different moral customs and conceptions in the idealistic affective milieu, in the intellectual world of the working duty and in the humane middle conditions of both. But everywhere are dangers and facilities, different and even in the opposite sense, but surely they are everywhere.

The most happy and morally most successful state of the human mind is undoubtedly that which permits or gives most *parallelism in love and duty*. That theoretical system which contradicts the real necessities very seriously in its magnetic tendencies and which therefore aggravates the natural difficulties of the human duties instead of extenuating them—must be considered as a bad and deplorable philosophical or religious method in the sense of our present existence. It is the sentimental task of the theoretical idea to be adaptable to the practical intellectual necessities, not to destroy the individual happiness of the personal unity of the human mind in resisting the inevitable necessities of the fate.

Virtue is just the harmonious moral state between these two opposite poles of the ideal-sentimental or divine enthusiasm and the intellectual necessity or duty. The probability of virtue is, therefore, so much greater as the one-sidedness of one of these prevalent factors may be less. The strong one-sided idealism with its extreme claim of obeisance, with the exceeding energetic uplifting desire creates the most powerful individual sentimental will, the most pronounced desire for ideal happiness at the expense of everything else which it has decided to sacrifice for this affective passion of its heart and creates, therefore, in the sense of virtue the most difficult tensions and oscillations producing heroism and vices, highest deeds and sin, wars, quarrels, victories and defeats, exultations and suffering, but never that serious and persevering middle stage of the human mind and habits which we call virtue. The strong, stiff and ruthless accentuation of the extreme idealism in its most pronounced sentimental one-sidedness is, therefore, not inclined at all to produce the happy, sure basis of practical quiet virtue and morality. The idealistic spoiling education has implanted into the heart much too ambitious desires for happy subjective ideal fulfillments which the practical life with its intellectual and material necessities never will be able to recognize or to respect.

The fixation of the uplifting ideal eagle to the real world by the infliction of the *Ten Commandments* or the commandments of the churches is interesting. The first thing is the fact that any moral or historic systems never undertake to create strong contradictions between idealism and reality, between the individual desire for happiness and the objective necessity of the life. Can the objective necessity of society, or ought it to be formulated by any previous systematic commandments? The objective necessities of the life produce themselves coming out from the competition of countless ever changing circumstances and they form in that manner always new exterior moral necessities which never were before and do not come again afterwards . The most mischievous thing happening on earth is the establishment of any philosophical, religious or theological system which discredits the real duty out-coming from the intellectual social necessisty of the life. Even if in the case of emergency the ideal religion throws the weight of her authority in the injunction of definite intellectual commandments on the scale of the social reality, this is doubtful for two reasons. First, and above all, because the individual acts according to his heart and love and less efficiently according to the objective necessity. The most efficient way is always this of the heart and not of the intelligence. Now, if the historic religion has too divergent directions from the inclination of the real necessities, it is no more able to persuade the human heart to real duties because it is hypnotized by the beauty and greatness, and not willing to part from the idealistic one-sided promises. And even if necessity forces the fulfillment of real respects upon the individual's activity, he is not at all able to do proficient real work, because the ideal desire takes away the psychic energy in a far and very magnetic direction. The second reason is the incompetency and incapability of the psychological ideal accent to regulate the minute objective reality, leading to failure. We are wrong, and will be soon taught, if we think that the objective world and its multiple necessities are very docile to any ideal suggestion. Idealism is blind for the necessitiees of the real world, it disregards and scorns the minute inevitable values of the categoric circumstances and asserts therefore always that things are possible in the real world which prove to be impossible and hurt and destroy in this way the bold experimental individual. The sentimental idealism avails itself of the human disposition as the instrument of its experiences attempting the most possible ideal inspiration of the material and intellectual world, but crushing and killing continuously the most hopeful and most gifted individual by the desperation of the real misfortune which follows the too bold audacity of ideal penetration into the real intellectual and material world. There is a limit. But idealism and enthusiasm do not know limits. They are blind in the direction of the height and of the depth, but they sacrifice the peculiar idealistic realistic disposition of the human nature and individual at the extreme boundaries of their active abysses. The predecessors of the success and of the enlargement of the ideal dominion must perish in material unsuccessfulness and in the lack of the habitual traditional morality.

Ideal subjective love should end in objective social duty and objective duty in genial ideal love. These two poles should stay always in a kind of harmonious equilibrium in the human life. We see in this point always the most serious divergencies. The human nature always is inclined to turn over to one extreme in an absolute manner. But what is more unreasonable and more dangerous because of unhappy relapses and material ruinous danger than the absolute idealist and what more despicable, petty and insignificant than the complete effusion of the personal life-force into the multiple objective world of small respects and real duties? The real morality lies here again in the middle. It is the peculiar virtuous activity and attitude of the personal feelings and understanding guiding the individual carefully between the blind arrogance of self-centred egoism and the theistic enthusiasm and the mean depression of the material exclusiveness.

We see, of course, here again that the more gifted individual is much more likely to be moral in a stable sense. He has more vista to join at the same time ideal will and conception and to be enough understood in the detailed reality to be successful in his practical actions. There must be at the same time and always real and ideal respects. But they must be moderate, not too far away from each other in order not to make the destruction of the individual personal unity by suffering, hypocrisy, lack of will power and inefficiency.

The TEN COMMANDMENTS represent the decree to express the absolute ideal will and the real necessities of our human nature in one short legislative resumé and compromising crystallization. They relate partly to the ideal will of our nature and partly to the intellectual relations of our social necessities. According to the idealistic views, the three first commandments relating to the idealistic activity of the human heart are on the whole commandments of agreeableness and only in so far exacting sacrifices as possibly the individual utilitarian egoism has to retire before the jealous magnetic energy of the terminal idealism. The seven following commandments have on the contrary in a sense the character of compulsatory restriction of our individual egoistic and ideal divine natural disposition. In the first part of the series of the Ten Commandments we have the emphasis of the terminal symbolization, in the second part, the conditional formulation of our practical behaviour in the world, owing to the intellectual social circumstances, which, however, as we said, are continually changeable and must be in this degree adaptable to the life, if they will have the claim of lasting authority. The Ten Commandments are indeed, on the whole, more or less well adapted to the necessities of the life; they contain in the roughest way about those practical exactions which lie at the very root of our social conditions and are until now not very much changed, though seemingly in different commandments, the most thorough and serious necessities of change are in preparation threatening over the head of the present society like dark clouds from which soon the lightnings of revolution, war and social destruction could be discharged. Wars and revolutions may be the consequence of social wrongs, of lacking interpretation of the most general natural laws of mutual moral relations, may they be brought about by national mutually cheating manoeuvres or by whole artificial systems in business or personal life by which the first and radical moral principles are circumvened and excluded.

The sharp symbolization of the notion of the divine idealism is besides all its advantages in itself very dangerous, because it attracts by its sharp monodetermination the individual magnetic power of the gifted believer much too much, spoiling in this the personal equipment of the individual in relation to himself and to the surrounding society which both suffer and are relatively and compensatorily neglected. There must be comprising respect for terminal ideal conclusions of all our life in the outside universe, but the monopunctual humanized symbolization is most dangerous for many reasons as we pointed out over and over again.

The love and the respect for the parents commanded in the *fourth commandment* is up to a certain degree most natural and in accordance with the affective individual's will of existence. But who will decide where and how strongly the diverging will of the idealistic child starts to resist the human imperfection and faults of his parents who are relative as the child himself? Where will the idealistic pride of the child thwart the real dominion of the parental authority? It thinks to have done the best service to his ideal God because of having carried through his idealistic wilful conceptions of wrong and right? Here we have already the commencement of the "unnecessary" tragedy of the human life of the idealist who is thrown into serious troubles, contradictions and tensions by the compulsatory obedience to his parents, whilst by his divine uplifting pride he is most independent at an early age of their personal authority which means to him an accidental and subordinate condition questionable in the life of the absolute ideal accent ruling his mind. Who is my father and mother? He who does the will of my Father.

This special condition comes out much more in the *fifth commandment*. This commandment does at least away with the wrong supposition that the idealistic type on behalf of his intentional condition, is the great lover and friend of humanity. Its tenor is eloquent and tragic enough, being so modest and draconic in the reserved optimism: Thou shalt not kill. Here we have the confession of the embittered mentality likely to come about among people who are too much convinced of their rights and the wrong of the others, a condition which occurs most seriously and most dangerously in the high tension of the self-centered idealistic will with its sharp monodetermination. In this we have again an unnecessary strong antagonism between idealism and reality. Suffering, inefficacy and unhappiness will be the result in every case where not a very strong total life-force or a deep speculative energy guarantees a better solution of the problem of the life of the neighbor and one-self.

The *sixth commandment* is especially interesting. The sexual desire is the arch-competitor of the terminal idealism. It exists and is one of the strongest inclinations of human nature. The sexual function throws the terminal idealist from the top of the tower of his proud tendencies to the next lower story, but he remains still on the idealistic height of humanity, looking towards the ideal future of later generations and of following evolutionary development. Idealistic and sexual desires have the nearest connection in goals, ways and tendencies; the extreme terminal idealism may be the very best educator and predecessor to strong sexual idealistic desires and is able to insinuate even an undesirable degree of hypercultivation of sexuality in its ideal desire and in the psychodynamic way to it. There are moral paradoxes in their relations underlying the whole view of the future population of a culture. It is the intellectual and real side of sexuality which has the function of a strong necessary damping power on this desire every moment in a position to burst out into the flames of intellectual and social destruction. The monogamic conception of the sexual life may be the best expression of real and economic conditions, but not at all the consequence of extreme idealistic conceptions which, on the contrary, mean by no means a facilitation, but a serious and heavy aggravation of the duty of the monogamic sexuality. Extreme idealism creates deep love, sense and susceptibility for beauty, strong sentiments, kindling from the individual towards the terminal symbol, easy change of intellectual representation, in a sense, and aids, therefore, the idealistic individual to switch easily from the object to different, more perfect and more instigating objects of his sexual desire. The extraordinary sharp contradiction to this temperamental exhaustibility in the sixth commandment of the church is, therefore, so much more fatal and disturbing for the quiet psychological temperamental performance of the extreme idealistic individual. It has often practically the effect of a pitfall or an open mouth of a wild beast into which the believing idealistic individual has been driven most thoroughly by sentimental idealistic conceptions and from which he can no more be delivered, suffering and aching, therefore, much more than the more moderate and more realistic people educated far away from the fascinating power of elevating idealism.

The foundation of the *seventh commandment* is the just apportionment of the real and ideal possessions of the world in material goods and in the good reputation, honor and power which everybody needs coming into this world and being obliged to perform a certain degree of accumulation of material acquisition and authority around his individual magnetic kernel. In this point the extreme sincere idealist is in the case to have too many difficulties. He is principally educated to scorn these goods of the world, and has at the same time the necessity to have and to use them more than anybody. The spiritualized type has not the means of the aggressive realist and the energetic defence against the attacks of his realistic competitor and adversary and has, therefore, in this realm the greatest real difficulties coming from his one-sided idealistic conceptions which are not congruant with the real necessities of the life.

The intellectual world cheats this commandment too easily: the idealistic legislation is not in a position to do away with trust and other companies and all kinds of tricks of the modern capitalism, which all intend to conduct the material riches of the world and the power of the public opinion into the channel and possession of a few audacious, unscrupulous realistic people. The theoretical law is always made by the idealistic extreme systems so that the great thieves are free, whilst the small ones are hanged. The churches in spite of their radically good intentions were never able to overcome the real tricks of the intellectual society.

It is due to the organisatory impotence of the sentimental character of the church that it is at a loss to do away with these individual intentions, not being able to look inside of the psychic function, principally optimistic, and yet being only concerned with the exterior civil legislation which is so far away from the thorough possibility of perfect justice and social equality.

The *eighth commandment* is perhaps the deepest and most thorough trial and run of a moral law, because it is based on the truth and consequence of our sentiments in the most general way. It unrolls the deepest and most complicated laws of psychological relations between the real objective intellectual life and the ideal sentiments; it exacts the harmonious logical connection of real performing duty and of sincere ideal sentiments at the same time. It exacts the most pronounced proof of personal strength and the most covering energetic real activity, the fact of continual comparison of the terminal intentions and of the present real circumstances, the serious trial to relate both to each other in logical consequence and consistence. But just the extreme distance of both the two standpoints of the idealistic and realistic view with their pronounced sharpness, which are not always practically compatible within the relativity of all human truth in the objective and ideal sense, induce the individual to transgress the limits of the absolute veracity and create difficulties in the psychological attitude of truth which are much more insuperable than they are in the experience of any other more moderate type.

Nobody will be so thoroughly and in such a humiliating way compelled to belie his highest principles as the great idealist. If he does not, he will perish by the weight and the truth of the objective reality whose prey his individual existence will be. Christ was the most pronounced or elaborated example of this heroic idealism which destroyed his individuality because he clang most thoroughly and consequently to his one-sided sentimental truth. His idealistic absolutism was thwarted by the real conditions of his intellectual human existence, and if he was the most splendid sacrifice for the general human hopes and universal claims, he on the other side had to pay the tribute to the relativity of human nature in the real destruction of his categoric personal existence.

The *ninth and tenth commandment* have the intention to stabilise the sexual and material possession, not to permit any individual displacement as to the wife or the material good of anybody: both right, but also both too narrow and too definite prescriptions, because circumstances may occur, where nature craves inevitably for changes of these conditions.

But there is indeed the urge for most thorough moral meditations given in the ninth and tenth commandment of Christianity and Judaism. The degree and the possibility of becoming moralised is dependent on the degree and the natural possibility of becoming accustomed to something. Moral discipline, civilisation and culture mean altogether a state of mind and habits where a human collectiveness agrees in the acceptance of certain intellectual formulas which are definitely expressed in legal notions. Our capability of accepting these historic formulas, our habitability and amenability to the ruling laws of a country is deciding as to how much we can be able of morality and loyalty in the sense of this special culture. From the standpoint of the local culture the question of our morality is just a question of our affective temperament in that sense that the too vivid psychodynamic development of the human nature, like a quick physiological oxydation, as it were, creates habits very quickly and thoroughly, but being soon disgusted of, leaves and changes them therefore. This individual psychorhythmic peculiarity, how quickly and how long any individual is able to form, to retain and to appreciate his habits, is perhaps the most thoroughly deciding point of the moral value of any individual. Howsoever has more need of changing intellectual principles than the average person, be it in intellectual philosophy and religious dogmas, in sexual intercourse or material possession, is of course more exposed not to be the lasting adherant of any legal localised morality. This individual will likely earlier or later apostatize from the stiff tenor of the old immovable legal and moral statements and will progress to other novel, perhaps more perfect, in every case for him surely more inviting and individually more attractive intellectual expressions of ideal values. This behaviour, in the sense of the legal fixation of the past historic conception which encroaches on the present, may be forcedly deemed as wrong and criminal. But we must not forget that every present legislation and every historic moral order has its necessary limits. It is one of the innumerable links of human psychological evolution, one of the ever changing waves or one of the falling leaves in the autumn which have all their time of existence and highest culmination, but have also their time to fall and to alternate with subsequent later similar developments.

There is of course the question whether the need of quick moral and legal changes of the individual has to be put on account of his personal temperamental disposition or of the insufficiency of the intellectual system or of both and how much of each part. May climate, descendency, race and other factors have a great influence on the quickness and changeability of our psychodynamic rhythms which are of course in nearest connection and perfect parallelism with the physiological, bodily oxygenability of the blood, they are as well in nearest connection with the character of religious education and its principles. The strong bluffing power of the sharp symbolism creates the angry and quick temperament of the mind, going ahead most energetically and thoroughly in the individual psychic action towards ideal conclusiveness, but also in everything else, in morality, in sexuality, even in the physiological functions of the body as well. The strong *Latin* fervent peculiarity and the slow northern performances in everything are put together with the climate: they may be: yet there is surely above all the peculiar philosophical background which is also responsible for this special difference of the Latin and *Teutonic* character and their specific morality. The religious education comes in for a great deal in the foundation of the specific formulation of the rhythmic temperament of all nations and ages.

The moral values of the northern and southern countries are essentially different. The northern type keeps more the formalistic intellectual and exterior faithfulness to his theoretic principles, the southern Latin individual puts more stress on the sentimental direction and loses so easily the formalistic dogmaticism. We may also say the reverse and prove it without difficulty (all extremes touch), but on the whole the first kind of conception may be the better one. The sophistication of the Latin type from any kind of partly wrong conception is generally much quicker: he digests the psychological experience with much more speed, being first more bluffable and gullible; he commits the wrongest faults in exaggerated enthusiasm, but is for this reason cured at a time, when the slower psychodynamic temperament of his northern brother starts only with the work of first distinctions of the roughest outline of the system presented to him by fate, history and religious founders. The reformation of older systems prove in the eyes of the sophisticated Latin type only, how little the northern race was able to recover from former principles. We see, therefore, how much the Germanic type is inclined to the lasting morality in the legal sense, because he sticks a long time closely to his formulas and needs much more time, many centuries often, to look through their weaknesses, because he did not love enough his strong needs and not desire enough his positive values from the beginning. The Latin type on the contrary is so thorough in sincere enthusiasm and ideal sway and love of any offered moral and legal system that he too soon is disappointed in discovering the imperfections which hurt his feelings. For he took the system as the expression of his sentimental intention in life, whilst the intellectual Teutonic type rather would conceive, up to a certain degree, the idealism as the logical terminal consequence of his legal system. One is more idealist, the other realist. So one of these two types is more moral in the sentiments and in the thoroughness of his speculative intentional conceptions, the other more in the intellectual minute expressions, in the most petty conscientiousness and in the persevering faithfulness to any given historic moral and legal tenets.

Morality is also a temperamental question in that sense that it exacts the most careful intellectual formalism which often practically has nothing to do with the sincere intention and sentiments of the individual, is rather in a certain compensatory relation to them, being possibly the mere consequence of logical habitual exterior development and the result of social and circumstantial compulsion of the visible surface of the world. So the exterior historic representation of the morality, the LAW, is often far away in its tyrannical habitual weight from what is right and wrong and therefore not at all just and careful enough in its judgments. The merely intellectual development of the legal morality is most hurtful to humanity. Any law which has lost the connection with the individual responsibility and the personal sentimental touch is nothing else than a cruel gallows where also some innocent may be hanged. The paragraph that lack of knowledge of a law is no excuse, is of course the most upsetting moral statement possible, because it is "immoral".

The most honestly sentimental individual is possibly the worst knower and minute observer of the literal intellectual tenets of the moral legal statements of the world. The most refined intellectual interpreter and explainer of the last shades of the moral laws, being most able to move on the polished floor of the intellectual legislation (qui s'excuse s'accuse) is perhaps the most shameless rascal individually without any sentimental respects nor knowledge. So we see here once more the unshakable law of compensation peeping everywhere through all possible clefts of the human fate. The most ideal type, full of deepest and best sentiments, is most easily caught in the pitfalls of formalistic incorrectness because of his detailed blindness and ignorance of the law; the greatest scoundrel with the most questionable conceptions of good and bad, on the contrary is, according to his experience and attention to the most minute interpretation of the legislative paragraphs, often the most victorious man in any law-court. The idealist has truth and greatness, but in a potential state, whilst the others understand to use the smaller amount of the right they possess and destroy therefore by their practical intellectual activity and habitual skill the most prominent, but inadaptable strength of divine authoritative accumulation and concentration. This is the general fate of the one-sided idealist who has good intentions and best sentiments being the source and authority of right himself and of legislation as well, but has not developed his inner strength until the last exterior instrumental organisation of intellectual and legal defence. Only this last state of development has the possibility of being useful in the practical social life. But we must not forget on the other hand that times, circumstances and more intellectual conditions and necessities of the world change continually, whilst the busy lawyer and moralist stick too long to their historically and traditionally crystallised paragraphs. They have according to this fact sunk into them all their life-force and lost compensatorily their sentimental judgment.

It is the minute precision of the law which checks its adaptability to all special cases and persons. The more general the law is, the more thorough and lasting value will it have in its elastic and adaptable nature, but the much more easy will it be for the individual and the special situation of any case to switch between its rough claws: reversely the most elaborate law with the most detailed and intimate remarks and determinations has the least chance to live a long time; for the refined circumstances for which it is made, change soon, and moreover, all individual cases, not exactly suitable for this preconceived legal situation, are not concerned with this exclusive law. For this reason we understand that the old ten commandments are of long lasting possibility. They are formulated in the broadest way referring only to the most general and human psychological and intellectual relations. They have therefore the possibility to keep for a very long time their practical valitity. They have the vista to live very long, because they are general and not individual in advance, because they are freed from all that warm human blood of the special adaptation to the intellectual circumstances and experiences which is so richly infused into the world's legal court. The religious law has therefore in its idealistic relationship a strong authoritative back-bone and in its more general relations more vista of lasting validity, whilst the civic law in its sharp and exceedingly multiple intellectual necessity is much more intruding, much more critical, but also much more ready and efficient in the real life, has, however, so much more the disadvantage of possible injustice, of undeserved sentimental ignorance and of serious wrong because it is more active and determined. The strong intellectual emphasis of the legal paragraph is of course exceedingly dangerous. First this paragraph has the chief meaning of being the reflection and the intellectual representative of philosophical ideas which ought to be behind its formulation. It has therefore to find out the defendent's connection and relation to this philosophical basis and sentimental atmosphere being behind the legal expressions. In the practical case the most progressed law naturally does perhaps not suit the psychological situation for the necessary solution which involves always quite special intellectual and psychological features which rightly must be treated and justified in an individual way, according to their character. It is moreover difficult in itself in the examination of the parties of any legal action, to find out the different objective circumstances, as they were and are in any social entanglement or collision of individual interests. The false witnesses are more frequent than it is generally expected or feared. The compulsatory obligation of swearing at the Bible supposes the belief in it (but the very Bible exacts never to swear, but only to say yes and no) and may be, even in believing people, the antagonistic competition with many other deeper convictions or rights in the sentimental direction challenged by the legal imperfect temptation, and even duty and character may be seriously at stake. The noble idealist in any case says the truth, so swearing is not necessary to him, whilst the scoundrel accepts this comfortable cloak in order to receive credit and to say so the things favorable to his advantage, with equal belief. The one's word is as good as the other's.

The lawyer himself with the characteristic sentimental sophistication of the intellectual people, expects as a rule the logical consequent support of his professional interests connected with his victorious issue and with the defeat of the contrary claim. The deepest and most weighty things in psychological quarrels and intricacies are, in addition, not expressable or explainable in words; they are not even known and recognised by the quarreling individuals themselves, not speaking of the intellectual refined knowers of the legal paragraphs, who seem to be very wise in the eyes of the exterior appearance, and may be very stupid in the light of the deepest truth and facts of psychological and philosophical relations which, however, rule the whole universal and individual life and right. These are therefore very often compensatorily non-amenable to the detailed intellectualist. It is quite different to be able to distinguish in the language of the legal intellectuality the smallest offences against the social conventions, or to have the most attentive ear for the deepest philosophical meaning and sense pervading the whole universal, human and individual fate with clear, but very subdued emphasis, easily overheard in the noise of the intellectual legal paragraphs. But only the justice equipped with the most susceptible and subtle ear for the deepest psychological connections and with the necessary respect and outlook for their mutual causation, is in a position to be the capable and definite *judge*. If the lawyer in general has the more scientific and general task of the circumstantial detailed proofs according to the letter of the legal paragraph, and if he in his disagreeable hard work is exposed to all kinds of errors, brought about owing to his own personal and political ambition, intellectual shortsightedness or superficiality and to his earning desire and necessity, to the unreliability of his clients and false witnesses, to the tricks of circumstances and to the inadaptability of his antiquated or otherwise unfitting laws, then it is indeed, as the help in the eleventh hour, the role of the finally deciding judge to look through this complicated net or cobweb of confusing intellectual dates and to use the subtle ear for the sentimental interspheric glorious music, sounding in a reserved, but determined majesty from the deepest wells of the psychological life, from the digressing root of quarrelling individuals. Legal actions are, in spite of all, almost always the issue of previous sentimental disagreements. The deep affective antagonism is mostly the reason if not the subject of exterior quarrels. This is the cause, why colliding interests cannot be put right by the concerned people themselves: for these thorough disagreements they cannot understand each other. The smallest things and most insignificant circumstances are picked up and engrossed incredibly by quarrelling individuals, owing to the deep affective differences and non-parallelisms which they expect and strive to carry through in the exaggeration of superficial non-conformities.

LIE, slanders, misrepresentations and exaggerations are very frequent in legal actions, because every party has a quite different point of view in its egotistic and sentimental attitude. Lie in itself may so be defined as the subjective conception and the special affective relationship of the intellectual objectivity to a personal standpoint or the projection of the individual intention or philosophical conviction into the outside real world. The lawyer very often may not be aware of his and other's misrepresentation of the objective truth, because he is guided by the affective sway of his temperament and of his desire to accept the outside circumstances in a light favorable to his best personal sentiments and convictions. Quod volumus credimus libenter. Objective truth in a quarrel of two individuals is a rare and difficult thing. Both represent the situation wrong in the desire to gain their case, both are misled by their egotistic passion and by the instinctive fear of their personal vital energy so that they easily distract the objective real facts, and it is again the question of the definite judgment to compare, to analyze and to reduce the double and opposite one-sidedness and to find out, in the comparison, the objective right and the intellectual truth as well. It is of course even for the shrewdest or most honest defending representative of any legal action most difficult to get rid of the one-sided sentimental attitude of his client. Sympathetic participation with the sentiments of the confident client is too natural than not to have the most pronounced seductive effect on the investigating lawyer. He may be often indeed the continually cheated victim of his clients who instil on him the interests and the point of view of their one-sidedness, and he has received the cheap task to fix and to express these views in the intellectual letter of the legal paragraph. So two quite opposite stand-points, both wrong because both subjective, arise and develop into an intellectual system, supported and elaborated by scientific men, and it is again the terminal battle, where these two formidable adversaries meet and look to defeat each other. It is again the cause of the idealism to reduce the intellectual law to the sentimental value, to strip them from their accidental and exterior intellectuality and to decide in favor of that individual who is nearer the objective and human truth, and the more valuable, most important sentimental depth is that which can be better understood as well in the light of the intellectual legislation. It is again the greater total amount of life-force which likely will gain the battle of right and wrong, because probably the more gifted individual has, if there is a normal middle disposition of intellectual and affective elaboration, at the same time the deeper and more fundamental sentiments and the larger objective truth. The judge has to investigate both and has to find out and to compare the individual predilection for objective intellectual and ideal sentimental emphasis. The more provable objectivity may be wrong because of lack of deep sentimental rights and so the deepest sentimental sincerity may be easily overthrown because of intellectual unprovabilities or formalistic legal inadaptability.

What is CONSCIENCE? This word points out that somebody has a certain knowledge of something. In our life we receive knowledge by experience and learning and we call our brain with its memory the place of the recollection of all our former personal and phylogenetic real experiences. If we call our *brain* the historic concentration or, if we will, the armouries of all the phylogenitic instruments for necessary actions of defence and of fight, put to our disposal by our ancestors, then we might call the *heart* the seat of our conscience. Our conscience is the recollection or anticipation of the interspheric magnetic experiences of our affective nature. The conscience has like the brain and recollection in regard to the intelligence with the means of ideas, in the way of feeling the role of guidance and correction of our actions and psychological and intellectual tendencies. There is the question whether the conscience is the sentimental accompaniment of our intellectual educational habits and inheritance, or whether it is the consequence of the former magnetic experiences of our sentimental idealistic mind before its human incarnation or, third, whether it is to be conceived as the divine anticipation of present and future universal magnetic harmonies and repulsions. The conscience has indeed the effect of the continual correction and *re-instradation* of our intentions and actions in regard to farthest actions and intentions being repulsed from the universal magnetic flow as soon as there is some non-parallelism in individual inclinations and universal magnetism. Good conscience means the harmony of the universal magnetic disposition or inheritance of our heart with the real actions of our intelligence and our corporeal organism with its urges. The function of the human brain lies perhaps between the animal appetite of the merely physiological inclinations of our corporeal nature and our sublime conscientious refinement. Our intellectual recollection protects us and checks us from many actions which seem good to the animal part of our natural instincts, whilst again the conscience withdraws from many practical actions which would be permitted by the intellectual gift and the memory. There are strong contradictions between psyiological animal instincts and intellectual recollecting judgment, but also between the last and the conscience as there are also special bonds of intimacy between them in every combination.

Remorses are offences of our magnetic universal dispositions by real non-conformity of our actions. But on the other hand the importance of the conscience can be superestimated, because we know that it can be educated wrongly. It can be spoiled or almost killed, modified and changed by educational influences. Somebody, owing to natural disposition, inheritance or education, may have remorses, in one case, where the other one has not, and one may condemn seriously which the other one of different character and education acknowledges as reasonable and good. It results from this fact that the conscience at least partly, and for a great deal, must be able to be educated and communicated and formed during the individual's life, that its magnetic ideal attraction has not even the meaning of absolute exclusive validity, because it is also the production of arbitrary educational influences on the soul, perhaps even more than the intellectual memory which is based on categoric experiences.

The notion of conscience is of course one of the most interesting and important. It is able to create and to discard great expectations and hopes of the human idealist according as we choose our attitude towards it. There is no doubt that the rise and existence of our conscience has categoric relations and is influencible by them. But there is further also no doubt that some remainder of an unchangeable basis of conscience lies under all these influences which hardly has been built up by personal experience nor can be entirely extinguished by them. There are features in the psychology of the conscience which excell by far everything which has ever been experienced by humanity in its intellectual real life, it recalls potentialities of the heart or rather more releases most distanced desires of our psychic nature looking in the reflection of our consciousness like the lost paradise, showing the highest wings of our future ideal aspirations. Our ideal mind has always like a seed of a flower a strong thriving energy in the direction of its generating eternal developing growth. The root of the conscience is the safe-guard of this "longitudinal" universal growth of our human nature, as it were, whilst the intellectual memory means the defence of the intellectual and real peripheric horizon of our displayed life.

Light, multiplicity, visibility and brains are in nearest connection, but also on the other hand, night, darkness, imagination, fear, sentiments and conscience. For this reason the awakening of the remorses in the night and their thorough vanishing with the first rays of the early sunshine in the morning. For this reason the sentimental objections and hyperemphasis of the importance of any intellectual experiences, if we happen to be alone, because we have the magnetic freedom to get rid of all surrounding attractions and distractions, our experiences and circumstances which would have a correcting, extenuating and modifying influence on our conceptions. Everything, every idea we have in our life is surrounded by the frame of a whole net of categoric conditions and can only be judged rightly if taken in this natural connections. The action of our conscience supposes that we have taken our experiences out from their natural intellectual frame and exposes them one by one to the flashlight of the concentrated sentimental attention, puts them in connection with eternal values and desires and creates in this ultimate projection proportions and relations which do fit the terminal dispositions, but perhaps not at all the present mediocre possibility of our real-ideal life and nature. The conscience has in this connection the meaning of affective one-sidedness of our human nature which is inclined to look at things from the angle of sharp affective concentration though it is forced to perform its functions in the life under the real dispersion of the multiple intellectual circumstances and distractions. Here we have the explanation why the practical life and the noisy world with its countless real opportunities and necessities can be greatest enemies of our conscience. It is the distraction and multiforme diversion of our interests which take away, owing to the law of compensation, our deep monosymbolic monoattentions and scatter it over the whole ranges of our necessary sensorial and categoric human experiences.

We have in the conscience the conscious representative of our monopunctual affective disposition which refers everything as soon to the universe in its monodetermined shooting organisation, as it is undisturbed in its natural meditation and can follow its peculiar inclination. This happens compulsatorily in the night and in the solitude, when the habitual multisensorial enlargement of the human psychopupil is relaxed and when the concentrated attention of the human soul rushes compensatorily on the fiery wings of its monosymbolic enthusiastic disposition towards the abyss of the universal divinity.

So strong conscience is more frequent in the individual who commits mistakes in the practical life. The strong central affective attention draws the individual observation from the peripheric detail and makes therefore the multiple objective conscientiousness difficult. The sharply intellectual individual on the contrary who has the inclination to stick perseveringly and minutely to all peripheric detailed duties of the life, does not only need so much, though also, the conscientious control of the central affective criticism, but would owing to shortcoming of energy not be able to do so. The first type represents the idealist with the strong inclination of mental monoattention, of intentional criticism from one standpoint and affective sentimental judgment with compensatory negligence of the peripheric reality which must be also the object of the conscientious judge, whilst the second type on the contrary means just the minute, refined conscientious performer of the objective reality and its duties, who at the same time is less careful about the central sentimental criticism of his actions, but does and achieves them indeed well and perfectly, nevertheless, or exactly for this reason. So we see that the conscientious sentimental type has not the power to fulfill himself his strict universal prescriptions whose respect he exacts so thoroughly in all consequences from his neighbour, and that the realist who does not care about deepest sentimental attitude is possibly the most thorough observer of the most minute and consequent human duties. In this sense years ago an idealistic parson told me: We have the better principles and the others are the better men. This means indeed enough. He meant: we idealists have the conscience and the others fulfil its practical exactions. People of the world do not think and speak so much about conscience, but they execute its insinuations exactly because they do not care so much about its powerful attraction. All really good and great things in our life must go on subconsciously. The artless virtue of the unassuming real worker and moderate intellectualist is so great because it does not relate in a conscious way, its deeds to the values of spirit, of highest greatness, divine importance and monodetermined conscience. The hyperemphasised idealistic type is not able to work patiently, perseveringly and "conscientiously," because he refers every detail too much to great values, lavishes therefore his magnetic forces in exhausting investigations, and has exaggerated expectations and consecutive disappointments. All these things are indeed always compensatory questions which rule the whole world and the whole psychology.

The human heart is the inexhaustible source of the UN-WRITTEN LAWS. There is no limit and no boundaries of unwritten laws in the good human life. He who is convinced of the fact that he has expressed the whole contents of his duties in the intellectual precision of legal expressions, may be sure that he is seriously morally sick. Whosoever thinks that the golden ray of the universal truth and love and justice can be put or caught into the small letters of our human legal contrivances, must be blind indeed. The tragedy of our life is just given in the terrible disproportion between the rights and legal facts of our socia. possibility and the unwritten sentimental values which we ought to express and are not able to. Whosoever is not thrilled and humiliated, at the same time, by this gaping difference, is not a man. To be able to become composed within the legal frame of any historic philosophical or historic religious system is the proof of a very ungifted and ruthless heart. There are not only countless question marks in every case of our real intellectual and legal life, but the whole collection of our legal culture, of our intellectual experimental development has, therefore, perhaps not even started to deal with the most thorough and most deciding legal questions of the human fate and life. And nevertheless the law acts, the

individual considered as criminal and sinner is condemned and
the general public is quiet because the legal court has done its conscientious duty. But within the doomed individual there may be a
whole world of universal important forces and unwritten laws
which nobody else ever was able to express, there are titanic battles
and terrible heroic fights which nobody ever expressed or was able
to put down in letters or laws and whose expressions the exterior
deeds however are. Can we so do justice to the greatest heroes,
the saints and prophets of our race? Is it enough for our satisfaction and quietness to know that the present footing of our habitual
exterior morality and its laws is powerful and crushes everybody
who seriously would resist it? Are we all so cowardly that we
never stand up and cry courageously for the right of the hidden
unwritten laws of our loving universal sentiments? How often
may the well-developed man be able to condemn his brother without blushing? There are greater and minor duties and the fulfilment of the greater task should excuse the small mistakes.

PUNISHMENT must in this connection be a most disagreeable thing for the judge. How can we know that anybody
must be punished? Do you think that we indeed are able to find
out that he really deserves the punishment? Can we exactly
know how the man called criminal came to do the action which
we call bad? Is there any judge on earth who is superficial enough
not to put serious question marks behind whatsoever judgment of
his in the sense not of the smallest relative, but greatest absolute
truth which any defendant has the right to enjoy? It must be
something of the most dreadful things therefore, to have received
the role to justice a fellowman. And even if he deserves a punishment which we never can prove thoroughly enough in the psychological sense, how can we dare crush any individual owing
to dispositions and inclinations which we have ourselves also? In
condemning anybody definitely, and expelling him from the social
life do we not hurt most seriously our own human nature from
which the worst criminal never is able to go away? This idea of
the gospel is indeed one of the greatest and most remarkable:
Judge not, that ye be not judged.

Punishment is no definite criterion for right and wrong. But
it settles once more the position of the leaseholder of the ruling
right. The individual is not only the highest culmination of right
and greatness, but also the localization of their deepest depression.
If perhaps society is wrong, in a sense, in carrying through its conviction in an exclusive and punishing way, the criminal surely is
not free from the reproach to make the attempt to crystallize and

materialize his views by force and violence. But he is weaker in power, loses therefore the battle; he is more one-sided and unbalanced owing to his personal shortcomings, whilst society has mature, broadened and mediated judgment and order. Yet confusion of right and power is an idea we are overcoming to-day. There is no doubt that what we call crime and what is decried and punished in public, often is the only helper of higher justice and broader humanity. Our deepest conscience often admires the "criminal" in a moment when he is abandoned and punished. The divine nature of any hatred even against the worst criminal, is most questionable. Our social legislation has to become better, otherwise we have the shame that the "criminal" is alone the courageous helper against irreligious, social morality. Many a "criminal" confuses right with violence, and afterwards the law confuses power with right. But the kernel of the question is not settled that way. Formulated power and spiritual right cannot be confused.

We have always the bitter fight between the universal idealistic conception and the real intellectual crystallisation of the legal fixation of the life. There is one incessant struggle of the two different stand-points, both of which have their serious objections. But for the present moment it is always the intellectual precision which gains. It is the antiquated tradition in its legal precision which possesses the real power, overthrows and crushes the helpless claims of the endless universal rights and truth. But the latter can not be killed or excluded forever. The root of all our difficulties is an inextricable coil of contradictory misunderstandings. The best truth can be brought to the scaffold and its individual representative may be beheaded, but its unwritten laws will develop the same during centuries and ages, in patient laborious courage humanity will be more freed from the fetters of narrow traditional legislation, and there will be at last the moment, when universal love and highest educational skill will be the solution of any crime, instead of social revenge and cruelty as we have them at the psychological basis of any legal action of today. Nobody shall be able at any rate to fall out from the frame of the social love, as little as he surely is able to switch from the harmonious concert of the universal progress and ideal resurrection.

Not only the individual ought to have pardon for digressive moral conceptions by a lenient, cautious and unprejudiced society, which has to learn from every legal complication as the possible further enlargement of the law, but society itself should progress in moral growth, truth and thoroughness; it should correct and develop its legal expressions and notions always again, because there is no stability and can not be in the representation of the principles of truth, right and morality. The law is always a reflection of the degree of universal development of the truth and morality of a nation. The exterior intellectual circumstances change always individually, the laws have to be correct and completed according to the continual richness of additional experiences made with the so-called or real criminal.

But there are waves of compensation everywhere, difficulties we may look and investigate in a direction whatsoever. The most idealistic fixation of legislation has just determined so definitely every right and wrong in the strong conviction of its self-confidence that it puts the capital punishment at the heading of its legislation, and has all features of theoretical partiality according to a whole system, never according to the minute circumstances of the case or of the person or actions of the concerned people. It is the category and the heading of the crime which determines its gravity.

The *scientific basis of the legislation* has the opposite danger of lack of conclusiveness. There is so much to be careful about and there are so numberless detailed cliffs where the conscientious mind could stumble in its right efficacy of justice, in the scientific opinion, that it is very hard and difficult to come to any practical sentence and conclusion. So the speculative self-confident *theological jurisprudence* turns out to be most efficient in producing strong, clear and exciting real facts, spreading much terror and maintaining great authority by fear, whilst the intellectual law on the contrary, just because of its detailed scientific conscientiousness and correctness, is considered to be weak in the opinion of the sensational mob or general public inclined to cruelty and revenge. The strong inclination for most clear language, ideas and facts is of course very understandable and natural as goal, but they are so much less possible in the practical life as our digging work toward absolute truth and justice is more serious. The clearer, more resolute the revenues of our human thinking are, the more they are in danger to be bold and inconsiderate in favour of objective truth and circumstances, but also at the expense of future universal expectations. It is true, however, that human nature has the need of clear conclusiveness and of right and wrong, but it is sure that there can scarcely be anything more difficult than the combination of the subjective, absolute speculative and objective, intellectual justice, reliable and logical in all most detailed real relations. Can there be compromises and bargaining in holiest and deepest convictions? But this is the highest degree, where real success was able to climb up to the present day.

If we were indeed most *humane,* not bribed by any theoretical legal paragraphs nor puzzled by the tiring and doubtful multiplicity of the real intricacy, of which we are tempted to be rid at last, then we would indeed find that there is nothing more difficult in the world than justice. How can we judge anybody even if he seems to be the worst criminal in the superficial eyes of the world, if we are not able to know surely neither all intellectual peripheric circumstances nor the deep psychological causal connections of the persons in question? And if we will be sincere we must admit that we indeed almost never are in a position to know neither one nor the other. Protection, fear, self-consciousness, suggestibility, laziness, exultation, hypocrisy, a whole host of faults are ready to trouble the justice of those who are given the power to execute.

It is indeed very agreeable and comfortable to have conclusiveness, to receive clear results, definite right or, for many, wrongs in life, in the world and in the law-court, but it is surely rather the proof of great superficiality and of lack of consciousness on the other side, if we are most ready and able to believe that there is ever a case in jurisprudence, where all right is on one and all wrong on the other side. Truth and humanity means careful reservedness as to the conclusiveness of any decision and clear statements. Heavy sentences may be mostly artificial products of a theoretically crushing personal will putting together into a connecting system of right and wrong what never is entirely together in any case but only fragmentarily, one party being right in this point and wrong in another one and vice versa. A legal court may be considered up to a certain degree as the *theatrical artificial* logical elaboration of right and wrong where the lawyer with his intellectual instruments looks to develop a whole play in his favor starting from some existing points of support. There is only the consolation that there are two opposite tendencies and that there is finally a judge looking through the tendencious representations and performances of either. But the lawyer in the court is on the whole very near the poetical author of any play, he combines and compiles, drops and arraignes the circumstances of the case of his client just so that they impress most thoroughly the attendants to the favor and the right of the client and most possibly in disfavour of the opponent. The barrister indeed finds also, as well as the poetical author, only fragments of right and causality in everyone of his cases, one is right here and wrong there, one has the question and the need and the other the answer and the fulfilment, but never entirely, never perfectly logically neither in the psychology of the clients and in their exterior circumstances, just as everywhere divided, fragmentary and doubtful. Conclusiveness and clearness are precious stones to which we strive seriously in our life, and we have to do so because they are the necessary hygienic pillows of our physiological psychological peace, the resumé of our conscientious detailed work, the "conscientious" terminal reaction of our activity. But if it is the excellent spirit of the dramatic author and of the theatre to give to us the impression of the possible conclusiveness of right and wrong, and of the hideous and the beautiful in logical psychological fulfilment and to make us quiet, happy and hopeful in this strong and deep well of idealizing *invigoration,* then on the other side we must indeed think, that in a legal action there is not the question of an artistic theatrical representation and suggestive manoeuvres, but of the veal and woe of supreme human destinies, of wife and children, of human honour, of the dignity of the ideal divinity as it is manifested in every individual. It is therefore in spite of all seriously objectionable, in advance, from the moral standpoint to arrange, or permit any theatrical representation and elaboration in the battle about human destinies and honours. The public authorities should defend just these *worst tournaments* about the very root of the human social right of existence, and the lawyer, instead of being induced to make the best out of his egotistical necessities and objective compulsions, should be kept away from the horrible "immorality" of his professional conception instead of being forced to exhibit and emphasize his cases in public. It is easier to criticise than to find perfection. But still——

Who would be the best judge? The one-sided idealist, the speculatively involved individual would be much too narrow, too absolute and exclusive for being just, not cautious and conscientious enough as to the real happening circumstances. The extreme scientific intellectualist would be on the contrary far from sentimental thoroughness and sufficient respect for the ideal intentions of the individual and would cling too much to petty exterior characteristics which never could explain everything, and hit perhaps even less the point of "right" and "wrong" than the speculative conception of jurisprudence. It is not the speculative sentimental divine nor the sharply analysing real critic that are the best judges, but the *humane* individual full of kind feelings and scientific orders at the same time. The modern psychiatrician and the more independent modern protestant divine may be closest to these exactions. There is no question about the sympathy of the cruel public psychology in legislation, there can-not be any question about personal ambition and money-making success of the barrister, but only of the best possible humane sentence, adapted to the whole dignity, greatness and significance of the human life and nature, deciding about the destiny of defendant and plaintiff.

Are then legal actions really necessary? Must necessarily one be right and the other wrong? Is there not mostly the question how bold, blind, egotistical and passionate somebody can be, or how much he is confident, how much he is able to crush his possibly honest kinder and poorer brother with the power of his passion and money? Are these not horrible things? And then the lawyers and the whole court of learned and earning people greedy of drawing out most possible money from the immorality of quarrelling people. The greatest crime is in this connection the very idea of quarrelling and of starting a legal action. He who is narrow and exclusive enough not to discuss in benevolent compromising manner with his neighbour, is the essential criminal and ought to be punished for this fault thoroughly and duly. Could there not be a serious previous instance which with a thorough effort ought to have an inquiry concerning both parts (The Justice of the Peace of today in European countries and in America is only a weak trial of reconciliation). There could be found out just in advance the relative bad or good will of the quarreller and there could be stated accordingly who is the blinder egotist and the more irreconciliable quarreller. The intelligent and psychic Justice of the Peace in this conception could, according to his observation, just catch the anti-social rebel; he could easily discover the worse and better character and could, equipped with legal power, from the beginning decide thoroughly. The development of legal actions creates all kinds of damages and shames in the moral direction, defamation and lowering of human standards, since the terrible power of money entices many a scoundrel to start legal actions because he indeed knows by experience that he may succed in the struggle against the immaterial ideal sentiments which so easily become dumb before the chair of the judge. Christ is the most significant representative of this fact.

As long as we have the fact that it is chiefly the monopoly of the possession to carry through the legal actions in a thorough way, to buy the "cleverest" and most audacious lawyers, as long as the poor in advance is not able to be duly represented in every law-court with the same emphasis as the rich, as long as any previous generous pardon, given to our neighbour in a written way, can be abused afterwards against ourselves, if the offender turns out to assail us with a legal action, we indeed are not entitled to speak of a well ordered reflection of humanity in our legislation.

As long as the cheater can be defeated best by over-cheating and the better excels in silence and punishment, as long as the word of Schiller is true: "Der beste Mensch kann nicht in Frieden leben, wenn es dem boesen Nachbar nicht gefaellt," this earth cannot be a desirable home for the sincere idealist.

We forget to grumble about the law if we need its assistance ourselves. Even if it is a two-edged sword, abused by many a hypocritical wrong-doer against the security of honest people, we must keep in mind that this sword works against the abuser himself, if his dishonest methods are discovered. Our objections were directed against the conception of the infallibility of any legislative construction; it can be abused and is misrepresented just against the most sincere and honest person by twisting lies, perjurious tricks and other insidious manipulations. This is the risk of the most necessary and inevitable legislation. In the practical life there are perhaps not as many who surpass the written law with their noble intentions and high aspirations, as those who try to hurt the honest man outside the law in a direct criminal way. Against this kind of danger the existence of the legislation is intended. It checks the private misfortune by the strong arm of the public moral and efficient help. There we may enjoy the favor of justice and individual protection and there we may learn to appreciate the safeguard given to us by means which are stronger than our personal real power. There are two sides in everything.

WE may wander in the CENTRAL CEMETERY of VIENNA for hours, rambling through the maze of countless rows of graves different in taste, form, artistic quality and outfit, according to the social standing and the means of the dead and their relatives. Even size and location of the monuments and graves change also, according to their circumstances at life-time, the poor citizens slumbering for ever in the stereotypical rectangular tombs with the simple black cross of wood, in the outskirts of the cemetery, whilst the wealthy and more outstanding deceased lie in variable and richer groups toward the centre. Even death was not in a position to do away with the questionable differentiation of material possession, exterior names, insignificant distinctions and temporal haphazards which are difficult enough in life and make a pitiful impression in the scent of the universal common love.

All these thoughts disapear, when we approach the centre of the large grave-yard. We pass through groups of monuments high like houses, impressive looking with brazen lions holding in a grim clutch historic flags of gone-by famous days. These monuments are ornamented and surrounded in their perennial peace with refined art work, dignifying bushes, willows looking compassionate with drooping boughs, hanging twigs and trembling leaves. The dark green needles of delicate life-trees and slender ceders exhale an inspiring fragrance. There lie famous generals, great politicians and others who had been brilliant during the long and old Austrian Hungarian monarchy and in the extraordinarily glorious history of the outstanding capital of Vienna. All those great political leaders, the most important capitalists, high financers and organizers sleep there quietly in their monuments covered with emphatic inscriptions giving all their honors, titles and credentials in huge and long gilded letters. But all is over for them. There is seldom a name, in spite of the glorious monuments pointing to great riches and power, of which the stranger ever heard.

Only in the very centre of the cemetery, in the bull's of this central disposition, we meet names of imperishable fame, stars which cannot be extinguished from the memory of mankind, but which send forth the blazing light of their ever shining and enligthening fame through all ages and centuries, seeming new every morning and blowing the trumpets of human resurrection, eternal hope and confidence all the time with a shaking intensity and puzzling emphasis. Whilst all others round about, king or duke or millionnaire, trying to grasp and hold the remembrance of hastening time with their bright and splendid monuments, just slowly sink altogether to the dust of oblivion as their bodies decay into ashes, these centrally located heroes seem to look through their modest and decent monuments in victorious confidence, resisting all neglecting and crumbling progression of time and the fact of being worn out and forgotten by others. They are about a dozen all emphasizing the perennial glory of each other, and we are deeply impressed and feel to stand on one of the most sacred spots where we ever stood in our life. There are assembled the immortal Beethoven and Mozart. Mozart's monument reminds us of his unknown "poor" grave in Salzburg, where he was shovelled like a beggar, and it expresses the desire to give him back the honour of dwelling in the middle of the illustrious circle of these greatest geniuses. What an ingrateful humanity! - There we meet besides the monuments of Schubert, Haydn, Grillparzer, the first dramatist of the German tongue after Schiller, a citizen of Vienna, Anastasius Gruen, Robert Hamerling, Suppe, Strauss and some others who replenish the world with their glory and will keep their high acknowledgement for ever. What could be more thrilling than to stand in the middle of these great prophets, leaders, heroes and martyrs of a rich old culture, having sacrificed all to the noblest and highest desires of their hearts! And if we think of those sweet and kindly musicians Schubert and Mozart and of Grillparzer, how they starved almost to death for their great and pure idealism little acknowledged and rewarded by their contemporaries, what will be more deeply felt and more sincere than our reverent tear and the true and full act of affection for those heroes of humanity, of whom we receive still to-day our best, but who received nothing from their time!

So we recognize that there are scarcely a dozen out of a long and great national culture, chosen not to fall through the wholes of the sieve of our perennial commemoration. Not only the poor citizen never mentioned even during his life-time by public fame, reposing now under the modest black cross for ever, but also the rich and important public man famous at his period, fell through the openings of oblivion of the unforgiving progression of history. What an accusation peers from those huge and glittering monuments of the numerous generations of the rich dead, confirming their impossibility to prevent them from being wiped out from the lasting human recollection! This shame is more emphasized than that of the poor forgotten who at least had never the exterior means to advertise and attract our attention!

What an indescribable honour and proof of worthiness, on the other side, if the nations are groping for the shadows of others in desperate admiration, long after they have gone, if they had rejected or ignored them at life-time, buried their remains like those of the last in some forgotten corner, and now they erect monuments of public worship, as it happened to Mozart, to their symbolic names, since they muddled in vain to find their real bodies ! Oh they crave to pretend the presence of the despised hero among the august company, where he belongs, in order to cover their own negligence of a former period! What a greatest resurrection after a life of most humiliating sacrifices, after the *courage to hang on to the last, in faithfulness, to the maturation of his best individuality!* Death, where is thy sting! Capitalism, where is thy victory! . . . *et omnia vanitas* . . .